WOMEN, AUTOBIOGRAPHY, THEORY

Wisconsin Studies in American Autobiography

William L. Andrews
General Editor

WOMEN, AUTOBIOGRAPHY, THEORY

A Reader

Edited by

Sidonie Smith

and

Julia Watson

The University of Wisconsin Press

The University of Wisconsin Press
2537 Daniels Street
Madison, Wisconsin 53718

3 Henrietta Street
London WC2E 8LU, England

5   4   3   2   1

Printed in the United States of America

A list of the sources for the chapters appears on pages 491–493.

Library of Congress Cataloging-in-Publication Data
Women, autobiography, theory: a reader / edited by Sidonie Smith &
     Julia Watson.
          538 pp.   cm.—(Wisconsin studies in American autobiography)
          Includes bibliographical references and index.
          ISBN 0-299-15840-3 (cloth: alk. paper).
          ISBN 0-299-15844-6 (paper: alk. paper)
          1. American prose literature—Women authors—History and
     criticism—Theory, etc.   2. Women authors, American—Biography—
     History and criticism.   3. Women—United States—Biography—History
     and criticism.   4. Women and literature—United States—History.
     5. Autobiography—Women authors.   I. Smith, Sidonie.   II. Watson,
     Julia, 1943–   .   III. Series.
     PS366.A88W636   1998
     818'.540809492072—dc21   97-39731

*To the centuries of women autobiographers
whose writing inspires our theorizing.*

Contents

Contents

Contents

Contents

Acknowledgments

Our primary debt in this project is to William L. Andrews, executive editor of Wisconsin Studies in American Autobiography, who proposed, several years ago, that we write a book situating women's autobiography in historical and theoretical frameworks. As we thought about his suggestion, we realized that the time had come for a wide-ranging reader that would reflect two decades of extraordinary critical scholarship on women's autobiography. As more and more courses on women's personal narratives are offered on campuses both nationally and internationally, we hope that a reader in theory to both supplement and "map" this activity will contribute to its growth.

We are also indebted to scholarly conversations among members of the Division of Autobiography, Biography, and Life Writing (and its Special Session predecessors) and the Division of Women's Studies in Language and Literature of the Modern Language Association, as well as to stimulating exchanges at many conferences focused on autobiography over the last decade. Ultimately this collection builds on the legacy of several distinguished anthologies that carved out the field of women's autobiography and on the work of pioneering feminist scholars. Although no single book could include this important work in its entirety, we have tried in this reader to capture its diversity and complexity.

Mary Elizabeth Braun has been an enthusiastic, consistently supportive, and resourceful editor throughout the project's development. Shirley Neuman and Françoise Lionnet, with characteristic scholarly expertise and collegial generosity, offered insightful suggestions on expanding the topical scope of the book and addressing diverse audiences.

We are grateful for research monies in support of this project provided to Sidonie Smith by the University of Michigan and to Julia Watson by the University of Montana and by the National Endowment for the Humanities for a productive summer seminar directed by James Phelan.

And, as always, we appreciate the support of our families, who helped us scramble to collaborate across states and continents.

WOMEN, AUTOBIOGRAPHY, THEORY

Introduction: Situating Subjectivity in Women's Autobiographical Practices

Sidonie Smith and Julia Watson

*The subject . . .—female autobiographies, memoirs, letters and diaries—repre-
sents one of those cases of maddening neglect that have motivated feminist
scholarship since 1970. This body of writing about the self has remained invisible, systematically ignored in the studies on autobiography that have proliferated in the past fifteen years.*
                    —Domna C. Stanton, *The Female Autograph* (vii)

*There are four ways to write a woman's life: the woman herself may tell it, in
what she chooses to call an autobiography; she may tell it in what she chooses to
call fiction; a biographer, woman or man, may write the woman's life in what
is called a biography; or the woman may write her own life in advance of living
it, unconsciously and without recognizing or naming the process. . . . Women of
accomplishment, in unconsciously writing their future lived lives, or, more recently, in trying honestly to deal in written form with lived past lives, have had
to confront power and control. Because this has been declared unwomanly, and
because many women would prefer (or think they would prefer) a world without evident power or control, women have been deprived of the narratives, or
the texts, plots, or examples, by which they might assume power over—take
control of—their own lives.*
                    —Carolyn G. Heilbrun, *Writing a Woman's Life* (11, 16–17)

After two decades of a ferment of activity in theorizing women's autobiography, it seems important to attempt, not an overview of, but a guide to, the field as it has evolved. This collection proposes a set of categories, however provisional, overlapping, and contingent, to focus key issues in scholarship. Some categories are formalist, such as genre and history; others indicate terrains of debate, such as experience, subjectivities, and sexualities. The essays we have selected for inclusion were not necessarily the most influential ones at the time of their publication; but they *now* foreground concepts and pose questions helpful for *practicing* the critical activity of theorizing women's autobiography. This collection does not claim to be a history. Rather, it aims to capture the complex interplay of multiple theoretical critiques as they have motivated a discussion of women's autobiography. The history of women's autobiography studies is yet to be written—and the dust has nowhere near settled.

As a guide for mapping the field of women's autobiography, this introduction has several goals:

- to *locate parameters* in the theory of women's autobiography by identifying how critics have read it in relation to dominant autobiographical theory;
- to *order the field* by surveying the "stages" of critical activity in women's autobiography, from theories of gendered experience, to theories of difference, to the proliferation of differences that inform postmodern and postcolonial theorizing;
- to *identify significant theoretical interventions* that have helped reframe critical perspectives on women's autobiography;
- to *reflect on the contributions* of the essays included in this volume; and
- to *propose prospects for future inquiry* in feminist critical investigation.

But before launching into this study, we want to emphasize that this is a book necessarily without a conclusion. Think of it as a set of tools— or building blocks, guides, recipes—for enabling your own entry into the activity (and the self-reflexivity) of theorizing women's autobiography. As a map for the perplexed, the skeptical, the uninitiated, the jaded, we hope it will aid readers in discovering and valuing the rich ferment of feminist critical activity that has excited and sustained scholars and contributed to the ever-increasing production, "rediscovery," and analysis of women's life writings.

Our Introduction is in five interrelated parts: Part 1 discusses the emergence of theories of women's autobiography as a series of critical moments; part 2 considers theoretical perspectives on subjectivity that have led to the reformulation of women's autobiography; part 3 discusses prospects for theorizing; part 4 considers the future of women's autobiography as a field; and part 5 offers summary remarks on the project and the contributors.

Part 1: The Emergence of Theories of Women's Autobiography

> The problem for the female autobiographer is, on the one hand, to resist the pressure of masculine autobiography as the only literary genre available for her enterprise, and, on the other, to describe a difficulty in conforming to a female ideal which is largely a fantasy of the masculine, not the feminine, imagination.
>
> —Barbara Johnson, *A World of Difference* (154)

Prehistory—Laying the Groundwork of a Women's Tradition

As we approach the millennium it is remarkable that, although women have written autobiographically for many centuries and published autobiographies throughout the twentieth century that are widely read, advertised by book clubs, and taught in university courses, the criticism of women's autobiography as a genre is barely two decades old. Women's autobiographical writing, seldom taken seriously as a focus of study before the seventies, was not deemed appropriately "complex" for academic dissertations, criticism, or the literary canon. The phrase "Read this only to yourself," used by one of the diarists discussed by Elizabeth Hampsten, named the "bind" that readers confronted in discovering their "bond" to women's autobiography. Academic and popular historians alike regarded it as at best a mine of biographical information and salty citations and deemed it too windy and unreliable—since life stories "stretch" the truth—to be worthy of critical investigation. Those who took autobiography seriously, critics such as Georg Misch, Georges Gusdorf, and William Spengemann, restricted their focus to the lives of great men—Augustine, Rousseau, Franklin, Goethe, Carlyle, Henry Adams—whose accomplished lives and literary tomes assured their value as cultural capital.

The status of autobiography has changed dramatically in the intervening decades, both within and outside the academy. Women's autobiography is now a privileged site for thinking about issues of writing at the intersection of feminist, postcolonial, and postmodern critical theories. Processes of subject formation and agency occupy theorists of narrative and, indeed, of culture as never before. If feminism has revolutionized literary and social theory, the texts and theory of women's autobiography have been pivotal for revising our concepts of women's life issues—growing up female, coming to voice, affiliation, sexuality and textuality, the life cycle. Crucially, the writing and theorizing of women's lives has often occurred in texts that place an emphasis on collective processes while questioning the sovereignty and universality of the solitary self. Autobiography has been employed by many women writers to write themselves into history. Not only feminism but also literary and cultural theory have felt the impact of women's autobiography as a previously unacknowledged mode of making visible formerly invisible subjects.

The growing academic interest in women's autobiography may be the result of an interplay of political, economic, and aesthetic factors. The growth of gender, ethnic, and area studies programs to address the interests of new educational constituencies has created a demand for texts that speak to diverse experiences and issues. Too, publishers have discovered that recovering and publishing women's life stories is a profitable enterprise. Autobiographies by women and people of color introduce stirring narratives of self-discovery that authorize new subjects who claim kinship in a literature of possibility. Most centrally, women reading other women's autobiographical writings have experienced them as "mirrors" of their own unvoiced aspirations. Critic Barbara Christian, for example, wrote of her excitement when, as a graduate student in 1967, she first read the autobiographical novel *Brown Girl, Brownstones* by Paule Marshall: "[it] was not just a text; it was an accurate and dynamic embodiment both of the possibilities and improbabilities of my own life. In it I as subject encountered myself as object. . . . It was crucial to a deeper understanding of my own life" (197).

This interest in women's autobiographical practices as both an articulation of women's life experience and a source for articulating feminist theory has grown over several decades and was acknowledged as a field around 1980. Activity was evident on three interrelated fronts that we will explore: building the archive of women's writing, claiming models of heroic identity, and revising dominant theories of autobiography.

Building the Archive of Women's Writing

In the fifties and sixties, several women's memoirs became best-sellers; some were by prominent or "notorious" women, others by unknown writers who created compelling life stories. Critic Carolyn Heilbrun, author of the best-selling *Writing a Woman's Life*, noted, "Only in the last third of the twentieth century have women broken through to a realization of the narratives that have been controlling their lives. Women poets of one generation—those born between 1923 and 1932—can now be seen to have transformed the autobiographies of women's lives, to have expressed, and suffered for expressing, what women had not earlier been allowed to say" (60). By incorporating hitherto unspoken female experience in telling their own stories, women revised the content and purposes of autobiography and insisted on alternative stories.

The translation of Simone de Beauvoir's multivolume autobiography—*Memoirs of a Dutiful Daughter, The Prime of Life,* and others—was important for its interrogation of the category of "woman" in the making of self-consciousness. Anais Nin's multivolume *Diaries* combined self-exposure and literary experimentation. A generation of girls grew up reading *The Diary of Anne Frank* and *I Never Promised You a Rose Garden* (Joanne Greenberg). Mary McCarthy's *Memories of a Catholic Girlhood,* first serialized in magazines in the fifties, was acclaimed as life writing of high seriousness by the eastern establishment. Lillian Hellman's three memoirs, *An Unfinished Woman, Pentimento,* and *Scoundrel Time,* were lionized as best-sellers and incorporated in films. And the McCarthy-Hellman feud, aired on the Dick Cavett talk show in January 1980, in which McCarthy remarked of Hellman's autobiographical texts that "Every word she writes is a lie, including 'and' and 'the,'" not only nurtured popular interest in famous lives but also exposed knotty issues of truth and lying in self-representation. An emerging generation of African American women, coming of age during the years of the civil rights movement and the later Black Power movement, published autobiographical narratives through which they staked out a place within political or artistic movements and explored the complex legacies of racial and sexual exploitation. Anne Moody's *Coming of Age in Mississippi* and Maya Angelou's *I Know Why the Caged Bird Sings* were among many writings that introduced African American women autobiographers to a broader American audience.

By the seventies the bravado self-assertions of some feminist critics were widely heard. Germaine Greer in *The Female Eunuch* and Shulamith Firestone in *The Dialectic of Sex* interwove autobiographical and theoretical writing to demonstrate that the personal is political; Kate Millett, in *Sexual Politics* and in her later autobiographical works *Flying* and *Sita,* took this posture to a limit in claiming experience as the foundation of theory. And Angela Davis used her life story, *An Autobiography,* not only to expose the reach of racism in the United States, but to make her case for the necessity of a radical politics that included a critique of misogyny within the writings of Black Power activists.

Influential early feminist literary critics focused on the intersection of women's lives and their writing in studies that sought to map a women's tradition and to legitimate feminist scholarship. Widely available books such as Mary Ellmann's *Thinking about Women,* Ellen Moers' *Literary Women,* and Elaine Showalter's *A Literature of Their Own* interrogated the history of patriarchy and the invisibility of women's texts and voices in dominant literary and academic culture. These early feminist critics pointed out that an extensive women's literary tradition had existed for centuries, especially if one turned to supposedly "marginal" genres— memoir, journal, diary, the many modes of private autobiographical writing. Moers' fifty-page list of women writers and their works mapped a female tradition that generated innumerable studies. In recovering the long-out-of-print writings of women over centuries and framing them as a tradition rather than as "marginal" or "failed" efforts to write master narratives for male audiences, these pioneering critics cracked literary history wide open.

The archive of women's writing was also built through the recovery of earlier women's texts, above all by historians and bibliographers. In numerous ways women historians redirected the attention of their discipline from large-scale political events to the social history of everyday subjects and practices. Historians such as Mary Beth Norton, Rayna Rapp, Ann Douglas, Nancy Cott, and Carroll Smith-Rosenberg used archival materials such as diaries, journals, and unpublished autobiographical narratives to rethink a rich record of women's histories. Bibliographies of women's writing were genuinely a work of cultural excavation. In addition to Ellen Moers' annotated list of women's published writings, women could turn to Louis Kaplan's *A Bibliography of American Autobiographies,* listing over six thousand works before 1945 and, in the eighties, to its extension to contemporary times that included many writings by women, *American Autobiography, 1945–1980,* edited by Mary Louise Briscoe, Lynn Z. Bloom, and Barbara Tobias. Though a bibliography of American women's autobiography would not appear until 1983, in Patricia K. Addis' *Through a Woman's "I,"* the groundwork was laid for exploring the vast and neglected storehouse of women's personal writing and revaluing women's "place."

Claiming Models of Heroic Identity

As early feminist literary critics developed courses on "Women in Literature" and "Images of Women," autobiographical texts often supplemented fictionalized accounts of women's lives. Critic Patricia Meyer Spacks in *The Female Imagination* read life writing analytically rather than as simply a mirror of women writers' lives. Exploring what she called the "characteristic patterns of self-perception" that "shape the creative expression of women," Spacks used autobiographies to probe what shapes the "female imagination" (1). Spacks's influential book historicized a tradition encompassing four centuries and many genres, including diaries, journals, and autobiographies. Her rubrics suggested a history of gradual artistic and personal liberation for "selves in hiding": "Finger Posts," "The Artist as Woman," and "Free Women" discovering creative spaces for female self-expression. Spacks emphasized women's struggle to assert a "positive" identity and focused on self-mastery and the dangers of "relational" female self-

definition, although she largely omitted texts by women of color, which now limits the usefulness of her study (267).

Germaine Brée was also an influential critic of women's autobiography. Her 1976 essay "George Sand: The Fictions of Autobiography" made an early call for reading a woman's personal narrative as a separate genre and a means for a writer to autobiographically "think back through her mothers" (441). In women's autobiographies students found models of heroic womanhood absent from their own education, as suggested by the title of Lynn Z. Bloom's 1978 essay "Promises Fulfilled: Positive Images of Women." To develop a feminist pedagogy teachers sought these positive models of women who had creatively talked back to patriarchs, defied, resisted, in short, been empowered through writing their lives. In a literary canon and a Western tradition that had "othered" women, whether as goddesses or demons, on pedestals or in back rooms, this effort to reclaim women's lives and discover how women would speak "in their own words" was an essential initiatory gesture. Without excavating and revaluing the buried texts of women's autobiography, the critical ferment of the last twenty years could not have occurred.

Revising Theories of Autobiography

With the loosening of formalist New Criticism's hold on literary scholarship, several critics began reading autobiographies as literary texts, rather than documentary histories. But the typologies, accounts, and theories of autobiography continued to dismiss, erase, and misidentify women's autobiographical texts. For example, Georges Gusdorf's "seminal" essay "Conditions and Limits of Autobiography," published in French in 1956 (and widely known through its publication in English in the Olney collection, 1980), defended autobiography as an "art" and "representative" of the best minds of its time because it "recomposes and interprets a life in its totality" (38).[1] But, like Georg Misch in his earlier three-volume *History of Autobiography,* Gusdorf configured autobiography as unquestionably white, male, and Western: "the artist and the model coincide, the historian tackles himself as object . . . he considers himself a great person" (31).[2] Wayne Shumaker in 1954 discussed some women's autobiographical texts in his history of autobiography in England, but ascribed to them "feminine" qualities that marginalized their contributions to the development of the genre. By the end of the seventies the growing critical interest in autobiography studies was evidenced by several texts that would remain influential throughout the decade for theorizing autobiography, notably the dissemination of French critic Philippe Lejeune's theory of the autobiographical pact, James Olney's collection of essays, *Autobiography: Essays Theoretical and Critical,* and studies of American autobiography by William Spengemann and Albert Stone. In the Olney anthology one essay, by Mary G. Mason, focused on women's autobiography and another, by Louis Renza, discussed the significance of a woman's autobiographical text (*The Life* of Saint Teresa of Avila) without foregrounding gender issues. In Spengemann women were absent from the tradition of autobiography mapped. Only Stone made a sustained attempt to address the intersection of race, class, and gender in the American tradition by focusing on many women's and ethnic, notably African American, autobiographies.

Around 1980: First Forays—Theories Based on Women's Experience

Around 1980 the criticism of women's autobiography necessarily came of age. It was clear that new theories and generic definitions were required to describe the women's writing that had been recovered and was being produced. Why? Gradually, it became clear to many feminist critics that academic scholars were complicit in broader cultural practices that valued women's writing only in terms of, and as the "other" of, men's writing. In publication, at conferences, in scholarly overviews, references to women's writing were often uninformed or condescending. Throughout the 1980s feminist critics intervened in what they saw as traditional reading practices that assumed the autobiographer to be male and reproduced cultural stereotypes of differences between men and women.

The 1979 collection of excerpts from British and American women's autobiographies *Journeys: Autobiographical Writings by Women,* edited by Mary G. Mason and Carol Hurd Green, mapped a skeletal canon. Mason's introduction proposed a women's autobiographical tradition rooted in four texts, the late-medieval life writings of Margery Kempe and Julian of Norwich and the self-effacing histories of others penned by Margaret Cavendish and Anne Bradstreet. Mason's essay, expanded as "The Other Voice" in Olney's collection, became the basis for much later theorizing of women's autobiography. It argued that women's alterity informs their establishment of identity as a relational, rather than individuating, process: "[T]he self-discovery of female identity seems to acknowledge the real presence and recognition of another consciousness, and the disclosure of female self is linked to the identification of some 'other'" (Olney, 210). Mason used an essentialized "woman" as an internally coherent gender distinction. And she contrasted the flamboyant self-staging of "the drama of the self" (210) in a male text, Rousseau's *Confessions,* with the relational self-presentations of these four women writing "radically the story of a woman" (235). Later critics, notably Susan Stanford Friedman, would productively expand Mason's argument for relationality by appeal to psychoanalytic theory and multicultural texts.

Even more influential in 1980 was the first anthology of essays in the field, *Women's Autobiog-*

raphy: Essays in Criticism, edited by Estelle C. Jelinek. The fourteen essays, most on white twentieth-century literary autobiographers in the British and American traditions, inaugurated sustained critical inquiry into women's experience as the basis of their autobiographical practice. Several essays called for either expanding the literary canon of autobiography or establishing an alternative canon of women's writing (Suzanne Juhasz, Annette Kolodny, Sidonie Smith and Marcus Billson). Jelinek's introduction called for diverse kinds of analysis to be brought to reading women's autobiography: "the historical, the social, the psychological, and the ethnic," as well as "rhetorical, poststructuralist, and Jungian" analyses (x). Jelinek primarily used gender, uninflected by class, ethnicity, genres, or life cycle, to define women's autobiography, and paid little attention to geographic or political locations. She argued that differences between the sexes are manifest in both the content and the style of autobiography (xi) and may be ascribed to the long-term restriction of women to the private, personal world and the prevailing view that women's lives are too "insignificant" to be of literary interest (4).

Jelinek contrasted the autobiographies of women and men on several points: At the level of content, she argued, men distance themselves in autobiographies that are "success stories and histories of their eras" focused on their professional lives (10), while women's life writings emphasize personal and domestic details and describe connections to other people (10). At the level of life scripts, men aggrandize themselves in autobiographies that "idealize their lives or cast them into heroic molds to project their universal import" (14–15). Women, by contrast, seek to authenticate themselves in stories that reveal "a self-consciousness and a need to sift through their lives for explanation and understanding," employing understatement to mask their feelings and play down public aspects of their lives (15). At the level of temporality, men shape the events of their lives into coherent wholes characterized by linearity, harmony, and orderliness (16). Irregularity, however, characterizes the lives of women and their texts, which have a "disconnected, fragmentary ... pattern of diffusion and diversity" in discontinuous forms because "the multidimensionality of women's socially conditioned roles seems to have established a pattern of diffusion and diversity when they write" (17). For Jelinek, women's narratives mime the everyday quality of their lives—their life writings are "analogous to the fragmentary, interrupted, and formless nature of their lives" (19). That is, a pattern of discontinuity consistently characterizes women's autobiography just as it marks their lives.

Jelinek's argument about women's discontinuous narrative textuality asserted a model of coherence for men's autobiographies that, from the perspective of the late nineties, seems difficult to maintain for the autobiographical writings of, say, Richard Wright and James Baldwin, as well as Augustine, Rousseau, and Franklin. Not only was this model of women's autobiography mimetic in form and expressive in content for women's lives; it also assumed that "experience" is unproblematically "real" and "readable," and can be captured transparently in language expressing the truth of experience. Jelinek's "Introduction" had a manifesto quality in its essentializing of gendered experience to the exclusion of other differences in women's autobiographies and its sweeping analogy between lives and texts.

Several critics in the Jelinek collection, however, gestured toward a more temperately theorized view of writing and analyzed texts such as *The Woman Warrior* that became crucial for exploring women's autobiography. The most significant impact of the Jelinek collection was that a vigorous group of feminist critics *claimed* women's autobiography as a field of cultural study and went on to extended studies of the field or of particular autobiographers.

A focus on women's experience as the true feminist "content" of women's autobiography and the transparent "expression" of their lives enabled critics' intervention in autobiography, but it essentialized woman. The approaches to women's autobiography that we have discussed tend to be based on experiential models that are vertical and foreground certain moments in the life cycle—childhood, adolescence, marriage/career, aging (for example, Spacks's analysis of "the female imagination" in the life cycle). Such models oppose all women to all men and set up a structure of resistance and self-authorization through collective critique and political action based on assumed universal subordination.

Clearly, the analysis of Second Wave feminism, which read women's lives as inextricably embedded in patriarchy—understood as a general, ahistorical, transcultural system of social organization through which men maintained domination over women—informed the experiential model of women's autobiography. Another foundational tenet of Second Wave feminism, the egalitarian sisterhood of all women as a collectivity undifferentiated in its subordination, is also evident in early analyses of women's autobiography, where the "we" of women was asserted unproblematically.[3] That assumption would later be severely critiqued in autobiographical writings by women of color who had been rendered invisible in these accounts and who would write autobiographically to announce their differences in an irreducible plurality of voices.

Nonetheless, certain provocative questions were posed by first-stage theorists of women's autobiography: To what extent is women's autobiography characterized by the frequency of nonlinear or "oral" narrative strategies, unlike the master narratives of autobiography that seem to pose stable, coherent self-narratives? To what extent is it characterized by frequent digression, giving readers the impression of a fragmentary, shifting narrative voice, or indeed a plurality of voices in dialogue? Is the subject in women's autobiography less firmly bounded, more "fluid"? If in women's autobiography writers often authorize their texts by appeal to the authority of experience rather than by public achievement or historical significance, should this privileging of the personal and domestic be gendered female? To what extent can it be ascribed to class and cultural moment or to an alternative rhetoric of the familiar style within the essay tradition?

Second Stage—Theorizing Beyond the Experiential in Women's Autobiography

In the wake of Jelinek's 1980 collection, several influential books appeared throughout the eighties that, in offering readings of particular texts and laying the groundwork for a women's countercanon, gradually revised and expanded the conceptual terms she had laid out. By the end of the decade none of Jelinek's definitional parameters remained uncontested.[4]

Two American critics well versed in French feminism and the French literary tradition, Nancy K. Miller and Domna C. Stanton, drawing on the early work of Germaine Brée, laid important groundwork for revising gender essentialism in the light of Second Wave theories of difference. They argued, in different ways, that theorizing in women's autobiography should not simply invert the exclusionary logic of the dominant tradition, but, instead, map women's dialectical negotiations with a history of their own representation as idealized or invisible. In "Toward a Dialectics of Difference" Miller critiqued the universalization of maleness as humankind in the literary canon and called for a gendered reading of genre. Refusing the "fiction" of a degendered reading, she urged critics to "read for difference," in a "diacritical gesture," and argued for reading as "a movement of oscillation which locates difference in the negotiation between writer and reader" (56).

Domna C. Stanton's collection *The Female Autograph* (1984), which announced itself as "a 'conversation' between writers and critics across cultural and temporal boundaries," cast a wide net for women's autobiography, with essays on women autobiographers from tenth-century Heian Japan to twentieth-century Palestine. Its spirit of inclusionary breadth indicated the expansion of boundaries, historically, generically, and in media, that critics of women's autobiography were pursuing in the decade. Stanton's lead essay, " Autogynography: Is the Subject Different?" critiqued the essentialism of first-stage criticism and theorized in terms of multiple differences of the subject. Stanton rehearsed with droll rapidity dozens of denunciatory comments by male critics about women's autobiographical texts and female textuality, positioning herself like Woolf's narrator in *A Room of One's Own*, at the margin of the literary world. Stanton's "I" asked why women's lives are suppressed in literary history and proposed a new nomenclature of "autogynography" for the separate genre of women's autobiography. In mapping a textual tradition of women's life writing, Stanton tried both to circumvent gender essentialism and to resist appropriation by the dominant tradition of autobiographical theory.

One of the emerging and enduring debates in theorizing women's autobiography, as Marjanne E. Goozé pointed out, is how narrowly or broadly to construct the field of autobiographical texts. Some early essays and collections argued strongly for an inclusionary scope of "women's personal literature of the self," in Margo Culley's phrase ("Women's," 13). The Hoffmann and Culley collection, *Women's Personal Narratives* (1985), included women's letters, diaries, journals, and oral histories to expand the canon of women's writing. Culley's

title, "Women's Vernacular Literature: Teaching the Mother Tongue," announced the essay's agenda. Likewise, Hoffmann called for reading the writings of non-professional women to discover "the modes of verbal art practiced by most women who use language to give shape and meaning to their experiences" (1). These essayists asserted that the interrelational and conversational purposes of women's writing distinguish it from men's "rhetorical" purposes (Elouise Bell, 168).

An inclusionary view of women's personal writing was also emphasized in *Interpreting Women's Lives: Feminist Theory and Personal Narratives* by the Personal Narratives Group (1989). The group, including ten scholars in the literary and social sciences, gathered together essays that offered multidisciplinary perspectives—from anthropology, sociology, history, political science, as well as literary disciplines—on a wide range of women's personal narratives drawn from everyday life venues such as abortion activism and from developing as well as developed countries. Electing to speak of "narrative forms" rather than the genre of autobiography, the Group called for exploring women's narratives as sources for our understanding of gendered identity: "Women's personal narratives embody and reflect the reality of difference and complexity and stress the centrality of gender to human life . . . [they] provide immediate, diverse, and rich sources for feminist revisions of knowledge" (263). While it is beyond the scope of this Introduction to survey the ever-growing literature on women's personal narratives in the social sciences, clearly work on personal writing has become increasingly interdisciplinary. For example, the collection *Investigating Subjectivity: Research on Lived Experience*, edited by Carolyn Ellis and Michael G. Flaherty (1992), explored personal stories as a mode of incorporating the investigator's reflexivity.

Other theorists of women's autobiography

called for a primary focus on the genre of auto-biography, in order to read women's writing within, and against, the master narratives of the West. In 1986, in *The Tradition of Women's Autobiography*, Estelle C. Jelinek proposed to set forth a two-thousand-year-old tradition. But unfortunately this book, in its sparse documentation and focus on the white Euro-American tradition, demonstrated the limits of first-stage theorizing as surely as her 1980 collection had shown its strengths.

The late eighties saw a breakthrough in numerous studies of women's autobiography. Two books in particular proposed theories centered in women's textuality and the history of women's cultural production rather than simply a gendered identity. In 1987 Sidonie Smith's *A Poetics of Women's Autobiography* argued that, in an androcentric tradition, autobiographical authorization was unavailable to most women. Historically absent from both the public sphere and modes of written narrative, women were compelled to tell their stories differently, and had done so, at least since medieval autobiographer Margery Kempe (*Poetics,* 50). Smith asserted that any theory of female textuality must recognize how patriarchal culture has fictionalized "woman" and how, in response, women autobiographers had challenged the gender ideologies surrounding them in order to script their life narratives. Smith posed key questions for reading a woman's autobiography: How does she authorize her claim to writing? how does she negotiate the gendered fictions of self-representation? how is her literary authority marked by the presence or absence of her sexuality as subject of her story? Smith was particularly interested in the historical specificity of the double-voiced structure of women's narratives as it reveals the tensions between their desire for narrative authority and their concern about excessive self-exposure.

In *Autobiographical Voices: Race, Gender, Self-Portraiture* (1989), Françoise Lionnet staked out an intercultural territory of writing by women of color and proposed a theory of *métissage* to articulate how marginalized subjects voice their lives. Lionnet argued that as historically silenced subjects, women and colonized peoples create "braided" texts of many voices that speak their cultural locations dialogically. *Métissage,* viewing autobiography as a multi-voiced act, emphasized orality and the irreducible hybridity of identity. In privileging difference, plurality, and voices, Lionnet asserted that not only new subjects but new kinds of subjects were emerging, and that "traditional" autobiographies could be read differently as well.

In many ways Smith's and Lionnet's theories shared an interest in the rhetoric of women's self-presentation. Centering their investigations on histories of women's subjectivities in dialogue with one another, rather than as adjunct to a tradition of "high" literature, their books set forth frameworks to assert women's autobiography as a legitimate field of analysis and practice.

The year 1988 saw the publication of two collections that were also influential for women's autobiography. In *Life/Lines: Theorizing Women's Autobiography* Bella Brodzki and Celeste Schenck gathered essays that read First World traditions of autobiography against postcolonial forms such as the *testimonio* (Doris Sommer), and diverse sexualities in the coming out story (Biddy Martin), as well as expanding the concept of autobiographical textuality to women's films, painted self-portraits, and poetry. Insisting on a more globalized concept of women's writing that ranged from Native American to Egyptian to Québecois texts, Brodzki and Schenck theorized explicitly as well as editorially. They reasserted the *bios* that Domna Stanton had excised in her notion of "auto-gynography," and called for a revision of post-structuralist theory, to assert "the imperative situating of the female subject in spite of the postmodernist campaign against the sovereign self" (14). Urging attention to female specificity against both feminist essentialism and "pure textuality," Brodzki and Schenck argued for a kind of theorizing that allows the female reader the "emotional satisfaction" of a referential world of women's lives (14).

Another 1988 collection, *The Private Self*, edited by Shari Benstock, with essays examining a wide range of women's narrative forms, includes two influential essays that contextualized female subjectivity in very different ways. Susan Stanford Friedman, in "Women's Autobiographical Selves: Theory and Practice," focused on "relationality" in women's autobiography as an expression of the "fluid boundaries" they experience psychologically. Shari Benstock, in "Authorizing the Autobiographical," offered a Lacanian reading of women's textuality as "fissures of female discontinuity" exemplified in the writing of Virginia Woolf. (These theorizings of subjectivity are explored in part 2 of this Introduction.)

Carolyn Heilbrun's *Writing a Woman's Life* (1988) was an important milestone in women's autobiographical criticism because it called the attention of a larger public to the field. Advertised by book clubs, taught in many women's studies courses, and used as a reference by readers uneasy with more "academic" feminist theory, Heilbrun's study was both inclusionary and deliberately nontheoretical. On the other hand, in analyzing women's coming to voice for a wide female readership, she focused on women's *lives* rather than their texts; for "we are in danger of refining the theory and scholarship at the expense of the lives of women who need to experience the fruits of research" (Heilbrun, 20). Heilbrun explored the recent past when women had begun to assert power and control—"only in the last third of the twentieth century have women broken through to a realization of the narratives that have been controlling their lives" (Heilbrun, 60)—rather than previous centuries of silencing in a patriarchal literary tradition, when this realization was encoded, often obliquely, in the long and rich history of women's self-representations. *Writing a Woman's Life* is a valuable resource for examining the lives of women in the West who have written autobiography in this century, and its focus has been complimented by many theorists in this decade writing on the lives and autobiographies of women writers throughout the world.

If Heilbrun sought to find an autobiographical thread in many kinds of women's writing, Rita Felski's *Beyond Feminist Aesthetics* (1989) provided an alternative model for exploring women's personal narratives broadly in a European, notably Germanic, frame. Critiquing the gender essentialism of much feminist writing, Felski foregrounded the social contexts of a wide range of women's confessional narratives that enforce gender-based identifications and examined their discursive practices. Revisionist in intent and focused on the intersection of politics and personal narrative, Felski's book helpfully extended the text-based focus of such work in German women's autobiography as Katherine Goodman's *Dis/Closures: Women's Autobiography in Germany between 1790 and 1914* (1986) and anticipated the ambitious reading of women's autobiographical practices sketched by Barbara Kosta in *Recasting Autobiography: Women's Counterfictions in Contemporary German Literature and Film* (1994). Similarly, for French and francophone women's autobiography Leah D. Hewitt, in *Autobiographical Tightropes* (1990), mapped concerns that yoke writers of personal narrative such as Nathalie Sarraute, Monique Wittig, and Maryse Condé, who had not previously been linked as generic practitioners, and argued that "they all openly adopt dialogic patterns to sustain the figure of an interactive subject" (194).

Specifying Location—Materialist and Difference Theorists

While many theorists of women's autobiography worked primarily in generic terms, important explorations of women's writing were also grounded in analyses of specific historical periods. Notably Felicity Nussbaum's *The Autobiographical Subject* (1989) on eighteenth-century women's writing and Regenia Gagnier's *Subjectivities* (1991) on nineteenth-century British working-class writing performed close readings of neglected texts of women's writing and provided materialist analyses of culture to situate forgotten women's traditions within established periods of literary history, thereby revising the terms of subjectivity. In-depth analysis of Victorian women's autobiography by critics such as Mary Jean Corbett, in *Representing Femininity: Middle-Class Subjectivity and Victorian and Edwardian Women's Autobiography,* and Linda H. Peterson, in "Institutionalizing Women's Autobiography: Nineteenth-Century Editors and the Shaping of an Autobiographical Tradition," called attention to the multiplicity and variety of women's autobiographical writings during a period when most were supposed to be outside public life.

The important work of reclaiming African American autobiography also contributed to amplifying the canon and honing the critical lens of women's autobiography theory. Jean Fagan Yellin's revival of Harriet Jacobs' *Incidents in the Life of a Slave Girl,* long ascribed to Lydia Maria Child, and the restoration of Zora Neale Hurston's *Dust Tracks on a Road* and her other writings under the aegis of Alice Walker[5] are two cases in point; the current range and status of the field are unthinkable without these texts. Searching analyses by, among others, William L. Andrews, Joanne M. Braxton, Hazel V. Carby, Frances Smith Foster, and Nellie Y. McKay, of Jacobs', Hurston's, and other African American women's autobiographical writings, have reframed the foundations of American women's autobiography. Braxton's *Black Women Writing Autobiography: A Tradition within a Tradition* mapped interrelationships among texts that, ten years earlier, had been out of print and known to few scholars.

Similarly, for Asian American writing, the proliferating critical scholarship on Maxine Hong Kingston's *The Woman Warrior* inspired examination of narratives of immigration and theorizing of specific national identities, hybridity, and generationally distinct histories. Studies of Asian American women's writing by Shirley Geok-lin Lim, Amy Ling, and Sau-ling Cynthia Wong, among others, have insightfully explored both the reception of Hong Kingston and the renegotiation of immigrant autobiography in second-generation Asian American women's writing.

The anthologizing, dissemination, and theorizing of ethnic identity in women's autobiography continue in a productive ferment, led by such critics as Tey Diana Rebolledo and Lourdes Torres on U.S. Latina women's autobiographies, Hertha D. Sweet Wong on Native American oral narratives and autobiographies, and Anne E. Goldman on working-class writing. Many other critics have contributed as well to the study of ethnic women's autobiographies. This critical explosion has rewritten the terms of American autobiography and arguably dislodged the novel as the master narrative of American literature. We call readers' attention to the pivotal role of such critics as William L. Andrews, Henry Louis Gates, Jr., Houston Baker, Ramon Saldívar, Genaro Padilla, John Beverley, Greg Sarris, and Arnold Krupat, whose theoretical interventions in autobiographies of women of color have made major contributions to revising the canon and the methods of literary history in the Americas.

Both American literature and autobiography studies have long existed in a state of willed ignorance about Canadian writing, but in women's autobiography valuable resources now exist for textual and comparative study. *Essays on Life Writing,* the collection of essays edited by Marlene Kadar (1992), Helen Buss's *Mapping Our Selves: Canadian Women's Autobiography in English* (1993), and the special issue on Canadian autobiography edited by Shirley Neuman for *Essays on Canadian Writing* (1997) have addressed this need in recent years. Julia V. Emberley's *Thresholds of Difference* (1993) foregrounded ethnographic issues in oral histories and written narratives of indigenous Canadian women writers. These studies of Canadian women's autobiographical writing helpfully complicate notions of "American" autobiography.

While most American critics lack the linguistic skill to engage the wealth of women's autobiographical writing being produced or revived in Mexico and the countries of Latin America and the Caribbean, feminist critics of autobiography including Doris Sommer, Debra Castillo, Amy Katz Kaminsky, Cynthia Steele, and Sylvia Molloy for writing in Spanish and Portuguese, and Françoise Lionnet, Elisabeth Mudimbe Boyi, VéVé Clark for French Caribbean, as well as many other critics, attest to a vigorous and nuanced tradition that includes collective histories and *testimonios,* as well as other genres of self-reflexivity.

The number and variety of collections on women's autobiography have increased during the nineties. *American Women's Autobiography: Fea(s)ts of Memory,* edited by Margo Culley (1992), assessed four centuries of women's personal narratives and, in her extensive bibliographical essay, proposed an eclectic view of women's self-reflexive writing. The University of Wisconsin Press series on American autobiography, notably in *American Autobiography: Retrospect and Prospect,* edited by Paul John Eakin (1992), has provided overviews in wide-ranging critical essays with extensive bibliographies. In that volume, critics Blanche H. Gelfant, on autobiographies of twentieth-century public women, and Carol Holly, on women's nineteenth-century autobiographies of affiliation, identified important subgenres of women's life writing. The essays in Susan Groag Bell and Marilyn Yalom's collection, *Revealing Lives* (1990), claimed that autobiographical texts are historical lenses through which readers may seek "evocations" of human beings and the mythologizing they do as they shape their life stories. Several of the essays selected by the editors deliberately blurred the distinction between biography and autobiography in employing gender as a lens for investigating life writing as a strategic response. An extreme and suggestive case is that of Charlotte Salomon, German painter-autobiographer and Holocaust victim, discussed by Mary Lowenthal Felstiner, who subsequently published a gripping biography of the artist in 1994.

Theorizing Women's Autobiography in the Wake of Postcolonialism and Postmodernism

For many new scholarly explorations, however, postcolonialism and postmodernism have become the dual focus, as the intellectual turn toward postcolonial studies in the eighties provoked serious engagement with women's status as multiply colonized in many parts of the world. Sidonie Smith and Julia Watson in *De/Colonizing the Subject: The Politics of Gender in Women's Autobiography* (1992) and Françoise Lionnet and Ronnie Scharfman in *Post/Colonial Conditions: Exiles, Migrations, and Nomadisms* (1993, two volumes) gathered essays that mapped emergent literatures and reframed women's issues and subjectivities at diasporic sites on the Asian, African, Australian, and American continents. Along with Lionnet's *Postcolonial Representations* (1995) and Barbara Harlow's earlier *Resistance Literature* (1987), these studies proposed issues and examined practices that relate subjectivity to the material and economic conditions of women's lives, recasting the terms of theories rooted in Anglo-American autobiography. Similarly, the publication and translation of women's autobiographies on a global scale have given new impetus to international and indigenous feminist movements.

Postmodernist theorizing has also stimulated new analytical tools and generated collections, such as Kathleen Ashley, Leigh Gilmore, and Gerald Peters' *Autobiography and Postmodernism* (1994), that dedicate considerable attention to women's autobiography. Some postmodernist critics have proposed new rubrics—for example, Leigh Gilmore's "autobiographics" or Jeanne Perreault's "autography"—to subvert the hold of the term "autobiography" and renegotiate the definition of "woman" as a writing subject. Similarly, Sidonie Smith, in *Subjectivity, Identity, and the Body* (1993), explored the relationship between subjectivity and autobiographical practice by posing questions about how women, excluded from official discourse, use autobiography to "talk back," to embody subjectivity, and to inhabit and inflect a range of subjective "I's." Such critiques of women's autobiography, informed by the theoretical discourses of feminism and postmodernism, have strategically opened new doors for the articulation and analysis of women's autobiographical practices in a global framework.

Before 1980 James Olney could sum up the activity in women's autobiography thus: "As several recent bibliographical publications attest, Women's Studies courses have a sizeable autobiographical literature to draw on, but theoretical and critical writing is for the most part yet to come" ("Autobiography," 16). And come it did, with an extensive body of critical writing that would lead Paul John Eakin to state in 1995: "[T]he serious and sustained study of women's autobiography . . . is the single most important achievement of autobiography studies in the last decade" ("Relational," 7).

Part 2: Theorizing Subjectivity

The gender balance of autobiographical history cannot be corrected simply by adding more women to the list; basic suppositions about subjectivity and identity underlying autobiographical theories have to be shifted.
—Laura Marcus, *Auto/Biographical Discourses* (220)

In this section we map various theoretical approaches to women's autobiography in order to establish a context for the essays that follow. To do so, we recast the history we have just sketched and, in this part, present a set of responses by theorists of women's autobiography to major theoretical currents of the eighties that changed the terms of the field. We want to emphasize here that feminist critics do not slavishly adhere to a particular theoretical line. They actively engage, critique, and modify theoretical models even as they import certain ideas and vocabularies into their reading practices. They also change their theoretical minds, so to speak. As they reflect upon responses to their analyses or as they read the work of other theorists and critics working in the field or in related—or even unrelated—fields, they formulate new ways of approaching the texts they take up.

Theories of Difference: Ego Psychology

By the early eighties the ferment of feminist and poststructuralist critical theory had brought a range of influences to bear upon women's autobiography. Above all, the psychological or psychoanalytical category of "sexual difference" elicited reformulations of what it meant to be "woman." In the United States the work of Nancy Chodorow was influential in rethinking the early dynamics of the mother-daughter relationship and their implications for creatively reframing the discussion of women interdisciplinarily. Chodorow, a psychologist specializing in ego psychology, took existing analyses of the "basic sex differences in personality" between girls and boys and postulated that "feminine personality comes to define itself in relation and connection to other people more than masculine personality does. That is, in psychoanalytic terms, women are less individuated than men and have more flexible ego boundaries" (44). This notion of "relationality" would have long-term implications for theorizing female subjectivity in autobiography.

Chodorow pursued the differentiating process of ego development before the oedipal stage that Sigmund Freud had described as formative of the (male) autonomous individual. She argued that the mother identifies differently with her boy and girl children. Because she is "a person who is a woman and not simply the performer of a formally defined role" (47) the mother "identif[ies] anticipatorily" with her daughter and therefore confounds for the daughter the process of separation and individuation. By contrast, the boy child turns away from the mother to the father in an identification that is positional rather than personal. In that process a boy learns to define himself as "that which is not feminine or involved with women . . . by repressing whatever he takes to be feminine inside himself, and importantly, by denigrating and devaluing whatever he considers to be feminine in the outside world" (50). As the boy turns away from the mother to identify with his father, he must enforce an emotional break, a rupture in identification, and impose a scheme of difference. A girl, by contrast, comes to develop more fluid ego boundaries than a boy because she does not have to resist her early identification with the mother or undergo a rupture. Therefore she develops less of a desire to sense her difference from the mother. "Feminine identification is based not on fantasied or externally defined characteristics and negative identification," wrote Chodorow, "but on the gradual learning of a way of being familiar in everyday life, and exemplified by the person . . . with whom she has been more involved. It is

continuous with her early childhood identifications and attachments" (51). That is, rather than a firm, differentiated boundary the girl child develops a fluid interface between self and others.

For literary critics reading avidly in the burgeoning interdisciplinary field of women's studies, Chodorow's theory of difference was attractive. Eventually a critique of her theory would emerge: that she hypostasized the difference between a universal boy and a universal girl, ignoring differences within communities; that she universalized the developmental process by giving only superficial attention to cultural practices not located in the twentieth-century West; that, consequently, her call for a political solution was naive. But in the early eighties Chodorow's psychoanalytic framing of difference was persuasive for scholars trying to define perceived differences in men's and women's narratives because it offered a foundational category informed by depth psychology and language acquisition theories. Her discussion of women's developmental difference also accounted for the formation of women's social roles within patriarchy. Linking vertical (psychological) and horizontal (social) axes, Chodorow's hypothesis moved beyond observed particulars of adult experience and "roles."

Chodorow's emphasis on women's relationality informed thinking about women's difference among many early theorists. Although her argument was not specifically linked to Chodorow's work, Mary G. Mason, in "The Other Voice: Autobiographies by Women Writers," stressed that female identity is grounded in relationship and produces textual self-presentations that contrast with masculine self-representations. Mason's "set of paradigms" for women's life writing involved the postulation of an "other" toward, through, and by whom women come to write themselves, whether that other is "God," for instance, or a "husband." The work of Chodorow was also important in encouraging literary critics to shift their focus from how daughters relate to "patriarchal" fathers to how they are connected to their mothers and the larger community of women.

Susan Stanford Friedman, in "Women's Autobiographical Selves: Theory and Practice," incorporated Chodorow's hypothesis to postulate that women have more "flexible or permeable ego boundaries" (72–82, in this volume). Friedman fused her emphasis on the interconnectedness of women's interpersonal relationships with an analysis drawn from Sheila Rowbotham's politically grounded focus on the importance of female community for women's self-definition. Friedman compellingly summarized the significance of her argument for a "difference" theory of women's autobiography: "[a woman's] autobiographical self often does not oppose herself to all others, does not feel herself to exist outside of others, and still less against others, but very much with others in an interdependent existence that asserts its rhythms everywhere in the community" (79, in this volume). By invoking examples from African American and lesbian women autobiographers, Friedman expanded not only the theoretical framework of the field but also its repertoire of exemplary texts. Her essay's emphasis on women's "relationality" and community has remained pivotal for a decade.

If terms such as female relationality and fluidity promised theorists of women's autobiography a more enlightened model for exploring and revaluing women's experiential histories, some have since cautioned against privileging these characteristics as innate to women's experience rather than as culturally conditioned responses. Considering theories of maternal identification, Jessica Benjamin warns of the dangers of a "one-sided revaluing of women's position; freedom and desire might remain an unchallenged male domain, leaving us to be righteous and de-eroticized, intimate, caring, and self-sacrificing" (Benjamin, 85; quoted in Marcus, 220).

Theories of Difference:
Lacan and French Feminisms

Theoretical models based on the authority of experience assume the transparency of language. But this assumption of transparency has long been challenged by groups of theorists who, influenced by structural linguistics, problematize the relationship of the signifier to the signified and the relationship of the subject to language. In the early eighties feminist theorists began to draw upon the work of the French psychoanalyst Jacques Lacan in order to sort through the particular dynamics of the young girl's entry into language and thus of woman's relationship to the symbolic order of words. Rethinking the Freudian psychoanalytic paradigm, Lacan redirected attention to what he described as the "mirror stage," critical to the subject's entry into language.

In the mirror stage the child comes to recognize its image in the looking glass; but as it looks in the glass it sees its image as an other. On the one hand, this image as other gives back to the child the semblance of a coherent identity. On the other hand, through acknowledgment of its image, the child mis/recognizes itself as a unified subject. This moment of mis/recognition is precisely the moment when the divided subject comes into being. As Elizabeth Grosz notes in discussing Lacan, "the subject recognizes itself at the moment it loses itself in/as the other. The other is the foundation and support of its identity, as well as what destabilizes or annihilates it" ("Contemporary," 44). This "loss" is the mark of "lack"—the incomplete identification of subject and other. "That," the child says to itself, is "me"! And thus the "I" becomes split. The split in the subject inaugurated by the entrance into language generates the sense of an ever elusive grasping toward self-presence that is forever unachievable. For the split in the subject can never be sutured. Thus, Lacan proposes, the coherent, autonomous self is indeed a fictive construct, a fantasy of the fully present subject in language.

The Lacanian "subject," established under and through the entry into the symbolic realm of language (what Lacan called the Law of the Father), is a masculine subject. Claiming the phallus as the transcendental signifier, Lacan rewrote the Freudian drama of castration by assigning to the phallus the compensatory promise of dominance in the symbolic realm. For the phallus is signifier for the intervention of the father and his "laws" in the desire of the child. With the entry into language—the realm of the law, what Susan Sellers described as "the pre-established order within which the child must take up its appointed place" (46)—the subject takes up a sexed position as either male or female. In this process "woman" becomes a reified cultural Other to the phallic masculine Subject—"the fantasised object (Other) that makes it possible for man to exchange and function" (Sellers, 47). Sexual difference is foundational, implicated in the entry into language.

Lacan's theorizing of the split subject, the privileged phallus, sexual difference, the function of the capital-O Other, and the Law of the Father has had a profound impact on feminist theories of the subject. For instance, the old notion of "self" has been redefined as an illusory ego construct (a fiction, a phantasm) and displaced by the new concept of "the subject," always split, always in the process of constituting itself through its others. As a result the fundamental terms invoked in discussions of autobiography have shifted as attention has been directed to the etiology of sexual difference, the relationship of the subject to its constitutive others, and the rhetorics of the self.

Lacanian theory has been refracted by a host of subsequent theorists who in turn have influenced the reading of women's autobiographies. From France came the work of the French feminists, among them Luce Irigaray, Hélène Cixous,

and Julia Kristeva, three theorists who have responded in markedly different ways to Lacan. In her militant manifesto "Laugh of the Medusa," Hélène Cixous urged women to resist their silencing within the Law of the Father and to "steal" the language in order to write *toward* their difference, difference that has been mis/identified in the Law of the Father. This new language would be, according to Cixous, a writing of and from the body.

For Luce Irigaray, representation is always representation within the "logic of the same" precisely because the subject is constitutively masculine. If the history of metaphysics and of representation in the West has been a history of the violent mis/representation of woman in "phallogocentrism," or what she labeled metaphorically a logic of solids, then what is required is a sustained critique of the "logic of the same"—the specular logic through which "man" projects onto the surface of "woman" her "lack" and his fullness in alterity. What is also required is the creation of a language alternative to specularity through which women can articulate their difference, their desire. This nonphalllogocentric language she metaphorizes as the logic of fluids, a logic emergent from women's different sexuality. It is a sexuality transgressive of stable boundaries, unity, sameness.

Julia Kristeva, rethinking Lacan's notion of the "symbolic" realm, proposed a presymbolic realm she calls "the semiotic." For Kristeva the realm of the semiotic is the space of *jouissance,* the nonverbal effluence of subjectivity that lies outside the Law of the Father, outside logocentric thinking and practices of representation. The eruptions of the semiotic signal the eruption of the irrational, that which must be suppressed in order for the subject to imagine itself as coherent, unified, autonomous. Because the self is a fiction sustained by the very practices of representation, its fictiveness can be glimpsed in the shadows of the semiotic, in the gaps, in nonsense, in puns, in pleasurable rhythms, all of which erupt from the unconscious (or preconscious) to disrupt meaning. As a strategy for resisting the Law of the Father, Kristeva thus proposes a politics of negativity. In response to the force of identifications, the subject can resist by insisting "I am not this and I am not this." Critically, Kristeva locates the figure of the preoedipal mother in the domain of the semiotic. Hers is the powerful mother not yet diminished and denigrated by association with castration.

There have been significant critiques of psychoanalytically-based approaches to sexual difference. An unnuanced psychoanalytic logic is a universalizing, indeed essentializing logic, despite claims to the contrary, since it assumes the sexual difference of two oppositional sexes as foundational, implicated in the entry into language. For some as well, psychoanalytic logic has the effect of hypostasizing temporality because it proposes a "tragic" narrative paradigm of human psychosexual development that reinforces the impossibility of change and of communication, thus begging the question of the subject's agency.

The rereadings of Lacan (and Freud) enacted by Cixous, Irigaray, and Kristeva have had tremendous importance for the reading of women's autobiography. They provide a way to confront the entrenched hold of patriarchal structures by locating them deep within the unconscious and the subject's foundational relationship to language. They provide a way of understanding the complexity of female positioning as a split subject within the symbolic order and its logic of representation. They provide terms for understanding how the female subject mis/recognizes herself as a coherent subject. They encourage readers to look for gaps and silences in texts, to read away from coherence—in fact, to become skeptical about such previously accepted notions in autobiography theory as the linearity of narrative and a unified concept of selfhood.

They provide a vocabulary for exploring the relationship of women to language, to systems of representation, to the mother, to the body. Since the intervention of the French feminists in psychoanalytic theories, critics have discovered in women's autobiographical texts strategies for writing the subject "other"-wise. Finally, all three theorists explored, in poetic and playful engagements with theory, possibilities for alternative languages. Their appeal to writing the body and to exploring diverse writing practices has prompted others to develop alternative critical styles. In fact, we might trace the current interest in personal criticism in part to the experimental texts of Irigaray, Cixous, and Kristeva.

Thus in the eighties, several theorists of autobiography adapted the work of Lacan and the French feminist theorists even as they remained skeptical of the extremist pronouncements issuing from France regarding the erasure of the author-function in the text. In "Writing Fictions: Women's Autobiography in France," Nancy K. Miller approached the issue of women's self-writing by asking: "Who is speaking? And in whose name?" (46). In "Autogynography: Is the Subject Different?" Domna C. Stanton asked a series of sophisticated questions about the writing woman and her autobiographical practices, proposing that the splitting of woman's subjectivity must be understood in the context of her "different status in the symbolic order": "Autogynography," concluded Stanton, "dramatized the fundamental alterity and non-presence of the subject, even as it asserts itself discursively and strives toward an always impossible self-possession. This gendered narrative involved a different plotting and configuration of the split subject" (140, in this volume). In "Authorizing the Autobiographical," Shari Benstock looked to Lacan's "mirror stage" as a figure through which to trace how the definition of writing is loosened from self-consciousness toward the *un*conscious. Even as the autobiographical act gestures toward a desire for the "self" and "self-image" to "coincide," the act, especially for women who "question" the authority of the Law of the Father, leads not to the inscription of a unitary self but to the self decentered or elided by "the fissures of female discontinuity" (152, in this volume). And in "Mothers, Displacement, and Language in the Autobiographies of Nathalie Sarraute and Christa Wolf," Bella Brodzki worked to reframe a Chodorovian focus on the mother/daughter dyad through the psychoanalytic notion of displacement. For Brodzki the compelling figure haunting the texts of women autobiographers is the figure of the lost mother. The daughter's representation (already a displacement) of the past loss involves her in a complex struggle with this loss that "initiates the metonymic chain of substitute objects of desire, some more productive than others" (158, in this volume).

Subject Matters: Althusser and Foucault

For many critics, psychoanalytic claims about female subjectivity, whether made in the wake of the ego psychology of Chodorow or the split subject of Lacan, too quickly and thoroughly erased the very real imprint of history itself. For materialist historians, subjectivist psychoanalysis universalized sexual difference and ignored the very different material circumstances of people's lives over time.

Concurrently, then, throughout the eighties important work was done by scholars concerned about situating the autobiographical subject in her historical specificity. Some critics turned to the work of French political theorist Louis Althusser, whose concept of ideology attempted to infuse Marxist economic determinism with the dynamic imprint of cultural formations. Althusser understood the social subject as a subject of ideology—not ideology in the narrow sense of propaganda but ideology in a broad sense of the pervasive and inescapable cultural formations of the dominant class (what he termed "state apparati"). As a way of understanding how ideology works to conform the subject, Althusser differentiated "Repressive State Apparatuses" (RSAs) from "Ideological State Apparatuses" (ISAs). RSAs are more coercive state institutions such as the military, the police, the judicial system. ISAs are less overtly coercive institutions—social services, educational institutions, the family, and cultural formations, such as the institution of "literature" and modes of popular culture. Both RSAs and ISAs "hail" the subject who enters them, calling her to a certain subject position. In this sense she is "interpellated" as a certain kind of subject through the ideology that informs and reproduces the institution. Critically, the "individual" understands herself as "naturally" self-produced precisely because the processes of interpellation are hidden, obscured by the practices of institutions. The subject, then, is invested in and fundamentally mystified by her own production. An ideological critique of her engagement in the state apparati is required to understand her own social formation, though such a critique will not undo it.

Althusser's analysis of ideology and interpellation contributed to feminist critiques of the West's romance with the free, autonomous "individual." For the Althusserian critique understood that "individual" to be a function of ideology. Students of Althusser directed attention to the ways in which historically specific cultural institutions provide ready-made identities to subjects. "Autobiography" becomes one such literary institution in the West. It has its traditions (or history); it participates in the economics of production and circulation; and it has its effects—that is, it functions as a powerful cultural site through which the "individual" materializes. Althusser's theory of ideology and subject formation sets the stage for political readings and for the politicization of subjectivity; that is, for readings that attend to the ways in which literary genres are complicit in reproducing dominant ideologies.

Michel Foucault was also influential for feminist theorists concerned with developing a materialist praxis. Unlike Althusser, Foucault came to understand power not as monolithic or centripetally concentrated in official and unofficial institutions; rather power (with a small *p*) is culturally pervasive, centrifugally dispersed, localized. For Foucault there is no "outside" of power; power is everywhere and inescapable. And it is "discursive," that is, it is embedded in all the languages of everyday life and the knowledges produced at everyday sites. Discourses function as so many "technologies of self" through which the subject materializes. To understand the technologies of self the theorist must attend to several aspects of historical practice: the historical specificity of discourses, historically situated ways of knowing and figuring the world, historically specific regimes of truth. And "history" itself must be redefined as a "genealogical" investigation into the historical emergence of concepts about persons through which knowledge claims are produced. Genealogical inquiry thus becomes what Lee Quinby termed "desacralization," the exposure of local disruptions, contradictions, inconsistencies in the production of regimes of truth (xii–xiii).

Foucault's emphases on the discursivity of texts, on historically specific regimes of truth/knowledge, and on genealogy have had a profound impact on scholars studying women's autobiographical practices. They have used Foucauldian analyses to critique the notion of women's experience, the romance of the "authentic" woman's voice, and the recourse to transparent notions of the "truth" of autobiographical experience and the "truth teller" status of the autobiographer. In her essay "Experience," for example, Joan W. Scott challenged the foundational status of experience as a ground of analysis. She called for the historicizing of "experi-

ence" and for reading experiential categories of identity as "contextual, contested, and contingent" if we are to analyze productively how individuals think of, come to know, and represent themselves in its terms (68, in this volume). "Experience," she writes, "is at once always already an interpretation *and* is in need of interpretation" (69, in this volume).

As neither Althusser nor Foucault addressed issues of gender, however, scholars of women's autobiography have had to critique their theories even as they use them to ground their analyses. To read women's autobiographical texts is to attend to the historically and culturally specific discourses of identity through which women become speaking subjects. Scholars have explored which discursive practices determine the kind of subject who speaks, the forms of self-representation available to women at particular historical moments, the meaning they make of their experiential histories. Such readings encourage us to think about women's texts—as we do about any texts—as sites for the re/production of knowledge.

Leigh Gilmore, in *Autobiographics*, examined autobiography as a Foucauldian "technology of the self" engaged with the discourses of truth telling and lying as it has authorized some "individual" identities and reproduced gendered identity. Focusing on noncanonical women's texts of self-representation, Gilmore argued for a counter practice of "autobiographics" that would emphasize the writing of multiple, contradictory experimental identities as a means to locate the autobiographical as a "point of resistance" (184, in this volume). And Felicity A. Nussbaum's reading of eighteenth-century British autobiographical writing in the two essays excerpted in this volume ("The Ideology of Genre" and "The Politics of Subjectivity") emphasized, à la Althusser and Foucault, "the materiality of ideology" and explored "the way in which conflictual discourses are yoked together within ideology to encourage bourgeois subjects to (mis)recognize themselves" (*Autobiographical*, 10). At the scene of autobiographical writing, Nussbaum argued, conflicting concepts of identity are played out as writing subjects, among them variously marginalized women of the eighteenth century, negotiate the politics of subjectivity through generic expectations and contradictions.

In a quite different manner but one also informed by Foucault's interrogation of the confession as a technology of self, Rita Felski's "On Confession" interrogated the "sincerity" and transparency of confessional discourse, particularly recent feminist confessional discourses, to think about how autobiographies accommodate "new" or counterknowledges. For Felski, a feminist recourse to confessional narrative signals a conscious mix of the personal and the political, which are held in tension out of a "concern with the representative and intersubjective elements of women's experience" (84, in this volume). Confession thus becomes a means of creating a new feminist audience to perform the impossible—a validation of the female experience narrated in the text.

As they have invoked Foucault and Althusser with a difference, scholars of autobiography have had to tackle head-on the issue of human agency. Althusser made a space for the agency of the subject through "science," the development of an objective analysis of the effects of ideological interpellation. The earlier work of Foucault seemed to make no space for the agency of the subject; discursive subjection was total; power was all. Dissatisfied with a problematic scientific objectivity, on the one hand, or total subjection on the other, critics began to pose questions aimed at probing the agency of the subject. How can the subject come to know itself differently? Under what conditions can the subject exercise any kind of freedom, find the means to change? Scott, in a sense speaking for many feminist historians theorizing women's everyday and social history, offered a way of making space for agency by insisting that subjects, simultaneously implicated in contradictory and conflicting discursive calls, discover or glimpse spaces through which to maneuver, spaces through which to resist, spaces for change.

Questions of agency became central to discussions of women's autobiography. How does the woman autobiographer negotiate a discursive terrain—autobiography—that has been until recently a primarily masculine domain? How do discourses of identity differentiate the narrative scripts of normative masculinity and femininity? How does the narrator take up and put off contradictory discourses of identity? How does she understand herself as a subject of discursive practices? How does she come to any new knowledge about herself? What has been "repressed" in the narrative, which dis/identifications erased? By locating autobiographical subjects in a historically embedded context and probing the conditions for gaining agency, critics have reframed the discussion of women's "experience" as nonessentialized.

A thick materialist analysis offers yet another line of inquiry. In "A Feminist Revision of New Historicism to Give Fuller Readings of Women's Private Writing," Helen M. Buss turned to the reading strategies of New Historicist theory and practice, specifically "thick description," to render more complex her approach to the personal diaries of a nineteenth-century British Canadian woman, Isabel West. Revising New Historicism for a feminist project, Buss locates her diarist among conflicting ideologies and the silence at the limits of patriarchal language in a way that renovates West for new readers.

Feminist theorists attentive to the material circumstances of real women's lives also look at the production and circulation of texts, that is, at the commodification of narrative genres and the ways in which women's literary production

23

is part of economic systems of exchange. British scholars have been especially concerned with the class status of the autobiographer. For these scholars the following questions are motivating: Who is writing? Where is she positioned within the socioeconomic field? How does her class status affect the way she negotiates autobiographical discourses? Who are her readers? How do autobiographical narratives function in the context of class politics and consciousness?

Regenia Gagnier, in "The Literary Standard, Working-Class Autobiography, and Gender," discussed the importance of socioeconomic status and mobility in her analysis of gender in nineteenth-century working-class autobiographies. Many women's working-class autobiographies, Gagnier argues, employ middle-class narratives of self, with their norms of familial, romantic, and financial success, at great psychic cost to the writer. The clash of enfranchised middle-class norms and disenfranchised working-class circumstances produces "narratives of disintegrated personality" that tell a counternarrative of the cost of individualistic ideology for those positioned at its margin. Employing a class analysis to read Victorian women's autobiography, Mary Jean Corbett, in "Literary Domesticity and Women Writers' Subjectivities," explored how women autobiographers "master their anxiety about being circulated, read, and interpreted only by carefully shaping the personae they present, and more especially, by subordinating their histories of themselves to others' histories" (255, in this volume). As they do so these women writers, who achieved public celebrity through work, forge "new concepts of history and subjectivity" as emergent "in and through all individuals" rather than in the "great man." The popular idiom of memoir enabled them to position themselves as astute "observers" of the familial and social scenes even if they sometimes chafed under the contradictions of publicity.

In "Stories," by contrast, Carolyn Kay Steedman positions subjects as "classed" in a complex way that informs her materialist reading of her own and her mother's lives. The personal interpretations of the past that autobiographical stories tell are often in conflict with a culture's ideology because "class and gender, and their articulations, are the bits and pieces from which psychological selfhood is made" (244, in this volume). Locating herself and her mother in a problematic relationship to the particulars of mid-twentieth century London, she reads their lives *against* the norms of British working-class autobiography and refuses any straightforward act of historical interpretation.

We have traced separate trajectories for psychoanalytic and materialist theories of the female subject, but ever more frequently theorists have sought to bridge the gap between them. Teresa de Lauretis, for example, has made a productive intervention for theorists of women's writing practices by reading materialist and psychoanalytic critiques through one another. De Lauretis claimed that the psychoanalytic concept of the unconscious (the repressed) can be reconceptualized as a site of cultural dis/identifications (the repository of culturally unsanctioned identifications). As a result, she radically revised psychoanalytic theory, without jettisoning it, through attention to cultural and historical specificity.

Interrogating "Woman," Multiplying Differences

To historicize experience is to erode the holding power of the concept of the universal "woman" of psychoanalytic modes of analysis. But the most urgent and invested critique of universal woman came from those women of color who focused attention on the cultural productions of subjects marginalized by virtue of their race and/or ethnicity. As they established a communal tradition and proposed countertexts to the canon, women of color argued the instrumental role of autobiographical writing in giving voice to formerly silenced subjects. Thus another set of motivating questions generated new ways of approaching autobiographical texts: What alternative traditions of women's autobiographical writing are there? How is the canon of (predominantly white) women's writing disrupted and revised by a focus on texts by women of color?

Numerous scholars of women's autobiography, in the United States and throughout the world, have been engaged in exploring a range of texts and theorizing the difference of their differences. Some of those critics are included in this volume, and their work gestures toward the work of other critics as well. In "The Narrative Self: Race, Politics, and Culture in Black American Women's Autobiography," Nellie Y. McKay suggested that African American women's writing needs to be read within a historically inflected paradigm attentive to the imbrication of gender and race. In the nineteenth-century slave and spiritual narratives, McKay argued, African American women asserted models of selfhood distinct from those of both middle-class white women and African American men. In the twentieth century, however, their autobiographical practice has valued variously the experience of growing up black in a racist world, as writers both chart and resist victimization while moving beyond protest narrative to autobiographically bear witness to the costs of their psychic and political survival.

Reading Asian women's autobiographical texts in "Semiotics, Experience, and the Material Self: An Inquiry into the Subject of the Contemporary Asian Woman Writer," Shirley Geok-lin Lim pointed to the importance of multiple marginalities, of gender, ethnicity, nationality, and linguistic community, that continue to characterize the Asian woman writer's cultural status. But she mined this positionality through her engagement with her own experiential history and the cultural expectations of passivity—which she approached through Julia Kristeva's notion of the "semiotic," secured as it is in the materiality of the body.

In "Immigrant Autobiography: Some Questions of Definition and Approach," Sau-ling Cynthia Wong called for a more historicized and ethnically specific approach to reading the genre, pointing out that the norms of autobiographies of Americanization are Eurocentric. In contrast, the narratives of many Chinese immigrants emphasize pre-American experience and assign nonutopian meanings to an America in which the autobiographer is "more a guide than an adventurer." Hertha D. Sweet Wong argues, in "First-Person Plural: Identity and Community in Native American Women's Autobiography," that "relationality" and "community" signify different practices and values in Native American and feminist contexts. Wong maps an inquiry into the possible "double relationality" of Native women and proposes terms for reading their autobiographical writing as something other than a foreclosed narrative of tragic loss.

Scholars writing on Chicana and Latina women's writing address a rich autobiographical tradition that encompasses nineteenth-century histories as well as a proliferation of contemporary voices. In "The Construction of the Self in U.S. Latina Autobiographies," Lourdes Torres read Latina autobiographical writing as both revolutionary and subversive. Latina autobiographers, appropriating a new literary space in which they can assert mestiza identity and theorize a politics of language and experience, write the contradictions of their multiple identities in ways that enable other women of color to reshape the paradigms and politics of identity in narrative.

In rethinking autobiographical narratives in terms of the politics of difference, scholars have necessarily developed a critique of Western individualism and the expectation that narrative lives conform to dominant cultural models of identity. They have also challenged theories that posit a universal woman—implicitly white, bourgeois, and Western—and that presume to speak on her behalf. This challenge has been aggressively directed at white feminists who complacently assume the "white" woman as normative; but it gestures as well to the need for collective affiliation with women of many and diverse differences. In *This Bridge Called My Back,* for instance, editors Cherríe Moraga and Gloria Anzaldúa brought over fifty voices together to insist on the inextricability of multiple differences. In doing so, the writers in *Bridge* challenged the white academic feminist establishment's allegiance to a privileged sexual difference and a white Western "woman." They exposed as well the untheorized access to power of white academic feminists.

In proposing accounts and countercanons of women's autobiography, theorists of difference have explored alternative notions of subjectivity based not on the unique individual but rather on complex collective identifications. That collective identity may be an indigenous one or the kind of diasporic, "pan"-collectivity posited by such critics as Gayatri Spivak and Chandra Talpade Mohanty. Theorists of difference foreground such questions as the following: Who is speaking? How are they already spoken for through dominant cultural representations? What must they do to be heard? By focusing on such questions, theorists of difference provide the terms to articulate how dominant cultural values have been internalized by oppressed subjects. Major explorations of "difference" occur in autobiographies by North American women of color, such as *Borderlands/La Frontera* by Gloria Anzaldúa, *Loving in the War Years* by Cherríe Moraga, *Bloodlines* by Janet Campbell Hale, *Among the White Moon Faces* by Shirley Geok-lin Lim, and *The Sweeter the Juice* by Shirlee Taylor Haizlip.

These challenges by women of color to a white feminist theory of autobiography were launched as identity claims and from collective practices located outside the academy—in urban centers, among collectives and movements. Because critique is inseparable from resistance to dominant modes, new modes of writing were necessary to ground theory in experience, including reading experience. The language of *Loving in the War Years,* for instance, or of *Borderlands/La Frontera,* is language engaged with the meanings, mythologies, conflicts, and contradictions of experiential history. At work to give voice and words to personal history and to map the intersection of personal and public spheres of meaning, writers such as Moraga and Anzaldúa revise the meaning of "theorizing" about subjectivity. They make explorations of what Sidonie Smith has termed the "Autobiographical Manifesto" in her piece of the same name. Their theorizing does not announce itself as "theory," high, dry, and hermetically sealed. It is theory at the bone and in the flesh. Autobiographical manifestos issue hopeful calls for new subjects even as they look back through critical lenses at the sources of oppression and conflictual identifications.

Women writing about multicultural practices repeatedly caution against reifying any simple model of difference as adequate to explore the complexity of lived or narrative "lives." As Marianne Hirsch suggested, "Subjects are constituted and differentiated in relation to a variety of screens—class, race, gender, sexuality, age, nationality, and familiality—and they can attempt to manipulate and modify the functions of the image/screen" (120). This call to complexity in theorizing of difference multiplies these differences and raises a new issue of priority among heterogeneous differences. If differences are multiple and asymmetrical, who bears the difference? "It was a while before we came to realize that our place was the very

multiple sites of identity and emphasizing the collectivity of subjects who talk back to Western concepts of the autonomous individual, these and many other theorists of postcolonial writing make clear how postcolonial texts have intervened to reframe the terms of subjectivity.

New terms have emerged to capture the complex vectors of de/colonization and of multicultural subjectivity. A variety of adjectives designate subjects of the "in-between," such as hybrid, marginal, migratory, diasporic, multicultural, border, minoritized, mestiza, nomadic, "third space." Each term carries its own historical and theoretical valences. All name aspects of the complex conditions of subjectivity in the late-twentieth-century world. As they ponder this complexity, postcolonial critics of autobiography draw attention to narrative practices in diverse global locations, from the writing practices of indigenous Australians to the narratives of African American women identifying themselves with the black diaspora; from the stories of the First Peoples of Canada to the narrative testimony of Bessie Head in South Africa; from the intellectual autobiographies and memoirs of postcolonial intellectuals living in the West to the resistance literature of the imprisoned, the institutionalized; from the narratives of the immigrants to the New Europe to the narratives of diasporic Chinese. Each of these instances of narrative voicing calls for a careful focus upon the site of de/colonization in its historical, material, and national specificity.

Developing reading practices attentive to these migratory subjects in all their diversity has led theorists to develop new models of transnationalism and transculturation. It has also spurred incisive critiques of readings framed by Western interpretive approaches. And it has led to a shift from the term "women's autobiography" to terms such as "women's autobiographical practices," "women's personal narratives," "women's lifewriting." This shift away from the word *autobiography* marks a shift away from an uncritical Western understanding of the subject of autobiography.

Postcolonial theory remains contentious and fractured; it is not monolithic. There are critiques coming from within of the problematic basis upon which postcolonial theorists found their analyses. There are critiques of the very term "postcolonial." For the idea of time as separated into precolonial, colonial, and postcolonial periods is itself caught in a teleological framing of history that always privileges the moment of Western encounter. The critique of Western values as purely Western takes away the transformative agency of cultures as well as their active transformation of inherited Western values as those values are incorporated through indigenous traditions.

And the reification of the voice of the "authentic" indigenous subject can promote a new form of nativism, as Sara Suleri cautioned in "Woman Skin Deep: Feminism and the Postcolonial Condition." Concerned to "dismantle the iconic status of postcolonial feminism" with its recourse to identity politics, Suleri cautioned that the invocation of the "postcolonial Woman" has the effect of erasing the specific historical contexts in which subjects are forced to understand their experience. She distrusted such identity politics because of its embrace of an unproblematized experience and the "local voice" of the autobiographical "as a substitute for any theoretical agenda that can make more than a cursory connection between the condition of postcolonialism and the question of gendered race" (122, in this volume).

Françoise Lionnet argued, however, that it remains crucial for critics to analyze and represent "the subjective experience of muted groups within social structures that rarely allow them to speak as subjects and agents of knowledge," and to retain an "awareness of the multicultural, multiracial dimensions of various strands of feminism inside and outside the academy" (*Post-colonial*, 188). We include here an excerpt from Assia Djebar's *Women of Algiers in Their Apartment*, with her caution in mind. The noted Algerian novelist wrote her identity as a subject under erasure, colonized by the politics of imperialism, the practices of the harem, and the métissage of languages, in "Forbidden Gaze, Severed Sound." Speaking the silences of Algerian women's lives, she gave voice to collective "fragments of ancient murmuring" (342, in this volume) to "embody" future conversations among women.

Theories of Heteroglossia and Heterogeneity

Theorists in the late seventies and early eighties argued the difference of women's voices. Notably, Carol Gilligan's influential *In a Different Voice* distinguished a "woman's" voice from a "man's" voice in an effort to better understand the differential ethical development of girls and boys. Boys' values she describes as rule-oriented, agonistic, goal directed; girls' values as communal, contextual, relational. The effect of Gilligan's theory of different "voices" was to assign to women an ethical high ground by appeal to a standard drawn from their own experience, not derived from the "universal" experience of men. Subsequent feminist theorists, suspicious of feminist "metanarratives," pointed to the essentializing and universalizing effects of this way of understanding difference in voice (Fraser and Nicholson, 33). Gilligan's notion of a different voice for women was thus fraught with problems for theorizing women's autobiographical practices; but theorizing women's voices—without recourse to a universalizing metanarrative—continued to be an issue.

Throughout the eighties critics employing the familiar metaphors "coming to voice" and "voicing female subjectivity" looked to the resonant theoretical framework provided by Mikhail Bakhtin, who elaborated the concepts of dialog-ism and heteroglossia. Arguing that "every word is directed towards an answer," Bakhtin claimed "the internal dialogism of the word." Words, that is, are argumentative. They are also always full of play, "plung[ing]," as he says, "into the inexhaustible wealth and contradictory multiplicity" of meanings. For Bakhtin language is the medium for consciousness; thus he understands subjectivity as dialogical in that it is always implicated in "the process of social interaction." Since social groups have their languages, each member of the group becomes conscious in and through that language. But because of what he calls heteroglossia, the proliferation of languages, words, meanings that "mutually supplement one another, contradict one another and [are] interrelated dialogically" (quoted in Henderson, 344, in this volume), the subject speaks through multiple voices. The utterance of the subject is irreducibly dialogic, contestatory, heteroglossic.

According to Mae Gwendolyn Henderson, Bakhtin's theory links "psyche, language, and social interaction" (345, in this volume). The concept of heteroglossia provides a means to join theories of consciousness to theories of culture and to refocus questions of textuality. The individual's language is always language permeated by the voices of others, voices out of the sociocultural field. Dialogism supports the claim that there are always other voices in the text, that even the most monologic of texts can be read for heteroglossia and that the autobiographical subject is a subject of the play of voices.

Dialogism has been particularly illuminating for discussions of women's autobiographical voices. Thinking about heteroglossia and about the social constitution of consciousness enables theorists to get away from the naive notion of the primary text and its hidden or "latent" subtext. Heteroglossia assumes a pervasive and fundamental heterogeneity to human subjectivity. The text is multivocal because it is a site for the contestation of meaning. Numerous critics have argued for the multivoicedness of women's autobiographical texts as a crucial way to reframe issues of agency and ideological interpellation. By this tactic they avoid the paralyzing polarization of the total determination of the subject, on the one hand, or the total freedom of the subject to make meaning, on the other.

The heteroglossia of language and consciousness is not specific to women's texts as opposed to men's texts, nor is it specific to a particular genre. Thus the notion of the dialogism of the word precludes theorizing any essential or universal difference. It becomes problematic to speak of an "authentic" voice of some universal "woman." The voice of the narrator is a dialogical voice through which heterogeneous discourses of identity cross the tongue. To paraphrase Bakhtin, the word in one's mouth is always somebody else's word. Therefore the reader must be careful not to discredit certain texts as somehow "inauthentic," or in a different (read "not right") voice.

The theorizing of Lionnet and Mae Gwendolyn Henderson, in different ways, demonstrates the enabling potential of theories of heteroglossia in discussions of women's autobiography. Lionnet's concept of *métissage,* put forth in "The Politics and Aesthetics of Métissage," has been influential for reading a wide variety of women's personal narratives. This "braiding" of voices addresses such issues as the agency of postcolonial francophone and anglophone women writers mixing indigenous and colonial languages. Lionnet reframed writing as voice, privileging orality and the incorporation of extra-(Euro)literary forms in women's texts as she reflected on the "muted" cultural status of women in many traditional cultures. Similarly, Henderson, in "Speaking in Tongues: Dialogics, Dialectics, and the Black Woman Writer's Literary Tradition," emphasized "glossalalia" and the multiple voices in which black women writers enunciate a complex subjectivity that employs the discourse of the other(s) and as Other contests

dominant discourses (347, in this volume). For these critics women's "coming to voice" has taken on new theoretical potential that need not be essentializing.

Theorizing the Everyday and Cultural Studies

Everyday kinds of writing in personal venues such as the diary and the journal have long fascinated literary critics interested in women's autobiographical writing and in the relationship of texts to women's material lives. In their inclusionary and democratizing projects, these theorists of dailiness focus on differentiating the kinds of subjects who speak in letters, diaries, journals, memoirs. And they rethink issues of temporality, noting the apparent discontinuity in diurnal forms.

In her "Introduction" to *A Day at a Time,* Margo Culley attended to the critical importance of the audience, either real or implied, addressed by the diary writer. For Culley the pages of the diary become "a kind of mirror before which the diarist stands assuming this posture or that" (219, in this volume). Moreover, the ongoing effect of time in the diary means that the outcome of time is unknown by both diarist and reader, so that self-positioning is always in flux. Similarly, using the letters of eighteenth-century women to explore "Female Rhetorics," Patricia Meyer Spacks emphasized the ways in which self-revelation, assumed in the writing of personal forms, conflicts with the ideology of normative femininity as self-effacing. Thus, women letter writers develop strategies of deflection, preoccupation with others, protestations of insignificance, or identification with women as a collectivity, that enable them to engage in the self-assertion of epistolary correspondence.

Up until the 1990s, feminist critics who focused on forms of dailiness confronted criticism that these modes had a secondary or marginal status as literature. But since the end of the eighties, the methods and models of cultural studies have been brought to bear on forms of dailiness and generated theories of the everyday constructions of experience. The variety of approaches to women's inscriptions of dailiness is evident in the recent collection *Inscribing the Daily: Critical Essays on Women's Diaries,* coedited by Suzanne L. Bunkers and Cynthia A. Huff. Contributors to this collection considered the different audiences for diaries; the diary as fragments; the broadened textual boundaries of diaries into which women insert various materials; and the intertextualities of diaries by family members.

As Jerome Bruner has argued persuasively, everyday life can be understood as an ongoing narrative negotiation. Life narratives are articulated in collaborative everyday projects, such as family stories and interactions. Or, as the contributors to our collection *Getting a Life: Everyday Uses of Autobiography* suggested, people "get a life" that conforms them to particular institutions (medical, social services, the academy, etc.) and practices (such as narrating the self-help or intimate presexual or "Personals" version of one's life) in diverse social contexts. Michel de Certeau has theorized the significance of "everyday" negotiations as tactics of social groups and noted how self-signification proliferates in an era of advanced capitalism.

The projects of cultural studies are diverse; but in general they signal a move away from privileging "high" literary forms and toward the reading of all kinds of cultural production as textual. Culture is, in its broadest sense, understood as an ever-negotiated site of conflict. And so popular forms become endlessly productive venues for the social constitution of subjects and for their everyday resistances. Thus cultural studies, opening flexible spaces for the serious explorations of alternative modes of self-writing, has revitalized discussions of many kinds of women's textual practices.

The implications of cultural studies approaches for women's autobiography are only beginning to be realized. Linda Martín Alcoff and Laura Gray-Rosendale have explored the conservative and the liberatory effects of what they call "survivor discourse," a discourse emergent in popular culture venues such as television talk shows and self-help groups. Biddy Martin has pointed to the social uses and the everyday politics of coming-out narratives. Other cultural critics have become fascinated with contemporary visual practices, performance art, talk show confessions. Asking us to read all kinds of texts as autobiographical, cultural critics require us to refine our mode of reading.

Concerned with the rush to privilege women's collective "we" as an alternative to the reification of the singular individual, Anne E. Goldman, in "Autobiography, Ethnography, and History: A Model for Reading," attended to "those impulses toward self-presencing which I believe remain an essential characteristic of life writings" (288, in this volume). She looked particularly at the autobiographical writings of working-class white women and women of color in order to understand how autobiographical narrators negotiate the pressures of the "I" and the "we," how they "maneuver between autobiographical and political-cultural texts," how they pursue self-presence as they "represent" a collectivity (290, in this volume).

The autobiographical thus becomes an aspect of textuality rather than a narrowly defined generic practice about lives lived chronologically.

Personal Criticism

In 1988 Jane Tompkins issued a manifesto of sorts to literary critics and theorists in her essay entitled "Me and My Shadow"—get real and get personal. Nancy K. Miller has theorized the need for and the significance of "Getting Personal." "Personal criticism," she explained on her opening page, "entails an explicitly autobiographical performance within the act of criticism. Indeed, getting personal in criticism typically involves a deliberate move toward self-figuration, although the degree and form of self-disclosure of course vary widely" (1). Miller, who distinguished personal from autobiographical criticism, acknowledged its "internal signature" as self-authorizing while criticizing Tompkins' essay as finally turning its back on theory (2–4).

Personal criticism is widely practiced by women, in homage to the textual practices they work on but also as integral to their efforts to reframe the critical act through feminist pedagogy and praxis. It is in part a response to the sterile evacuation of the personal voice in what has by now become institutionalized as theoretical discourse. The critic who gets personal may critique the claim to universal judgment and the objectivity of any universal critical "I." Getting personal also becomes an occasion for the critic/theorist to examine her relationship to the object of study, for a white critic to examine her vexed relationship to issues of unequal power as they affect her reading of texts by women of color, for the psychoanalytic critic to turn the lens of psychoanalytic praxis upon her own critical enterprise. For some it becomes a means to theorize personal experience, or, in the words of Joan Scott, to see experience not only as an interpretation but as in need of interpretation. Thus personal criticism facilitates the reading of personal experience and theory through each other.

As a critical gesture personal criticism aims to bridge the troubling gap between academic feminists and feminist activists. It is a search for a wider audience, a broader conversation, ideally on more honest and equal terms. Thus, as Gayle Greene noted, such writing works toward "a clearer sense of responsibility to a social movement . . . to revitalize some important connections—between ourselves and our audience, our writing and its effects" (20). For some, asserting the importance of engaged writing becomes a way of assuming certain characteristics of what Antonio Gramsci called the "organic intellectual" within the academy (normally a site of critical disengagement).

One of the most productive and widely circulated practitioners of personal criticism has, of course, been bell hooks. In several volumes of autobiographical essays and in the essay in this volume, "writing autobiography," hooks made essay writing a way of both "talking back" and "talking to myself." Moving between a personal "I" and a collective "we," hooks infused cultural critique with her own responses and politics. The directness of her writing has won her a wide and enthusiastic following, but also sharp criticism, from, for example, Sara Suleri in this volume.

In redirecting attention from the object of inquiry to the critic's responses to the object, personal criticism can overwrite the subject of inquiry as the theorist's textual preoccupation becomes herself. At its worst it can resort to willful abandonment of theory for a simplistic identity politics. In a—personally narrated—dissent from personal criticism as critical practice, Linda S. Kauffman asserted: "Writing about yourself does not liberate you, it just shows how engrained the ideology of freedom through self-expression is in our thinking" ("Long," 133). But for the autobiographer, contextualizing her life narrative as personal criticism attentive to the norms of narrative self-disclosure may enable a more nuanced space for writing the self. Nancy Mairs, in *Remembering the Bone House*, insisted on an integration and eroticization of body and mind precisely in inscribing her experience of disability in the "house" of her past, of memory, to address the commonality of experience. "Our stories utter one another" (473, in this volume).

Queering the Scene, Undoing "Woman"

In 1980 Adrienne Rich's influential essay "On Compulsory Heterosexuality and Lesbian Existence" appeared, challenging the norm of heterosexuality as natural or chosen. Throughout the seventies Monique Wittig articulated her reading of the lesbian as the third sex, neither the one nor the other, in essays such as "The Straight Mind" and "The Mark of Gender" and novels including *Les Guérillères* and *The Lesbian Body*. Women in particular were called by these authors to reexamine their unreflective assumption of heterosexuality as a norm and homosexuality as perverse or diminished sexuality. Coming-out narratives proliferated, and autobiographies of sexual experimentation became more explicit, as autobiographers investigated the relationship of personal and social experience. In "Lesbian Identity and Autobiographical Difference(s)," Biddy Martin argued that lesbianism must no longer be theorized as "an identity with predictable contents." Rather it should be understood as "a position from which to speak" that "works to unsettle rather than to consolidate the boundaries around identity" (390, in this volume).

While many postcolonial autobiographers, according to Julia Watson in "Unspeakable Differences: The Politics of Gender in Lesbian and Heterosexual Women's Autobiographies," would resist placing sexuality at the center of women's affiliations, contestations around sexuality have emerged as a crucial ground for theory. Watson interrogated the unspeakable as a category "used to designate sexual differences that remain unspoken, and therefore invisible" (393, in this volume). While lesbian desire has until recently been one potent cultural unspoken, so too, suggested Watson, has heterosexual desire remained unspoken. Assumed as normative, that unspeakable desire has functioned to block intercultural affiliations among women.

If difference theorists reinterpreted sexual orientation as relational positionality rather than fixed identity marker, the nineties have brought a retheorizing of debates on sexuality. Queer studies erupted on the academic scene to shift the terms of debate from sexual difference to issues of "performativity." Theorists such as Judith Butler argued against any simplistic recourse to the essentialized differences of identity politics. In an attempt to "retain" the "explanatory force" of psychoanalysis, Butler, in the "Introduction" to *Bodies That Matter,* used the term "performativity" to capture the provisional and political nature, the "gender trouble," of identity formation. She defined performativity as the "power of discourse to produce effects through reiteration" (368, in this volume). For Butler, an "I" does not precede the social construction of gender identity; the "I" comes into being through that social construction: "The subject is produced in and as a gendered matrix of relations" (371, in this volume). Social construction is always a process of "reiterated acting" (9). Thus bodies "materialize," but the body is not "site or surface"; rather the body is *a process of materialization that stabilizes over time to produce the effect of boundary, fixity, and surface we call matter* (372, in this volume). Identity is always coming into being through reiteration and being unfixed through the "gaps and fissures" that emerge "as the constitutive instabilities in such constructions, as that which escapes or exceeds the norm" (373, in this volume).

If gender identity, and identity more generally, is a reiterative process of coming into being and simultaneously failing to cohere, then masculinity and femininity are not fixed attributes of the "self." "Woman" is effectively a style of the flesh, a materialization, that can also be dematerialized, in unconscious and conscious iterations. For queer theorists challenging the notion that there are any differences that are "natural," man, woman—the most "natural" of human categories—are styles of the body. Nor are femininity and masculinity monolithic differences, coherent and unified. There are many styles of masculinity and femininity, specific to different times, places, and sociocultural locations.

In queer theory the very materiality of the body becomes a site of social construction and conflict. Thus queer theorists challenge any recourse to the body or to the direction of desire as the ground of essential difference. Once again, we find the critique of identity politics—signified by the shift from "lesbian" identity to "queer" identity, the former rooted in a theory of essential sexual difference, the latter in a theory of the performativity of difference. Queer theory proposes a thoroughgoing rhetorical sense of self, a notion of self that has influenced theorists of subjectivity more generally. Sidonie Smith, for example, drew upon theories of performativity in her essay on "Performativity, Autobiographical Practice, Resistance" (108–15, in this volume). Thus queer theory unfixes the relationship of gender identity to sexed body, and gender performance to gender identity. Yvonne Yarbro-Bejarano has, however, cautioned that queer theory's emphasis on performative gender "does not actively factor in how racial formations shape the 'performance' of gender and sexual identity" (129), thus pointing to an ongoing debate.

Deconstructing concepts of gendered voices, gendered bodies, and gendered texts, queer theory has influenced the ways in which women's autobiographical texts are currently being read. The terms of analysis now focus on autobiographical identity as performative. Such an approach undercuts earlier theoretical investments in certain kinds of autobiographical fixities. For instance, claims based on the binary opposition of man/woman are put into question as multiple gender positions are made available. Kate Bornstein's 1995 book *Gender Outlaw: On Men, Women, and the Rest of Us* captured this resistance to any fixed style of the body. A transgendered performance artist, Bornstein intertwined a personal narrative with a journey through theories of sexual identity in order to challenge the reader to resist the notion of any essential concept of masculinity and femininity. In Bornstein's narrative the usual meanings of identity are evacuated: "My identity becomes my body which becomes my fashion which becomes my writing style. Then I perform what I've written in an effort to integrate my life, and that becomes my identity, after a fashion" (1).

Bodies and Desire

Any theorizing of the body in the West takes up the history of the polarization of thought and feeling that assigned the "natural" and "feeling" body to women and the higher capacities of reason to man, a polarization especially pronounced in Enlightenment thinking and its philosophical legacies. The materiality of bodies was erased by the Cartesian identification of being with consciousness, rationality with a disembodied self-consciousness. Man thus projects onto what Irigaray called the "flat mirror" of woman a material groundedness from which he can launch into dematerialized speculation, the transcendental space of pure thought. Thoroughly saturated with her materiality, which is a sign of her diminished humanity, woman struggles to become bodiless as well, but for different reasons.

Theorists interested in the body seek to retrieve the body from its disembodied, denatured status and to relocate it in the subject. Some, influenced by psychoanalysis, do so by tracking the play of desire across the female body. Others seek to theorize female desire outside the model of psychoanalysis. Still others analyze how the materiality of the female body has been overwritten by—but also necessarily embedded in—social practices. In doing so they look to the histories of specific women's bodies. Still others challenge the notion of any unified body by exploring the multiplicity of embodiments. Indeed, Kauffman suggested that the late twentieth century is witnessing a paradigm shift from the specular body to the body staged as spectacle, its insides and outsides exhibited for consumption ("Bad").

Thus theorists interested in women's autobiography have begun to read for the ways in which the body emerges in, disrupts, redirects narrative practices. For if economic and political realities are played out quite literally on the bodies of women, the signature of the political is erased when the reader does not attend to the body in the text. Readers can resist being complicit in the denial of desire to women or the denigration of the body of women by attending to the ways in which narrative is about desire, embodiment, and the material conditions of women's lives and "lives." But in theorizing the body, readers must discover strategies for taking back the (narrative) body in such a way as not to participate in the consignment of women to their bodies.

In this volume, Shirley Neuman's exploration of the phantasmatic male body, "Autobiography, Bodies, Manhood," insists that all, and not just women's, texts be read as sites of bodily inscription and desire. Fascinated by the erasure of the material body that characterizes so much of Western autobiography, Neuman considers "one anomalous moment in which a masculine body ruptures and exceeds the discursive effacement of the corporeal which is characteristic of autobiography" (416, in this volume). Reading the body as simultaneously a material and cultural site on which the nonalignment of biological sex and gender is played out, Neuman looks at the autobiographical writings of Herculine Barbin, the nineteenth-century hermaphrodite about which so much has been written. She does so to tease out in that "rare autobiography which represents the body" the degree to which the narrating subject reproduces normative cultural meanings of sexed bodies and the degree to which s/he resists such cultural inscriptions

(416, in this volume). And in "Mystical Bodies and the Dialogics of Vision," Laurie Finke historicizes medieval mystical bodies to provide a framework for reading how women writers negotiate their constrained and devalued bodily status as they rewrite mystical experience to give themselves agency as visionaries.

Practical Theorizing

In this section we have been tracing the interplay between major theoretical interventions of the last two decades and theories of women's autobiography. But in fact women writing the autobiographical have always engaged in theorizing identity. This interplay between theory and autobiographical writing has intensified in recent years as women offer versions of theory in practice.

Feminist writers have used autobiographical forms, for example, to show how the personal is political. Adrienne Rich has mined the possibilities of poetry, the personal essay, and analysis in her explorations of lesbian identity and women's culture. Audre Lorde extended the mix of autobiography and critique toward the new form of "biomythography" to carve out a writing space expansive enough for her house of difference. Cherríe Moraga and Gloria Anzaldúa combined poetry and essay, Spanish and English, to probe and reimagine the cultural meanings of collective mythologies and the personal politics of border subjects. Related anthologies of women's writing, such as Anzaldúa and Moraga's *Making Face, Making Soul/Haciendo Caras,* reasserted the interweaving of personal narrative and the theorizing of difference. Other subjects of American multiculture, such as Maxine Hong Kingston, Janet Campbell Hale, and Meena Alexander, have written in quest of their voices within the vexed legacies of multiple cultural traditions. Shuttling the "black Atlantic," Michelle Cliff turned her experiential history as a subject of post/colonial education into the autobiographical novels *No Telephone to Heaven* and *Abeng*. Carolyn Kay Steedman, in her "genealogical" *Landscape for a Good Woman*, combined autobiographical remembering, biographical case study, and theoretical essay in order to retheorize the working-class subjectivity of her good-enough mother. In Portugal the three Marias engaged in a collaborative narrative of coming of age in a society that represses feminine assertion and denies women's voices. In Germany Christa Wolf repeatedly investigated her childhood as a site for exploring the collective German history of National Socialism and resisting arbitrary assignments of guilt based on political identification. Monique Wittig and Nathalie Sarraute in France, Oriana Falacci in Italy, Elena Poniatowska in Mexico, Bessie Head in Botswana, Nigerian-born Buchi Emecheta in London, Algerian-born Assia Djebar in France have all employed a blend of analytical critique and personal disclosure in shaping feminist voices that resist any easy ideological position. Authorizing their political critiques of women's subjection by appeal to personal experience, they show the resilience and persuasiveness of autobiographical writing as cultural critique.

Women's autobiography has also become a collection of generic possibilities. A wide and growing range of narrative projects have generated new or hybrid forms for addressing diverse audiences—forms such as pathography, collective histories, collaborative life writing projects, testimonial and witnessing, manifesto, bilingual projects, survival narratives, performance art, ethnography, scriptotherapy, and legal testimony. In "Autography/Transformation/Asymmetry," for instance, Jeanne Perreault, mining the possibilities of hybrid writing practices, coined the term "autography" to call attention to the writing of the feminist self as an ongoing negotiation of the shifting boundaries of the "I" and the "we" of feminist collectivity. Through the negotiation of "I" and "we," the autogra-

pher resists "monadic" subjectivity to engage "in a (community of) discourse of which she is both product and producer" (194, in this volume). These autobiographical occasions generate new reading practices, practices that refuse any simplistic notion of autobiography as a master narrative of the bourgeois subject. It is not surprising, then, that much of the energy devoted to theorizing subjectivity has come out of the practitioners and the readers who engage women's autobiographical texts.

In summary, we suggest that the real legacy of the last twenty years in women's autobiographical theorizing has been the emergence of a heterogeneous welter of conflicting positions about subjectivity and the autobiographical. To the degree that autobiography studies is a contested field, it offers an enabling history through which students can gain confidence and flexibility as readers and can honor the richness of women's autobiographical practices.

Part 3: Prospects for Theorizing Women's Autobiography

Theorists of women's autobiography have occupied a special place in calling for new autobiographical practices and critiques adequate to the texts of women's lives while exposing the blind spots, aporias, complicities, and exclusions in dominant theorizing of the subject. This collection examines the alternatives proposed by theorists of women's autobiography. But the range of possibilities has by no means been exhausted. We foresee many options for scholars interested in autobiographical studies and in theories of women's autobiography to pursue—and our list is only partial.

Relationality, across genders and genres, deserves further exploration. The notion of "fluid boundaries" claimed in early theorizing by Friedman and Mason as characteristic of women's autobiography, in distinction to all others, and typical of all women's autobiography—across ethnicity, class, sexuality, age, historical periods—has been challenged by Hertha Wong, Nancy K. Miller, and Paul John Eakin, among others, in their inquiries about how *all* autobiography may be relational. What links exist between self-narrating and representation of an autobiography's others? How, and in what terms, should relationality be redirected and reappropriated for feminist theory? How else might gendered aspects of women's subjectivity be described?

Autobiographical ethics includes a host of issues about how and what subjects and audiences know of each other, and how they comport themselves. The ethics of self- and family revelation within the autobiography, the positioning of audiences during and after the subject's lifetime, the subject's relation to biographical accounts and extratextual evidence are areas that deserve further scrutiny. What would a feminist ethics of autobiography look like? As Doris Sommer suggested in a recent essay on Elena Poniatowska and the testimonial novel, the relationship between (woman) informant and (woman) narrator, like that between writer and reader, may be neither symmetrical nor unmanipulated. Indeed an informant may resist being "consumed" by an interlocutor's mediation. A writer attentive to issues of difference can acknowledge ethical problems in conversations of social unequals, can write so as to resist the "complicity between narrator and reader," acknowledging the social inequities of lives and the privilege of her own authority as author ("Taking," 914).

Narratology, or the telling of a life as a semiotic encoding and a transaction between writer and readers, has as yet been insufficiently theorized in women's autobiography. Perhaps this is due in part to the current interest in voice and the body, or the cachet of psychoanalytic and Foucauldian readings. Moreover, issues of performativity now obscure issues of narratology. But we might think more carefully about the textual features that distinguish autobiography from the novel or other forms of nonfiction, especially in light of the tendency of people to use "novel" and "autobiography" interchangeably when they discuss personal narratives. What does it mean for readers to blur the distinction, to read novelistically? The work of Philippe Lejeune on the autobiographical pact can be helpful here; but we would have to consider how Lejeune's concept of the pact might need to be modified in feminist practices.

The relationship of national identity formation and autobiographical narrative deserves sustained examination. As Benedict Anderson aptly noted, nations are "imagined communities." Communities of people create and sustain narratives about the bases for their existence as distinct collectivities, and autobiography, at least in the West, has functioned as a potent vehicle for such narratives. For theorists of multiculture and of postcoloniality, including several in this volume, "national" identity is a deeply problematic category of meaning because national myths are founded upon the discourses of the "other," the "alien." This logic of alterity becomes the means through which national borders are established, policed, and breached. The gendered aspects of this logic are everywhere in evidence in debates about the nation and national identity. Readings of women's autobiographical texts need to attend to the complex ways in which narrators engage myths of national identity and represent themselves as national and/or unnational subjects.

The building of archives and documentary collections needs to continue. The archive of women's autobiographical history already recovered in the last few decades has transformed the field, establishing a rich legacy. Expanding the archive by incorporating works formerly regarded as "merely personal" and extraliterary will make available to scholars and students a broader range of texts—including diaries, letters, journals, memoirs, travel narratives, meditations, cookbooks, family histories, spiritual records, collages, art books, and others.

Memory, the project for the millennium, has now come to preoccupy scholars from all areas of the academy—from philosophers to neuroscientists, from cultural critics to psychologists, from quantum theorists to poets. Increasingly, scholars are studying the making and unmaking of memory—personal, collective, biochemical. Since autobiography unfolds in the folds of memory, there are projects to be found in probing the limits of remembering, the politics of remembering, the communal effects of remembering, and the ways in which remembering confuses our expectations of linearity and spatiality, of poetics and thematics in narrative. Moreover, commitment to the imperatives of testimony, as Shoshana Felman argued in her work on testimony, requires us, as teachers and scholars, to develop radical pedagogies that can facilitate encounters between readers and the texts of unspeakable horror.

In the nineties the project of recovering and validating memories of sexual abuse and psychic trauma through writing, which has authorized much women's autobiographical narrative, is being vigorously debated on several fronts. Feminist therapist and theorist Janice Haaken, in "The Recovery of Memory, Fantasy, and Desire: Feminist Approaches to Sexual Abuse and Psychic Trauma," offered a critique of the stakes involved in debates on recovered memory and considered the implications of theories of memory for reading women's narratives of victimization and survival (352–61, in this volume). Her project is directed at the "recovery" of conflictual discourses and fantasies in women's stories.

Theorizing travel turns our attention to issues of mobility, location, and zones of transit.

We might argue that all theory is in transit, or that all subjects are in transit, shifting from one identity to another. This is to say that mobility is the condition for the stabilities of identification. To approach autobiographical texts with this focus on travel and mobility stimulates a provocative set of questions. What is subjectivity in transit? How do different kinds of mobility affect self-representational practices—the mobility of forced displacement, for example, or of emigration, immigration, exile? What are the personal and political costs to the autobiographer of homesteading and of homelessness? How do autobiographical subjects negotiate strangeness— whether the strangeness of language, behaviors, cultures, histories, gender differentiation, sexualities? And how does interest in mobility stimulate attention to borders—between places, spaces, identities, destinies—and to the crossings and recrossings of those borders?

Spatiality, rather than temporality, as a focus of critical reading practices has been proposed by Susan Stanford Friedman as particularly appropriate to women's texts. "Spatialization emphasizes the psychodynamic, interactive, and situational nature of narrative processes; it also provides a fluid, relational approach that connects text and context, writer and reader" ("Spatialization," 82). For Friedman, drawing on Kristeva's notion of a text as an "'intersection of textual surfaces,'" spatialized readings allow readers to construct a "story" of the interactive play between narrative surface and a text's palimpsestic depths (83). Bringing a spatialized reading strategy to analyses of women's autobiography, which have usually emphasized temporal succession, may bring new attention to their texture and new interpretations of apparent incoherences.

Interdisciplinary studies of personal narratives that draw analytical frameworks from sociology, history, psychology, anthropology, religion, medicine, and many other disciplines will produce more nuanced readings of autobiographical texts. The separate studies of first-person narratives that have gone on within fields such as ethnography, oral history, communications, and performance studies offer revolutionary possibilities for recontextualizing autobiographical writing in specific contexts.

Theorizing a new episteme implicated in the technological revolution will reform concepts of the subject and of narrative practices, as Donna Haraway's "A Manifesto for Cyborgs" has suggested. Cyborg identity, embodying both nature and "other," belongs neither wholly to nature nor to culture and subverts all certainties (Balsamo, 33). The mode of production of modernity elicited "identities as autonomous and (instrumentally) rational"; but new communications technologies form subjects as "unstable, multiple, and diffuse," with a revolutionary fluidity of identity (Poster, 87). What has been called the "explosion of narrativity" in cyberspace calls for new theories of the relationship between human and machines. As we are drawn further into technology, we may find ourselves revising our notions of the autobiographical subject and of narrativity itself (Poster, 91, 93–94).

The therapeutics of writing autobiography has engaged feminist critics and calls for further theorizing. Writing and reading autobiography have long been regarded by psychoanalytic practitioners as instruments of healing, in the ongoing search to find and recognize one's story. Similarly, pathography, the writing of illness narratives as both "cure" and consolation, has created a body of literature that is only beginning to be read by such critics as Anne Hunsaker Hawkins, Mary Elene Wood, Suzette Henke, and Marilyn Chandler.

New modes of women's self-representation invite revision of models of women's subjectivity. For example, to read Generation X writer Elizabeth Wurtzel's *Prozac Nation*, we need to attend to the modulation of consciousness by psychotropic drugs. In the case of the oral collaborative narratives of *taasu* among nonliterate Wolof West African village women discussed by Lisa McNee, the autobiographical involves neither the solitary individual, writing, nor a "life" in the usual Western sense. This proliferation of autobiographical genres is not simply additive, for forms such as these confuse how we have understood the terms "woman" and "autobiography."

Part 4: The Future of Women's Autobiography

At this historical moment little can be asserted about women's autobiography without qualification. Whether to read the "women" in women's autobiography as referring to writers, subjects, readers, communities, performances, or other entities and processes is under debate. Indeed, as Jeanne Perreault suggested, an alternate concept such as "autography" may be desirable to designate a kind of life writing practiced by women that continually calls its own boundaries and activity into question. Virtually every critic of women's autobiography has challenged or modified its perceived definitional parameters to fit an evolving feminist sense of subjects in process.

Given the directions that much recent feminist and postfeminist theorizing has taken, the subject of study here, women's autobiography, may itself have become suspect. All of the features once claimed as hallmarks of women's autobiography—nonlinear narrative, fragmented textuality, relationality, the authority of experience—have been challenged as gender essentialism, from within feminist theory, as the essays in this volume suggest, and from outside it. For example, Nancy K. Miller suggested that the model of identity through alterity associated with women's autobiography by some early theorists operates in the autobiographical performances of some recent male authors as well. She asked if "we might not more usefully *expand* the vision of the autobiographical self as connected to a significant other and bound to a community rather than restrict it through mutually exclusive models". . . . "When we return to male-authored texts in the light of patterns found in female-authored texts—reading *for* connection, for the relation to the other—we may want to revise the canonical views of male autobiographical identity altogether" ("Representing," 4, 5). That is, to what extent and in what ways does the category of women's autobiography continue to be a useful generic descriptor for women's autobiographical texts and for the *experience* of reading them? Reading other autobiographical texts? As certain postfeminists also argue, isn't it time to move beyond this preoccupation with woman, women, and women's "this" or "that"? And hasn't the continuing proliferation of theoretical accounts of "difference" undermined any solid ground for focusing separately on women's texts?

While we recognize the need to continually critique cultural constructions of "woman" and of "difference," we also recognize the utility and the importance of continuing to focus on the cultural production of women. As Denise Riley advised, we have to act as if "women" exist even as we continue to resist the fixedness of particular forms of "woman" and "femininity" (Riley, 112). Or, as Friedman pointed out in a recent essay, the new geography of identity insists that we think about women writers in relation to a fluid matrix instead of a fixed binary of male/female or masculine/feminine ("Beyond," 13). A more flexible critical practice will not regard gender difference as a priori and immutable. It will "guard against using male writers or masculinity as fixed foils, as categorical Others whose static nature allows for the identification of female diversity and difference" ("Beyond," 22).

Rather, feminist criticism needs to consider how gender intersects with other components that comprise identity. Such a focus permits us to locate ourselves even as the theoretical grounds underneath us continue to shift. There is much to be gained by opening up the questions raised in these essays to all texts. As we pursue a feminist theory of women's autobiographical practices, we might simultaneously pursue a critique of autobiographical practice generally. We hope that this collection offers a set of ideas for engaging in such projects.

Part 5: The Contributors and the Project

We are two feminist critics who have worked in autobiography studies for over twenty years and have ourselves moved through successive inquiries and reassessments of several positions that we trace here. We came to the subject at about the same time that the subject came to the academy. Sidonie's early work, coming out of the social movements of the late sixties, focused on African American autobiography, its traditions, its politics, and its narrative poetics. It had gone unremarked by her dissertation advisor and by herself that her dissertation on African American autobiography included no discussion of women's texts. That would come later. In the mid-seventies growing political and intellectual preoccupations motivated her shift to concerted engagement with women's autobiographical narratives, as part of the process of revisioning literary studies and theorizing women's practices. Julia's early work was in exploring and theorizing Renaissance self-writing (Montaigne's *Essays*) at a time when her mentors focused on neither women's writing nor autobiography. In the early eighties she realized that there was a common thread among her interests in the self, feminist theory, and women's writing, and that it focused on the emerging field of women's autobiography. She began to teach, lecture, and write on autobiography in both women's writing and the Western tradition generally. As the field has grown and changed in the nineties each of us has redefined her interests more globally and interdisciplinarily.

Clearly we were formed by and in the world of the academy in the United States, and much of the work cited here has come out of that world. This collection, however, aims to draw upon disparate sources and include essays theorizing self-representational texts from diverse global locations, from the *testimonio* of Rigoberta Menchú to Shirley Geok-lin Lim's experience of growing up in colonial Malaysia. The essays are organized as conversations on shared topics from diverse perspectives. For example, the essays of Mason, Suleri, Lionnet, and Henderson probe different aspects and registers of voice. The relationship between the unconscious and language is framed variously in essays by Stanton, Brodzki, and Benstock. The material specificity of the autobiographical subject emerges in quite different contexts in essays by Gagnier, Steedman, and Nussbaum. Readers may want to use a different organizational rubric for grouping the essays, for instance, their dates of publication or their topic areas or the kinds of autobiographical texts they foreground.

All but one of the essays in this volume (Hertha D. Wong's) have been previously published. We were reluctant to use excerpted rather than full versions of most essays and chapters, but pragmatic considerations dictated this choice. Had we printed essays in their entirety, we would have been more restricted in the number of essays we could include. Our dilemma was, how to compile a collection that demonstrates the lucidity and complexity of critical analysis of women's autobiography and includes a sufficient number of essays to indicate the range and scope of those critiques? We opted for a wide variety of approaches and a relatively large number of theorists in a book that would be attractive—and affordable—for classroom use. Essays have been edited to preserve the integrity of their theoretical arguments. We hope that readers will pursue other work by those theorists they find particularly helpful in their development of reading strategies. And we hope that our bibliography will stimulate teachers and readers to acquire, read, and learn from the prodigious and productive scholarship in theorizing women's autobiography.

Like paintings in a museum exhibit or patches on a quilt, putting together diverse perspectives on the same topic brings all of them into sharper focus. If new understandings are achieved by this mixture of essays and categories and new discussion provoked, our goal will have been accomplished.

Notes

1. See "Autobiography and the Cultural Moment" by James Olney for a more complete history of autobiography studies prior to 1980.

2. It is worth noting that early literary critic Anna Robeson Burr, unlike her male compatriots, took women's autobiography seriously and listed numerous works by women in her bibliography; but she did not attend to issues of gender.

3. Although the first efforts to theorize women's autobiography occurred in the seventies and early eighties, they should not be confused with First Wave feminism, which usually refers to movements for women's suffrage between 1890 and 1920. Second Wave feminism dates from the early 1970s. In *The Dictionary of Feminist Theory* Maggie Humm notes such hallmarks of the Second Wave as the slogan "The personal is political," the celebration of a women-centered perspective, and declarations of a feminist movement aimed at radical transformation of patriarchy and the creation of a feminized world (198). For an introduction to and readings in Second Wave feminist analyses, see Linda Nicholson, ed., *The Second Wave: A Reader in Feminist Theories.*

4. For a helpful discussion of ten major books on theorizing women's autobiography between 1980 and 1990, see Marjanne E. Goozé, "The Definitions of Self and Form in Feminist Autobiography Theory." The texts Goozé explores are discussed here, along with some she overlooks (Felski, Nussbaum, Hewitt). Goozé argues that these eighties critiques share a concern with the interrelation of self and form in women's writing (414). She reads women's autobiography theory as theorizing the female subject between French and American feminisms and between two male traditions, the humanist view of autonomous unified selves, and the postmodern view of de-centered, split selves. Goozé's reservation about theorizing of women's autobiography in the eighties, namely that much of it equates "the de-centered self of postmodernism" with "a woman's self which defines itself in terms of interconnectedness to others and mutual interdependence," is a provocative one for theorists (425). Our discussion is indebted to Goozé's careful readings and helpful distinctions among theorists as we incorporate her observations and carry them forward to critiques in the nineties.

5. Novelist and critic Alice Walker was also an important force in the recognition of multiple women's textualities. In *In Our Mothers' Gardens* she distinguished herself from white feminists as a "womanist" who, in autobiographical essays such as "When the Other Dancer Is the Self," asserted the inextricability of her experience of political marginalization and personhood.

Works Cited

Addis, Patricia K. *Through a Woman's 'I': An Annotated Bibliography of American Women's Autobiographical Writings, 1946–1976.* Metuchen, NJ: Scarecrow, 1983.

Alcoff, Linda Martín, and Laura Gray-Rosendale. "Survivor Discourse." In *Getting a Life: Everyday Uses of Autobiography,* ed. Sidonie Smith and Julia Watson. Minneapolis: University of Minnesota Press, 1996. 198–225.

Allen, Paula Gunn. *Sacred Hoop: Recovering the Feminine in American Indian Traditions.* Boston: Beacon Press, 1986.

Althusser, Louis. *Essays on Ideology.* London: Verso, 1984.

Anderson, Benedict. *Imagined Communities: Reflections on the Origin and Spread of Nationalism.* London: Verso, 1983.

Andrews, William L. *To Tell a Free Story: The First Century of Afro-American Autobiography, 1760–1865.* Urbana: University of Illinois Press, 1986.

Anzaldúa, Gloria, and Cherríe Moraga, eds. *Making Face, Making Soul/Haciendo Caras: Creative and Critical Perspectives by Women of Color.* San Francisco: Aunt Lute Foundation Books, 1990.

Ashley, Kathleen, Leigh Gilmore, and Gerald Peters, eds. *Autobiography and Postmodernism.* Amherst: University of Massachusetts Press, 1994.

Baker, Houston A., Jr. *Workings of the Spirit: The Poetics of Afro-American Women's Writing.* Chicago: University of Chicago Press, 1991.

Bakhtin, M. M. *The Dialogic Imagination: Four Essays.* Austin: University of Texas Press, 1981.

Balsamo, Anne. *Technologies of the Gendered Body: Reading Cyborg Women.* Durham: Duke University Press, 1995.

Bell, Elouise. "Telling One's Story: Women's Journals Then and Now." In *Women's Personal Narratives: Essays in Criticism and Pedagogy,* ed. Leonore Hoffmann and Margo Culley. New York: Modern Language Association, 1985. 167–76.

Bell, Susan Groag, and Marilyn Yalom, eds. *Revealing Lives: Autobiography, Biography, and Gender.* Albany: State University of New York Press, 1990.

Benjamin, Jessica. "A Desire of One's Own: Psychoanalytic Feminism and Intersubjective Space." In *Feminist Studies/Critical Studies,* ed. Teresa de Lauretis. London: Macmillan, 1988.

Bennett, Paula. "Lesbian Poetry in the United States, 1890–1990: A Brief Overview." In *Professions of Desire: Lesbian and Gay Studies in Literature,* ed. George E. Haggerty and Bonnie Zimmerman. New York: Modern Language Association, 1995. 98–112.

Benstock, Shari. "Authorizing the Autobiographical." In *The Private Self: Theory and Practice of Women's Autobiographical Writings,* ed. Benstock. Chapel Hill: University of North Carolina Press, 1988. 10–33. Excerpted in this volume.

Benstock, Shari. *The Private Self: Theory and Practice of Women's Autobiographical Writings,* Chapel Hill: University of North Carolina Press, 1988.

Beverley, John. *Against Literature.* Minneapolis: University of Minneapolis Press, 1993.

Blodgett, Harriet. *Capacious Hold-All: An Anthology of Englishwomen's Diary Writings.* Charlottesville: University Press of Virginia, 1991.

Blodgett, Harriet. *Centuries of Female Days: English-women's Private Diaries.* New Brunswick, NJ: Rutgers University Press, 1988.

Bloom, Lynn Z. "Promises Fulfilled: Positive Images of Women in Twentieth-Century Autobiography." In *Feminist Criticism: Essays on Theory, Poetry, and Prose,* ed. Cheryl Brown and Karen Olson. Metuchen, NJ: Scarecrow Press, 1978. 324–38.

Bornstein, Kate. *Gender Outlaw: On Men, Women, and the Rest of Us.* New York: Routledge, 1994.

Boyce Davies, Carole. *Black Women, Writing and Identity.* London and New York: Routledge, 1994.

Braxton, Joanne. *Black Women Writing Autobiography: A Tradition within a Tradition.* Philadelphia: Temple University Press, 1989.

Breé, Germaine. "George Sand: The Fictions of Autobiography." *Nineteenth-Century French Studies* 4 (1976): 438–49.

Brinker-Gabler, Gisela, and Sidonie Smith, eds. *Writing New Identities: Gender, Nation, and Immigration in Contemporary Europe.* Minneapolis: University of Minnesota Press, 1996.

Briscoe, Mary Louise, Lynn Z. Bloom, and Barbara Tobias. *American Autobiography, 1945–1980: A Bibliography.* Madison: University of Wisconsin Press, 1982.

Brodzki, Bella. "Mothers, Displacement, and Language in the Autobiographies of Nathalie Sarraute and Christa Wolf." In *Life/Lines: Theorizing Women's Autobiography,* ed. Bella Brodzki and Celeste Schenck. Ithaca: Cornell University Press, 1988. 243–59. Excerpted in this volume.

Brodzki, Bella and Celeste Schenck, eds. *Life/Lines: Theorizing Women's Autobiography,* Ithaca: Cornell University Press, 1988.

Bruner, Jerome. "Life as Narrative." *Social Research* 54 (1987): 11–32.

Bruss, Elizabeth W. *Autobiographical Acts: The Changing Situation of a Literary Genre.* Baltimore: Johns Hopkins University Press, 1976.

Bunkers, Suzanne L., and Cynthia A. Huff, eds. *Inscribing the Daily: Critical Essays on Women's Diaries.* Amherst: University of Massachusetts Press, 1996.

Burr, Anna Robeson Brown. *The Autobiography, A Critical and Comparative Study.* Boston: Houghton Mifflin, 1909.

Buss, Helen M. "A Feminist Revision of New Historicism to Given Fuller Readings of Women's Private Writing." In *Inscribing the Daily: Critical Essays on Women's Diaries,* ed. Suzanne L. Bunkers and Cynthia A. Huff. Amherst: University of Massachusetts Press, 1996. 86–103. Excerpted in this volume.

Buss, Helen M. *Mapping Ourselves: Canadian Women's Autobiography in English.* Montreal and Kingston: McGill-Queen's University Press, 1993.

Butler, Judith. *Bodies That Matter.* New York: Routledge, 1993. Excerpted in this volume.

Butler, Judith. *Gender Trouble: Feminism and the Subversion of Identity.* New York: Routledge, 1990.

Carby, Hazel V. *Reconstructing Womanhood: The Emergence of the Afro-American Woman Novelist.* New York: Oxford University Press, 1987.

Castillo, Debra A. *Talking Back: Toward a Latin American Feminist Literary Criticism.* Ithaca: Cornell University Press, 1992.

Castro-Klarén, Sara and Beatriz Sarlo, eds. *Women's Writing in Latin America: An Anthology.* Boulder: Westview Press, 1991.

Césaire, Aimé, *Discourse on Colonialism.* Trans. Joan Pinkham. New York: MR, 1972.

Chandler, Marilyn R. *Dwelling in the Text: Houses in American Fiction.* Berkeley: University of California Press, 1991.

Cheung, King-kok. *Articulate Silences: Hisaye Yamamoto, Maxine Hong Kingston, Joy Kogawa.* Ithaca: Cornell University Press, 1993.

Cheung, King-kok. *Asian American Literature: An Annotated Bibliography.* New York: Modern Language Association of America, 1988.

Chodorow, Nancy. *The Reproduction of Mothering: Psychoanalysis and the Sociology of Gender.* Berkeley: University of California Press, 1978.

Christian, Barbara. "Being the Subject and the Object: Reading African-American Women's Novels." In *Changing Subjects: The Making of Feminist Literary Criticism,* ed. Gayle Greene and Coppelia Kahn. New York: Routledge, 1993. 195–200.

Cixous, Hélène. "The Laugh of the Medusa." In *New French Feminisms,* ed. Elaine Marks and Isabelle De Courtivron. New York: Schocken Books, 1981. 245–64.

Corbett, Mary Jean. "Literary Domesticity and Women Writers' Subjectivities." In *Representing Femininity: Middle-Class Subjectivity and Victorian and Edwardian Women's Autobiography.* New York: Oxford University Press, 1992. Excerpted in this volume.

Cott, Nancy. *The Bonds of Womanhood: "Woman's Sphere" in New England, 1780–1835.* New Haven: Yale University Press, 1977.

Culley, Margo. "Women's Vernacular Literature: Teaching the Mother Tongue." In *Women's Personal Narratives: Essays in Criticism and Pedagogy,* ed. Leonore Hoffmann and Margo Culley. New York: Modern Language Association, 1985.

Culley, Margo. *American Women's Autobiography: Fea[s]ts of Memory.* Madison: University of Wisconsin Press, 1992.

Culley, Margo, ed. *A Day at a Time: The Diary Literature of American Women from 1764 to the Present.* New York: Feminist Press, 1985. Excerpted in this volume.

Davidson, Cathy N., and Linda Wagner-Martin, eds. *The Oxford Companion to Women's Writing in the United States.* New York: Oxford University Press, 1995.

De Certeau, Michel. *The Practice of Everyday Life.* Trans. Steven Rendall. Berkeley: University of California Press, 1984.

De Lauretis, Teresa. "Eccentric Subjects: Feminist Theory and Historical Consciousness." *Feminist Studies* 16, no. 1 (1990): 115–50.

Djebar, Assia. "Forbidden Gaze, Severed Sound." *Women of Algiers in Their Apartment.* Trans. Marjolijn de Jager. Charlottesville: University of Virginia Press, 1992. 133–54.

Douglas, Ann. *The Femininization of American Culture.* New York: Knopf, 1977.

Eakin, Paul John. *American Autobiography: Retrospect and Prospect.* Madison: University of Wisconsin Press, 1992.

Eakin, Paul John. "Relational Selves, Relational Lives: The Story of a Story." In *True Relations: Essays on Autobiography and the Postmodern,* ed. G. Thomas Couser and Joseph Fichtelberg. Westport, CT: Greenwood Press, 1998. 63–81.

Ellis, Carolyn, and Michael G. Flaherty, eds. *Investigating Subjectivity: Research on Lived Experience.* Newbury Park, CA: SAGE Publications, 1992.

Ellmann, Mary. *Thinking about Women.* New York: Harcourt, Brace & World, 1968.

Emberley, Julia V. *Thresholds of Difference: Feminist Critique, Native Women's Writings, Postcolonial Theory.* Toronto: University of Toronto Press, 1993.

Fanon, Frantz. *Black Skin, White Masks.* Trans. Charles Lam Markmann. New York: Grove Press, 1967.

Farwell, Marilyn R. "The Lesbian Narrative: 'The Pursuit of the Inedible by the Unspeakable.'" In *Professions of Desire: Lesbian and Gay Studies in Literature,* ed. George E. Haggerty and Bonnie Zimmerman. New York: Modern Language Association, 1995.

Felman, Shoshana, and Dori Laub. *Testimony: Crises in Witnessing in Literature.* New York: Routledge, 1992.

Felski, Rita. "On Confession." *Beyond Feminist Aesthetics: Feminist Literature and Social Change.* Cambridge: Harvard University Press, 1989. 86–121. Excerpted in this volume.

Finke, Laurie A. "Mystical Bodies and the Dialogics of Vision." In *Maps of Flesh and Light: The Religious Experience of Medieval Women Mystics,* ed. Ulrike Wiethaus. Syracuse: Syracuse University Press, 1993. 28–44. Excerpted in this volume.

Firestone, Shulamith. *The Dialectic of Sex: The Case for Feminist Revolution.* New York: Morrow, 1970.

Foster, Frances. *Witnessing Slavery: The Development*

of Ante-bellum Slave Narratives. Westport, CT: Greenwood Press, 1979.

Foucault, Michel. The History of Sexuality. Trans. Robert Hurley. New York: Pantheon Books, 1978.

Foucault, Michel. Language, Counter-Memory, Practice: Selected Essays and Interviews. Ed. Donald F. Bouchard and Sherry Simon. Ithaca: Cornell University Press, 1977.

Foucault, Michel. Technologies of the Self: A Seminar with Michel Foucault. Ed. Luther H. Martin, Huck Gutman, and Patrick H. Hutton. Amherst: University of Massachusetts Press, 1988.

Frank, Anne. The Diary of a Young Girl. Garden City, NJ: Doubleday, 1952.

Fraser, Nancy, and Linda J. Nicholson, eds. Social Criticism without Philosophy: An Encounter between Feminism and Postmodernism. Minneapolis: University of Minnesota Press, 1988.

Friedman, Susan Stanford. "'Beyond' Gynocriticism and Gynesis: The Geographics of Identity and the Future of Feminist Criticism." Tulsa Studies in Women's Literature 15 (Spring 1996): 13–40.

Friedman, Susan Stanford. "Spatialization: A Strategy for Reading Narrative." Narrative (1993): 75–86.

Friedman, Susan Stanford. "Women's Autobiographical Selves: Theory and Practice." In The Private Self: Theory and Practice of Women's Autobiographical Writings, ed. Shari Benstock. Chapel Hill: University of North Carolina Press, 1988. 34–62. Excerpted in this volume.

Gagnier, Regenia. "The Literary Standard, Working-Class Autobiography, and Gender." In Revealing Lives: Autobiography, Biography, and Gender, ed. Susan Groag Bell and Marilyn Yalom. Albany: State University of New York Press, 1990. 115–30. Excerpted in this volume.

Gagnier, Regenia. Subjectivities. New York: Oxford University Press, 1991.

Gates, Henry Louis, Jr. Bearing Witness: Selections from African-American Autobiography in the Twentieth Century. New York: Pantheon Books, 1991.

Gates, Henry Louis, Jr. Reading Black, Reading Feminist: A Critical Anthology. New York: Meridian Books, 1990.

Gates, Henry Louis, Jr. The Signifying Monkey: A Theory of Afro-Amerian Literary Criticism. New York: Oxford University Press, 1988.

Gates, Henry Louis, Jr., and K. A. Appiah, eds. Zora Neale Hurston: Critical Perspectives Past and Present. New York: Amistad (Distributed by Penguin USA), 1993.

Gelfant, Blanche. "Speaking Her Own Piece: Emma Goldman and the Discursive Skeins of Autobiography." In American Autobiography: Retrospect and Prospect, ed. Paul John Eakin. Madison: University of Wisconsin Press, 1992. 253–66.

Gilligan, Carol. In a Different Voice: Psychological Theory and Women's Development. Cambridge: Harvard University Press, 1983.

Gilmore, Leigh. Autobiographics: A Feminist Theory of Women's Self-Representation. Ithaca: Cornell University Press, 1994. Excerpted in this volume.

Goldman, Anne E. "Autobiography, Ethnography, and History: A Model for Reading." "Take My Word": Autobiographical Innovations by Ethnic American Working Women. Berkeley: University of California Press, 1996. xv–xxxv. Excerpted in this volume.

Goodman, Katherine. Dis/Closures: Women's Autobiography in Germany between 1790 and 1914. New York, Bern: Peter Lang, 1986.

Goozé, Maryanne E. "The Definitions of Self and Form in Feminist Autobiography Theory." Women's Studies 21 (1992): 411–29.

Gramsci, Antonio. A Gramsci Reader: Selected Writings, 1916–1935. Ed. David Forgacs. London: Lawrence and Wishart, 1988.

Greenberg, Joanne. I Never Promised You a Rose Garden. Garden City, NY: Holt, Rinehart & Winston, 1964.

Greene, Gayle, and Coppelia Kahn, eds. Changing Subjects: The Making of Feminist Literary Criticism. New York: Routledge, 1993.

Greer, Germaine. The Female Eunuch. New York: McGraw-Hill, 1971.

Grosz, Elizabeth. "Contemporary Theories of Power and Subjectivity." In Feminist Knowledge: Critique and Construct, ed. Sneja Gunew. London: Routledge, 1990.

Grosz, Elizabeth. *Space, Time, and Perversions: Essays on the Politics of Bodies.* New York: Routledge, 1995.

Grosz, Elizabeth. *Volatile Bodies: Toward a Corporeal Feminism.* Bloomington: Indiana University Press, 1994.

Grosz, Elizabeth, and Elspeth Probyn, eds. *Sexy Bodies: The Strange Carnalities of Feminism.* London and New York: Routledge, 1995.

Gusdorf, Georges. "Conditions and Limits of Autobiography." In *Autobiography: Essays Theoretical and Critical,* ed. & trans. James Olney. Princeton: Princeton University Press, 1980. 28–48.

Haaken, Janice. "The Recovery of Memory, Fantasy, and Desire in Women's Trauma Stories: Feminist Approaches to Sexual Abuse and Psychotherapy." *Signs* 21, no. 4 (Summer 1996): 1069–94. Excerpted in this volume.

Hampsten, Elizabeth. *Read This Only to Yourself: Writings of Midwestern Women, 1880–1910.* Bloomington: Indiana University Press, 1982.

Haraway, Donna. "A Manifesto for Cyborgs: Science, Technology, and Socialist Feminism in the 1980s." In *Feminism/Postmodernism,* ed. Linda J. Nicholson. New York: Routledge, 1990. 190–233.

Harlow, Barbara. *Barred: Women, Writing, and Political Detention.* Middletown, CT: Wesleyan University Press, 1992.

Harlow, Barbara. "From a Women's Prison: Third World Women's Narratives of Prison." *Feminist Studies* 12 (Fall 1986): 502–24. Excerpted in this volume.

Hawkins, Anne Hunsaker. *Reconstructing Illness: Studies in Pathography.* West Lafayette, IN: Purdue University Press, 1993.

Heilbrun, Carolyn G. *Writing a Woman's Life.* New York: W. W. Norton, 1988.

Hellman, Lillian. *Pentimento.* Boston: Little, Brown, 1973.

Hellman, Lillian. *Scoundrel Time.* Boston: Little, Brown, 1976.

Hellman, Lillian. *An Unfinished Woman.* Boston: Little, Brown, 1969.

Henderson, Mae Gwendolyn. "Speaking in Tongues: Dialogics, Dialectics, and the Black Woman Writer's Literary Tradition." In *Changing Our Words: Essays on Criticism, Theory, and Writing by Black Women,* ed. Cheryl A. Wall. New Brunswick, NJ: Rutgers University Press, 1989. 116–42. Excerpted in this volume.

Hewitt, Leah D. *Autobiographical Tightropes.* Lincoln: University of Nebraska Press, 1990.

Hirsch, Marianne. "Masking the Subject: Practicing Theory." In *The Point of Theory: Practices in Cultural Analysis,* ed. Mieke Bal and Inge E. Boer. New York: Continuum, 1994. 109–24.

Hoffmann, Leonore, and Margo Culley, eds. *Women's Personal Narratives: Essays in Criticism and Pedagogy.* New York: Modern Language Association, 1985.

Hogan, Rebecca. "Diarists on Diaries." *a/b Auto/Biography Studies* 2, no. 2 (1986): 9–14.

Holly, Carol. "Nineteenth-Century Autobiographies of Affiliation: The Case of Catharine Sedgwick and Lucy Larcom." In *American Autobiography: Retrospect and Prospect,* ed. Paul John Eakin. Madison: University of Wisconsin Press, 1992. 216–34.

hooks, bell [Gloria Watkins]. "An Interview with Bell Hooks by Gloria Watkins: No, Not Talking Back, Just Talking to Myself, January 1989." *Yearning: Race, Gender and Cultural Politics.* Boston: South End Press, 1990. 215–23.

hooks, bell [Gloria Watkins]. "Writing Autobiography." *Talking Back: Thinking Feminist, Thinking Black.* Boston: South End Press, 1989. 155–59. Excerpted in this volume.

Huff, Cynthia. *British Women's Diaries: A Descriptive Bibliography of Selected Nineteenth-Century Women's Manuscript Diaries.* New York: AMS Press, 1985.

Huff, Cynthia. "Textual Boundaries: Space in Nineteenth-Century Women's Manuscript Diaries." In *Inscribing the Daily: Critical Essays on Women's Diaries,* ed. Suzanne L. Bunkers and Cynthia A. Huff. Amherst: University of Massachusetts Press, 1996. 123–38.

Hull, Gloria T., et al. *All the Women Are White, All the Blacks are Men, but Some of Us Are Brave: Black Women's Studies.* Old Westbury, NY: Feminist Press, 1982.

Humm, Maggie. *The Dictionary of Feminist Theory.* Columbus; Ohio State University Press, 1990.

Hurston, Zora Neale. *Dust Tracks on a Road: An Autobiography.* Urbana: University of Illinois Press, 1970.

Irigaray, Luce. *Speculum of the Other Woman.* Trans. Gillian C. Gill. Ithaca: Cornell University Press, 1985.

Irigaray, Luce. *This Sex Which Is Not One.* Trans. Catherine Porter and Carolyn Burke. Ithaca: Cornell University Press, 1985.

Jelinek, Estelle C. *The Tradition of Women's Autobiography: From Antiquity to the Present.* New York: Twayne, 1986.

Jelinek, Estelle C. *Women's Autobiography: Essays in Criticism.* Bloomington: Indiana University Press, 1980.

Johnson, Barbara. *A World of Difference.* Baltimore: Johns Hopkins University Press, 1987.

Kadar, Marlene. *Essays on Life Writing: From Genre to Critical Practice.* Toronto: University of Toronto Press, 1992.

Kadar, Marlene. "Whose Life Is It Anyway? Out of the Bathtub and into the Narrative." In *Essays on Life Writing: From Genre to Critical Practice,* ed. Kadar. Toronto: University of Toronto Press, 1992. 152–61

Kaminsky, Amy Katz. *Reading the Body Politic: Feminist Criticism and Latin American Women Writers.* Minneapolis: University of Minnesota Press, 1993.

Kaplan, Caren. "Resisting Autobiography: Out-Law Genres and Transnational Feminist Subjects." In *De/Colonizing the Subject: The Politics of Gender in Women's Autobiography,* ed. Sidonie Smith and Julia Watson. Minneapolis: University of Minnesota Press, 1992. 115–38. Excerpted in this volume.

Kaplan, Louis, et al. *A Bibliography of American Autobiographies.* Madison: University of Wisconsin Press, 1962.

Kauffman, Linda S. "Bad Girls and Sick Boys: Inside the Body of Fiction, Film, and Performance Art." In *Getting a Life: Everyday Uses of Autobiography,* ed. Sidonie Smith and Julia Watson. Minneapolis: University of Minnesota Press, 1996. 27–46.

Kauffman, Linda S. "The Long Goodbye: Against Personal Testimony, or An Infant Grifter Grows Up." In *American Feminist Thought at Century's End: A Reader,* ed. Linda S. Kauffman. Cambridge and Oxford: Blackwell, 1993. 258–78.

Kosta, Barbara. *Recasting Autobiography: Women's Counterfictions in Contemporary German Literature and Film.* Ithaca: Cornell University Press, 1994.

Kristeva, Julia. *The Kristeva Reader.* Ed. Toril Moi. New York: Columbia University Press, 1986.

Kristeva, Julia. "My Memory's Hyperbole." In *The Female Autograph,* ed. Domna C. Stanton. New York: New York Literary Forum, 1984. 219–35.

Krupat, Arnold. *For Those Who Come After: A Study of Native American Autobiography.* Berkeley: University of California Press, 1985.

Krupat, Arnold. *Native American Autobiography: An Anthology.* Madison: University of Wisconsin Press, 1994.

Lacan, Jacques. *Feminine Sexuality.* Ed. Juliet Mitchell and Jacqueline Rose. Trans. Jacqueline Rose. London: Macmillan, 1982.

Lacan, Jacques. *The Language of the Self: The Function of Language in Psychoanalysis.* Trans. Anthony Wilden. Baltimore: Johns Hopkins University Press, 1968.

Lacan, Jacques. *The Seminar of Jacques Lacan.* Ed. Jacques-Alain Miller. New York: W. W. Norton, 1988.

Lejeune, Philippe. "The Autobiographical Pact." In *On Autobiography,* ed. Paul John Eakin. Minneapolis: University of Minnesota Press, 1989. 3–30.

Lim, Shirley Geok-lin. "Semiotics, Experience, and the Material Self: An Inquiry into the Subject of the Contemporary Asian Woman Writer." *Writing S. E./Asia in English: Against the Grain, Focus on Asian-English Literature.* London: Skoob Books, 1994. 3–39. Excerpted in this volume.

Ling, Amy. *Between Worlds: Women Writers of Chinese Ancestry.* New York: Pergamon Press, 1990.

Ling, Amy, and Wesley Brown, eds. *Visions of America: Personal Narratives form the Promised Land.* New York: Persea Books, 1993.

Lionnet, Françoise. "The Politics and Aesthetics of Métissage." *Autobiographical Voices: Race, Gen-*

der, *Self-Portraiture.* Ithaca: Cornell University Press, 1989. 1–30. Excerpted in this volume.

Lionnet, Françoise. *Postcolonial Representations.* Ithaca: Cornell University Press, 1995.

Lionnet, Françoise, and Ronnie Scharfman, eds. *Post/Colonial Conditions: Exiles, Migrations, and Nomadisms.* New Haven: *Yale French Studies* 82, 83, 1993.

Lorde, Audre. *Zami: A New Spelling of My Name.* Trumansberg, NY: Crossing Press, 1982.

Mairs, Nancy. "The Way In." *Remembering the Bone House: An Erotics of Place and Space.* New York: Harper and Row, 1989. 1–11. Excerpted in this volume.

Marcus, Laura. *Auto/Biographical Discourses.* Manchester: Manchester University Press, 1994.

Martin, Biddy. "Lesbian Identity and Autobiographical Difference(s)." In *Life/Lines: Theorizing Women's Autobiography,* ed. Bella Brodzki and Celeste Schenck. Ithaca: Cornell University Press, 1988. 77–103. Excerpted in this volume.

Mason, Mary G. "The Other Voice: Autobiographies by Women Writers." In *Autobiography: Essays Theoretical and Critical,* ed. James Olney. Princeton: Princeton University Press, 1980. 207–35. Excerpted in this volume.

Mason, Mary G., and Carol Hurd Green, eds. *Journeys: Autobiographical Writings by Women.* Boston: G. K. Hall, 1979.

McCarthy, Mary. *Memories of a Catholic Girlhood.* New York: Harcourt Brace, 1957.

McKay, Nellie Y. "The Journals of Charlotte L. Forten-Grimké: Les Lieux de Mémoire in African-American Women's Autobiography." In *History and Memory in African-American Culture,* ed. Genevieve Fabré and Robert O'Meally. Oxford: Oxford University Press, 1994. 261–71.

McKay, Nellie Y. "The Narrative Self: Race, Politics, and Culture in Black American Women's Autobiography." In *Feminisms in the Academy,* ed. Domna C. Stanton and Abigail J. Stewart. Ann Arbor: University of Michigan Press, 1995. 74–94. Excerpted in this volume.

McNee, Lisa. "Autobiographical Subjects." *Research in African Literatures* 28, no. 2 (1997): 83–101.

Milani, Farzaneh. "Veiled Voices: Women's Autobiography in Contemporary Iran." In *Women's Autobiography in Contemporary Iran,* ed. Afsaneh Najmabadi. Cambridge: Harvard University Press, 1990. 2–17.

Miller, Nancy K. "Representing Others: Gender and the Subjects of Autobiography." *differences* 6, no. 1 (1994): 1–27.

Miller, Nancy K. "Teaching Autobiography." *Getting Personal.* New York: Routledge, 1991. 121–42. Excerpted in this volume.

Miller, Nancy K. "Toward a Dialectics of Difference." In *Women and Language in Literature and Society,* ed. Sally McConnell-Ginet, Ruth Borker, and Nelly Furman. New York: Praeger, 1980. 258–73.

Miller, Nancy K. "Writing Fictions: Women's Autobiography in France." In *Life/Lines: Theorizing Women's Autobiography,* ed. Bella Brodzki and Celeste Schenck. Ithaca: Cornell University Press, 1988. 45–61.

Millett, Kate. *Flying.* New York: Knopf, 1974.

Millett, Kate. *Sexual Politics.* Boston: New England Free Press, 1968.

Millett, Kate. *Sita.* New York: Farrar, Straus & Giroux, 1977.

Misch, Georg. *History of Autobiography.* Trans. E. W. Dickes. 2 vols. 1907. Rpt. London: Routledge and Kegan Paul, 1950.

Moers, Ellen. *Literary Women.* Garden City, NY: Doubleday, 1976.

Mohanty, Chandra Talpade, Ann Russo, and Lourdes Torres, eds. *Third World Women and the Politics of Feminism.* Bloomington: Indiana University Press, 1991.

Moody, Anne, *Coming of Age in Mississippi.* New York: Dial Press, 1968.

Moraga, Cherríe. *Loving in the War Years.* Boston: South End Press, 1983.

Moraga, Cherríe, and Gloria Anzaldúa, eds. *This Bridge Called My Back: Writing by Radical Women of Color.* New York: Kitchen Table Press, 1981.

Neuman, Shirley. "Autobiography, Bodies, Manhood." In *Autobiography and Questions of Gender,* ed. Neuman. London: Frank Cass, 1991. 137–65. Excerpted in this volume.

Neuman, Shirley, ed. *Essays on Canadian Writing*

60 (Winter 1996). Special issue on Canadian autobiography.

Nicholson, Linda, ed. *The Second Wave: A Reader in Feminist Theories.* New York: Routledge, 1997.

Nin, Anaïs. *The Diary of Anaïs Nin.* New York: Swallow Press, 1966–80.

Norton, Mary Beth, and Carol Ruth Berkin, eds. *Women of America: A History.* Boston: Houghton Mifflin, 1979.

Nussbaum, Felicity A. *The Autobiographical Subject.* 2d ed. 1989; Baltimore: John Hopkins University Press, 1995.

Olney, James. "Autobiography and the Cultural Moment." In *Autobiography: Essays Theoretical and Critical,* ed. James Olney. Princeton: Princeton University Press, 1980. 3–27.

Olney, James. *Autobiography: Essays Theoretical and Critical.* Princeton: Princeton University Press, 1980.

Padilla, Genaro M. *My History, Not Yours: The Formation of Mexican American Autobiography.* Madison: University of Wisconsin Press, 1993.

Pascal, Roy. *Design and Truth in Autobiography.* Cambridge: Harvard University Press, 1960.

Perreault, Jeanne. "Autography/Transformation/Asymmetry," *Writing Selves: Contemporary Feminist Autography.* Minneapolis: University of Minnesota Press, 1995. 1–30. Excerpted in this volume.

Personal Narratives Group. *Interpreting Women's Lives: Feminist Theory and Personal Narratives.* Bloomington: Indiana University Press, 1989.

Peterson, Linda. "Victorian Autobiography." In *The Culture of Autobiography: Constructions of Self-Representation,* ed. Robert Folkenflik. Stanford: Stanford University Press, 1993. 80–103.

Poster, Mark. "Postmodern Virtualities." *SAGE* 1, nos. 3–4 (1995): 79–95.

Quinby, Lee, ed. *Genealogy and Literature.* Minneapolis: University of Minnesota Press, 1995.

Raiskin, Judith L. *Snow on the Cane Fields: Women's Writing and Creole Subjectivity.* Minneapolis: University of Minnesota Press, 1996.

Raoul, Valerie. "Women and Diaries: Gender and Genre." *Mosaic* 22.3 (1989): 57–65.

Rebolledo, Tey Diana. *Women Singing in the Snow: A Cultural Analysis of Chicana Literature.* Tucson: University of Arizona Press, 1995.

Renza, Louis. "The Veto of the Imagination: A Theory of Autobiography." In *Autobiography: Essays Theoretical and Critical,* ed. James Olney. Princeton: Princeton University Press, 1980. 268–95.

Riley, Denise. *"Am I That Name?": Feminism and the Category of "Women" in History.* Minneapolis: University of Minnesota Press, 1988.

Saldivar, Ramón. *Chicano Narrative: The Dialectics of Difference.* Madison: University of Wisconsin Press, 1990.

Sarris, Greg. *Keeping Slug Woman Alive: A Holistic Approach to American Indian Texts.* Berkeley: University of California Press, 1993.

Sarris, Greg. *Mabel McKay: Weaving the Dream.* Berkeley: University of California Press, 1994.

Scott, Joan C. "Experience." In *Feminists Theorize the Political,* ed. Judith Butler and Joan C. Scott. New York: Routledge, 1993. 22–40. Excerpted in this volume.

Sellers, Susan. *Language and Sexual Difference.* New York: St. Martin's Press, 1991.

Showalter, Elaine. *A Literature of Their Own: English Women Novelists from Brontë to Lessing.* Princeton: Princeton University Press, 1977.

Shumaker, Wayne. *English Autobiography: Its Emergence, Materials, and Forms.* Berkeley: University of California Press, 1954.

Smith, Sidonie. "Performativity, Autobiographical Practice, Resistance." *a/b: Auto/Biography Studies* 10, no. 1 (1995): 17–31. Excerpted in this volume.

Smith, Sidonie. *A Poetics of Women's Autobiography: Marginality and the Fictions of Self-Representation.* Bloomington: Indiana University Press, 1987.

Smith, Sidonie. "Autobiographical Manifestos." *Subjectivity, Identity, and the Body.* Bloomington: Indiana University Press, 1993. 154–82. Excerpted in this volume.

Smith, Sidonie, and Julia Watson, eds. *De/Colonizing the Subject: The Politics of Gender in Women's Autobiography.* Minneapolis: University of Minnesota Press, 1992.

Smith, Sidonie, and Julia Watson, eds. *Getting a Life: Everyday Uses of Autobiography.* Minneapolis: University of Minnesota Press, 1996.

Smith-Rosenberg, Carroll. *Disorderly Conduct: Visions of Gender in Victorian America.* New York: Knopf, 1985.

Sommer, Doris. "No Secrets: Rigoberta's Guarded Truth." *The Real Thing: Testimonial Discourse and Latin America,* ed. Georg M. Gugelberger. Durham: Duke University Press, 1995. 51–72.

Sommer, Doris. "'Not Just a Personal Story': Women's *Testimonios* and the Plural Self." In *Life/Lines: Theorizing Women's Autobiography,* ed. Bella Brodzki and Celester Schenck. Ithaca: Cornell University Press, 1988. 107–30.

Sommer, Doris. "Taking a Life: Hot Pursuit and Cold Rewards in a Mexican Testimonial Novel." *Signs* 20, no. 4 (1995): 913–40.

Spacks, Patricia Meyer. *The Female Imagination.* New York: Avon Books [Knopf], 1972.

Spacks, Patricia Meyer. "Female Rhetorics." In *The Private Self: Theory and Practice of Women's Autobiographical Writings,* ed. Shari Benstock. Chapel Hill: University of North Carolina Press, 1988. 177–91. Excerpted in this volume.

Spengemann, William C. *The Forms of Autobiography: Episodes in the History of a Literary Genre.* New Haven: Yale University Press, 1980.

Spivak, Gayatri Chakravorty. "Can the Subaltern Speak?" In *Marxism and the Interpretation of Culture,* ed. Cary Nelson and Lawrence Grossberg. Urbana and Chicago: University of Illinois Press, 1988. 271–313.

Stanton, Domna C. "Autogynography: Is the Subject Different?" In *The Female Autograph,* ed. Stanton. New York: New York Literary Forum, 1984. 3–20. Excerpted in this volume.

Stanton, Domna, ed. *The Female Autograph.* New York: New York Literary Forum, 1984.

Steedman, Carolyn Kay. "Stories." *Landscape for a Good Woman: A Story of Two Lives.* New Brunswick: Rutgers University Press, 1987. 5–24.

Steele, Cynthia. *Politics, Gender, and the Mexican Novel, 1968–1988: Beyond the Pyramid.* Austin: University of Texas Press, 1992.

Stone, Albert E. *Autobiographical Occasions and Original Acts: Versions of American Identity from Henry Adams to Nate Shaw.* Philadelphia: University of Pennsylvania Press, 1982.

Suleri, Sara. "Woman Skin Deep: Feminism and the Postcolonial Condition." *Critical Inquiry* 18 (Summer 1992): 758–66. Excerpted in this volume.

Tompkins, Jane. "Me and My Shadow." In *Gender and Theory: Dialogues on Feminist Criticism,* ed. Linda S. Kauffman. New York: Basil Blackwell, 1989.

Torres, Lourdes. "The Construction of the Self in U.S. Latina Autobiographies." In *Third World Women and the Politics of Feminism,* ed. Chandra Talpade Mohanty, Ann Russo, and Lourdes Torres. Bloomington: Indiana University Press. 271–87. Excerpted in this volume.

Walker, Alice. "When the Other Dancer Is the Self." *In Search of Our Mother's Gardens: Womanist Prose.* San Diego: Harcourt Brace Jovanovich, 1983.

Warhol, Robyn, and Diane Price-Herndl, eds. *Feminisms.* New Brunswick, NJ: Rutgers University Press, 1991.

Watson, Julia. "Unspeakable Differences: The Politics of Gender in Lesbian and Heterosexual Women's Autobiographies." In *De/Colonizing the Subject: The Politics of Gender in Women's Autobiography,* ed. Sidonie Smith and Julia Watson. Minneapolis: University of Minnesota Press, 1992. 139–68. Excerpted in this volume.

Wittig, Monique. *The Straight Mind and Other Essays.* Ed. and foreword by Louise Turcotte. Boston: Beacon Press, 1992.

Wong, Hertha D. Sweet *Sending My Heart Back Across the Years: Tradition and Innovation in Native American Autobiography.* New York: Oxford University Press, 1992.

Wong, Sau-ling Cynthia. "Immigrant Autobiography: Some Questions of Definition and Approach." In *American Autobiography: Retrospect and Prospect.* Ed. Paul John Eakin. Madison: University of Wisconsin Press, 1992. 142–70.

Wong, Sau-ling Cynthia. *Reading Asian American Lit-*

erature: From Necessity to Extravagance. Princeton: Princeton University Press, 1993.

Wood, Mary Elene. The Writing on the Wall: Women's Autobiography and the Asylum. Urbana: University of Illinois Press, 1994. 142–70.

Wurtzel, Elizabeth. Prozac Nation. Boston: Houghton Mifflin, 1994.

Yarbro-Bejarano, Yvonne. "Expanding the Categories of Race and Sexuality in Lesbian and Gay Studies." In Professions of Desire: Lesbian and Gay Studies in Literature, ed. George E. Haggerty and Bonnie Zimmerman. New York: Modern Language Association, 1995. 124–35.

Yellin, Jean Fagan. Introduction. Incidents in the Life of a Slave Girl, by Harriet A. Jacobs. Cambridge: Harvard University Press, 1987.

PART I
Experience and Agency

White. But also woman.

As such, insecure in relation to most of the value systems that regulate culture. Wanting to be both whore and madonna. Both good and bad. Traditional and a rebel. To be a wife-and-mother, and to shake up the establishment. Drawn to the feminist image, still attached to the feminine mystique. Wanting to be loved for both. And in permanent trouble on account of both.

To make matters even more divisive, both French and English.

White woman speaks with forked tongue: this writer writes in two languages, and about literature in two languages.

White woman speaks with forked tongue: this writer wants to find out, through writing, why she writes. She writes fiction as well as criticism. The two seep into each other. She writes as academic, straining towards theory, and as woman. Sometimes she allows everything she is to filter through into writing, and then she becomes frightened of what she's done, and she pushes it under. And the voice that grapples with reality oozes into the texts that try to be at one remove, the structures that the critical voice has erected.

. . . Over a period of time, eight years or so, it has become increasingly clear that only by allowing my voice to fork, by letting the autobiographical or the fictional surface into my thinking about something else, somebody else, by diversifying and personalizing the discourse, letting the French interfere with the English, do I ever manage to be at all adequate to the occasion, or true to myself. It seemed a pity that what had developed into a genuine practice, one that had its own logic, and purpose, and could be useful to others also in search of a different voice, a more inclusive and exploratory way of writing about literature or women's issues, should be scattered all over the place. This book is an attempt to put it together.

Forked tongues are, after all, rooted in one throat. And the serpent has ever been the friend of woman. . . .

—Nicole Ward Jouve, *White Woman Speaks with Forked Tongue: Criticism as Autobiography* (London and New York: Routledge, 1991), xiii–ix

The strength of these pictures—but sight was always then so much mixed with sound that picture is not the right word—the strength anyhow of these impressions makes me again digress. Those moments—in the nursery, on the road to the beach—can still be more real than the present moment. This I have just tested. For I got up and crossed the garden. Percy was digging the asparagus bed; Louie was shaking a mat in front of the bedroom door. But I was seeing them through the sight I saw here—the nursery and the road to the beach. At times I can go back to St. Ives more completely than I can this morning. I can reach a state where I seem to be watching things happen as if I were there. That is, I suppose, that my memory supplies what I had forgotten, so that it seems as if it were happening independently, though I am really making it happen. In certain favourable moods, memories—what one has forgotten—come to the top. Now if this is so, is it not possible—I often wonder—that things we have felt with great intensity have an existence independent of our minds; are in fact still in existence? And if so, will it not be possible, in time, that some device will be invented by which we can tap them? I see it—the past—as an avenue lying behind; a long ribbon of scenes, emotions. There at the end of the avenue still, are the garden and the nursery. Instead of remembering here a scene and there a sound, I shall fit a plug into the wall; and listen in to the past. I shall turn up August 1890. I feel that strong emotion must leave its trace; and it is only a question of discovering how we can get ourselves again attached to it, so that we shall be able to live our lives through from the start.

—Virginia Woolf, "A Sketch of the Past," in *Moments of Being* (London: Hogarth Press, 1985), 67

1 Experience

Joan W. Scott

Becoming Visible

There is a section in Samuel Delany's magnificent autobiographical meditation, *The Motion of Light in Water*,[1] that dramatically raises the problem of writing the history of difference, the history, that is, of the designation of "other," of the attribution of characteristics that distinguish categories of people from some presumed (and usually unstated) norm.[2] Delany (a gay man, a black man, a writer of science fiction) recounts his reaction to his first visit to the St. Marks bathhouse in 1963. He describes standing on the threshold of a "gym-sized room" dimly lit by blue bulbs. The room was full of people, some standing, the rest "an undulating mass of naked male bodies, spread wall to wall." "My first response," he writes, "was a kind of heart-thudding astonishment, very close to fear."

> I have written of a space at certain libidinal saturation before. That was not what frightened me. It was rather that the saturation was not only kinesthetic but visible. (173)

Watching the scene establishes for Delany a "fact that flew in the face" of the prevailing representation of homosexuals in the 1950s as isolated perverts, subjects gone awry. The "apprehension of massed bodies" gave him (as it does, he argues, anyone, "male, female, working or middle class") a "sense of political power."

> [W]hat *this* experience said was that there was a population—not of individual ho-

mosexuals . . . not of hundreds, not of thousands, but rather of millions of gay men, and that history had actively and already, created for us whole galleries of institutions, good and bad, to accommodate our sex. (174)

The sense of political possibility is frightening and exhilarating for Delany. He emphasizes not the discovery of an identity, but a sense of participation in a movement; indeed it is the extent (as well as the existence) of these sexual practices that matters most in his account. Numbers—massed bodies—constitute a movement and this, even if subterranean, belies enforced silences about the range and diversity of human sexual practices. Making the movement visible breaks the silence about it, challenges prevailing notions, and opens new possibilities for everyone. Delany imagines, even from the vantage point of 1988, a future utopian moment of genuine sexual revolution ("once the AIDS crisis is brought under control").

> That revolution will come precisely because of the infiltration of clear and articulate language into the marginal areas of human sexual exploration, such as this book from time to time describes. . . . Now that a significant range of people have begun to get a clearer idea of what has been possible among the varieties of human pleasure in the recent past, heterosexuals

and homosexuals, females and males will insist on exploring them even further. . . . (175)

By writing about the bathhouse Delany seeks not, he says, to "romanticize that time into some cornucopia of sexual plenty," but rather to break "absolutely sanctioned public silence" on questions of sexual practice, to reveal something that existed but that had been suppressed. The point of Delany's description, indeed of his entire book, is to document the existence of those institutions in all their variety and multiplicity, to write about and thus to render historical what has hitherto been hidden from history.

A metaphor of visibility as literal transparency is crucial to his project. The blue lights illuminate a scene he has participated in before (in darkened trucks parked along the docks under the West Side Highway, in men's rooms in subway stations), but understood only in a fragmented way. "No one ever got to see its whole" (174). He attributes the impact of the bathhouse scene to its visibility: "You could see what was going on throughout the dorm" (173). Seeing enables him to comprehend the relationship between his personal activities and politics. "[T]he first direct sense of political power comes from the apprehension of massed bodies." Recounting that moment also allows him to explain the aim of his book: to provide a "clear, accurate, and extensive picture of extant public sexual institutions" so that others may learn about and explore them. Knowledge is gained through vision; vision is a direct, unmediated apprehension of a world of transparent objects. In this conceptualization of it, the visible is privileged; writing is then put at its service.[3] Seeing is the origin of knowing. Writing is reproduction, transmission—the communication of knowledge gained through (visual, visceral) experience.

This kind of communication has long been the mission of historians documenting the lives of those omitted or overlooked in accounts of the past. It has produced a wealth of new evidence previously ignored about these others and has drawn attention to dimensions of human life and activity usually deemed unworthy of mention in conventional histories. It has also occasioned a crisis for orthodox history, by multiplying not only stories, but subjects, and by insisting that histories are written from fundamentally different—indeed irreconcilable—perspectives or standpoints, no one of which is complete or completely "true." Like Delany's memoir, these histories have provided evidence for a world of alternative values and practices whose existence gives the lie to hegemonic constructions of social worlds, whether these constructions vaunt the political superiority of white men, the coherence and unity of selves, the naturalness of heterosexual monogamy, or the inevitability of scientific progress and economic development. The challenge to normative history has been described, in terms of conventional historical understandings of evidence, as an enlargement of the picture, a corrective to oversights resulting from inaccurate or incomplete vision, and it has rested its claim to legitimacy on the authority of experience, the direct experience of others, as well as of the historian who learns to see and illuminate the lives of those others in his or her texts.

Documenting the experience of others in this way has been at once a highly successful and limiting strategy for historians of difference. It has been successful because it remains so comfortably within the disciplinary framework of history, working according to rules which permit calling old narratives into question when new evidence is discovered. The status of evidence is, of course, ambiguous for historians. On the one hand, they acknowledge that "evidence only counts as evidence and is only recognized as such in relation to a potential narrative, so that the narrative can

of lessons gained from the past, but it also referred to a particular kind of consciousness. This consciousness, in the twentieth century, has come to mean a "full, active awareness" including feeling as well as thought. The notion of experience as subjective witness, writes Williams, "is offered not only as truth, but as the most authentic kind of truth," as "the ground for all (subsequent) reasoning and analysis" (128). According to Williams, experience has acquired another connotation in the twentieth century different from these notions of subjective testimony as immediate, true, and authentic. In this usage it refers to influences external to individuals—social conditions, institutions, forms of belief or perception—"real" things outside them that they react to, and does not include their thought or consideration.[10]

In the various usages described by Williams, "experience," whether conceived as internal or external, subjective or objective, establishes the prior existence of individuals. When it is defined as internal, it is an expression of an individual's being or consciousness; when external, it is the material upon which consciousness then acts. Talking about experience in these ways leads us to take the existence of individuals for granted (experience is something people have) rather than to ask how conceptions of selves (of subjects and their identities) are produced.[11] It operates within an ideological construction that not only makes individuals the starting point of knowledge, but that also naturalizes categories such as man, woman, black, white, heterosexual, or homosexual by treating them as given characteristics of individuals.

Teresa de Lauretis's redefinition of experience exposes the workings of this ideology:

Experience [she writes] is the process by which, for all social beings, subjectivity is constructed. Through that process one places oneself or is placed in social reality

and so perceives and comprehends as subjective (referring to, originating in oneself) those relations—material, economic, and interpersonal—which are in fact social, and, in a larger perspective, historical.[12]

The process that de Lauretis describes operates crucially through differentiation; its effect is to constitute subjects as fixed and autonomous, and who are considered reliable sources of a knowledge that comes from access to the real by means of their experience.[13] When talking about historians and other students of the human sciences, it is important to note that this subject is both the object of inquiry—the person one studies in the present or the past—and the investigator him- or herself—the historian who produces knowledge of the past based on "experience" in the archives or the anthropologist who produces knowledge of other cultures based on "experience" as a participant observer.

The concepts of experience described by Williams preclude inquiry into processes of subject construction; and they avoid examining the relationships between discourse, cognition, and reality, the relevance of the position or situatedness of subjects to the knowledge they produce, and the effects of difference on knowledge. Questions are not raised about, for example, whether it matters for the history they write that historians are men, women, white, black, straight, or gay; instead "the authority of the 'subject of knowledge' [is established] by the elimination of everything concerning the speaker."[14] His knowledge, reflecting as it does something apart from him, is legitimated and presented as universal, accessible to all. There is no power or politics in these notions of knowledge and experience.

An example of the way "experience" establishes the authority of the historian can be found in R. G. Collingwood's *The Idea of History*, the 1946 classic that has been required reading in historiography courses for several generations. For Collingwood, the ability of the historian to "reenact past experience" is tied to his autonomy, "where by autonomy I mean the condition of being one's own authority, making statements or taking action on one's own initiative and not because those statements or actions are authorized or prescribed by anyone else."[15] The question of where the historian is situated—who he is, how he is defined in relation to others, what the political effects of his history may be—never enters the discussion. Indeed, being free of these matters seems to be tied to Collingwood's definition of autonomy, an issue so critical for him that he launches into an uncharacteristic tirade about it. In his quest for certainty, the historian must not let others make up his mind for him, Collingwood insists, because to do that means

> giving up his autonomy as an historian and allowing someone else to do for him what, if he is a scientific thinker, he can only do for himself. There is no need for me to offer the reader any proof of this statement. If he knows anything of historical work, he already knows of his own experience that it is true. If he does not already know that it is true, he does not know enough about history to read this essay with any profit, and the best thing he can do is to stop here and now. (256)

For Collingwood it is axiomatic that experience is a reliable source of knowledge because it rests on direct contact between the historian's perception and reality (even if the passage of time makes it necessary for the historian to imaginatively reenact events of the past). Thinking on his own means owning his own thoughts, and this proprietary relationship guarantees an individual's independence, his ability to read the past correctly, the authority of the knowledge he produces. The claim is not only for the his-

torian's autonomy, but also for his originality. Here "experience" grounds the identity of the researcher as an historian.

Another, very different use of "experience" can be found in E. P. Thompson's *Making of the English Working Class,* the book that revolutionized social and labor history. Thompson specifically set out to free the concept of "class" from the ossified categories of Marxist structuralism. For this project "experience" was a key concept. His notion of experience joined ideas of external influence and subjective feeling, the structural and the psychological. This gave Thompson a mediating influence between social structure and social consciousness. For him experience meant "social being"—the lived realities of social life, especially the affective domains of family and religion and the symbolic dimensions of expression. This definition separated the affective and the symbolic from the economic and the rational. "People do not only experience their own experience as ideas, within thought and its procedures," he maintained. "[T]hey also experience their own experience *as feeling . . .*"[16] This statement grants importance to the psychological dimension of experience, and it allows Thompson to account for agency. Feeling, Thompson insists, is "handled" culturally as "norms, familial and kinship obligations, . . . values or . . . within art and religious beliefs." At the same time it somehow precedes these forms of expression and so provides an escape from a strong structural determination: "For any living generation, in any 'now,'" Thompson asserts, "the ways in which they 'handle' experience defies prediction and escapes from any narrow definition or determination" (171).[17]

And yet in his use of it, experience, because it is ultimately shaped by relations of production, is a unifying phenomenon, overriding other kinds of diversity. Since these relations of production are common to workers of different ethnicities, religions, regions, and trades, they necessarily provide a common denominator and they emerge as a more salient determinant of "experience" than anything else. In Thompson's use of the term, experience is the start of a process that culminates in the realization and articulation of social consciousness, in this case a common identity of class. It serves an integrating function, joining the individual and the structural and bringing together diverse people into that coherent (totalizing) whole which is a distinctive sense of class (170–71).[18]

The unifying aspect of experience excludes whole realms of human activity by simply not counting them as experience, at least with any consequences for social organization or politics. When class becomes an overriding identity, other subject positions are subsumed by it, those of gender for example (or, in other instances of this kind of history, race, ethnicity, and sexuality). The positions of men and women and their different relationships to politics are taken as reflections of material and social arrangements rather than as products of class politics itself.

In Thompson's account class is finally an identity rooted in structural relations that pre-exist politics. What this obscures is the contradictory and contested process by which class itself was conceptualized and by which diverse kinds of subject positions were assigned, felt, contested, or embraced. As a result, Thompson's brilliant history of the English working class, which set out to historicize the category of class, ends up essentializing it. The ground may seem to be displaced from structure to agency by insisting on the subjectively felt nature of experience, but the problem Thompson sought to address isn't really solved. Working-class "experience" is now the ontological foundation of working-class identity, politics, and history.[19]

This use of experience has the same founda-

tional status if we substitute women or African-American or lesbian or homosexual for working-class in the previous sentence. Among feminist historians, for example, "experience" has helped to legitimize a critique of the false claims to objectivity of traditional historical accounts. Part of the project of some feminist history has been to unmask all claims to objectivity as an ideological cover for masculine bias by pointing out the shortcomings, incompleteness, and exclusiveness of "mainstream" history. This has been achieved by providing documentation about women in the past which calls into question existing interpretations made without consideration of gender. But how authorize the new knowledge if the possibility of all historical objectivity has been questioned? By appealing to experience, which in this usage connotes both reality and its subjective apprehension—the experience of women in the past and of women historians who can recognize something of themselves in their foremothers.

Judith Newton, a literary historian, writing about the neglect of feminism by contemporary critical theorists, argues that women, too, arrived at the critique of objectivity usually associated with deconstruction or the New Historicism. This feminist critique "seemed to come straight out of reflection on our own, that is, [on] women's experience, out of the contradictions we felt between the different ways we were represented even to ourselves, out of the inequities we had long experienced in our situations."[20] Newton's appeal to experience seems to bypass the issue of objectivity (by not raising the question of whether feminist work can be objective), but it rests firmly on a foundational ground (experience). In her work the relationship between thought and experience is represented as transparent (the visual metaphor combines with the visceral) and so directly accessible, as it is in historian Christine Stansell's insistence that "social practices" in all their "immediacy and entirety" constitute a domain of "sensuous experience" (a prediscursive reality directly felt, seen, and known) that cannot be subsumed by "language."[21] The effect of these kinds of statements, which attribute an indisputable authenticity to women's experience, is to establish incontrovertibly women's identity as people with agency. It is also to universalize the identity of women and so to ground claims for the legitimacy of women's history in the shared experience of historians of women and those women whose stories they tell. In addition, it literally equates the personal with the political, for the lived experience of women is seen as leading directly to resistance to oppression, to feminism.[22] Indeed, the possibility of politics is said to rest on, to follow from, a pre-existing women's experience.

"Because of its drive towards a political massing together of women," writes Denise Riley, "feminism can never wholeheartedly dismantle 'women's experience,' however much this category conflates the attributed, the imposed, and the lived, and then sanctifies the resulting melange."[23] The kind of argument for a women's history (and for a feminist politics) that Riley criticizes closes down inquiry into the ways in which female subjectivity is produced, the ways in which agency is made possible, the ways in which race and sexuality intersect with gender, the ways in which politics organize and interpret experience—the ways in which identity is a contested terrain, the site of multiple and conflicting claims. In Riley's words again, "it masks the likelihood that . . . [experiences] have accrued to women not by virtue of their womanhood alone, but as traces of domination, whether natural or political" (99). I would add as well that it masks the necessarily discursive character of these experiences.

But it is precisely the discursive character of experience that is at issue for some historians, because attributing experience to discourse

seems somehow to deny its status as an unquestionable ground of explanation. This seems to be the case for John Toews, writing a long review article in the *American Historical Review* in 1987, called "Intellectual History after the Linguistic Turn: The Autonomy of Meaning and the Irreducibility of Experience."[24] The term "linguistic turn" is a comprehensive one used by Toews to refer to approaches to the study of meaning which draw on a number of disciplines, but especially on theories of language "since the primary medium of meaning was obviously language" (881). The question for Toews is how far linguistic analysis has gone and should go especially in view of the poststructuralist challenge to foundationalism.

By definition, he argues, history is concerned with explanation; it is not a radical hermeneutics, but an attempt to account for the origin, persistence, and disappearance of certain meanings at "particular times and in specific sociocultural situations" (882). For him explanation requires a separation of experience and meaning; experience is that reality which demands meaningful response. "Experience" in Toews's usage is taken to be so self-evident that he never defines the term. (This is telling in an article that insists on establishing the importance and independence—the irreducibility—of "experience." The absence of definition allows experience to take on many resonances, but it also allows it to function as a universally understood category—the undefined word creates a sense of consensus by attributing to it an assumed, stable, and shared meaning).

Experience for Toews is a foundational concept. While recognizing that meanings differ and that the historian's task is to analyze the different meanings produced in societies and over time, Toews protects "experience" from this kind of relativism. In so doing he establishes the possibility for objective knowledge and so for communication among historians, however diverse their positions and views. This has an effect (among others) of removing historians from critical scrutiny as active producers of knowledge.

Since the phenomenon of experience itself can be analyzed outside the meanings given to it, the subjective position of historians then can seem to have nothing to do with the knowledge they produce. Toews's "experience" thus provides an object for historians that can be known apart from their own role as meaning makers, and it then guarantees not only the objectivity of their knowledge, but their ability to persuade others of its importance. Whatever diversity and conflict may exist among them, Toews's community of historians is rendered homogeneous by its shared object (experience). But as Ellen Rooney has so effectively pointed out, this kind of homogeneity can exist only because of the exclusion of the possibility that "historically irreducible interests divide and define . . . communities. . . . "[25] Inclusiveness is achieved by denying that exclusion is inevitable, that difference is established through exclusion, and that the fundamental differences that accompany inequalities of power and position cannot be overcome by persuasion. In Toews's article no disagreement about the meaning of the term "experience" can be entertained, since experience itself lies somehow outside its signification. For that reason, perhaps, Toews never defined it.

Even among those historians who do not share all of Toews's ideas about the objectivity or continuous quality of history, writing the defense of "experience" works in much the same way: it establishes a realm of reality outside of discourse and it authorizes the historian who has access to it. The evidence of experience works as a foundation providing both a starting point and a conclusive kind of explanation, beyond which few questions need to or can be asked. And yet it is precisely the questions precluded—questions about discourse, difference, and subjectivity, as well as about what counts as experience and who gets to make that determination—that would enable us to historicize experience, to reflect critically on the history we write about it, rather than to premise our history upon it.

Historicizing "Experience"

How can we historicize "experience"? How can we write about identity without essentializing it? Answers to the second question ought to point toward answers to the first, since identity is tied to notions of experience, and since both identity and experience are categories usually taken for granted in ways that I am suggesting they ought not to be. It ought to be possible for historians to, in Gayatri Spivak's terms, "make visible the assignment of subject-positions," not in the sense of capturing the reality of the objects seen, but of trying to understand the operations of the complex and changing discursive processes by which identities are ascribed, resisted, or embraced and which processes themselves are unremarked, indeed achieve their effect because they aren't noticed.[26] To do this a change of object seems to be required, one which takes the emergence of concepts and identities as historical events in need of explanation. This does not mean that one dismisses the effects of such concepts and identities, that one does not explain behavior in terms of their operations. It does mean assuming that the appearance of a new identity is not inevitable or determined, not something that was always there simply waiting to be expressed, not something that will always exist in the form it was given in a particular political movement or at a particular historical moment.

The fact is "black" has never been just there either [writes Stuart Hall]. It has always been an unstable identity, psychically, culturally and politically. It, too, is a narrative, a story, a history. Something constructed, told, spoken, not simply found. People now speak of the society I come from in totally unrecognizable ways. Of course Jamaica is a black society, they say. In reality it is a society of black and brown people who lived for three or four hundred years without ever being able to speak of themselves as "black." Black is an identity which had to be learned and could only be learned in a certain moment. In Jamaica that moment is the 1970s.[27]

To take the history of Jamaican black identity as an object of inquiry in these terms is necessarily to analyze subject positioning, in part at least, as the effect of discourses that placed Jamaica in a late-twentieth-century international-racist political economy; it is to historicize the "experience" of blackness.[28]

Treating the emergence of a new identity as a discursive event is not to introduce a new form of linguistic determinism, nor to deprive subjects of agency. It is to refuse a separation between "experience" and language and to insist instead on the productive quality of discourse. Subjects are constituted discursively, but there are conflicts among discursive systems, contradictions within any one of them, multiple meanings possible for the concepts they deploy.[29] And subjects have agency. They are not unified, autonomous individuals exercising free will, but rather subjects whose agency is created through situations and statuses conferred on them. Being a subject means being "subject to definite conditions of existence, conditions of endowment of agents and conditions of exercise."[30] These conditions enable choices, although they are not unlimited. Subjects are constituted discursively, experience is a linguistic event (it doesn't happen outside established meanings), but neither is it confined to a fixed order of meaning. Since discourse is by

definition shared, experience is collective as well as individual. Experience is a subject's history. Language is the site of history's enactment. Historical explanation cannot, therefore, separate the two.

The question then becomes how to analyze language, and here historians often (though not always and not necessarily) confront the limits of a discipline that has typically constructed itself in opposition to literature. (These limits have to do with a referential conception of language, the belief in a direct relationship between words and things). The kind of reading I have in mind would not assume a direct correspondence between words and things, nor confine itself to single meanings, nor aim for the resolution of contradiction. It would not render process as linear, nor rest explanation on simple correlations or single variables. Rather it would grant to "the literary" an integral, even irreducible, status of its own. To grant such status is not to make "the literary" foundational, but to open new possibilities for analyzing discursive productions of social and political reality as complex, contradictory processes.

The reading I offered of Delany at the beginning of this essay is an example of the kind of reading I want to avoid. I would like now to present another reading—one suggested to me by literary critic Karen Swann—as a way of indicating what might be involved in historicizing the notion of experience. It is also a way of agreeing with and appreciating Swann's argument about "the importance of 'the literary' to the historical project."[31]

For Delany, witnessing the scene at the bathhouse (an "undulating mass of naked male bodies" seen under a dim blue light) was an event. It marked what in one kind of reading we would call a coming to consciousness of himself, a recognition of his authentic identity, one he had always shared, would always share with others like himself. Another kind of reading, closer to Delany's preoccupation with memory and the self in this autobiography, sees this event not as the discovery of truth (conceived as the reflection of a prediscursive reality), but as the substitution of one interpretation for another. Delany presents this substitution as a conversion experience, a clarifying moment, after which he sees (that is, understands) differently. But there is all the difference between subjective perceptual clarity and transparent vision; one does not necessarily follow from the other even if the subjective state is metaphorically presented as a visual experience. Moreover (and this is Swann's point), "the properties of the medium through which the visible appears—here, the dim blue light, whose distorting, refracting qualities produce a wavering of the visible," make any claim to unmediated transparency impossible (Swann, 4). Instead, the wavering light permits a vision beyond the visible, a vision that contains the fantastic projections ("millions of gay men" for whom "history had, actively and already, created . . . whole galleries of institutions") that are the basis for political identification (Delany, 174). "In this version of the story," Swann notes, "political consciousness and power originate, not in a presumedly unmediated experience of presumedly real gay identities, but out of an apprehension of the moving, differencing properties of the representational medium—the motion of light in water" (4).

The question of representation is central to Delany's memoir. It is a question of social categories, personal understanding, and language, all of which are connected, none of which are or can be a direct reflection of the others. What does it mean to be black, gay, a writer, he asks, and is there a realm of personal identity possible apart from social constraint? The answer is that the social and the personal are imbricated in one another and that both are historically variable. The meanings of the categories of identity change and with them possibilities for thinking the self:

[A]t that time, the words "black" and "gay"—for openers—didn't exist with their current meanings, usage, history. 1961 had still been, really, part of the fifties. The political consciousness that was to form by the end of the sixties had not been part of my world. There were only Negroes and homosexuals, both of whom—along with artists—were hugely devalued in the social hierarchy. It's even hard to speak of that world. (Delany, 242)

But the available social categories aren't sufficient for Delany's story. It is difficult, if not impossible, to use a single narrative to account for his experience. Instead he makes entries in a notebook, at the front about material things, at the back about sexual desire. These are "parallel narratives, in parallel columns" (29). Although one seems to be about society, the public, the political, and the other about the individual, the private, the psychological, in fact both narratives are inescapably historical; they are discursive productions of knowledge of the self, not reflections of either external or internal truth. "That the two columns must be the Marxist and the Freudian—the material column and the column of desire—is only a modernist prejudice. The autonomy of each is subverted by the same excesses, just as severely" (212). The two columns are constitutive of one another, yet the relationship between them is difficult to specify. Do the social and economic determine the subjective? Is the private entirely separate from or completely integral to the public? Delany voices the desire to resolve the problem: "Certainly one must be the lie that is illuminated by the other's truth" (212). And then he denies that resolution is possible since answers to these questions do not exist apart from the discourses that produce them.

If it *is* the split—the space between the two columns (one resplendent and lucid with the writings of legitimacy, the other dark and hollow with the voices of the illegitimate)—that constitutes the subject, it is only after the Romantic inflation of the private into the subjective that such a split can even be located. That locus, that margin, that split itself first allows, then demands the appropriation of language—now spoken, now written—in both directions, over the gap. (29–30)

It is finally by tracking "the appropriation of language . . . in both directions, over the gap," and by situating and contextualizing that language that one historicizes the terms by which experience is represented, and so historicizes "experience" itself.

Conclusion

Reading for "the literary" does not seem at all inappropriate for those whose discipline is devoted to the study of change. It is not the only kind of reading I am advocating, although more documents than those written by literary figures are susceptible to such readings. Rather, it is a way of changing the focus and the philosophy of our history, from one bent on naturalizing "experience" through a belief in the unmediated relationship between words and things, to one that takes all categories of analysis as contextual, contested, and contingent. How have categories of representation and analysis—such as class, race, gender, relations of production, biology, identity, subjectivity, agency, experience, even culture—achieved their foundational status? What have been the effects of their articulations? What does it mean for historians to study the past in terms of these categories; for individuals to think of themselves in these terms? What is the relationship between the salience of such categories in our own time and their existence in the past? Questions such as these open consid-

eration of what Dominick LaCapra has referred to as the "transferential" relationship between the historian and the past, that is, of the relationship between the power of the historian's analytic frame and the events that are the object of his or her study. And they historicize both sides of that relationship by denying the fixity and transcendence of anything that appears to operate as a foundation, turning attention instead to the history of foundationalist concepts themselves. The history of these concepts (understood to be contested and contradictory) then becomes the evidence by which "experience" can be grasped and by which the historian's relationship to the past she writes about can be articulated. This is what Foucault meant by genealogy:

If interpretation were the slow exposure of the meaning hidden in an origin, then only metaphysics could interpret the development of humanity. But if interpretation is the violent or surreptitious appropriation of a system of rules, which in itself has no essential meaning, in order to impose a direction, to bend it to a new will, to force its participation in a different game, and to subject it to secondary rules, then the development of humanity is a series of interpretations. The role of genealogy is to record its history: the history of morals, ideals, and metaphysical concepts, the history of the concept of liberty or of the ascetic life; as they stand for the emergence of different interpretations, they must be made to appear as events on the stage of historical process.[32]

Experience is not a word we can do without, although it is tempting, given its usage to essentialize identity and reify the subject, to abandon it altogether. But experience is so much a part of everyday language, so imbricated in our narratives that it seems futile to argue for its expulsion. It serves as a way of talking about what happened, of establishing difference and similarity, of claiming knowledge that is "unassailable."[33] Given the ubiquity of the term, it seems to me more useful to work with it, to analyze its operations and to redefine its meaning. This entails focusing on processes of identity production, insisting on the discursive nature of "experience" and on the politics of its construction. Experience is at once always already an interpretation *and* is in need of interpretation. What counts as experience is neither self-evident nor straightforward; it is always contested, always therefore political. The study of experience, therefore, must call into question its originary status in historical explanation. This will happen when historians take as their project *not* the reproduction and transmission of knowledge said to be arrived at through experience, but the analysis of the production of that knowledge itself. Such an analysis would constitute a genuinely nonfoundational history, one which retains its explanatory power and its interest in change but does not stand on or reproduce naturalized categories.[34] It also cannot guarantee the historian's neutrality, for the choice of which categories to historicize is inevitably "political," necessarily tied to the historian's recognition of his/her stake in the production of knowledge. Experience is, in this approach, not the origin of our explanation, but that which we want to explain. This kind of approach does not undercut politics by denying the existence of subjects; it instead interrogates the processes of their creation, and, in so doing, refigures history and the role of the historian, and opens new ways for thinking about change.[35]

NOTES

A longer version of this paper appeared in *Critical Inquiry* 17 (Summer 1991): 773–97. I am grateful for their critical advice to Judith Butler, Christina Crosby, Nicholas Dirks, Christopher Fynsk, Clifford Geertz, Donna Haraway, Susan Harding, Gyan Prakash, Donald Scott, William Sewell, Jr., Karen Swann, and Elizabeth Weed.

1.   Samuel R. Delany, *The Motion of Light in Water: Sex and Science Fiction Writing in the East Village, 1957–1965* (New York: New American Library, 1988). Citations from this book are indicated in the text.

2.   Martha Minow, "Foreword: Justice Engendered," *Harvard Law Review* 101 (November 1987): 10–95.

3.   On the distinction between seeing and writing in formulations of identity, see Homi K. Bhabha, "Interrogating Identity," in *Identity: The Real Me,* ICA Documents (London) 6 (1987): 5–11.

4.   Lionel Gossman, "Towards a Rational Historiography," *Transactions of the American Philosophical Society* 79, no. 3 (1989): 26.

5.   On the "documentary" or "objectivist" model used by historians, see Dominick LaCapra, "Rhetoric and History," in LaCapra, *History and Criticism* (Ithaca: Cornell University Press, 1985), 15–44.

6.   On vision as not passive reflection, see Donna Haraway, "Situated Knowledges," typescript, 9, and Donna Haraway, "The Promises of Monsters; Reproductive Politics for Inappropriate/d Others," unpublished paper, Summer 1990, 9. See also Minnie Bruce Pratt, "Identity: Skin Blood Heart," in *Yours in Struggle: Three Feminist Perspectives on Anti-Semitism and Racism* (Brooklyn, NY: Long Haul Press, 1984), and the analysis of Pratt's autobiographical essay by Biddy Martin and Chandra Talpade Mohanty, "Feminist Politics: What's Home Got to Do with It?" in Teresa de Lauretis, *Feminist Studies/Critical Studies* (Madison: University of Wisconsin Press, 1986), 191–212.

7.   I am grateful to Judith Butler for discussions on this point.

8.   Fredric Jameson, "Immanence and Nominalism in Postmodern Theoretical Discourse," in *Postmodernism, or, The Cultural Logic of Late Capitalism* (Durham: Duke University Press, 1991), 199.

9.   Raymond Williams, *Keywords* (New York: Oxford University Press, 1983), 126–29. My discussion in this paragraph paraphrases much of Williams's definition. Citations are indicated in parentheses in the text.

10. On the ways knowledge is conceived "as an assemblage of accurate representations," see Richard Rorty, *Philosophy and the Mirror of Nature* (Princeton: Princeton University Press, 1979), especially 163.

11. Homi Bhabha puts it this way: "*To see* a missing person, or *to look* at Invisibleness, is to emphasize the subject's *transitive* demand for a *direct* object of self-reflection; a point of presence which would maintain its privileged enunciatory position *qua subject,*" in "Interrogating Identity," 5.

12. Teresa de Lauretis, *Alice Doesn't* (Bloomington: Indiana University Press, 1984), chapter 6, "Semiotics and Experience," 159.

13. Gayatri Spivak describes this as positing a metalepsis, that is, substituting an effect for a cause. See Gayatri Chakravorty Spivak, *In Other Worlds: Essays in Cultural Politics* (New York: Routledge, 1987), 204.

14. Michel de Certeau, "History: Science and Fiction," *Heterologies: Discourse on the Other,* trans. Brian Massumi (Minneapolis: University of Minnesota Press, 1986), 218.

15. R. G. Collingwood, *The Idea of History* (New York: Oxford University Press, 1956), 274–75. Citations are indicated in parentheses in the text.

16. E. P. Thompson, *Making of the English Working Class* (New York: Vintage, 1963), 171.

17. Raymond Williams's discussion of "structures of feeling" takes on some of these same issues in a more extended way. See his *The Long Revolution* (New York: Columbia University Press, 1961) and the interview about it in Raymond Williams, *Politics and Letters: Interviews with New Left Review* (London: Verso, 1989), 156–74. I am grateful to Chun Lin for directing me to these texts.

18. On the integrative functions of "experience," see Judith Butler, *Gender Trouble: Feminism and the Subversion of Identity* (New York: Routledge, Chapman and Hall, 1990), 22–25.

19. For a different reading of Thompson on experience, see William Sewell, Jr., "How Classes Are Made: Critical Reflections on E. P. Thompson's Theory of Working-Class Formation," in *E. P. Thompson: Critical Perspectives,* ed. Harvey J. Kaye and Keith McClelland (Philadelphia: Temple University Press, 1990); see also Sylvia Schafer, "Writing about 'Experience': Workers and Historians Tormented by Industrialization," unpublished paper, May 1987.

20. Judith Newton, "History as Usual? Feminism and the 'New Historicism,'" *Cultural Critique* 9 (1988): 93.

21. Christine Stansell, "Response," *International Labor and Working Class History* 31 (Spring 1987): 28. Often this kind of invocation of experience leads back to the biological or physical "experience" of the body. See, for example, the arguments about rape and violence offered by Mary Hawkesworth, "Knowers, Knowing, Known: Feminist Theory and Claims of Truth," *Signs* 14, no. 3 (Spring 1989): 533–57.

22. This is one of the meanings of the slogan "the personal is the political." Personal knowledge (i.e., experience) of oppression is the source of resistance to it. For critiques of this position, see Chandra Talpade Mohanty, "Feminist Encounters: Locating the Politics of Experience," *copyright* 1 (Fall 1987): 32; and Katie King, "The Situation of Lesbianism as Feminism's Magical Sign: Contests for Meaning and the U.S. Women's Movement, 1968–1972," *Communication* 9 (1986): 65–91. Catharine MacKinnon's work is probably the best example of the uses of "experience" Mohanty, King, and I are criticizing; see her *Feminism Unmodified: Discourses on Life and Law* (Cambridge: Harvard University Press, 1987).

23. Denise Riley, *"Am I That Name?" Feminism and the Category of "Women" in History* (Minneapolis: University of Minnesota Press, 1988), 100.

24. John Toews, "Intellectual History after the Linguistic Turn: The Autonomy of Meaning and the Irreducibility of Experience," *American Historical Review* 92, no. 4 (October 1987): 879–907.

25. Ellen Rooney, *Seductive Reasoning: Pluralism as the Problematic of Contemporary Theory* (Ithaca, NY: Comell University Press, 1989), 5–6.

26. Gayatri Spivak, "A Literary Representation of the Subaltern: A Woman's Text from the Third World," *In Other Worlds,* 241.

27. Stuart Hall, "Minimal Selves," in *Identity: The Real Me,* ICA Documents (London) 6 (1987): 45. See also Barbara J. Fields, "Ideology and Race in American History," in *Region, Race and Reconstruction,* ed. J. Morgan Kousser and James M. McPherson (New York: Oxford University Press, 1982), 143–77. (Fields's article is notable for its contradictions: the

way, for example, that it historicizes race while naturalizing class and refusing to talk at all about gender.)

28. An excellent example of the historicizing of black women's "experience" is Hazel Carby, *Reconstructing Womanhood: The Emergence of the Afro-American Woman Novelist* (New York: Oxford University Press, 1987).

29. For discussions of how change operates within and across discourses, see James Bono, "Science, Discourse, and Literature: The Role/Rule of Metaphor in Science," in *Literature and Science: Theory and Practice,* ed. Stuart Peterfreund (Boston: Northeastern University Press, 1990), 59–89. See also Mary Poovey, *Uneven Developments: The Ideological Work of Gender in Mid-Victorian England* (Chicago: University of Chicago Press, 1988), 1–23.

30. Parveen Adams and Jeff Minson, "The Subject of Feminism," *m/f* 2 (1978): 52. On the constitution of the subject, see Michel Foucault, *The Archaeology of Knowledge* (New York: Harper and Row, 1972), 95–96; Felicity A. Nussbaum, *The Autobiographical Subject: Gender and Ideology in Eighteenth-Century England* (Baltimore: Johns Hopkins University Press, 1989); and Peter de Bolla, *The Discourse of the Sublime: Readings in History, Aesthetics, and the Subject* (Oxford and New York: Basil Blackwell, 1989).

31. Karen Swann's comments on this paper were presented at the Little Three Faculty Colloquium "The Social and Political Construction of Reality," Wesleyan University, 18–19 January 1991. The comments exist only in typescript. The reference cited here is p. 5.

32. Michel Foucault, "Nietzsche, Genealogy, History," *Language, Counter-Memory, Practice,* ed. Donald F. Bonchard and Sherry Simon (Ithaca, NY: Cornell University Press, 1977), 151–52.

33. Ruth Roach Pierson, "Experience, Difference and Dominance in the Writings of Women's History," unpublished paper, 1989, 32.

34. Conversations with Christopher Fynsk helped clarify these points for me.

35. For an important attempt to describe a post-structuralist history, see Peter de Bolla, "Disfiguring History," *Diacritics* 16 (Winter 1986): 49–58.

2 Women's Autobiographical Selves: Theory and Practice

Susan Stanford Friedman

In his seminal essay "Conditions and Limits of Autobiography" (1956), Georges Gusdorf writes that "autobiography is not possible in a cultural landscape where consciousness of self does not, properly speaking, exist" (30). The cultural precondition for autobiography, Gusdorf argues, is a pervasive concept of individualism, a "conscious awareness of the singularity of each individual life," a self-consciousness that is "the late product of a specific civilization," by which he means the post-Renaissance Western societies (29). Gusdorf is often identified as the dean of autobiographical studies, particularly for his cogent articulation of the theoretical foundations of a formerly marginalized genre of writing. His contributions are undeniable, especially his assertion that autobiographical selves are constructed through the process of writing and therefore cannot reproduce exactly the selves who lived.[1]

However, the individualistic concept of the autobiographical self that pervades Gusdorf's work raises serious theoretical problems for critics who recognize that the self, self-creation, and self-consciousness are profoundly different for women, minorities, and many non-Western peoples. The model of separate and unique selfhood that is highlighted in his work and shared by many other critics establishes a critical bias that leads to the (mis)reading and marginalization of autobiographical texts by women and

minorities in the processes of canon formation. The fundamental inapplicability of individualistic models of the self to women and minorities is twofold. First, the emphasis on individualism does not take into account the importance of group identity for women and minorities. Second, the emphasis on separateness ignores the differences in socialization in the construction of male and female gender identity. From both an ideological and psychological perspective, in other words, individualistic paradigms of the self ignore the role of collective and relational identities in the individuation process of women and minorities. The concepts of female selfhood in the work of feminist theorists Sheila Rowbotham and Nancy Chodorow, in contrast, are grounded in a recognition of the historically generated differences between men and women. Application of their theories of women's selfhood to women's autobiographical texts—particularly those by women who also belong to racial, ethnic, sexual, and religious minorities—illuminates the unfolding narratives of women's life writing and thereby revises the prevailing canons of autobiography.

Gusdorf's concept of autobiography is premised on a model of the self that he identifies as endemically Western and individualistic. The "metaphysical conditions" for the development of autobiography are ripe in a society that fosters "the curiosity of the individual about himself, the wonder he feels about the mystery of his own destiny" (31). Gusdorf associates this curiosity with the Copernican revolution—an odd connection, as the impact of Copernican astronomy was to diminish man's centrality in the cosmos, not to enhance it. After the Copernican revolution, "henceforth, man knows himself a responsible agent: gatherer of men, of lands, of power, maker of kingdoms or of empires, inventor of laws and of wisdom. He alone adds consciousness to nature, leaving there the sign of his presence" (31). Gusdorf thus associates "presence" and self-consciousness with the rise of the European empires and the related phenomenon of the Industrial Revolution, with its constitution of highly polarized public and private spheres. Autobiography is the literary consequence of the rise of individualism as an ideology, according to Gusdorf. As a genre, it also represents the expression of individual authority in the realm of language. The "sign" to which Gusdorf refers is, literally and literarily, the "mark" or "imprint" of man's power: his linguistic, psychological, and institutional presence in the world of letters, people, and things.

Gusdorf contrasts the culture in which autobiography can develop with cultures where autobiography does not exist at all or exists only as a cultural "transplant" from Western societies. Autobiography does not develop endemically in cultures where "the individual does not oppose himself to all others; [where] he does not feel himself to exist outside of others, and still less against others, but very much *with* others in an interdependent existence that asserts its rhythms everywhere in the community . . . [where] lives are so thoroughly entangled that each of them has its center everywhere and its circumference nowhere. The important unit is thus never the isolated being" (29–30). For Gusdorf, the consciousness of self upon which autobiography is premised is the sense of "isolated being," a belief in the self as a discrete, finite "unit" of society.

Man must be an island unto himself. Then, and only then, is autobiography possible.[2]

Gusdorf's emphasis on the individual as an "isolated being" is not idiosyncratic. Similarly individualistic paradigms pervade other critical approaches to autobiography as diverse as historical, generic, poststructuralist, and psychoanalytic. According to James Olney, for example, the autobiographer is "surrounded and isolated by his own consciousness, an awareness grown out of a unique heredity and unique experience. . . . Separate selfhood is the very motive of creation" (*Metaphors*, 22–23). Although Olney argues that the autobiographer creates a self in the very act of seeking it, he nonetheless invokes Plato in positing the self as a "teleological unity" whose metaphors of circularity represent "the isolate uniqueness" of the individual (20–22). An autobiography projects "a single, radical and radial energy originating in the subject center, an aggressive, creative expression of the self, a defense of individual integrity in the face of an otherwise multiple, confusing, swarming, and inimical universe" (15).[3]

Although psychoanalytic critics would disagree with Olney's Neoplatonic concept of the teleological self, they share with his approach an ultimate presumption of the self as distinct from all others. In contrast to the theories of Olney and Gusdorf, psychoanalysis focuses on the development of the self as it forms through intense interaction with others, particularly the mother and father. Consequently, psychoanalytic critics of autobiography often focus their analysis on the way in which self-creation in the text explores or recapitulates the writer's past interplay with his or her parents. Nonetheless, psychoanalytic models of the autobiographical self remain fundamentally individualistic because the healthy ego is defined in terms of its ability to separate itself from others.

According to psychoanalytic theory, psychological development moves from identification to separation. The child's ego develops as it comes to realize its difference first from the mother and then from the external world in general. Sigmund Freud wrote that "an infant at the breast does not as yet distinguish his ego from the external world as the source of the sensations flowing in upon him" (*Civilization*, 13–14). But this lack of "boundary" between itself and the external world yields eventually to the "reality principle"—that is, the child gradually learns to "separate off an external world from itself," to see itself as distinct from all others (14–15).[4] In Jacques Lacan's theory, the child's separation of himself from his mother is followed by the mirror stage and a narcissistic identification first with his own image and then with others like him. The child knows himself as a separate entity by seeing his whole shape in the mirror and identifying that false image with a sense of a distinct and coherent identity. As the Oedipal phase supplants the early narcissistic sense of self, that child continues the process of self-construction through the acquisition of symbolic systems, preeminently language itself. To Lacan, the self constructed through language is also false, like the image in the mirror. This theory of the ego's inherent falseness represents a departure from Freud. But as with Freud, Lacan's concept of ego formation is based on the assumption that the ego results from a process that moves away from fusion and toward separation.

These theories of ego formation often lead psychoanalytic critics of autobiography to decode the narrative as the ego's movement away from early fusion with the mother and toward the establishment of sharp boundaries between the self and others. In "Autobiography and Psycho-Analysis," for example, Bruce Mazlish states that autobiography is a "consciously shaped *literary production*" similar to the interpretive process of psychoanalysis. In both analysis and autobiography, "the self is seen as a de-

veloping entity, changing by definable stages" (36, 28). Influenced by a Lacanian model, Jeffrey Mehlman sees the narcissistic and Oedipal stages of development inscribed into the narratives of autobiography. The failures of Narcissus and Oedipus prefigure the impossible task of the autobiographer to reach a "real self." All autobiography is "necessarily fictive"; it creates a self whose very coherence is the sign of its falseness and alienation—just as the child's image in the mirror is false (*A Structural Study of Autobiography*, 35–39). A number of other critics like Willis Buck, Gerald Kennedy, and Gregory Ulmer further apply to autobiography Lacanian and structuralist concepts of the self as a fictive entity constituted in images or words that cannot refer back to the "real" world because of the inherently nonreferential nature of all signs.[5] This focus on the autobiographical self's nonreferentiality nonetheless presumes, along with Gusdorf and Olney, that this false entity created in the text is distinct, separate from all others.

Although Gusdorf, Olney, Mehlman, and many others have greatly advanced our understanding of autobiography, their related individualistic paradigms for the self have obscured the presence and significance of women's autobiography in literary tradition. In fact, Gusdorf's description of the culture in which autobiography is impossible serves as a far better theoretical point of departure, one that re-places the works of women at the center of the autobiographical canon. His description of a culture without the necessary preconditions for autobiography is uncannily akin to the marginalized cultures of women. A slight alteration of his statement will serve the purposes of reversal: Autobiography is possible when "the individual does not feel *herself* to exist outside of others, and still less against others, but very much *with* others in an interdependent existence that asserts its rhythms everywhere in the community . . . [where] lives are so thoroughly entangled that each of them has its center everywhere and its circumference nowhere. The important unit is thus never the isolated being." The very sense of *identification, interdependence,* and *community* that Gusdorf dismisses from autobiographical selves are key elements in the development of a woman's identity, according to theorists like Rowbotham and Chodorow. Their models of women's selfhood highlight the unconscious masculine bias in Gusdorf's and other individualistic paradigms.

In *Woman's Consciousness, Man's World,* Rowbotham examines the role of cultural representation and material conditions in the formation of "woman's consciousness" of self. Building on *The Second Sex,* Rowbotham explores the significance for woman's sense of self of Simone de Beauvoir's assertion that woman is not born, but made. A woman cannot, Rowbotham argues, experience herself as an entirely unique entity because she is always aware of how she is being defined *as woman,* that is, as a member of a group whose identity has been defined by the dominant male culture. Like Lacan, Rowbotham uses the metaphor of mirrors to describe the development of woman's consciousness. But her mirror is the reflecting surface of cultural representation into which a woman stares to form an identity: "The prevailing social order stands as a great and resplendent hall of mirrors. It owns and occupies the world as it is and the world as it is seen and heard" (27). That mirror does not reflect back a unique, individual identity to each living woman; it projects an image of WOMAN, a category that is supposed to define the living woman's identity.

The cultural hall of mirrors—the repositories of representation—does not reflect back a unique individual when a man stands before its mirrors either. The cultural categories MAN, WHITE, CHRISTIAN, and HETEROSEXUAL in Western societies, for example, are as significant for a man of the dominant group as they are for a woman at the margins of culture. Isolate individualism is an illusion. It is also the privilege of power. A white man has the luxury of forgetting his skin color and sex. He can think of himself as an "individual." Women and minorities, reminded at every turn in the great cultural hall of mirrors of their sex or color, have no such luxury. Quoting Georg Simmel, Lynn Sukenick emphasizes the significance of group identity for women's consciousness of self:

> If we express the historic relation between the sexes crudely in terms of master and slave, it is part of the master's privileges not to have to think continuously of the fact that he is the master, while the position of the slave carries with it the constant reminder of his being a slave. It cannot be overlooked that the woman forgets far less often the fact of being a woman than the man of being a man. (28)

The emphasis on individualism as the necessary precondition for autobiography is thus a reflection of privilege, one that excludes from the canons of autobiography those writers who have been denied by history the illusion of individualism.

Women's sense of collective identity, however, is not only negative. It can also be a source of strength and transformation. As Rowbotham argues, cultural representations of woman lead not only to women's alienation, but also to the potential for a "new consciousness" of self (26–46). Not recognizing themselves in the reflections of cultural representation, women develop a dual consciousness—the self as culturally defined and the self as different from cultural prescription:

> But always we were split in two, straddling silence, not sure where we would begin to find ourselves or one another. From this division, our material dislocation, came the experience of one part of ourselves as

strange, foreign and cut off from the other which we encountered as tongue-tied paralysis about our own identity. We were never all together in one place, were always in transit, immigrants into alien territory. . . . The manner in which we knew ourselves was at variance with ourselves as an historical being-woman. (31)

This description of women's double consciousness directly parallels W. E. B. Du Bois's identification of dual consciousness for blacks living in a dominant white culture.[6] In *The Souls of Black Folk,* Du Bois wrote: "The Negro . . . is gifted with second-sight in this American world,—a world which yields him no true self-consciousness, but only lets him see himself through the revelation of the other world. It is a peculiar sensation, this double consciousness, this sense of always looking at one's self through the eyes of others, of measuring one's soul by the tape of a world that looks on in amused contempt and pity. One ever feels his twoness" (30). Du Bois's and Rowbotham's metaphors of reflection, invisibility, and silence are useful for understanding the process of alienation in the identities of any group existing at the margins of culture: women in a man's world; blacks in a white world; Jews in a Christian world; lesbians and gays in a heterosexual world; the havenots in a world of haves.

Like Du Bois, Rowbotham says women can move beyond alienation through a collective solidarity with other women—that is, a recognition that women as a *group* can develop an alternative way of seeing themselves by constructing a group identity based on their historical experience:

In order to create an alternative an oppressed group must at once shatter the self-reflecting world which encircles it and, at the same time, project its own image onto history. In order to discover its own iden-

tity as distinct from that of the oppressor it has to become visible to itself. All revolutionary movements create their own ways of seeing. But this is a result of great labour. People who are without names, who do not know themselves, who have no culture, experience a kind of paralysis of consciousness. The first step is to connect and learn to trust one another. . . . Solidarity has to be a collective consciousness which at once comes through individual self-consciousness and transforms it. (27, 29)

In taking the power of words, of representation, into their own hands, women project onto history an identity that is not purely individualistic. Nor is it purely collective. Instead, this new identity merges the shared and the unique. In autobiography, specifically, the self created in a woman's text is often not a "teleological entity," an "isolate being" utterly separate from all others, as Gusdorf and Olney define the autobiographical self. Nor is the self a false image of alienation, an empty play of words on the page disconnected from the realm of referentiality, as a Lacanian and post-structuralist critic of autobiography might say. Instead, the self constructed in women's autobiographical writing is often based in, but not limited to, a group consciousness—an awareness of the meaning of the cultural category WOMAN for the patterns of women's individual destiny. Alienation is not the result of creating a self in language, as it is for Lacanian and Barthesian critics of autobiography. Instead, alienation from the historically imposed image of the self is what motivates the writing, the creation of an alternate self in the autobiographical act. Writing the self shatters the cultural hall of mirrors and breaks the silence imposed by male speech.

Whereas Rowbotham focuses on ideology and institutions, Chodorow examines the psychology of gender socialization within the family. Although her emphasis is different from Rowbotham's, Chodorow's approach also suggests that the concept of isolate selfhood is inapplicable to women. Using and revising psychoanalytical objects-relations theory from a feminist perspective, she argues that "growing girls come to define themselves as continuous with others; their experience of self contains more flexible or permeable ego boundaries. Boys come to define themselves as more separate and distinct, with a greater sense of rigid ego boundaries and differentiation. The basic feminine sense of self is connected to the world, the basic masculine sense of self is separate" (169). "Girls," she writes, "come to experience themselves as less differentiated than boys, as more continuous with and related to the external object-world and as differently oriented to their inner object-world as well" (167). By "object," Chodorow does not mean "things," but rather people. Women's "object-world" remains "a more complex relational constellation than men's. . . . Masculine personality, then, comes to be defined more in terms of denial of relation and connection (and denial of femininity), whereas feminine personality comes to include a fundamental definition of self in relationship" (169). Chodorow's theory of differential gender identity highlights the unconscious equation of masculine selfhood with human selfhood in the concept of isolate identity proposed by writers like Gusdorf and Olney. Basing an examination of women's autobiography on the relational model of female selfhood in Chodorow's work, we can anticipate finding in women's texts a consciousness of self in which "the individual does not oppose herself to all others," nor "feel herself to exist outside of others," "but very much with others in an interdependent existence."[7]

What leads to the different sense of self in men and women, Chodorow suggests, is the importance of mother-child relationships. Following a general psychoanalytic approach, Chodorow regards the family structure, in which the mother or one woman is the primary caretaker of the child, as a universal phenomenon, although she departs from conventional theory in insisting that universal mothering is culturally, not biologically, determined (3–5, 11–39). Chodorow's premise obscures important cultural variations in the caretaking of children, but her description of mother-child relationships is nonetheless useful for the study of women's autobiography. The mother is the child's first love "object," according to the psychoanalytic theories Chodorow uses. During the Oedipal phase, the boy learns to repress that love, identify with his father, and separate himself from his mother: "Mothers experience their sons as a male opposite. Boys are more likely to have been pushed out of the preoedipal relationship, and to have had to curtail their primary love and sense of empathetic tie with their mother. A boy has engaged, and been required to engage, in a more emphatic individuation and a more defensive firming of experienced ego boundaries" (166–67). Girls, on the other hand, retain that primary attachment to their mothers even as they pass into the Oedipal phase, according to Chodorow: "Mothers tend to experience their daughters as more like, and continuous with themselves. Correspondingly, girls tend to remain part of the dyadic primary mother-child relationship itself. This means that a girl continues to experience herself as involved in issues of merging and separation, and in an attachment characterized by primary identification and the fusion of identification and object choice" (166). The mother-daughter relationship remains central to the ongoing process of female individuation, according to Chodorow. This is particularly true of lesbian women, for whom, she argues, the love of women is an extension of their love for their mothers. "Lesbian relationships," Chodorow writes, "do tend

to recreate mother-daughter emotions and connections" (200).[8]

Rowbotham's conceptualization of collective
alienation, consciousness, and formation of new
identities through reclamation of language and
image provides a richly suggestive framework
for approaching the individual life stories in
autobiographies by women and minorities. So
does Chodorow's model of female individuation, with its emphasis on women's relational
sense of self and the ongoing influence of the
mother-daughter relationship. Although no critics of autobiographies by women and minorities
have explicitly used the theoretical formulations
of Rowbotham or Chodorow, some have been
working along parallel lines. Often themselves at
the margins of criticism because of the texts they
discuss, a few of these critics have noted the role
that group consciousness—both alienated and
potentially transformative—sometimes plays in
the construction of personal histories. In "In
Search of the Black Female Self," Regina Blackburn argues that black women autobiographers
use the genre to redefine "the black female self
in black terms from a black perspective" (147).
Blackburn adapts Stephen Butterfield's discussion of black consciousness in *Black Autobiography in America* for her interpretation of how
black women integrate their racial and sexual
identities into their individual life stories. As
Butterfield writes:

> The "self" of black autobiography . . . is
> not an individual with a private career, but
> a soldier in a long, historic march toward
> Canaan. The self is conceived as a member
> of an oppressed social group, with ties and
> responsibilities to the other members. It is
> a conscious political identity, drawing sus-
> tenance from the past experience of the
> group. . . . The autobiographical form is
> one of the ways that black Americans have
> asserted their right to live and grow. It is a

bid for freedom, a beak of hope cracking
the shell of slavery and exploitation. (2–3)

Similarly, Bernice Johnson Reagon identifies
black women's autobiographical writing as "cultural autobiography" because the story of a
black woman's selfhood is inseparable from her
sense of community. She writes: "We are, at
the base of our identities, nationalists. We are
people builders, carriers of cultural traditions,
key to the formation and continuance of culture" (81).[9]

Mary Mason's pathbreaking introduction to
Journeys: Autobiographical Writings by Women
does not use Chodorow's developmental model
of female selfhood, but Mason argues in a related vein that women's sense of self exists within
a context of a deep awareness of others. "Wom-
en do not present the 'self' on a dramatic scale
where a battle of opposing forces is played out"
(xiv), she argues, in opposition to the models
of autobiography based in the example of Saint
Augustine's *Confessions*. "Nor do women," she
continues, "use a Rousseauean version of the
confession," in which "characters and events
exist only to become part of the landscape of
the hero's self-discovery" (xiv). Instead, wom-
en's autobiographical writings often include "the
real presence and recognition of another consciousness. . . . While de Beauvoir argues that
men have cast women into the role of 'the other'
existing only in relation to the male identity,
women, as revealed in our selections, seem to
recognize the full autonomy of the 'other' (in
this case the male) without destroying their own
sense of self" (xiv). Mason's theory that many
women's autobiographies create the female self
by exploring her relation with a fully rendered
Other is consistent with Chodorow's description
of the "more complex relational constellation"
of women's emotional lives.[10]

Building on the work of critics like Blackburn,
Butterfield, and Mason, I want to explore the

usefulness of Rowbotham's ideological focus on collective consciousness and Chodorow's psychoanalytical focus on relational gender identity for a psycho-political reading of women's autobiographical writings. The complementary models Rowbotham and Chodorow propose for women's selfhood are not equally relevant for all autobiographies, but they provide illuminating perspectives on both thematic and formalistic elements in a range of women's autobiographical writing. Although women often do not situate the self in Rowbotham's overtly political context, their awareness of group identity as it intersects with individual identity is pervasive. Instead of seeing themselves as solely unique, women often explore their sense of shared identity with other women, an aspect of identity that exists in tension with a sense of their own uniqueness. Although few women autobiographers express a fully psychoanalytic model of the self's development, Chodorow's concept of women's fluid ego boundaries and the importance of mother-daughter relationships is useful in understanding the unfolding self in women's writing. . . .

[Friedman proceeds to offer readings of autobiographical writings by Anäis Nin, Charlotte Perkins Gilman, Isbella Leitner, Ntozake Shange, Paule Marshall, H. D. (Hilda Doolittle), Gertrude Stein, and Maxine Hong Kingston. Her conclusion follows.]

Women's autobiography comes alive as a literary tradition of self-creation when we approach its texts from a psycho-political perspective based in the lives of women. Historically, women as a group have never been the "gatherer of men, of lands, of power, maker of kingdoms or of empires," to echo Gusdorf once again. Instead, they have been the gathered, the colonized, the ruled. Seldom the "inventor of laws and of wisdom," they have been born into those inventions—all the more so if their race, religion, class, or sexual preferences also marginal-

ized them. Nonetheless, this historical oppression has not destroyed women's consciousness of self. As Rowbotham says, woman have shattered the distorting identities imposed by culture and left "the sign" of their "presence" in their autobiographical writings. Their signs, however, remain marginal or even untranslatable when they are placed in a context in which individuation is defined as the separation of the self from all others. Individualistic paradigms do not take into account the central role collective consciousness of self plays in the lives of women and minorities. They do not recognize the significance of interpersonal relationships and community in women's self-definition, nor do they explain the ongoing identification of the daughter with her mother. Rowbotham's historical and Chodorow's psychoanalytic models, on the other hand, offer a basis for exploring the self as women have constituted it in their writings. To echo and reverse Gusdorf once more, this autobiographical self often does not oppose herself to all others, does not feel herself to exist outside of others, and still less against others, but very much with others in an interdependent existence that asserts its rhythms everywhere in the community.

Notes

For their criticism and bibliographic help, I am indebted to Nellie McKay, Elizabeth Hirsh, Marilyn Young, and Steven Feierman. A version of this essay was presented at the Modern Language Association meeting in December 1984.

1. See also Pascal for an important early statement on autobiographical self-construction.

2. Gusdorf's "pre-conditions for autobiography" do not take into account the phenomenon of non-Westem autobiographies. Many of these predate contact with the West, and others are connected to indigenous traditions that should not be dismissed as "transplanted." For Asian and African autobiogra-

phies, for example, see Muraski, Bowring, Shen, Honig, Curtin, Wright, and Cunnison. Gusdorf also does not recognize the importance of early Christian spiritual autobiographies for the later secular genre. See, for example, Augustine and Pomerleau. His dating particularly ignores the early autobiographical writings of women. See, for example, Hildegard's *Vita* (1160s); Margery Kempe's *The Book of Margery Kempe* (early 1400s); Sor Juana's *La Respuesta* (1691); Glückel's *The Memoirs of Glückel of Hameln* (1689–1719); Alice Thornton's *The Autobiography of Mrs. Alice Thornton* (late seventeenth century); Kempe's *Book* is the first extant autobiography in English.

3. Many other valuable studies of autobiography also assume an individualistic model of the self. See for example Bruss, Buck, Gunn, Jay, Lejeune, Mazlish, Pascal, Spengemann, and Weintraub. These excellent studies draw their examples from an overwhelmingly white, male canon. Stone is an important exception. Although he emphasizes the "linkage of individualism, democratic pluralism, and autobiography," his valuable study of American "cultural narratives" extensively incorporates the work of women and minorities (9). In stressing the impact of cultural history and heritage on autobiography, he has moved away from a concept of the self as a purely isolate entity.

4. See also Neumann (5–195) for a Jungian version of Freud's emphasis on separation in the individuation process.

5. See also Mazlish, Mehlman.

6. According to Paul Lauter, Rowbotham is familiar with Du Bois's concept of double consciousness (conversation with Lauter).

7. Stone also refers to Chodorow's concept of women's relational identity in his chapter on women's autobiographies, but only to dismiss it, not to use it. He argues that such relational definitions are ideological, the kind of "social myth" which must be abandoned if we are to understand women's texts. See also Gilligan and Peck for discussion of the impact of relational models of female selfhood for understanding women's experience. Gilligan's application of Chodorow's model to gender differences in ethical development should prove especially useful for understanding autobiography, since life stories so often involve ethical crises.

8. For discussion of the pre-Oedipal period and lesbianism, see Freud, "Femininity," and Friedman and DuPlessis. For a lesbian critique of this pre-Oedipal model for adult lesbian relationships, see the papers from the panel entitled "Mothering Theory in Lesbian Writing," Division of Gay Studies, Modern Language Association meeting, December 1986.

9. See also Taylor.

10. See also Mason, "The Other Voice," and Billson and Smith. For important applications of Chodorow's concept of women's relational identity to women's fiction and poetry, see Gardiner and Ostriker.

Works Cited

Augustine, Saint. *Confessions*. Trans. Albert C. Outler. Philadelphia: Westminster Press, 1955.

Billson, Marcus K., and Sidonie A. Smith. "Lillian Hellman and the Strategy of the 'Other.'" In Jelinek, 163–79.

Bowring, Richard. "The Female Hand in Heian Japan: A First Reading." In Stanton, 55–62.

Broner, E. M. *Her Mothers*. Berkeley: Berkeley Medallion, 1975.

Blackburn, Regina. "In Search of the Black Female Self: African-American Women's Autobiographies and Ethnicity." In Jelinek, 133–48.

Bruss, Elizabeth W. *Autobiographical Acts: The Changing Situation of a Literary Genre*. Baltimore: Johns Hopkins University Press, 1976.

Buck, William R, Jr. "Reading Autobiography." *Genre* 13 (Winter 1980): 477–98.

Butterfield, Stephen. *Black Autobiography in America*. Amherst: University of Massachusetts Press, 1974.

Chodorow, Nancy. *Psychoanalysis and the Sociology of Gender*. Berkeley: University of California Press, 1978.

Cunnison, Ian. "History and Genealogies in a Conquest State." *American Anthropologist* 59 (1957): 20–31.

Cunnison, Ian. "Perpetual Kinship: A Political Institution of the Lulapula Peoples." *Rhodes-Livingston Journal* 20 (1956): 28–48.

Curtin, Philip, ed. *Africa Remembered: Narratives by West Africans from the Era of the Slave Trade*. Madison: University of Wisconsin Press, 1967.

Du Bois, W. E. B. *The Souls of Black Folk.* 1903. Rpt. in *Black Voices: An Anthology of Afro-American Literature,* ed. Abraham Chapman. New York: New American Library, 1968.

Freud, Sigmund. *Civilization and Its Discontents.* 1930. Trans. James Strachey. New York: Norton, 1961.

Freud, Sigmund. "A Difficulty in the Path of Psychoanalysis." 1917. In *Standard Edition of Sigmund Freud,* ed. James Strachey. London: Hogarth Press, 1955. 17: 137–44.

Freud, Sigmund. "Femininity." 1933. In *New Introductory Lectures,* trans. James Strachey. New York: Norton, 1965. 112–35.

Freud, Sigmund. "On Narcissism." 1914. In *General Psychological Theory: Papers on Metapsychology,* ed. Philip Rieff. New York: Collier, 1963.

Friedman, Susan Stanford. *Penelope's Web: Gender, Modernity, H.D.'s Fiction.* Cambridge: Cambridge University Press, 1990.

Friedman, Susan Stanford, and Rachel Blau DuPlessis. "'I Had Two Loves Separate': The Sexualities of H.D.'s *Her.*" *Montemora* 8 (1981): 7–30.

Gardiner, Judith Kegan. "On Female Identity & Writing by Women." *Critical Inquiry* 8 (Winter 1981): 347–61.

Gilligan, Carol. *In a Different Voice: Psychological Theory and Women's Development.* Cambridge: Harvard University Press, 1982.

Glückel. *The Memoirs of Glückel of Hameln.* Trans. Marvin Lowenthal. New York: Schocken, 1977.

Gunn, Janet Varner. *Autobiography: Toward a Poetics of Experience.* Philadelphia: University of Pennsylvania Press, 1982.

Gusdorf, Georges. "Conditions and Limits of Autobiography." 1956. Trans. James Olney. In Olney, *Autobiography,* 28–48.

Hildegard of Bingen. *Vita.* Excerpted in *Women Writers of the Middle Ages: A Critical Study of Texts from Perpetua (d. 203) to Marguerite Porete (d. 1310).* Ed. Peter Dronke. Cambridge: Cambridge University Press, 1984. 144–201, 231–64.

Honig, Emily. "Private Issues, Public Discourse: The Life and Times of Yu Luojin." *Pacific Affairs* 57 (Summer 1984): 252–64.

Jelinek, Estelle C., ed. *Women's Autobiography: Essays in Criticism.* Bloomington: Indiana University Press, 1980.

Jay, Paul. *Being in the Text: Self-Representation from Wordsworth to Roland Barthes.* Ithaca: Cornell University Press, 1984.

Juana Ines de la Cruz, Sor. *La Respuesta.* 1691. In *A Woman of Genius: An Intellectual Autobiography of Sor Juana Ines de la Cruz.* Trans. Margaret Sayers Peden. Salisbury: Lime Rock Press, 1982.

Kempe, Margery. *The Book of Margery Kempe.* In *By a Woman Writt: Literature from Six Centuries By and About Women.* Ed. Joan Goulianos. London: New English Library, 1973. 3–20.

Kennedy, Gerald. "Roland Barthes, Autobiography, and the End of Writing." *Georgia Review* 35 (Summer 1981): 381–400.

Lacan, Jacques. *Ecrits: A Selection.* Trans. Alan Sheridan. New York: Norton, 1977.

Lejeune, Philippe. "Autobiography in the Third Person." *New Literary History* 9 (1977): 27–50.

Mason, Mary G. "The Other Voice: Autobiographies of Women Writers." In Olney, *Autobiography,* 207–35.

Mason, Mary G., and Carol Hurd Greed, eds. *Journeys: Autobiographical Writings by Women.* Boston: G. K. Hall, 1979.

Mazlish, Bruce. "Autobiography and Psychoanalysis: Between Truth and Self-Deception." *Encounter* 35 (October 1970): 28–37.

Mehlman, Jeffrey. *A Structural Study of Autobiography: Proust, Leiris, Sartre, Levi-Strauss.* Ithaca: Cornell University Press, 1974.

Muraski, Shikibu. *The Tale of Genji.* Trans. Arthur Waley. New York: Modern Library, 1960.

Neumann, Erich. *The Origins and History of Consciousness.* Trans. R. F. C. Hull. Princeton: Princeton University Press, 1954.

Olney, James, ed. *Autobiography: Essays Theoretical and Critical.* Princeton: Princeton University Press, 1980.

Olney, James, ed. *Metaphors of Self: The Meaning of Autobiography.* Princeton: Princeton University Press, 1972.

Pascal, Roy. *Design and Truth in Autobiography.* London: Routledge and Kegan Paul, 1960.

Peck, Teresa. "Attachment and Separation Mold Women's Experience." *Women's Studies Research Center Newsletter* 5 (Winter 1984): 5.

Pomerleau, Cynthia S. "The Emergence of Women's Autobiography in England." In Jelinek, 21–38.

Reagon, Bernice Johnson. "My Black Mothers and Sisters or On Beginning a Cultural Autobiography." *Feminist Studies* 8 (Spring 1982): 81–95.

Rowbotham, Sheila. *Woman's Consciousness, Man's World.* London: Penguin, 1973.

Shange, Ntozake. *For colored girls who have considered suicide / when the rainbow is enuf: a choreopoem.* New York: Bantam, 1977.

Shen Fu. *Six Chapters in a Floating Life: The Autobiography of a Chinese Artist.* Trans. Shirley M. Black. New York: Oxford University Press, 1960.

Spengemann, William. *The Forms of Autobiography: Episodes in the History of a Literary Genre.* New Haven: Yale University Press, 1980.

Stone, Albert E. *Autobiographical Occasions and Original Acts: Versions of American Identity from Henry Adams to Nate Shaw.* Philadelphia: University of Pennsylvania Press, 1982.

Sukenick, Lynn. "On Women and Fiction." In *The Authority of Experience: Essays in Feminist Criticism,* ed. Arlyn Diamond and Lee R. Edwards. Amherst: University of Massachusetts Press, 1977. 28–44.

Taylor, Gordon O. "Voices from the Veil: Black American Autobiography." *Georgia Review* 35 (Summer 1981): 341–61.

Thornton, Alice. "The Autobiography of Alice Thornton." Excerpted in Goulianos, 31–53.

Ulmer, Gregory L. "The Discourse of the Imaginary." *Diacritics* 10 (March 1980): 61–75.

Weintraub, Karl J. "Autobiography and Historical Consciousness." *Critical Inquiry* 1 (June 1975): 821–48.

Wright, Marcia. *Women in Peril.* Lusaka: University of Zambia, 1984.

Wright, Marcia. "Women in Peril: A Commentary on the Life Stories of Captives in Nineteenth-Century East-Central Africa." *African Social Research* 20 (December 1975): 800–819.

3 On Confession

Rita Felski

. . . In examining the influence of feminism on women's autobiography, I focus upon the confession, a distinctive subgenre of autobiography which has become prominent in recent years, and whose importance in the context of feminism is clearly related to the exemplary model of consciousness-raising. The term "confession" has occasionally acquired slightly dismissive overtones in recent years. No such connotation is intended here; I use "confession" simply to specify a type of autobiographical writing which signals its intention to foreground the most personal and intimate details of the author's life. Francis Hart writes: "'Confession' is personal history that seeks to communicate or express the essential nature, the truth of the self."[1] Like consciousness-raising, the confessional text makes public that which has been private, typically claiming to avoid filtering mechanisms of objectivity and detachment in its pursuit of the truth of subjective experience. Examples of recent women's writing which can be regarded as conforming to this description include the following: in the United States, Alice Koller, *An Unknown Woman* (1982), Audre Lorde, *The Cancer Journals* (1980), Kate Millett, *Flying* (1974) and *Sita* (1977); in West Germany, Svende Merian, *Der Tod des Märchenprinzen* (The death of the fairytale prince) (1980), Judith Offenbach, *Sonja* (1980), Verena Stefan, *Häutungen* (Shedding) (1975), Karin Struck, *Klassenliebe* (Class love) (1973) and *Kindheits Ende* (Childhood's end) (1982); in France, Marie Cardinal, *The Words to Say It* (1975); in the Netherlands, Anja Meulen-

belt, *The Shame Is Over* (1980); and in England, Ann Oakley, *Taking It Like a Woman* (1984).[2]

Although a number of differences exist among these texts both formally and ideologically, they share an explicit rhetorical foregrounding of the relationship between a female author and a female reader and an emphasis upon the referential and denotative dimension of textual communication rather than its formal specificity. These features distinguish them from more consciously stylized and "literary" examples of twentieth-century women's autobiography by such writers as Simone de Beauvoir, Janet Frame, Lillian Hellman, Mary McCarthy, and Nathalie Sarraute. The questioning of self is frequently inspired by a personal crisis which acts as a catalyst: cancer (Lorde), crippling neurosis (Cardinal), the death or departure of a lover (Millett, Offenbach). Whereas [Estelle] Jelinek argues that "neither women nor men are likely to explore or to reveal painful and intimate memories in their autobiographies,"[3] this is clearly *not* the case in feminist confessional literature, which explicitly seeks to disclose the most intimate and often traumatic details of the author's life and to elucidate their broader implications. I am less interested in a detailed thematic interpretation of individual examples of this recent feminist autobiographical writing than in a consideration of the logic of confessional discourse as such in relation to its recent appropriation by the women's movement, mapping out the ambivalent status of this pursuit of self-identity. The question which arises is whether this confessional writing is an indispensable aspect of a process of critical self-understanding which constitutes part of feminism's emancipatory project, or whether, as Richard Sennett suggests, the current fascination with intimacy and self-discovery engenders an ever more frantic pursuit for a kernel of authentic self which continually eludes one's grasp: "Expression is made contingent upon authentic feeling, but one is always plunged into the narcissistic problem of never being able to crystallize what is authentic in one's feelings."[4] In this sense, the confession poses in exemplary fashion the problem of the relationship between personal experience and political goals within feminism as a whole. . . .

[Felski considers the limitations of a "purely formal definition of autobiography" and suggests how contemporary feminist writing confuses the boundaries between fiction and autobiography.]

. . . Recent years have seen the publication of large numbers of feminist texts which are written in an unrelativized first-person perspective, are strongly confessional, and encourage reader identification. This alone does not unambiguously mark the text as autobiography (as [Phillip] Lejeune points out, such features can be imitated by the novel), but they occur within a context of *reception* which encourages an interpretation of the text as the expression, in essence, of the views and experiences of the writing subject. Thus the women's movement has been influential in "personalizing" the literary text by emphasizing its autobiographical dimension. Feminist literature is often marketed in such a way as to foreground the persona of the author through the inclusion of photographs and biographical details which link the text to the life and act as a guarantee of its authenticity. Evelyne Keitel, discussing the reception of feminist confessional literature in West Germany, suggests that it is typically read as a truthful account of the author's experiences which is used as a springboard by readers from which to examine and compare their own experiences. The text is read less for its own sake, as a literary construct, than for its content in relation to its similarities and differences to the reader's own life. Reception, in other words, is strongly functional and often collective; Keitel refers to the use of such texts as Merian's *Der Tod des Märchenprinzen* as a basis for group discussions by women on the subject of their own sexual experiences.[5]

What, then, are the reasons for this blurring of the distinction between autobiography and fiction in feminist literature? Feminist confession exemplifies the intersection between the autobiographical imperative to communicate the truth of unique individuality, and the feminist concern with the representative and intersubjective elements of women's experience. In other words, the shift toward a conception of communal identity which has emerged with new social movements such as feminism brings with it a modification of the notion of individualism as it is exemplified in the male bourgeois autobiography. It is for this reason that Oakley feels free to invent some of the characters in her autobiography, for, as the publisher's blurb states: "In this honest, somewhat painful and absorbing account of her life . . . every woman will find some reflection of her own personality and feelings."[6] The obligation to honest self-depiction which constitutes part of the autobiographical contract is here mitigated by the feminist recognition that it is the representative aspects of the author's experience rather than her unique individuality which are important, allowing for the inclusion of fictive but representative episodes from the lives of women. The fact that the authors discussed write autobiographies explicitly and self-consciously *as women* is of central importance as an indication of the shifting conceptions of cultural identity which are in turn echoed in the changing forms and functions of autobiography. . . .

The autobiographical writing inspired by the

women's movement differs . . . from the traditional autobiography of bourgeois individualism, which presents itself as the record of an unusual but exemplary life. Precisely because of this uniqueness, the eighteenth-century autobiography claims a universal significance. Feminist confession, by contrast, is less concerned with unique individuality or notions of essential humanity than with delineating the specific problems and experiences which bind women together. It thus tends to emphasize the ordinary events of a protagonist's life, their typicality in relation to a notion of communal identity. "The legitimation for reporting these experiences lies precisely in their correspondence to other life histories, and all individual traits appear blurred or disguised, in order to emphasize their general validity and applicability."[7]

On the one hand, the autobiographical status of the text is important in guaranteeing its truthfulness as the depiction of the life, and more important, the inner feelings of a particular individual. On the other, it is the *representative* aspects of experience, rather than those that mark the protagonist/narrator as unique, which are emphasized in relation to a notion of a communal female identity. It is for this reason that feminist confession is sometimes deliberately ambiguous in its use of proper names, seeking to minimize the specificity of its content as the depiction of the life of a single individual and to emphasize its exemplary status, while still retaining the claim to historical truthfulness and authenticity which form part of the autobiographical contract. As Oakley writes in *Taking It Like a Woman*, "it would be arrogant to suppose I'm unique; I'm not."[8]

Keitel suggests that this kind of autobiographical writing, precisely because of its combination of "authenticity" and representativeness, has played an important role in the self-definition of social movements in the 1970s and 1980s, serving as an identifying point of reference in much the same way as political theory (the work of

Marcuse, for example) was a rallying point for the New Left in the 1960s. By writing autobiographical narratives centered on personal experience, authors avoid "theoretical abstraction"; there exists within contemporary social movements, feminism included, an ambivalence toward theory which extends from a legitimate critique of the kind of arid leftist theorizing which remains oblivious to personal relationships and their exploitative aspects, to an uncritical celebration of "feeling" and a problematic anti-intellectualism. Confessional writing, then, proceeds from the subjective experience of problems and contradictions as encountered in the realm of everyday life. At the same time, however, feminist confession selects out those aspects of experience which are perceived to possess a representative significance in relation to the audience of women it wishes to reach. Through the discussion of, and abstraction from, individual experience in relation to a general problematic of sexual politics, feminist confession thus appropriates some of the functions of political discourse. It is instrumental in the delineation of a group identity through the establishment of norms, formulates elements of a more general feminist critique, and concretizes aspects of the aims and interests of the women's movement: "The lyrical self articulated in these texts always perceives itself as part of a collective, whose experiences constitute its norms and on behalf of whose members it speaks."[9]

The Forms of Confession

Structurally, it is possible to make a rough division of feminist confession into two main groups. The first can be defined as conforming more or less closely to the journal form, that is, an open-ended structure written in the present tense, in which the author records the details of daily events as they occur. The second, to be discussed below, offers a retrospective and thus more clearly synthetic account of part or all of the author's life history from the standpoint of the writing present. . . .

The confessional diary . . . often shores up its claims to authenticity and truthfulness by consciously distinguishing itself from the category of literature. Aesthetic criteria are rejected as irrelevant: a conscious artistic structure is in fact suspect insofar as it implies distance and control rather than an unmediated baring of the soul. [Karin] Struck writes, "I think of the word 'fiction' and immediately see in front of me a frosted plane of glass, behind which a child is lying that can't be touched or visited. Fiction *is* remoteness, distance, separation." [10] The more obviously "literary" the text—the more clearly it signals its fictional status through such textual features as irony, parody, and self-reflexivity, extended use of symbolic and "poetic" language, or elaborated narrative structures—the less likely the reader is to respond to the text as the authentic self-expression of an authorial subject. It is for this reason that feminist confession often imitates such personal, nonliterary forms as the diary or the letter in the attempt to regulate the potential open-endedness of the literary text. It attempts, in other words, to achieve the reverse of the defamiliarization which Russian formalism identified as the key function of literature, in order to inspire a process of involvement and identification by persuading readers that they are reading an intimate communication addressed to them personally by the author.

On a structural level the diary is episodic and fragmented, depicting events as they occur rather than attempting to select and organize in terms of any unifying vision. . . . Through this kind of structure, the confession seeks to emphasize its status as reflecting and contingent on lived experience, rather than as a self-contained literary artifact. The author shares with her audience an uncertainty as to the final outcome of the text, which is determined by external factors rather than the logic of aesthetic form. . . .

The second main type of confessional text employs a structure based on retrospective narration and is less obviously concerned with inclusiveness and the depiction of every detail of daily events. . . . The need for an exhaustive rendering of every detail of experience is less overriding in these texts. With the benefit of hindsight, it becomes possible to focus on those moments which have been revealed as turning points in the development of a life history. Such moments are typically defined in terms of personal relations: the loss of a lover, the experience of childbirth, the death of a parent. The depiction of the author's life frequently coincides with the narrative of a conversion to feminism, but an obviously teleological structure is usually avoided. . . .

In general, then, the feminist confession seeks to reduce the patterning and organization of experience which characterizes historical narrative, its structure is episodic and fragmented, not chronological and linear. The organizing principle of the text is provided by the associations of the experiencing subject. While foregrounding the consciousness of this writing self, however, the feminist confession simultaneously encodes an audience. It self-consciously addresses a community of female readers rather than an undifferentiated general public. This sense of communality is accentuated through a tone of intimacy, shared allusions, and unexplained references with which the reader is assumed to be familiar. The implied reader of the feminist confession is the sympathetic female confidante and is often explicitly encoded in the text through appeals, questions, and direct address. The importance of the reader's role is directly related to the belief that she will understand and share the author's position. . . .

The formal features of feminist confession are thus closely related to the social function which it is intended to serve, encouraging a particular form of interaction between text and audience. They typically include an unrelativized first-personal narrative perspective, a thematic concentration upon feelings and personal relationship, and frequent reliance upon an informal and nonliterary style which establishes a relationship of intimacy between author and reader, and a tendency to deemphasize the aesthetic and fictive dimension of the text in order to give the appearance of authentic self-expression.

[Felski then looks at the emergence of the diary form in the eighteenth century and the value placed on "the appearance of authenticity" which depended upon an intimate relationship between narrator and reader. She concludes this section of her essay by emphasizing that "the adoption of the confessional mode by contemporary feminism . . . raises a number of questions regarding the emancipatory value of writing about the self, which can be elucidated by tracing the historically determined shift in the meaning and function of confession."]

The Dialectic of Confession

Autobiography in the modern sense, as a literary genre predicated upon the possibility and legitimacy of self-knowledge, first emerges as a distinctive form in the eighteenth century. Rousseau's *Confessions* is usually held up as the first example of autobiography as a celebration of unique individualism, and thus fundamentally different from earlier texts, such as the confessions of Saint Augustine or the life of Saint Teresa, in which self-analysis is valued not for its own sake but as a means of exposing the fallibility of humanity and affirming the ultimate authority of a divine knowledge beyond the individual's grasp.[11] Protestantism's emphasis on the importance of the individual struggle for salvation prepared the way for the self-consciousness necessary for autobiography proper; the flourishing of Pietism in Germany and Puritanism in England in the seventeenth century encouraged an active interest in self-scrutiny and spiritual introspection, often in the form of diaries in which every detail of daily thoughts and actions was recorded and examined for its moral and spiritual meaning.

Autobiography, then, develops out of the genre of the religious confession; there is a gradual shift from a form of self-analysis which seeks out sin and transgression in the context of adherence to a religious orthodoxy to an exploration of intimacy, emotion, self-understanding as aspects of a nascent bourgeois subjectivity. The one English word "confession" is ambiguous in that it covers this shift in meaning and function which is expressed in German by three different words: *Beichte, Geständnis, Bekenntnis.* Confession as *Beichte* or *Geständnis* refers to an institutionalized form of confession to religious or legal authority through the acceptance of individual culpability for transgression and the enactment of penance: "Confession is part of a moral-legal syndrome of practices and beliefs which include certain key concepts (the conscience, the self, interior guilt, sin)."[12] As such, as Mike Hepworth and Bryan Turner note, confession can be seen to operate as a mechanism of social control, a reaffirmation of social order and the status quo through acknowledgment of individual deviance. Yet confession acquires a more positive meaning in the development of bourgeois society; as the enforcement of confession through religious law increasingly gives way to voluntary affirmations of faith and of the self, so the confession comes increasingly to symbolize a private assertion of freedom which may challenge rather than simply conform to existing social norms. Literary confession since the eighteenth century is primarily concerned not with the admission of guilt and the appeal to a higher authority, but rather with the affirmation and exploration of free subjectivity. Yet this attempted emancipation of the self can expose a self-defeating dialectic in which the history of confession as *Beichte,* as subjection to external authority, returns in new form. For the "authentic self" is itself very much a social product, and the attempt to assert its privileged autonomy can merely underline its profound dependence upon the cultural and ideological systems through which it is constituted. The more frantic the search for an inner self, for a kernel of meaning untouched by a society rejected as oppressive and alienating, the more clearly subjectivity is revealed to be permeated by and dependent upon those very symbolic constraints from which it seeks to liberate itself. In other words, the act of confession can potentially exacerbate rather than alleviate problems of self-identity, engendering a dialectic in which the production of ever more writing as a means to defining a center of meaning merely serves to underscore the alienation of the subject even as it seeks to overcome it.

If feminist confession is considered in this light, the interpenetration of the subjective with the social and ideological domains emerges at a number of levels. Most obviously, the social constitution of the inner self manifests itself in the ambivalent self-image of women writers, which reveals the powerful psychological mechanisms by which gender ideologies are internalized. It is clear that autobiographical writing by oppressed groups will be particularly prone to conflicts and tensions. On the one hand, the depiction of one's life and experiences as a woman, a black person, a homosexual, can be a potentially liberating process insofar as it expresses a public self-acceptance and a celebration of difference. Oakley, while writing, "I want to surpass my femininity,"[13] and offering a critical account of the negative aspects of female socialization, nevertheless reaffirms in her autobiography the value and importance of many aspects of women's lives. Lorde uses her self-image as a black lesbian feminist as a source of strength in the face of cancer, wishing to see herself as "a fighter resisting rather than as a passive victim suffering."[14]

On the other hand, the internalized cultural values which define specific identities as marginal, inferior, or deviant can come to the surface in feelings of anxiety and guilt. Regina Blackburn, analyzing a number of autobiographies by black women writers, shows that black identity generates ambivalent feelings, that it can be a source of pride but just as easily give rise to a sense of shame and self-hatred.[15] This phenomenon of a strongly negative self-image can be a particular problem for women, whose socialization typically endows them with feelings of inadequacy. Discussing the autobiographies of well known and publicly successful women, Patricia Meyer Spacks comments upon their self-deprecatory stance: "They use autobiography, paradoxically, partly as a mode of self-denial."[16]

This negative pattern in which attempted self-affirmation reverts back into anxiety and self-castigation is a recurring one in at least some examples of feminist confession. Millett, for one, is contemptuous of her own emotional responses, speaking of "debility, weakness, loss. All the hateful, the despicable traits. Dependence most of all, a paralyzing, humiliating dependence."[17] German authors Struck and Offenbach are particularly prone to self-accusation. "It's almost embarrassing, how often I use the word 'guilt' in these notes,"[18] admits Offenbach, who refers to the particular problems caused by "homosexual self-hatred."[19] Feminism appears ironically to accentuate guilt rather than resolve it by providing an ideal of autonomy which the author is unable to emulate. Thus Struck savagely condemns her own "slimy dependency."[20] The central metaphor of *Kindheits Ende* is the author's perception of herself as a child, and her consequent self-castigation for her own immaturity. Both she and Offenbach continually censure their own behavior, defining themselves as obsessive and neurotic. Any insight gained through the act of confession does not appear to be translated into action, but merely generates increased feelings of guilt in the author at the extent of her own failings: "Then I think, how sick and tired I am of it; it's always the same reproduction of the same person who suffers, but who never draws conclusions for action from this suffering. I should stop suffering some time, I think, then there'd be something new to talk about."[21] Of course, the very point of the feminist confession is to confront the more unpalatable aspects of female experience as general problems, not to present idealized images of women as positive role models. Nevertheless, such passages are an indication that the project of self-disclosure as a means to self-emancipation may be more fraught with difficulties than it first appears.

The Critique of Narcissism

These difficulties in turn expose a broader and more general problematic at the very heart of confession: the belief that self-examination and self-disclosure can provide a source of truth and meaning in a society whose public values and institutions no longer possess any such authority. This conviction is of course a defining feature of bourgeois subjectivity; the development of capitalism brings with it individual emancipation from the authority of tradition, but only at the cost of alienation from a social environment which can no longer provide unquestioningly accepted values and systems of belief. Hence the preoccupation with the self and the personal sphere in bourgeois culture. . . .

. . . [T]he critique of [narcissistic preoccupation with the self by such writers as Christopher Lasch[22] and Richard Sennett] is helpful insofar as it correctly identifies the potentially self-defeating logic of a striving for authenticity which seeks to deny all mediating social and symbolic structures by uncovering a kernel of pure self-identity. The unconditional demand for intimacy, confronted with the intolerable reality of alienation and lack, reverts back into anxiety and self-hatred. The goal of the confession is to strip away the superficial layers of convention and to expose an authentic core of self, of meaning as fully present to itself. Yet the more frantically this true subjectivity is pursued, the more elusive it appears; the greater the desire for intimacy and spontaneity, the more clearly the act of writing is revealed as the most alienated of activities. Feminist confession is by no means exempt from this dialectic of intimacy and alienation, which constitutes a defining feature of subjectivity as such. Indeed, because of women's socialization toward intimacy, and because ideologies of "feminine" sincerity and spontaneity continue to mark at least some examples of contemporary women's writing, feminist confession often reveals particularly clearly the contradictions between the desire for total intimacy and union, which seeks to erase all boundaries between desire and its object, and the act of writing as a continuing deferral of any such identity. . . .

Intimacy and Alienation

The longing for intimacy emerges as a defining feature of the feminist confession at two interconnected levels: in the actual representation of the author's own personal relationships and in the relationship between author and reader established by the text. . . .

In one sense . . . the feminist confession documents the failure of intimacy. Yet clearly the production of the text itself functions as an attempted compensation for this failure, generating in the relationship between reader and author the erotic mutuality which cannot otherwise be realized. Writing, seemingly the most isolated of activities, becomes the means to the creation of an ideal intimacy. As Offenbach notes of her own text, the confession is a cry for love, allowing the author to express powerful emotional feelings to an unknown reader without fear of rejection. The writing self is profoundly dependent upon the reader for validation, specifically the projected community of female readers who will understand, sympathize, and identify with the author's emotions and experiences.

As a consequence, the boundaries between text and life can become blurred, and writing becomes both a medium of, and a substitute for, personal relations. Offenbach, for instance, describes in *Sonja* how she reads another confessional autobiography and falls obsessively in love with its author; although an actual meeting ends in disaster, a similar and more successful relationship begins in the same way, with Offenbach falling in love with a woman after reading her autobiography. Sensitive to criticism that such behavior might be considered odd, she writes: "Isn't that after all a way of getting to know another person really very closely, perhaps a lot better than if you simply meet and have a talk?" . . .[23]

The ambivalence of autobiography as both the ultimate truth of the author's life and as a mere simulacrum which can never fully encapsulate the reality of which it speaks is clearly apparent in the contemporary fascination with confession. It is as if the written text has acquired the function of guaranteeing the author's identity. . . .

Feminist confession thus seeks to affirm a female experience which has often been repressed and rendered invisible by speaking about it, by writing it into existence. The act of writing promises power and control, endowing subjective experience with authority and meaning. Millett writes: "My notebook . . . has become my friend, solace, obsession. I will live in it, in the ability to record experience which makes me more than its victim. . . . Magical transformation of pain into substance, meaning, something of my own."[24] Yet this status of the text as the validation for a life is double-edged; the more emphatically it defines its function as the communication of the real, the more clearly the unbridgeable gap between word and referent is exposed. Thus Millett immediately contradicts her earlier statement: "The notebook assumes its real aspect, an untidy scribble without meaning or body or direction. The cheapest illusion."[25] Feminist confession swerves between the affirmation of the truth of its own discourse and the recognition of the text's insufficient status, the lack of identity of the text and the life. The consciousness of this discrepancy can generate ever more writing in the attempt to fill the gap, an extravagant piling up of protestations of feeling as a means of intensifying the reality of the text. The confessions of Offenbach and Struck in particular are full of repeated references to love, guilt, pain, anxiety, hatred, as if the constant reiteration of such words will bring the text closer to its goal of transparent self-disclosure. Yet the more words that are generated by the confessional text, the more clearly it reveals itself as infinitely extendable, an endless chain of signifiers that can never encapsulate the fullness of meaning which the author seeks and which would put an end to writing itself.

This lack of identity between the text and the life, experience and its representation, is of course a central problem of autobiography, and, in a broader sense, of literature itself. "Writing perpetually stands in for a reality it can never encompass."[26] Moreover, not only does the life call into question the authority of the text, but the text begins to undermine the reality of the life. Although the confession is chosen to convey immediacy and spontaneity, the very process of recording intrudes upon that which is being recorded and changes it. "If you record a day of your life, does the decision to do so change the shape of that day? . . . Do you change the balance, distort the truth?" asks Millett.[27] Life itself is revealed as literary material awaiting process-

ness."[32] Lorde's text exemplifies the continuing importance of confessional writing as long as privatized areas of shame, fear, and guilt continue to exist in women's lives. The author confronts the issue of breast cancer on both personal and social levels, exploring the emotions experienced before and after surgery, but also examining the politics of the American medical establishment and the trivialization of breast cancer as a cosmetic rather than a health problem. . . .

A feminist critique of the political aims, themes, and techniques of feminist confession has been articulated by Sigrid Weigel. Whereas more consciously stylized, fragmented, and "literary" forms of writing can serve the function of estranging and calling into question gender identity, Weigel argues, feminist confession generates the illusion of a "natural" female self and is both aesthetically and politically naive, confirming the existing prejudices of readers rather than challenging them. Weigel suggests that feminist confession typically results in cathartic self-reproach rather than critical self-analysis and is essentially harmless, "without any transformative social impact."[33] In turn, the prevalence of feminist confessional writing risks encouraging a pejorative dismissal of "women's literature" by the reading public as a whole as typically lachrymose and self-indulgent.

Weigel's critique has a certain validity, particularly in relation to German feminist literature, which forms the basis of her analysis and which has become strongly identified with the confessional genre. Whereas *Häutungen* was instrumental in challenging existing reader expectations and breaking the silence about women's experience of sexuality, it has been followed by a flood of confessional texts in a similar vein, which often appear to confirm rather than challenge the prejudices of female readers, reiterating gender stereotypes and often indulging in little more than self-pity and self-justification.

Merian's *Der Tod des Märchenprinzen*, for example, reveals a remarkably blinkered moral self-righteousness in its representation of femininity as victimhood, espousing a dogmatic conviction regarding the absolute authority of female subjective experience. As a counter-example, however, one can cite *The Cancer Journals*, which offers acute insights into the anguish and the politics of cancer while avoiding self-pity and simplistic judgments. Similarly, *An Unknown Woman* and *The Words to Say It* exemplify the potential value of confession as a process of critical reflection upon the construction of female subjectivity, illuminating the deeply ingrained passivity, dependency, and anxiety to please which frequently shape the female psyche, while revealing the potentially liberating effects of recognizing and calling into question such psychological mechanisms. Cardinal writes, "Day after day since my birth, I had been made up: my gestures, my attitudes, my vocabulary. My needs were repressed, my desires, my impetus, they had been dammed up, painted over, disguised and imprisoned."[34]

As a result, it becomes difficult to pronounce any one final judgment upon feminist confession as a genre, either to celebrate it as radically subversive or simply to reject it as self-indulgent and naive. It is certainly true, as Weigel argues, that feminist confession can at times reproduce images of women uncomfortably close to the stereotypes feminist theorists are attempting to challenge: a belief in the moral superiority of female expressiveness, an assumption that women's language is more "authentic" than that of men. Against this, however, it can also be noted that the dividing line between a repressive stereotype and an empowering symbol of cultural identity is often a very narrow one. The creation and affirmation of symbolic identities constitutes a recurring need on the part of marginalized social groups, fulfilling a desire for self-validation in the face of the hostility of a dominant culture. . . .

As [Jeffrey] Weeks emphasizes, the significance of identity politics can only be adequately assessed by examining the needs it fulfills for particular social groups at a given historical moment.[35] Feminist confession is not a self-generating discourse to be judged in abstraction from existing social conditions; it exemplifies a simultaneous interrogation and affirmation of gendered subjectivity in the context of notions of communal identity generated by new social movements. Feminist literature addresses a potential "we" and challenges contemporary perceptions of the alienated anonymity of the individual in mass society by means of an appeal to a notion of oppositional community based upon the shared bond of gender linking author and reader. It may appear easy to expose the naiveté of such an attempt to reclaim literature for the purposes of intersubjective communication in a society in which texts are regarded as commodities to be regulated by the impersonal demands of the market, and where subjectivity is itself increasingly depicted as a mere effect of technologized communication networks, of fetishized images of pseudoindividuality manufactured and circulated by the mass media. Yet any such sweeping vision of one-dimensionality constitutes a gross oversimplification, ignoring the complex and contradictory nature of contemporary social relations as expressed in the current reemergence of forms of resistance and dissent embodied in autonomous social movements. Feminist literature *has* been an instrumental force in the creation of a feminist "counter-public sphere," an oppositional discursive space within contemporary society defined in terms of a notion of gender identity perceived to unite all participants. Confessional writing has been central to this sphere, as it has played out an anxious, often uneasy struggle to discover a female self, a struggle which is by no means free of contradiction but which constitutes a necessary moment in the self-definition of an oppositional community.

Notes

1. Francis Hart, "Notes for an Anatomy of Modern Autobiography," *New Literary History* 1 (1970): 491.

2. In the case of texts written in a language other than English, I have cited translations whenever these are readily available. All other translations are my own.

3. Estelle C. Jelinek, "Introduction: Women's Autobiography and the Male Tradition," in *Women's Autobiography: Essays in Criticism,* ed. Jelinek (Bloomington: Indiana University Press, 1980), 10.

4. Richard Sennett, *The Fall of Public Man* (New York: Knopf, 1977), 267.

5. Evelyne Keitel, "Verständingungstexte—Form, Funktion, Wirkung," *German Quarterly* 56, no. 3 (1983): 439.

6. Ann Oakley, *Taking It like a Woman* (London: Jonathan Cape, 1984). See the back cover of the Fontana 1985 paperback edition.

7. Keitel, 436.

8. Oakley, 2.

9. Keitel, 447.

10. Karin Struck, *Kindheits Ende: Journal einer Krise* (Frankful am Main: Suhrkamp, 1982), 497.

11. James Goodwin, "Narcissus and Autobiography," *Genre* 12 (1979): 82.

12. Mike Hepworth and Bryan S. Turner, *Confession: Studies in Deviance and Religion* (London: Routledge and Kegan Paul, 1982), 8.

13. Oakley, 57.

14. Audre Lorde, *The Cancer Journals* (1980; rpt. London: Sheba Feminist Publishers, 1985), 65.

15. Regina Blackburn, "In Search of the Black Female Self: African-American Women's Autobiographies and Ethnicity," in Jelinek, 149–162.

16. Patricia Meyer Spacks, "Selves in Hiding," in Jelinek, 132.

17. Kate Millett, *Sita* (London: Virago, 1977), 136.

18. Judith Offenbach, *Sonja: Eine Melancholie*

für Fortgeschrittene (Frankfurt am Main: Suhrkamp, 1980), 264.

19. Ibid., 236.

20. Struck, 387.

21. Ibid., 297.

22. Christopher Lasch, *The Culture of Narcissism: American Life in an Age of Diminishing Expectations* (New York: Norton, 1979).

23. Offenbach, 291.

24. Millett, 137.

25. Ibid.

26. Terry Eagleton, *The Rape of Clarissa: Writing, Sexuality and Class Struggle in Samuel Richardson* (Oxford: Basil Blackwell, 1982), 44.

27. Millett, 272–73.

28. Sennett, 334.

29. Wendy Martin, "Another View of the 'City upon a Hill': The Prophetic Vision of Adrienne Rich," in *Women Writers and the City: Essays in Feminist Lit-* *erary Criticism,* ed. Susan Merrill Squier (Knoxville: University of Tennessee Press, 1984), 261.

30. Offenbach, 98.

31. Oakley, 2.

32. Lorde, 1.

33. Sigrid Weigel, "'Woman Begins Relating to Herself': Contemporary German Women's Literature (Part One)," *New German Critique,* no. 31 (1984): 82. See also Jutta Kolkenbrock-Netz and Marianne Schuller, "Frau feministischer Praxis," in *Entwürfe von Frauen in du Literatur des 20. Jahrhunderts,* ed. Irmela von der Luhe (Berlin: Argument, 1982).

34. Marie Cardinal, *The Words to Say It,* trans. Pat Goodheart (Cambridge, MA: Van Vactor and Goodheart, 1983), 164.

35. Jeffrey Weeks, *Sexuality and Its Discontents: Meanings, Myths and Modern Sexualities* (London: Routledge and Kegan Paul, 1985), 189.

4 The Narrative Self: Race, Politics, and Culture in Black American Women's Autobiography

Nellie Y. McKay

From their earliest writings in the West, autobiography was sufficiently central to African Americans that they made it the genre of preference in the development of black literary culture. In the eighteenth and nineteenth centuries, displaced Africans found it critical in gaining the language they needed to enter white debates on the humanity of Africans, and to challenge western European discourses on freedom and race. They believed that in mastering the literacy and the language of their enslavers they could prove to their oppressors and to sympathetic white readers that people with black skins were as intelligent as other groups.[1] Since then the life story (or portions of it) has been the most effective forum for defining black selfhood in a racially oppressive world.

For race (which also implied class) was the crucial ground on which relations of power developed between black and white people in eighteenth- and nineteenth-century America, making blackness and U.S. citizenship virtually antithetical to each other and the power relations in race and politics together central to both secular and religious black autobiographical narrative. Challenging white hegemony, black autobiographers used narrative to fight their battle against chattel slavery and to engage in the search for political and psychological freedom for all black people. For the black writer did not and could not participate in an ideology of self that separated the self from the black community and the roots of its culture. Consequently, the personal narrative became a historical site on which aesthetics, self-confirmation of humanity, citizenship, and the significance of racial politics shaped African-American literary expression.

Black autobiographers almost always focus on the racial authentication of self. Their narratives begin from a stated (sometimes disguised) position that establishes and asserts the reality of self through experience. Critic Craig Werner believes that the internal pressure for self-authentication in the black narrative originates in the African American's awareness of a contingent "self": an ever shifting social construct that makes it impossible for powerless people to take the self for granted (Werner, 209). As signifying metaphors, in black words printed on white pages from a black perspective, black life stories announced authentic selves secure in their individual worth, group pride, and the humanity of black people. The texts were linguistic achievements affirming a rejection of white-imposed denigration of the black self and, in the best of American traditions, making proud assertions of a new identity. Early black autobiographers appropriated the master's tools to write themselves into being and their community into freedom (Werner, 204). Using the white oppressor's language and black cultural tropes (like masking), they transformed the racially inferior, abstract African self of the master's text into the ultimately triumphant black experiential self. These selves, inhabitants of the slave and spiritual self-stories, were the legacy of twentieth-century autobiographers as different as W. E. B. Du Bois, Richard Wright, and Maya Angelou. For the autonomous black self in the United States is the achievement of a racial and/or sexual self that is the product of mediation through peculiar experiences of oppression and survival (Andrews, 1–31). But, while the struggle for agency on these terms is central to the black self in narrative, that is not its end: for there is no monolithic representation of black identity, and the richness of the autobiographical tradition includes its multiplicity and complexity of narrative strategies and its various forms of self-representation that delineate differences among and between black women and men.

This study assumes gender as a force in black women's stories interrogating the narratives of black male sexism, white female racism, and white patriarchal authority. For, in spite of the racial and class oppression black women share with black men and the gender oppression they share with white women, they see themselves differently from black men and white women. On one hand, white people drove black slave women, punished them as severely as men, and valued them like men for their productive labor. In addition, women's worth as property included their reproductive value and sexual availability to white men, activities that forced them to be victims of unrelenting sexual abuses, many even bearing children for white and black men at the same time. On the other hand, nineteenth-century ideologies of white womanhood enabled white women, from their own subordinate po-

sition, to negotiate a relationship with patriarchy that joined their class interests with those of white men and actively discouraged them from forging alliances with black women (Carby, 17–18). Thus, in the struggle against oppressive sexual and racial authority, the black female self stands at once alongside and apart from white women and black men, joined to the struggles of each but separated from both in a system that still privileges whiteness and maleness. From this complex angle of vision the black female narrative self makes of black female identity an exploration of differences from—and limits of loyalty to—black men and all others.

Differences in how black women and men see themselves, want to be perceived, and exploit the circumstances and opportunities available to them to assert autonomy in the world were apparent from the earliest autobiographical texts from which black female and male selves emerged. For instance, most slave autobiographers identify a dramatic moment when the slave in the self and the self in the slave confront each other and the self overcomes the slave. For example, the transformation from "slave" to "man" occurred, Frederick Douglass tells us, in a public moment of high drama, when he uses physical force to refuse to be further brutalized by his temporary master, Edward Covey (Douglass, 89–105). Douglass declares that from that time, though he was still technically a slave, his relationship to white power changed. It was only a matter of time before he engineered his own freedom from the hateful and hated institution. Douglass expresses the triumph of self in gendered terms, recognizing himself as a man in his victory over Covey.

Conversely, Linda Brent, the persona of female slave Harriet Jacobs's *Incidents in the Life of a Slave Girl*, metamorphoses from helpless slave girl to woman with some control over her life (also a gendered transformation) with her secret determination to resist the sexual harassment of her owner, Dr. Flint. In both texts these events are alike in their focus on concrete experiences that link the selves in the texts to the writers of the texts. They also parallel each other in that it is their status as slaves (race and class) that generates their oppression. However, gender makes the difference to these characters in their development from passive slaves to conscious human agents. For his moment of self-recognition the virile Douglass selects a public confrontation with his master, contesting relations of force. The imminent danger in his situation (Covey might have killed him for resisting the whipping and for striking a white man) increases his male heroic stature in a struggle of wills turned into one over manhood.

In a reversal of this situation, in the cross-racial sexual relationship between the nubile young female slave and her master, the fifteen-year-old Brent chooses to challenge her oppressor in private. For one thing, she knew her success depended on leaving his public image as master intact. In addition, any revelation of her dilemma, even to those closest to her, would have compromised her standing in the community, increasing her sexual vulnerability. Her subsequent concealment in the crawl space of her grandmother's house and her life in seclusion as a fugitive after she escaped the South are extensions of links between privacy and female survival that intimately connect to experiential differences between black women and men in search of dignity and selfhood. Brent's presentation of her life during and after her enslavement includes a portrait of the constricted physical and psychological spaces allotted to black women and contrasts sharply with Douglass's audacious statement of "walking away from slavery," followed by his meteoric rise to abolitionist spokesman par excellence. For most of her story Brent remained within the domestic sphere, while Douglass had considerable mobility, even as a slave.[2] But in the outcome of her

efforts to forge her own freedom Brent's strategies deserve great applause. Her political insights, her ingenuity in thwarting her master, and her ultimate success in depriving him of power over her life make her text extremely significant in the larger struggle for black freedom. It is also noteworthy that as a seemingly helpless orphaned teenage girl, Brent believed that she was not completely a victim (no doubt from observing her grandmother's life) and that it was in her power to manipulate her erstwhile abused womanhood in the struggle against white male power. Such comparison of the narrative selves in Douglass's and Brent's texts reveals some of the differences in black male and female psychological developments toward agency as slaves unshackled themselves from a system designed to rob them of selfhood. For men, agency was the power of self in the public image of manhood; for women, it was a self-recognition of their ability to manipulate the power in the self even when they were in otherwise powerless situations.

This is not to suggest that some slave women did not frontally attack the slave system. But, with notable exceptions, many were constrained by confinement to their owner's households as workers and nurturers of their own children and those of others, including those of their masters, and by a deep sense of loyalty to family and community. As a consequence, fewer engaged in "macho" tactics that would have put them and others at greater risk than came with day-to-day life. One exception to this pattern was the fair-skinned Ellen Craft, who, accompanied by her dark-skinned husband disguised as her slave, daringly escaped by passing herself off as a white southern gentleman traveling for reasons of ill health. Harriet Tubman, well-known for her bold missions of rescue, was another. After her escape North, Tubman returned to the South several times and led dozens of slaves to freedom. The courage of women like Craft and Tubman indicate that female slaves did not fear to challenge the system boldly, but the oppressiveness they experienced of sex and gender roles influenced them to engage in more cautious modes of resistance.

In spiritual narratives black women also constructed their identities differently from men.[3] In their move for independence a number of free nineteenth-century black women rejoiced in their transformation from uneducated menial laborers to professionals when they became itinerant preachers and/or missionaries. Ideological conflicts over women's roles in the black church hierarchy restricted their access to the clergy, but this did not deter them. They confronted, contested, and engaged black male perceptions of entitlement to exclusive power in the religious life, challenged black male gender oppression, and created a new place for themselves in their communities. Their faith grounded in spiritual beliefs and biblical doctrine, they fought battles for self-hood and independent black womanhood on the religious frontier and discovered new and affirming identities in claims to self-authority. They, too, used autobiography to express and record the history of black women's liberation. (Foster, 128–29; McKay, "Nineteenth-Century," 141–52).

Other kinds of texts also shed light on the conflict of free nineteenth-century black women and their assertions of self as women in a restrictive world. For example, *A Narrative of the Life and Travels of Mrs. Nancy Prince* (1850), the work of a free-born Massachusetts black woman (born 1799), focuses on Prince's travels in Russia, Europe, and Jamaica. The common center in these varied women's narrative constructions (slave, spiritual, and travel narratives) of their lives revolves around their survival in the face of racial and sexual oppression, pride in their achievements, and their celebrations of self in male and female communities of support and affection. Drawing on resources inside of themselves and their communities, the selves in these narratives asserted control over how they saw and presented themselves to the world outside.[4] They were conscious of strength in spite of great adversity and used those insights against the difficulties they faced.

Early black male autobiographers also celebrated liberated selves in their texts but, in contrast to women, almost always in public stories of individual masculine heroism explicitly enacted to recuperate the manhood they lost to white patriarchy as slaves. For African enslavement in the West and European colonialization of Africa cost black men—holders of economic and political power over women, children, and weaker men in their homelands—the power to exercise dominance over others. Thus, white patriarchy rendered African men powerless (like women), psychologically emasculating them and effecting a symbolic relational change in their sexual status to the systems of power. Also, Reconstruction institutionalized racism as a force in the social fabric of American life, and reinforced the subordinate status of black men.[5] In reaction to this perception of loss, black male concepts of manhood, since slavery, developed in conformity to the western European paradigm (almost universally accepted by men) with domination ("power over" others) as its most important component: power over women, over less powerful men, economic and political power. Consequently, the long history of violent confrontation between black male powerlessness and white male power, from slavery to the present, has deep roots in the black male quest to recover a black manhood that, unfortunately, is predicated on the exercise of power and control outside of the self.[6] No comparable aspect of a search for womanhood exists in black women's stories, although black women in slavery lost control over their productive and reproductive labor and, since Reconstruction, have suffered the racial and sexual oppression of institutionalized racism, sexism, and classism. Their losses appear not to have destroyed their senses of themselves as women.

The identity construction of black women in autobiography thus comes out of a separate tradition from black men's. For twentieth-century black women identity is grounded in models of nineteenth-century black women who passed on to their generations the most vital lesson of their experiences: black womanhood was not static or a single ideal. The selves in the stories of the early foremothers reveal black female identity as a process of ongoing reinvention of self under the pressures of race, class, and gender oppression. While one cannot overestimate the damaging effects of black and white, male and female dominance on black women's agency, the group turned away from absolute victim status by rejecting other-determined and unachievable (for them) models of womanhood to shape its identity out of its own self-definition. For example, slave or free-born nineteenth-century black women, as members of a white-designated inferior racial group, knew that the conditions of their lives denied them access to the construct of white womanhood. As a result, they set about the task of reconstructing selves out of the only reality they could claim: their experiences and the need to survive.[7] Sojourner Truth's well-known declaration that in spite of the brutalization she suffered in slavery she was still a woman (Akron, Ohio, 1851) remains one of the most militant assertions of self-assuredness of black womanhood and black women's rejection of the model of white womanhood. And, instead of lamenting their inability to be like white women, or other patriarchal efforts to defeminize them through such stereotypes as the mammy and the whore, Truth and other women like her focused attention on how to survive and how to enable others (black men and children) to do likewise. For that it was necessary to maintain flexibility in determining their survival strategies but also to define "true black womanhood" through race-centered analyses that promoted "uplift" for the entire black group. The black female narrative tradition thus evolved from the process of reinventing the self out of the specificities of each black woman's experiences. The narratives of Brent and others of her time illustrate that black survival (their own and that of others), not the quest to recuperate lost selves, motivated these women's active subversion of black victimization. They turned to their own resources and discovered a power within their powerlessness that enabled them to resist the devastating impact of white power over the black self.[8]

Twentieth-century daughters and granddaughters of earlier "scribbling" black women continue to write themselves through issues of individual and collective survival in a world that still denigrates blackness and privileges maleness over femaleness. Among the writings of this group there is a visible trend that extends the implications of nineteenth-century self-assuredness of black womanhood into a complex recognition of different levels of power in the self, even under the racist and sexist conditions of modern American life. The single most pronounced aspect of these narratives is in their narrators's rejection of black victim status in favor of a self-empowered black female self at the center of their identity. To examine this trend, this study focuses on the autobiographies of Zora Neale Hurston, Marian Anderson, and Lorene Carey. These three women came of age at different times in this century, their experiential narrative selves are strikingly different from one another, but through the strategies of identity construction they create narrative selves who assume a measure of ownership of their lives. The narratives in this study, published during periods when major black male writers had race-representative black selves exploding against their victimization by white racism, present female narrators that are less psychologically embattled and more in control of their lives than male narrators. These women make of the black self-story a mechanism that adds their own revolutionary dimension to a now long and culturally significant tradition. This tradition rejects some accepted black cultural conventions and sees autobiography as a weapon in the continuing search for black freedom, thus reinforcing the centrality of the tradition. Each writer presents a self that, to quote Toni Morrison, is "solitary and representative" (339), both individual and a member of the "tribe." Above all, each writer rejects the discourse of racist and/or sexist definitions of the black self and seeks to empower black people to take control of their lives. . . .

Zora Neale Hurston's autobiography, *Dust Tracks on a Road,* published in 1942, is a fascinating transgressive construction of a black female narrative self. In a subversion of the race-representative text of oppression, *Dust Tracks* breaks with some of the rhetorical patterns of the slave narrative tradition in favor of a strategy that frees black autobiography from the ideological supremacy of race. In contrast, Hurston's racial tolerance was not in conflict with her identification with black culture. In fact, in foregrounding her identity in the richness and emotional security of the preurban nonmaterialistic black culture of her "village," she offered an alternative (positive) perspective on the black experience. In representing black people for the most part as emotionally independent of white people, with control over their lives, and in suggesting her protagonist's greater harmony with the white world than most blacks and whites were aware of, she refuted the representativeness of the black racial protest text and challenged the patriarchal text of Euro-American white discourse on black life. Faced with black group demoralization inscribed in the texts on both sides of black-white relations, Hurston used *Dust Tracks* to invent a narrative identity that rejected the primacy of slave history and the supremacy of white racism over black lives. At the same time, in her use of dazzling metaphors in the

black idiom and stories of the colorful exploits of the folk, she maintained allegiance to her community.

Looking closely at the inner life of the community, *Dust Tracks* was the first secular autobiography by a black woman that explicitly addressed personal tensions between black women and men and highlighted the sexism of black men and their domination of women.[9] In her own home, as a child, the textual Hurston was aware of parental conflicts and her mother's marital unhappiness. She also observed ill treatment other women received at the hands of their husbands and lovers as well as black male efforts to silence women, especially by excluding their voices from ritual storytelling sessions—the combmunity's most significant group activity. She acclaimed the folk culture but did not deny the subordinating effects of black male authority on women. Her discussions of black male sexism were most personal in her choice to end her marriage, rather than sacrifice her career on the altar of a love that required her to accept male domination. But *Dust Tracks* is more than a revision of the racial/sexual self in black narrative. Hurston does not only break with—or expand—earlier patterns in personal narrative; she strengthens women's tradition of valorizing peer group and intergenerational bonds between black women.

Dust Tracks liberated her identity from the straitjacket of racial struggle and replaced it with black womanhood in negative and positive inter- and intraracial and sexual group relationships and encounters. Although most of her peers saw her strategy as a betrayal of the community's political agenda for black writing, Hurston's text boldly inscribed a revolutionary alternative for women's narrative into the black tradition. As autobiography, it expanded the boundaries of the slave narrative tradition and examined previously unexplored gender conflicts and tensions between black women and men. Her use of folk language and traditions reinforced connections between the educated protagonist of her text and the people of her village and lessened the gap between the city and the country in black cultural expression. *Dust Tracks* was groundbreaking, leading the way to other self-empowering creative inventions of narrative identities that enrich the black autobiographical tradition.

Singer Marian Anderson's autobiography, *My Lord, What a Morning* (1956), appeared shortly before the mass demonstrations and civil disobedience of the 1960s and in the wake of *Brown v. Board of Education* (1954). It is doubtful that Anderson ever heard of Hurston or read *Dust Tracks on a Road*. But, while the circumstances of these women's lives were different, strategies of identity construction in their autobiographies make Anderson's text a direct descendant of Hurston's. For, like her predecessor, she rejected the black victim self and did not postulate race and class (the text does little with gender considerations) as obstacles that have the ultimate power to determine the destiny of black people who worked hard and willed themselves to succeed. . . .

As the narrative of a black woman in white America, *My Lord, What a Morning* is as troublesome to some as Hurston's *Dust Tracks*. Between her birth at the turn of the century and the book's publication, just past its midpoint, Anderson lived through momentous world events that must have seriously affected her outlook on life, but that she never mentions in *My Lord*. Even the Daughters of the American Revolution's (DAR) refusal to permit her to sing in Constitution Hall in 1939 and the triumph of her Easter morning concert at Lincoln Memorial are treated without fanfare or the credit due their importance as history. The self in *My Lord, What a Morning* does not indulge in emotional feelings: neither hurt nor anger, arrogance or even pride in her achievements over the course of her extraordinary musical career.[10] Analogically,

the text is a site that envelops, almost entirely, Marian Anderson's positive journey through the silken cocoon of the world of music.

Following in the footsteps of Hurston, Anderson's autobiography does not protest white racism through the black victim. But there are differences between the selves created by each woman in her narrative. Unlike Hurston, whose text makes clear that there is no cultural gap between the folk culture and the educated urbanized protagonist, Anderson in her single-minded focus on concert music suggests a separation between her and the concerns of her group. Even her inclusion of spirituals as standard parts of her repertoire does not dispel the impression that Anderson (although the lesser academic of the two women) loses the connection that the college-educated intellectual Hurston maintained with the roots of black culture.[11]

While it can reasonably be argued that Anderson's apparent separation from her cultural roots has links to the demands for undivided loyalty that a successful career in opera—the music of high culture—made on her, I believe other political motives were at work here. For, although Anderson openly supported no ideological platform and avoided overt political involvement, she was not apolitical, and, in spite of her fame and achievements, she cared deeply about the welfare of the black community. The self-presentation in *My Lord* was a deliberate rhetorical strategy growing out of political intentions she had for this work.

In her focus on her art Anderson's protagonist empowered herself to achieve success in an oppressive society and at the same time to avoid painful displays of impotent anger. This was the message she wanted to give to a young black audience. But how does one achieve this level of self-empowerment?

Self-confidence, beginning at an early age, is one of the fundamental elements in the text's recipe for engendering power in the self in the white world. She was very young when she made her decision to be a classical concert singer, and she was alone in her choice, without role models to emulate. Although she had the emotional support of her family, none of them was able to counsel or advise her. That aloneness reverberates in the silences in her autobiography. Yet there is no doubt that she knew what she wanted, and she used that knowledge along with personal commitment and the determination to work hard toward her goals. . . .

Self-confidence is linked to a Victorian concept of human dignity in Anderson's text. In its stylistic presentation, its language, content, and silences, dignity is the signature of *My Lord*. Dignity embodies, among other qualities, the self-control to refrain from publicly expressing rancorous anger and to endure great hardships without complaint. The textual mother—whom the textual daughter reports never complained and never expressed anger—has the same kind of personal dignity that the narrative self in this book espouses. In her instructions to young black people coming of age in the 1950s, the narrator strives to convey the value of that dignity through her own success.

Making of silence a companion to dignity enabled Anderson's protagonist to focus almost entirely on the high artistic life. On the one hand, her ideal must have disappointed black readers, who expected militant political narrators in black autobiography, while, on the other, it confounded white racists, who expected only barbaric emotionalism from African Americans. As author of her text, Anderson declares to both groups that there is no single black self. To protect further the image of dignity and self-control she crafts for herself, the protagonist of *My Lord* does not associate herself with black protest movements, although her agenda is similar to many of theirs. Such deliberate strategic actions make this autobiography as political a document as Richard Wright's or any in the school

of more overt protest literature. Written against the white text of black people's inability to achieve through hard work, patience, and dignity and against the black text of the dehumanized black brute of Wright's *Native Son* and the angry young man of James Baldwin's *Notes of a Native Son*, *My Lord, What a Morning* joins *Dust Tracks on a Road* to rewrite the narrative of the victimized racial self and to produce a self-empowered survivor of race, politics, and gender oppression.

Zora Neale Hurston and Marian Anderson were successful pioneers who early in their lives did not perceive race or gender as insurmountable barriers to how they chose to live in the world. Both wrote narratives rejecting the impotence of black group victim status for the possibilities of individual agency. Although Hurston later discovered limits to her ability to control her destiny, her narrative is a monument to the ideal of autonomy and success achieved by a few and a sign—a promise by the side of the road for younger women like Lorene Carey.[12]

Born in Marian Anderson's home city in 1957, more than half a century after the "First Lady," Lorene Carey is a member of the first black post–civil rights generation in America. Her autobiography, *Black Ice* (1991), appeared almost fifty years after *Dust Tracks on a Road* and thirty-five years after *My Lord, What a Morning*. She may not have read Anderson's autobiography, but she was familiar with the accomplishments of the black woman whom large numbers of white people across the world and almost all other black people knew by name and whom, more than all others, middle-class Philadelphians held in enormous esteem. . . .

In addition to the social and institutional changes of the 1960s and 1970s, Carey's black middle-class background offered her many advantages that were foreclosed to Hurston and Anderson in their young years. *Black Ice* covers a very short period in the life of its young protagonist, only the two years in the mid-1970s that Carey spent in New England at the exclusive St. Paul's School in Concord, New Hampshire; then it moves ahead seventeen years to the time when she explores her memory of that past time. Here she attempts to recapture her youthful feelings of St. Paul's School and to recreate the self that survived those experiences. Her return to the school after fifteen years (as teacher and later as a member of the Board of Trustees) and her need to write this book were part of her effort to reclaim the girl she left behind for a long time in New Hampshire, hoping to forget her. To go back was to accept the meaning of "old rage and fear, ambition, self-consciousness, love, curiosity, energy, hate, envy, compulsion [and] fatigue"; to end her denial of these feelings while there (4). Unlike Hurston and Anderson, she admits to the unreliability of memory and the uncertainty of "truth" in her reconstruction of self. Also unlike them, she seeks to reconcile the racial self: to claim her American identity in its entirety, a unity denied black people in the United States for generations.[13]

But, while Carey's complex interrogation of the racial self in the white world and tensions in intrafamilial relationships signals new advances in the development of black autobiography, she is reticent to probe issues of violence between black women and men, much like most of her female predecessors. Most notably, her neglect to explore her ambivalence surrounding the rape she suffers is an unfortunate silence in an otherwise open story.

Through generations of black women writing-the-self in the United States, the center of their life stories remains black survival. Lorene Carey's book is no exception. Amid the pain of the St. Paul's school experiences, one of the elements this protagonist credits for her survival was her family's "narratives," including her great grandfather's, which spoke to her "honestly about growing up black in America" (6).

She writes, "[the narratives] burst into my silence, and in my head, they shouted and chattered and whispered and sang together. I am writing this book to become part of that unruly conversation . . . "(6); and "Without the stories and the songs, I am mute" (237).

Like Hurston's and Anderson's, Lorene Carey's story is a narrative that speaks to growing up black in America and surviving beyond the victimization of whiteness. But while *Dust Tracks* casts the black-white conjunction mainly in positive terms, and *My Lord* muffles it, *Black Ice* foregrounds race and still avoids embracing the tenets of the popular protest black literature of the 1940s and 1950s. Carey's story confronts head-on the hurt and the pain that is the price blacks pay for claiming their racial selves in their American lives. As a new-generation black woman survivor, the self in the text refuses to deny or keep secret the trauma of becoming that self without compromising her dignity. In this respect *Black Ice* breaks new ground and is a "story not to pass on."[14] It is painful and healing as it brings together the complex, inseparable strands of the American/African-American self: "I began writing about St. Paul's School when I stopped thinking of my prep-school experience as an aberration from the common run of black life in America" (6). *Black Ice,* a new story in a venerable tradition of resistance, sings its own song of black liberation which also embraces the challenge to survive by transforming the would-be victim of race and sex into a self-empowered free self.

Hurston, Anderson, Carey, and generations of black women writers use multiple strategies to tell their stories in fiction, autobiography, poetry, drama, and the personal essay. These stories shape black female identity in such a way that the self, however invented, is a witness against the racism, sexism, and classism of the master text and not its absolute victim. Black women writers who participate in this self-affirmation do not compromise their racial and/

or gender integrity by rejecting a tradition that isolates and centralizes the worst effects of racism on black people in narrative. Whatever their strategies of self-construction, active resistance to oppression of all kinds has been at the center of the history of black women's lives in this country from slavery to the present time. These narratives are as politically significant as more overt modes of protest. Black women's stories need to be heard and accorded their rightful place in the tradition. . . .

Notes

1. The relationship between the acquisition of literacy and the black challenge to racial oppression in the eighteenth and nineteenth centuries significantly contributed to the development of African-American written traditions and the making of the Afro-American self in America at that time. Somewhat mistakenly, many slaves even believed that literacy, forcibly denied them by their masters and the law in some regions, would lead to—or actually was—freedom. The seriousness with which they held these beliefs can be readily understood by looking at their determination to acquire the rudiments of reading and writing, even at the risk of life and limb. Their awareness that the Western debate over the humanity of Africans included the issue of their intellectual capability to learn to read and write, even as that instruction was withheld from them, made the stakes in achieving literacy more than an intellectual activity. Thus, when former slaves made "Written by Him/Herself" a part of their texts, the words were a declaration of immense personal and group pride in physical and psychological survival.

2. This does not suggest that all male slaves enjoyed the kind of sanctioned mobility that Douglass did. In fact, Douglass was permitted more mobility than the majority of male slaves, including those who rose to prominence after their escape from bondage.

3. During the antebellum period spiritual narratives were written by free blacks, some of whom were former slaves.

4. One of the remarkable attributes of American slaves was how little each of them appeared to have internalized a lack of her or his self-worth. The sense

of value in the self kept alive their hopes for release from undeserved bondage and fueled the fires of their efforts to struggle against slavery. For slave women their realization of the interlocking nature of race and gender oppression forced them to greater self-dependency in order to survive. Central to the will to survive was the knowledge that others, especially children, could not survive unless they did. This sense of responsibility for the future of the race, handed down from one generation of women to the next, together with the support that emanated from within the women's community, was among the most important of internal resources on which slave women drew to sustain themselves and help those who depended on them.

5. The horrendous racial oppression of black men is a fact. A number of good studies focus on the effects of institutionalized racism on the status of the group in America since the end of the Civil War. Although slavery was brutal before that time, racial violence and white supremacy after the war combined to intimidate all black people in an even more bloody way than before. In the late nineteenth and first third of the twentieth century the lynching of black men was the most potent weapon that white men used to reinforce their racial supremacy. See, for instance, Hall; Finkelman; McGovern; and Tolnay and Massey.

6. I am grateful to Kimberly Benston (following the May 1991 conference on politics and culture at Harvard University at which this essay was first presented) for suggesting the need to discuss differences between male and female identity formation; and to Stanlie James, Florencia Mallon, Nell Irvin Painter, Judylyn Ryan, and Craig Werner, who were my sounding boards as I worked through the concept of lost black manhood in comparison to the greater security black women have in their black womanhood and the relationship between black women's identity and their strategies for survival. I also thank Nanci Calamari, student and friend, for her useful and perceptive reading of the first draft of the final version of this essay.

7. Although reality, like experience, is mediated by the subjectivity of one's perceptions of day-to-day life and the circumstances of that life, for nineteenth-century black people in America, experience filtered through memory, as unreliable as that is, in addition to a strong faith in ultimate justice and a sense of their

own human value, offered the only ground on which they could develop a theory of who they were as human beings.

8. My argument is that, although black women share race and class with black men, issues of sexual exploitation make identity construction between the two groups different. At the same time, conditions of slavery and discriminations of race, sex, and class made it impossible for nineteenth-century black women to have access to the identity of the "cult of true womanhood." The survival of all black people required of them an all-inclusive theory of "true black womanhood." Poet Nikki Giovanni believes that black women are the only "group that derives its identity from itself" (Giovanni, 144). Conversely, I argue, the degree to which black male narratives focus on racial oppression against them by white men reinforces the notion that black men perceive black freedom as the struggle for power vested in Western images of manhood.

9. In nineteenth-century spiritual narratives tensions between black women and men occur largely over the women's right to preach. In other kinds of autobiography black women, until Hurston, foregrounded race in their autobiographies to represent to the world a racially solid front with black men. Hurston shows, however, that even in Edenic Eatonville black women were not treated as equals by black men, and she does not hesitate to condemn sexism by black men in her own and other women's lives.

10. Black women's autobiographies are well-known for silences regarding their private lives, from silences about sexuality to ones concerning feelings on social subjects. In this way Anderson's narrative is not singular. What makes her stand out, however, is her reticence even in how she expresses her sense of joy over her successes. Far from appearing to be the superstar she really was, she tells her story with an understatement that makes it seem that others with her ambition can succeed as easily as she did. This posture is what partly led me to conclude that she saw her audience for the book as one not sufficiently worldly-wise to be overwhelmed by her accomplishments and for whom she could be a good role model.

11. I am grateful to Paul Lauter for pointing out to me that even Anderson's musical renditions of the spirituals have much in common with her operatic production.

12. Hurston's literary fortunes began to fall in the late 1940s and continued to do so in the following decade. She continued to write but was unable to find publishers for her works. Ill health also plagued her in the 1950s, and in 1959, without resources and suffering from a stroke, she entered a welfare nursing home in Florida, where she died in 1960. She was buried in an unmarked grave. In the early 1970s writer Alice Walker, following the discovery of Hurston's most outstanding novel, *Their Eyes Were Watching God* (1937), went on a pilgrimage to "find Zora." In the place where she might be buried Walker left a plaque inscribed to the woman whom she called "a genius of the South." Hurston's literary fame is now worldwide, and she is often referred to as the foremother of late-twentieth-century black women writers.

13. In 1903, in his classic work, *The Souls of Black Folk*, W. E. B. Du Bois first wrote of the "double consciousness" of African Americans. The American black, he said, was not allowed "true self-consciousness" and always felt her or his "twoness"—"an American, a Negro; two souls, two thoughts, two unreconciled strivings; two warring ideals in one dark body" (45). Furthermore, he noted, "the history of the American Negro is the history of this strife,—this longing to attain self-conscious manhood [*sic*], to merge his double self into a better and truer self" (45). Carey attempts to find what Du Bois would have called the black American true self-consciousness. Interestingly, some contemporary theories in black literature argue for double consciousness as a positive aspect of the black experience.

14. Toni Morrison uses this phrase toward the conclusion of her Pulitzer Prize–winning novel *Beloved* (1987): "It is not a story to pass on." The syntax suggests the fiction is not to be retold and perhaps is best forgotten, but in reality Morrison intends the exact opposite: it is one to be remembered, one not to be passed over.

Works Cited

Anderson, Marian. *My Lord, What a Morning*. Intro. Nellie Y. McKay. Madison: University of Wisconsin Press, reprint 1992.

Andrews, William L. *To Tell a Free Story: The First Cen-*

tury of Afro-American Autobiography, 1760–1865. Urbana: University of Illinois Press, 1986.

Baldwin, James. *Notes of a Native Son.* New York: Beacon Press, 1955.

Carby, Hazel. *Reconstructing Womanhood: The Emergence of the Afro-American Woman Novelist.* New York: Oxford University Press, 1987.

Carey, Lorene. *Black Ice.* New York: Knopf, 1991.

Douglass, Frederick. *Narrative of the Life of Frederick Douglass, An American Slave, Written by Himself.* 1845. Ed. Benjamin Quarles. Cambridge: Harvard University Press, 1960.

Du Bois, W. E. B. *The Souls of Black Folk.* 1903. Intro. Nathan Hare and Alvin Poussaint. New York: New American Library, 1964.

Du Bois, W. E. B. *The Philadelphia Negro.* Philadelphia: University of Pennsylvania Press, 1899.

Finkelman, Paul, ed. *Lynching, Racial Violence, and Law.* New York: Garland, 1992.

Foster, Frances. "Neither Auction Block nor Pedestal: The Life and Religious Experience of Jarena Lee, A Colored Lady.'" In *The Female Autograph,* ed. Donna Stanton. Chicago: University of Chicago Press, 1984. 126–51.

Giddings, Paula. *When and Where I Enter: The Impact of Black Women on Race and Sex in America.* New York: William Morrow, 1984.

Giovanni, Nikki. *Gemini: An Extended Autobiographical Statement on My First Twenty-Five Years of Being a Black Poet.* New York: Viking Press, 1971.

Hall, Jacqueline Doud. *Revolt Against Chivalry: Jess Daniel Ames and the Women's Campaign against Lynching.* New York: Columbia University Press, 1979.

Hurston, Zora Neale. *Dust Tracks on a Road.* 1942. 2d ed. Intro. Robert Hemenway. Urbana: University of Illinois Press, 1984.

Hurston, Zora Neale. *Their Eyes Were Watching God.* 1937. Foreword by Mary Helen Washington. New York: Harper and Row, 1990.

Jacobs, Harriet A. *Incidents in the Life of a Slave Girl, Written by Herself.* 1861. Ed. Jean Fagan Yellin. Cambridge: Harvard University Press, 1987.

Larsen, Nella. *Quicksand.* New York: Knopf, 1928.

McGovern, James R. *Anatomy of a Lynching: The Killing of Claude Neal.* Baton Rouge: Louisiana State University Press, 1982.

McKay, Nellie Y. "An Interview with Toni Morrison." *Contemporary Literature* 24 (Winter 1983): 413–29.

McKay, Nellie Y. "Nineteenth-Century Black Women's Spiritual Autobiographies: Religious Faith and Self-Empowerment." In *Interpreting Women's Lives: Feminist Theory and Personal Narratives,* ed. Personal Narratives Group. Bloomington: University of Indiana Press, 1989. 139–54.

Morrison, Toni. *Beloved.* New York: Knopf, 1987.

Mosselle, Mrs. N. F. *The Work of the Afro-American Woman.* 1894. Intro. Joanne Braxton. New York: Oxford University Press, 1988.

Prince, Nancy Gardener. *A Black Woman's Odyssey through Russia and Jamaica: The Narrative of Nancy Prince.* 1850. Princeton: Markus Wiener Publishers, 1989.

Tolnay, Stewart, and James Massey. "Legal Execution of Blacks as Social Control in the Cotton South, 1890–1929." *Social Security Quarterly* (September 1992): 627–44.

Walker, Alice. "Looking for Zora." *In Search of Our Mothers' Gardens.* New York: Harcourt Brace Jovanovich, 1983. 93–116.

Werner, Craig. "On the Ends of Afro-American 'Modernist' Autobiography." *Black American Literature Forum* 24, no. 2 (Summer 1990): 203–20.

Wright, Richard. *Black Boy.* New York: Harper and Row, 1945.

Wright, Richard. *Native Son.* New York: Harper and Row, 1940.

5 Performativity, Autobiographical Practice, Resistance

Sidonie Smith

Performativity is thus not a singular "act," for it is always a reiteration of a norm or set of norms, and to the extent that it acquires an act-like status in the present, it conceals or dissimulates the conventions of which it is a repetition.
—Judith Butler, *Bodies That Matter*

Autobiography and Performativity

Every day, in disparate venues, in response to sundry occasions, in front of precise audiences (even if an audience of one), people assemble, if only temporarily, a "life" to which they assign narrative coherence and meaning and through which they position themselves in historically specific identities. Whatever that occasion or that audience, the autobiographical speaker becomes a performative subject.

This is another way of suggesting that autobiographical telling is not a "self-expressive" act. The theory of self-expression that has driven various strands of autobiography theory assumes that self-identity emerges from a psychic interiority, located somewhere "inside" the narrating subject. There it lies in a state most coherent, unified, evidentiary, even expectant, awaiting transmission to a surface, a tongue, a pen, a keyboard. Through such media the essence of this inner self can be translated into the metaphorical equivalence in language, into strings of words and narrative sequences. This theory of autobiography assumes an ontological and integumentary relationship of interiority to bodily

surface and bodily surface to text as well as the identity (synonymity) of the I before the text, the I of the narrator, and the I of the narrated subject.

But the "self" so often invoked in self-expressive theories of autobiography is not a noun, a thing-in-itself, waiting to be materialized through the text. There is no essential, original, coherent autobiographical self before the moment of self-narrating. Nor is the autobiographical self expressive in the sense that it is the manifestation of an interiority that is somehow ontologically whole, seamless, and "true." For the self is not a documentary repository of all experiential history running uninterruptedly from infancy to the contemporary moment, capacious, current, and accessible. The very sense of self as identity derives paradoxically from the loss to consciousness of fragments of experiential history. Benedict Anderson suggests that this "estrangement" from our experiential history necessitates "a conception of personhood, *identity* . . . which, because it cannot be 'remembered,' must be narrated" (204).

Autobiographical narration begins with amnesia, and once begun, the fragmentary nature of subjectivity intrudes. After all, the narrator is both the same and not the same as the autobiographer, and the narrator is both the same and not the same as the subject of narration. Moreover, there are many stories to be told and many different and divergent storytelling occasions that call for and forth contextually marked and sometimes radically divergent narratives of identity.

In each instance, then, narrative performativity constitutes interiority. That is, the interiority or self that is said to be prior to the autobiographical expression or reflection is an *effect* of autobiographical storytelling. What Judith Butler says of gender performativity can be reframed in terms of autobiographical performativity: "Within the inherited discourse of the metaphysics of substance, gender proves to be performative—that is, constituting the identity it is purported to be. . . . There is no gender identity behind the expressions of gender; that identity is performatively constituted by the very 'expressions' that are said to be its results" (*Gender*, 24–25). And those expressions of interiority are effects produced through the action of public discourses, among them the culturally pervasive discourses of identity and truthtelling that inform historically specific modes, contexts, and receptions of autobiographical narrating (see Gilmore, *Autobiographics*, 1–15).

Such discourses might well be understood, à la Michel de Certeau, as hegemonic "strategies" for the cultural reproduction of normative selves (xviii–xx). They function as culturally credible means of making people "believers" in deep selves. For, as de Certeau recognizes,

To make people believe is to make them act. But by a curious circularity, the ability to make people act—to write and to machine bodies—is precisely what makes people believe. Because the law is already applied with and on bodies, "incarnated" in physical practices, it can accredit itself and make people believe that it speaks in the name of the "real." It makes itself believable by saying: "This text has been dictated for you by Reality itself." (148)

Autobiographical storytelling becomes one means through which people in the West believe themselves to be "selves." In this way, autobiographical storytelling is always a performative occasion, an occasion through which, as Butler argues in theorizing performativity, the "power of discourse . . . produce[s] effects through reiteration" (20).

De Certeau and others trace this conjunction of bourgeois subjectivity and disciplined bodies to various effects of post-Enlightenment culture. Emergent capitalist economies and new republican nations encouraged and required persons to understand themselves to be equal, free, autonomous, and rational subjects, "individuals." But such free individuals in turn required disciplining through an internally generated program of self-scrutiny.[1] Thus the bourgeois reification of self-regulation assumed an interiorized self to be regulated. To this self was assigned depth beneath/inside the surface of the body, what was sometimes considered synonymous with "soul."

But the specificities of flesh determined the degree and kind of interiority assigned the self-regulating subject. Interiority became an effect, and not a cause, of the cultural regulation of always already identified bodies, bodies that were sexed and gendered, bodies that were racialized, bodies that were located in specific socioeconomic spaces, bodies that were deemed unruly or grotesque. Interiority, in complicated ways, became the effect of the surface politics of the body, its physical characteristics, gestures, behaviors, location. And the cultural affirmation of a normative "self" became an effect of the evacuation of unruly heterogeneity within the individual and within the body social and politic. Thus autobiographical storytelling emerged as one powerful means of constituting bourgeois subjects and thereby regulating both bodies and selves. Autobiographical storytelling also became a culturally potent means through which this Enlightenment self was situated in what the West understood as "historical time." As Dipesh Chakrabarty notes, historical time is understood as "a natural homogeneous secular calendrical time." It is time necessary to the modernist master narrative of development and progress, a time, picking up Chakrabarty again, "without which the story of human evolution/civilization—a single human history, that is—cannot be told" (431).[2]

Autobiography and Disidentification

Consider then the "mise en scène" of autobiographical performativity. The "scene" is at once a literal place, a location, and also a moment in history, a (sociopolitical) space in culture. Permeating the scene are all those many and nonidentical discourses that comprise the sense of the "credible" and the "real." Then there is the "audience" or the implied reader. An audience implies a community of people for whom certain discourses of identity and truth make sense. The audience comes to expect a certain kind of performativity that conforms relatively comfortably to criteria of intelligibility. Thus a specific recitation of identity involves the inclusion of certain identity contents and the exclusion of others; the incorporation of certain narrative itineraries and intentionalities, the silencing of others; the adoption of certain autobiographical voices, the muting of others. But audiences are never simple homogeneous communities. They

are themselves heterogeneous collectives that can solicit conflicted effects in the autobiographical subject.

And so the cultural injunction to be a deep, unified, coherent, autonomous "self" produces necessary failure, for the autobiographical subject is amnesiac, incoherent, heterogeneous, interactive. In that very failure lies the fascination of autobiographical storytelling as performativity. For Butler the failure signals the "possibility of a variation on [the] repetition" of "the rules that govern intelligible identity." "The injunction *to be*" a particular kind of subject, she continues,

> produces necessary failures, a variety of incoherence configurations that in their multiplicity exceed and defy the injunction by which they are generated. Further, the very injunction to be a given [subject] takes place through discursive routes: to be a good mother, to be a heterosexually desirable object, to be a fit worker, in sum, to signify a multiplicity of guarantees in response to a variety of different demands all at once. The coexistence or convergence of such discursive injunctions produces the possibility of a complex reconfiguration and redeployment. (*Gender*, 145)[3]

It is as if the autobiographical subject finds him/herself on multiple stages simultaneously, called to heterogeneous recitations of identity. These multiple calls never align perfectly. Rather they create spaces or gaps, ruptures, unstable boundaries, incursions, excursions, limits and their transgressions.

How might we understand these disruptions? Rethinking the role of the unconscious and its relationship to feminist consciousness, Teresa de Lauretis calls this disruptive space the space of *disidentification* (125–27). The unconscious might be understood as the repository of all the experiences and desires that cannot be identi-fied with the symbolic realm and its laws of citationality, those calls to take up normative subject positions. And Butler reminds us that this power of the symbolic ("the domain of so-cially instituted norms" [*Bodies,* 182]) to effect citationality is installed in what Freud referred to as the super-ego or the conscience ("the in-teriorized judge . . . the psychic agency of reg-ulation" [*Bodies,* 181]). The unconscious thus becomes the repository of surplus, of excess, of unbidden and forbidden performativity. Re-pository of that which is not speakable, not in-telligible, not credible, the unconscious is an interiority of disidentifications nested inside the interiority of the identifying subject, an effect of an effect (or what J. Paul Eakin describes as "a construct of a construct," "a story of a story" [102,120]). This domain of the excluded, according to Butler, "haunt[s] signification as its abject borders or as that which is strictly foreclosed: the unlivable, the nonnarrativizable, the traumatic" (*Bodies,* 188).

Yet this process of identification and disiden-tification is on-going. As a result there can be no fixed or essential preconstitutive identity. Identifications become what Chantal Mouffe de-scribes as "nodal points" or "fixations" which "limit the flux of the signified under the sig-nifier" (371). This "dialectics of fixity/non-fixation" generates practices that can be unfix-ings of imposed systems of identification.

In the midst of the "strategies" of what de Certeau calls the "strong" ("whether the strength be that of powerful people or the vio-lence of things or of an imposed order" [xix]) a specific autobiographical subject seizes the oc-casion to effect a timely adjustment of the norm. de Certeau calls such interventions the "tactic" of the weak through which habitable spaces are staked out, through which ruptures in disci-plined interiority are effected. "The weak," he

contends, "must continually turn to their own ends forces alien to them. This is achieved in the propitious moments when they are able to com-bine heterogeneous elements . . . ; the intellec-tual synthesis of these given elements takes the form, however, not of a discourse but of the de-cision itself, the act and manner in which the opportunity is 'seized'" (xix). Through tactical dis/identifications the autobiographical subject adjusts, redeploys, resists, transforms discourses of autobiographical identity.

The history of an autobiographical subject is the history of recitations of the self. But if the self does not exist prior to its recitations then autobiographical storytelling is a recitation of a recitation. Ultimately, as Jerome Bruner has ar-gued, the life as lived experientially is itself per-formative. The living of a life becomes the effect of the life as narrated.

Now I turn to performative moments in and performative aspects of . . . Gertrude Stein's *The Autobiography of Alice B. Toklas* (1933), and Cherríe Moraga's *Loving in the War Years* (1983). My comments are not meant to be readings of the texts as such; they are meant to explore the textual implications of the autobio-graphical performativity mapped out in these opening comments. . . .

Gertrude's Alice
(Being and Possessing)

In turning to Gertrude Stein's *The Autobiogra-phy of Alice B. Toklas* I want to consider the per-formative nature of the entire autobiographical enterprise.

About six weeks ago Gertrude Stein said it does not look to me as if you were ever going to write that autobiography. You know what I am going to do. I am going to write it for you. I am going to write it as

111

simply as Defoe did the autobiography of Robinson Crusoe. And she has and this is it. (252)

Quite simply Stein undermines the basis upon which what Philippe Lejeune describes as the "autobiographical pact" is founded: the self-identify of the subject of the autobiographical narrative and the autobiographical speaker. We might call this a first-person biography or a second-person auto/biography or un/collaborative storytelling. The subversive nature of Stein's "camp" autobiography (Gilmore, "Signature") reveals the fantasy which sustains "traditional," or what Stein would call "paternal," autobiography. In the ruse of conclusion Stein's tour de force confuses the differentiation of identities, roles, and performances.

Thus the trick in the ending becomes thick with meaning. As many have noted, in their long-term relationship, Stein assumed the role of "husband" to Toklas's "wife," the lesbian couple thereby reiterating the normative heterosexual model of domesticity. With this context in mind we can unpack the implications of the autobiographical project. One woman, Stein, who assumes the positionality of "husband" in the heterosexual couple, speaks as another woman, "Toklas," who assumes the positionality of "wife." Stein, that is, puts on the identity of "wife." But something excessive happens when a woman performs femininity; as Mary Russo suggests: "To put on femininity with a vengeance suggests the power of taking it off" (224). Thus a disjunction occurs between the sexed body (Stein as biological female), gender identity (Stein as "husband"), and gender performance (Stein as "Toklas"/the culturally credible "wife"). Body/identity/gender are rendered non-identical.

Stein also camps up the performativity of gendered narrative expectations. The autobiography of Alice B. Toklas begins with the failure of

Toklas to perform her "wifely" duty. In other words, the "wife" fails to enact the rituals of "wifehood." As a result, the husband takes on the "wife's" duty. As "Alice" then, Stein reiterates a conventional wife's tale, the narrative of the husband's public "life." In this sense the narrating Stein puts on "femininity" as she narrates a normative "feminine" story (a biography rather than an autobiography). But neither the "wife" nor the "husband" functions as a unified narrator. And so this narrative ventriloquation not only sustains the notion of a "feminine" narrative—the "wifely" tale is finally told, after all—but also subverts it—the "husband" tells it as a "wife," but the "husband" is "him"self a "her"self. "There is no there there," as Stein said of Oakland.

The very autobiographical recitation that promises to shore up gender identity becomes its very undoing. And so the notion of autobiography as expressive of a gendered "self" is here undermined through Stein's emphasis on the performative nature of identity. Stein's ventriloquation disrupts the stabilities of "feminine" and "masculine" narratives as it disrupts the normative alignment of interiority to bodily surface to gender performance in the context of compulsory heterosexuality. Heterosexual coupling becomes here a fiction both re-sited and dis-located in the camped-up performance and the performativity of sexual norms.

Cherríe Moraga and Her Malinché

The second text I want to consider is Cherríe Moraga's *Loving in the War Years*. In this personal/political compendium of multiple genres,[4] Moraga explores through poetry, essays, memory fragments, myths, the complex relationship of the surface of bodies, the construction of interiority, and the specific inscription of history. As I have noted elsewhere the body moves through all the disparate forms intermixing in this text, fragmented into specific parts and pieces, crossed by desires, overwritten by cultural inscriptions and discourses, but most particularly the discourse of female treachery and betrayal signified by the body and the history of La Malinché (Smith, 139–46). The Chicana lesbian is rendered as the cultural grotesque assigned an "unnatural" body, a disruptive, corrupting body, and thus a traitorous interiority.

Moraga explores her experiential history of passing, passing across her racial identities, disappearing into the Anglo in her or reasserting the Chicana in her. "I was 'la guera'" she writes "—fair-skinned. Born with the features of my Chicana mother but the skin of my Anglo father, I had it made. . . . Everything about my upbringing (at least what occurred on a conscious level) attempted to bleed me of what color I did have" (51). The materiality of her specific body and the historical conditions of her experiential history enforce upon her the ways in which racial identity can be performative. But she also explores another kind of passing, the passing of the lesbian girl/woman as a heterosexual "woman." She discovers the ways in which she learned to perform as a heterosexual woman in a cultural context that joined treachery to lesbian desire. Moraga's incisive analysis reveals the complexities of identity formation and deformation. It isn't that identity is totally disjoined from the surface politics of the body; it is that identity, produced by complex cultural locations, is at once culturally overdetermined and manipulable. Paradoxically identity is dis/identity.

It is precisely the possibility of "passing" in doubletime that unmasks the regulatory fictions disciplining the Chicana body. The internalization of cultural fantasies of gender identity (for instance, the cultural fantasy invoked by the very name La Malinché as a negative fantasy, as the "woman" not to be) creates a conflicted interiority that produces necessary failures. The dis-

comforts of dis/identifications, the increasing gaps in stable identifications, prompt the increasing awareness, awareness gained through the very acts of writing, that interiority is an effect of social discourses: "But at the age of twenty-seven it is frightening to acknowledge that I have internalized a racism and classism where the object of oppression is not only someone *outside* my skin but the someone *inside* my skin" (54). Refusing to remain in the "passing" lane, Moraga confronts the disabling judgments that had become what Butler terms "the psychic agency of regulation" (*Bodies,* 181).

The experiential and cultural histories of the lesbian body provide Moraga with a means to confront the cultural injunctions that enforce a specific gender/racial/class interiority. This desire is an "excess" in the system, an excess De Lauretis describes as "a *resistance to* identification rather than unachieved identification" or "a *dis-identification* with femininity that does not necessarily revert or result in an identification with masculinity but, say, transfers to a form of female subjectivity that exceeds the phallic definition" (126). Moreover this desire becomes a material window opening onto the social construction of a disabled and disempowered interiority as well as a point of view used to resist that disempowerment. This excessive space stretches open interiority and thereby motivates a changed consciousness, an awareness of the performative effects of the discourses of identity culturally provided her.

Speaking autobiographically as a Chicana lesbian is itself a "variation" on the repetition of "rules that govern intelligible identity, e.g., that enable and restrict the intelligible assertion of an 'I'" (Butler, *Gender,* 145). For the very assertion of that identity signals a failure to *be* a "woman" within both Chicano and Anglo cultures. In making intelligible a culturally unintelligible subject, Moraga deconstructs the normative identity founding multiple communities. The diverse autobiographical writings incorporated in the text entitled *Loving in the War Years* marks the performativity of identity as differences.

Conclusion

I have tried in these brief readings to illuminate various aspects of autobiographical performativity and resistance. The moments signal the making and unmaking of identities and thus undermine the foundational myth of autobiographical storytelling as self-expressive of an autonomous individualism. . . . Stein and Moraga each in their different ways register the degrees to which the white Euro/American norm is recited by those persons it positions as self-consolidating others. Yet since the performative interiority of the autobiographical subject can be many and conflicted "effects," they also mark interventions in normative identifications with stagings of incommensurable differences that re-site those norms. Writing from eccentric cultural positions, . . . Stein and Moraga take up autobiographical storytelling in order to critique the regulatory effects of the West's romance with bourgeois individualism. They occupy an "I" and in doing so scramble the boundary markers delimiting the sites of the included and the excluded. In effect, these narratives become sites where a complex and disruptive theorizing of autobiographical performativity takes place.

Notes

1. For an incisive analysis of the construction of an interiorized female subjectivity in conduct books written at the end of the eighteenth and beginning of the nineteenth century, see Armstrong, esp. chap. 1.

2. Chakrabarty calls history "this gift of modernity to many peoples" (433).

3. Please note that I have substituted the word "subject" for "gender" in the original.

4. On the intermixing of generic forms in writings by women of color, see Emberley (163).

Works Cited

Anderson, Benedict. *Imagined Communities: Reflections on the Origin and Spread of Nationalism.* London: Verso, 1991.

Armstrong, Nancy. *Desire and Domestic Fiction: A Political History of the Novel.* New York: Oxford, 1991.

Bruner, Jerome. "Life as Narrative." *Social Research* 54 (1987): 11–32.

Butler, Judith. *Bodies That Matter.* New York: Routledge, 1993.

Butler, Judith. *Gender Trouble: Feminism and the Subversion of Identity.* New York: Routledge, 1990.

Chakrabarty, Dipesh. "Marx after Marxism: History, Subalternity, and Difference." *Meanjean* 3 (Spring 1993): 429–45.

De Certeau, Michel. *The Practices of Everyday Life.* Trans. Steven F. Rendall. Berkeley: University of California Press, 1984.

De Lauretis, Teresa. "Eccentric Subjects: Feminist Theory and Historical Consciousness." *Feminist Studies* 16 (Spring 1990): 115–50.

Eakin, Paul John. *Touching the World: Reference in Autobiography.* Princeton: Princeton University Press, 1993.

Emberley, Julia V. *Thresholds of Difference: Feminist Critique, Native Women's Writings, Postcolonial Theory.* Toronto: University of Toronto Press, 1993.

Gilmore, Leigh. *Autobiographics: A Feminist Theory of Women's Self-Representation.* Ithaca: Cornell University Press, Excerpted in this volume. 1994.

Gilmore, Leigh. "Signature of Lesbian Autobiography: 'Gertrice/Altrude.'" In *Autobiography and Questions of Gender,* ed. Shirley Neuman. London: Frank Cass, 1991. 56–75.

Goffman, Erving. *Gender Advertisements.* New York: Harper, 1976.

Lejeune, Philippe. "The Autobiographical Pact." In *On Autobiography,* ed. Paul John Eakin. Trans.

Katherine Leary. Minneapolis: University of Minnesota Press, 1989. 3–30.

Moraga, Cherríe. *Loving in the War Years: lo que nunca paso por sus labios.* Boston: South End, 1983.

Mouffe, Chantal. "Feminism, Citizenship, and Radical Democratic Politics." In *Feminists Theorize the Political,* ed. Judith Butler and Joan W. Scott. New York: Routledge, 1992. 369–84.

Russo, Mary. "Female Grotesques: Carnival and Theory." In *Feminist Studies/Critical Studies,* ed. Teresa de Lauretis. Bloomington: Indiana University Press, 1986. 213–29.

Smith, Sidonie. *Subjectivity, Identity, and the Body.* Bloomington: Indiana University Press, 1993.

Stein, Gertrude. *The Autobiography of Alice B. Toklas.* New York: Random, 1960.

6 Woman Skin Deep: Feminism and the Postcolonial Condition

Sara Suleri

Given the current climate of rampant and gleeful anti-intellectualism that has overtaken the mass media at the present time, both literary and cultural interpretive practitioners have more than ample reason to reassess, to reexamine, and to reassert those theoretical concerns that constitute or question the identity of each putatively marginal group. There are dreary reiterations that must be made, and even more dreary navigations between the Scylla and Charybdis so easily identified in journalism as a conflict between the "thought police" on the one hand and the proponents of "multiculturalism" on the other. As readers of mass culture, let us note by way of example the astonishing attention that the media has accorded the academy: the Gulf War took up three months of their time, whereas we have been granted over a year of headlines and glossy magazine newsworthiness. Is our anathema, then, more pervasive than that of Saddam Hussein? In what fashion is the academy now to be read as one of the greatest sources of sedition against the new world order? The moment demands urgent consideration of how the outsideness of cultural criticism is being translated into that most tedious dichotomy that pits the "academy" against the "real world." While I am somewhat embarrassed by the prospect of having to contemplate such a simplistic binarism, this essay seeks to question its own cultural parameters by situating both its knowledge and its ignorance in relation to the devastating rhetoric of "us and them" that beleaguers issues of identity formation today. Grant me the luxury, then, of not having to supply quotation marks around several of the terms employed, and—since the time of life is short—an acknowledgement that the "we" to which I am forced to take recourse is indeed very, very wee.

The sustained and trivializing attack on what is represented as academic self-censorship cannot be segregated from current reformulations of cultural identities: the former will continue to misconstrue deliberately questions of marginality into solutions of frivolity, or cultural criticism into tyrannical clichés about the political correctness of the thought police. And, if the debate on multiculturalism simply degenerates into a misplaced desire for the institution of rainbow coalition curricula, its shadow will fall in all heaviness on those disciplines most responsible for producing the kind of rhetoric that is presently castigated for its political rectitude. Discursive formations that question canonical and cultural censors, in other words, are precisely the ones to be singled out as demonstrative of the academy's spinelessly promiscuous submission to "correctness." The list of public enemies thus produced is hardly surprising: our prostitution is repeatedly characterized by intellectual allegiances to the identity of postcoloni-alism, of gender, of gay and lesbian studies, and finally, of the body. The academy has subcul-tured itself out of viable existence, we are told, and the subtextual moral that attends such jour-nalistic cautionary tales is almost too obvious to merit articulation: if thy left hand offendeth thee, cut it off.

Since none of us are partial to being lopped, the only resort appears to be a two-tiered re-sponse to the anti-intellectualism that is our "fin de siècle" fate. First—as has been clear for at least the last year—the world lies all before us; we have and must continue to respond. While much of the material that has appeared in the popular press is so low-grade as to disqualify it-self as discourse, the academy must persist in making a resolute attempt to present some firm alternative opinions within those very columns. On a very simplistic and pragmatic level, if we must be freaks, let us be freaks with a voice. It may well be that this effort at articulation will yield some useful readings of the peculiar iden-tity of the professional academic: how plural are we in our constructions of singularity; and how singular in our apprehensions of the plural? The second tier of any sustained response consists of an attempt to engender within the academy an overdue exchange about the excesses and the limitations that marginal discourses must inevi-tably accrue, even as they seek to map the ulti-mate obsolescence of the dichotomy between margin and center. For until the participants in marginal discourses learn how best to critique the intellectual errors that inevitably accompany the provisional discursivity of the margin, the monolithic and untheorized identity of the cen-ter will always be on them. The following read-ings seek an alignment with the second strate-gic tier to contain anti-intellectualism—that is, an essay into the methodology through which contemporary academic discourse seeks to de-

contaminate itself of territorial affiliations and attempts instead to establish the proliferating and shifting locations of the margins of cultural identities.

1

The specific margin that is my subject is one most virulently subjected to popular parodies and to the label of irrational rectitude: the work conducted around theoretical intersec-tions of feminism and gender studies. It would be unproductive to demonstrate that journal-ists are shoddy readers, or that the "elevation" of Camille Paglia's words to the pages of a soft-core porn magazine is in fact quite apposite with her discourse. An alternative margin might be found in the tensions incipient within the criti-cal practice itself: are the easy pieties that ema-nate from the anti-thought-police press in any way implicit in academic discourse on this keen cultural problem? Is girl talk with a difference, in other words, at all responsible for the parodic replays that it has engendered in the scurrilous imaginations of North American magazines? If the academy chooses to be the unseen legislator through which cultural difference is regulated into grouped identities of the marginal, then an urgent intellectual duty would surely be to sub-ject not merely our others but ourselves to the rigors of revisionary scrutiny.

If you will allow me some further space-clearing generalizations, I would claim that while current feminist discourse remains vexed by questions of identity formation and the con-comitant debates between essentialism and con-structivism, or distinctions between situated and universal knowledge, it is still prepared to grant an uneasy selfhood to a voice that is best de-scribed as the property of "postcolonial Wom-an." Whether this voice represents perspectives as divergent as the African-American or the postcolonial cultural location, its imbrications of race and gender are accorded an iconicity that is altogether too good to be true. Even though the marriage of two margins should not necessarily lead to the construction of that contradiction in terms, a "feminist center," the embarrassed privilege granted to racially encoded feminism does indeed suggest a rectitude that could be its own theoretical undoing. The concept of the postcolonial itself is too frequently robbed of historical specificity in order to function as a preapproved allegory for any mode of discursive contestation. The coupling of *postcolonial* with *woman*, however, almost inevitably leads to the simplicities that underlie unthinking celebrations of oppression, elevating the racially female voice into a metaphor for "the good." Such metaphoricity cannot exactly be called essentialist, but it certainly functions as an impediment to a reading that attempts to look beyond obvious questions of good and evil. In seeking to dismantle the iconic status of postcolonial feminism, I will attempt here to address the following questions: within the tautological margins of such a discourse, which comes first, gender or race? How, furthermore, can the issue of chronology lead to some preliminary articulation of the productive superficiality of race?

Before such questions can be raised, however, it is necessary to pay some critical attention to the mobility that has accrued in the category of postcolonialism. Where the term once referred exclusively to the discursive practices produced by the historical fact of prior colonization in certain geographically specific segments of the world, it is now more of an abstraction available for figurative deployment in any strategic redefinition of marginality. For example, when James Clifford elaborated his position on travelling theory during a recent seminar, he invariably substituted the metaphoric condition of postcoloniality for the obsolete binarism between anthropologist and native.[1] As with the

decentering of any discourse, however, this reimaging of the postcolonial closes as many epistemological possibilities as it opens. On the one hand, it allows for a vocabulary of cultural migrancy, which helpfully derails the postcolonial condition from the strictures of national histories, and thus makes way for the theoretical articulations best typified by Homi Bhabha's recent anthology *Nation and Narration*.[2] On the other hand, the current metaphorization of postcolonialism threatens to become so amorphous as to repudiate any locality for cultural thickness. A symptom of this terminological and theoretical dilemma is astutely read in Kwame Anthony Appiah's essay "Is the Post- in Postmodernism the Post- in Postcolonial?"[3] Appiah argues for a discursive space-clearing that allows postcolonial discourse a figurative flexibility and at the same time reaffirms its radical locality within historical exigencies. His discreet but firm segregation of the postcolonial from the postmodern is indeed pertinent to the dangerous democracy accorded the coalition between postcolonial and feminist theories, in which each term serves to reify the potential pietism of the other.

In the context of contemporary feminist discourse, I would argue, the category of postcolonialism must be read as a free-floating metaphor for both cultural embattlement and historicity of race. There is no available dichotomy that could neatly classify the ways in which such a redefinition of postcoloniality is necessarily a secret sharer in similar reconfigurations of feminism's most vocal articulation of marginality, or the obsessive attention it has recently paid to the racial body. Is the body in race subject or object, or is it more dangerously an objectification of a methodology that aims for radical subjectivity? Here, the binarism that informs Chandra Mohanty's paradigmatic essay "Under Western Eyes: Feminist Scholarship and Colonial Discourses" deserves particular consideration. Where Mohanty engages in a particular critique of "Third World Woman" as a monolithic object in the texts of Western feminism, her argument is premised on the irreconcilability of gender as history and gender as culture. "What happens," queries Mohanty, "when an assumption of 'women as an oppressed group' is situated in the context of Western feminist writing about third world women?" What happens, apparently, begs her question. In contesting what she claims is a "colonialist move," Mohanty proceeds to argue that "Western feminists alone become the true 'subjects' of this counterhistory. Third World women, on the other hand, never rise above the debilitating generality of their 'object' status."[4] A very literal ethic underlies such a dichotomy, one that demands attention to its very obviousness: how is this objectivism to be avoided? How will the ethnic voice of womanhood counteract the cultural articulation that Mohanty too easily dubs as the exegesis of Western feminism? The claim to authenticity—only a black can speak for a black; only a postcolonial subcontinental feminist can adequately represent the lived experience of that culture—points to the great difficulty posited by the "authenticity" of female racial voices in the great game that claims to be the first narrative of what the ethnically constructed woman is deemed to want.

This desire all too often takes its theoretical form in a will that claims a theoretical basis most clearly contravened by the process of its analysis. An example of this point is Trinh Minh-ha's treatise, *Woman, Native, Other*,[5] which seeks to posit an alternative to the anthropological twist that constitutes the archaism through which nativism has been apprehended. Subtitled *Writing Postcoloniality and Feminism*, Trinh's book is a paradigmatic meditation that can be essentialized into a simple but crucial question: how can feminist discourse represent the categories of "woman" and "race" at the same time? If the languages of feminism and ethnicity are to escape an abrasive mutual contestation, what novel idiom can freshly articulate their radical inseparability? Trinh's strategy is to relocate her gendering of ethnic realities on the inevitable territory of postfeminism, which underscores her desire to represent discourse formation as always taking place after the fact of discourse. It further confirms my belief that had I any veto power over prefixes, *post-* would be the first to go—but that is doubtless tangential to the issue at hand. In the context of Trinh's methodology, the shape of the book itself illuminates what may best be called the endemic ill that effects a certain temporal derangement between the work's originary questions and the narratives that they engender. *Woman, Native, Other* consists of four loosely related chapters, each of which opens with an abstraction and ends with an anecdote. While there is a self-pronounced difference between the preliminary thesis outlined in the chapter "Commitment from the Mirror-Writing Box" and the concluding claims in "Grandma's Story," such a discursive distance is not matched with any logical or theoretical consistency. Instead, a work that is impelled by an impassioned need to question the lines of demarcation between race and gender concludes by falling into a predictable biological fallacy in which sexuality is reduced to the literal structure of the racial body, and theoretical interventions within this trajectory become minimalized into the naked category of lived experience.

When feminism turns to lived experience as an alternative mode of radical subjectivity, it only rehearses the objectification of its proper subject. While lived experience can hardly be discounted as a critical resource for an apprehension of the gendering of race, neither should such data serve as the evacuating principle for both historical and theoretical contexts alike. "Radical subjectivity" too frequently translates into a low-grade romanticism that cannot recognize its discursive status as *pre-* rather than *post-*. In the concluding chapter of Trinh's text, for example, a section titled "Truth and Fact: Story and History" delineates the skewed idiom that marginal subjectivities produce. In attempting to proclaim an alternative to male-identified objectivism, Trinh-as-anthropologist can only produce an equally objectifying idiom of joy:

> Let me tell you a story. For all I have is a story. Story passed on from generation to generation, named Joy. Told for the joy it gives the storyteller and the listener. Joy inherent in the process of storytelling. Whoever understands it also understands that a story, as distressing as it can be in its joy, never takes anything away from anybody. (119)

Given that I find myself in a more acerbic relation both to the question of the constitution of specific postcolonialisms and to the question of a more metaphoric postcolonial feminism, such a jointly universalist and individualist "joy" is not a term that I would ordinarily welcome into my discursive lexicon. On one level, its manipulation of lived experience into a somewhat fallacious allegory for the reconstitution of gendered race bespeaks ascendence—and an attendant evasion—of the crucial cultural issues at hand. On a more dangerous level, however, such an assumption serves as a mirror image of the analyses produced by the critics of political rectitude. For both parties, "life" remains the ultimate answer to "discourse." The subject of race, in other words, cannot cohabit with the detail of a feminist language.

Trinh's transcendent idiom, of course, emanates from her somewhat free-floating understanding of "postcoloniality": is it an abstraction into which all historical specificity may be subsumed, or is it a figure for a vaguely defined ontological marginality that is equally applicable to all "minority" discourses? In either case, the categories of both "woman" and "race" assume the status of metaphors, so that each rhetoric of oppression can serve equally as a mirrored allegory for the other. Here, *Woman, Native, Other* is paradigmatic of the methodological blurring that dictates much of the discourse on identity formation in the coloring of feminist discourse. To privilege the racial body in the absence of historical context is indeed to generate an idiom that tends to waver with impressionistic haste between the abstractions of postcoloniality and the anecdotal literalism of what it means to articulate an "identity" for a woman writer of color. Despite its proclaimed location within contemporary theoretical—not to mention post-theoretical—discourse, such an idiom poignantly illustrates the hidden and unnecessary desire to resuscitate the "self."

What is most striking about such discursive practices is their failure to confront what may be characterized best as a great enamorment with the "real." Theories of postcolonial feminism eminently lend themselves to a reopening of the continued dialogue that literary and cultural studies have—and will continue to have—with the perplexing category known as realism, but at present the former discourse chooses to remain too precariously parochial to recognize the bounty that is surely its to give. Realism, however, is too dangerous a term for an idiom that seeks to raise identity to the power of theory. While both may be windmills to the quixotic urge to supply black feminism with some version of the "real," Trinh's musings on this subject add a mordantly pragmatic option to my initial question: "what comes first, race or gender?" Perhaps the query would be more finely calibrated if it were rephrased to ask, "What comes first, race, gender, or profession?" And what, in our sorry dealings with such realisms, is the most phantasmagoric category of all?

According to *Woman, Native, Other*, such a triple bind can be articulated only in order to declare that bonding is all. An opening section of that text is in fact titled "The Triple Bind"; it attempts to outline the alternative realism still to be claimed by the postcolonial feminist mentality:

> Today, the growing ethnic-feminist consciousness has made it increasingly difficult for [the woman of color who writes] to turn a blind eye not only to the specification of the writer as historical subject . . . but also to writing itself as a practice located at the intersection of subject and history—a literary practice that involves the possible knowledge (linguistical and ideological) of itself as such. (6)

Here the text evades the threat of realism by taking recourse to the "peaceable" territory of writing, on which all wars may be fought with each discursive contingency in deployment. While writing may serve as a surrogate for the distance between subject (read self) and history, Trinh unwittingly makes clear her academic appreciation of alterity: the female writer, or the third person "she" that haunts her text, "is made to feel she must choose from among three conflicting identities. Writer of color? Woman writer? Or woman of color? Which comes first? Where does she place her loyalties?" (6). The hierarchy of loyalties thus listed illustrates the danger inherent in such cultural lists: the uneasy proclamation with which *Woman, Native, Other* sets out to be the "first full-length study of postfeminism" (according to the book's jacket) is a self-defeating project, for feminism has surely long since laid aside the issue of an individualized female loyalty as its originating assumption. If race is to complicate the project of divergent feminisms, in other words, it cannot take recourse to biologism, nor to the incipient menace of rewriting alterity into the ambiguous shape of the exotic body.

The body that serves as testimony for lived experience, however, has received sufficient interrogation from more considered perspectives on the cultural problems generated by the dialogue between gender and race, along with the hyperrealist idiom it may generate. Hazel Carby helpfully advocates that

> black feminist criticism [should] be regarded critically as a problem, not a solution, as a sign that should be interrogated, a locus of contradictions. Black feminist criticism has its source and its primary motivation in academic legitimation, placement within a framework of bourgeois humanistic discourse.[6]

The concomitant question that such a problem raises is whether the signification of gendered race necessarily returns to the realism that it most seeks to disavow. If realism is the Eurocentric and patriarchal pattern of adjudicating between disparate cultural and ethnic realities, then it is surely the task of radical feminism to provide an alternative perspective. In the vociferous discourse that such a task has produced, however, the question of alternativism is all too greatly subsumed either into the radical strategies that are designed to dictate the course of situated experience, or into the methodological imperatives that impel a work related to *Woman, Native, Other* such as bell hooks's *Talking Back: Thinking Feminist, Thinking Black.*

While the concept of "talking back" may appear to be both invigorating and empowering to a discourse interested in the reading of gendered race, the text *Talking Back* is curiously engaged in talking to itself; in rejecting Caliban's mode of protest, its critique of colonization is quietly narcissistic in its projection of what a black and thinking female body may appear to be, particularly in the context of its repudiation of the genre of realism. Yet this is the genre, after all, in which African-American feminism continues to seek legitimation: hooks's study is predicated on the anecdotes of lived experience and their capacity to provide an alternative to the discourse of what she terms patriarchal rationalism. Here the unmediated quality of a local voice serves as a substitute for any theoretical agenda that can make more than a cursory connection between the condition of postcolonialism and the question of gendered race. Where hooks claims to speak beyond binarism, her discourse keeps returning to the banality of easy dichotomies: "Dare I speak to oppressed and oppressor in the same voice? Dare I speak to you in a language that will take us away from the boundaries of domination, a language that will not fence you in, bind you, or hold you? Language is also a place of struggle."[7] The acute embarrassment generated by such an idiom could possibly be regarded as a radical rhetorical strategy designed to induce racial discomfort in its audience, but it more frequently registers as black feminism's failure to move beyond the proprietary rights that can be claimed by any oppressed discourse.

As does Trinh's text, hooks's claims that personal narrative is the only salve to the rude abrasions that Western feminist theory has inflicted on the body of ethnicity. The tales of lived experience, however, cannot function as a sufficient alternative, particularly when they are predicated on dangerously literal professions of postcolonialism. *Yearning: Race, Gender, and Cultural Politics,* hooks's more recent work, rehearses a postcolonial fallacy in order to conduct some highly misguided readings of competing feminisms within the context of racial experience. She establishes a hierarchy of color that depressingly segregates divergent racial perspectives into a complete absence of intellectual exchange. The competition is framed in terms of hooks's sense of the hostility between African-American and Third World feminisms:

The current popularity of post-colonial discourse that implicates solely the West often obscures the colonizing relationship of the East in relation to Africa and forgets that many Third World nationals bring to this country the same kind of contempt and disrespect for blackness that is most frequently associated with white western imperialism. . . . Within feminist movements Third World nationals often assume the role of mediator or interpreter, explaining the "bad" black people to their white colleagues or helping the "naive" black people to understand whiteness. . . . Unwittingly assuming the role of go-between, of mediator, she re-inscribes a colonial paradigm.[8]

What is astonishing about such a claim is its continued obsession with a white academy, with race as a professional attribute that can only reconfigure itself around an originary concept of whiteness. Its feminism is necessarily skin deep in that the pigment of its imagination cannot break out of a strictly biological reading of race. Rather than extending an inquiry into the discursive possibilities represented by the intersection of gender and race, feminist intellectuals like hooks misuse their status as minority voices by enacting strategies of belligerence that at this time are more divisive than informative. Such claims to radical revisionism take refuge in the political untouchability that is accorded the category of Third World Woman, and in the process sully the crucial knowledge that such a category has still to offer to the dialogue of feminism today.

The dangers represented by feminists such as hooks and Trinh is that finally they will represent the profession as both their last court of appeal and the anthropological ground on which they conduct their field work. The alternative that they offer, therefore, is conceptually parochial and scales down the postcolonial condition in order to encompass it within North American academic terms. As a consequence, their discourse cannot but fuel the criticism of those who police the so-called thought police, nor is it able to address the historically risky compartmentalization of otherness that masquerades under the title of multiculturalism. Here it is useful to turn to one of the more brilliant observations that pepper Gayatri Spivak's *The Post-Colonial Critic.* In concluding an interview on multiculturalism, Spivak casually reminds her audience that

> if one looks at the history of post-Enlightenment theory, the major problem has been the problem of autobiography: how subjective structures can, in fact, give objective truth. During these same centuries, the Native Informant [was] treated as the objective evidence for the founding of the so-called sciences like ethnography, ethnolinguistics, comparative religion, and so on. So that, once again, the theoretical problems only relate to the person who knows. The person who *knows* has all of the problems of selfhood. The person who is *known,* somehow seems not to have a problematic self.[9]

Lived experience, in other words, serves as fodder for the continuation of another's epistemology, even when it is recorded in a "contestatory" position to its relation to realism and to the overarching structure of the profession.

While cultural criticism could never pretend that the profession does not exist, its various voices must surely question any conflation of the professional model with one universal and world historical. The relation between local and given knowledge is obviously too problematic to allow for such an easy slippage, which is furthermore the ground on which the postcolonial can be abused to become an allegory for any one of the pigeonholes constructed for multiculturalism. Allow me to turn as a consequence to a local example of how realism locates its language within the postcolonial condition, and to suggest that lived experience achieves its articulation not through autobiography, but through that other third-person narrative known as the law.

2

I proffer life in Pakistan as an example of such a postcolonial and lived experience. Pakistani laws, in fact, pertain more to the discourse of a petrifying realism than do any of the feminist critics whom I have cited thus far. The example at hand takes a convoluted postcolonial point and renders it nationally simple: if a postcolonial nation chooses to embark on an official program of Islamization, the inevitable result in a Muslim state will be legislation that curtails women's rights and institutes in writing what has thus far functioned as the law of the passing word. The Hudood Ordinances in Pakistan were promulgated in 1979 and legislated in 1980, under the military dictatorship of General Mohammad Zia-ul-Haq. They added five new criminal laws to the existing system of Pakistani legal pronouncements, of which the second ordinance—against *Zina* (that is, adultery as well as fornication)—is of the greatest import. An additional piece of legislation concerns the law of evidence, which rules that a woman's testimony constitutes half of a man's. While such infamous laws raise many historical and legal questions, they remain the body through which the feminist movement in Pakistan—the Women's Action Forum—must organize itself.

It is important to keep in mind that the formulation of the Hudood Ordinances was based on a multicultural premise, even though they were multicultural from the dark side of the moon. These laws were premised on a Muslim notion of *Hadd* and were designed to interfere in a postcolonial criminal legal system that was founded on Anglo-Saxon jurisprudence. According to feminist lawyer Asma Jahangir, the Hudood Ordinances were promulgated to bring the criminal legal system of Pakistan in conformity with the injunctions of Islam. . . . Two levels of punishments are introduced in the Ordinances. Two levels of punishment and, correspondingly, two separate sets of rules of evidence are prescribed. The first level or category is the one called the "Hadd" which literally means the "limit" and the other "Tazir," which means "to punish."[10]

The significance of the *Hadd* category is that it delineates immutable sentences: *Tazir* serves only as a safety net in case the accused is not convicted under *Hadd*. These fixed rules are in themselves not very pretty: *Hadd* for theft is amputation of a hand; for armed robbery, amputation of a foot; for rape or adultery committed by married Muslims, death by stoning; for rape or adultery committed by non-Muslims or unmarried Muslims, a hundred public lashes (24). While I am happy to report that the *Hadd* has not yet been executed, the laws remain intact and await their application.

The applicability of these sentences is rendered more murderous and even obscenely ludicrous when the immutability of the *Hadd* punishments is juxtaposed with the contingency of the laws of evidence. If a man is seen stealing a thousand rupees by two adult Muslim males, he could be punished by *Hadd* and his hand would be amputated. If an adult Muslim stole several million rupees and the only available witnesses were women and non-Muslims, he would not qualify for a *Hadd* category and would be tried under the more free-floating *Tazir* instead. "A gang of men can thus rape all the residents of a women's hostel," claims Jahangir with understandable outrage, "but [the] lack of ocular evidence of four Muslim males will rule out the imposition of a Hadd punishment" (49). Such a statement, unfortunately, is not the terrain of

rhetoric alone, since the post–Hudood Ordinance application of the *Tazir* has made the definition of rape an extremely messy business indeed.

Here, then, we turn to *Zina*, and its implications for the Pakistani female body. The Hudood Ordinances have allowed for all too many openings in the boundaries that define rape. Women can now be accused of rape, as can children; laws of mutual consent may easily convert a case of child abuse into a prosecution of the child for *Zina*, for fornication. Furthermore, unmarried men and women can be convicted of having committed rape against each other, since a subsection of the *Zina* offense defines rape as "one where a man or a woman have illicit sex knowing that they are not validly married to each other" (58). In other words, fornication is all, and the statistics of the past few years grimly indicate that the real victims of the Hudood Ordinances are women and children, most specifically those who have no access to legal counsel and whose economic status renders them ignorant of their human rights.

Jahangir cites the example of a fifteen-year-old woman, Jehan Mina, who, after her father's death, was raped by her aunt's husband and son. Once her pregnancy was discovered, another relative filed a police report alleging rape. During the trial, however, the accused led no defense, and Mina's testimony alone was sufficient to get her convicted for fornication and sentenced to one hundred public lashes. That child's story is paradigmatic of the untold miseries of those who suffer sentences in Muslim jails.

Let me state the obvious: I cite these alternative realisms and constructions of identity in order to reiterate the problem endemic to postcolonial feminist criticism. It is not the terrors of Islam that have unleashed the Hudood Ordinances on Pakistan, but more probably the United States government's economic and ideological support of a military regime during that bloody but eminently forgotten decade marked by the "liberation" of Afghanistan. Jehan Mina's story is therefore not so far removed from our current assessment of what it means to be multicultural. How are we to connect her lived experience with the overwhelming realism of the law? In what ways does her testimony force postcolonial and feminist discourse into an acknowledgment of the inherent parochialism and professionalism of our claims?

I will offer a weak bridge between the two poles of my rhetorical question: a poem by the feminist Pakistani writer Kishwar Naheed. Her writing has been perceived as inflammatory, and she has been accused of obscenity more than once. The obscenity laws, or the Fahashi laws, are another story altogether. Once they were passed, they could not be put in print because the powers that be declared them to be too obscene. The poem below, however, is one that could easily earn the poet a prison sentence in contemporary Pakistan:

. . . . It is we sinful women
who come out raising the banner of truth
up against barricades of lies on the highways
who find stories of persecution piled on each
    threshold
who find the tongues which could speak have
    been severed. . . .

It is we sinful women.
who are not awed by the grandeur of those
    who wear gowns
who don't sell our bodies
who don't bow our heads
who don't fold our hands together.[11]

We should remember that there remains unseen legislation against such poetry, and that the *Hadd*—the limit—is precisely the realism against which our lived experience can serve as a metaphor, and against which we must continue

to write. If we allow the identity formation of postcolonialism to construe itself only in terms of nationalism and parochialism, or of gender politics at its most narcissistically ahistorical, then let us assume that the media has won its battle, and the law of the limit is upon us.

Notes

1. James Clifford's course, "Travel and Identity in Twentieth-Century Interculture," was given as the Henry Luce Seminar at Yale University, fall 1990.

2. See *Nation and Narration,* ed. Homi K. Bhabha (New York, 1990).

3. See Kwame Anthony Appiah, "Is the Post- in Postmodernism the Post- in Postcolonial?" *Critical Inquiry* 17 (Winter 1991): 336–57.

4. Chandra Talpade Mohanty, "Under Western Eyes: Feminist Scholarship and Colonial Discourses," in *Third World Women and the Politics of Feminism,* ed. Mohanty, Ann Russo, and Lourdes Torres (Bloomington, IN, 1991), 71.

5. See Trinh T. Minh-ha, *Woman, Native, Other: Writing Postcoloniality and Feminism* (Bloomington, IN, 1989); hereafter cited in the text.

6. Hazel V. Carby, *Reconstructing Womanhood: The Emergence of the Afro-American Woman Novelist* (New York, 1987), 15

7. bell hooks [Gloria Watkins], "On Self-Recovery," *Talking Back: Thinking Feminist, Thinking Black* (Boston, 1989), 28.

8. bell hooks, *Yearning: Race, Gender, and Cultural Politics* (Boston, 1990), 93–94.

9. Gayatri Chakravorty Spivak, "Questions of Multiculturalism," interview by Sneja Gunew (30 Aug. 1986), *The Post-Colonial Critic: Interviews, Strategies, Dialogues,* ed. Sarah Harasym (New York, 1990), 66.

10. Asma Jahangir and Hina Jilani, *The Hudood Ordinances: A Divine Sanction?* (Lahore, Pakistan, 1990), 24; hereafter cited in the text.

11. Kishwar Naheed, "We Sinful Women," in *Beyond Belief: Contemporary Feminist Urdu Poetry,* trans. Rukhsana Ahmad (Lahore, Pakistan, 1990), 22–23.

PART II
Subjectivities

Writing can be therapeutic and autobiographical writing even more so, as it affords one a kaleidoscopic view of one's life. For instance, it was only when I started writing these autobiographical episodes that one question that had been nagging me for a very long time seemed to be answered. Why, oh why, do I always trust men, look up to them more than to people of my own sex, even though I was brought up by women? I suddenly realized that all this was due to the relationship I had with my mother.

My mother, Alice Ogbanje Ojebeta Emecheta, that laughing, loud-voiced, six-foot-tall, black glossy slave girl, who as a child suckled the breasts of her dead mother; my mother who lost her parents when the nerve gas was exploded in Europe, a gas that killed thousands of innocent Africans who knew nothing about the Western First World War; my laughing mother, who forgave a brother that sold her to a relative in Onitsha so that he could use the money to buy ichafo siliki—*silk head ties for his coming-of-age dance. My mother, who probably loved me in her own way, but never expressed it; my mother, that slave girl who had the courage to free herself and return to her people in Ibusa, and still stooped and allowed the culture of her people to re-enslave her, and then permitted Christianity to tighten the knot of enslavement.*

She never understood the short, silent, mystery daughter she had. Words said that she died not blessing me. That hurt, it did hurt and for twenty years I carried the hurt. But on going back to Ibusa in 1980, and seeing the people she lived with and the place she was buried, then the image of that tall, lanky, black woman nicknamed 'Blakie the black' seemed to loom over me. Then I felt the warmth of her presence, then I knew right there inside me that my mother did not die cursing me.

—Buchi Emecheta, *Head above Water* (Oxford: Heinemann, 1994), 3

. . . You've got it, then. She moves, walks, lies down, sits, eats, sleeps, drinks. She can laugh and cry, dig sand pits, listen to fairy tales, play with dolls, be frightened, happy, say mama and papa, love and hate and say her prayers. And all with deceptive authenticity. Until she strikes a false note, a precocious remark—less than that: a thought, a gesture—exposing the limitation for which you had almost settled.

Because it hurts to admit that the child—aged three, helpless, alone—is inaccessible to you. You're not only separated from her by forty years; you are hampered by your unreliable memory. You abandoned the child, after all. After others abandoned it. All right, but she was also abandoned by the adult who slipped out of her, and who managed to do to her all the things adults usually do to children. The adult left the child behind, pushed her aside, forgot her, suppressed her, denied her, remade, falsified, spoiled and neglected her, was ashamed and proud of her, loved her with the wrong kind of love, and hated her with the wrong kind of hate. Now, in spite of all impossibility, the adult wishes to make the child's acquaintance.

—Christa Wolf, *Patterns of Childhood,* trans. Ursule Molinaro and Hedvig Rappot
(New York: Farrar, Straus and Giroux, 1980), 7

7 Autogynography: Is the Subject Different?

Domna C. Stanton

"The impulse towards autobiography may be spent," so says the "I" in *A Room of One's Own,* as she narrates autobiographically "the story" of two days she spent "combing the shelves" of libraries, reading texts and metatexts in preparation for a discourse on women in fiction.[1] Fifty years later, the reader who would emulate Woolf's rhetorical strategy could never reach a similar conclusion about autobiography and its criticism. That reading "I," which is "only a convenient term for someone who has no real being" (4), would need a figurative lifetime to consume the autobiographies on library shelves. The total far exceeds the number of titles contained in the 2,868 pages of Georg Misch's *History of Autobiography,* which closes with the Renaissance, or even in the additional 1,000 pages Misch's students compiled, which do not include the twentieth century.[2] And, leaving aside the primary texts, the autobiographical scholar would require more than two symbolic days to peruse the body of critical literature that has grown by leaps and bounds since 1968. A cursory look at the criticism published during the past fifteen years reveals a dramatic change in the discursive status of autobiography, a mode of writing traditionally considered marginal, generically inferior. Thus, where Stephen Shapiro was still trying to validate what he termed "the dark continent of literature" in 1968, in 1980, Barrett J. Mandel aptly entitled his study "Full of Life Now."[3] Even

this phrase, however, does not convey the recent assertion that autobiography lies at the very center of modernist concerns. As William C. Spengemann has written: "the modernist movement away from representational discourse toward self-enacting, self-reflexive verbal structures and the critical theories that have been devised to explain this movement conspire to make the very idea of literary modernism synonymous with that of autobiography."[4]

And yet, if a female reader were to take down from the shelves the bulk of those critical volumes, she would be forced to conclude that women had written virtually no autobiographies. In traditional and "new" literary history, on both sides of the ocean, this "I"—whom I could name, after Woolf, "Mary Beton, Mary Seton, Mary Carmichael . . . any name you please, it is not a matter of any importance" (5)—would find women's autobiographies conspicuous by their absence. Not a single study in Mehlman's *A Structural Study of Autobiography* (1971), Bruss's *Autobiographical Acts* (1976), Spengemann's *The Forms of Autobiography* (1980), or Lejeune's influential *L 'Autobiographie en France* (1971), *Le Pacte Autobiographique* (1975), and *Je est un autre* (1980).[5] None, moreover, in the special issues on autobiography of such journals as *Genre* nos. VI 1 and 2 (1973), *Modern Language Notes* (1978), *Esprit Créateur* (1980), *or Poétique* (1983). At best, an isolated study or chapter in Butterfield's *Black Autobiography in America* (1974), Stone's *Autobiographical Occasions and Original Acts* (1982), and *Autobiography: Essays Theoretical and Critical,* edited by Olney (1980). Within this new realm of autobiographical criticism, woman still remained "the dark continent," in replication of the status that Freud ascribed to her over half a century ago.

What did that ghostly absence mean, I asked, looking as did Mary Beton, at "the blank spaces" on those shelves? (54). Did it signal, once again, and despite over a decade of feminist studies, the collective repression of women? Even in phallocratic terms, it made no sense. How could that void be reconciled with the age-old, pervasive decoding of all female writing as autobiographical? One answer, I thought, turning away from those "empty shelves" (54), was that "autobiographical" constituted a positive term when applied to Augustine and Montaigne, Rousseau and Goethe, Henry Adams and Henry Miller, but that it had negative connotations when imposed on women's texts. It had been used, I realized, as I moved through the stacks toward the French collections, to affirm that women could not transcend, but only record, the concerns of the private self; thus, it had effectively served to devalue their writing. Accordingly, over the centuries, the anonymous seventeenth-century *Portuguese Letters* had been called autobiographical, spontaneous, natural when ascribed to a woman, but fictive, crafted and aesthetic, when attributed to a man.[6] As with George Sand, whose fictions had been notoriously branded as autobiographical, critical reactions to Colette's work represented a dramatic case of the autobiographical wielded as a weapon to denigrate female texts and exclude them from the canon.

To be sure, women had iterated this predominant reading of their writing. Was it, perhaps, a cliché, a convention to which they subscribed to gain some currency in the marketplace?, I wondered, taking down Colette's *Break of Day:* "Man, my friend," I read, "you willingly make fun of women's writings because they can't help being autobiographical."[7] And yet, more aggressively, Beauvoir chastized the autobiographical narrowness and narcissism of female writing in *The Second Sex:* "it is her own self that is the principal—sometimes the unique subject of interest to her."[8] This view had led the future author of five remarkable volumes of memoirs to declare: "there are . . . sincere and engaging feminine autobiographies, but none can compare with Rousseau's *Confessions* and Stendhal's *Souvenirs d'égotisme*" (668). Was this a provocation for women to engage in self-transcending political and philosophical questions or a reflection of the androcentrism of *The Second Sex?*

However complex the reasons for this self-devaluation, it was clearly not women who had determined the repression of autobiographies by the second sex, I countered, turning angrily to make my way to that post Woolfian "room of our own" we call Women's Studies. Here I was sure to find the secondary sources for my text on autobiographical writing by women—what I would term *autogynography.* But my search yielded only one item in the card catalogue: Jelinek, Estelle C., ed., *Women's Autobiography: Essays in Criticism* (Indiana, 1980). Turning to the preface, I read the opening lines with growing discouragement:

> The idea for this collection came to me in 1976 when I was writing my dissertation on the tradition of women's autobiography. I found practically no criticism on women's autobiographies, except for that on Gertrude Stein's, and so had no way of comparing ideas with other critics to see if they were coming to the same or different conclusions I had. Working alone, I wrote that dissertation . . . but vowed to encourage such criticism by compiling this col-

lection so that those working in the field could communicate with one another and individual articles would not be lost in journals in disparate places, but seen as a whole and as a distinct school of criticism. (ix)

Three years later, the situation had hardly changed. Surely there had to be more than the few "individual articles" I too managed to locate in "disparate places." And just as surely, there had to exist a vast number of autogynographies, dating back to early periods, which those articles, written mostly on nineteenth- and twentieth-century texts, did not begin to enumerate. Yes, I decided, as I carted a highly disproportionate number of gynocentric and androcentric studies to the library desk, it was time to return to my own room and, by letter and phone, from friends and from strangers, try to unearth the primary and secondary sources I would need to write my text.

The search for primary sources—and here I am telescoping more than a few days—revealed the existence of important but unexplored autogynographies, contemporary with or even predating the earliest productions of men canonized by literary history. Scholars who claimed, for example, that English autobiography developed in the eighteenth century invariably neglected to consider the works of Laetitia Pilkington, Teresia Constantia Phillips, and Frances Anne Vane, which privileged confessions of feeling and influenced the content and form of both autobiographies and novels. In the rare instances when they were cited, these texts were dismissed as "frigidly sentimental chronicles," their authors branded as "dishonest and libertine women."[9] Similarly, in a work on "English beginnings" of autobiography in the seventeenth century, William Matthews mentioned the "modernism" of the Duchess of Newcastle's *True Relation of My Birth, Breeding and Life*

(1656), though he treated text and author with contempt; and he ignored the *Memoirs* of Lady Ann Fanshaw, though he cited them in passing as "the first of the two lives types."[10] By contrast, Mary Mason declared the *Book of Margery Kempe* (1432) "the first full autobiography in English by anyone male or female," and earlier still, Julian of Norwich, author of *A Shewing of God's Love* (c. 1300), the first Englishwoman to "speak out about herself."[11] England was not an isolated instance, I discovered, as my archaeological quest progressed. Elaine Johnson and Amy Kaminsky, for example, insisted that the fifteenth-century *Written Document* of Doña Leonor Lópes de Córdoba was not only the "first work by a known woman writer" in Spain, but that country's "first autobiography." Yes, that was more like it, I thought. But what of the non-Western world, which, critics claimed, lacked a concept and thus a literature of the individual self. Happily, I learned of Richard Bowring's research on the Heian period in Japan (794–1185). Women, who were forbidden to use Chinese, the language of the male elite, had authored a group of "introspective writings" that constituted, along with *The Tale of Genji*, the major texts of the period. From this perspective, Bowring claimed that the opening sentence of the famous *Tosa Diary* (935)—"A daily record, that preserve of men; but might not a woman produce one too, I wonder, and so I write"—penned by the male poet and grand arbiter of taste, Ki no Tsurayuki, did not involve merely a playful act of sexual substitution. Man was trying to reclaim or usurp a female literary role that was becoming entrenched, argued Bowring; thus Ki no Tsurayuki, adopting a strategy of negation or reversal, proclaimed man preeminent and woman the nascent intruder.[12]

Here was an emblem provided by the East, of the strategies used by Western literary historians to efface autogynography! Indeed, this remarkable Japanese example tended to confirm Cynthia Pomerleau's contention that "the idea that oneself, one's feelings . . . were properly and innately worth writing about was essentially a female idea" (Jelinek, 28), one that men may have usurped and proclaimed their own by obscuring women's texts. To be sure, it was a speculative, even paranoid, reading; only the dogged pursuit of the gynarchaeological enterprise in different cultures, races, and classes would validate the theory or, in all likelihood, attenuate it. Still, it was a seed to sow in my text, perhaps in the introduction, where the need for an a-mazing journey, to use Mary Daly's demystificatory term, should be emphasized. This, however, did not resolve the matter of my text. How was I to treat the subject of autogynography when the primary and secondary sources were only beginning to emerge? Of necessity, as the Woolfian "I" had insisted, my text would contain doses of fiction and opinion (4) that could have some validity but make no claim to "the essential oil of truth" (25). Yes, I decided, leafing through *A Room of One's Own*, I could start by evaluating theories and studies of autobiography in those many gynoless volumes that now stood on my bookshelves before tackling the question of the specificity of women's texts in the few "individual articles" by feminist scholars. Then, perhaps, I might be able to say something, however partial and inconclusive, on the subject of autogynographical difference.

It will surely come as no surprise that beyond their tacit agreement to exclude women's texts, critics disagreed about the specific nature and substance of autobiography. The explorations that had dramatically altered the status of autobiography had also bred controversy and confusion. Typically, Professor Y—as I chose to call the more valid critic after/against the misogynistic Professor Von X of *A Room of One's Own* (31ff.)—confronted this confusion in his opening paragraph: "As the number of people writing about autobiography has swelled," he wrote, "the boundaries of the genre have expanded proportionately until there is virtually no written form that has not either been included in some study of autobiography or else been subjected to autobiographical interpretation" (Spengemann, xii). Where Professor Z— as I dubbed the less valid critic—propounded arbitrary and unconvincing criteria to differentiate "classic," "formal," or "true" autobiographies from memoirs, confessions, or diaries, Professor Y maintained that there was "no way to bring autobiography to heel as a literary genre with its own proper form, terminology and observances." [13] However, the generic fixation was not so easily exorcised; instead, it was displaced onto new thematic or discursive categories such as oratorical, dramatic, philosophical, or poetic autobiographies. [14] It transpired, too, in such formulations as "a genre without conventions" or in the expressed hope of arriving at a generic definition in the future, while speaking in the present "as if we knew what it were." [15] More covertly, an ambivalent desire both to relinquish and to maintain generic certainty emerged in the closely related texts of Bruss and Lejeune. Although she began by proclaiming genre a nominalist fiction, Bruss also upheld it as the set of stable conventions in a community that help define what is permitted a writer and expected of a reader; and she elaborated a set of "rules" that distinguish autobiography from other illocutionary acts in a cultural context. [16] But in view of the confusion among critics, one would have to conclude that autobiography did not exist today, despite all titular or subtitular evidence to the contrary. Like Bruss, Lejeune affirmed the generic specificity of autobiography on the basis of a pact or contract between the author and the reader; at the same time, he inveighed against the essentialist and authoritarian nature of the generic impulse, which he compared to a restricted club, even a pure race, from which all deviations are branded aberrations or aborted failures.[17] Yes, this exposure of the implications of genre is salutory, I thought; but ultimately E. S. Burt is right: "the whole project of defining autobiography generically is what needs to be abandoned."[18] That radical gesture would meet with continued resistance, however, for it would confound Professor Z's system of hierarchies and oppositions, in which the generic, as the French *genre* suggested, was inextricably linked to the genderic.

Well-intentioned, Professor Y opposed any prescriptive definitions, but his text invariably contained a minimal statement that raised troubling questions. Thus the seemingly innocuous definition, "a biography of a person written by himself,"[19] veiled the uncertain meaning and relation of the terms *person* and *himself,* and displaced the content of autobiography onto the undefined *biography*. There was, however, a difference between the autobiographic and the biographic text, which quickly came to mind: the first can never inscribe the death of the speaking subject, the terminus of life, which theoretically the second can describe. Autobiography, then, was necessarily un-ended, incomplete, fragmentary, whatever form of rhetorical closure it might contain. Of course, how much or how little of this partial *bio* an autobiography should properly contain, not even Professor Z tried to tell me. Sensitive to the variabilities and complexities of its narrative modes, Professor Y observed that autobiography might appear to privilege chronological linearity, but that it tended "toward discontinuous structures . . . with disrupted narrative sequences and competing foci of attention" (Bruss, 64). Indeed, an autobiography, I agreed, was a heterogeneous mixture of *discours* and *histoire,* to use Benveniste's terms,[20] the personal and the historico-cultural, the elegiac and the picaresque, the illustrative and the reflective. It might be structured around a crisis or moment of transformation; it could have

explicit or implicit didactic or epistemological aims for the narratee or the narrator, but its thematic base, insisted Professor Y, was "all inclusive."[21] Inevitably, I reflected, the specific texture of an autobiography also represents the mediation of numerous contextual factors: a particular intertext, such as Rousseau's *Confessions* for George Sand and other nineteenth-century autobiographers; or a set of intertexts, such as hagiographies for Margery Kempe and conversion narratives for Quaker and Puritan women. More broadly, every autobiography assumes and reworks literary conventions for writing and reading. And its texture is ultimately determined by the way in which meaning can be signified in a particular discursive context, an (ideo)logical boundary that always already confines the speaking subject.

Although Professor Y was largely indifferent to such matters, he did grapple with the status of the past that the speaking subject narrates, a question laden with ideological implications. Occasionally, he spoke of the recuperation or even the re-creation of the past with the help of a selective or unconscious memory, and here he resembled Professor Z. But Professor Y also declared that the past was never a presence, only an absence; thus its textual substance necessarily involved a creation, an invention at the moment of enunciation. "The way in which the illusion of the past is presented," he said, ". . . is the 'form' the life takes."[22] In this perspective, the facts of the invented past had an undecidable status, according to Professor Y; they produced, through a set of conventions similar to those of the realistic novel, the effect or impression of a referential narrative; facts, he argued, were artifacts.[23] Such a notion of facticity, I recognized, was leading Professor Y away from Professor Z's belief in the truth-value of autobiography, which centuries of writers had claimed for their texts, or even some undefinable alloy of "design and truth," as Roy Pascal put it.[24] Yes, this theory of facticity heralded the ficticity of autobiography, I concluded, turning the page of his study to find these words: "in effect [it is] a novel written in the present with one's life as its subject. Not all fiction is autobiographical," Professor Y conceded, "but on this deeper level all autobiography is fiction."[25] Or, as Lejeune stated, internally, there is "no difference between an autobiography and an autobiographical novel."[26]

To speak of the autobiographical text as fiction did not, however, resolve the issue of the identity of the subject or its referential status, a problem that Professor Y's phrase "one's life" encapsulated. Whose life was it anyway, I wondered. Professor Y insisted that the narration by a subject of enunciation—most often, but not always, selected to be "I"[27]—about the past self or selves as object of enunciation could not, by definition, display the unity, coherence, or self-presence that mark the Western myth of subjecthood. If Professor Z objected to such views as post modernist and anachronistic to the notion of the subject in earlier times, Professor Y countered that he necessarily read with contemporary eyes and that, from his vantage point, the very nature of the autobiographical project involved a splitting of the subject. That split perdured even as the past, heterogeneous self or selves moved discontinuously forward to the present moment of enunciation in an apparent desire for self-possession and one-ness; as Lejeune observed, the autobiographical subject "becomes simple only at the moment when the narrator speaks of his own present narration."[28] Despite his insistence on a self-reflexive structure and the inscription of the myth of the self, Lejeune could not give up the referential ghost or the identity of the subject, I realized, rereading his often-cited definition of autobiography: "a retrospective narrative in prose that a real person makes of his own existence when he emphasizes his individual life, especially the story of his personality."[29] This identity between a real person,

the narrator, and the object of narration was the basis for his autobiographical pact between author and reader. Lejeune was clearly right to privilege the reader, who served as the autobiographer's muse, said Professor Y,[30] and even, I ventured, determined the very configuration of the speaking subject. But Lejeune transformed the reader into a transcendent authority, a kind of policing force who could purportedly verify the fulfillment of the contract or pronounce the work a fraud. No less troubling was the underlying notion of a self-identical entity, which Lejeune considered an "immediately perceived fact" but which evoked, to his critics, the Cartesian principle of self-evidence or the spectre of Derridean phallogopresence. Thus in a disarming, autographic text, Lejeune had recently acknowledged certain imperfections or limitations of his theories and shifted his focus to the miming of a contract and the play of identity.[31]

What had not changed, however, was Lejeune's avowed belief in truth-value and the identity of the proper name, which he regarded as the "profound subject of autobiography."[32] Although Lejeune confused the proper name in the text with the authorial signature, the notion elicited ambivalent reactions, which I, as feminist reader, could not resolve. On the one hand, "author" spelled the phallic myth of authority, not to speak of the patriarchal institutions of property and law. On the other, I wondered uncomfortably, what would the elimination of the signature mean for women autobiographers, whose texts had yet to be explored, acknowledged, and included in the literary and critical canons. Better to bracket that question, I decided in frustration, putting the androcentric volumes back on the shelf. Perhaps I could tackle the problem more knowledgeably once I had examined the gynocentric studies of autobiography. Yes, it was time—the days were in fact passing—to take down from my shelf that small body of work—the individual articles, the

couple of books, and the unpublished texts—
that friends and strangers had helped me compile, and determine, in light of the issue Professors Y and Z had raised, what heuristic claims
could be made at this discursive moment for the
difference of autogynography.

Difference was much on her mind, I realized, as
soon as I began to read the feminist scholar. Unlike Professors Y and Z, who seemed indifferent
to anyone but the generic and hegemonic "he,"
the feminist scholar—why not call her F.S.?—
strove to find generic differences, as Jelinek's
preface confirmed: "It has been gratifying," she
said, "to read all the essays sent to me and to
discover that the critics are substantiating our
contention that there is a literary tradition in
which women write autobiography that is different from that by men" (xi–xii). Implicitly, however, that assertion of difference was based on a
preselected corpus of male autobiographies and
a preestablished set of common traits. A troubling but familiar sign of the generic fixation, I
thought, now transposed to a generic formula:
Male = X, ergo Female = non-X + W. Besides,
wasn't such a notion of difference premature
when the archaeological quest for autogynographies has just begun to make headway? Still, any
single text can suggest constructs, to be tested
out on other texts, I thought, looking through
the work of F.S. for discussions of formal differences. One opposition appeared repeatedly:
men's narratives were linear, chronological, coherent, whereas women's were discontinuous,
digressive, fragmented (17–19). This was the
same narrative shape that Didier had discovered
in Sand's *My Life,* a form Anaïs Nin likened to
"a crazy quilt, all in bits."[33] And yet, women
also wrote linear narratives, as Lynn Bloom and
Orlee Holder observed in re-viewing several
twentieth-century texts.[34] Moreover, narrative
discontinuity was integral to Professor Y's conception of autobiography; and fragmentariness

was the matrix of Beaujour's study of the "auto-
portrait" from Augustine to Leiris.[35] Indeed, I
reflected, discontinuity and fragmentation constitute particularly fitting means for inscribing
the split subject, even for creating the rhetorical
impression of spontaneity and truth.

If there existed a specifically female type of
narrative discontinuity, more detailed and focused analysis would have to reveal it, I concluded, turning now to the question of autogyn-
ographic content. Here, too, a binary opposition
recurred that associated the female with personal
and intimate concerns, the male with professional achievement[36]—a replication, it seemed,
of the private/public, inner/outer dichotomies
that mark generic differences in our symbolic
system. But here, too, I could object that Professor Z upheld the "personal" *Confessions* of
Rousseau as the origin of modern autobiography and that Lejeune made "the history of the
individual personality" central to his definition.
To be sure, I could also cite autogynographies
that were anything but "personal," but what
precisely did the term mean: a particular type of
introspective and affective analysis? a certain
quantity and quality of detail? Although a domestic "dailiness," to use Kate Millett's word,
often permeated autogynographies, the concept
of the personal was a function of changing conventions, which determined the said and, more
important, the unsaid, such as the desires and
the experiences of the female body. Thus, even
the violence of rape was consistently silenced
in nineteenth century female slave narratives,
Francis Smith Foster had said on the phone. Reserved or "decorous communication," as Nancy
K. Miller put it, any autobiography imposed decided limits on the intimate revelations of the
narrating "I," which were conveyed to readers
by omissions or by explicit statements, such as
that of St. Theresa: "I wish I had also been allowed to describe clearly and in full detail my
grave sins and wicked life . . . [but] I have been

137

subjected to severe restrictions [by my confessors] in the matter."[37] Intrasubjectively, the self-censoring speaker invariably displayed impulses toward both exposure and concealment. Or, perhaps, what was said made room for the not-said, as Colette's *Break of Day* seemed to suggest: "[By divulging] to the public love-secrets and amorous lies and half-truths . . . she manages to hide other important and obscure secrets" (62). Women's "personal" or "intimate" autographs, then, remained partial inscriptions of what Spacks called "selves in hiding."[38]

Some feminist critics defined the personal in women's autobiographies as a primary emphasis on the relation of self to others. However, this relatedness was traced to the dependence imposed on women by the patriarchal system, or then it was upheld as a fundamental female quality.[39] In the parental relation, moreover, both father and mother appeared alternatively as privileged terms. According to Spacks, the father-daughter bond dominated the works of Laetitia Pilkington, Charlotte Charke, and Fanny Burney, while the mother was depicted in negative terms that verged, in Hester Thrale's diary, on matrophobia.[40] And yet, matrilinealism prevailed in the autographs of Sand and Colette and, as Demetrakopoulous showed, in such diverse twentieth-century works as Mead's *Blackberry Winter*, Hellman's *Pentimento*, Angelou's *I Know Why the Caged Bird Sings*, and Kingston's *The Woman Warrior*.[41] To be sure, no one had yet compared the relation to the mother in female and male autobiographies, a bond that Professor Y regarded as crucial (Stone, 147). Still, it seemed valid that this relation would have particular meanings for the female subject, since her mother symbolized both an origin that is same and different, and subsequently, a mirror of the possibilities of becoming. Analogously, I thought, a different narrative thread must inscribe the double identification of the maternal "I" with her child, as the self she had been and

the other who had been within her. However, this privileged relation also allowed authors from Anne Bradstreet to Margaret Oliphant to present their texts as records for their children and thus to legitimize or naturalize their writing. It was difficult, then, to separate a manifestation of female difference from a strategic conformity to cultural norms. Indeed, over and beyond children, the central role ascribed to husband or mate, in autographs ranging from the Duchess of Newcastle's *True Relation* to the memoirs of Hellman and Beauvoir, could signal either a special female relatedness and/or an acquiescence to the dominant sex through which the female is meant to define and confine the self in our symbolic order.

More than the ambiguous inscription of multiple personal relations, the autogynographical narrative was marked by conflicts between the private and the public, the personal and the professional. As F.S. observed, there was a systematic tension between the conventional role of wife, mother, or daughter and another, unconventional self that had ambition or a vocation. This dual and contradictory impulse, which Professor Z had first located in Lady Ann Fanshawe's seventeenth-century text, was displayed much earlier in the "two equally demanding identities" of wife-mother and pilgrim-mystic that structured the *Book of Margery Kempe*.[42] That "divided consciousness" and the "rhetoric of uncertainty" that conveyed it, as Spacks put it, recurred in various forms throughout the centuries, down to the autographs of Eleanor Roosevelt and Golda Meir.[43] A similar tension underlay Elizabeth Cady Stanton's *Eighty Years and More*, in which, as Jelinek showed, the "I" kept returning to the public career, even though the stated intention was to present "the story of my private life as wife and earnest reformer, as an enthusiastic housekeeper, proud of my skill in every department of domestic economy, and as the mother of seven children" (71–72). So doing, the speaking subject strove and failed to present the unitary and ordinary self of wife and mother.

Beyond professional aspirations there was, I believed, a fundamental deviance that pervaded autogynographies and produced conflicts in the divided self: the act of writing itself. For a symbolic order that equates the idea(l) of the author with a phallic pen transmitted from father to son places the female writer in contradiction to the dominant definition of woman and casts her as the usurper of male prerogatives.[44] Internalized, this generic "horizon of expectations," to paraphrase Jauss,[45] generated a particular self-consciousness about the fact of writing often manifested in a defensive or justificative posture. "Because I am a woman, ought I therefore to believe that I should not tell you of the goodness of God?" asks the "I" in Julian of Norwich's *Showings*, proceeding to use the insignificant hazelnut as a metaphor for God's perfection and the value of her own narrative (Mason, 216). As this example also revealed, however, the speaking "I" constituted the reading "you" as the representation of society's view of women and thus as the personification of the writing interdiction. Analogously, although the eighteenth-century *Narrative of the Life of Mrs Charlotte Charke* was defiantly dedicated to the self, the reader was still encoded as the amused critic of the eccentric female speaker: "those that like to laugh I know will encourage me; and, I am certain, there is none in the World MORE FIT THAN MYSELF TO BE LAUGHED AT. I confess myself an odd Mortal, and believe I need no Force of Argument, beyond what has already been said, to bring the whole Globe terrestrial into that Opinion."[46] Forgoing such self-mockery, the female "I" could resort to more conventional means of attenuating the deviance or, in Fanny Burney's case, the sin of writing: she could cast her text in the ethical frame of a spiritual journey, a search for virtue and goodness, or the fulfillment of a duty,[47] semes that

found a latter-day expression as therapy for the speaker in the diaries of Anaïs Nin.

Although the injunction against writing had somewhat lifted for some women in some contemporary places,[48] autogynography, I thought, had a global and essential therapeutic purpose: to constitute the female subject. In a phallocentric system, which defines her as the object, the inessential other to the same male subject—that *The Second Sex* had proved beyond a doubt—the *graphing* of the *auto* was an act of self-assertion that denied and reversed woman's status. It represented, as Didier had said of Sand's *My Life*, the conquest of identity through writing (562). Creating the subject, an autograph gave the female "I" substance through the inscription of an interior and an anterior. And yet, the symbolic specificity of woman as the inessential other also helped explain why the female self was textually constructed through the relation to mother and father, mate and child. This "delineation of identity by way of alterity," as Mason put it, was nowhere more clearly illustrated than in the *True Relation* of the Duchess of Newcastle:

> I hope my readers will not think me vain for writing my life, since there have been many that have done the like, as Caesar, Ovid and many more, both men and women, and I know no reason I may not do it as well as they: but I verily believe some censuring Readers will scornfully say, why hath this Lady writ her own life? since none care to know whose daughter she was or whose wife she is, or how she was bred, or what fortunes she had, or how she lived, or what humour or disposition she was of? I answer that it is true, that it is to no purpose to the Readers, but it is to the Authoress, because I write for my own sake, not theirs; neither did I intend this piece for to delight, but to di-

vulge; not to please the fancy but to tell the truth, lest after-ages should mistake, in not knowing I was daughter to one Master Lucas of St. Johns, near Colchester, in Essex, second wife to the Lord Marquis of Newcastle; for my Lord having had two wives, I might easily have been mistaken, especially if I should die and my Lord marry again.[49]

In this remarkable passage, the "I" asserted that she "writ her own life" "for [her] own sake," out of a need to differentiate the self from others, only to show that its constitution and individuation predicated reference and relatedness to others: father and husband, and beyond, less "censuring Readers" of "after-ages." It was no mere coincidence, then, that three centuries later, Beatrice Webb's *The Partnership* began with a chapter entitled "The Other." Beyond the surface theme of marital happiness, the title suggested both the affirmation of the female as subject and the recognition that one cannot exist without the other.[50] The female "I" was thus not simply a texture woven of various selves; its threads, its life-lines, came from and extended to others. By that token, this "I" represented a denial of a notion essential to the phallogocentric order: the totalized self-contained subject present-to-itself.

Because of woman's different status in the symbolic order, autogynography, I concluded, dramatized the fundamental alterity and nonpresence of the subject, even as it asserts itself discursively and strives toward an always impossible self-possession. This gendered narrative involved a different plotting and configuration of the split subject, which the androcentric Professor Y wholly ignored, although he had begun to consider the problematics of subjecthood. Indeed, I reflected, surveying my differing bookshelves, Professor Y seemed ready, in a few instances at least, to undermine the notion of identity, whereas F.S., at this discursive moment, appeared determined to affirm and maintain it. What scenarios underlay those contrasting tendencies, I wondered, leaning back in my chair. One possible explanation was that Professor Y was feeling paralyzed by the identity that the symbolic order bestowed (or imposed) upon him, whereas F.S. was still struggling, in that recently constructed room of her own, to assert an identity that was denied her. To be sure, there were exceptions, most notably among women with French connections, who considered the unitary subject inimical to the feminist enterprise. By and large, however, F.S. did not seem willing to accept Gertrude Stein's pronouncement that identity "destroys creation," whereas masterpieces derive from "knowing there is no identity and producing while identity is not."[51] Moreover, in contrast to Stein's *Autobiography of Alice B. Toklas,* a text that openly rejects the "autobiographical pact" of identity between a real person, the subject, and the object of enunciation, the valorized notion of female identity in most readings by F.S. was conjoined with an explicit or implicit belief in the referentiality and truth-value of autogynographies as "honest records of the moment," or of women's "inner lives."[52] It was almost as if—and here I was speculating again—the feminist scholar's own identity depended on the referential reality of the woman in the text, as if that woman was the same and different other through whom F.S. needed to construct and relate her self. Still, I thought, glancing at the corpus I had now finished reading, the notion of romances, of fictions, of "imagined selves" had appeared in a couple of "disparate places"[53] and there was no predicting the future shape of our room.

It was nonetheless clear that F.S. was not going to help me confront the question of the status and the significance of the female signature. And yet, I thought anxiously, as I put the gynocentric studies back on the shelf, I cannot end my text without shifting focus from the *auto* in the *graph* to its author, and exploring, however ambivalently or abortively, the importance of her/his gender and referentiality. To broach these issues, I would have to look beyond autobiographical criticism, since Professor Y, with his generic he, was oblivious to their problematics. In the one pertinent article I had found, Professor Y envisaged the death of the author, after Derrida and most especially Foucault, who declared that this relatively recent manifestation of the system of private property served to constrain the proliferation of new meanings and readings.[54] Yes, I said, the name of the female author has consistently generated restricted and distorted readings,[55] when her texts were not, as autogynographies had been, simply banned from consideration; in that sense, Foucault was right, although he never spoke of women. Because of that gender-bound discursive situation, however, in which I was engaged, I had to privilege and promote the female signature, make it visible and prominent, or else endure and insure more of the phallocentric same. The elimination of the signature, Nancy K. Miller had warned in a debate with Peggy Kamuf (who assumed a Foucaultian stance), could even spell a return to female anonymity.[56] In this perspective, I could argue that at this symbolic moment the female signature, unlike the generic fixation, had liberating rather than constraining effects, although there was always the risk of reconfirming, as Kamuf emphasized, the very systems and institutions we wished to undermine.

More problematic by far was the question of the referential status of the signature. To be consistent with my textual, nonreferential approach to the female subject, I should view the signature as a name that comprised various semes of gender, ethnicity, or class and that evoked various cultural and literary associations. Did it matter, after all, on the signifying plane, whether the

name affixed to *Life's Adventure* (Woolf, 98) was Mary Carmichael or Mary McCarthy? And yet, as the names George Sand and Pauline de Réage illustrated, a signature could always be counterfeit.[57] Given that uncertainty, I could take the signature at its face value and promote, with Peggy Kamuf and Mary Jacobus, Derridean and Kristevan notions of the "feminine" as a modality open to both men and women;[58] but that I resisted, for it involved recourse to abstract and essentialist predefinitions, rather than the heuristic exploration of sexual/textual differences. Even less satisfactory as a solution, however, was a return to Lejeune's pact and to a policing reader who could purportedly confirm anatomical truth. Yes, I realized, pacing the room in frustration, I was at an impasse. My text would leave an unresolved contradiction. But why not? I asked, sitting back at my desk; contradictions were emblematic of broad discursive problems; and I was, it appeared, in good company. Jacobus, for instance, rejected the idea of the gendered signature, but she also unconsciously used it when she contrasted Mary Shelley to all the rivalrous male authors she cited. And although Foucault said with Beckett that it does not matter who is speaking, he also promoted certain male writers as "founders of discursivity" (154), thus confirming by his own practice that the author had not, and perhaps could not, at present be eliminated. At the very least, then, I should clearly mark the contradiction in my text—no less overtly than the divided female subject in the autograph—before I exposed my illogical belief that the gender of the author did make a difference, at this discursive point in time.

"What should that difference be?" asked the "I" in *A Room of One's Own,* just before she proceeded to imagine and affirm the distinct difference of the sentence, sequence, theme, and sensibility of Mary Carmichael's *Life's Adventure* (81ff.). And yet, I realized, reading Woolf's last chapter a last time, Mary Beton had ultimately retreated into an incandescent vision of androgyny, an ideal that, in our system, would guarantee the female anonymity she decried. To be sure, although I had not reached any inspired conclusions, I had something to say about the different subject of and in the female autograph, a tentative, exploratory idea that other readings by F.S. and, perhaps, even Professor Y would revise. I want to cast my own text in the interrogatory mode, I decided, taking out a blank sheet of paper and writing: *Autogynography: Is the Subject Different?* And instead of a formal closure, I would leave my text unended, open it to a critical reading by appropriating a passage from Woolf: "Lies will flow from my lips, but there may perhaps be some [valid statement] mixed up with them; it is for you to seek out [this statement] and to decide whether any part of it is worth keeping. If not, you will, of course, throw the whole of it into the waste paper basket and forget all about it" (4).

Notes

A first draft of this essay was presented at the colloquium on New Directions in Women's Biographies and Autobiography sponsored by the Project on Women and Social Change, Smith College, June 12–17, 1983.

1. Virginia Woolf, *A Room of One's Own* (New York: Harcourt, Brace and World, 1929), 83.
2. Georg Misch, *Geschichte der Autobiographie,* 4 vols. (Frankfurt am Main: Schulte und Bulmke, 1946–69).
3. Stephen A. Shapiro, "The Dark Continent of Literature: Autobiography," *Comparative Literature Studies* 5 (1968): 421–54; Barrett J. Mandel, "Full of Life Now," in *Autobiography: Essays Theoretical and Critical,* ed. James Olney (Princeton: Princeton University Press, 1980), 49–72.
4. William C. Spengemann, *The Forms of Autobiography: Episodes in the History of a Literary Genre* (New Haven: Yale University Press, 1980), xvi.

5. See, however, Philippe Lejeune, "Women and Autobiography at Author's Expense," in *The Female Autograph,* ed. Domna C. Stanton (New York: New York Literary Forum, 1984), 205–18. And, in a recent conversation, Lejeune told me he is undertaking a systematic survey of women's autobiographies of the nineteenth and twentieth centuries.
6. See Peggy Kamuf, "Writing like a Woman," in *Women and Language in Literature and Society,* ed. Sally McConnell-Ginet, Ruth Borker, and Nelly Furman (New York: Praeger 1980), 284–99.
7. Colette, *Break of Day,* trans. Enid McLeod (New York: Farrar, Straus and Cudahy, 1961), 19.
8. Simone de Beauvoir, *The Second Sex* (New York: Vintage Books, 1974), 655.
9. Wayne Shumaker, *English Autobiography: Its Emergence, Materials, and Form* (Berkeley: University of California Press, 1954), 23–24. See also Estelle Jelinek, "Introduction," *Women's Autobiography: Essays in Criticism* (Bloomington: Indiana University Press, 1980), 2–5.
10. William Matthews, "Seventeenth-Century Autobiography," paper read at the William Andrews Clark Memorial Library (Los Angeles: University of California, 1973), 14.
11. Mary G. Mason, "The Other Voice: Autobiographies of Women Writers," in Olney, 207, 209.
12. See the texts of Bowring, Kaminsky and Johnson in Stanton *Female Autograph.*
13. James Olney, "Autobiography and the Cultural Moment: A Thematic, Historical, and Bibliographical Introduction," in Olney, 4.
14. See Spengemann, and William Howarth, "Some Principles of Autobiography," in Olney, 83–114.
15. Michael G. Cooke, "'Do You Remember Laura?' or the Limits of Autobiography," *Iowa Review* 9, no. 2 (1978): 68; Georges May, *L'Autobiographie* (Paris: Presses Universitaires de France, 1979), 12.
16. Elizabeth W. Bruss, *Autobiographical Acts: The Changing Situation of a Literary Genre* (Baltimore: Johns Hopkins University Press, 1976).
17. Philippe Lejeune, *Le Pacte Autobiographique* (Paris: Seuil, 1975), passim, but especially 311–45.
18. E. S. Burt, "Poetic Conceit: The Self-Portrait and Mirrors of Ink," *Diacritics* 12, no. 4 (Winter 1982): 19.

19. Jean Starobinski, "The Style of Autobiography," in Olney, 73.

20. Emile Benveniste, *Problèmes de linguistique générale,* vol. 2 (Paris: Gallimard, 1974), 237–50.

21. Howarth, 87.

22. Mandel, 64.

23. Louis A. Renza, "The Veto of the Imagination: A Theory in Autobiography," in Olney, 269.

24. Roy Pascal, *Design and Truth in Autobiography* (Cambridge: Harvard University Press, 1960).

25. Burton Pike, "Time in Autobiography," *Comparative Literature* 28 (1976): 337.

26. Lejeune, "Le Pacte Autobiographique," *Poétique* 14 (1973): 147.

27. See, however, Lejeune's "Autobiography in the Third Person," *New Literary History* 9, no. 1 (Autumn 1977): 26–50, and Julia Kristeva's first person plural autograph, "My Memory's Hyperbole," in Stanton *Female Autograph,* 219–35.

28. Lejeune, "Le Pacte Autobiographique," 167.

29. Lejeune, *Le Pacte Autobiographique,* 139.

30. Renza, 293.

31. See Michael Ryan, "Self-Evidence," *Diacritics* 10, no. 2 (Summer 1980): 2–16; and Lejeune, "Le Pacte Autobiographique (bis)," *Poétique* 66 (November 1983): 416–34.

32. Lejeune, "Le Pacte Autobiographique," 163; "Le Pacte Autobiographique (bis)."

33. Béatrice Didier, "Femme, identité, écriture: A Propos de *L'Histoire de ma vie* de George Sand," *Revue des Sciences Humaines* 168, no. 4 (1977): 661–76; Anaïs Nin is quoted in Albert R. Stone, *The American Autobiography: A Collection of Critical Essays* (Englewood Cliffs, NJ: Prentice Hall, 1981), 192; see also Annette Kolodny, "Towards a Theory of Form in Feminist Autobiography: Kate Millett's *Flying* and *Sita,* Maxine Hong Kingston's *The Woman Warrior,*" in Jelinek, 221ff.

34. Lynn Bloom and Orlee Holder, "Anaïs Nin's Diary in Context," in Jelinek, 208ff.; see also Patricia Meyer Spacks, *Imagining a Self: Autobiography and Novel in Eighteenth-Century England* (Cambridge: Harvard University Press, 1976), 161ff.

35. Michel Beaujour, *Miroirs d'encre: Rhétorique de l'auto-portrait* (Paris: Seuil, 1980).

36. See Jelinek's "Introduction: Women's Autobiography and the Male Tradition," and Patricia

Meyer Spacks' "Selves in Hiding," both in Jelinek, 10, 113.

37. Nancy K. Miller, "Women's Autobiography in France: For a Dialectics of Identification," in McConnell-Ginet, Borker, and Furman, 268; Saint Theresa is quoted in Renza, 284.

38. Spacks, "Selves in Hiding," 112–32.

39. Ibid., 122, and Spacks, *Imagining a Self,* 73; Stone, 196.

40. Spacks, *Imagining a Self,* 74–78, 164; "Reflecting Women," *Yale Review* 63 (1973): 33. On matrophobia, see also Mary Fleming Zirin's contribution in Stanton *Female Autograph.*

41. Stephanie Demetrakopoulos, "The Metaphysics of Matrilinealism in Women's Autobiography . . . ," in Jelinek, 180–206. See also Lynn Z. Bloom, "Heritages: Discussions of Mother-Daughter Relationships in Women's Autobiographies," in *The Lost Tradition: Mothers and Daughters in Literature,* ed. Cathy N. Davidson and E. M. Broner (New York: Ungar, 1980), 281–302.

42. See Matthews, 14; Mason, 211, 221.

43. Spacks, "Reflecting Women," 37; "Selves in Hiding," 112–32.

44. See Sandra Gilbert and Susan Gubar, *The Madwoman in the Attic* (New Haven: Yale University Press, 1979).

45. Hans-Robert Jauss, "Littérature médiévale et théorie des genres," *Poétique* 1, no. 1 (1970): 91.

46. Quoted in Spacks, *Imagining a Self,* 82.

47. Ibid., 59ff.

48. See Elizabeth Winston's analysis of some English and American women's autobiographies after 1920 in "The Autobiographer and Her Readers: From Apology to Affirmation," in Jelinek, 93–111.

49. Mason, 231; Margaret, Duchess of Newcastle, "A True Relation of My Birth, Breeding and Life," *The Lives of William Cavendish, Duke of Newcastle and of his Wife, Margaret Duchess of Newcastle,* ed. Mark Antony Lover (London: John Russell, 1892), 309–10.

50. Beatrice Webb, *Our Partnership* (Cambridge: Cambridge University Press, 1975). For a woman-centered manifestation of this idea, see Luce Irigaray, "And the One Doesn't Stir Without the Other," trans. Hélène Wenzel, *Signs: Journal of Women in Culture and Society* 7, no. 1 (Autumn 1981): 60–67.

51. Quoted in James E. Breslin, "Gertrude Stein

and the Problems of Autobiography," in Jelinek, 150.

52. Demetrakopoulos, 208; Mary G. Mason and Carol H. Green, eds., *Journeys: Autobiographical Writings by Women* (Boston: G. K. Hall, 1979), vii.

53. E.g., Didier; Miller; Spacks, *Imagining a Self;* and Germaine Bree, "George Sand: The Fictions of Autobiography," *Nineteenth-Century French Studies* 4, no. 4 (Summer 1976): 438–49.

54. Michael Sprinker, "Fictions of the Self: The End of Autobiography," in Olney, 322ff. Michel Foucault, "What Is an Author?" in *Textual Strategies,* ed. Josue V. Harari (Ithaca: Cornell University Press, 1979), 141–60.

55. See Jonathan Culler, "Reading as a Woman," *On Deconstruction: Theory and Criticism after Structuralism* (Ithaca: Cornell University Press, 1982), 43–64.

56. Peggy Kamuf and Nancy K. Miller, "Dialogue," *Diacritics* (Summer 1982): 42–53.

57. See Jacques Derrida, "Signature Event Context," trans. Jeffrey Mehlman and Samuel Weber, *Glyph* 1 (1977): 172–96

58. Kamuf and Miller, 42–47; Mary Jacobus, "Is There a Woman in This Text?" *New Literary History* 14, no. 1 (1982): 117–41.

8 Authorizing the Autobiographical

Shari Benstock

I suggest that one could understand the life around which autobiography forms itself in a number of other ways besides the perfectly legitimate one of "individual history and narrative": we can understand it as the vital impulse—the impulse of life—that is transformed by being lived through the unique medium of the individual and the individual's special, peculiar psychic configuration; we can understand it as consciousness, pure and simple, consciousness referring to no objects outside itself, to no events, and to no other lives; we can understand it as participation in an absolute existence far transcending the shifting, changing unrealities of mundane life; we can understand it as the moral tenor of the individual's being. Life in all these latter senses does not stretch back across time but extends down to the roots of individual being; it is atemporal, committed to a vertical thrust from consciousness down into the unconscious rather than to a horizontal thrust from the present into the past.*
—James Olney, "Some Versions of Memory" (emphasis added)

In this extended definition of "the life around which autobiography forms itself," James Olney has accounted for nearly all the concerns addressed by the essays in [*The Private Self*]. In one way or another each contributor has taken up the issues enumerated here: the assertion that autobiography is "transformed by being lived through the unique medium of the individual"; the assumption that the individual bears "special, peculiar psychic configuration"; the belief that autobiography represents "consciousness, pure and simple . . . referring to no object outside itself, to no events, and to no other lives" and that it transcends "the shifting, changing unrealities of mundane life"; the supposition that "life . . . does not stretch back across time but extends down to the roots of individual being," moving in "a vertical thrust from con-

sciousness down into the unconscious rather than . . . a horizontal thrust from the present into the past." These essays take up such premises in order to revise them, to rethink the very coincidence of "ontology" and "autobiography." That each of these premises should prove an "issue" in the essays that follow derives, I think, from the primary contexts of their writing—the concerns with gender, race, class, and historical and political conditions in the theory and practice of women's autobiographical writings.

How does writing mediate the space between "self" and "life" that the autobiography would traverse and transgress? One definition of autobiography suggests that it is an effort to recapture the self—in Hegel's claim, to know the self through "consciousness" (Gusdorf, 38). Such a claim presumes that there is such a thing as the

145

"self" and that it is "knowable." This coming-to-knowledge of the self constitutes both the desire that initiates the autobiographical act and the goal toward which autobiography directs itself. By means of writing, such desire presumably can be fulfilled. Thus the place to begin our investigation of autobiography might be at the crossroads of "writing" and "selfhood."[1]

Initiating Autobiography

The autobiographical perspective has . . . to do with taking oneself up and bringing oneself to language.
—Janet Varner Gunn, *Autobiography*

If the autobiographical moment prepares for a meeting of "writing" and "selfhood," a coming together of method and subject matter, this destiny—like the retrospective glance that presumably initiates autobiography—is always deferred. Autobiography reveals gaps, and not only gaps in time and space or between the individual and the social, but also a widening divergence between the manner and matter of its discourse. That is, autobiography reveals the impossibility of its own dream: what begins on the presumption of self-knowledge ends in the creation of a fiction that covers over the premises of its construction. Georges Gusdorf has argued that "the appearance of autobiography implies a new spiritual revolution: the artist and model coincide, the historian tackles himself as object" (31). But in point of fact, the "coincidence" of artist and model is an illusion. As Jacques Lacan has noted, the "mirror stage" of psychic development that initiates the child into the social community and brings it under the law of the Symbolic (the law of language as constituted through society) serves up a false image of the child's unified "self." This unity is imposed from the outside (in the mirror reflection) and is, in Ellie Ragland-Sullivan's words, "asymmetrical, fictional, and artificial." As Ragland-Sullivan

continues, the "mirror stage must, therefore, be understood as a metaphor for the vision of harmony of a subject essentially in discord" (26–27). The "discord" that gives the lie to a unified, identifiable, coterminous self has been built up out of the images, sounds, and sensory responses available to the child during the first six months or so of its life; it is called the unconscious, or that which derives from an experience of "self" as fragmented, partial, segmented, and different. The developing child drives toward fusion and homogeneity in the construction of a "self" (the *moi* of Lacan terminology) against the effects of division and dissolution. The unconscious is thus not the lower depths of the conscious (as in Olney's description of it) but rather an inner seam, a space between "inside" and "outside"—it is the space of difference, the gap that the drive toward unity of self can never entirely close. It is also the space of writing, which bears the marks and registers the alienating effects of the false symmetry of the mirror stage.

Here I bracket some considerations about a developing self with particular reference to divisions between the soma and psyche and to mirrors.

In Virginia Woolf's "A Sketch of the Past," her effort at writing her memoirs, she comments at length on her relation to mirrors, remembering crucial events from her childhood in which mirrors played some part:

> There was a small looking-glass in the hall at Talland House. It had, I remember, a ledge with a brush on it. By standing on tiptoe I could see my face in the glass. When I was six or seven perhaps, I got into the habit of looking at my face in the glass. But I only did this if I was sure that I was alone. I was ashamed of it. A strong feeling of guilt seemed naturally attached to it. (*Moments*, 67–68)

Woolf lists various reasons for this shame—that she and Vanessa were "tomboys" and that "to have been found looking in the glass would have been against our tomboy code" (68); or that she inherited "a streak of the puritan," which made her feel shame at self-regard or narcissistic behavior. From a readerly perspective, neither of these reasons seems adequate to the kind of shame she clearly felt before the looking glass, a shame that lasted her entire life. Further on in this memoir, she continues her commentary on female beauty: "My mother's beauty, Stella's beauty, gave me as early as I can remember, pride and pleasure" (68). She declares that her "natural love for beauty was checked by some ancestral dread," then clarifies and qualifies her perceptions: "Yet this did not prevent me from feeling ecstasies and raptures spontaneously and intensely and without any shame or the least sense of guilt, so long as they *were disconnected with my own body*" (68; emphasis added).

Slowly, as though with dread, Woolf comes to "another element in the shame which I had in being caught looking at myself in the glass in the hall" (68). She declares that she was "ashamed or afraid" of her own body. The memory of the hallway with its looking glass is overlaid by another memory of that same hallway, a scene that may well have been reflected for her in the very looking glass of which she speaks. This memory is of George Duckworth raising her onto the slab outside the dining room and "there he began to explore my body":

I can remember the feel of his hand going under my clothes; going firmly and steadily lower and lower. I remember how I hoped that he would stop; how I stiffened and wriggled as his hand approached my private parts. But it did not stop. His hand explored my private parts too. I remember resenting, disliking it—what is the word for so dumb and mixed a feeling?

It must have been strong, since I still recall it. This seems to show that a feeling about certain parts of the body; how they must not be touched; how it is wrong to allow them to be touched; must be instinctive. (69)

Sexual abuse adds itself to the shame of looking at the face in the mirror. Or perhaps sexual abuse actually preceded the shame of looking in the glass. Woolf's memories, as we shall see, do not announce their sequence; their timing always contradicts the logical sequence of conscious thought and action, escaping the dating of calendars and clocks. In recounting the scene with George Duckworth, Woolf does not claim to have discovered the reason for her shame at looking at her own face, she admits to having "only been able to discover some possible reasons; there may be others; I do not suppose that I have got at the truth; yet this is a simple incident; and it happened to me personally; and I have no motive for lying about it" (69). The layers of conscious recall and justification overlap each other, their movement inexorably marked by the semicolons of these clauses that march her back to the moment in the hallway, just as her circuitous "tunneling" method of finding her way back to the past had brought her to the scene with George Duckworth from another direction—from the reflection of her own face in the mirror.

Woolf has one more comment on the "mirror stage" of her own sexual and psychic development:

Let me add a dream; for it may refer to the incident of the looking-glass. I dreamt that I was looking in a glass when a horrible face—the face of an animal—suddenly showed over my shoulder. I cannot be sure if this was a dream, or if it happened. Was I looking in the glass one day when something in the background moved, and seemed to me alive? I cannot be sure. But

I have always remembered the other face in the glass, whether it was a dream or a fact, and that it frightened me. (69)

Two things presumably occur at the mirror stage: a realization (even if it cannot yet be verbalized) of wholeness, completeness, in an image that contradicts the intuited understanding that the child is still fragmented, uncoordinated, and not yet experiencing bodily reactions through a kind of psychic "wholeness"; and a shock of awareness that the image (which may be seen not in a mirror, but rather in a parent's or a sibling's face) is that of an other—someone or something unlike and unconnected to the infant. The mirror stage marks a differentiation that is potentially frightening, a moment that cannot be recaptured through memory as such, a moment that hangs in a space that is neither dream nor fact, but both. The mirror stage marks both the exceptional and the common; it is a stage common to us all, but within our experience—and this experience exists outside and beyond memory—this stage marks us as exceptional, differentiated. What should be communicated in this moment is a wholeness, an integration that is present in the image but not yet apparent in experience. For Woolf such an experience—really an aftershock of trauma—recorded both differentiation and a psychic/somatic split. A mysterious, frightening, unknown shame clouds the mirror; the other face in the mirror marks dread.

In a definition of the autobiographical act that strikingly recapitulates the effects of Lacan's mirror stage, Georges Gusdorf has written: "Autobiography . . . requires a man to take a distance with regard to himself in order to reconstitute himself in the focus of his special unity and identity across time" (35). The effect of such a distancing and reconstituting is precisely the effect of the mirror stage: a recognition of the alienating force within the specular (the "regard") that leads to the desperate shoring-up of

the reflected image against disintegration and division. What is reinforced in this effort is the *moi,* the ego; what is pushed aside (or driven into the darkened realms of the repressed) is the split in the subject (who both "is" and "is not" the reflected image) that language effects and cannot deny. Man enforces a "unity and identity across time" by "reconstituting" the ego as a bulwark against disintegration; that is, man denies the very effects of having internalized the alienating world order. One such "denial" is autobiography itself, at least as it is defined by Gusdorf, who would place random reflections on self and society, such as diaries, journals, and letters, in a category separate from (and prior to—the sources for) the self-conscious autobiography in which the writer "calls himself as witness for himself" (29).

For Gusdorf, autobiography "is the mirror in which the individual reflects his own image" (33); in such a mirror the "self" and the "reflection" coincide. But this definition of autobiography overlooks what might be the most interesting aspect of the autobiographical: the measure to which "self" and "self-image" might not coincide, can never coincide in language—not because certain forms of self-writing are not self-conscious enough but because they have no investment in creating a cohesive self over time. Indeed, they seem to exploit difference and change over sameness and identity: their writing follows the "seam" of the conscious/unconscious where boundaries between internal and external overlap. Such writing puts into question the whole notion of "genre" as outlined by the exclusionary methods of Gusdorf's rather narrow definition of the autobiographical. And it is not surprising that the question of "genre" often rides on the question of gender.[2]

Psychic health is measured in the degree to which the "self" is constructed in separateness, the boundaries between "self" and "other" carefully circumscribed. From a Gusdorfian perspective, autobiography is a re-erecting of these psychic walls, the building of a linguistic fortress between the autobiographical subject and his interested readers: "The autobiography that is thus devoted exclusively to the defense and glorification of a man, a career, a political cause, or a skillful strategy . . . is limited almost entirely to the public sector of existence" (36). Gusdorf acknowledges that "the question changes utterly when the private face of existence assumes more importance" (37), but he suggests that "the writer who recalls his earliest years is thus exploring an enchanted realm that belongs to him alone" (37). In either kind of autobiography, the writing subject is the one presumed to know (himself), and this process of knowing is a process of differentiating himself from others.[3] The chain-link fence that circumscribes his unique contributions is language, representative of the very laws to which this writing subject has been subjected; that is, language is neither an external force nor a "tool" of expression, but the very symbolic system that both constructs and is constructed by the writing subject. As such, language is both internal and external, and the walls that defend the *moi* are never an entirely adequate defense network against the multiple forms of the *je*.

If the linguistic defense networks of male autobiographers more successfully keep at bay the discordant *je*, it may be because female autobiographers are more aware of their "otherness." Like men, we are subjected to the phallic law, but our experience of its social and political effects comes under the terms of another law— that of gender. Ragland-Sullivan comments that "the early mother is internalized as the source of one's own narcissism, prior to the acquisition of individual boundaries, while the father's subsequent, symbolic role is that of teaching these boundaries—he is a limit-setter. As a result, the father is later both feared and emulated, since his presence has taught the infant about laws

and taboos" (42). Language itself, as Lacan has shown, is a defense against unconscious knowledge (Ragland-Sullivan, 179). But it is not an altogether successful defense network, punctuated as it is by messages from the unconscious, messages that attempt to defeat this "fencing-off" mechanism; indeed, there is no clearly defined barrier between the conscious and the unconscious. Fenced in by language, the speaking subject is primordially divided.[4]

This division is apparent as well in writing, and especially in autobiographical writing. Denial of the division on the part of some theoreticians of autobiography, however, is itself a symptom of autobiographical writing—a repeated but untranslated, unconscious message. This message is directed at the culture from the position of the Other, by those who occupy positions of internal exclusion within the culture—that is, by women, blacks, Jews, homosexuals, and others who exist on the margins of society. A frequent spokesperson for those who have been denied full rights within the society on the grounds of gender, Virginia Woolf also questioned the limits of genre, with particular regard to autobiography. In 1919, at age thirty-seven, she was particularly concerned with these issues, thinking to what use she might put her diary and at what point in her life she would begin writing her memoirs. She begins by suggesting that "this diary does not count as writing, since I have just re-read my year's diary and am much struck by the rapid haphazard gallop at which it swings along, sometimes indeed jerking almost intolerably over the cobbles" (*Diary*, 20 January 1919). But the next sentence justifies this fast-paced method as preserving that which "if I stopped and took thought . . . would never be written at all," that which "sweeps up accidentally several stray matters which I would exclude if I hesitated, but which are the diamonds of the dustheap." Thinking of her future self at age fifty, Woolf conjures up on the diary page an image of herself, wearing reading glasses, poring over the pages of the past in preparation for the writing of her memoirs. Many years later, when Woolf was fifty-eight, she placed her memoir writing even further in the future, commenting in her diary: "I may as well make a note I say to myself: thinking sometimes who's going to read all this scribble? I think one day I may brew a tiny ingot out of it—in my memoirs" (19 February 1940). The "brewing" method would seem to be reductive—to eliminate the dross and save the gold.

Woolf did not live to write her memoirs, and the bulk of the autobiographical Virginia Woolf exists in her diary and letters, forms whose generic boundaries she extended and reconstructed. The diary, for instance, was constantly reexamined as a cultural artifact, as a living presence, as a necessary exercise for her fatigued mind, as a secret place (she found it impossible to write in it, for instance, if anyone else were in the room). She used the diary to pose theoretical and practical questions of writing, a place where the very definitions of writing might be reexamined:

There looms ahead of me the shadow of some kind of form which a diary might attain to. I might in the course of time learn what it is that one can make of this *loose, drifting material of life*; finding another use for it than the use I put it to, so much more consciously and scrupulously, in fiction. What sort of diary should I like mine to be? Something loose knit and yet not slovenly, *so elastic that it will embrace anything, solemn, slight or beautiful that comes into my mind*. I should like *it to resemble some deep old desk, or capacious hold-all*, in which one flings a mass of odds and ends without looking them through. I should like to come back, after a year or two, and *find that the collection had sorted itself and*

refined itself and coalesced, as such deposits so mysteriously do, into a mould, transparent enough to reflect the light of our life, and yet steady, tranquil compounds with the aloofness of a work of art. The main requisite, I think on re-reading my old volumes, *is not to play the part of censor*, but to write as the mood comes or of anything whatever; since I was curious to find how I went for things put in haphazard, and found the significance to lie *where I never saw it at the time*. (20 April 1919; emphasis added)

Setting aside momentarily the question of what Woolf might have done with the materials she later rediscovered in the "hold-all" of the diary, we can readily see that her efforts at defining the diary's form in the broadest terms possible ("so elastic that it will embrace anything, solemn, slight or beautiful that comes into my mind") and assigning the sorting, refining, and coalescing of such deposits into "a mould, transparent enough to reflect the light of our life," radically redefines the whole autobiographical project. Woolf does not conceive of such an undertaking in terms that Augustine, Rousseau, Montaigne, Proust, or Sir Leslie Stephen would recognize. She removes herself—that is, her self conceived as a censor—from this enterprise, discredits the notion of "self-consciousness" (indeed, she argues for the importance of the thoughtless, the loose, the unrestrained, the *un*conscious), and refrains from all efforts to shape, sort, or subordinate this material to her will. She rather systematically cuts out from under herself the props that hold up her authority as an *author*, turning authority back to the matter that constitutes her "subject"—and that subject is not necessarily the "self" of traditional autobiography. Woolf gives power to conscious artifice through fiction, a creation that also bears a relation to the "loose, drifting material of life." But for the purposes of memoir writing, she wishes to conceive of a different form and purpose—a conception that is infinitely deferred, as her own death puts an end to the project. That such a project would have followed the unconscious, would have followed the seam of writing itself, is undeniable, as . . . sections from *Moments of Being* . . . demonstrate.

> It took me a year's groping to discover what I call my tunnelling process, by which I tell the past by installments as I have need of it. This is my prime discovery so far; and the fact that I've been so long finding it proves, I think, how false Percy Lubbock's doctrine is—that you can do this sort of thing consciously. (*Diary*, 15 October 1923)

Later she comments, "as far as I know, as a writer I am only now writing out my mind" (20 March 1926), in a turn of phrase that suggests multiple relations between "mind" and "writing." In 1933, she notes "how tremendously important unconsciousness is when one writes" (29 October 1933). Such commentaries on the workings of the mind ally themselves with others that address questions of narrative method and artistic systems. On 25 September 1929, she writes in the diary: "Yesterday morning I made another start on *The Moths* [later retitled *The Waves*] . . . and several problems cry out at once to be solved. Who thinks it? And am I outside the thinker? One wants some device which is not a trick." And on 2 October 1932, in an entirely different context, she writes in irritation at reading D. H. Lawrence's published letters of what she calls his "preaching" and "systematizing": "His ruler coming down and measuring them. Why all this criticism of other people? Why not some system that includes the good? What a discovery that would be—a system that did not shut out." The relation of the conscious to the unconscious, of the mind to writing, of the in-

side to the outside of political and narrative systems, indicate not only a problematizing of social and literary conventions—a questioning of the Symbolic law—but also the need to reconceptualize form itself.

In other words, where does one place the "I" of the autobiographical account? Where does the Subject locate itself? In definitions of autobiography that stress self-disclosure and narrative account, that posit a self called to witness (as an authority) to "his" own being, that propose a double referent for the first-person narrative (the present "I" and the past "I"), or that conceive of autobiography as "recapitulation and recall" (Olney, 252), the Subject is made an Object of investigation (the first-person actually masks the third-person) and is further divided between the present moment of the narration and the past on which the narration is focused. These gaps in the temporal and spatial dimensions of the text itself are often successfully hidden from reader and writer, so that the fabric of the narrative appears seamless, spun of whole cloth. The effect is magical—the self appears organic, the present the sum total of the past, the past an accurate predictor of the future. This conception of the autobiographical rests on a firm belief in the *conscious* control of artist over subject matter; this view of the life history is grounded in authority. It is perhaps not surprising that those who cling to such a definition are those whose assignment under the Symbolic law is to *represent* authority, to represent the phallic power that drives inexorably toward unity, identity, sameness. And it is not surprising that those who question such authority are those who are expected to submit to it, those who line up on the other side of the sexual divide—that is, women.[5] The self that would reside at the center of the text is decentered—and often is absent altogether—in women's autobiographical texts. The very requirements of the genre are put into question by the limits of gender—

which is to say, because these two terms are etymologically linked, genre itself raises questions about gender.[6]

Fissures of Female Discontinuity

Alas, my brothers,
Helen did not walk
upon the ramparts,
she whom you cursed
was but the phantom and the shadow thrown
of a reflection

—H.D., *Helen in Egypt*

How do the fissures of female discontinuity display themselves, and what are their identifying features? On what authority can we ascribe certain forms of discontinuity to the female rather than to the male, assigning them as functions of gender rather than of social class, race, or sexual preference? One might remark that such issues are not raised—either directly or indirectly—by those texts that form the tradition of autobiographical writings in Western culture. The confessions of an Augustine or a Rousseau, the *Autobiography of Thomas Jefferson,* or the *Education of Henry Adams* do not admit internal cracks and disjunctures, rifts and ruptures. The whole thrust of such works is to seal up and cover over gaps in memory, dislocations in time and space, insecurities, hesitations, and blind spots. The consciousness behind the narrative "I" develops over time, encompassing more and more of the external landscape and becoming increasingly aware of the implications of action and events, but this consciousness—and the "I" it supports—remains stable. The dissection of self-analysis premises the cohesion of a restructured self. Any hint of the disparate, the disassociated, is overlooked or enfolded into a narrative of synthesis. This "model" of autobiography, a product of the metaphysic that has structured Western thinking since Plato, repeated itself with

unsurprising frequency until the early twentieth century—until the advent of what we now term Modernism put into question the organic, unifying principles of artistic creation that had reasserted themselves with such force in the nineteenth century.

The influence of Freud's discovery of the unconscious cannot be discounted in the unsettling of the "I" that had heretofore stood at the center of narrative discourse. (In accounting for this "unsettling" of self-unity, one must also consider the political and social effects of World War I, the advent of industrial mechanization, the loss of belief in God, the fall of colonial empires, and the changing status of women and minorities, all of which altered the cultural landscape against which literature was produced in the early years of the twentieth century. We live today in a world that has been constructed out of these changes: nearly all the changes that discomposed the complacent world of 1910 have been culturally assimilated, except perhaps the full force of Freud's discoveries. Predictably, its effects are most tenaciously resisted precisely where they are most evident: in language—in speech and writing.) The instability of this subject is nowhere more apparent than in women's writing of this period, in texts by Djuna Barnes, Isak Dinesen, H.D., Mina Loy, Anaïs Nin, Jean Rhys, Gertrude Stein, and Virginia Woolf, writing that puts into question the most essential component of the autobiographical—the relation between "self" and "consciousness." The simultaneous exploration of the autobiographical and probing of self-consciousness in works by each of these writers suggests not that they knew their Freud better than T S. Eliot, James Joyce, Ezra Pound or W B. Yeats, but that as women they felt the effects of the psychic reality Freud described more fully than did men. Gender became a determining issue at the point at which culture (broadly defined in both its psychic and social terms) met aesthetic principles.

As I have argued elsewhere, female Modernism challenged the white, male, heterosexual ethic underlying the Modernist aesthetic of "impersonality" (e.g., the transformation of the textual "I" from the personal to the cultural).[7] It is this white, male, heterosexual ethic that poststructuralist critics have exposed behind the facade of a supposedly apolitical artistic practice.[8] Post-structuralism has taught us to read the politics of every element in narrative strategy: representation; tone; perspective; figures of speech; even the shift between first-, second-, and third-person pronouns. In identifying the "fissures of female discontinuity" in a text, for example, we also point toward a relation between the psychic and the political, the personal and the social in the linguistic fabric.[9]

Notes

1.   Olney's "Some Versions of Memory" examines the *bios* at the center of this word without attention to the terms that enclose it—auto/graphy. In particular, this essay fails to mention that without *graphé* autobiography would not exist—that is, it is known only through the writing.

2.   Gusdorf's essay, "Conditions and Limits of Autobiography," opens with the declaration: "Autobiography is a solidly established literary genre" (28). James Olney's later essay in the same volume suggests "the impossibility of making any prescriptive definition for autobiography or placing any generic limitations on it at all" (237). Indeed, whether autobiography can be circumscribed within generic definitions is an important issue in autobiography studies. To date, however, there has been no rigorous investigation of the question of genre in relation to autobiography.

It is important to note that for Gusdorf autobiography is a genre that belongs to men, whose public lives it traces. Women are denied entrance to this writing for reasons examined in Susan Friedman's essay in this volume.

3.   The "subject presumed to know" is a Lacanian construction belonging not, as one might expect, to the conscious realm of thinking (as "the one consciously in control") but to the unconscious. This subject is "supposed" precisely because the speaking (or writing) subject senses a lack in itself, and supposes, in Ellie Ragland-Sullivan's terms, that "'something' somewhere knows more than he or she. That 'something' furnishes the speaker with the authority for a given opinion" (172). The sense of an internal division, the claim of an authority from "elsewhere" (in the Other residing in the unconscious), problematizes the assigning of authority in the speaking/writing situation. Both meanings of "suppose" are at work here: to believe, especially on uncertain or tentative grounds; to expect or require, to presume.

4.   This division cannot be "healed"; identity itself rests in this division, the effects of the working of the unconscious. Ragland-Sullivan comments: "Humans have an unconscious because they speak; animals have no unconscious because they do not speak. Since Lacan views repression and verbal symbolization as concurrent processes, which both mark the end of the mirror stage and create a secondary unconscious, we can look for answers to the self/ontology riddle in the transformational processes that mark repression" (173). For a particularly cogent reading of the effects of this division in women's writing, see Buck.

5.   Not only women are included in this group, but all humans who—for whatever reasons—are not seen to represent authority. Psychosexual identity often does not coincide with biological sexuality, and thus male homosexuals fall into this grouping (and female homosexuals resist its effects), as do all others considered powerless and marginal—blacks, Jews, the economically deprived, and so on.

6.   For an exhaustive analysis of the relation of genre and gender, see Jacques Derrida, "La Loi du Genre/The Law of Genre" which traces the etymological transferences of the two terms, and my essay "From Letters to Literature," which traces the effects of this law on one literary genre.

7.   See Benstock, "Beyond the Reaches of Feminist Criticism" and *Women of the Left Bank*; DeKoven, *A Different Language*; DuPlessis, *Writing beyond the Ending*; Friedman, "Modernism of the Scattered Remnant" and *Psyche Reborn*; Friedman and DuPlessis, "'I Had Two Loves Separate'"; Gubar, "Blessings in Disguise" and "Sapphistries"; Kolodny, "Some

Notes on Defining a 'Feminist Literary Criticism'";
Marcus, "Laughing at Leviticus" and "Liberty, Sorority, Misogyny"; and Stimpson, "Gertrice/Altrude."

8. Special reference needs to be made to the work
of Roland Barthes, Hélène Cixous, Jacques Derrida,
Jacques Lacan, Michel Foucault, and Julia Kristeva.
Interestingly, each of these people is excluded in one
way or another from the dominant national discourse
(French, white, male heterosexual); each sees himself
or herself as (or is seen as being) an "outsider." This
outsidership—which takes various forms and exerts
varying effects over the "subjects" that these writers
choose to discuss and the ways in which they discuss
them—has been overlooked entirely by those critics
who claim that collectively these people constitute a
hegemonic power.

9. Lacan's reading of Freud teaches us that the social constructs the personal: "In 'The Agency of the
Letter' (1957) Lacan says that there is no original or
instinctual unconscious. Everything in the unconscious gets there from the outside world via symbolization and its effects" (Ragland-Sullivan, 99). This
discovery by Freud and its patient explication by Lacan have been systematically disregarded by most
American interpreters of this work, especially by
American feminists who ground their objections to
Lacan's reading on the presumption that it separates
the unconscious and the social or that it gives the unconscious the power (through the phallic signifier) to
construct the external environment.

Works Cited

Benstock, Shari. "Beyond the Reaches of Feminist
Criticism: A Letter from Paris." *Tulsa Studies
in Women's Literature* 3 (1984): 5–27. Rpt. in
Issues in Literary Scholarship, ed. Shari Benstock. Bloomington: Indiana University Press,
1987. 7–29.

Benstock, Shari. "From Letters to Literature: *La Carte
Postale* in the Epistolary Genre." *Genre* 18 (Fall
1985): 257–95.

Benstock, Shari. *Women of the Left Bank: Paris, 1900–
1940.* Austin: University of Texas Press, 1986.

Broe, Mary Lynn, ed. *Silence and Power: A Reevaluation of Djuna Barnes.* Carbondale: Southern Illinois University Press, 1991.

Brown, Cheryl L., and Karen Olson, eds. *Feminist
Criticism: Essays on Theory, Poetry and Prose.*
Metuchen: Scarecrow, 1978.

Buck, Claire. "Freud and H.D.—Bisexuality and a
Feminine Discourse." *m/f* 8 (1983): 53–66.

DeKoven, Marianne. *A Different Language: Gertrude
Stein's Experimental Writing.* Madison: University of Wisconsin Press, 1983.

Derrida, Jacques. "La Loi du Genre/The Law of
Genre." Trans. Avital Ronell. *Glyph* 7 (1980):
202–32.

Doolittle, Hilda [H.D.]. *Helen in Egypt.* New York:
New Directions, 1961.

DuPlessis, Rachel Blau. *Writing beyond the Ending:
Narrative Strategies of Twentieth-Century Wom-
en Writers.* Bloomington: Indiana University
Press, 1984.

Friedman, Susan Stanford. "Modernism of the 'Scat-
tered Remnant': Race and Politics in H.D.'s
Development." In *Feminist Issues in Literary
Scholarship,* ed. Shari Benstock. Bloomington:
Indiana University Press, 1986. 208–31 .

Friedman, Susan Stanford. *Psyche Reborn: The Emergence of H.D.* Bloomington: Indiana University
Press, 1981.

Friedman, Susan Stanford, and Rachel Blau DuPlessis.
"'I Had Two Loves Separate': The Sexualities of
H.D.'s *Her.*" *Montemora* 8 (1981): 7–30.

Gubar, Susan. "Blessings in Disguise: Cross-Dressing
as Re-Dressing for Female Modernists." *Massachusetts Review* 22 (1981): 477–508.

Gubar, Susan. "Sapphistries." *Signs* 10 (1984): 43–62.

Gusdorf, Georges. "Conditions and Limits of Autobiography." In Olney, *Autobiography,* 28–48.

Heilbrun, Carolyn G., and Margaret R. Higgonet, eds.
The Representation of Women in Fiction. Baltimore: Johns Hopkins University Press, 1983.

Kolodny, Annette. "Some Notes on Defining a 'Feminist Literary Criticism.'" In Brown and Olson,
37–58.

Marcus, Jane. "Laughing at Leviticus: *Nightwood* as
Woman's Circus Epic." In *Silence and Power: A
Reevaluation of Djuna Barnes,* ed. Mary Lynn
Broe. Carbondale: Southern Illinois University
Press, 1991. 221–51.

Marcus, Jane. "Liberty, Sorority, Misogyny." In Heilbrun and Higgonet, 60–97.

Olney, James, ed. *Autobiography: Essays Theoretical*

and Critical. Princeton: Princeton University Press, 1980.

Olney, James. "Some Versions of Memory/Some Versions of Bios: The Ontology of Autobiography." In Olney, *Autobiography,* 236–67.

Perry, Ruth, and Martine Watson Brownley. *Mothering the Mind.* New York: Holmes and Meier, 1984.

Ragland-Sullivan, Ellie. *Jacques Lacan and the Philosophy of Psychoanalysis.* Urbana: University of Illinois Press, 1986.

Stimpson, Catharine R. "Gertrice/Altrude: Stein, Toklas, and the Paradox of the Happy Marriage." In Perry and Brownley, 123–29.

Woolf, Virginia. *The Diary of Virginia Woolf.* Ed. Anne Olivier Bell. 5 vols. New York: Harcourt Brace Jovanovich, 1977–84.

Woolf, Virginia. *Moments of Being.* Ed. Jeanne Schulkind. New York: Harcourt Brace Jovanovich, 1976.

9 Mothers, Displacement, and Language

Bella Brodzki

To appropriate by means of the word has been a divine privilege rarely accorded women. Although every speaking and writing subject is in a sense a stranger in a strange land, the feeling of power derived from even provisional occupation of a certain linguistic or textual space (often confused with virtual possession) has been a characteristically masculinist delusion.[1] If in linguistic terms "I" is a shifter reflecting the figure of enunciation only in the instance of enunciation and carrying no transcendent status,[2] then staking out and negotiating the perilous terrain of autobiography not only challenges the notion "I am s/he who says I" but—more important still—constitutes a veritable transgression of discursive as well as literary boundaries. Of course, transgression is in the eye of the transgressor as well as the beholder. To be susceptible to the power of transgression (while using it) means to be both within the space where the Law prevails and beyond the point at which it makes a difference.

Whether male or female, the autobiographer is always a displaced person. To speak and write from the space marked self-referential is to inhabit, in ontological, epistemological, and discursive terms, no place. Nothing but the rhetorical nature of literary language (and our desire to have all autobiographical acts be perforce performative utterances) guarantees the self-authenticating simpler mode of referential-

ity that autobiography is assumed at once to depend upon and to provide. Of all literary genres, autobiography is the most precariously poised between narrative and discourse or history and rhetoric. Invoking Nietzsche, Paul de Man makes the perverse point: "Death is a displaced name for a linguistic predicament, and the restoration of mortality by autobiography . . . deprives and disfigures to the precise extent that it restores."[3] Self-representation is the effect of a constructed similarity or equivalence between identity and language, an attempt to cast in fixed terms the self-reflexive, discontinuous shifts in modality and perspective, temporal and spatial, that are inherent in human experience—in a word, being—and to ground them in a single subjectivity. And to make this attempt is to confront the limitations of language head on.[4]

While the interrelated phenomenological and rhetorical aspects of alienated or displaced subjectivity interest me here, my particular considerations are the political and cultural implications of displacement and their bearing on diverse literary strategies in women's autobiographies. In the case of the female autobiographer who is compelled to strive for modes of expression and self-representation in a patriarchal world not generous enough to make room for her, "double displacement" is both a way of reading and writing and a way of life.[5] As Maxine Hong Kingston starkly renders the gender-specific prison house of language, "There is a Chinese word for the female I—which is slave. Break the women with their own tongues!"[6] Thus, to be a woman and to speak is already to submit to the phallocentric order while gloriously contradicting it, to serve as the very sign of transgression itself. Here we are only a step away from the Kristevan notion of woman as "eternal dissident,"[7] which has irresistible revolutionary appeal, even though the equation is both too simple and too self-congratulatory: it is as if every time "woman" opens her mouth she (emblematically) speaks, as Josette Féral puts it, "this perpetual displacement which underlines her impossible choices . . . a displacement that stresses these multiples that constituted her and which by their co-existence assure this requestioning and this subversion of which she is the principal driving force."[8] There is an inherent danger in the kind of seductive thinking which allows a concept or a thematics of representation to be affixed to an identity already inscribed in / by the discourse of the dominant culture rather than to a linguistic (or historical) process, especially when what is explicitly at stake is the very concept of unrepresentability.

Modernists (in general) and postmodernists (in particular) have employed the metaphor of displacement to refer to the human condition (in general) and to diacritical and avant-garde practice (in particular); feminist theorists must take diacritical practice one step farther and continually displace "woman" as the metaphor for displacement or divest the movement of the energy that generates it and the context that specifically shapes it. Certainly it is the point at which rhetorical strategies and political practice converge wherein lies the greatest potential for transformations of the dominant structure, but it is also at that same point of convergence where self-deception and co-optation by that structure are most likely to be involved. Such a signifying act would displace signification itself: "It's no accident: women take after birds and robbers just as robbers take after women and birds. They go by, fly the coop, take pleasure in jumbling the order of space, in disorienting it, in changing around the furniture, dislocating things and values, breaking them all up, emptying structures, and turning propriety upside down."[9]

The autobiographies on which this essay will focus—Nathalie Sarraute's *Childhood* and Christa Wolf's *Patterns of Childhood*—struggle with the complicitous (and not always revolutionary) relationship between displacement and language. The struggle, represented by each narrator's/protagonist's linguistic disability or instability and cultural disorientation, pivots on one figure or object: her mother. Emblematic of the way language itself obscures and reveals, withholds and endows, prohibits and sanctions, the mother in each text hovers from within and without. Still powerful and now inaccessible (literally or figuratively), she is the pre-text for the daughter's autobiographical project. Indeed, these autobiographical narratives are generated out of a compelling need to enter into discourse with the absent or distant mother. As the child's first significant Other, the mother *engenders* subjectivity through language; she is the primary source of speech and love. And part of the maternal legacy is the conflation of the two. Thereafter, implicated in and overlaid with other modes of discourse, the maternal legacy of language becomes charged with ambiguity and fraught with ambivalence. In response (however deferred), the daughter's text, variously, seeks to reject, reconstruct, and reclaim—to locate and recontextualize—the mother's message.[10]

Classically, the autobiographical project symbolizes the search for origins, for women a search for maternal origins and that elusive part of the self that is coextensive with the birth of language. At this point in my discussion the reader might suspect that this narrative-strategy-become-intro/retrospective-journey has delivered her back to the familiar (if forgotten) intra-uterine space called the womb, to that interior place where all conversations are fulfilling and speech is always adequate to the task it is called upon to perform. In this ontogenetic version of the creation story, speech is not necessary at all, because everything that passes between the symbiotic couple is osmotically communicated and understood: the matrix is there where there is no representation because there is no lack.

Mother lack, and all that it implies, comes later. In spite of her "best" critical defenses, the reader will recognize, mirrored in a projection of the autobiographer's "deepest" intentions, her own desire to return to the preexilic state of union with the mother. To be exiled from the maternal continent is to be forever subjected to the rules of a foreign economy for which one also serves as the medium of exchange. Women have devised many strategies for accommodating this loss which, in psychoanalytic terms, initiates the metonymic chain of substitute objects of desire, some more productive than others. As Luce Irigaray expresses it, "A woman, if she cannot in one way or another, recuperate her first object, that is the possibility of keeping her earliest libidinal attachments by displacing, is always exiled from herself."[11] Yet, however strong our need for maternal origins, it is important to keep in mind, in the words of Jean Laplanche, that "we never have at our disposal anything but what is patently observable. The constitutive is reconstructed from the constituted, or in any event from a constitutive process which is not primal, but derived; and that of course, is the definitive impasse in every quest for origins."[12] I am arguing against a thriving brand of feminist criticism (call it womb criticism) that seeks to replace or subvert phallic criticism—not only because a return to origins is impossible but because I think we should carefully consider the theoretical and political consequences of ideal-

izing the maternal as a category even as each of us negotiates her way within a specific and complex mother-daughter configuration. What is at issue here is not the ideological justification for transforming the paradigm of paternity that exploits and represses the maternal or revoking patriarchal privilege in all its manifestations but rather the idea that in order to bring back the mother from Irigaray's "dark continent of the dark continent"[13] we must mystify her. Clearly, matriarchal myths serve very different real and symbolic functions from those served by patriarchal ones, for both women and men, but some of the inherent dangers of privileging principles are the same, and it is the ideology of the same that feminists need to subvert and work to transfigure.[14]

The narratives of Sarraute and Wolf, while matrocentric, are resolutely antinostalgic. They call into question the assumption of an unmediated presence embodied in/by the mother and an unproblematical relation to the maternal origin, while disclosing a genealogy of matronymic displacement and attempting to situate themselves within a genealogy as part of their overall strategy. They remind us that the autobiographical space is not to be taken for granted or assumed as a given; that "natural" is a cultural construct; and that motherhood is both an experience and an institution.[15]

The pervasive conflict between an overwhelming compulsion to address and an equally strong internal resistance against self-disclosure underscores what I have described as the transgressive nature of the autobiographical enterprise in general and women's autobiographies in particular. Engaged in a relentless self-interrogation (with all the political connotations of that word left intact) of the oft-times distressing, and oft-times exhilarating, indeterminacy of female psychic and moral boundaries, a matrocentric autobiography necessarily involves guilt and fear of (self)betrayal.

By the very act of assuming the autobiographical stance the narrators perceive themselves to be "sinners" certainly, but they present themselves first and foremost as having been "sinned" against—by their mothers and, as Wolf's text suggests, by the patriarchal structures that have made her mother an unknowing collaborator with male authority.

Notes

1. The appropriation of meaning as a form of empowerment, says Peggy Kamuf, is an attempt to "contain an unlimited textual system, install a measure of protection between this boundlessness and one's own power to know, to be this power and to know that one is the power." Peggy Kamuf, "Writing Like a Woman," in *Women and Language in Literature and Society,* ed. Sally McConnell-Ginet, Ruth Borker, and Nelly Furman (New York: Praeger, 1980), 298.

2. Emile Benveniste, *Problems in General Linguistics,* trans. Mary Elizabeth Meek (Miami: University of Miami Press, 1971). For an analysis of the problematics of split subjectivity and split intentionality inherent in autobiography, see Louis Renza, "The Veto of the Imagination: A Theory of Autobiography," in *Autobiography: Essays Theoretical and Critical,* ed. James Olney (Princeton: Princeton University Press, 1980), 268–95. For a discussion of the provocative connections between linguistic and specular subjectivity, see Elizabeth W. Bruss, "Eye for I: Making and Unmaking Autobiography in Film," in Olney, 296–320; and Catherine Portuges, "Seeing Subjects: Women Directors and Cinematic Autobiography," in *Life/Lines: Theorizing Women's Autobiography,* ed. Bella Brodzki and Celeste Schenck (Ithaca: Cornell University Press, 1988), 338–50.

3. Paul de Man, "Autobiography as De-facement," *MLN* 94 (Dec. 1979): 930.

4. A lucid and succinct presentation of Nietzsche's philosophical critique of the subject can be found in the introduction to Paul Jay's *Being in the Text* (Ithaca: Cornell University Press, 1984), 28–29.

5. See Gayatri Chakravorty Spivak, "Displacement and the Discourse of Woman," in *Displacement: Derrida and After,* ed. Mark Krupnick (Bloomington: Indiana University Press, 1983), 169–95. See also Jonathan Culler, *On Deconstruction* (Ithaca: Cornell University Press, 1983), 43–64; and Nancy K. Miller, "Writing Fictions: Women's Autobiography in France," in Brodzki and Schenck, 45–61.

6. Maxine Hong Kingston, *The Woman Warrior: Memoirs of a Girlhood among Ghosts* (New York: Random House, 1977), 56.

7. Julia Kristeva, *Polylogue* (Paris: Seuil, 1977).

8. Josette Féral, "Towards a Theory of Displacement," *Sub-Stance* 32 (1981): 52–64. Féral's discussion strongly echoes the work of Kristeva, as well as Hélène Cixous and Luce Irigaray, on strategies of displacement in women's writing and feminist theory.

9. Hélène Cixous, "The Laugh of the Medusa," trans. Keith Cohen and Paula Cohen, *Signs* 1 (1976): 875–93.

10. For an extensive and perceptive review of the theoretical and fictional literature on the mother-daughter relationship, see Marianne Hirsch, "Mothers and Daughters," *Signs* 7 (Autumn 1981): 200–22. See also *The (M)other Tongue: Essays in Feminist Psychoanalytic Interpretation,* ed. Shirley Nelson Garner, Claire Kahane, and Madelon Sprengnether (Ithaca: Cornell University Press, 1985).

11. Luce Irigaray, "Women's Exile," *Ideology and Consciousness* 1 (1977): 76.

12. Jean Laplanche, *Life and Death in Psychoanalysis,* trans. Jeffrey Mehlman (Baltimore: Johns Hopkins University Press, 1976), 128–29.

13. Luce Irigaray, *Corps à corps avec la mère* (Paris: Editions de la Pleine Lune, 1981). I am quoting from an unpublished translation, "Body-to-Body against the Mother," trans. and ed. Carole Sheaffer-Jones et al. (Manuscript, 1985), 34.

14. Domna Stanton also argues this point—in far more elaborate theoretical terms—in the third section of her excellent essay "Difference on Trial: A Critique of the Maternal Metaphor in Cixous, Irigaray and Kristeva," in *The Poetics of Gender,* ed. Nancy K. Miller (New York: Columbia University Press, 1986), 157–82.

15. Adrienne Rich, *Of Woman Born* (New York: Norton, 1976).

10 The Politics of Subjectivity *and* The Ideology of Genre

Felicity A. Nussbaum

From "The Politics of Subjectivity"

The prevailing views of the eighteenth-century subject, those views that we have long associated with common sense, assume that knowledge is the product of experience and that a universal human nature exists outside the confines of history. In other words, each individual participates in a transhistorical human nature that is distinguished from the nature of other species by its ability to make ethical decisions and its reverence for the past; most important, human consciousness is assumed to be uniformly capable of making symbols. In spite of its universality, humanism, as it was understood in its various manifestations in eighteenth-century England, tolerates contradictions within its ideological frame, for it relies on a dualist concept of a split human nature that is paradoxical and even inconsistent. In fact, humanism assumes that moral duplicity is fundamental to the uniform nature of man. As Paul Fussell puts it: "To the humanist, inconsistency is necessarily Man's lot: to expect consistency from him is to deny by implication the paradoxical dualism that makes him man." [1]

This humanist model further encompasses the notion that the pursuit of happiness is man's goal, and his failure to achieve it can only be a failure of will. Man's will is free, so liberated that Samuel Johnson argues strongly against the rul-

ing passion or other inherently determinative forces on character. We are capable of controlling our own desires. He writes in the *Rambler,* "Nature will indeed always operate, human desires will be always ranging; but these motions, though very powerful, are not resistless; nature may be regulated, and desires governed; and to contend with the predominance of successive passions, to be endangered first by one affection, and then by another, is the condition upon which we are to pass our time, the time of our preparation for that state which shall put an end to experiment, to disappointment, and to change." [2] In Johnson's interpretation, what is changeless in our nature is the insatiability of human desire, for men resemble each other more than they differ. But that capacity for change is always circumscribed by the universal equalizer, death, and by the changelessness of eternity. In short, eighteenth-century humanism allows for inconsistencies within individual consciousness and between man and society. But the divisions are sufficiently knotted together so that any individual identity may finally become explicable and comprehensible, its essence pregiven and known and its plenitude displayed.

In analyzing these familiar eighteenth-century assumptions of the "self" through postmodern theory, we can rethink the autobiographical subject to interrupt our notions of a coherent, stable human self who originates and sustains the meaning of his experience. I want to first define more fully the autobiographical subject that is at issue here, and then turn to consider the conflictual discourses in circulation in particular eighteenth-century texts. Of particular relevance for redefining the concept of narrative consciousness in autobiographical texts is Émile Benveniste's distinction between the "I" who speaks and the "I" who is spoken. For Benveniste, language constructs subjectivity, and in turn subjectivity writes language: "*I* refers to the act of individual discourse in which it is pronounced, and by this it designates the speaker."[3] Benveniste proposes a split subject: "It is in and through language that an individual constitutes himself as a *subject,* the I who is uttering the present instance of the discourse"[4] between the agent of speech and the subject engendered in discourse, speaking and spoken. The "I" is a shifter, always changing its referent in time and space. The split subject, then, allows for the recognition that the "I" who is writing is distinct from the "I" who is written about. This disparity between parts of the "self" has also been taken up in contemporary psychoanalytic theory by Jacques Lacan, who, in his rereading of Freud, has decentered the self as we have known it since Descartes.[5]

Bridging the social and the psychic to theorize the way the fragmented subject is articulated within discourse, Lacan argues that the subject is constructed in language. No longer the origin of meaning, knowledge, and action, the individual consciousness in its infancy is both as diffuse and as unified as a broken egg—the "*hommelette*" of Lacan's formulation. For Lacan, universal symbolic categories describe and define the human subject through its developmental stages when it loses its androgynous unity and shifts from the diffuse infant to a subject who differentiates herself or himself from the

(mother) parent. The human subject, moving through the imaginary stage of identification and duality, sees an ideal image reflected in the mirror and simultaneously recognizes and misrecognizes that image. That mirror stage or movement into the symbolic realm is the beginning of the "self" dividing from itself. According to Lacan's system, the mirror stage also marks the moment of the production of the unconscious—of the unspoken and unsaid—as well as the foundation of desire. In a reinterpretation of Freud's *fort-da* story, the child's entrance into power relations comes at the moment of attempting to gain control over an object that has disappeared from view. And finally there is Lacan's stage of signification, in which the subject emerges into language. In order to enter into society, the child must begin to learn and manipulate language. The entrance into the symbolic is also the moment of recognition of the sexual split, of the split into a gendered subjectivity.

While Lacan's premise that there is no unmediated experience or access to reality without the use of a sign system is useful, his theory of language is inadequate to a politically viable critique of autobiographical writing because it isolates the subject from the real, confining it forever to the realm of signification. Lacan's theories conceptualize a contradictory subject who nevertheless seems freed from history and culture, one who is entrapped and incapable of change. Lacan pays little attention to the ways in which the symbols that describe the individual's emergence into language and identity are themselves produced within ideology. That is, the Lacanian subject, without being sufficiently embedded in the economic and the political, erases the variations of particular sociocultural formations. This lacuna can be circumvented in part by attending more specifically to the particular historical situations of the specific discourses that produce the subject, and to the production of "individual" desire at the conjunction of these discourses. For the politically situated subject, consciousness is less the origin and center of meaning than the reproduction of social and historical relations. Discourses, too, then, participate in these relations rather than remaining only expressive products of an individual self, and a single consciousness is no longer perceived to be the originating impulse. Thus, I find an emphasis on a discursive subject placed in its historical specificity more productive than a universal symbolic system that explains all subjects through time. In addition, Lacan's discourse of universal difference, of binary opposition that replicates a transhistorical heterosexual sex/gender system with its fixed hierarchies, poses serious difficulties for feminist criticism because it cannot address the material conditions of oppression based on gender.

In other words, we feel compelled as writers of ourselves and readers of autobiographies to construct a "self," but that interest in a closed, fixed, rational, and volitional self is fostered within a historically bound ideology. One consequence of the subject's entering into the culture's language and symbol system is a subjectivity placed in contradiction among dominant ideologies while those ideologies simultaneously work to produce and hold in place a unified subject. In order to preserve the existing subject positions, individual subjects are discouraged from attending to the ways in which the discourses are incongruent. We *believe* that the different positions make an autonomous whole, but the *feeling* that we are constant and consistent occurs because of ideological pressures for subjects to make order and coherence. Though we have confidence that the conflicting positions will add up to a whole, it is partially that we attend to the particular memories that match the available codes and make us believe in a fundamental unity. If human subjects give heed instead to inconsistencies, the reformu-

lated "self," an intersection of competing discourses, may seem less obviously continuous and explicable. As Mieke Bal has described subjectivity, "The discourses [that language] produces are (located in) common places, be it institutions, groups or, sometimes, and by accident, individuals. Those common places are the places where meanings meet."[6] All the moments may not fit, and the subject positions may strain against each other. In short, the emergence of language takes place within a system of semiotic power relations to displace the universality of human nature and to substitute a historically located subject. Autobiographical texts, then, may specifically resist a self made whole by humanist ideology, Cartesian philosophy, or Christian theology. Thus, a model of multiple discursive formations which calls a historically located individual subject into being proves more flexible for producing new ways of regarding gender, identity, and narrative.

In order to locate this subject of power, we may then ask whose interests the production of this autobiographical subject serves. Marx's notion of ideology as "false consciousness" would emphasize the way in which ideology is opposed to what is true, and it would seem to be the possession of a ruling class that is then imposed on the underclasses. That is, the ideology is in the hands of the dominant class, and power moves from that class downward.[7] There are, however, important alternative ways of viewing ideology. In his landmark essay "Ideology and Ideological State Apparatuses" (1971), Althusser attempts to account for the position of the subject of power in relation to material practices.[8] In that essay, Althusser defines interpellation as a process by which the subject comes to recognize itself as it is hailed in language. For Althusser, ideology functions to disguise the real conditions of the production of the subject: "Ideology represents the imaginary relationship of individuals to their real conditions of existence."[9] The subject produced in capitalist societies is one ready to claim that it is the free author of its own "expression," but because ideology obscures the conditions of its production, the subject cannot recognize the real conditions of its subjection. If we follow these assumptions, the autobiographical subject would believe in its agency to express and know and regulate itself without discerning the economic and political powers that limit its expression.

In any sociocultural situation, Althusser further argues, multiple contradictory forces are at play in the formation of material and discursive practices. Rather than the individual's being the source of her or his own language and ideas, ideological state apparatuses (ISAs) such as the church, the family, and the educational system produce that consciousness and assign systems of meaning which individuals absorb and adopt. The individual also unwittingly reproduces the conditions that allow the institutional state apparatuses to persist in their assignments of meaning. Ideological practices, he argues, are inscribed in the rituals and other material practices of everyday existence. The agency for these practices is widely scattered because the ISAs are not the product of any one class or monolithic power group. While literature, for example, may be the attempt of one class to control another, it may also subtly voice several contradictory codes at one time. Ideology then interpellates or constitutes individuals as subjects, defining and confining them in part, so that they achieve "free" recognition of their subject positions.

For Althusser, the social formation is not simply a reflection of the economic, but is produced by multiple conflictual levels that are themselves "relatively autonomous." While the economic level is determinative in the last instance for Althusser, as it was for Marx, other elements of the social formation (the family, state, religion) may dominate at a given moment. Though Althusser does not take up the issue of gender, his formulation enables the possibility of other revolutionary forces, such as feminism, gaining hegemony and transforming ideology.

It is the materiality of ideology which I want to stress here, as well as the way in which ideology is not monolithic or exclusively aligned with a particular class as the only hegemonic force. Everything need not have a direct economic cause or reflect the economic interests of a class, as in reductionist versions of Marxism. Antonio Gramsci, for example, usefully argues for a more interactive notion of class hegemony as an ensemble of social relations articulated together, "a process of class relations in which concrete and determinate struggles for cultural, economic and political power or jurisdiction represent the decisive terrain of specific historical analysis." [10] That is, though the economic has powerful effects, the ideological, economic, and political are mutually determining forces within which subjects are produced. In this way, the economic is productive of the real rather than merely reflective of a reality that is already given. These social relations work to reproduce existing relations, but oppositional force is situated in the subjugated which may find avenues to make itself known. Nonhegemonic ideologies may contest dominant ideologies and make the contradictions felt. For Gramsci, domination or power may come through ideological struggle rather than being exerted exclusively by one class upon another. Recent theories of ideology, then, may regard ideology as a "material matrix of affirmations and sanctions," as a system of assent to regulation, produced within ideological struggle. [11] We cannot say with conviction that a particular ideology is the uncomplicated possession or product of a particular class, such as the aristocracy or the working class; nor can we say that a particular ideology belongs exclusively to one gender. In the definition I am using here, ideology is itself a set of conflictual practices and class antagonisms that legitimate exploitation and its favored modes of production. In other words, though class may be more intensely constitutive for men, or gender more crucial for women, at particular historical moments, these are applied asymmetrically. In perpetual struggle and subject to co-optation by particular political programs, ideologies may elide contradictions in the interests of declaring a "self" that matches hegemonic ideologies about the individual in culture. The interstices between them may encourage imagined alternatives to the status quo as ideologies vie for dominance in the determinative order of intelligibility within textual practices. It is here, in the contradictions within the materials of culture, that we may locate the oppositional subject necessary for a materialist feminist politics. Such a project, then, requires a model of ideology which acknowledges contradiction within it in order to allow subjects to misrecognize themselves in prevailing ideologies and to intervene in producing new knowledge.

Particularly important for regarding this reformulated subject of ideology is the way in which "meaning" is produced at the conjunctions of conflicting discourses. Michel Pêcheux's theories of transformation of the subject place particular emphasis on theorizing the way that human subjects take up language within power relations. He argues that once we abandon the notion that words have transhistorical meanings, we begin to see how their meanings shift and slip in the crevices between discourses as they are deployed at particular times. Pêcheux writes that "words, expressions, propositions, etc. change their meaning according to the positions held by those who use them, which signifies that they find their meaning by reference to those positions." [12] In a given social formation, then, at a particular historical moment, the power of certain discourses to determine knowledge may be uneven, and an ensuing struggle occurs in human subjects, in texts, and in the management of those texts. Pêcheux has argued that individuals

may readily accept the ways they are interpellated in society, and are then defined as "good." Or they may counteridentify, refusing and acting against the available subject positions. A third alternative is that they may disidentify, in which case a "transformation-displacement of the subject form may take place." [13] Such disidentification may occur because such subjects are held in subject positions that are incompatible, and the ideologies are brought into contestation. "Disidentification" in text or in the world may make visible the previously invisible aspects of ideology that produce subjects, and new positions may be made available through which change may be effected.

It is not only relevant that language means in relation to itself and its linguistic system, but that language practices, and thus meanings may vary radically according to the subject position of its users and the extent to which they are enabled to contest dominant ideologies. In an example of disidentification, though the underclass and the female gender may use the same words as the dominant class and possessors of male privilege, they may be dismissed from the category "knowledge." In addition, especially pertinent to materialist feminism is Diane Macdonell's insight that different domains of language use exist and are taken up in relation to each other—they are interactive and even transgressive. [14] The human subject, she suggests, is one location of the *interdiscourse,* or the place where these conflictual discourses meet. Those who control meanings of words and concepts are empowered, though resistance to that power may occur at the intersections of conflicting discourses. For example, women's scandalous memoirs in eighteenth-century England are a collectivity of discourses aimed at mocking masculine privilege and at libeling the dominant classes; but at the same time, the female memoirists usurp the language of the oppressors to redefine dominant notions of their disreputable characters and of their inferior status.

I am suggesting, then, that these theoretical notions of the subject make it possible to read eighteenth-century autobiographical writing as one textual location where women and men, privately and publicly, experiment with interdiscourses and the corresponding subject positions to broach the uncertainties of identity. Autobiographical writing allows the previously illiterate and disenfranchised to adopt a language sufficiently acceptable to be published, and, at the same time, it enables them to envisage new possibilities in the interstices between discourses or to weave them together in new hybrid forms. In its public and private manifestations, autobiographical writing is a discursive and material practice in which gendered subjectivity is constructed, confirmed, and sabotaged. Such texts may work simultaneously for and against the ideologies of identity which prevail. They may sometimes seem to resolve certain manifest contradictions in order to affirm the humanist self, but just as often the texts may be read as subverting hegemonic formulations of identity, thus arrogating the power to change dominant knowledges regarding the human subject.

By stepping outside narrative conversion models and privately experimenting with other forms, the autobiographical writers at once form the private self necessary for an emergent market economy and produce a space for interrogating received assumptions about identity. The period from 1660 to 1800 might be read then not as the movement toward the formation of a human subject who is the source of his own meanings but, rather, as one crucial period for representing and revisioning the experience of human subjects in formation, subjects constructed in multiple conflicting domains, through which the ideologies of the "self" are made known.

In eighteenth-century England, "identity," "self," "soul," and "person" were dangerous and disputed formations, subject to appropriation by various interests. Heated rhetorical battles were waged throughout the century after Locke's *An Essay Concerning Human Understanding* (2nd. ed. 1694), in which the issues at stake were the meaning that each word would be granted and the implications of those words for the individual's legal, moral, and spiritual responsibility in relation to church and state. The controversy concerning identity set out these imperatives in order to fix identity and to recoil from the heretical notions of skepticism. Here I will argue that these competing discourses of identity are redundantly in evidence from the end of the seventeenth century until they wear themselves out with repetition by the 1790s. The intensity, diversity and duration of the controversy indicate that the issues they touched were vitally linked to the social formation. Autobiographical writing, though seeming to be a benign search for an essential "self," affords first a private occasion and later a public forum for attempting to resolve these problems.

From "The Ideology of Genre"

The diary and journal . . . are representations of reality rather than failed versions of something more coherent and unified. In spite of the fact that the diary and other serial narratives imitate traditional and emergent generic codes (romance, epic, drama, comedy, tragedy), by being written in "private" they affect to escape preexisting categories, to tell the "truth" of experience. By eschewing known narrative codes and opting for discontinuity and repetition, diaries and journals often attempt to seem spontaneous, and thus avoid assigning meaning or a hierarchy of values. The diarist pretends simply to transcribe the details of experience, but clearly some events are more important to the narrative "I" than others, and the minute particulars of an interiority increasingly become the diarist's focus. In addition, the diary usually claims that it is secret, in spite of its apparent invitation to the "self"—and perhaps others—to read it at a later date or after the diarist's death. Finally, the diary produces a sincere yet changeable narrator and reader, whether self or other, who delights in smoothing over the contradictory strands in the text. In sum, the eighteenth-century diary produces and reflects an individual who believes she or he is the source and center of meaning; it inscribes the dominant ideologies of empiricism and humanism while it also, through its discontinuous and fragmentary form, may disrupt the ideologies it seems to espouse.

These prenarrative and antinarrative forms serve certain ideological functions in culture and history. Autobiographical texts in the period issue from the culture as much as the individual author, and as marginalized versions of identity and experience, they contest the culture's more public and institutionalized constructs of reality. Remarkably unfixed texts that were only infrequently published during the eighteenth century, they invalidate our expectations of narrative. Far from being incidental to eighteenth-century identity, revisions and changes were crucial to its reproduction. But the emergence and proliferation of these various forms raise further questions about notions of reality in the eighteenth century, as well as questions about whose interests the production of a private much-revised subjectivity reinforces.

In short, a rethinking of the ideologies of genre in the eighteenth century must include the recognition that eighteenth-century English diaries and self-biographies existed in multiple versions, seldom reached the public eye during the life of the author, and often remained unpublished until later centuries. The mid-eighteenth century, then, cleared a public space for writers and readers of documents about the private "self." What had seemed private to the early eighteenth century had become a desirable commodity by the end of the century, but the prac-

tice of diary writing was believed to wane as its publication became a conventional, if sometimes disreputable, practice.

If private autobiographical writing constituted a place for experimentation and sabotage of prevailing class and gender categories, as well as political and religious doctrines, it does not however escape the familiar ways of making meaning in a given historical moment. That is, diaries can only be relatively autonomous from the culture they inhabit, for there is no truly private language or practice. The subject of serial autobiography is a subject positioned within struggles to claim individual difference, autonomy, freedom, and privacy. Writing oneself in autobiographical text, even in asserting the existence of a private self, is complicit in the political and economic production of that subject. Private autobiographical writing in the eighteenth century serves the purposes of various institutions in anchoring a self-regulating body of individuals who perceive themselves to be autonomous and free. But it also functions to articulate modes of discourse that may disrupt and endanger authorized representations of reality in their alternative discourses of self and subject. As such, it poses tentative textual solutions to unresolvable contradictions, largely within the private sphere. An eighteenth-century serial autobiography, read through the ideology of genre, is the thing itself rather than a failed conversion narrative or an incipient realist novel.

Notes

1. Paul Fussell, *The Rhetorical World of Augustan Humanism: Ethics and Imagery from Swift to Burke* (Oxford: Clarendon Press, 1965), 121.

2. Samuel Johnson, *Rambler* 151, 27 August 175 I, in *The Rambler*, ed. W. J. Bate and Albrecht B. Strauss, *The Yale Edition of the Works of Samuel Johnson* (New Haven: Yale University Press, 1969), 5:42.

3. Emile Benveniste, *Problems in General Linguis-*

tics, trans. Mary Elizabeth Meek (Coral Gables, FL.: University of Miami Press, 1971), 226. Benveniste claims, however, the status of "objective testimony" for the subject speaking about himself. For theories of the semiotic subject, see Rosalind Coward and John Ellis, *Language and Materialism: Developments in Semiology and the Theory of the Subject* (London: Routledge and Kegan Paul, 1977).

4. Benveniste, 224.

5. Jacques Lacan, *The Language of the Self: The Function of Language in Psychoanalysis,* trans. Anthony Wilden (Baltimore: Johns Hopkins University. Press, 1968). Julian Henriques, Wendy Hollway, Cathy Urwin, Couze Venn, and Valerie Walkerdine provide a provocative analysis of the self's historicity in *Changing the Subject: Psychology, Social Regulation, and Subjectivity* (New York: Methuen, 1984). See also Paul Smith, *Discerning the Subject,* Theory and History of Literature Series 55 (Minneapolis: University of Minnesota Press, 1988).

6. Mieke Bal, "The Rhetoric of Subjectivity," *Poetics Today* 5, no. 2 (1984): 343. See also Catherine Belsey's important study, *The Subject of Tragedy: Identity and Difference in Renaissance Drama* (London: Methuen, 1985): "Subjectivity is discursively produced and is constrained by the range of subject-positions defined by the discourses in which the concrete individual participates. Utterance—and action—outside the range of meanings in circulation in a society is psychotic. In this sense existing discourses determine not only what can be said and understood, but the nature of subjectivity itself, what it is possible to be" (5).

7. For a discussion of ideology, see Raymond Williams, *Marxism and Literature* (Oxford: Oxford University Press, 1977), esp. 55–71.

8. Louis Althusser, "Ideology and Ideological State Apparatuses (Notes toward an Investigation)," *Lenin and Philosophy and Other Essays* (New York: Monthly Review Press, 1971), 127–87.

9. Althusser, 162.

10. Antonio Gramsci, *Selections from the Prison Notebooks,* ed. and trans. Quintin Hoare and Geoffrey Nowell Smith (New York: International Publishers, 1971), 161. For discussions of the complexities of post-Althusserian Marxism, see especially *Rethinking Ideology. A Marxist Debate,* ed. Sakari Hanninen and Leena Paldan (New York and Bagnolet, France: International General, 1983); and Terry E. Boswell, Edgar V. Kiser, and Kathryn A. Baker, "Recent Developments in Marxist Theories of Ideology," *Insurgent Sociologist* 13 (Summer 1986): 5–22.

11. Boswell, Kiser, and Baker, 20. The formulation of affirmations and sanctions and their effectivity derives from Göran Therborn, *The Ideology of Power and the Power of Ideology* (London: New Left Books, 1980). Ernesto Laclau and Chantal Mouffe, *Hegemony and Socialist Strategy* (London: Verso, 1985), also address the question of how to articulate together a "relative autonomy of ideology and the determination in the last instance by the economy" within a historical materialism that regards ideology as productive of the real. See also Chantal Mouffe, "Hegemony and Ideology in Gramsci," in *Gramsci and Marxist Theory,* ed. Mouffe (London: Routledge and Kegan Paul, 1979).

12. Michel Pêcheux, *Language, Semantics, and Ideology: Stating the Obvious,* trans. Narbans Nagpal (London: Macmillan, 1982), 112.

13. Pêcheux, 159.

14. Diane Macdonell, *Theories of Discourse: An Introduction* (Oxford: Blackwell, 1986). V. N. Volosinov, in *Marxism and the Philosophy of Language,* trans. L. K. Matejka and R. Titunick (New York: Seminar, 1930), earlier emphasized the social construction of language in regarding discourses as historically and culturally produced. See also Pierre Machérey, *A Theory of Literary Production,* trans. Geoffrey Wall (London: Routledge and Kegan Paul, 1978).

11 First-Person Plural: Subjectivity and Community in Native American Women's Autobiography

Hertha D. Sweet Wong

Early theorists of women's autobiography often defined the difference between men's and women's self-narrations through the framework of relationality and individuality. In particular, female subjectivity was posited as relational, while male subjectivity (represented as universal) was said to be individual. Theorists of Native American autobiography (and culture) have also marked indigenous difference through the relational versus individual grid. American Indian subjectivity has been defined as relational, while European (or universal Western) subjectivity has been presented as individual. While feminists and Native Americanists often rely on this oppositional model, they generally do so without much awareness of each other. Although I continue to find relational identity a useful descriptor, I want to resist the reductive oppositionality of this framing of difference through a brief reading of two autobiographies by Native North American women informed by a discussion of the following set of questions. If we were to accept the above account of relationality, certain questions arise about its parameters. If female and Native subjectivities are both relational, does that mean a Native woman is doubly relational? And what would "doubly relational" look like? Might such formulations lead to reductive conflations such as: Since

women are relational because of nature and culture and Native men and women are relational because of cultural norms associated with communality, women are somehow indigenized and/or Native cultures are feminized. In short, in terms of relationality, is Woman to Man as Native to Western? And if so, is female erased for the two groups Man and Western? Are feminist and Native Americanist concepts of relationality really equivalent? Not all concepts of relationality are equal. When a Native woman writes or speaks in the first-person singular, who else is crowded into that "I"? Who are her relations? And is that speaking/writing subject a product of her Native culture(s) (as well as of the larger U.S. culture) or an invented figure of the female indigene commodified by the dominant culture? Theorists of Native relationality tend to discuss relational subjectivity as associated with cultural grounding and as linked to family, community, and expansive geocentric kinship networks, as distinguished from theorists of female relationality who often consider it as associated with biopsychological and gender socialization and as connected to family and community. Questions about relational subjectivity, then, naturally lead to considerations of community. If "community" is central to female and Native relational subjectivity, what or who is the community?

How is community represented in the self-narrations of Native women? This set of questions frames a large project, only some of which can be addressed here.

Subjectivity in Community

Many critics have written about the now familiar distinction, a highly generalized distinction, between Native American and European American notions of subjectivity. Despite diverse cultures, languages, and histories, indigenous people, it is said, have a notion of self as communal or relational, while European(s)/Americans, at least since the Romantic period, envision identity as individual and autonomous. Generally, Native people see themselves as connected to an entire network of kinship relations with family, clan, community, earth, plant and animal life, and cosmos, while Western non-Natives envision themselves as separate from such relations. In many indigenous contexts, it is understood that to speak or write about oneself, calling attention to one's own accomplishments (as is often the case in autobiography), reveals a poor upbringing (displaying an inappropriate and exaggerated individuality that may diminish communal values), while in many Western contexts to announce oneself directly is considered straightforward and honest.

But to say that in self-narrations Westerners write in first-person singular and indigenous people write (or speak) in the first-person plural oversimplifies. Mikhail Bakhtin's notion of the polyvocality of what only appears to be a singular voice challenges any monolithic construction of identity that does not acknowledge its own plurality. In fact, Bakhtin replaces the paradigm of individuality—with its insistence on a unified, stable, autonomous, essential, and representable self—with a notion of a multivocal self—constituted by "the forms of the ideological environment" and characterized as multiple, shifting, and relational (Medvedev and Bakhtin, 14). Bakhtin's revised definition of subjectivity is helpful for those who find Western individualism insufficient. Similarly, I am not interested in perpetuating yet another binary opposition—in this case, Native relationality/Western autonomy—but in reconfiguring this opposition as points on a spectrum or points on a circle, images that might better reveal multiple and diverse subject positions within both sets of culture groups and challenge monolithic (and reductive) representations of cultural identity.

My point is that numerous kinds of relational subjectivities are possible, that a subject is not either individual or relational, but may be more or less individual or more or less relational in diverse contexts, and that subjectivity is not determined entirely by either biological or social-cultural discourses. Although cultures do indeed have dominant and dominating orientations that shape subjectivity, individuals or groups within those cultures may not always conform to them. Within Western communities, farmers, for instance (or anyone who lives closely with the seasonal cycles and relies on a network of reciprocal obligations for survival), may have a *type* of relational identity just as some feminists claim that women often do, in part because of women's ties to biological rhythms such as childbearing or to socially inscripted patterns like domestic labor and child rearing. Similarly, in some indigenous cultures, there are appropriate occasions to exercise individuality—articulating personal achievements to attest to the right to speak at a council or practicing "traditional" arts with innovations (just as storytellers may tell well-known stories, but with their own unique styles).

In her critique of Western individualism at the center of autobiography, Susan Stanford Friedman reveals how "[i]ndividualistic paradigms of the self ignore the role of collective and relational identities in the individuation process of women and minorites" (72, in this volume). Models promoting individualism, she concludes, overlook the significance of "a culturally imposed group identity for women and minorities" and the "differences in socialization in the construction of male and female gender identities" 72, in this volume). The implication of Friedman's model (which she continues to revise)[1] is that a kind of universal female collectivity exists despite our diverse social, economic, racial, cultural positionalities. But like many women of color, Native American women, in general, are far less likely than European American women to define themselves in gender-based terms and are often suspicious of "mainstream" feminisms that reflect neither their sociopolitical concerns nor their historical positions within their own nations. With notable exceptions, instead of identifying as a (universal) woman, a Native woman is far more likely to define herself by tribal, national, or cultural affiliation. For some, the material conditions of being Indian in the United States (or Canada) outweigh gender considerations; for others, it is neither desirable nor feasible to focus on gender as if gender might be separated from a cultural web of significance. Gender, after all, is constructed differently within diverse sociocultural contexts. For a number of women, to (re)claim a Native identity may be to locate what Paula Gunn Allen (*Sacred*, 2–3) describes (albeit generally) as "gynocratic" (woman-centered) traditions—both those suppressed or eradicated by years of internal colonization and those ongoing. Reconnecting to tribal myths and practices (as many Native writers have done) for some women is specifically reconstituting diminished female power. But while it may be true that many Native women are multiply marginalized, it is also true that some women continue to hold secure positions of power within their own cultures (both indigenous and U.S./Canadian). Polarized concepts of gender identity (that insist that one

is either relational or individual) are not adequate because subjects exist in kaleidoscopic relation to multiple, simultaneously overlapping positionalities. Native women, by virtue of culture and gender, are multiply relational subjects. But forced to choose, Native women often feel obligated to insist on Native over female identity. Of course, this self-defining takes place in the context of a larger critical assault on marginalized subjectivities. For as Linda Hutcheon points out, "The current post-structuralist/post-modern challenges to the coherent, autonomous subject have to be put on hold in feminist and post-colonial discourses, for both must work first to assert and affirm a denied or alienated subjectivity: those radical postmodern challenges are in many ways the luxury of the dominant order which can afford to challenge that which it securely possesses" (130–31). David L. Moore suggests that instead of the "tragic modern imperial self" or "the tragicomic postmodern pawn," indigenous subjectivities offer "alternative choices" (371) of what I will call nonoppositional relationality.

What underlies some of the discussion about indigenous models of self, though, at least as this discussion has been addressed to Native American autobiography, is a profound and persistent tendency to impose a historical fixity on Native people. And this, in part, is tied to notions of authenticity. According to a discredited but still persistent belief (derived from a Romantic model of contact as contamination), "authentic" Natives are those who are furthest from the "corrupting" influences of Western civilization, those people (usually "elders") closest to the cultural condition (or at least that state as imagined by cultural critics) during (or preferably prior to) European contact. "Authentic" Indians, according to this thinking, don't wear Reeboks, drive minivans, eat sushi, or write best-selling novels. Not surprisingly, contemporaneity and class dominate this list. "Authentic" Indians, viewed from this perspective, cannot live in the late twentieth century, nor can they be "successful," economically or otherwise. Trinh Minh-ha makes this point for many women of color when she describes how some members of the dominant society both invent and legislate authenticity: "They, like their anthropologists whose specialty is to detect all the layers of my falseness and truthfulness, are in a position to decide what/who is 'authentic' and what/who is not. No uprooted person is invited to participate in this 'special' wo/man's issue unless s/he 'makes up' her/his mind and paints her/himself thick with authenticity" (88). "Authenticity," then, becomes a performance, a mask, yet another commodity. And though the discussion of authenticity is, as Jana Sequoya points out, "a 'red herring' discourse, . . . it has real consequences for contemporary American Indian people" (451). Many Native women writers directly challenge the dominant (mis)representations of American Indians and the Native and non-Native border patrols of Indian authenticity. Mixed-blood Hopi poet Wendy Rose phrases it bluntly when she announces: "There is nothing authentic or nice about my past" (261). I can think of no other group whose cultural "authenticity" is judged by whether they are living in the ways of their ancestors (ways that sometimes, at least as they circulate within academic circles and the popular media, are too often imagined from deeply ingrained stereotypes). Many Native people today do indeed carry on "traditional" cultural practices, but they are informed citizens of the late twentieth century, not relics of a distant (and often idealized) past.

The tendency to define "authentic" indigenes as those linked to ancient tradition is due, in part, to the historical link between Native Americans and ethnographers. Ethnographers and others who have studied Native cultures have participated, however unintentionally, in transforming living Native people into commodities, what Su-

san Danly calls "museum artifacts" and Alexander Nemerov refers to as "marketable products." Historically, such practices contributed to a national rationale for dispossessing indigenous people of land; to a national tragic narrative that allowed non-Natives to pity and condemn the supposedly "vanishing" Indian (as Roy Harvey Pearce, Richard Slotkin, and more recently Arnold Krupat have discussed); and to the construction of "replacement relics," as Nemerov has pointed out, contaminated though they may be by participation in the commodifying process, for a spiritually anemic, increasingly technologically dominant society. What links these efforts is the desire to recuperate a lost (or soon to be disappearing) past (never mind that such a past may have existed only as an imagined construction of a dominant society). Contemporary Native women must be multiply resistant. As indigenous people, they still must resist being perpetually frozen in the past as anthropological objects of study and, at the same time, resist performances of "authentic" Indianness (that is, taking on, and thus perpetuating, stereotypical representations of nativity); as women they must negotiate whatever gender identities are available within their particular cultures and resist being rendered invisible within the larger cultures of the United States or Canada.

For many Native American women reclaiming their own histories and cultures is not a Romantic retreat to a lost past, but a political strategy for cultural (and national) survival and personal identity. A Native autobiographer, whether a speaking or writing subject, often implies, if not announces, the first-person plural—we—even when speaking in the first-person singular. "We" often invokes a (sometimes the) Native community. Unlike the idea of indigenous subjectivity, however, the notion of community, assumed in a first-person-plural construction of identity, has remained relatively uninterrogated. What is meant precisely when someone invokes generally "the Indian community" or even, more specifically, "the Navajo community" as if a monolithic, stable center of homogeneous beliefs and attitudes stood behind the speaker?

Community

Too often invoked as a monolithic center of identity, belief, and culture and used to legitimate the speaker/writer, community, like subjectivity, is linked to authenticity. Questions about authenticity involve more than arguments about what constitutes a "legal" or "genuine" (blood quantum or tribal enrollment, for instance) Indian; they include discussions of what counts as a legitimate home/land/community for Indian subjects. As with definitions of subjectivity, there is no consensus about the meaning of community transculturally. Iris Young criticizes what she describes as a widespread "ideal of community" propounded by many U.S. academics and activists because it perpetuates "a normative model of social organization" (320 n. 1). Although community is "an understandable dream," Young says, "expressing a desire for selves that are transparent to one another, relationships of mutual identification, social closeness and comfort," it is "problematic" (300). Using deconstructive tools, she critiques feminist formulations of this ideal community, in part because of their totalizing impulses—suppressing differences within the group and excluding others from membership. Young seeks to replace the ideal of community with a model of "the unoppressive city," defined as "openness to unassimilated otherness," and based on a "politics of difference" (319). Her project, as she readily admits, assumes a variety of idealized conditions—all people enjoying material plenty, a clean and well-maintained physical environment, and meaningful work or thoughtful care—that make it difficult to see it

as anything more than a utopian vision. Although her unrealizable and universalist notion of community is not a solution to the problematics of community, Young's careful analysis of the way the concept has been deployed by feminists is applicable, at least in part, to some formulators of Native identity who also sacrifice diverse indigenous subjectivities in the name of (pan)tribal nationalism.

The word *community,* from the Latin noun *communitas,* refers to "fellowship, a community of relations or feelings." By medieval times, according to the *Oxford English Dictionary,* it was used to refer to a "body of fellows or fellow towns-men." While in English the word was first associated with people joined by similar feelings and came to mean a gathering of people in the same vicinity, in many indigenous contexts community is more likely to refer to a host of kinship networks and geocentric relations, extending beyond human beings to include vegetable and animal life. For both non-Native and Native American, though, community has to do with having something in common: shared residence in a specific locality; shared interests; shared history; shared political structure.

Each individual participates in a variety of simultaneous and overlapping communities—social, political, linguistic, and religious communities, for example—yet the myth of a singular, unified, self-defining community (with obvious parallels to the fiction of a singular, unified, self-constructing subject) is still apparent. This is especially true for those "communities" that have been besieged by colonialism and its aftereffects. I want to emphasize here, however, that there are quite tangible and pragmatic reasons to posit a unified community, a strategic political positioning to counter colonial conditions, such as ongoing struggles to secure native national sovereignty, for instance.

But communities, like most social bonds, are largely imagined, claims Benedict Anderson, "because the members of even the smallest nation will never know most of their fellow members . . . yet in the minds of each lives the image of their communion" (6). While I am not convinced that communities are imagined solely because individual members can never know "their fellow members" firsthand, I find Anderson's focus, even with his perspective of Western historiography, on how communities imagine themselves into nationalisms worth consideration. Although I am interested in relating the idea of community as it has been invoked and used in Native American autobiography to the articulation of Native nationalisms—indigenous, sovereign nations within the United States—my focus here will be on how the idea of community has been used in various recurrent ways by Native American women autobiographers.

Sometimes, for instance, "community" refers to a specific geographical locale or people or history; at others, it is used to call up the image of an extensive and monolithic pan-Indian or international indigenous movement. The contemporary notions of community circulated in Native American autobiography are not merely continuations or retrievals of ongoing "traditional" thoughts and practices, but, in many cases, particularly when deployed by Native mixed-blood women writers, a conscious strategy to understand what over two hundred years of colonial rule has disassembled and, by so doing, to resist the official tragic narrative of Indian loss and disappearance.

Autobiography

For this discussion I will focus on how community has been assumed, invoked, or constructed in two autobiographical texts collected and written in the 1980s: *Life Lived like a Story: Life Stories of Three Yukon Elders* (1990) in which anthropologist Julie Cruikshank has translated and edited the life stories of Angela Sidney, Kitty Smith, and Annie Ned, all of Athapaskan and Tlingit ancestry; and *I Tell You Now: Autobiographical Essays by Native American Writers* (1987) edited by Brian Swann and Arnold Krupat. This pair reflects two ongoing modes of Native North American autobiography: collaborative life histories in which Native persons speak their personal/cultural narratives to (usually) non-Native amanuenses/editors who translate, transcribe, and edit the narratives; and autobiographical texts written by Native people. While many ethnographic autobiographies have been criticized for the unequal power relations that result in the literary colonization of the speaking subject, Cruikshank insists that the three Yukon women with whom she worked had clear and strong ideas, as well as active input, into how their stories were shaped and circulated.

In the narratives of the three Yukon elders, collected and edited by Cruikshank, community is assumed, not announced. In the autobiographical essays, solicited by Swann and Krupat, and written by various mixed-blood Native writers, on the other hand, community is often being sought. The Yukon elders share a long history in a vast but well-defined region, while most of the Native writers are part of an internal Indian diaspora, removed from historical and cultural homelands. The difference in how community is constituted may be generational as well. Sidney, Smith, and Ned were "born in the southern Yukon territory around the turn of the century" (Cruikshank, ix). Two of them were youngsters during the Klondike Gold Rush (1896–98), and all were alive during the construction of the Alaska Highway in 1942–43. In contrast, the eldest of the Native writers included in the Swann/Krupat collection is Mary TallMountain who was born in 1918, almost a generation later than the women of the Yukon. The Yukon elders are community educators whose authority comes from years of lived experience and whose primary audience is their own residential community, while the Native writers are generally academics—writers, professors, etc.—whose authority comes from their professional status and whose audience is unspecified. The differences in the way community is presented in these texts might also be attributed to regional, historical, and cultural considerations. Indigenous people in the far North have different patterns of contact with outsiders, and though they have been moved, they have not been displaced, as most of the writers in the Swann-Krupat anthology have been.

Angela Sidney, for instance, begins her self-narration by telling a brief history of her nation—the Deisheetan nation. More precisely, she shares her clan history, which is "narrated as a travelogue" (Cruikshank, 347). Next, she tells her Shagoon or family history in the "traditional" way—that is, as she describes it, "first my own history—that's the same as my mother's in Indian way—then my dad's, then my husband's" (37). She includes also the origin myth of her people. She does not even get to her birth until page 52 (and then it is buried in a long list of her brothers and sisters arranged by birth order). For Sidney self is related not to an imagined community, but to a very tangible one that consists of an extensive network of relationships temporally and spatially. And community, in this instance, includes genealogy and precise geography articulated through a variety of characteristic discursive strategies—mythic, historical, and familial narratives. The women are not merely located within a narratively mapped geography, they are rooted in it.

In addition, individuals from diverse geographies throughout the entire region are linked by travel and kinship (through trade, hunting, marriage, and clan affiliation). Significantly, Cruikshank discusses the importance of toponyms, of place names that map not only geography, but relationships (of trade, hunting, travel, and spirituality). Each of the early sections concludes

with Sidney, who has traveled to a distant community, acknowledging relationship with that community. "I know now the truth," Sidney explains to a man from Ross River whose community uses the same names as her own: "'You must be our people'" (41).

All three women narrators include myth, history, and teaching stories as central structural components of their life stories. This structure challenges canonical Western notions of autobiography in several ways: it replaces the model of an autonomous individual narrating a single (and singular) life with a relational subjectivity narrating an individual (but affiliated) life; and it extends the autobiographical project temporally by stretching the boundaries of one person's life (no longer just from birth to death) and insisting on the mythic and historical networks of identity formation. Community and its values, restraints, and obligations are woven into the narratives so that they do not need to be explained, except to clarify to a younger Native readership (their primary audience, as the women see it) as well as to non-Natives. At such moments, the women become "autoethnographers,"[2] translating their perspectives to the culturally uneducated within their communities and to cultural others outside. For these women, community is a place (actually many places), a people (actually many people), and a history (told over a long period by many voices), all linked by a network of narrative. A variety of rhetorical moves serve as markers of identity clearly situating the women in place and history (space and time). For Angela Sidney, Kitty Smith, and Annie Ned, relational identity rooted in community is not a Romantic concept, but a lived experience. For many indigenous women, though, community must be consciously constructed.

In the autobiographical essays in *I Tell You Now*, community is seen as place (earth, land, reservation, neighborhood), people (relatives, clans, neighbors), and history as well, but more consistently as a place, a people, a history *lost*. Many of the Native writers anthologized by Swann and Krupat focus on loss or destruction of land, broken lineages, and lack of access not only to the histories and stories of their people, but to their own personal histories. The predominant theme is how the writers define themselves as American Indians by selecting and arranging the fragments of myth, history, and identity they inherit. More than genetic inheritance or cultural practice, Native American identity, for many of the autobiographers, demands an act of will and creativity; an act of reinterpretation and reclamation to assert a lost or threatened but felt relationality. Memory and relationship to place are central to this process. Many contributors to the volume, especially the men, position themselves primarily as "subjects of loss" (93). "I tried to grasp something I could not name," explains Jim Barnes, "something I knew was gone forever" (89). Duane Niatum explains that the central theme of his art is "the quest for the meaning of survival of loss" (136). Loss, then, is shared by all, but especially by mixed-blood, displaced writers. By returning to a specific (geographical or historical) place via memory or travel (and with a healthy dose of Romantic redemptive imagination), they recollect or imagine the precise dimensions of their loss (of land, language, culture, identity) in writing.

While acknowledging loss in her essay "The Autobiography of a Confluence," Paula Gunn Allen does not focus upon it. She does not limit her notion of community to land or people or history, but, like the Yukon elders (only quite self-consciously), links her Native female subjectivity to a network of all. What links the land, people, and history in her essay are spatial networks (in particular, highways) and temporal networks (the stories, what some might refer to as gossip)[3] that link people over time and space.

In her autobiographical essay Allen literally maps her past, present, and future, all linked by three central themes: "the land, the family, the road" (Swann and Krupat, 145). Allen describes the Southwest (where she grew up on the Cubero Land Grant, in New Mexico) as "the confluence of cultures" (145). Allen's New Mexico is not simply the tricultural state (Nativos, Chicanos, and Anglos) as it has been called in travel brochures, but a mixture of "Pueblo, Navajo and Apache, Chicano, Spanish, Spanish-American, Mexican-American . . . Anglo" including "Lebanese and . . . Lebanese-American, German-Jewish, Italian-Catholic, German-Lutheran, Scotch-Irish-American Presbyterian, halfbreed (that is, people raised white-and-Indian), and Irish-Catholic" (145). Situating herself at the house she grew up in, Allen's persona scans the horizon, noting the mountain to the north, the hills to the east, and the paved road to the south. She follows the road, which hugs the contours of the land, in this case along the arroyo, until it joins the "San Jose River, eventually meeting the Rio Puerco, which, in its turn, joins the Rio Grande" on its way south to Mexico and the Gulf (146). Returning to the road, she follows it from Albuquerque east through Tijeras Canyon, stopping to point to Texas, Oklahoma, the Plains, and the East beyond.

In the next section, she sets out on the road again, guiding the reader along Old Highway 66 (146), noting landmarks:

> If you go right on the old highway out of Cubero, from the cattle guard southwest of the village, you will pass King Cafe and Bar, where the wife shot the husband a few years ago and got out on $10,000 bail; next comes Budville, once owned by that infamous Bud, who was shot in a robbery. The main robber-murderer later married Bud's widow. They were living happily

ever after, the last I heard, and it served old Bud right. Or so most people around there believed. . . . (148)

She points out the Dixie Tavern, the Villa (that includes a cafe, motel, and general store), Bibo's, and many others. These are not historical or geographical landmarks (not the "important" sites noted on maps or travel guides), but places where people gather, just off the highway, for rest and replenishment. What is particularly striking, though, is that these places are inhabited by people and stories, both past and present. Allen's detailed descriptions of the land are interspersed with those of the landmarks. Occasionally, she will stop at the top of a hill, for instance, and describe the vista. All are connected not only by the road, but more important by the stories about those who live there past and present.

In this section also she turns west, describing key towns like Grants, Milan, Gallup. Just as she conjures up the monolithic East at the conclusion of the last section, she describes the West embodied as California. Her metaphorical geographical mapping almost complete, she moves on to mapping her dreams. By the end of the essay, having mapped her physical, cultural, and spiritual geography, she describes herself as living in "the confluence"—the space between West and East, North and South—the coming together of many cultures. The Road "has many dimensions," she says; "it exists on many planes; and on every plane it leads to the wilderness, the mountain, as on every plane it leads to the city, to the village, and to the place beneath where Iyatiku[4] waits, where the four rivers meet, where I am going, where I am from" (154). Here she provides an image of overlapping communities; notes her ability to reside in or traverse them (unlike some others who feel stuck outside of or between communities); links past and future with the autobiographical present; reconciles opposites; and illustrates that the first-person

construction is always plural, shaped by familial, historical, and cultural narratives arising from the precise physical and spiritual geography of community.

These two sets of autobiographies suggest a few of the ways notions of subjectivity and community are being constructed and represented by Native American women speakers and writers. In contrast to the Yukon women's relationality, which provides a complex grid for their individual narratives, Allen's individuality seems to frame an affiliated subjectivity that is at least partially constructed in the very activity of autobiography. A loosely Bakhtinian notion of multivocality helps to articulate an indigenous woman's first-person-plural subjectivity that is evident both temporally (in the myths, histories, genealogies, and gossip that link the so-called prehistoric to the contemporary and highlight their interrelation) and spatially (in the site-specific narratives that situate individuals in a shared landbase and link travelers over great distances) throughout these autobiographies. All the autobiographers suggest a loss, or, in the case of the Yukon women, a fear of loss, of community (a homeland, people, language, and history) and a consequent loss of identity. Unlike the Native male autobiographers in the Swann-Krupat anthology who lament an irrecoverable loss and the inaccessibility of a rich past in the diminished present, Angela Sidney, Kitty Smith, Annie Ned, and Paula Gunn Allen describe a tangible network of extended communities (numerous sites of interaction and overlap) with clear but traversable boundaries. Inflecting it with their own experiences and interpretations, the Yukon women describe a very real community held together over a vast geographic region made accessible via a network of narrative trails; while Allen and many of the other women autobiographers more self-consciously construct an "ideal of community" that combines the specificity of a particular tribe and landbase with the generality of pan-Indianism and mobility. For

Sidney, Smith, and Ned, Native American female subjectivity and community are inherited and assumed; for Allen they are actively (re)-constructed. Not surprisingly, both sets of autobiographies seem to foreground indigenous identity, leaving female subjectivity an (almost) unmarked category. But a feminist conclusion that Native women are rendered doubly invisible would be mistaken. Perhaps cultural or national identity is emphasized because the immediate demands of cultural preservation are more acute than gender concerns. Perhaps gender is not emphasized because the autobiographers assume (rather than announce) female centrality (from Sidney's tracing the beginnings of her life story in her mother's story to Allen's noting of gynocratic myth). Rather than present reductive oppositional subjectivities, these Native women autobiographers illustrate two of the variously constituted, multiply relational identities possible for Native North American women and the manifold communities with which they are affiliated. They make it clear that any discussion of (Native) women's autobiography (and the subjectivity it constitutes) must resist positing a generalized female or Native relationality or a monolithic community in favor of working toward understanding the diverse and shifting trajectories they simultaneously reflect and construct.

Notes

1. In a paper presented to the Narrative Literature Conference in Park City, Utah (April 1995), Friedman reconsidered her earlier model in light of such critiques. Similarly, recently both Paul John Eakin and Nancy K. Miller have argued that all subjectivity (and thus all autobiography) is relational. While I believe that to be true, I am interested in examining what distinguishes as well as what connects different types of relationality.

2. Françoise Lionnet defines "autoethnography" as "the defining of one's subjective ethnicity as mediated through language, history, and ethnographical analysis" (99). Mary Louise Pratt uses the term also.

3. Leslie Marmon Silko insists that Pueblo people "make no distinction between types of story—historical, sacred, plain gossip—because these distinctions are not useful when discussing the Pueblo experience of language" (53).

4. In *The Sacred Hoop*, Allen explains that "Iyatiku, Corn Woman, [is] the mother goddess of the Keres" (17) known also as "Earth Woman" (45).

Works Cited

Allen, Paula Gunn. "The Autobiography of a Confluence." In *I Tell You Now: Autobiographical Essays by Native American Writers*, ed. Brian Swann and Arnold Krupat. Lincoln: University of Nebraska Press, 1987. 143–154.

Allen, Paula Gunn. *The Sacred Hoop: Recovering the Feminine in American Indian Traditions.* Boston: Beacon Press, 1986.

Anderson, Benedict. *Imagined Communities: Reflections on the Origin and Spread of Nationalism.* Rev. ed. 1983. New York: Verso, 1991.

Cruikshank, Julie, ed., with Angela Sidney, Kitty Smith, and Annie Ned. *Life Lived like a Story: Life Stories of Three Yukon Elders.* Lincoln: University of Nebraska Press, 1990.

Danly, Susan. "Delegations and Degradation: Alexander Gardner's Photographs of North American Indians," in *An Enduring Interest: The Photographs of Alexander Gardner,* ed. Brooks Johnson. Norfolk, Virginia: The Chrysler Museum, 1991.

Friedman, Susan Stanford. "Women's Autobiographical Selves: Theory and Practice." In *The Private Self: Theory and Practice of Women's Autobiographical Writings,* ed. Shari Benstock. Chapel Hill: University of North Carolina Press, 1988. Excerpted in this volume.

Hutcheon, Linda. "Circling the Downspout of Empire." In *The Post-Colonial Studies Reader,* eds. Bill Ashcroft, Gareth Griffiths, Helen Tiffin. New York: Routledge, 1995. 130–35.

Krupat, Arnold. *For Those Who Come After: A Study of Native American Autobiography.* Berkeley: University of California Press, 1985.

Lionnet, Françoise. *Autobiographical Voices: Race, Gender, Self-Portraiture*. Ithaca: Cornell University Press, 1989.

Medvedev, P. N., and Mikhail Bakhtin. *The Formal Method in Literary Scholarship: A Critical Introduction to Sociological Poetics*. Trans. Albert J. Wehrle. Baltimore: Goucher College Series, 1978.

Minh-ha, Trinh T. *Woman, Native, Other: Writing Postcoloniality and Feminism*. Bloomington: Indiana University Press, 1989.

Moore, David L. "Myth, History, and Identity in Silko and Young Bear: Postcolonial Praxis." In *New Voices in Native American Literary Criticism*, ed. Arnold Krupat. Washington, D.C.: Smithsonian Institution Press, 1993. 370–395.

Nemerov, Alexander. "The Indian Portraits of Elbridge Ayer Burbank: Science and Stereotype." Paper delivered at the Modern Language Association Convention, December 1995.

Pearce, Roy Harvey. *Savagism and Civilization: A Study of the Indian and the American Mind*. 1965. Baltimore: Johns Hopkins University Press, 1967.

Pratt, Mary Louise. *Imperial Eyes: Travel Writing and Transculturation*. New York: Routledge, 1992.

Rose, Wendy. "Neon Scars." In Swann and Krupat, 252–61.

Sequoya, Jana. "How (!) Is an Indian? A Contest of Stories." In *New Voices in Native American Literary Criticism*, ed. Arnold Krupat. Washington, D.C.: Smithsonian Institution Press, 1993. 453–73.

Silko, Leslie Marmon. "Language and Literature from a Pueblo Indian Perspective." *Yellow Woman and a Beauty of the Spirit: Essays on Native American Life Today*. 1981. New York: Simon and Schuster, 1996. 48–59.

Slotkin, Richard. *Regeneration through Violence: The Mythology of the American Frontier, 1600–1800*. Middletown, CT: Wesleyan University Press, 1973.

Swann, Brian, and Arnold Krupat, eds. *I Tell You Now: Autobiographical Essays by Native American Writers*. Lincoln: University of Nebraska Press, 1987.

Young, Iris Marion. "The Ideal of Community and the Politics of Difference." In *Feminism/Postmodernism*, ed. Linda J. Nicholson. New York: Routledge, 1990.

PART III
Modes and Genres

*The Making of Americans is a very important thing and everybody ought to be read-
ing at it or it, and now I am trying to do it again to say everything about everything,
only then I was wanting to write a history of every individual person who ever is or
was or shall be living and I was convinced it could be done as I still am but now
individual anything as related to every other individual is to me no longer interesting.
At that time I did not realize that the earth is completely covered over with every one.
In a way it was not then because every one was in a group and a group was separated
from every other one, and so the character of every one was interesting because they
were in relation but now since the earth is all covered over with every one there is
really no relation between any one and so if this Everybody's Aubiography is to be the
Autobiography of every one it is not to be of any connection between any one and any
one because now there is none.*

      —Gertrude Stein, *Everybody's Autobiography* (New York: Random House, 1937), 99

12 Autobiographics

Leigh Gilmore

. . . The subject of autobiography, upon which so much scrutiny has recently focused, can be more accurately described as the object of production for the purposes of cultural critique. This object has been produced as *possessing* attributes whose meaning must be *acquired* for the requirements of legibility in the broadest sense, that is, for us to be read as subjects. Thus the ways in which an autobiography variously acknowledges, resists, embraces, rejects objectification, the way s/he learns, that is, to interpret objectification as something less than simply subjectivity itself marks a place of agency. It is in this act of interpretation, of consciousness, that we can say a woman may exceed representation within dominant ideology. She exceeds it not because she possesses some privileged relation to nature or the supernatural. Rather, the discourses and practices that construct subjectivity through hierarchy must always be defended, their boundaries guarded, their rights maintained. Within these discourses exist unruly subjects who are unevenly objectified and who represent identity in relation to other values and subjectivities. In other words, if feminist theory describes women as "objects of exchange" in order to analyze social organization and to reveal the constitutively delimited sphere of possibility for women, my work builds from that critique to analyze how women use self-representation and its constitutive possibilities for agency and subjectivity to become no longer primarily subject to exchange but subjects who exchange the

position of object for the subjectivity of self-representational agency.

The question of gender, then, cannot be explored mainly through the compulsory lumping together of all male-authored texts, on one side, and all female-authored texts on the other. Instead, I think, the question can usefully be enjoined at a more specific level, at the level of each text's engagement with the available discourses of truth and identity and the ways in which self-representation is constitutively shaped through proximity to those discourses' definition of authority. As useful as more monolithic claims about "men's" and "women's" autobiography have been to feminists during this crucial historical period in the institutionalization of feminism, generalizations about gender and genre in autobiography naturalize how men, women, and the activity of writing an autobiography are bound together within the changing philosophies of the self and history. As a hedge against this tendency, I will attempt to chart the terrain—the discourses of self-representation—differently by looking to noncanonical texts in order to understand how and in what ways women's self-representation occurs and in relation to what cultural institutions and forms it is written. To do so, I shift simultaneously within two critical discourses: feminist criticism and autobiography studies, and the differing temporalities of their subjects in relation to the differing possibilities of finding them. These discourses can be taken as different legends for a map that is still being drawn, and they should demonstrate that women's self-representational writing is bound up in still other discourses. . . .

I offer the term *autobiographics* to describe those elements of self-representation which are not bound by a philosophical definition of the self derived from Augustine, not content with the literary history of autobiography, those elements that instead mark a location in a text where self-invention, self-discovery, and self-representation emerge within the technologies of autobiography—namely, those legalistic, literary, social, and ecclesiastical discourses of truth and identity through which the subject of autobiography is produced. Autobiographics, as a description of self-representation and as a reading practice, is concerned with interruptions and eruptions, with resistance and contradiction as strategies of self-representation.

A text's autobiographics consist in the following elements in self-representational writing, or writing that emphasizes the autobiographical *I*: an emphasis on writing itself as constitutive of autobiographical identity, discursive contradictions in the representation of identity (rather than unity), the name as a potential site of experimentation rather than contractual sign of identity, and the effects of the gendered connection of word and body. Autobiographics gives initial conceptual precedence to positioning the subject, to recognizing the shifting sands of identity on which theories of autobiography build, and to describing "identity" and the networks of identification. An exploration of a text's autobiographics allows us to recognize that the *I* is multiply coded in a range of discourses: it is the site of multiple solicitations, multiple markings of "identity," multiple figurations of agency. Thus, autobiographics avoids the terminal questions of genre and close delimitation and offers a way, instead, to ask: Where is the autobiographical?[1] What constitutes its representation? The *I*, then, does not disappear in-

to an identity-less textual universe. Rather, the autobiographicality of the *I* in a variety of discourses is emphasized as a point of resistance in self-representation.

I think of autobiographics operating within texts that have not been seen as autobiographies and occurring in the margins of hegemonic discourses within cultural texts, in the social spaces carved in the interstices of institutions, and so it is there that the terms of a different reading and retextualization of the subject of autobiography must be located. It is there also that we may begin to think about agency. Thus, the traditional construction of autobiography may be pressured further by my refusal to produce a critical study that differs from its predecessors and contemporaries in content only. A study of autobiographics allows for removing the following writers, among others, from interpretive contexts in which their works are canonized, though not as autobiography: Julian of Norwich, Gertrude Stein, Monique Wittig, and Minnie Bruce Pratt. These writers removed themselves in material and psychological ways from a social economy in which they would function as objects of exchange through self-representational practices and social and political acts and choices, and they represented their identities through an emphasis on the *I* that contrasts with the *I* in the traditional forms or epistemologies they restructure. . . .

Even as feminist theory has unsettled and inspired self-representation, self-representation has challenged theory in a reciprocal reworking of subjectivity, identity, and politics. Three texts exemplify the reworking of disciplinary and discursive boundaries and the energizing relations among politics, theory, and self-representation in feminist discourse. Through three figures or sites of feminist self-representation, I would like to read for the autobiographical as that which resists static identity categories. Donna Haraway's "Manifesto for Cyborgs" (1985), Patricia Williams's *Alchemy of Race and Rights: Diary of a*

Law Professor (1991), and Minnie Bruce Pratt's "Identity: Skin Blood Heart" (1984) represent identity in specific networks rather than in entities or essences traditionally associated with women and feminists. All construe consciousness, identity, agency, and experience as key terms in the discourse of self-representation.

In "A Manifesto for Cyborgs: Science, Technology, and Socialist Feminism in the 1980s," Donna Haraway goes adventuring as a feminist subject in a discourse of truth that has seemed nearly implacable to feminism: science.[2] In her essay, Haraway offers "an ironic political myth faithful to feminism" (65) which uses the figure of the cyborg to explicate the complexity of feminists' positions within discourses of truth and identity. Haraway offers the cyborg as the subject of feminist political self-representation; it "is our ontology; it gives us our politics" (66). It is a hybrid of machine and organism, recognizable as a fiction, a science fiction, and as a creature of social reality. Here, Haraway uses "social reality" in a specific and expansive sense; for her, social reality is "our most important political construction, a world-changing fiction" (65). The potential of this myth lies in its relation to history, its past tenses and possible futures revealed through a present-tense identity. The specter of faithfulness is raised in proximity to blasphemy. Irony and potent effects of blasphemy, which Haraway is careful to distinguish from apostasy, offer feminism both "a rhetorical strategy and a political method" (65). It is important to focus on the irony in this "ironic political myth faithful to feminism" (66), especially in the confessional context I have discussed, for some may accuse Haraway of capitulating the contested ground of female identity and opting for an unrecognizable, unrealistic hybrid like the cyborg. The end result of Haraway's manifesto should not be capitulation, nor do I think this is the result implicit in it. Saying "I am a cyborg" is different from saying "I am a woman" in some ways but not logically, in a politics of identity, for it makes visible what was not previously recognizable.

What is the cyborg's experience, agency, and identity? How can it be a self-representational fiction for feminists? We are all cyborgs, according to Haraway, poised in this identity on the cusp of the twenty-first century: "We are all chimeras, theorized and fabricated hybrids of machine and organism; in short, we are cyborgs" (66). And Haraway likes it here, blurring the boundaries between natural and fabricated, human and machine, material and fantasy. The cyborg breaks with all previous mythologies of identity, all critical narratives, their ontology and epistemology. Most important, the cyborg confounds the possibility and desirability of a myth of origin founded on an originary whole or an identifying split. Cyborg identity becomes possible at the end of the twentieth century through breakdowns along three boundaries that previously structured identity and made it knowable: the human/animal boundary, the human-animal/machine boundary, and the physical/nonphysical boundary. This is our experiential past with respect to the concept of identity.

In this context, what are the possibilities for agency? The cyborg's agency lies in social relations and the identities it can access through heteroglossic naming. It is not surprising that cyborg affinity is based not in blood relations but in choice, but what Haraway uses the image of the cyborg to explore and to name is the extent to which its world already exists. She asks, "And who counts as 'us' in my own rhetoric? Which identities are available to ground such a powerful political myth called 'us,' and what could motivate enlistment in this collectivity?" (72–73). Affirming this already multiple collectivity, Haraway eschews any of the categories the cyborg—itself a powerful fiction—reveals as fictitious. Agency is made possible for Haraway when women are linked through affinity, not identity, for political purposes. The cyborg, then, is ultimately a political identity that emerges in relation to a collectivity that mirrors its own hybrid identity; here, coalitions represent the body politics of the cyborg. Identity is thereby conserved as a political category. Irony enables the cyborg's political agency within confessional technologies. The cyborg's faithfulness to feminism and faithlessness to gender distinguish its confessional project: the cyborg's confessors are positioned as scientists, as feminists, as consumers and producers of hybrid identities, that is, as already implicated in discourses that take identity seriously (a precondition for irony).

In *The Alchemy of Race and Rights: Diary of a Law Professor*, Patricia Williams locates identity at the boundary of historical possibility, legal representation, and political rhetoric.[3] Like Haraway's cyborg, Williams's alchemist lives in a world whose past is distinctly undeserving of nostalgia. In her first chapter, "The Brass Ring and the Deep Blue Sea: (some parables about learning to think like a lawyer)," Williams presents her aims for her book through a dialogue with her sister. As Williams ticks off her theoretical goals, her sister agitates, "But what's the book *about*?" (6). As Williams explains, the book is not so much *about* something as it is itself a way of *doing*, and Williams puts the emphasis on writing as action: "I would like to write in a way that reveals the intersubjectivity of legal constructions, that forces the reader both to participate in the construction of meaning and to be conscious of that process" (7–8). Her writing is an attempt "to create a genre of legal writing to fill the gaps of traditional scholarship" (7).

The current genre of legal writing, as well as the practice and, as Williams suggests, the teaching of law, makes her identity "oxymoronic." This category is the negative version of the hybridity Haraway celebrates in the cyborg, and it lives by the law of genre. Williams describes it: "I am a commercial lawyer as well as a teacher

of contract and property law. I am also black and female, a status that one of my former employers described as being 'at oxymoronic odds' with that of commercial lawyer" (6). Identity categories are at stake here because, in rhetorical terms, they are property, they are the properties of the person, and they define persons as property. Most significant, they are discursive constructions in discourses with normative predispositions. How else could one be "at oxymoronic odds" with oneself? The presumed objectivity of legal language flattens out the meaning of people's lives, and as it does so it fails to render them knowable to themselves and others. Williams, I think, sees this flattening out as a distortion that undermines the possibilities of justice, for it disallows the self-representation of the one whose evidence is always, in part, identity. Clearly, it will take an alchemist to produce this new writing, one who does not fear prosecution under the law of genre ("genres are not to be mixed").

Williams's use of confessional technologies can be seen through her invocation of a community that constructs meaning along with the writer. I think there is productive tension between her goals to force "the reader both to participate . . . and to be conscious of that process" and "to create a genre of legal writing." I see that tension as autobiographical; that is, the genre of legal writing is profoundly concerned with property rights, by which African Americans have been construed through slavery as property. Williams seeks to create a genre concerned with putting the disenfranchised "voice" and "self" into a legal discourse that has itself been one of the major instruments through which disenfranchisement was codified and rendered enforceable. What is at stake . . . is the development of the anecdotal as a far-reaching representational style concerned with the self and the extent to which it can be thought to be its own possession. The connection between identity and ownership affects legal discourse, for it focuses on the implication of being "a subject before the law" for self-representation.

The historical and cultural specificity of racial identity informs Williams's writing. By contextualizing African-American identities with legal notions of property, she explains that for Africans brought to the emerging United States as slaves, the conditions for preserving and reconstructing "identity" were violently constrained: the only possible legal identity was as property. The legacy of racism for African Americans, as Williams points out, is evident in the language of identity. She specifies her own use of this language: "A final note about some of my own decisions on categories: I wish to recognize that terms like 'black' and 'white' do not begin to capture the rich ethnic and political diversity of my subject. But I do believe that the simple matter of the color of one's skin so profoundly affects the way one is treated, so radically shapes what one is allowed to think and feel about this society, that the decision to generalize from such a division is valid" (256). As an identity category, "blackness" is not all, but all that it signifies is crucial to convey: "While being black has been the most powerful social attribution in my life, it is only one of a number of governing narratives or presiding fictions by which I am constantly reconfiguring myself in the world" (256).

In an essay titled "On Being the Object of Property," Williams frames an inquiry into property law with a historical and personal anecdote about the self and ownership. Just before her first day of law school, Williams's mother reminds her of her family history. Williams's knowledge of her mother's side of the family begins with her great-great-grandmother Sophie, who was purchased when she was eleven years old by a lawyer named Austin Miller. Williams has the document that is probably the contract of sale for her great-great-grandmother: "It is a very simple but lawyerly document, describing her as 'one female' and revealing her age as

eleven; no price is specified, merely 'value exchanged'" (17). Miller impregnates Sophie, whose daughter Mary, Williams's grandmother, is taken from her to be brought up as a house servant. "While I don't remember what I was told about Austin Miller before I decided to go to law school, I do remember that just before my first day of class my mother said, in a voice full of secretive reassurance, 'The Millers were lawyers, so you have it in your blood'" (216). Identity, then, figured through the powerful symbol of blood, is bound up in a network of coerced histories, violently colonized persons, and rapes, but also, as Williams emphasizes, in the ambivalent legacy of her own success and demonstrated talents, of disenfranchisement and reclamations.

For Williams, the discourse of self-representation enacted in *The Alchemy of Race and Rights* remains centrally concerned with the significance of "truth" to identity. A series of experiential anecdotes emphasizes that to be seen as black and female by various institutions is already to have been placed in a position of defense, a position in which one is the transgressor, the liar, the criminal. Other subject positions are available, however, within the kind of writing Williams produces as an intervention in the connection of race-gender-identity-violence. For her, identity is forged in a crucible and the process is alchemical, mysterious; the third term between race and rights which produces an autobiographical identity is neither simply nor eternally given.[4] Autobiographical identity is expressed as Williams confounds boundaries, her political and imaginative goal in this book, and wages battles over their meanings and who will decide them.

Minnie Bruce Pratt's long essay "Identity: Skin Blood Heart" is a critique of the feminist nostalgia for an identity discourse and its place within contemporary technologies of autobiography.[5] Given the title, one might expect an essentialist view of female identity located in the body; however, Pratt considerably revises the conjunction of "skin blood heart" through a critical anatomization of anti-Semitism, racism, and homophobia. Like Williams, Pratt has received a racist and sexist indoctrination in which blood figured as a powerful symbol. She casts a critical eye on how her identity as a white, Christian, southern woman was constructed; she examines what she now understands as the networks in which identity is enmeshed, where the lures of racist and heterosexist identification lie, and offers the history of her resistance to the privileges of her former home. Pratt describes herself as being propelled into political consciousness when she came out as a lesbian and lost her two sons to her husband in a custody battle in which her mother threatened to testify against her.

Pratt's understanding of "experience," "consciousness," and "identity" as aspects of political self-representation offers a dynamic model of feminist agency. Pratt suggests that the subject of self-representation is *experience,* understood as "an exhausting process, this moving from the experience of the 'unknowing majority' (as Maya Angelou called it) into consciousness" ("Identity," 12). When experience is further specified as "an ongoing process by which subjectivity is constructed semiotically and historically,"[6] then it cannot be thought to simply accumulate, its dynamism defined through sheer bulk. It doesn't just add up. Rather, experience connotes a profoundly political, emotional, intellectual, and imaginative response, a series of alterations, differences, and repositionings in relation to sameness. The temporality of experience understood in this way is not exclusively or primarily linear, not additive or iterative but potentially transformative of the meaning of time. It does, however, engage this potential in specific cultural, historical, and narrative terms. Constitutive of feminist change are narratives of change, and Pratt offers a narrative of "consciousness" changing which foregrounds the re-

lationship between "truth" and "lies" through the figure, place, and experience of home.

Marcia Aldrich and I have elsewhere discussed the centrality of "home" to Pratt's revisionary politics, but I would repeat here that Pratt constructs the home as a duplicitous site of acculturation which violently binds differences together under the sign of the same (as in the white, Christian family, and the construction of "our" people and "our" women who must be protected by "our" men from a malevolent black "them").[7] She explains how the stability of home is rendered through this violence and so wields its power through its continuous reproduction and the suppression of its reality. The identity enforced and experienced within this "home" is in large part refused, though it is precisely what Pratt must labor to understand in order not to be compelled by either the pull of nostalgia or the unknowing that comes from trying to raise one's own consciousness by analogy to someone else's oppression. To say "I am not what I was" and "I was not what I am," as Pratt does, locates identity on the move. Identity acts. It acts in relation to skin, to blood, and to heart, and the process of finding this relationship is itself an act of identity. But it is not final. The identity network, figured through the body as "skin blood heart," offers a dynamic model of self-representation: How do I know myself and how am I known by others? by skin? by blood? do I know myself by heart?

As a feminist with home truths to tell, Pratt reworks confessional technologies through critical revision: she is seeing experience from an altered perspective and repositions herself to tell the truth rather than to have it told to her by father, mother, community, or husband. Her goal is to use the mode of truth telling to "get a little closer to the longed-for but unrealized world, where we are each able to live, but not by trying to make someone less than us, not by someone else's blood or pain: yes, that's what I'm trying to do with my living now" ("Identity," 13). Pratt's "living now" is represented in "Identity" as moments of "speaking to" in which a truth is communicated not only in the content but in the quality of the exchange. These stand as confessional moments in which listener and speaker are joined in the production of truths that will reconstruct the world as an altogether different "home," one in which it will be possible to "tell the truth" from a subject position not based on exclusion, violent differentiation, or the compulsory masking of identities in the face of punitive institutions and identity authorities. It is necessary to speak what Pratt calls the "stark truth" (14) in order to create a context in which it can be heard: "This listening is one way of finding out how to get to the new place where we all can live and speak to each other for more than a fragile moment" (14). Pratt recognizes the provisional nature of her confessional project, her refusal of nostalgia compels such an understanding, and she records the false starts and missteps in an effort to "expand my constricted eye" (17). She explains her perspective and enunciatory position: "I am speaking my small piece of truth, as best I can. . . . I'm putting it down for you to see if our fragments match anywhere, if our pieces, together, make another larger piece of the truth that can be part of the map we are making together to show us the way to get to the longed-for world" (16).

Pratt's description of her method exemplifies what I have been trying to convey through my exploration of autobiographics. The extent to which confessional technologies continue to operate in the discourses of truth and identity has put women writers on notice, but these technologies have also been negotiated in a variety of ways by writers who find other positions from which to tell the "truth." I have looked to women who intervene in the linkage of "lying"

and "women," who refuse the violence of gender identity compelled by dominant discourses of self-representation in order to put themselves into their texts through the agency of re-membering. If autobiography provokes fantasies of the real, then autobiographics explores the constrained "real" for the reworking of identity in the discourses of women's self-representation.

Notes

1. See Celeste Schenck, "All of a Piece: Women's Autobiography and Poetry," in Bella Brodzki and Schenck, eds., *Life/Lines: Theorizing Women's Autobiography* (Ithaca: Cornell University Press, 1988), 281–305.

2. Donna Haraway, "A Manifesto for Cyborgs: Science, Technology, and Socialist Feminism in the 1980s" in *Feminism/Postmodernism*, ed. Linda J. Nicholson. New York: Routledge, 1990. 190–233.

3. Patricia J. Williams, *The Alchemy of Race and Rights: Diary of a Law Professor* (Cambridge: Harvard University Press, 1991).

4. In *Sexing the Cherry* (New York: Vintage, 1991), Jeanette Winterson explains alchemy through an analogy to imaginative processes: "The alchemists have a saying, '*Tertium non data*': the third is not given. That is, the transformation from one element to another, from waste matter into best gold, is a process that cannot be documented. It is fully mysterious. No one really knows what effects the change. And so it is with the mind that moves from its prison to a vast plain without any movement at all. We can only guess at what happened" (150).

5. Minnie Bruce Pratt, "Identity: Skin Blood Heart," in *Yours in Struggle: Three Feminist Perspectives on Anti-Semitism and Racism*, by Elly Bulkin, Minnie Bruce Pratt, Barbara Smith (Brooklyn, New York: Long Haul Press, 1984).

6. Teresa de Lauretis, *Alice Doesn't: Feminism, Semiotics, Cinema* (Bloomington: Indiana University Press, 1984), 182.

7. Leigh Gilmore and Marcia Aldrich, "Writing Home: 'Home' and Lesbian Representation in Minnie Bruce Pratt," *Genre* 25 (Spring 1992): 25–46.

13 Autography/Transformation/Asymmetry

Jeanne Perreault

In the fact that the subject is a process *lies the possibility of transformation.*
— Catherine Belsey, "Constructing the Subject: Deconstructing the Text"

For silence to transform into speech, sounds and words, it must first traverse through our female bodies.

— Gloria Anzaldúa, *Making Face, Making Soul*

"I" and "we" are the most important words in the writing(s) of contemporary feminism, continuously transformed and reenacted as feminists claim the rights of self-definition. This process of transformation, these texts, works actively and explicitly in the context of feminist communities, communities that are, I will argue, inextricable from discourses of selfhood. Throughout this study, textual enactments of an "I" and the boundaries of "we" are in play as elements of inquiry, as territories to be claimed and disclaimed, as constructions or as essences. Feminist writers of all races, sexualities, and classes interrogate discourses of power, identity, and experience as alternative discourses become available through the speaking of greater numbers of women.[1] The feminist texts effected by this process of self writing make the female body of she who says "I" a site and source of written subjectivity, investing that individual body with the shifting ethics of a political, racial, and sexual consciousness. These intersecting layers of mediation inform feminist autography. One

of my aims is to explore in the writing of self how the continual revision of these categories (self/community/identity) is central to the way in which feminism makes itself continuously meaningful.

In referring to the texts of signficant contemporary feminist writers as "autographies," I am naming a kind of writing that can and should be identified in order to foreground the suggestive and flexible processes of both *autos* and *graphia*. Much contemporary self-writing does not fall within the parameters of familiar modes of "I" writing (autobiography, life writing, memoirs, etc.), and various feminist theorists and critics have been grappling with unwieldy generic terminology that does not seem to fit women's texts. Here, I read Audre Lorde, Adrienne Rich, Kate Millett, Patricia Williams, and others, looking to textual configurations of a subjectivity precisely articulated in the varied forms that I call "autography."[2] In autography, I find a writing whose effect is to bring into being a "self" that the writer names "I," but whose parameters and boundaries resist the monadic. Writing "I" has been an emancipatory project for women, and a crucial one in the evolution of contemporary American[3] feminism. This study addresses who and what is meant by that written "I" as an element in the "we" of feminist communities, and takes up problems of feminist articulations of self and writing in the context of current debates on subjectivity. Although I rehearse some of the arguments of contemporary theorists, my focus is on the texts that explicitly make the process of being a self contiguous with the inscription of selfhood. The forms I examine here, including poems, "meditations," and journals, share some common ground: each writer names herself "I" and "feminist," and reveals that the process of self-in-the-making is made available to the reader. Autography, then, as I conceive it, invites the reader to reconsider the imbrications of subjectivity, textuality, and community.

The American feminist exists in a context of intense, almost obsessive, ideology of attention to "the individual." She is informed by a passion for social justice and a will toward discerning how that might be enacted. Recent discussions of multiplicity of "selves," or the deconstruction of the figure of the indivisible "self," have not so much undermined the valorizing of selfhood as extended it, giving the "selves" a share in the belief in the rights of the individual. These perspectives underlie the struggle to find a "voice," a place from which to speak, and the continual revising of feminist discourses is the most secure of feminism's practices. It is in the mutable, capacious space and time of the written (that is, the public, published) text that feminist discourses of selfhood, "freedom," and ethics recombine under, or through, the sign of "I." My readings of what I am calling autography look to writers whose feminism is embodied, historically precise, self-reflective, and communally shaped: Audre Lorde's *The Cancer Journals;* the later prose and poetry of Adrienne Rich; Kate Millett's *The Basement: Meditations on a Human Sacrifice;* and Patricia Williams's *The Alchemy of Race and Rights: Diary of a Law Professor.* Even if we think that feminism may be about many other things than the subjectivity of the feminist,[4] the importance of this "subject" in feminist discourse can hardly be overestimated, and it is her varied voice that we find in feminist autography. Throughout this study I demonstrate how each writer traces the discursive boundaries of her identity, and illustrate the impossibility of imposing a metadiscourse on the texts of feminist subjectivity.

Categories and Communities

Feminist theorists of autobiography and life writing have been grappling with modes of expression that evade the familiar narrative of life events. Simultaneously, and not coincidentally, discussions of "identity" and subjectivity, and ongoing reconsiderations of categories of "women" and "feminism," push literary and feminist theory in new directions. One way in which autography differs from autobiography is that it is not necessarily concerned with the process or unfolding of life events, but rather makes the writing itself an aspect of the selfhood the writer experiences and brings into being. In their generically unfixed literary productions, contemporary feminist autographers have been enacting subjectivity in multiple and various ways. These writers make "I" and "we" signify both continuity with an ongoing life in a body and a community, and dissociation within that life—gaps, amputations, silences. That self-in-the-making defies, and affirms, some of the most provocative aspects of contemporary theory and reinforces the tentative proposals of feminist theorists that a new kind of subjectivity is evolving.

The texts produced by this process simultaneously reshape female subjectivity and agency while reinscribing the possibility, experience, and value of being a "self." The problematics of these concepts—subjectivity, agency, self—form the basis of a writing of self whose parameters are relentlessly mobile. The woman who speaks "I" in feminist autography seems to have anticipated the procedure that Denise Riley suggests for theorists: "Instead of veering between deconstruction and transcendence, we could try another train of speculations: that 'women' is indeed an unstable category, . . . that feminism is the site of the systematic fighting-out of that instability" (Riley, "Am I That Name?" 5). Riley is addressing the issue from the perspective of those talking *about* women. My concern, however, is the voice of she who writes in the body of a woman, when "I" and "woman" (the singular of "women," not the blank screen of historical specularities and speculations) are embraced as unstable categories, territories to be inhabited, claimed, or reclaimed—not colonized, but worked and revised. Tania Modleski speaks of "a way to hold on to the category of woman while recognizing ourselves to be in the *process* (an unending one) of *defining and constructing the category*" (20). A category in process does not cease to be a category.[5]

The central questions for feminists are these: Who will construct the categories into which "I" and "we" fit ourselves? Whose words will we attend to? Whose texts will we honor? Audre Lorde declares, "If we don't name ourselves we are nothing" ("Interview," 19). Here, Lorde predicates being upon naming: those who are named by others have no way to exist in and for themselves. Yet the "we" is somehow in existence, known to itself, available for the naming. Audre Lorde frames a "we" that situates her clearly among those who are vulnerable to being named from the outside and thus, paradoxically, created for others' purposes while being eliminated for their own. Lorde's assertion addresses

one of the ongoing sites of negotiation in the making of a movement. The processes that the texts of self-writing enact are not solitary or sovereign, and any discussion of a feminist "I" must take into account the register of "we," a contested zone that resists definition but asserts its own existence. Cherríe Moraga says:

> Our strategy is how we cope—how we measure and weigh what is to be said and when, what is to be done and how, and to whom and to whom and to whom, daily deciding/risking who it is we can call an ally, call a friend (whatever that person's skin, sex, or sexuality). We are women without a line. We are women who contradict each other. (Moraga and Anzaldúa, xix)

Here Moraga, as a woman of color speaking with other women of color, asserts the identity that ensues as lives are enmeshed with those of others for self-defense and social transformation. Allies and friends are not assumed, but decided upon; and the decision is made daily, provisionally. To be "women without a line" is to eschew a correct line, to see borderlines as mobile, and to take responsibility for coping. Strategy is no abstraction. Moreover, contradiction does not destroy "we-ness" in Moraga's view; rather, it is necessarily part of a subjectivity that is discursive *and* embodied. The subject Moraga configures (here, both agent and topic) anticipates what Teresa de Lauretis calls a "feminist concept of identity." This is de Lauretis's definition: "a political-personal strategy of survival and resistance that is also, at the same time, a critical practice and a mode of knowledge" (9). Both de Lauretis and Moraga use the word "strategy," thereby asserting identity as purposeful, intentional practice, and a "mode of knowledge," a "daily deciding" that is necessarily provisional, modifying action and being modified in a dialectic of everydayness.[6] As these definitions suggest, identity is valued as mobile and transformational, communal as well as private.

This problematic of subjectivity is complexly implicated in an identity politics that must confront the issues of representation when to "represent" means to speak for, to speak about, and, most troublingly, to speak as. "Identity politics" as a politically effective principle was first explicitly articulated in "The Combahee River Collective Statement" when socialist Black lesbian feminists asserted the specificity of their experience and oppression as the basis of their political organizing. The Collective reports that Black women describe "feelings of craziness" until concepts allowing group identification are available (211). The "seemingly personal experiences" of sexist or racist abuses can be reframed as political when the "concepts of sexual politics [and] . . . racial politics" come together in antiracist, feminist practice and analysis (211–12). The issues, problems, and possibilities that arise in these assertions invite speculation about the intersection of experiences and discourses within the person. She who is feeling crazy is certainly (whatever else) feeling dislocated from her world. The discourse communities of which she is a part are inadequate to her "feeling" or "experience." It is this gap between the conceptual and the experiential that feminist self-writers (and theorists) explore as the zone most available for modification.

The forms of feminist autography are widely varied, generically unbounded, modifying ways of seeing the world and being selves in it. As available discourses of selfhood have been largely masculinist, the sense of self that the feminist writer has at any moment must be a mixture of contradictory and shifting configurations of personhood, and her interpretation of those configurations will inevitably refigure

both them and her "self." When "self" is written (whether that is understood to mean described, [re]presented, [re]created, articulated, or fixed), the distinction between the received models of selfhood and the "autobiographical impulse to self invention" can again be brought into play, to be revised, necessarily, in the next sentence (Eakin, 6). Paul Eakin looks to the "dialectical interplay between the autobiographical impulse to self-invention and received models of selfhood" (6), but he does not examine the degree to which a Western cultural imperative toward "selfhood" may include "self-invention." When "received models" of self are narrow and too uniform, self-invention may be an imperative.

The will toward self-making, in feminist textual practice, is multidimensional. Autography asserts a highly indeterminate feminism and an equally indeterminate notion of selfhood. As women write themselves, categories of difference (inner, outer, body, world, language) do not disappear, but take shape as "I" and in relation to "I." The shifts in relations between personal, body-specific identity and communal, or ideological, identity (the I who says we) both maintain ongoingness and require discontinuity. To the extent that "I" and "we" are imbricated in feminist autography, tracing the modulations of representation is the crux of feminist thought. The texts that are effected anticipate and extend the problematic of subjectivity. The feminist "self," then, exists in the particulars of feminist texts and not in any particular kind of text. Like all writing, feminist self-writing is informed by the experiences of the everyday, of the body, of the sites of contact with and isolation from the read-about and lived-in worlds. But that world as the writer lives it can be imagined, felt, and recognized only from the writing.

Most often in feminist texts the "self" is provisional, an exploration of possibility and a tentative grammar of transformations. Rather than treating "self" as a fixed notion, clearly conceptualized and needing only to be "expressed," the feminist writer of self engages in a (community of) discourse of which she is both product and producer. This interrelation of self and community is one of the most provocative issues in the writing of feminist subjectivity. Political or ideological consciousness takes into account the intersections of individual experience in its complexities of race, sexuality, class, ethnicity. The feminist writing of self, then, is part of creating new communities. Jane Marcus observes in women's self-writing a "structure that insists on the reader's response and sets the writer in conversation with her own community" and suggests that this will toward the discursive is the moving spirit of women's autobiography (141). Once again: as women write themselves they write the movement. The transformations of self, of community, and of material reality are brought to possibility and registered in the writing. . . .

Rather than figuring subjectivity as a "center" or "core" of a person, I read the texts of feminist autography as articulating not a site or a space, but an energy. It is this "I" that works for the social, material, and personal transformations that we know as feminism, seeking an alternative both to the suppression of difference that totalization implies and to the dissociations suggested by a fragmented subjectivity. Sidonie Smith observes that "endless fragmentation and a reified multiplicity" make the feminist subject an elusive being (188). She notes, "It is hard to coalesce a call to political action around a constantly deferred point of departure" (188). Feminist gestures toward cohesion may be grounded in the desire for a "point of departure" and, indeed, a point of arrival that embrace a process of transformation as a revolutionary concept, and as a feminist principle.

I situated "transformation" as epigraph to this chapter, and this book, in order to suggest how deeply embedded the idea and value of transformation are in the practice of feminist autography. If we agree that "no socio-political transformation is possible which does not constitute a transformation of subjects" (Kristeva quoted by Stanton, "Language," 74), we will agree with Catherine Belsey's observation about the intimate link between the social and the personal: "In the fact that the subject is a *process* lies the possibility of transformation" (50). The subject as and in process is central to what I have been discussing here. In Gayatri Spivak's definition of feminism, bodies are involved in action, whereas transformation seems to be primarily a mental phenomenon ("*against* sexism, where women unite as a biologically oppressed caste; and *for* feminism, where human beings train to prepare for a transformation of consciousness" [144]). Gloria Anzaldúa corrects the balance and returns us to women's bodies and the role of the body in transformations of consciousness and action: "For silence to transform into speech, sounds and words, it must first traverse through our female bodies" (xxii).

Transformation enters the discussion of writing the self in that it is the site of the mutable self engaging with language. When this multiple transformation includes the intention to effect social/cultural/political change, as an aspect of writing the self, feminist autography is quickened.

Notes

"Autography/Transformation/Asymmetry" is excerpted from the introductory chapter of Perreault's *Writing Selves: Contemporary Feminist Autography*.

1. I refer here to "numbers" of speakers: women of every community or context have, I believe, always been speaking, but only when some critical mass (or volume) is achieved does that "speaking" seem to be

heard. And it can be said to be "heard" when its effects make their way into a mainstream of institutional, public life (the media, the education system, the courts).

2. For other uses of this word see Ryan, 6; Gallop, 284; Stanton, *Female;* and Meese, 79.

3. Here, referring to the United States.

4. For my purposes, "a feminist" is she who claims the name—though obviously not all practices of feminists can be called feminist practices. As for "feminism," Gayatri Spivak's description of "the best of French feminism" continues to have the virtues of clarity, spaciousness, and inclusiveness: "against sexism, where women unite as a biologically oppressed caste; and *for* feminism where human beings train to prepare for a transformation of consciousness" (145).

5. Riley's sensitivity to naming is the basis of her study, and she is committed to a feminism that includes "female persons" and rejects a postfeminist indifference to "the stubborn harshness of lived gender" (3); her anxiety, however, about claiming the power of naming seems to lie at the heart of her insistence that women can exist only within quotation marks (as "women").

6. Readers should note Elspeth Probyn's discussion of distinctions between strategy and tactics. See *Sexing the Self,* esp. 86–107.

Works Cited

Anzaldúa, Gloria, ed. *Making Face, Making Soul. Haciendo Caras: Creative and Critical Perspectives by Women of Color.* San Francisco: Aunt Lute, 1990.

Belsey, Catherine. "Constituting the Subject: Deconstructing the Text." In *Feminist Criticism and Social Change: Sex, Class and Race in Literature and Culture,* ed. Judith Newton and Deborah Rosenfelt. New York and London: Methuen, 1985. 45–64.

Combahee River Collective. "A Black Feminist Statement." In *This Bridge Called My Back: Writings by Radical Women of Color,* ed. Cherríe Moraga and Gloria Anzaldúa. Watertown, MA: Persephone Press, 1981.

De Lauretis, Teresa. "Feminist Studies/Critical Studies: Issues, Terms, and Contexts." In *Feminist Studies/Critical Studies,* ed. Teresa de Lauretis. Bloomington: Indiana University Press, 1986. 1–20.

Eakin, Paul John. *Fictions in Autobiography: Studies in the Art of Self-Invention.* Princeton, NJ: Princeton University Press, 1985.

Gallop, Jane. "Writing and Sexual Difference: The Difference Within." In *Writing and Sexual Difference,* ed. Emily Abel. Chicago: University of Chicago Press, 1982. 283–90.

Jardine, Alice A. *Gynesis: Configurations of Woman and Modernity.* Ithaca: Cornell University Press, 1985.

Lorde, Audre. *The Cancer Journals.* San Francisco: Spinsters Ink, 1980.

Lorde, Audre. "An Interview with Karla Hammond." *American Poetry Review* (March/April 1980): 19.

Marcus, Jane. "Invincible Mediocrity: The Private Selves of Public Women." In *The Private Self: Theory and Practice of Women's Autobiographical Writings,* ed. Shari Benstock. Chapel Hill and London: University of North Carolina Press, 1988. 114–46.

Meese, Elizabeth. *(Sem)Erotics—Theorizing Lesbian: Writing.* New York: New York University Press, 1992.

Millett, Kate. *The Basement: Meditations on a Human Sacrifice.* New York: Simon and Schuster, 1979.

Modleski, Tania. *Feminism without Women: Culture and Criticism in a "Postfeminist" Age.* New York and London: Routledge, 1992.

Moraga, Cherríe and Gloria Anzaldúa. *This Bridge Called My Back: Writings by Radical Women of Color.* Watertown, MA: Persephone Press, 1981.

Neuman, Shirley, ed. *Prose Studies* 14, no. 2 (1991). Special Issue on Autobiography and Questions of Gender.

Probyn, Elspeth. *Sexing the Self: Gendered Positions in Cultural Studies.* London and New York: Routledge, 1992.

Riley, Denise. *"Am I That Name?" Feminism and the Category of "Women" in History.* Minneapolis: University of Minnesota Press, 1988.

Ryan, Michael. "Self-Evidence." Review of *Le Pacte*

Autobiographique, by Philip Lejeune. *Diacritics* (June 1980): 2–16.

Smith, Sidonie. "The Autobiographical Manifesto: Identitites, Temporalities, Politics." In Neuman, 186–212. Excerpted in this volume.

Spivak, Gayatri Chakravorty. *In Other Worlds: Essays in Cultural Politics.* New York and London: Methuen, 1987.

Stanton, Domna C. "Language and Revolution: The Franco-American Dis-Connection." In *The Future of Difference,* ed. Hester Eisenstein and Alice Jardine. New Brunswick, NJ: Rutgers University Press, 1980. 73–87.

Stanton, Domna C., ed. *The Female Autograph: Theory and Practice of Autobiography from the Tenth to the Twentieth Century.* Chicago: University of Chicago Press, 1984.

Williams, Patricia J. *The Alchemy of Race and Rights: Diary of a Law Professor.* Cambridge, MA, and London, England: Harvard University Press, 1991.

14 Sacred Secrets: A Strategy for Survival

Doris Sommer

The language-game of reporting can be given such a turn that a report is not meant to inform the hearer about its subject matter but about the person making the report.

—Wittgenstein, II.x

Rigoberta Menchú's secrets astonished me when I read her autobiographical testimony over ten years ago. Secrets seemed then, as they do now, the most noteworthy and instructive feature of her book, however one judges the validity of the information or the authenticity of the informant. Why should she make so much of keeping secrets, I wondered, secrets that don't have any apparent military or strategic value? The book, after all, is a public denunciation of murderous Indian removal politics in Guatemala, an exposé in an ethnographic frame. Yet throughout, Rigoberta claims that she purposely withholds cultural information. Is she a witness to abuse as an authentic victim, or is she being coy on the witness stand? The difference is significant, even if we will see that the alternatives are irreducibly tangled: Either she is a vulnerable vehicle for truth beyond her control, revealing information that compromises and infuriates the government; or she is exercising control over apparently irrelevant information, perhaps to produce her own strategic version of truth.

In what follows, a reference to Nietzsche will help to negotiate the distance between telling and troping, between relevant and irrelevant data. Then, lessons from Enrique Dussel, Paul Ricoeur, and the shades of Church-affiliated victims of Guatemalan death squads can remind us that bearing witness has been a sacred responsibility throughout Christianity, a responsibility that is related both etymologically and historically to martyrdom. I will suggest that Rigoberta glosses those lessons in her performance of ethically responsible survival. Her techniques include maintaining the secrets that keep readers from knowing her too well. One conclusion to be drawn is that giving and getting information should respect the cultural differences of an exchange that can produce alliances, if we are careful not to collapse positions into single-minded programs. Like the rhetorical figure of metonymy, alliance is a relationship of contiguity, not of metaphoric identification. To shorten the distance between writer and readers is what autobiographies do, in the game of mutual displacements that Paul de Man described as defacement. This invites identifications that make both positions unstable and finally make one of them redundant. Rigoberta is too smart to prepare her own removal, in the logic of meta-phoric evaporations of difference. Embattled Indians generally know that reductions are dangerous. Since the Conquest, *reducción* has been the name for violent pacification and for a defeated indigenous community controlled by Spanish masters.

Sympathy and Surveillance

But first we might notice that the audible protests of silence are, of course, responses to anthropologist Elisabeth Burgos Debray's line of questioning. If she were not asking what we must take to be impertinent questions, the Quiché informant would logically have no reason to refuse answers. From the introduction to *Me llamo Rigoberta Menchú* (1983), we know that the testimonial is being mediated at several levels by Burgos, who records, edits and arranges the information, so that knowledge in this text announces its partiality. The book, in other words, does not presume any immediacy between the narrating "I" and the readerly "you." Nor does Rigoberta proffer intimacy when she claims authorship for the interviews that remain catalogued under the interrogator's name (Britton and Dworkin, 214). Yet some readers have preferred the illusion of immediacy, deriving perhaps from certain (autobiographical?) habits of reading that project a real and knowable person onto the persona we are hearing, despite being told that the recorded voice is synthesized and processed, and despite the repeated reminders that our access is limited. Could the ardent interest, and our best intentions towards the informant, amount to construing the text as a kind of artless "confession," like the ones that characterized surveillance techniques of nineteenth century colonizers? For a recent and typical case of violation by sentimentality, consider the editors of *Autobiographical Essays by Native American Writers* who insisted that their contributors reveal and publish intimate information. "While our presentation of autobiographies of contemporary Native American writers may seem to testify to the congeniality of the autobiographical form to Indians today, the reality is finally much more complex. Thus, a contributor . . . movingly wrote in a covering letter: 'You should realize that focusing so intently on oneself like that and blithering on about your own life and thoughts is very bad form for Indians.'" In response to the reticence, the editors proudly report that they persisted and prevailed (Swann and Krupat, ix). Yet another example are the African American women who increasingly bring their experience more plainly into focus. Barbara Smith explains that part of the process is calling attention to the pain and the personal costs of telling.[1]

Maybe empathy for an informant is a good feeling that covers over a controlling disposition, what Derrida calls "an inquisitorial insistence, an order, a petition. . . . To demand the narrative of the other, to extort it from him like a secretless secret" (87). The possibility should give us pause. Natives who remained incalculable, because they refused to tell secrets, obviously frustrated the controlling mechanisms of colonial states (Bhabha, 99).

Rigoberta probably appreciated and deployed the aggressively passive ruse of leaving the interrogator unsatisfied, while her sentimental readers have missed the point. She too manages to frustrate unabashed demands for calculable confessions. One such frustration is recorded in Dinesh D'Souza's tirade against institutionalizing her testimonial in a required curriculum at Stanford University. He would surely have preferred scientific information about genuine Guatemalan Indians, stable objects of investigation. Instead he gets a protean subject of multiple discourses in Indian disguise (D'Souza, 71–73). Some of us, no doubt, would dismiss his inquisitorial demand for knowable essences. But my concern here is that the demand lingers in what passes for sentimental interest and solidarity. Sympathetic readers can be as reluctant as is D'Souza to doubt the sincerity of a life-story; they are reluctant, as well, to question their own motives for requiring intimate truth, even when they know that the life in their hands is a mediated text.

"What draws the reader to the novel," in Walter Benjamin's scornful observation, "is the hope of warming his shivering life with a death he reads about" (101). But novels seem unobliging today, given the sheer intellectual difficulty of important Latin American fiction since the "Boom" of the 1960s and 70s. Testimonials promise more warmth. In a strong case for the genre's distinctiveness, John Beverley argued that *testimonio* is poised *against* literature: that its collective denunciatory tone distinguishes testimony from the personal development narrative of standard autobiography. Testimonio allegedly erases the tracks of an elitist author who is mediating the narrative. This allows for a "fraternal or sororal" complicity between narrator and reader, in other words, a tighter bond of intimacy than is possible in manipulative and evasive narrative fiction (Beverley, 77, and generally chapters 4 and 5). I have already argued that the projections of presence and truth are less than generous here (Sommer, "Rigoberta's"). Empathy is hardly an ethical feeling, despite the enthusiasm for identifying with Others among some political activists, including some first-world feminists (See for example, Cornell, 97). In effect, the projections of intimacy invite appropriations once the stretch is shortened between writer and reader, in disregard of the text's rhetorical (decidedly fictional) performance of a politically safe distance. To close in on Rigoberta might be to threaten her authority and leadership.

The very fact that I am able to call self-critical attention to our culture-bound appetites is a sign that I have been reading Rigoberta. When I began, her forthright refusals to satisfy my interest woke me to the possibility that she was cultivating my interest so that I could feel the rebuff. Concerns about the text's authenticity— that is, transparency—seemed beside the point, as I began to appreciate its artful manipulations. Perhaps the informant was being more active and strategic than our essentialist notions of authenticity have allowed. The possibility triggered memories of other books that had refused intimacy, perhaps more subtly, so that their distancing tropes came into focus only then, as corollaries to Rigoberta's lesson. The unyielding tropes add up to a rhetoric of particularism that cautions privileged readers against easy appropriations of Otherness into manageable universal categories. Among those rhetorical moves, I remembered El Inca Garcilaso's introductory *Advertencias* about the difficulties of the Peruvian language, Juan Francisco Manzano's refusal to detail the humiliating scenes of Cuban slavery, "Jesusa Palancares"'s gruff dismissal of her interlocutor, and Toni Morrison's distinction between love and the demand for intimate confession, in *Beloved*. There were white authors, too, who theatricalized their incompetence to narrate colored lives across social asymmetries and cultural barriers: Cirilo Villaverde's *Cecila Valdés* (1882) and Cortázar's "The Pursuer" (1959); later, Vargas Llosa's *The Storyteller* (1987) would fit into the cluster of texts I now read more cautiously.

Why did we assume that our interest in the "Other" was reciprocated? Edward Said asked that question, at the public lecture, as he interrupted a sympathetic colleague who was asking how we could know the Orient better, and avoid the errors decried in *Orientalism*. Did we imagine that the desire was mutual, or that we were irresistible? Could we consider that the sympathy was not bilateral in an asymmetrical world? This possibility of non-requited interest is one lesson to be learned from the kind of textual resistance Rigoberta performs. The problems raised by presuming anything less than political inequality and cultural difference are both epistemological and ethical, problems that ring familiar now that postmodern skepticism has lowered the volume on masterly discourses in order to hear some competing, even incommensurate, voices.

Masterful reading is what some particularist narrators try to baffle. One is Rigoberta Menchú whose secrets can help to cordon off curious and controlling readers from the vulnerable objects of their attention. Secrecy is a safeguard to freedom, Emmanuel Levinas argues against Hegel who ridiculed it; it is the inviolable core of human subjectivity that makes interaction a matter of choice rather than rational necessity. "Only starting from this secrecy is the pluralism of society possible" (78–79). Menchú will repeat with Villaverde's contraband dealer in slaves, "Not everything is meant to be said" (Villaverde, 112). But her discretion is more subtle than his, and far less corrupt, since it is entirely possible that she is hiding very little. Perhaps, as I suggested, Menchú's audible silences and her wordy refusals to talk are calculated, not to cut short our curiosity, but to incite it, so that we feel our differences as frustrated intimacies.

Staged Standoffs

What I find so noteworthy about Rigoberta's testimonial, in contrast to most autobiographies, is that her refusals remain on the page after the editing is done. The refusals say, in effect, this document is a screen, in the double sense that Henri Lefebvre (78) uses the term: something that shows and that also covers up. From the beginning, the narrator tells us very clearly that she is not going to tell: "Indians have been very careful not to disclose any details of their communities" (*I, Rigoberta,* 9; in Spanish, 42). They are largely "public" secrets, known to the Quichés

and kept from us in a gesture of self-preservation. "They are told that the Spaniards dishonoured our ancestors' finest sons. . . . And it is to honour these humble people that we must keep our secrets. And no-one except we Indians must know" (13; in Spanish, 50. See also 17, 20, 59, 67, 69, 84, 125, 170, 188; in Spanish, 55, 60, 118, 131, 133, 155, 212, 275, 299). By some editorial or joint decision, the very last words of the testimonial are, "I'm still keeping secret what I think no-one should know. Not even anthropologists or intellectuals, no matter how many books they have, can find out all our secrets" (247; in Spanish, 377).

Readers have generally noticed the inevitable interference of the ethnographer in these transcriptions. And they have been predictably critical or disappointed at the loss of immediacy, perhaps with a resentment born of ardor that chafes at insulating frames that contain explosive life-stories. Most disturbing to many readers is probably Burgos Debray's Introduction, where she presumes to have shared intimacy and solidarity with Rigoberta as they shared nostalgic plates of black beans in Paris. Almost unremarked, however, but far more remarkable for being unanticipated, are the repeated and deliberate signs of asymmetry throughout Rigoberta's testimony. Either the informant, the scribe, or both were determined to keep a series of admonitions in the published text. Uncooperative gestures are probably typical of ethnographic interrogations, but they are generally deleted from the scientific reports as insignificant "noise." Here, however, scientific curiosity turns out to be impertinent, a conclusion we draw from the refusal to respond. And if she did not refuse decidedly and repeatedly, we might mistake her active negation for a passive inability. This contrast between the possibility of speech and an impossibility imposed by others is what Jean-François Lyotard adapts from Aristotle in order to distinguish between a plaintiff (who can attest to a crime against her) and a victim (who is silenced by her fear or is dismissed as irrelevant).[2] Are we being warned, by Rigoberta's active refusal, that curiosity may be an impulse to warm our cold bodies with the fuel of passionate and violated lives? Ironically, in the backhanded logic of metaleptic effects, our curiosity—the cause of Rigoberta's resistance—is a product of her performance. I wonder if she staged even more questions than she was asked, so that she could perform more refusals; this seductive possibility doesn't occur to Lyotard's legal logic.[3] Without refusing our putative interest often enough for us to notice, she could hardly have exercised the uncooperative control that turns a potentially humiliating scene of interrogation into an opportunity for self-authorization.

Nevertheless, the almost 400 pages of the original book are full of information. About herself, her community, traditional practices, the armed struggle, strategic decisions. Therefore, a reader may wonder why her final statement insists, for a last and conclusive time, that we "cannot know" her secrets. Why is so much attention being called to our insufficiency as readers? Does it mean that the knowledge is impossible or that it is forbidden? Is she saying that we are *incapable* of knowing, or that we *ought* not to know? My line of questioning is not entirely original, of course. It echoes the quandary that Nietzsche posed in a now famous posthumous work about the nature of language. If I repeat his dilemma here it is to highlight a particular textual strategy in Rigoberta's testimonial, to notice it and to respect its results.

Nietzsche begins his consideration of the possible truth value of language, including philosophical language that makes claims to truth, by wondering what our general criteria for validity are. The first, he says, is the identity principle: "We are unable to affirm and to deny one and the same thing." But he adds immediately, "this is a subjective empirical law, not the expression of any 'necessity' but only an inability. . . . The proposition therefore contains no criterion of

truth, but an imperative concerning that which should count as true" (quoted in de Man, *Allegories*, 119–20). In other words, the identity principle, which at least from Aristotle on has been the ground for logical claims to truth, merely *presupposes* that A equals A as an ethical restriction; it is a necessary beginning, a fiction that constructs a ground for systematic philosophical thinking. If the claims of philosophy are based on a fiction, there can evidently be no categorical difference between one kind of writing and another, between logic and literature. It is rather a difference of degree in self-consciousness. In literature, tropes are obviously constructed and fictional, while non-literary texts presume their tropes to be true. Yet language, Nietzsche argues, cannot absolutely affirm anything, without acknowledging that any affirmation is based on a collective lie. He concludes from this exposition that the difference between truth and fiction, philosophy and literature, constatives and performatives, philosophical persuasion and literary troping is finally undecidable.

How then are we to take Rigoberta's protestations of silence as she continues to talk? Are there really many secrets that she is not divulging, in which case her restraint would be true and real? Or is she performing a kind of rhetorical, fictional, seduction in which she lets the fringe of a hidden text show in order to tease us into thinking that the fabric must be extraordinarily complicated and beautiful, even though there may not be much more than fringe to show? If we happen not to be anthropologists, how passionately interested does she imagine the reader to be in her ancestral secrets? Yet her narrative makes this very assumption, and therefore piques a curiosity that may not have pre-existed her resistance. That is why it may be useful to notice that the refusal is performative; as I said, it constructs metaleptically the apparent cause of the refusal: our craving to know. Before she denies us the satisfaction of learning her secrets we may not be aware of any desire to grasp them. Another way of posing the alternatives is to ask whether she is withholding her secrets because we are so different and would understand them only imperfectly; or whether we should not know them for ethical reasons, because our knowledge would lead to power over her community.

Rigoberta continues to publicly perform this kind of silence, almost like a leitmotif. At an address delivered at the Political Forum of Harvard University, in April of 1994, she opened with some literally incomprehensible words for her audience. It was an incantatory flow pronounced between smiling lips under friendly eyes, words which a student asked her to translate during the question period. "No," was her polite response, "I cannot translate them." They were a formal and formulaic greeting in Quiché, she said, and they would lose their poetic quality in a different rendering. This speech act was not hostile, as I said; but it was distancing.

As in the case of Nietzsche's meditation on the nature of rhetoric in general, the choice between ethics and epistemology is undecidable. Because even if her own explicit rationale is the non-empirical, ethical rationale (claiming that we should not know the secrets because of the particular power attached to the stories we tell about ourselves) she suggests another reason. It is the degree of our foreignness, our cultural difference that would make her secrets incomprehensible to the outsider. We could never know them as she does, because we would inevitably force her secrets into our framework. "Theologians have come and observed us," for example, "and have drawn a false impression of the Indian world" (9, translation adjusted; in Spanish, 42).

Double Duty

Guatemalan Indians have a long history of being read wrong by outsiders who speak European languages. From the sixteenth century to the present, the Maya have been "Surviving Conquest," as a recent demographic analysis puts it. If some readers perceive a certain ahistorical inflection in Rigoberta's sense that the Spanish conquest is an event of the recent past, George Lovell might corroborate her sense of continuity in this new period of cultural genocide. "Viewed in historical perspective, it is disconcerting to think how much the twentieth century resembles the sixteenth, for the parallels between cycles of conquest hundreds of years apart are striking. Model villages are designed to serve similar purposes as colonial congregaciones— to function as the institutional means by which one culture seeks to reshape the ways and conventions of another, to operate as authoritarian mechanisms of resettlement, indoctrination, and control" (47; see also Manz). The less comprehension in/by Spanish, the better; it is the language that the enemy uses to conquer differences. For an Indian, to learn Spanish can amount to passing over to the other side, to the Ladinos, which simply means "Latin" or Spanish speakers. "My father used to call them 'ladinized Indians,' . . . because they act like *ladinos*, bad *ladinos*" (Menchú, *I, Rigoberta*, 24; in Spanish, 66). This kind of caution has managed to preserve Mayan cultural continuities, and the political solidarity it can activate, beyond the social scientific paradigms that have tried to account for it.[4]

All the theologians could not have been equally insensitive, however. Rigoberta, after all, became a Christian catechist devoted to the socially engaged spirit of liberation theology; and she continued to believe in a God who inspires political commitment, even after marxist comrades objected. Those objections surely underlined her determination to keep an autonomous distance from allies. Testimony itself, the very kind of juridically oriented narrative that she produces for us to read, is a Christian's obligation, as Paul

Ricoeur reminds us. He explains that from the moment God appeared directly to human beings, testimony has implied an investment of absolute value in historical, contingent, events (Ricoeur, 119). The Old Testament prophets had prepared the connection, with their divine intuitions of God's will. But it was the New Testament, where eternal truth irrupts into human history, that the juridical act of bearing witness obliged even average people to confront a defensive and punitive world (Ricoeur, 134). "When the test of conviction becomes the price of life, the witness changes his name; he is called a martyr. . . . *Martus* in Greek means witness" (Ricoeur, 129).

The root word also grounds Enrique Dussel's project to Latin Americanize ethical philosophy by way of lessons from theology of liberation: "He who opens himself to the other, is with him, and testifies to him. And that means *martyr*; he who 'testifies' to the other is a martyr. Because, before murdering the Other, totality will assassinate the one who denounced its sin against Otherness" (Dussel and Guillot, 29). One limitation of European, basically Levinasian, ethics, he objects, is that absolute and awe-inspiring Otherness leaves the philosopher paralyzed, too stunned and too cautious to do anything useful (Dussel and Guillot, 8–9). Another limitation is that in order to face Otherness, ethics turns its back to a long tradition of subject-centered ontology that has ravaged difference by reducing it to more of the same. For Levinas, in other words, to identify the Self *as* the subject of history would be self-serving. But, Dussel argues, if an inhospitable First World has always had its back turned to oneself, the discovery of Otherness at home is nothing less than liberating (Dussel and Guillot, 38). A Latin American ethics needs to be actively committed, not cautiously self-effacing. As a corollary, or rather as a precondition for activity, it needs to refocus the Levinasian asymmetry from this side of the re-

lationship between colonial centers and colonized peripheries.

Gayatri Spivak used to quip that if the subaltern could speak, she would be something else (*Post-Colonial*, 158). But more recently and more reflectively in collaboration with subaltern historians, Spivak has appreciated the "subject-effects" of subaltern eloquence ("Introduction," 12). It is the eloquence of what might be called a genre of "speech-acts" that inverts the relationship between tenor and vehicle (just as Self and Other change places from the center to the sidelines) and recognizes the acts of organized resistance as a narrative speech. For Dussel and Guillot, too, violence is the language of a "subaltern" committed philosophy. Liberation means reconstituting the Alterity of the Other in a fallen world where Cain has already murdered Abel (Dussel and Guillot, 27), a violated and violent world. "If there is no reply to domination, nothing happens; but if a reply is made, the war begins" (Dussel and Guillot, 18). At the end of his essay, in a climax after which words are insufficient, he repeats, "The war begins" (43).

From the comments by Ricoeur and Dussel, it would seem that a commitment to absolute imperatives requires physical self-sacrifice, that the discourse of subalternity is written in blood and in the statistics of martyrdom. On the other hand, sacrificial responsibility can be finessed, somehow. Maybe an immobilized posture of awe before so much responsibility can keep philosophy out of the fray; or maybe a purely rhetorical self-defense can slip off the mantle of martyr that witnessing would dress on its vehicles. In terms of Rigoberta's personal comportment, to recall the apparently incommensurable difference between vulnerable testimony and coy control, either she accepts the traditional Christian robe, or she designs disguises.

But Ricoeur confounds the polarity by adding another, mediating, term: it is the incorrigibly compromising term of our fallible human languages. Charged with a communicative duty imposed by absolute truth, language cannot avoid humanizing, not to say debasing, the message by interpreting it. There is no help for it; even sacred testimony passes through the contingency of interpretation. So, Ricoeur concludes, the only possible philosophy of testimony is hermeneutics, an interpretation (143). Testimony is hermeneutical in a double sense: it both gives a content to be interpreted, and calls for an interpretation; it narrates facts, and it confesses a faith during the juridical moments that link history to eternity (Ricoeur, 142).

Rigoberta apparently appreciates the double duty of testifying: the message of liberation pulls in one (ideal) direction, and the (earthly) medium of political persuasion pulls in another. To confuse the two would be worse than simply foolish. It might be disastrous to mistake unconditional demands for justice with what she evidently senses as sentimental interest from interrogators and readers. Their offers of solidarity may not stop to distinguish doing good from feeling good. The double challenge for this Christian leader, as new and as beleaguered as Christ's first witnesses, is to serve truth in ways that make a difference in the world. Testimony to that truth and coyness about how to convey it turn out to be voices in counterpoint. If we cannot hear the complexity, perhaps the inability is simply that, as Nietzsche would remind us, rather than a sign that contradictions cannot exist.

"J'accuse" rings loudly throughout the text, between the provocative, and protective, pauses of information flow. The pauses work in two directions, because it seems quite clear that Rigoberta's secrets are doubly strategic. They stop avid readers in their appropriative tracks, tracks that threaten to overstep the narrator's authority by assuming an unobstructed textual terrain. We have detoured here from the autobiographical meeting place where one particular life can become the potential experiences of others. Ri-

goberta Menchú's performance doesn't describe an isolated individual whom we can reproduce through readers who decide to pick her up. Her testimony is "not a personal story," as she makes clear from the first interview session; instead it is communal, grounded in collective memory and practices. The book grips the reader more than it gives. It demands responsibility more than it satisfies curiosity. An autobiography might not have stinted on giving the pleasure of vicarious fears and passions; but Rigoberta evidently understood that frustration has a political purpose. By stinting and explaining why, she can keep us ardently but respectfully engaged.

Notes

I would like to thank Luis Cifuentes, Bradley Epps, Antonio Benítez Rojo, Amrita Basu, and Jonathan Flatley for their encouragement.

1. Smith, 158: "It seems overwhelming to break such a massive silence. Even more numbing, however, is the realization that so many of the women who will read this have not yet noticed us missing either from their reading matter, their politics, or their lives."

2. Lyotard, #14: "Not to speak is part of the ability to speak, since ability is a possibility and a possibility implies something and its opposite. . . . To be able not to speak is not the same as not to be able to speak. The latter is a deprivation, the former a negation. (Aristotle, *De Interpretatione* 21 b 12–17; *Metaphysics* IV 1022 b 22ff.)"

3. Lyotard, #26. "Silence can indicate my incompetence to hear, the lack of any event or relevant information to recount, the unworthiness of the witness, or a combination of these."

4. See Nash, 9: "The rebellion attests to the extraordinary durability of distinctive cultures in Middle America. Anthropologists have attributed this persistence variously to indigenous withdrawal into zones of retreat, exploitation in the form of internal colonialism, and Catholic traditions imposed by the conquerors to encumber native groups with debts for religious celebrations. These earlier theories stressed

one side or the other of the dominant-subordinate hierarchy, with those maintaining the essentialist position emphasizing primordial cultural characteristics and those arguing domination from above emphasizing that forced acculturation has conditioned indigenous responses. Structuralists attacked the functionalism of those emphasizing the rational basis for distinctive indigenous characteristics, while their opponents challenged economic determinists for failing to recognize the preconquest ideological constructs manifested across wide regions.

"Protagonists on both sides of this older debate have shown that the persistence of distinct beliefs and practices among indigenous populations of the Americas arises from internal resources and from pressures exerted by the dominant group. Current debates are taking into account the combined force of antagonistic but interpenetrating relationships between *indígenas* and *ladinos* as they generate and sustain ethnic diversity . . . By looking inward at 'narrative strategies for resisting terror' (Warren *The Violence Within: Cultural and Political Opposition in Divided Nations* Boulder, Westview 1993), evoking dialogue between ancient and present traditions (Gossen and Leventhal 1989), and assessing the economic opportunities that condition their survival, researchers are constructing a theory that recognizes both the structural imperatives of the colonial and postcolonial systems encapsulating indigenous peoples and their own search for a base from which to defend themselves and generate collective action."

Works Cited

Alegría, Claribel, and D. J. Flakoll. *No me agarran viva: La mujer salvadoreña en lucha.* Mexico: Serie Popular Era, 1983.

Bakhtin, Mikhail M. *The Dialogic Imagination.* Trans. Michael Holquist and Caryl Emerson. Austin: University of Texas Press, 1980.

Barrios de Chungara, Domitila. *"Si me permiten hablar . . . ": Testimonio de Domitila, una mujer de las minas de Bolivia.* Ed. Moema Viezzer. Mexico: Siglo Veintiuno Editores, 1977, *Let Me Speak!* Ed. Moema Viezzer, trans. Victoria Ortiz. New York: Monthly Review Press, 1978.

Benjamin Walter. *Illuminations.* Edited and with an introduction by Hannah Arendt. Translated by Harry Zohn. New York: Schocken, 1969.

Bercovitch, Sacvan. *The Rites of Assent: Transformations in the Symbolic Construction of America.* New York: Routledge, 1993.

Bernard, H. Russell, and Jesús Salinas Pedraza. *Native Ethnography: A Mexican Indian Describes His Culture.* Newbury Park, CA: Sage, 1989.

Beverley, John. *Against Literature.* Minneapolis: University of Minnesota Press, 1993.

Bhabha, Homi K. *The Location of Culture.* New York: Routledge, 1994.

Britton, Alice, and Kenya Dworkin. "Rigoberta Menchú: 'Los indígenas no nos quedamos como bichos aislados, inmunes, desde hace 500 años. No. Nosotros hemos sido protagonistas de la historia.'" *Nuevo Texto Crítico,* no. 11 (1993).

Cornell, Drucilla. "What Is Ethical Feminism?" In Seyla Benhabib, Judith Butler, Drucilla Cornell, Nancy Fraser, *Feminist Contentions: A Philosophical Exchange.* Intro by Linda Nicholson. New York: Routledge, 1995.

Cortazar, Julio. *El Perseguidor y otros relatos.* Barcelona: Brugera, 1959.

De Man, Paul. *Allegories of Reading.* New Haven: Yale University Press, 1979.

De Man, Paul. "Autobiography as De-facement." *The Rhetoric of Romanticism.* New York: Columbia University Press, 1984.

Derrida, Jacques. "Living On: Border Lines." In *Deconstruction and Criticism,* ed. J. Derrida, P. de Man, J. Hillis Miller, H. Bloom, and G. Hartman. London: Routledge & Kegan Paul, 1979.

Diskin, Martin. "Anthropological Fieldwork in Mesoamerica: Focus on the Field" *Latin American Research Review* 30, no. 1 (1995): 163–75.

D'Souza, Dinesh. *Illiberal Education.* New York: Free Press, 1991.

Dussel, Enrique, and Daniel E. Guillot. *Liberación Latinoamericana y Emmanuel Levinas.* Buenos Aires: Editorial Bonum, 1975.

Gusdorf, Georges. "Conditions and Limits of Autobiography." In *Autobiography: Essays Theoretical and Critical,* ed. James Olney. Princeton: Princeton University Press, 1980. 28–48.

Jameson, Fredric. "Criticism in History." In *Weapons*

of Criticism: Marxism in America and the Literary Tradition, ed. Norman Rudich. Palo Alto, CA: Ramparts Press, 1976. 31–50.

Laclau, Ernesto. "Populist Rupture and Discourse." *Screen Education* 34 (Spring 1980): 87–93.

Laclau, Ernesto, and Chantal Mouffe. *Hegemony & Socialist Strategy: Towards a Radical Democratic Politics.* London: Verso, 1985.

Leduc, Violette. *La bâtarde.* Paris: Gallimard, 1964.

Lefebvre Henri. "Toward a Leftist Cultural Politics: Remarks Occasioned by the Centenary of Marx's Death." Trans. David Reifman. In *Marxism and the Interpretation of Culture,* ed. Cary Nelson and Lawrence Grossberg. Urbana: University of Illinois Press, 1988.

Leiris, Michel. *La règle du jeu.* 4 vols. Paris: Gallimard, 1948–76.

Lejeune, Philippe. *L'Autobiographie en France.* Paris: Armand Colin, 1971.

Lejeune, Philippe. "Le pacte autobiographique." *Poétique* 14 (1973): 137–62, esp. 160–62.

Lejeune, Philippe. *Le pacte autobiographique.* Paris: Seuil, 1975.

Levinas, *Ethics and Infinity.* Pittsburgh: Duquesne University Press, 1985.

Lovell, W. George. "Surviving Conquest: The Maya of Guatemala in Historical Perspective." *Latin American Research Review* 23, no. 2 (1988): 25–57.

Lugones, María, and Elizabeth Spelman. "Have We Got a Theory for You! Feminist Theory, Cultural Imperialism and the Demand for 'The Woman's Voice.'" *Women's Studies International Forum* 6 (1983): 573–81.

Lyotard, Jean-François. *The Differrend: Phrases in Dispute.* Trans. Georges Van Den Abbeele. Minneapolis: University of Minnesota Press, 1992.

Manz, Beatriz. *Refugees of a Hidden War: The Aftermath of Counterinsurgency in Guatemala.* Albany: State University of New York Press, 1988.

Manzano, Juan Francisco. *Autobiografía, cartas y versos de Juan Fco. Mainzano.* Habana: Municipio de la Habana, 1937.

Manzano, Juan Francisco. *The Autobiography of a Slave.* Ed. Ivan A. Schulman. Trans. Evelyn Picon Garfield. Detroit: Wayne State University Press, 1996.

Marks, Eklaine. "'I am my own heroine': Some Thoughts About Women and Autobiography in France." In *Teaching about Women in the Foreign Languages: French, Spanish, German, Russian,* ed. Sidonie Cassirer. Prepared for the Commission on the Status of Women of the MLA. Old Westbury: Feminist Press, 1975. 1–10.

Menchú, Rigoberta. *Me llamo Rigobereta Menchú.* Habana: Casa de las Americas, 1983.

Menchú, Rigoberta. *I, Rigoberta Menchú: An Indian Woman in Guatemala.* Edited and introduced by Elisabeth Burgos-Debray. Trans. Ann Wright. London: Verso, 1984.

Michaels, Walter Benn. "Race into Culture: A Critical Genealogy of Cultural Identity." *Critical Inquiry* 18 (Summer 1992): 665–85.

Molloy, Sylvia. *At Face Value: Autobiographical Writing in Spanish America.* Cambridge: Cambridge University Press, 1991.

Nash, June. "The Reassertion of Indigenous Identity: Mayan Responses to State Intervention in Chiapas." *Latin American Research Review* 30, no. 3 (1995): 7–41.

Poniatowska, Elena. *Hasta no verte Jesús mío.* Mexico: Editiones Era, 1969.

Ricoeur, Paul. "The Hermeneutics of Testimony." In *Essays on Biblical Interpretation,* ed. Lewis S. Mudge. Philadelphia: Fortress Press, 1980. 119–54.

Rosenblatt, Roger. "Black Autobiography: Life as the Death Weapon." In *Autobiography: Essays Theoretical and Critical,* ed. James Olney. Princeton: Princeton University Press, 1980. 166–75.

Sarmiento, Domingo Faustino. *Recuerdos de provincia.* 1850. Barcelona: Ramón Sopena, 1931.

Smith, Barbara. "Toward a Black Feminist Criticism." In *But Some of Us Are Brave: Black Women's Studies,* ed. Gloria Hall, Patricia Bell Scott, and Smith. New York: Feminist Press, 1982. 157–75.

Sommer, Doris. *One Master for Another: Populism as Patriarchal Rhetoric in Dominican Novels.* Lanham, MD: University Press of America, 1983.

Sommer, Doris. "Rigoberta's Secrets." *Latin American Perspectives* 18, no. 3 (1991): 32–50. Special Issue on Testimonials, ed. George Gugelburger.

Sommer, Doris. "Resisting the Heat: Menchú, Morrison, and Incompetent Readers." In *Cultures of United States Imperialism,* ed. Donald Pease and Amy Kaplan. Durham: Duke University Press, 1994. 407–32.

Spivak, Gayatri Chakravorty. Introduction. In Ranajit Guha and Gayatri Chakravorty Spivak, *Selected Subaltern Studies.* Foreword by Edward W. Said. Oxford: Oxford University Press, 1988.

Spivak, Gayatri Chakravorty. *The Post-Colonial Critic: Interviews, Strategies, Dialogues.* Ed. Sarah Harasym. New York: Routledge, 1990.

Steiner, George. *After Babel: Aspects of Language and Translation.* London and New York: Oxford University Press, 1975.

Swann, Brian, and Arnold Krupat. *I Tell You Now: Autobiographical Essays by Native American Writers.* Lincoln: University of Nebraska Press, 1987.

Vargas Llosa, Mario. *The Storyteller.* New York: Farrar, Straus, Giroux, 1989.

Vega, Garcilaso de la. *Comentarios reales de los incas.* Lima: Fondo de Cultura Económica, 1991.

Villaverde, Cirilo. *Cecilia Valdes.* Habana: Editorial Lex, 1953.

Wittgenstein, Ludwig. *Philosophical Investigations.* 1953. Trans. G. E. M. Anscombe. New York: Macmillan, 1968.

Yúdice, George. "Testimonio and Postmodernism (1991)." In *The Real Thing: Testimonial Discourse and Latin America.* Ed. Georg M. Gugelberger. Durham: Duke University Press, 1996 42–57.

15 Resisting Autobiography: Out-Law Genres and Transnational Feminist Subjects

Caren Kaplan

The Law of Genre

. . . In his essay "The Law of Genre," Jacques Derrida suggests that the institution of literature (in collusion with its siblings in Western humanism—philosophy, history, and so on) works a particularly duplicitous arrangement. The "law of genre" is based on a "counterlaw"; that is, the possibility of genre limits is always already undermined by the impossibility of maintaining those very limits. Yet the law of genre asserts that "genres are not to be mixed":

> As soon as the word "genre" is sounded, as soon as it is heard, as soon as one attempts to conceive it, a limit is drawn. And when a limit is established, norms and interdictions are not far behind: "Do," "Do not" says "genre," the word "genre," the figure, the voice, or the law of genre. . . . Thus, as soon as genre announces itself, one must respect a norm, one must not cross a line of demarcation, one must not risk impurity, anomaly or monstrosity.[1]

A brief glance at the history of autobiography criticism in the West confirms Derrida's thesis. Although genre criticism frequently consists of continual definition and redefinition, most autobiography criticism appears to be engaged in a vigorous effort to stabilize and fix generic boundaries. . . .

Adopting Derrida's version of genre production in the service of autobiography criticism poses both limits and possibilities. The limits of Western literary structures are abundantly obvious in the powerful elisions, co-optations, and experiments that constitute cultural margins. As counterlaw, or *out-law,* such productions often break most obvious rules of genre. Locating out-law genres enables a deconstruction of the "master" genres, revealing the power dynamics embedded in literary production, distribution, and reception.

Out-law genres in autobiographical discourse at the present moment mix two conventionally "unmixable" elements—autobiography criticism and autobiography as thing itself. Thus, in all the cultural productions that I will discuss, critical accountability is implicitly or explicitly a primary subject. These emerging out-law genres require more collaborative procedures that are more closely attuned to the power differences among participants in the process of producing the text. Thus, instead of a discourse of individual authorship, we find a discourse of situation; a "politics of location."[2]

I will examine a number of versions of the discourse of situation: expansions or revolutions of generic boundaries that rework and challenge conventional notions of critic and author (including prison memoir, testimonial literature, ethnographic writing, "biomythography," "cultural autobiography," and "regulative psychobiography"). I juxtapose these alternative genres not as a comprehensive list or complete map of global literary production that refers to the "autobiographical" tradition, but as an indication of a variety of reading and writing strategies in operation as the law of genre intersects with contemporary postcolonial, transnational conditions.

Resistance Literature: Women's Prison Memoirs as Out-Law Genre

Barbara Harlow uses the term "resistance literature" to describe a body of writing that has been marginalized in literary studies: writing marked by geopolitical situation.[3] As a global phenomenon, resistance literature is created out of political conflicts between Western imperialism and non-Western indigenous resistant movements. Resistance literature, therefore, breaks many of elite literature's laws: it is comparative but not always linked to a national language; it is overtly political, sometimes anonymous, always pressuring the boundaries of established genres. . . .

The choice of autobiography as a genre by women in nonmetropolitan or non-Western prisons will necessarily change the narrative structure itself to reflect what Harlow calls "secular critical consciousness."[4] The prison writing of Third World women does not automatically conform to conventional genre specifications, but "it does . . . propose alternative parameters for the definition and articulation of literary conventions."[5] Harlow names Bessie Head, Nawal al-Saadawi, Akhtar Baluch, Domitila Barrios de Chungara, Ruth First, and Raymonda Tawil

as writers whose works constitute an emerging genre that challenges and reworks dominant social structures. . . .

Harlow asserts that the texts she discusses rewrite "the social order to include a vision of new relational possibilities which transcend ethnic, class, and racial divisions as well as family ties."[6] This view of Third World women's writing as dynamic and synthetic unravels the polar opposition between Western feminism and non-Western women. Harlow deconstructs the gender-specific modernity of Western feminism as well as the monolithic, antimodern nationalism of non-Western women to propose transnational affiliations among liberation movements. Reading women's prison writing as resistance literature provides "new modes of affiliation" based on the "material conditions of people themselves."[7]

The critical consciousness produced by the reworking of a conventional genre such as autobiography in a specific relocation such as the experience of detainment creates genre destabilization. The essential categories of autobiography, especially as adopted by Western feminism in the last twenty years—the revelation of individuality, the chronological unfolding of a life, reflections and confessions, the recovery and assertion of suppressed identity—are utilized, reworked, and even abandoned. The primacy of the individual author whose mind is separate and unique is especially moribund in the context of Harlow's "women's prison." Ultimately, we read the rejection of purely aesthetic categories in favor of a worldly, politicized framework for narrative and cultural production in the texts that Harlow highlights in her work.

Once the author has been deconstructed in postcolonial and neocolonial contexts, the question remains how to situate the critic and, especially, the figure combining and managing the functions of translator, editor, and collaborator in the production of particular kinds of "autobiographical" discourse emerging from non-Western locations. The testimony of non-Western women that arrives in the West in book form requires new strategies of reading cultural production *as* transnational activity. Treating the "author" of the "testimonial" as an authentic, singular voice without acknowledging the mediations of the editors and market demands of publishing can result in new forms of exoticization and racism. The nature of the relationship between author and critic in the instance of testimonial writing is never simple or nonpolitical, and must always be charted.

Testimonial Literature and the Question of Authenticity

Testimonial literature, because it usually takes the form of first-person narrative elicited or transcribed and edited by another person, participates in a particularly delicate realm of collaboration. Like many emerging genres, *testimonio* (as this form of writing is called in Latin American contexts) has an out-law and an "in-law" function. As an out-law genre, testimonial literature is a form of "resistance literature"; it expresses transitional material relations in neo- and postcolonial societies and disrupts mainstream literary conventions. Testimonial literature highlights the possibilities for solidarity and affiliations among critics, interviewers, translators, and the subject who "speaks." As an in-law genre, *testimonio* may refer to colonial values of nostalgia and exoticization, values that operate via a discourse of "truth" and "authenticity." ...

Testimonio read as out-law genre provides a powerful critique of the colonial discourse inherent to Western feminist discussions of identity politics in autobiography. Doris Sommer's essay on *testimonio* and the concerns of feminist autobiography, "'Not Just a Personal Story': Women's *Testimonios* and the Plural Self," does not just contrast the singular "I" of conventional Western autobiography to the collective "I" of *testimonio*. Reading *I, Rigoberta Menchú* and *Let Me Speak! Testimony of Domitila, a Woman of the Bolivian Mines* as exemplary testimonial productions, requiring the collaboration of testifier, interviewer, and, sometimes, translator, Sommer emphasizes the difference between autobiographical and testimonial strategies of identification:

> The testimonial "I" does not invite us to identify with it. We are too different, and there is no pretense here of universal or essential human experience. . . . The singular represents the plural not because it replaces or subsumes the group but because the speaker is a distinguishable part of the whole.[8]

Thus, testimonial literature, by the very nature of its mode of production, calls attention to a process that is more often muted or invisible in autobiographical writing. . . .

The destabilizing effect of testimony comes through reading as well as through writing; that is, our responsibility as critics lies in opening the categories so that the process of collaboration extends to reception. Refusing to read testimonial writing by poor and imprisoned women *only* as autobiography links resistance literature to resistance criticism. The possibility of transnational feminist cultural production requires affiliations among prison memoir, life writing, political testimonial, autobiography, and ethnography. Each category is provisional and different in relation to specific struggles and locations. Learning to read the differences will engender the possibility of strategic similarities.

Ethnography and the Question of Authorship

Ethnographic writing shares issues of authorship and power with testimonial writing and the other forms considered here. All potential out-law genres are highly mediated. These genres are produced within the matrix of colonial and postcolonial discourses that discipline the humanities. Reading ethnographic writing as an out-law genre challenges the traditional hierarchy of objective scientist and native informant in mainstream anthropology and demystifies the "literary" classics of the field. Linking ethnography to the issues raised by prison memoir and testimonial literature deconstructs the nostalgia for perfect rapport between the fieldworker and the "Other."

The recent publication of a set of books that "read" the activity of "writing culture," drawing on the various interpretive strategies available to the literary critic (especially poststructuralist theories), has politicized the poetics of anthropology.[9] As a result, the role of the ethnographer as reader and writer has been destabilized and retheorized even as the position and subjectivity of the informant have come to be renegotiated. . . . [10]

Questions of power and the legacies of colonialism in ethnography as a written mode of production must be raised in texts that chart the encounters of Western and non-Western women. Kamala Visweswaran suggests that the first-person narrative is a logical form to convey the dilemmas and solutions of cross-cultural interaction, even as this mode leads to narratives of "imperfect rapport" that construct and support colonial discourse.[11] Visweswaran suggests that there is an entire genre of "confessional" first-person accounts written by Western women that has been ignored or rejected by conventional and experimental anthropologists, a genre that constitutes an important element in colonial discourse. To dismiss this literature as "too subjective" or "confessional" or even literarily uninteresting is to miss the political and cultural issues raised by the encounters between Western and non-Western women. Visweswaran

explains: "Questions of positionality more often than not confront female rather than male field workers, and the female ethnographer is more likely to be faced with a decision over which world she enters."[12]

. . . Visweswaran asserts that "a feminist anthropologist cannot assume the willingness of women to talk."[13] In his study of the construction of "autobiography" by both ethnographer and indigenous subject, Roger Keesing argues that scrupulous attention to the micropolitics of the "elicitation situation," the context of interviewer and interviewee, raises critical questions about how women's subjectivity is formed, reported, and interpreted. . . .

. . . Ethnography as autobiographical out-law genre, like testimonial writing, requires radical revisions of notions of individual authorship and authenticity. For the subject of ethnographic writing to circulate in transnational culture as "author," essentialist mythologies of identity and authorship must be challenged and bracketed in favor of reading strategies that acknowledge the complexities of power in the production of life writing from nonmetropolitan, non-Western locations. The stakes in developing nonexploitative political alliances between women from different parts of the world to produce documents that empower the subjects of ethnographic writing are very high. Feminists who are alert to power dynamics in identity politics will find in resistance literature and out-law genres useful models of multiracial, multinational, multiethnic, and polysexual struggle.

Biomythography: Lesbian Identities and Literary Production

One location of the struggle for multiple identification strategies in the field of late-twentieth-century Western culture is the cultural revolution of politicized sexual preference characterized by gay and lesbian liberation. In an effort to identify effective methods of representation that counter damaging stereotypes, some lesbian and gay writers have utilized autobiographical forms to varying extents, from conventionally celebratory to experimental forms. The construction of a political entity that can agitate for change in Western democratic social structures requires the support of cultural institutions such as literature. The construction of sexual identity and the creation of literary genres are linked by necessity in the process of cultural production. . . .

[Biddy Martin's] deconstruction of conventional assumptions of identity and genre [see her essay in this volume] can be found, as well, in Katie King's recent work on contemporary sexualities and debates about cultural production. In her essay "Audre Lorde's Lacquered Layerings: The Lesbian Bar as a Site of Literary Production," King highlights Lorde's term "biomythography" for her autobiographical memoir, *Zami*, as naming "a variety of generic strategies in the construction of gay and lesbian identity in the USA."[14] "Biomythography," King suggests, is "a writing down of our meanings of identity . . . with the materials of our lives."[15] The generic strategy of biomythography focuses on the process as well as the materials of autobiographical narrative without insisting on any one rule or form. As King writes:

> The generic strategies of the biomythography of lesbian and gay history currently include historical monograph and book, polemical critique, film and video and slide show, oral history, review essay, introspective analysis, academic/polemical anthology, novel and poem and short story, and undoubtedly others as well.[16]

. . . Biomythography as out-law genre requires a recognition of "layers of meanings, layers of histories, layers of readings and rereadings through webs of power-charged codes."[17]

In this particularized sense, "difference" becomes a material reality that can be charted. As King writes in another essay: "This doesn't mean that gay people have no interests in common: we do. But our coalitions and identities are in flux and appropriately so."[18] Making "maps" of changing affiliations and coalitions is part of the "work" of biomythography as text. The bridging of disparate and shifting concerns and identities raised in biomythography echoes the political affiliations forged through the coalition work that engenders transnational feminisms. The critique of identity politics (and the forms of autobiography that are attached to modern Western structures of identity) requires the reformulation of authorship and selfhood found in emerging out-law genres.

Rewriting Home: The Coalition Politics of Cultural Autobiography

Traditionally, Western autobiographical writing has participated in the literary construction of "home"; a process of generalizing the particular, fabricating a narrative space of familiarity, and crafting a narrative that links the individual to the universal. The homogenizing influence of autobiography genres identifies similarities; reading an autobiography involves assimilating or consenting to the values and worldview of the writer. Out-law genres renegotiate the relationship between personal identity and the world, between personal and social history. Here, narrative inventions are tied to a struggle for cultural survival rather than purely aesthetic experimentation or individual expression.

A concern with the "rapid disintegration of black folk experience" leads bell hooks to life writing and the complicated process of reworking the autobiographical genre.[19] In her essay "Writing Autobiography," hooks uses the genre to preserve and transmit experiences of black southern life. Autobiography, she argues, can counter some of the damaging effects of capitalism and middle-class cultural domination. Remembering experiences nonsynchronous with dominant culture, hooks contends, is the activity of cultural and personal survival. . . .

The joining of fragments in hooks's autobiographical process does not result in a seamless accommodation of generic rules. Rather, the process of delineating a narrative space of the coexistence of disparate parts underscores a productive tensions between homogeneity and difference. In her essay "Coalition Politics," Bernice Johnson Reagon argues that a distinction has to be made between "home" and "coalition"; a difference between the safety net of similarity and familiarity and the difficult but necessary terrain of diversity and unfamiliarity.[20] Writing a life story as both an affirmation of "home" and a declaration of affiliation through coalition work requires alternative versions of self, community, and identity, versions that may be read in the production of some kinds of out-law genres. . . .

Staying alive—cultural and personal survival—fuels the narrative engines of out-law genres. An oppositional relationship to writing and to genres such as autobiography requires the difficult embrace of unfamiliar narrative strategies as well as the validating insertion of your own familiar modes of expression and your own systems of signification. The histories of coalitions—their dynamism and their difficulties—can be charted as cultural autobiographies of communities in crisis and resistance. The struggle *in* writing remains to be read and recognized by literary criticism. First, it is necessary to read the narratives of coalition politics as cultural autobiographies. Second, personal histories that link the individual with particular communities at given historical junctures can be read as cultural autobiographies. The link between individual and community forged in the reading and writing of coalition politics de-

constructs the individualism of autobiography's Western legacy and casts the writing and reading of out-law genres as a mode of cultural survival.

Regulative Psychobiographies: Postcolonial Subjects

Even as the interaction of coalition work and diverse identities presents opportunities for the expression of "subaltern" subject positions, Gayatri Spivak suggests that there is another subject who is so under-represented as to be absent even from "emerging" out-law genres. Drawing on the work of June Nash and Maria Patricia Fernandez-Kelly, Spivak considers the difference between the colonial subject and a new international neocolonial subject who can be found in the proliferation of export-processing zones (otherwise known as EPZs).[21] EPZs, or "free-trade zones," have emerged as export-led industrialization has become the preferred mode of development since the mid 1960s. Protective trade barriers that worked in favor of individual nations such as the United States and Great Britain have been dismantled to construct the EPZs. The export-processing zones require a "free flow" of "capital and goods across national boundaries," thereby contributing to the creation of transnational culture.[22] Annette Fuentes and Barbara Ehrenreich report that the majority of the more than one million workers in EPZs are women, and that the preferred work force in the multinational-controlled plants and domestically owned subcontracting factories outside the EPZs is female.[23] This is the context for Spivak's analysis of the condition of women in transnational culture, "fractured by the international division of labor."[24]

Spivak describes a time when the traditional subject of colonialism was violently remolded by consumer capitalism. As territorial imperialism developed legal and social codes to legitimate the new colonial structure, the colonial subject entered the "struggle for individualism." [25] Drawing on Spivak's description of subaltern subject formation, I would argue that autobiographical expression, along with other cultural signposts of individualism, became part of the economy of colonialism, that is, part of the division of labor that produced subject positions and the artifacts of subjectivity. We can locate most resistance literatures and out-law genres on the borders between colonial and neocolonial systems, where subjectivity, cultural power, and survival are played out in the modern era. . . .

Can the critical practice of out-law genres, as defined so far, address this neocolonial subject? Are there out-law genres that interact with the new feudal mode of production in operation in the EPZs? Out-law genres challenge Western critical practices to expand their parameters and, consequently, shift the subject of autobiography from the individual to a more unstable collective entity. If the individual subject is not constituted in the social framework of the free-trade zones (in any of its traditional areas: law, psychology, medicine, and so on), what forms of cultural production work against domination and exploitation?

Since poststructuralist psychoanalytic theories of subject formation and object relations cannot adequately address the constitution of the neocolonial subject and her oppressors, Spivak argues, feminist critics must develop an alternative procedure, a more intensely collaborative method. The "narrative" form that must be invented is "regulative psychobiography": the expressions "that constitute the subject-effect of these women, give these women a sense of their 'I.'" [26] The model narratives that Spivak refers to as "regulative psychobiographies" are less obvious to "us" at the present moment. Spivak asks: "What narratives produce the signifiers of the subject for other traditions? . . . traces of this psychobiography can be found in the in-

digenous legal tradition, in the scriptures, and of course, in myth." [27]

In her study of women in the free-trade zones of Malaysia, Aihwa Ong found "four overlapping sets of discourses about factory women: corporate, political, Islamic, and personal." [28] If we embrace Spivak's project, the regulative psychobiographies produced in the Malaysian context that Ong studied, for example, would require a densely layered study, with input from people with various forms of expertise and knowledge. Spivak urges Western feminists to develop the skills and methods necessary for this multilayered coalition project. Without this effort, she warns, we will leave transnational knowledge in the hands of the military-industrial complex.

Transnational Feminism and the Politics of Culture

A discussion of autobiographical out-law genres in the postcolonial and neocolonial era of transnational capital leads us to a conception of collaborative work that can best be described by Katie King's term "feminist writing technologies." [29] Taking Spivak's collaborative conception of "regulative psychobiography" into consideration, "feminist writing technologies" suggests a global project that employs the efforts of many people, rather than the act of a single hand lifting pen to paper or an individual pressing the keys on a keyboard. "Feminist writing technologies" can transform cultural production from individualized and aestheticized procedures to collaborative, historicized, transnational coalitions. Yet, because the electronic communications technologies we use are literally made by women in the free-trade zones and our "sisters" in the assembly plants in the West, Western feminists must be alert to our participation in the international division of labor. Transnational feminisms are enabled by the very conditions that have created the "Third World female subproletariat," the neocolonial subject. Therefore, to quote Saralee Hamilton, "If feminism is going to mean anything to women all over the world, it's going to have to find new ways to resist corporate power internationally."[30]

In this world-system of asymmetrical participation in cultural and industrial production, the activities of writing and reading cannot remain neutral. These power dynamics construct genres and countergenres, including autobiography and criticism. Autobiography may not have enjoyed a central role in literary studies until recently, but its outsider status has not automatically aligned it with resistance. This essay has argued that resistance is a mode of historical necessity, that Western feminism must participate in this moment, and that the critical practice of outlaw genres challenges the hierarchical structures of patriarchy, capitalism, and colonial discourse. Reading prison memoir, *testimonio,* ethnography, "biomythography," cultural autobiography, "regulative psychobiography," and other challenges to the conventions of autobiography in an oppositional mode moves Western feminist criticism into transnational coalition work. Feminist criticism as activism, in an expanded transnational sense, will produce theories and methods of culture and representation grounded in the material conditions of our similarities and differences. The deconstruction of autobiography in transnational feminist criticism marks the constitution of "writing technologies" that can work *for* and *with* women so that the law of genre will no longer dominate the representation and expression of women from different parts of the world.

Notes

I would like to thank Katie King, Inderpal Grewal, and Eric Smoodin for invaluable conversations and inspiration.

1. Jacques Derrida, "The Law of Genre," trans. Avital Ronell, *Glyph* 7 (1980): 203–4.

2. Useful discussions of the "politics of location" can be found in Adrienne Rich, "Notes toward a Politics of Location," *Blood, Bread, and Poetry: Selected Prose 1979–1985* (New York: W. W. Norton, 1986), 210–31; Donna Haraway, "Situated Knowledges: The Science Question in Feminism and the Privilege of Partial Perspective," *Simians, Cyborgs, and Women: The Reinvention of Nature* (New York: Routledge, 1991), 183–201; Chandra Mohanty, "Feminist Encounters: Locating the Politics of Experience," *Copyright* 1 (Fall 1987): 35; and essays included in "Third Scenario: Theory and the Politics of Location," special issue, ed. John Akomfrah and Pervaiz Ichan, *Framework* 36 (1989): 4–96.

3. Barbara Harlow, *Resistance Literature* (New York: Methuen, 1987).

4. Barbara Harlow, "From the Women's Prison: Third World Women's Narratives of Prison," *Feminist Studies* 12 (Fall 1986): 508.

5. Harlow, *Resistance Literature,* 136.

6. Ibid., 142.

7. Ibid., 147–48.

8. Doris Sommer, "'Not Just a Personal Story': Women's *Testimonios* and the Plural Self," in *Life/Lines: Theorizing Women's Autobiography,* ed. Bella Brodzki and Celeste Schenck (Ithaca, NY: Cornell University Press, 1988), 108.

9. See George E. Marcus and Michael M. J. Fischer, eds., *Anthropology as Cultural Critique* (Chicago: University of Chicago Press, 1986); James Clifford and George E. Marcus, eds., *Writing Culture* (Berkeley: University of California Press, 1986); James Clifford, *The Predicament of Culture* (Cambridge: Harvard University Press, 1988).

10. See James Clifford, "On Ethnographic Authority," in *The Predicament of Culture* (Cambridge: Harvard University Press), 21–54.

11. See Kamala Visweswaran, "Defining Feminist Ethnography," *Inscriptions* 3/4 (1988): 27–46.

12. Ibid., 33.

13. Ibid., 37. See also Roger M. Keesing, "Kwaio Women Speak: The Micropolitics of Autobiography in a Solomon Island Society," *American Anthropologist* 87 (1985): 37.

14. Katie King, "Audre Lorde's Lacquered Layer-

ings: The Lesbian Bar as a Site of Literary Production," *Cultural Studies* 2 (1988): 331.

15. Ibid., 330.

16. Ibid., 331.

17. Ibid., 336.

18. Katie King, "Producing Sex, Theory and Culture: Gay/Straight ReMappings in Contemporary Feminism," in *Conflicts in Feminism,* ed. Marianne Hirsch and Evelyn Fox Keller (New York: Routledge, 1990), 82–101.

19. bell hooks, "Writing Autobiography," 431, in this volume.

20. Bernice Johnson Reagon, "Coalition Politics: Turning the Century," in *Homegirls: A Black Feminist Anthology,* ed. Barbara Smith (New York: Kitchen Table Women of Color Press, 1983).

21. June Nash and Maria Fernandez-Kelly, eds., *Women, Men and the International Division of Labor* (Albany: State University of New York Press, 1983). See also Annette Fuentes and Barbara Ehrenreich, *Women in the Global Factory* (Boston: South End, 1983).

22. Fuentes and Ehrenreich, 9.

23. Ibid., 11–12.

24. Gayatri Chakravorty Spivak, "The Political Economy of Women as Seen by a Literary Critic," in *Coming to Terms: Feminism, Theory, Politics,* ed. Elizabeth Weed (New York: Routledge, 1989), 219.

25. Ibid., 224.

26. Ibid., 227.

27. Ibid.

28. Aihwa Ong, "Colonialism and Modernity: Feminist Re-presentations of Women in Non-Western Societies," *Inscriptions* 3/4 (1988): 88.

29. See Katie King's works in progress, "Crafting a Field: Feminism and Writing Technologies" (presentation at Princeton University, 12 April 1990); "Feminism and Writing Technologies" (presentation at the annual meeting of the Modern Language Association, 28 December 1988).

30. Saralee Hamilton, coordinator of the AFSC Nationwide Women's Program, quoted in Fuentes and Ehrenreich, 59.

16 Introduction to *A Day at a Time: Diary Literature of American Women, from 1764 to 1985*

Margo Culley

Constructing the Self

As invaluable as women's life-records are as historical sources containing a kind of "truth" about women's lives not found in other places, we must remember that diaries and journals are texts, that is, verbal constructs. The process of selection and arrangement of detail in the text raises an array of concerns appropriately "literary," including questions of audience (real or implied), narrative, shape and structure, persona, voice, imagistic and thematic repetition, and what James Olney calls "metaphors of self."[1] The act of autobiographical writing, particularly that which occurs in a periodic structure, involves the writer in complex literary as well as psychological processes. It is a paradox that the process whose frequent goal is to establish self-continuity involves at its heart a dislocation from the self, or a turning of subject into object. Even in some of the earliest American women's diaries we can see this kind of "double consciousness," as the self stands apart to view the self. Rebekah Dickinson, a single woman living in Hatfield, Massachusetts, in 1787 is very much conscious of herself as different from those around her and she fills the pages of her journal with this sense of "otherness": ". . . wondered how my lot fell by my Self alone how it

Came about that others and all the world was in Possession of Children and friends and a hous and homes while i was so od as to Sit here alone . . ." She writes of herself being "as lonely as tho i was Cast out from all the rest of the People and was a gasing stock for the old and young to gaze upon."[2] In using her journal as a vehicle for religious self-examination, Dickinson knows herself as God would know her (completely, truly, and from within) and also views herself from the imagined position of those around her. The painful sense of "otherness" that fills the pages of this journal is born of her awareness of being alone as she experiences it subjectively, compounded by her sense that others view her as an odd object.

An important vehicle in this process of objectifying the self is the audience of the journal. Some journals, as we have seen, are intended for real audiences but in many more the audience is implied. In some instances, the diary itself takes on this role as it is personified. "Dear diary" is a direct address to an ideal audience: always available, always listening, always sympathetic. Charlotte Forten addresses this audience on the last day of 1856: "Once more my beloved Journal, who art become a part of myself,—I say to thee, and to the Old Year,—Farewell!" Later she writes: "And now farewell, farewell to thee! my dear old friend, my *Only confidant!—my* journal!" In another passage where she seems to be speaking to a loved one, she is also speaking to the diary itself. "What name shall I give to thee, oh *ami inconnue?* It will be safer to give merely an initial—A. And so, dear A., I will tell you a little of my life for the past two years."[3]

Others who have given their journals names include Helen Ward Brandreth, a young upper-class girl in New York state, who in 1876 begins her diary: "I have determined to keep a journal. I shall call it Fannie Fern." She cautions Fannie, questions her, and apologizes to her ("I am afraid that you will think me dead or that something awful has happened to me").[4] Carol Potter, who has written about this diary kept by her great-grandmother, says in her own diary: "Most people would laugh to think that a personal diary was of such significance to a person, but this one is to me. When Nellie [Brandreth] writes—my dearest darling Fan—over and over, I know how she felt about that little book. It was a friend and so is this dumpy little blue notebook. How I wish I had started in a really nice bound notebook. But one never knows what will become of a first meeting or even a few."[5]

A contemporary diarist who knows what the relationship between writer and journal may become writes: "This notebook becomes my own little cheerleader, conscience, reckoner. You said it, now do it, it yells—OK, OK. WHAT?? It says—what's holding you up? What's the paralysis?" (March 1, 1977). Two days later she writes: "This journal has become my friend, my compulsion also . . . I need this writing. It is saving me . . . releasing me . . . But there is no one here to hold me, to tell me it's alright and yes—you can do it!—Right about now I feel the biggest, grandest need to be mothered."[6]

The importance of the audience, real or implied, conscious or unconscious, of what is usually thought of as a private genre cannot be over-stated. The presence of a sense of audience, in this form of writing as in all others, has a crucial influence over what is said and how it is said. Friend, lover, mother, God, a future self—whatever role the audience assumes for the writer—that presence becomes a powerful "thou" to the "I" of the diarist. It shapes the selection and arrangement of detail within the journal and determines more than anything else the kind of self-construction the diarist presents. In naming her diary after the popular novelist Fanny Fern, Helen Ward Brandreth casts herself in its pages as the heroine of a piece of romantic fiction. She describes to "Fan" her "spooners," her flirtations, her engagement to the "wrong man," and her scheming to free herself for the "right man."

> I danced with him about six times; then he asked me to go out on the stoop with him. Of course I went and when we got out there he took off his glove and wanted to hold my hand. I resisted the temptation for awhile, but, O Fan, I am *so* ashamed; at last I yielded. My hand trembled so that I was afraid he would notice it. O Fan, Fan!! I will die if he marries Birdie, For he does like her more than anybody else. At present.[7]

As we read Brandreth's journal we can see how its pages contain not *self* in any total sense, but a self which is to some degree a fiction, a construction. Even Mary MacLane, who attempts to write *everything,* is aware of this phenomenon and the crucial role of audience in the process. "I am trying my utmost to show everything—to reveal every petty vanity and weakness, every phase of feeling, every desire. It is a remarkably hard thing to do, I find, to probe my soul to its depths, to expose its shades and half-lights." She later concludes: "I am in no small degree, I find, a sham—a player to the gallery."[8] Whether "the gallery" is the personified diary, a real or implied audience, all diarists are involved in a process, even if largely unconscious, of selecting details to create a persona. The presence of the "gallery" is strongly felt in the journal of Alice James, brilliant and tortured invalid, who casts herself in her journal as an ironic social satirist. In what Robert Fothergill calls "the unique instance in the genre of a self-presentation which is almost unremittingly comic,"[9] we see clearly the distance possible between the character created in the diary and the far more complex life lived.

The pages of the diary might be thought of as a kind of mirror before which the diarist stands assuming this posture or that. One might even draw analogies between the process of psychoanalysis and the process of periodic life-writing, where the transference is made to the pages of the journal. But unlike the many oral forms of self-presentation, the self-constructions in the pages of a diary are fixed in time and space, available to the diarist for later viewing. Evidence abounds in all periods that women read and reread their diaries, a reality that renders the self-construction and reconstruction even more complex. Some diarists record comments upon previous entries, some emend them, some copy over entire diaries and edit them. One Amherst, Massachusetts, woman in rewriting her diary omits an entire year and comments: "We had such a hard year in 1905 that I destroyed my diary did not want to read it—."[10] Mary Mac-Lane, very aware of the charged experience of encountering past selves in the pages of her journal, writes: "I write this book for my own reading. / It is my postulate to myself. / As I read it it makes me clench my teeth savagely: and coldly tranquilly close my eyelids: it makes me love and loathe Me, Soul and bones."[11] As modern psychoanalysis has demonstrated, such dialogue with aspects of the self is a potent process, capable of unlocking mysteries of the human psyche and becoming the occasion of profound knowledge, growth, and change.

This power may explain why numbers of diarists record that periodic life-writing becomes addictive. Even in some early diaries we find comments like that of Lydia Smith in 1805: "I find that my idle habit of scribbling interferes so much with all regularity that I have determined to relinquish it, tho not entirely, yet I must so constrain it as to pursue my duties and studies, etc. I must wean myself by degrees for I have not strength to quit at once."[12] For those who do not wean themselves from the writing, diaries may be kept for a lifetime, and in some cases seem to be understood as synonymous with the life itself. In 1899 knowing she is near death, Cynthia Carlton writes: "I am not very well. Tried to straighten diary."[13] And the well-known last entry in Alice James's journal is by her companion Katherine Loring, who writes: "One of the last things she said to me was to make a correction in the sentence of March 4th 'moral discords and nervous horrors.' This dictation of March 4th was rushing about in her brain all day, and although she was very weak and it tired her much to dictate, she could not get her head quiet until she had it written: then she was relieved . . ."[14] For these women it is almost as though the life cannot be ended until the diary is finished. After her death in 1848, Elizabeth Ann Cooley's husband makes this final entry in her journal: "This journal is done! The author being Elizabeth A. McClure died March 28, 1848. Tho happy in Christ Jesus being the only consolation left me!! She was 22 years 7 months and 12 days old."[15] In the spirit of the diarist, he does not begin the entry saying she has died, but that the journal is done.

This conflation of the journal and the life itself may indeed be an accurate rendering of a complex dialectic. Some evidence exists that the persona in the pages of the diary shapes the life lived as well as the reverse. As Mary MacLane comments: "I don't know whether I write this because I wear two plain dresses or whether I wear two plain dresses because I write it."[16] The statement makes one ask to what extent Helen Ward Brandreth "plots" the romantic episodes of her life in order that they be available to "Fannie Fern" and whether Alice James views the world as ironic social satirist *because* of the persona in her journal or vice versa. . . .

Time and Narrative Structures

While the novel and autobiography may be thought of as artistic wholes, the diary is always in process, always in some sense a fragment. That is not to say that diaries do not have distinct shapes, but that their shapes derive from their existence in time passing. Some are shaped by external events in the diarist's life, which, even from the writer's point of view, have a beginning, middle, and end. Courtship diaries ending with a marriage and travel diaries ending with the arrival at a destination are examples of such texts.

Because diaries are periodic in creation and structure, incremental repetition is an important aspect of the structure of most journals, and the dynamic of reading the periodic life-record involves attending to what is repeated. Repeated actions large and small build tension as they advance the "plot." Will beloved Sister Mary Ermeline in the convent school diary of Suzette Pierce be waiting in the hall again today? Will she take her arm again and speak of friendship and love? [17] Will the wagon train in the diary of Amelia Stewart Knight make it across this next, even more dangerous river?

The calendar year provides the structural rhythms of many diaries. Frequently diarists mark the end of each calendar year with repeated rituals; early diaries often end the year with a list of persons who died during that year, later ones with reflections and resolutions. Many women diarists mark holidays and personal anniversaries as does Mary Dodge Woodward:

Thanksgiving Day. This used to be a day of unusual gladness, for on this day Walter was born, and he has proved a great blessing to me. We used to try, after the fashion of New Englanders, to be all at home on Thanksgiving if it were possible. I have been very happy with my family around the table many years—how happy, I did not realize until that sad day on which the father was taken from us and I was left alone with the children. Never since then have all the children been with me on this day. It is our fourth Thanksgiving in Dakota. The turkey is roasted and eaten, and the day has gone; I am thankful. [18]

Time and the Reader

A novel creates a fictional world complete unto itself, while an autobiography or memoir looks back from a fixed point in time which is the terminus of the retrospective. A diary, on the other hand, is created in and represents a continuous present. And as we have seen, many diarists reread previous entries before writing a current one, creating a complexly layered present to which a version of the past is immediately available. From entry to entry, the text incorporates its future as it reconstructs its past.

While analogies may be drawn between the construction of self in a diary and an autobiography, and even between the creation of a persona in a diary and a novel, the unique demands made of the reader of a diary derive from its periodic creation and structure. The writer's relationship to "real time" and representation of "time passing" in the text itself create formal tensions and ironies not found in texts generated from an illusion of a fixed point in time. What is known as well as what is *unknown* to the writer underscores the unique dynamic of the periodic text. Further, what is known and unknown to the *reader* of the journal text determine the unusually active role demanded of that reader. Again, periodicity is the key phenomenon determining the relationship of the writer and the reader to the text, and to each other, within both real and imagined time.

While diaries may have narrative structures approximating those of other forms of verbal art—action moving toward an end creating anticipation around the question of what happens next—the obvious difference in the "plots" of diaries and those of most other narratives is that the novelist, poet, oral storyteller, or writer of an autobiographical memoir knows what happens next and directs the reader's response at every point. Most diaries, on the other hand, are a series of surprises to writer and reader alike, one source of the immediacy of the genre. For example, eighteen-year-old Helen Marnie Stewart kept a journal on her family's trip to Oregon in 1853. She writes: "it being raining the road is extremely slippy and there is very steep hills to go up and down and that makes it difficult and hard, there was neer us a grave that had been dug open and a women head was layin and a come sticking in her hair it seems rather hard."[19] Though the last line, indeed the understatement of the entire passage, suggests the extent to which Helen Stewart and her party had become inured to horror, the reader experiences something of the sharp intake of breath in coming unprepared upon the grave in the diary text that Helen Stewart felt in seeing it along the road.

Notes

1. James Olney, *Metaphors of Self: The Meaning of Autobiography* (Princeton: Princeton University Press, 1972).

2. From the manuscript diary of Rebekah Dickinson, 20 August 1787 and 22 August 1787. Used with permission from Betty Billings.

3. *The Journal of Charlotte Forten Grimke* (New York: Oxford University Press, 1988), 76, 100, 25.

4. From the typescript of the diary of Helen Ward Brandreth, 2 January 1876 and 2 October 1876, 1, 6.

5. From the manuscript diary of Carol Potter. Used with permission.

6. From a manuscript diary loaned to Margo Culley. Used with permission.

7. Brandreth, 27 June 1877, 12.

8. *I, Mary MacLane* (Chicago: Herbert S. Stone, 1902), 75, 133.

9. Robert A. Fothergill, *Private Chronicles: A Study of English Diaries* (London: Oxford University Press, 1974), 29.

10. Typescript of the diary of Eunice Williams Smith, Amherst, MA.

11. *I, Mary MacLane*, 141.

12. "Lydia Smith's Journal, 1805–1806," *Proceedings of the Massachusetts Historical Society* 48 (1914–15), 515.

13. *Cynthia: Excerpts from the Diaries of Cynthia Brown Carlton, 1841–1900, Burton, Ohio, in the Western Reserve*, ed. Margaret Patricia Ford (Privately printed, 1976), not paginated.

14. *The Diary of Alice James*, ed. Leon Edel (New York: Dodd, Mead, 1934) 232–33.

15. "From Virginia to Missouri in 1846: The Journal of Elizabeth Ann Cooley," ed. Edward D. Jervey and James E. Moss, *Missouri Historical Review* 60, no.2 (January 1966): 206.

16. *I, Mary MacLane*, 189.

17. The manuscript diary of Suzette Pierce, 1899–1900. Owned by Margo Culley.

18. Mary Dodge Woodward, *The Checkered Years*, ed. Mary Boynton Cowdry (Caldwell, Idaho: Caxton Printers, 1937), 104

19. "The Diary of Helen Stewart, 1853," typescript produced by the Lane County Pioneer-Historical Society, 6.

17 A Feminist Revision of New Historicism to Give Fuller Readings of Women's Private Writing

Helen M. Buss

Stephen Greenblatt, in describing the origins of his New Historicist practice, has said that he "began with the desire to speak with the dead" (quoted in Veeser, ix). Feminist scholars interested in finding the silenced voices of women in history and literature cannot begin merely with an effort to speak with the famous "dead" of men's historical and literary traditions. We hardly know who our dead are: what could they possibly say that was not conditioned and structured by their place inside the gender system that silenced them or allowed them to speak only in the limited and oppressive public scripts allowed to women? However, women's private writings, although not exempt from the interpellation of subjectivity by ideology, offer a rich source of insight into women's cultural and personal development for critics seeking a feminist New Historicist practice.

In turn, an awareness of New Historicist theory and practice in general can facilitate breathing new life into formerly ignored texts, can allow us to "speak with the dead." The most attractive aspect of New Historicist practice is its commitment to what Clifford Geertz, the anthropologist, calls "thick description in which an event or anecdote is 're-read . . . in such a way as to reveal through the analysis of tiny particulars the behavioral codes, logics and motive

forces controlling a whole society" (quoted in Veeser, xi). This is a particularly helpful strategy for a literary critic like myself, trained many years ago in the "close reading" techniques of the New Critics. My first reading experiences in archives showed me that the texts I read were open to such close readings, but the terminology I had learned, the location of such consciously used and overdetermined markers as metaphor, symbol, and allegory left me bereft of an adequate critical practice. "Thick description" allows me to use my training to a different purpose, not to identify the markers of a literary consciousness, but to read the trace of a human person constructing her identity in her historical, social, cultural, and gendered place.

Because New Historicists prefer a vocabulary derived from materialist theories, the use of terms such as "circulation," "negotiation," and "exchange" are common. The use of such terms allows me to bring the texts of women's personal writing and the private worlds they describe into the marketplace of public culture, where the personal and private can be seen as having the same cultural nuance and importance as the public lives of men and nations. Bringing these texts into such a marketplace also allows me to identify when female labor is subsumed, unrecognized, and thus unvalued by the public economy. Particularly useful is the term "moment of exchange," a term that can designate all kinds of exchanges of assets, of power, not only the economic exchanges of a public economy, but also the more symbolic and personal moments of a private economy. H. Aram Veeser observes: "Circulation involves not just money and knowledge but also . . . prestige—the 'possession' of social assets as evanescent as taste in home furnishings or as enduring as masculinity. The point is that such social advantages circulate as a form of material currency that tends to go unnoticed because it cannot be crudely translated into liquid assets" (xiv). Learning a critical practice that allows me to see that "symbolic exchanges" of talent, power, skills, nurturing, and labor are happening in public as well as private places and relationships, and that the effect and value of these exchanges pass between the domains, gives an awareness of critical importance to the reader of women's private writings.

As a researcher concerned with archival documents, I very quickly found the need for a critical practice that is interdisciplinary in nature, one that does not accept the traditional disciplinary divisions of the academy. Moreover, within the territory of literary theory, I need to meld reading strategies that are often seen as mutually exclusive. My own critical practice is particularly facilitated by exploring the relationship between New Historicism and poststructuralist literary analysis. As Richard Terdiman points out, despite their acknowledged differences, both activities are very concerned with the language of texts. Whereas "poststructuralists are moved by a concern with the constitutive, irreducible *play* of signifiers . . . new historicists [are moved by] a concern with their constitutive, irreducible *power*. Together, both tendencies counterpose themselves against strains of formalism which conceive language as *stable* and *absolute*" (225). As a feminist reader, my own discontent with linguistically based poststruc-

turalist practice has been with its lack of a political content. While attempting to inform my skills as a close reader with the insights of theorists who recognize the slippages of language, I have felt uncomfortable with the hermetically sealed nature of their critical practice, concerned as it often is with the play of language inside a text, without reference to the social setting of that language, the gendered nature of language usage, and indeed the real personal and political power that can come from the practice of certain discourses. New Historicism offers me a way of exploring how the "play of signifiers" in a text can reveal the writer's locations in the power systems of patriarchal language and institutions and how language facilitates and hampers her negotiation of her assets and value in that world.

In working with personal documents often not consciously constructed for a readership other than the writer and her intimates, I have been in the process of realigning my thinking about the deconstructive aspect of poststructuralist readings. Many deconstructionist readers treat the text as a patient, assuming their own superiority in knowledge and diagnostic ability. (My own reservations concerning deconstruction derive from my dislike of the metaphors of militarism and penetrating violence used by such writers as Christopher Norris in *Deconstruction*). Gayatri Chakravorty Spivak denies that the metaphor of physician-patient offers the best description of deconstructive practice: "I do not go into a text thinking to diagnose the absences because you leave a lot outside the door when you enter as a doctor. And after all, a doctor cannot read the text as the body of her mother, his wife, or her husband, or their lovers. This relationship of love, which is the deconstructive relationship—you cannot deconstruct something which is not your own language" (288). I find that the reader-text relationship Spivak describes is in the spirit of the best New Historicist research in which the text is not the "patient," but the "accomplice" of the reader (although I prefer to see myself as the text's accomplice). For a reader of archival documents, where the danger of "deformation" (as Philippe Lejeune names it in *On Autobiography* [207]) of the identity being investigated is plagued by the dissociation between the motives for writing the document, the motives for its archival acquisition, and the motives for studying it, a reading ethic that involves reader responsibility as well as reader pleasure, a sense of reciprocal activity of text and reader, a respect for the writer's subjectivity—in other words, an ethic of love—is essential.

The major concerns I have as a reader— my need for an interdisciplinary close reading strategy and a refreshed critical vocabulary, my need for a poststructuralist reading strategy informed by a consciousness of the social power of language, and a reader-response theory that is grounded in a feminist ethic—were first realized for me not through New Historicist scholarship but through feminist critics' insights. From the beginning of my archival research, critics and feminists working with women's personal writings have taught me how and what to read. Elizabeth Hampsten has taught me about new strategies of close reading with her advice on the "inventive patience" needed in examining women's accounts. Elizabeth Meese's decanonizing strategies and her infusion of feminist concerns into poststructuralist theory have been valuable in identification of the need to see language signification as both play and power. Gerda Lerner taught me how to see women's history as different from men's. As well, Suzanne Bunkers's work on reflexivity as a reading strategy and Patrocinio Schweickart's feminist reader-response theories carry with them the same identification of reader responsibility and accountability as does Spivak's identification of the "loving" possibility in deconstructive reading. While New Historicist scholars foreground similar concerns they are not the first to do

so. Critics using their insights should heed the warnings of feminists. Catherine Gallagher says that the women's movement is the teacher of the New Historicism in that feminist experience teaches that "the more 'personal' and 'mundane' the issues the more resistance to change we encounter" and that "the deepest, most inaccessible region of social formation [is] the formation of ourselves as gendered subjects" (42). As well, Elizabeth Fox-Genovese warns against uncritical adoption of New Historicist ideology: "Only in rare instances have new historicists embraced the full implications of [their] project. In most cases they have implicitly preferred to absorb history into the text of discourse without (re)considering the specific characteristics of history herself" (217). Like Fox-Genovese, I find that many New Historicists need to realize that a new understanding of what history is recognizes that "history must disclose and reconstruct the conditions of consciousness and action, with conditions understood as systems of social relations, including relations between women and men, between rich and poor, between the powerful and the powerless, among those of different faiths, different races, and different classes" (217).

The ethical and political agendas of feminists make them very aware that "assumptions and techniques [are] given different articulation depending on the politics of the practitioners" (Newton, 153), and New Historians are as likely as old historians to appropriate feminist research while eliding gender as a central issue in their projects. Judith Newton advises that feminists refocus New Historicist practice to recognize that "role anxiety" may be "role resistance," that the domestic sphere has values that are in tension with the public world, that race and sex as well as class construct women's roles differently than men's and that we need to access many "local sites" to access the nuance of power in ideologies (155).

Taking Newton's revisionary advice as mandate, I would revise, for the purposes of a feminist New Historicist reading, Veeser's five summary statements of the conditions of New Historical readings (my additions appear in italics).

1. every expressive act is embedded in a network of material practices, *and those practices are highly male-gendered practices that assume and subsume female labor without taking it into account;*

2. every expressive act of unmasking, critique and opposition uses the tools it condemns and risks falling prey to the practice they expose. *Therefore, to avoid reappropriation, feminists must self-consciously foreground their subversive use of those tools and the feminist ethical agendas that motivate their critiques, self-reflexively examining their own expressive acts;*

3. *although* literary and nonliterary "texts" circulate inseparably, *a new hegemony of privileged texts can emerge at any time, and only continued extension of what we consider as texts, and our awareness of the gendered nature of those texts, will resist hegemonic forces;*

4. *while* no discourse, imaginative or archival, gives access to unchanging truths nor expresses inalterable human nature, *the search for a fuller reading of female discourses will yield contextual truths that reveal the places of women in culture and history and the many possibilities of female subjectivity that will revise male models of truth and human nature;*

5. *although* a critical method and a language adequate to describe culture under capitalism participate in the economy they describe, *language can also inscribe social change if its users inform their critical method with a feminist ethical agenda.* (xi)

I can best illustrate how my revision of New Historicist theory and practice has affected my reading of women's private writing by doing my own "thick description" of a woman's text, in actuality three texts, the personal documents of the wife of a medical doctor practicing with the Northwest Mounted Police in the first decade of this century at Lesser Slave Lake in the Canadian Northwest Territories. Isabel West, her husband, Dr. Christopher West, and their three children lived in daily contact with aboriginal and Métis people who were suffering from severe culture shock in the wake of the arrival of white culture. As well, the Wests interacted on a daily basis with a fairly large contingent of British missionaries actively involved in the attempt to convert and assimilate aboriginal people to white religion. The different intended readership of the three texts—a retrospective account of the journey north written in a tone seemingly meant for at least a familial readership, a letter meant for an uncle's eyes only, and a personal diary kept during the years in the northern community seemingly meant for the eyes of the writer alone—alerts my reading immediately to the different subject positions such a woman must take if she is to survive in her world. The travel account is full of the modest language of a woman who must portray herself as nonheroic, while showing herself able to suffer hardship in silence for her husband's sake and her own respectability as a middle-class woman. But as well, such an intelligent, middle-class woman allows herself a certain humorous self-indulgence, showing that a witty but not too threatening sense of self, one always willing to be self-deprecating, exists underneath the modest, nonheroic exterior. When writing in her travel journal of the rough trail between Edmonton and the Athabasca River, she records the men's comments that she is not a "whining type of women" (3). She adds: "Evidentially they thought they were going to be burdened with a clinging vine, but I was young and healthy and a good sport, and what could not be cured had to be endured" (3). She does confess to a certain insecurity when she admits, "I certainly did not feel like a pioneer or heroine. I envied other women in four walls, with lights, warmth and security. Here were we, a few mortals in the open spaces, with only the sky above us and the damp earth beneath, surrounded by darkness and miles of uninhabited territory" (1).

Such references to the stereotypes of women as "clinging vine," "good sport," "pioneer," and "heroine" point to the several gender agendas that early twentieth-century, middle-class ideology offered women.[1] The "Cult of True Womanhood," emphasizing the virtues of piety, purity, submissiveness, and domesticity, was an important nineteenth-century ideal still felt by women in the early twentieth century (see Welter). For the purposes of my work, the economic place of this ideology is important. As Barbara Welter has pointed out, industrialized patriarchy separated the world into private and public spheres, denying the existence of much of the circulation of value and labor between the two. In the latter, men had little time for any values outside of profit values. More spiritual and moral values were placed in the realm of the home and its angel, woman, where men could retreat to a fine sense of the moral nature of their universe, while not letting that morality interfere with business.

Early in our century, Charlotte Perkins Gilman noted that this binary opposite of public/private spheres could force a woman into the position of "moral mother" who held incredibly high standards of ethical living with little or no power to enforce these standards. Although some women may have been able to use their position of moral mother to gain personal power covertly, Gilman's own life and her writing attest that this effort was often at great personal cost. This ideology was still strongly in force in North America when Isabel West went north. My own interest in nineteenth-century women's ideologies has led me to explore the way the "cult"

emerged in the more British-derived Canadian culture. Interestingly, Canadian pioneer men worshipped (seemingly in a nostalgic effort to recapture the old middle-class life in England) the image of the weak and delicate lady, the "clinging vine," even though their own wilderness lifestyles required the company of women more in the mold of the aboriginal and Métis women they took as their "country wives."[2]

Recently, Frances B. Cogan has contended that the image of the "submissive maiden" was not hegemonic, that it was accompanied and opposed by a doctrine of "real womanhood" that, although advocating a separate sphere for women, did not see them as weak but rather as "biologically equal (rationally as well as emotionally) and in many cases markedly superior in intellect to what passes for male business sense, scholarship, and theological understanding" (45). However, as Cogan herself points out, "real women," while distinguishing themselves from "true women," also "deliberately" separated themselves from feminists who demanded real political power for women: "Real Women survived but remained good daughters, good sisters, wives and mothers because in their own eyes they were important to family and to society" (5). Implicit in such a view (although not in Cogan's statement) is a belief that such a version of self involves being valued in one's "own eyes" but not necessarily in men's economics, while fulfilling the function of "good" woman in patriarchy. That is, the "real woman" like the "true woman" is one who fulfills all her relational functions lovingly while asking for none of the power that would make her love an effective moral force: the very double bind that Gilman explores in her work and life. My interest in the contending doctrines is not to validate one or the other varieties of female gendering, but rather to point out the variety of ideological self-definitions interpellating a woman like Isabel West. Indeed, while the detail of her diary certainly shows her as subject to these nine-teenth-century ideologies of gender, her mention of the "good sport" she hopes she is indicates that she is also subject to what I would identify as the new version of "true/real" womanhood of the twentieth century, a gendering of females as more active, boyish women, who are "good sports" and companions for their men, while not competing with them. This "cult," if I may name it that, culminates in our own time in the fitness ideals and anorexic body images offered young women; these images have at least as much ideological force and attendant illness as the earlier ideals of "submissive maidens" or "moral mothers."

Despite the various agendas and their pressures affecting Isabel West's experience as woman at the turn of the century, the account she gives of her journey north is the happy prelude to more difficult times. She reveals herself as an optimistic, well-educated woman of middle-class sensibility who disguises her fears with humor and an admirable attention to the detail of travel by York boat on the Athabasca River. The travel journal comments on their late arrival at their destination after many misadventures and discomforts and after their missionary reception committee had devoured the dinner meant for the travelers, in these words: "I agreed with my husband, it was very annoying to arrive looking like the Pilgrim Fathers to be met by a smiling band of missionaries arrayed in their summer raiment, full of goose and good intention" (11). The careful deference to male opinion and the equally careful humor that disguises the discomfort, fear, and displeasure and unladylike ravenous hunger of the traveler, are familiar to me from other travel accounts of middle- and upper-class Victorian women. The deferential humor allowed women both to show a correctly gendered face to the reader and to reveal some of their own courage and adaptability while "roughing it in the bush."[3]

When I am able to contrast the diplomacy of this semipublic account with the tones of the personal letter and the diary this woman kept in her years in the north, and when I inform these readings with a developing theory of her position in the economy of that place, a much more nuanced human subject emerges. I find a female person caught between two systems of colonial power, one represented by the missionaries, the other by her own husband, the medical doctor ministering to the aboriginal community, both missionaries and doctor convinced that their actions are for the good of that community, and both of them taking for granted the loyalty and labor of the middle-class white wife in the service of their systems.

In "The Political Function of the Intellectual" Michel Foucault has described the way in which certain intellectual systems have been established in Western culture, whereby individuals, otherwise without personal power, through their education and licensing inside certain systems take on the intellectual discourses and thus the power of these systems. In the small community of aboriginal persons, already culturally displaced by the activities of whites, their traditional systems of beliefs and medicines compromised by white diseases and white belief systems, the missionaries and the doctor represent powerful instruments of cultural dominance. Isabel West spends most of her time caught between the competing demands for the authority of white religion and of white medicine in the aboriginal community. Her position is complicated by the fact that she has local people working in her home; she cares about them, wants their friendship, feels guilty and frustrated when her care is of no use (or worse yet, is received without gratitude or rejected entirely). The reader needs to be aware of the various kinds of material and symbolic exchanges being undertaken, and attentive to the moments of exchange that are fraught with tension and ambiguity for this woman; her "assets," though often required, are not always valued or recognized. She sometimes resorts to blaming the victims, which allows her to avoid blaming her too often absent and overworked husband and allows her to avoid a direct recognition of her hardly concealed antipathy toward the missionaries. To lay blame on either is to declare herself a bad wife or a woman lacking in piety, a difficult self-definition for a woman who wants to be "good." Her husband and the missionaries represent the "intellectuals" who take on the power discourses of Western civilization. What Foucault's theory does not entirely account for is the way these intellectual systems require the implication as well as the imbrication of white female figures in the operation of their systems. This woman's diary, however, when used as a glass through which to view Foucaultian power systems, can offer additional insight into the male gendering of these power systems. They are dependent on a female subjectivity that labors for the system, but is not of the system, a female subjectivity that defers its own existence.

In a series of succinct diary entries made in the course of one winter week in 1906 we see graphically the condition of Isabel West living at the interface of these systems:

> Wednesday, 19 February (1900). Chris was to see the sick child on his way to Peace River last night, did not go. We were just starting over to see the child today when Mrs. Holmes [a missionary] came in and prevented us going, she thought the child was better because they did not go for her again. The child died tonight! I reproach myself I did not insist in spite of everything to go to the child. (2–3)

The conflict between who is to be the authority in the natives' lives, the doctor or the missionaries, emerges here in "Mrs. Holmes . . . prevented us going," because she assumes that she,

a member of the religious community, could offer authoritative opinion on when a doctor was needed. West and his wife accept her assumption of authority and power and the child dies, perhaps as a result of the contention in the power systems. But Isabel's reaction—"I reproach myself I did not insist in spite of everything"—is an assumption of personal guilt and is evidence of how burdensome and psychologically draining her sense of personal responsibility could be as a white wife and mother who has internalized a role definition of almost magical dimensions, as "moral mother" who holds herself responsible for events over which she has no power. But hidden behind the "in spite of everything" is also a suggestion that the situation may be even more complicated than the words make obvious. Encoded in the phrase "everything" is the possibility that there would be more involved than defying Mrs. Holmes in going to the sick boy.[4]

Would it be neglect of her own children? Would she have to defy her husband? Other community taboos? The politics of the small northern outpost, where the power/knowledge relationships are complex and subtle, lie just below the surface of this writing. In such an economy, where female labor is a value that goes unrecognized because it cannot be "crudely translated" into "liquid assets," or (in Foucaultian terms) into "intellectual power systems," Isabel West's distress and uncertainty are inevitable. Her continuing uncertainty as to her correct place and value in the economy seeks a solution in her diary entries:

> Thursday, 20 February. I acted badly and made a fuss over the child dying, Chris felt badly and I made him feel worse. I do not know how I am to stand it here. I cannot see them needing nursing and not nurse them and I must not neglect my own. If I stay with these people and my own come

to harm, I would never forgive myself. The girl I have [her housemaid] is thoroughly ignorant. (3)

"Acted badly" and "made a fuss" are rather strange expressions to use regarding a reaction to death. Is Isabel not supposed to care about the death of Indian children? From the construction of the first and second sentences it would seem the most important point about "acting badly" is that it made her husband feel worse. Perhaps she feels it is important to her that he remain as guilt free as possible in order to carry on his vital work as doctor. Perhaps grieving over the death of an aboriginal child is not being a "good sport," a good companion for her husband. Yet she failed to make a "fuss" when it would have done some good, the day before. Would that be also not to upset her husband? Or, perhaps she refused to behave emotionally or disagreeably in front of the missionary because of the precarious balance of power between white medicine and white religion in the lives of the aboriginal people and the embarrassing position she would have created for everyone if she had insisted on her husband's and/or her going to the child. Now she must bear the guilt of her double bind, the special location she has as moral mother at the heart of patriarchy. Made to feel a responsibility to participate at every moment of symbolic exchange in the small community where everyone knows everyone, she is at the same time powerless to control the effects of those exchanges. . . .

When reading personal documents, an informed consciousness of the power systems that are operational in such an economy is essential. However, reading strategies that take into account language's double nature are also necessary. Besides language's consciously apprehended referential uses and its function as power discourse, we need to explore language's ability to maximize some conditions of existence, to make their value real in the economy of a culture, and its ability to suppress and absent other conditions, to repress their existence into powerlessness and inarticulation. What language suppresses in Isabel West's diary is still present for the reader reading as a feminist New Historicist. It may be under "erasure" if we appeal to the linguistic theories of Derrida; it may be "encoded," awaiting "decoding" as some researchers of women's private writing claim; it may be present in the connotative possibilities of close reading that any trained literary critic has learned inside the traditional canons, but it is there, and it can be found by doing what I used to call, before I was exposed to a theoretical literary education, "reading between the lines."

I used to be told that "reading between the lines" was something that unsophisticated women such as myself did, women in search of messages, of depth, of richness, in accounts that were naive, nonliterary, incapable of nuance. Now that I have learned strategies of reading informed by a consciously interdisciplinary practice in which a "thick description" and a poststructuralist theory of language are put in the service of a feminist New Historicist agenda, I do not discard as amateurish the methodologies of my past, but attempt to make them more sophisticated by using the master's theories in a subversive manner. Thus I have used Foucault, not only to uncover the power systems of culture, but also to reveal the ways those power systems are gendered male and leave women outside power, while making women feel responsible for the smooth operation of such systems and guilty if they offer criticism of any of their functions.

Notes

1. When I outlined these "agendas" for an audience of academic and nonacademic women, several protested (with much of the audience nodding in

agreement) that these agendas have as much force to-day as they had in the nineteenth and early twentieth century, indeed, that only their style of ideological expression had changed.

2. See my "The Dear Domestic Circle," for an examination of the cult's effect on English immigrating women; and see Sylvia Van Kirk, "*Many Tender Ties*," for the effect on aboriginal and Métis women in Canada.

3. The phrase comes from the text *Roughing It in the Bush*, the title of Susanna Moodie's account of an English lady becoming a Canadian pioneer. This autobiographical account is, in many ways, the central text of women's literature in Canada.

4. The "encoded" nature of women's accounts is taken up by Bunkers in "Midwestern Diaries and Journals." She uses the word to describe the fact that the discourse of women's diaries often suggests other possibilities of meaning that individual women will not express because of the formal strictures on certain subjects or cannot express given the psychological and linguistic dictates of their time and place. Myers, in "The Significant Fictivity," discusses the kinds of "implicature" to be found in the encoded language in women's accounts.

Works Cited

Bunkers, Suzanne L. "Midwestern Diaries and Journals: What Women Were (Not) Saying in the Late 1800s." In *Studies in Autobiography*, ed. James Olney. Oxford: Oxford University Press, 1988. 190–210.

Bunkers, Suzanne L., ed. *"All Will Yet Be Well": The Diary of Sarah Gillespie Huftalen, 1873–1952*. Iowa City: University of Iowa Press, 1993.

Buss, Helen M. "'The Dear Domestic Circle': Frameworks for the Literary Study of Women's Personal Narratives in Archival Collections." *Studies in Canadian Literature* 14, no. 1 (1989): 1–17.

Cogan, Frances B. *All-American Girl: The Idea of Real Womanhood in Mid-Nineteenth-Century America*. Athens: Georgia University Press, 1989.

Foucault, Michel. "The Political Function of the Intellectual." *Radical Philosophy* 17 (1977): 12–25.

Fox-Genovese, Elizabeth. "Literary Criticism and the Politics of the New Historicism." In Veeser, *The New Historicism*, 213–24.

Gallagher, Catherine. "Marxism and the New Historicism." In Veeser, *The New Historicism*, 37–48.

Gilman, Charlotte Perkins. *Women and Economics: A Study of the Economic Relation between Men and Women as a Factor in Social Evolution*. 4th ed. London: Putnam; Boston: Small, Maynard, 1905.

Hampsten, Elizabeth. *"Read This Only to Yourself": The Private Writings of Midwestern Women, 1880–1910*. Bloomington: Indiana University Press, 1982.

Lejeune, Philippe. *Cher Cahier . . . : Témoignages sur le Journal Personnel*. Paris: Gallimard, 1990.

Lejeune, Philippe. *On Autobiography*. Ed. Paul John Eakin. Trans. Katherine Leary, Minneapolis: University of Minnesota Press, 1989.

Meese, Elizabeth. "The Languages of Oral Testimony and Women's Literature." *Women's Personal Narratives: Essays in Criticism and Pedagogy*, ed. Leonore Hoffmann and Margo Culley. New York: Modern Language Association of America, 1985. 18–28.

Moodie, Susanna. *Roughing It in the Bush, or Life in Canada*. Ed. Carl Ballstadt. CEECT edition. Ottawa: Carlton University Press, 1988.

Myers, Victoria. "The Significant Fictivity of Maxine Hong Kingston's *The Woman Warrior*." *Biography* 9, no. 2 (Spring 1986): 112–25.

Newton, Judith. "History as Usual? Feminism and the 'New Historicism.'" In Veeser, *New Historicism*, 152–67.

Norris, Christopher. *Deconstruction: Theory and Practice*. London: Routledge, 1986.

Spivak, Gayatri Chakravorty. "The New Historicism: Political Commitment and the Postmodern Critic." In Veeser, *New Historicism*, 277–92.

Terdiman, Richard. "Is There Class in This Class?" In Veeser, *New Historicism*, 225–30

Van Kirk, Sylvia. *"Many Tender Ties": Women in the Fur Trade Society in Western Canada, 1670–1870*. Winnipeg: Watson and Dwyer, n.d.

Veeser, H. Aram. Introduction. In Veeser, *New Historicism*, ix-xvi.

Veeser, H. Aram. *The New Historicism.* New York: Routledge, 1989.

Welter, Barbara. "The Cult of True Womanhood: 1820–1860." *American Quarterly* 18 (1996): 151–74.

West, Isabel. "Diary of Mrs. Christopher H. West (née Isabel Alice Sinclair Patterson) 1900–1909." 1906 Diary. File M1299. Glenbow Archives, Calgary, t. s. 19 pp.

West, Isabel. "Journey into the North." File M1299. Glenbow Archives, Calgary, t. s. 11 pp.

18 Female Rhetorics

Patricia Meyer Spacks

Personal letters, published, entice readers by fictions of self-revelation. In eighteenth-century England, much epistolary rhetoric encouraged such fictions. Letter writers—at least those whose communications have survived in print—proclaim to one another their sincerity and artlessness. "Now as I love you better than most I have ever met with in the world . . . ; so inevitably I write to you more negligently, that is more openly, and what all but such as love another will call writing worse." That comes from a letter from Alexander Pope to Jonathan Swift (28 Nov. 1729, Sherburn, 3). Samuel Johnson, with his usual bracing realism, suggested that friendships involving perfect self-revelation belonged to children, or to the Golden Age, but letters between intimates continued to insist on their own candor. Many that survive sound like works written with an eye to publication: Pope, Swift, and Walpole, with their artifices of naturalness, glance toward posterity. But whether the famous letters of the eighteenth century *construct* or *reveal* a self, they encourage readers to acknowledge a personality so compelling as to constitute selfhood.

For eighteenth-century women as letter writers, the notion of direct self-revelation and self-assertion would conflict with ideas about femininity deeply inscribed in the culture. A chilling passage in *Clarissa* suggests the female obligation to self-suppression. Aunt Hervey reproaches her niece for alluding to a suitor's "unworthiness": "Not so fast, my dear. Does not this look like setting a high value on yourself?"

(Richardson, 1:373). The high value may—as in Clarissa's case—accurately assess worth, but no speaker has the right to claim it for herself.

Eighteenth-century letters by women reflect and elucidate the conflict between the desire for self-assertion and the need for self-suppression, and they demonstrate strategies of deflection. Lady Mary Wortley Montagu, Mary Delany, and Elizabeth Carter, my three subjects, all conducted voluminous correspondences in which they worked out ways of understanding themselves: each set of letters reveals its own dominant theme of self-elucidation. But the writers also find ways to avoid the troubling threat of egotism. Female correspondence, their letters suggest, supplies means of evasive self-definition, and the sex of women letter writers informs their use of the epistolary form.

The twentieth-century reputations of Lady Mary, Delany, and Carter confirm the women's avoidance of excessive personal claims. Most people who now recognize the name of Elizabeth Carter dimly recollect Johnson's praise of her as one who could make good puddings as well as translate Greek. Lady Mary Wortley Montagu survives in present-day consciousness because Pope attacked her. The entry for Mary Delany in the *Concise Dictionary of National Biography* begins, "Friend of Swift." All three women lived prolonged lives (Carter died at eighty-nine, Delany at eighty-eight, Lady Mary at seventy-three) of various accomplishment: among other things, Carter translated Epictetus; Delany invented the paper mosaic, a mode of representing flowers with accuracy and beauty by layered shapes of colored paper; Lady Mary introduced small-pox inoculation into England. But their modern fame, such as it is, rests largely on their associations with distinguished men.

The women's published letters exist in different states of completeness and accuracy. Lady Mary Wortley Montagu, born earliest of the three (in 1689), has been most recently edited; her letters appeared in 1966 in unexpurgated, lucidly annotated form, comprising three volumes of correspondence beginning in her twentieth year and extending to a few weeks before her death. Lady Llanover, a descendant of Mary Granville Delany's sister Ann, produced six volumes of Delany's letters, each more than six hundred pages long, in 1861. The reverential tone of her preface conveys her high regard for her subject (born in 1700), but the editor fails to explain her editorial principles; we cannot know what has been silently omitted. At least equally reverential, and irritatingly self-satisfied about his severe censorship, the Reverend Montagu Pennington, nephew of Elizabeth Carter, published four volumes of her letters in 1809, only three years after her death (she was born in 1717). "Nothing has been added to any of the Letters," he assures his readers, "but a good deal has been left out of trifling chit-chat and confidential communications"—exactly what a modern reader might most wish to see. Moreover, Pennington prints only two specific sets of letters, one containing communications between Carter and Catherine Talbot, the other composed of letters from Carter to Elizabeth Vesey. He explains that Carter burned some of her letters and ordered others returned to their senders; he chooses from those remaining apparently on the basis of their moral and theological wisdom. . . .

The problem of egotism explicitly concerns all three of these women. When they write about their own actions, thoughts, or feelings, they worry about seeming too self-involved; often they deprecate the activities they report. Carter explains that she had read nothing except *Joseph Andrews* and Ariosto for some time, because she has been much involved "in the important affair of working a pair of ruffles and handkerchief." She has also developed a passion for dancing, but she assures her correspondent that she will soon move on to something new: "learning the Chinese language, or studying Duns Scotus and Thomas Aquinas." Then she apologizes for the paragraph she has just written: "I ought to beg your pardon for all this egotism, but after the description I have given you of my employments, you will easily imagine I am at a loss of a subject" (1 Jan. 1743, Pennington, 1:24, 25). She thus articulates a female problem: if one does nothing important and feels guilty at betraying self-concern, what can one write about? . . .

In an early letter to Ann, Delany complains about another correspondent who adopts too "cramped" and obscure an epistolary style. "The beauty of writing (in my opinion)," she concludes, "consists in telling our sentiments in an easy natural way" (14 Mar. 1728–29, 1:196). Almost a quarter of a century later, she complains because Ann has shown Samuel Richardson some of Delany's letters to her. "Indeed, such careless and incorrect letters as mine are to you, should not be exposed: were they put in the best dress I could put them into, they have nothing to recommend them but the warm overflowing of a most affectionate heart, which can only give pleasure to the partial friend they are addressed to" (17 Nov. 1750, 2:617). Stressing the importance of epistolary style, these comments also differentiate appropriate styles in relation to levels of intimacy. The "easy and natural" mode desirable in letters between friends provides an appropriate "dress" for the telling of sentiments—meaning, epistolary practice suggests, the expression of views about such matters as books and current political happenings. Only between extreme intimates can feeling be allowed simply to overflow, justifying "careless and incorrect" style, but also shaping letters inappropriate for any audience but the intended recipient. From a modern perspective, even Delany's most intimate letters sound highly controlled, sharply restraining their expression of personal feeling. But she manifestly experiences more freedom in writing her sister than in other correspondences; in that context she allows herself at least the possibility of focusing on her own emotions.

The conventions of female correspondence resemble those dominating its male counterpart. Women's letters almost ritualistically apologize for their own length; they reiterate ardent professions of friendship. Pope and Swift do the same thing, but because the women often apparently have less to write about, their conventional protestations assume a larger place in their letters. In her old age, Delany would offer lessons in "propriety" to her little grandniece, pointing out that propriety amounts to thoughtfulness, a way to demonstrate concern for others. The stylized aspects her letters share with those of other women express their status as communications dominated by consciousness of *the other*. Hence the special importance of self-subordination: concern for self must not be allowed to block sensitivity to the imagined needs of the recipient. Hence the insistent recurrence, within these texts, of rituals of politeness.

The ideology of self-subordination implies, among other things, suppression of narrative about the self. Even when these letter writers experience their own emotional dramas, they frequently fail to report them directly. Lady Mary, in her premarital letters to Wortley and in her later passionate correspondence with the young Italian Algarotti, with whom she fell in love in her middle age (he, bisexual in orientation, apparently preferred Lord Hervey), expresses her-

self rather like a literary heroine; she calls attention to the analogy between her situation and Clarissa's in a letter written late in her life. But she elides the aftermath of her romantic predicaments, hardly hinting at her unhappiness with her husband in letters to intimates and never revealing what has happened with Algarotti, much less how she feels about it. . . .

Why should a modern reader feel interested in women who avoid self-revelation and personal narrative, concern themselves obsessively with stylistic propriety, and fill their letters with courteous protestation? One may note in such phenomena evidence of familiar social attitudes toward women and of the internalization of these attitudes by the women themselves; that once said, why bother? In fact, these letters create an impression of vitality and emotional tension comparable to that generated by the fictional letters conveying the drama of such novels as *Pamela* and *Clarissa*. If real female letter writers eschew narratives focused on themselves and avoid direct outpourings of emotion, they nonetheless find ways of indirect self-dramatization, codes for revealing the self. . . .

Lady Mary states most directly a theme implicit in the stories all three women tell. Sounding like Mr. Bennet in *Pride and Prejudice*, she writes her sister, "I own I enjoy vast delight in the Folly of Mankind, and God be prais'd that is an inexhaustible Source of Entertainment" ([Sept. 1725], 2:56). The narrative energy of these female letters often derives from their loving rendition of mankind's—and womankind's—folly:

What a sad story of that vile Miss T. who has run away with Mr. O., and poor Mrs. O. *run mad,* and gone into the Bedlam! An intrigue was discovered last year, and hushed up, and Miss T. was more circumspect in her behavior, and it made no noise, but about a month ago she left her father's house under pretence of going to see her mother, she took her maid in the post-chaise with her, all her jewels, her best clothes, and £700, and went off to France; she was pursued but not overtaken. (Delany to Mrs. Dewes, undated, Llanover 3:452)

Delany loves such episodes; she reports many of them. Even Carter, despite her "insignificancy" ("I often secretly exult in the privileges that attend one's being suffered to go in and out of a room with as much silence, and as little ceremony as the cat" [14 Sept. 1754, 2:182]), and despite her editor's excisions, relates, for example, the tale of a rich man who shut himself up in his house, running to lock the door if he spied a human being nearby, and associating only with six "conversible" hogs (23 Jan. 1744, 1:48).

Such narratives substitute for narratives of the self—most strikingly, perhaps, in Delany's reports of her association with King George III and Queen Charlotte. Day after day, she renders in loving detail everything said and done at court and during royal visits, suppressing the fact of her own presence as much as possible, while yet emphasizing her powerful role as observer and narrator. In most of the anecdotes told by the other women, the tellers have not actually witnessed the events they report. Yet all, like Delany, assert by their narratives the traditional resources of women: to notice, to interpret, to tell.

The often scandalous stories incorporated in female correspondences help to define their reporters by the principle of differentiation—the women tell of lives led by other values and based on other assumptions than their own. They also satisfy forbidden wishes by brief vicarious excitement, reminding themselves of possibilities for the unconventional—if also, often, of the likelihood of retribution for deviation. And, of course, they enjoy the power of their knowledge and their telling, of being able to convey titillating information that their correspondent lacks. But their stories of male and female enactments of desire most forcefully convey their musings on the relative positions and possibilities accessible to men and women in their society. Their expedients for self-definition involve reflection on the same compelling subject.

The topic of women's position explicitly informs Lady Mary's project of self-definition. Characteristically her letters move from her own particular situation or that of another to meditations on the general— the social and psychological possibilities and limitations of the female. Lady Mary feels especially conscious of women's destiny of subordination; she cannot even choose an Italian tutor for herself but must accept her father's selection, since "'tis allwais the Fate of Women to obey" (to Frances Hewet, [13 Feb. 1710], Halsband, 1:21). Women have long been labeled frivolous, creatures of "trifling inclinations" (to Wortley, [28 Mar. 1710], 1:24); Lady Mary insists on her own difference. But she recurs frequently to the notion that Wortley cannot "esteem" her because he assumes her participation in the universal female weakness. She wishes that she could accept the fact that *all* men fail to esteem women; then she might rest content because her lover grants her wit and beauty and would not worry because he also assumes her folly and weakness ([25 Apr. 1710], 1:29). Writing to Bishop Gilbert Burnet, sending him her translation from a Latin version of Epictetus (unlike Carter, she had not mastered Greek), she comments that "Folly [is] reckon'd . . . our proper Sphere," and education is forbidden to women on the grounds that it makes them "tattling, impertinent, vain, and conceited" creatures. She will not argue, she says, for the equality of the sexes; she accepts the necessity of female submission. But she begs for the right to alleviate in herself the ignorance that allows women to be readily seduced, intellectually and morally (20 July 1710, 1:44, 45, 46).

These early statements set the tone for Lady Mary's utterances on the subject, typically marked by the same combination of announced resignation and ill-concealed resentment. Angry at Wortley, she acknowledges the wisdom of women who base their happiness on trifles because they, unlike her, yearn for what they can attain ([26 Feb. 1711], 1:83–84). Much later, to a woman friend (Barbara Calthorpe), she writes: "To say Truth, I have never had any great Esteem for the generality of the fair Sex, and my only consolation for being of the gender has been the assurance it gave me of never being marry'd to anyone amongst them." She adds, however, that she feels ashamed of her sex because of Lady Holderness's indiscreet marital plans (7 Dec. [1723], 2:33)—explicit evidence of how scandalous stories provoke thought about gender. In letters to her sister, Lady Mary poignantly recalls their early belief that marriage would solve all problems and childbearing would make one happy forever. She reflects on the world's tendency to generalize about her sex on the basis of a few women's reprehensible actions; she speaks insistently about the problem of interpretation, the way in which men understand all female responses as functions of women's sexuality. From the beginning, she has tried to separate herself from other women on the basis of her special intelligence, her unique "sincerity." Finally she accepts her participation in the female situation, advising her daughter about the education of girls, acknowledging the inevitability of disappointment, demonstrating the possibility of contentment despite the limited choices and limited resources inherent in the conditions of eighteenth-century womanhood. Even in this more resigned period of her life, however, she bursts out from time to time, as when she praises Francis Sydenham for his analysis of hysteria: "He clearly proves that your wise honourable spleen is the same disorder [a female hysteria]; but you vile usurpers do not only engross learning, power, and authority to yourselves, but will be our superiors even in constitution of mind" (to Sir James Steuart, [5 Sept. 1758], 3:171–72).

In her reflections about women, Lady Mary expresses the dilemmas of her own sense of specialness, her desire to declare her difference, and then her need at last to find what she shares with others of her kind. Mary Delany, compliant where Lady Mary was rebellious and leading a conventional rather than an ostentatiously original life, makes community her theme from the beginning—a more indirect way of thinking about women and of thinking about herself. Even her earliest letters to her sister emphasize the importance of "friendship." . . .

Delany's concern with relationships serves the same psychic purpose as Lady Mary's dwelling on the situation of her sex; both women thus confront the problem of their function in the world. In her earlier years Lady Mary occasionally published bits of poetry and prose—anonymously, sometimes employing a male persona—but she developed no real literary career. Her ne'er-do-well son made her feel a failure as a mother; her self-willed marriage hardly provided self-justification; her efforts to find romance in middle age proved disastrous. She could not hope to proclaim her worth by her accomplishments. The letters show her gradual reconciliation to a life dedicated more to being than to doing, reflecting on hers as a woman's fate. Delany, childless, kept herself constantly occupied. As the letters report, she did needlework, supervised the servants, endlessly copied other people's paintings, and created almost a thousand "paper mosaics" that were much praised by those who saw them. But she could not think of such work as supplying her life's meaning—meaning she found primarily in her human connections.

The thematic emphasis of Elizabeth Carter's letters to Catherine Talbot reflects yet another female strategy of self-presentation: constant disclaimers of the self's significance. Carter apologizes for the contents of her letters, characterizing them as "nonsense"; if she allows herself to move freely from one subject to another, she feels that she has imposed on her correspondent. The puddings Johnson praised have more problematic meaning for her: at the age of thirty, she reports an episode from her teens, when she "produced a pudding of a new invention, so overcharged with pepper and brandy that it put the whole family in a flame. The children all set up their little throats against Greek and Latin, and I found this unlucky event was like to prove my everlasting disgrace" (15 Sept. 1747, Pennington, 1:218). The children's association of domestic failure with intellectual preoccupation underlines Carter's anxiety about the propriety of her own concerns. She accuses herself of inability to make good use of time. "I am perpetually amusing myself with schemes of a hundred agreeable employments, which appear mighty practicable till I come to undertake them, and then, to my great mortification, I find it impossible to apply myself a single hour to any one thing without growing stupid, and feeling all manner of distempers" (29 Oct. 1747, 1:233). She suffers from bad nerves and headaches, but also, she says, from native dullness; she eagerly desires improvement, but feels a "tormenting incapacity of attaining it" (13 July 1748, 1:275). If she makes a joke about how the author of a play should assign his hero to some such quiet person as her or her correspondent, she immediately castigates herself for vanity. And so on.

This consistent self-deprecation is neither verbal tic nor mere convention. It reflects a profound "bashfulness" infecting the writer's entire life....

Shyness is a strategy of avoidance, protecting its victim from attracting one of the condescending lords of creation. Carter's reminiscence asserts a connection between suppressed female vanity, denied self-esteem, and repressed sexuality. Carter continues metaphorically to hang her head down, to deny her own importance, to experience social difficulties, and to refuse sexual connections. Like Delany, she writes passionately of her disinclination for marriage: "If I have suffered from the troubles of others, who have more sense, more understanding, and more virtues than I might reasonably have expected to find, what might I not have suffered from a husband! Perhaps be needlessly thwarted and contradicted in every innocent enjoyment of life: involved in all his schemes right or wrong, and perhaps not allowed the liberty of even silently seeming to disapprove them!" (21 May 1751, 2:29). She sees marriage, for a woman, as a situation of "voluntary dependence" and feels grateful to her father for allowing her to refuse it (28 Apr. 1750, 1:338). Her own "insignificant," private life strikes her as infinitely preferable.

Carter's protestations of insufficiency protect a treasured realm of private possibility. Occasionally she betrays resentment about the limiting rules of female decorum—after a lovely rural evening, for example, she cannot be allowed to walk home alone. But a sense of contentment emerges beneath her self-deprecations. . . .

Delany's primary concern with relationship, Lady Mary's obsession with the condition of women, Carter's proclamations of her own insignificance—such preoccupations help define the writers to themselves and locate them in the context of their society. The three women, despite their differences, share central concerns: female concerns. Their letters demonstrate not only the varied possibilities of self-presentation inherent in the epistolary act but also the degree to which self-exploration and self-presentation lead women to ruminate, implicitly or explicitly, on the special conditions of their sex.

Works Cited

Halsband, Robert, ed. *The Complete Letters of Lady Mary Wortley Montagu.* 3 vols. Oxford: Clarendon, 1966.

Llanover, Lady, ed. *The Autobiography and Correspondence of Mary Granville, Mrs. Delany.* 6 vols. London: Bentley, 1861.

Pennington, Montagu, ed. *A Series of Letters between Mrs. Elizabeth Carter and Miss Catherine Talbot, from the Year 1741 to 1770.* 4 vols. London: Rivington, 1809.

Richardson, Samuel. *Clarissa, or, the History of a Young Lady.* 4 vols. London: Dent, 1932.

Sherburn, George, ed. *The Correspondence of Alexander Pope.* 5 vols. Oxford: Clarendon, 1956.

PART IV
Histories

My life is history, politics, geography. It is religion and metaphysics. It is music and language. For me the language is an odd brand of English, mostly local, mostly half-breed spoken by the people around me, filled with elegance and vulgarity side by side, small jokes that are language jokes and family jokes and area jokes, certain expressions that are peculiar to that meeting of peoples who speak a familiar (to me) laconic language filled with question and comment embedded in a turn of phrase, a skewing of diction, a punning, cunning language that implies connections in diversity of syntax and perception, the oddness of how each of us seems and sees. It is the Southwest, the confluence of cultures, the headwaters of Mexico. It is multiethnic cowboy, with a strong rope of liturgy and classics tied to the pommel, a bedroll of dreams tied up behind, and a straight-shooting pistol packed along. It's no happenstance that the Gunn in my name has been good fortune, or that the Indians I knew growing up were cowboys. As most of the cowboys I knew were Indians—the others were Chicanos, Natives, and a few Anglos, though their idea of cowboy was mostly a big hat and western clothes (long before they found fashion in New York). Rednecks—Redskins: an odd thing, a dichotomy to Americans who go to movies and believe what they see, a continuum to others who take their history straight from life.

The triculture state, as New Mexico is often called, is more than three-cultured, as it works itself out in my life. It is Pueblo, Navajo and Apache, Chicano, Spanish, Spanish-American, Mexican-American; it is Anglo and that includes everything that is not Indian or Hispanic—in my case, Lebanese and Lebanese-American, German-Jewish, Italian-Catholic, German-Lutheran, Scotch-Irish-American Presbyterian, halfbreed (that is, people raised white-and-Indian), and Irish-Catholic; there are more, though these are the main ones that influenced me in childhood, and their influence was literary and aesthetic as well as social and personal. The land, the family, the road—three themes that haunt my mind and form my muse, these and the music: popular, country and western, native American, Arabic, Mexican, classical like operas and symphonies, especially Mozart, the Mass. The sounds I grew up with; the sounds of the voices, the instruments, the rhythms, the sounds of the land and the creatures. These are my sources, and these are my home.

—Paula Gunn Allen, "The Autobiography of a Confluence," in *I Tell You Now: Autobiographical Essays by Native American Writers*, ed. Brian Swann and Arnold Krupat (Lincoln: University of Nebraska Press, 1987), 145

The new mestiza *copes by developing a tolerance for contradictions, a tolerance for ambiguity. She learns to be an Indian in Mexican culture, to be Mexican from an Anglo point of view. She learns to juggle cultures. She has a plural personality, she operates in a pluralistic mode—nothing is thrust out, the good the bad and the ugly, nothing rejected, nothing abandoned. Not only does she sustain contradictions, she turns the ambivalence into something else. . . . This assembly is not one where severed or separated pieces merely come together. Nor is it a balancing of opposing powers. In attempting to work out a synthesis, the self had added a third element which is*

241

greater than the sum of its severed parts. That third element is a new consciousness—a mestiza consciousness—and though it is a source of intense pain, its energy comes from continual creative motion that keeps breaking down the unitary aspect of each new paradigm.

—Gloria Anzaldúa, *Borderlands/La Frontera: The New Mestiza*
(San Francisco: Aunt Lute Books, 1987), 79–80.

19 Stories

Carolyn Kay Steedman

The present tense of the verb to be *refers only to the present: but nevertheless with the first person singular in front of it, it absorbs the past which is inseparable from it. 'I am' includes all that has made me so. It is more than a statement of immediate fact: it is already biographical.*

—John Berger, *About Looking*[1]

This book is about lives lived out on the borderlands, lives for which the central interpretative devices of the culture don't quite work. It has a childhood at its centre—my childhood, a personal past—and it is about the disruption of that fifties childhood by the one my mother had lived out before me, and the stories she told about it. Now, the narrative of both these childhoods can be elaborated by the marginal and secret stories that other working-class girls and women from a recent historical past have to tell.

This book, then, is about interpretations, about the places where we rework what has already happened to give current events meaning. It is about the stories we make for ourselves, and the social specificity of our understanding of those stories. The childhood dreams recounted in this book, the fantasies, the particular and remembered events of a South London fifties childhood do not, by themselves, constitute its point. We all return to memories and dreams like this, again and again; the story we tell of our own life is reshaped around them. But the point doesn't lie there, back in the past, back in the lost time at which they happened; the only point lies in interpretation. The past is re-used through the agency of social information, and that interpretation of it can only be made with what people know of a social world and their place within it. It matters, then, whether one reshapes past time, re-uses the ordinary exigencies and crises of all childhoods whilst looking down from the curtainless windows of a terraced house like my mother did, or sees at that moment the long view stretching away from the big house in some richer and more detailed landscape. All children experience a first loss, a first exclusion; lives shape themselves around this sense of being cut off and denied. The health visitor repeated the exclusion in the disdainful language of class, told my mother exactly what it was she stood outside. It is a proposition of this book that specificity of place and politics has to be reckoned with in making an account of anybody's life, and their use of their own past.

My mother's longing shaped my own childhood. From a Lancashire mill town and a working-class twenties childhood she came away wanting: fine clothes, glamour, money; to be what she wasn't. However that longing was produced in her distant childhood, what she actually wanted were real things, real entities, things she materially lacked, things that a culture and a social system withheld from her. The story she told was about this wanting, and it remained a resolutely social story. When the world didn't deliver the goods, she held the world to blame. In this way, the story she told was a form of political analysis, that allows a political interpretation to be made of her life.

Personal interpretations of past time—the stories that people tell themselves in order to explain how they got to the place they currently inhabit—are often in deep and ambiguous conflict with the official interpretative devices of a culture. This book is organized around a conflict like this, taking as a starting point the structures of class analysis and schools of cultural criticism that cannot deal with everything there is to say about my mother's life. My mother was a single parent for most of her adulthood, who had children, but who also, in a quite particular way, didn't want them. She was a woman who finds no place in the iconography of working-class motherhood that Jeremy Seabrook presents in *Working Class Childhood*, and who is not to be found in Richard Hoggart's landscape. She ran a working-class household far away from the traditional communities of class, in exile and isolation, and in which a man was not a master, nor even there very much. Surrounded as a child by the articulated politics of class-consciousness, she became a working-class Conservative, the only political form that allowed her to reveal the politics of envy.

Many of these ambiguities raise central questions about gender as well as class, and the development of gender in particular social and class circumstances. So the usefulness of the biographical and autobiographical core of the book lies in the challenge it may offer to much of our conventional understanding of childhood, working-class childhood, and little-girlhood. In particular, it challenges the tradition of cultural criticism in this country, which has celebrated a kind of psychological simplicity in the lives lived out in Hoggart's endless streets of little houses.

It can help reverse a central question within feminism and psychoanalysis, about the reproduction of the desire to mother in little girls, and replace it with a consideration of women who, by refusing to mother, have refused to reproduce themselves or the circumstances of their exile. The personal past that this book deals with can also serve to raise the question of what happens to theories of patriarchy in households where a father's position is not confirmed by the social world outside the front door. And the story of two lives that follows points finally to a consideration of what people—particularly working-class children of the recent past—come to understand of themselves when all they possess is their labour, and what becomes of the notion of class-consciousness when it is seen as a structure of feeling that can be learned in childhood, with one of its components a proper envy, the desire of people for the things of the earth. Class and gender, and their articulations, are the bits and pieces from which psychological selfhood is made.

I grew up in the 1950s, the place and time now located as the first scene of Labour's failure to grasp the political consciousness of its constituency and its eschewal of socialism in favour of welfare philanthropism.[2] But the left had failed with my mother long before the 1950s. A working-class Conservative from a traditional Labour background, she shaped my childhood by the stories she carried from her own, and from an earlier family history. They were stories designed to show me the terrible unfairness of things, the subterranean culture of longing for that which one can never have. These stories can be used now to show my mother's dogged search, using what politics came to hand, for a public form to embody such longing.

Her envy, her sense of the unfairness of things, could not be directly translated into political understanding, and certainly could not be used by the left to shape an articulated politics of class. What follows offers no account of that particular political failure. It is rather an attempt to use that failure, which has been delineated by historians writing from quite different perspectives and for quite different purposes, as a device that may help to explain a particular childhood, and out of that childhood explain an individual life lived in historical time. This is not to say that this book involves a search for a past, or for what really happened.[3] It is about how people use the past to tell stories of their life. So the evidence presented here is of a different order from the biographical; it is about the experience of my own childhood, and the way in which my mother re-asserted, reversed, and restructured her own within mine.

Envy as a political motive has always been condemned: a fierce morality pervades what little writing there is on the subject. Fiercely moral as well, the tradition of cultural criticism in this country has, by ignoring feelings like these, given us the map of an upright and decent country. Out of this tradition has come Jeremy Seabrook's *Working Class Childhood* and its nostalgia for a time when people who were "united against cruel material privations . . . discovered the possibilities of the human consolations they could offer each other," and its celebration of the upbringing that produced the psychic structure of "the old working class."[4] I take a defiant pleasure in the way that my mother's story can be used to subvert this account. Born into "the old working class," she wanted: a New Look skirt, a timbered country cottage, to marry a prince.

The very devices that are intended to give expression to childhoods like mine and my mother's actually deny their expression. The problem with most childhoods lived out in households maintained by social class III (manual), IV and V parents is that they simply are not bad enough to be worthy of attention. The literary form that allows presentation of working-class childhood, the working-class autobiography, reveals its mainspring in the title of books like *Born to Struggle; Poverty, Hardship, But Happiness; Growing Up Poor in East London; Coronation Cups and Jam Jars*—and I am deeply aware of the ambiguities that attach to the childhood I am about to recount. Not only was it not very bad, or only bad in a way that working-class autobiography doesn't deal in, but also a particular set of emotional and psychological circumstances ensured that at the time, and for many years after it was over and I had escaped, I thought of it as *ordinary,* a period of relative material ease, just like everybody else's childhood.

I read female working-class autobiography obsessively when I was in my twenties and early thirties (a reading that involved much repetition: it's a small corpus), and whilst I wept over Catherine Cookson's *Our Kate* I felt a simultaneous distance from the Edwardian child who fetched beer barefooted for an alcoholic mother, the Kate of the title (I have to make it very clear that my childhood was really not like that). But it bore a relationship to a personal reality that I did not yet know about: what I now see in the book is its fine delineation of the feeling of being on the outside, outside the law; for Catherine Cookson was illegitimate.[5]

In 1928, when Kathleen Woodward, who had grown up in not-too-bad Peckham, South London, wrote *Jipping Street,* she set her childhood in Bermondsey, in a place of abject and abandoned poverty, "practically off the map, derelict," and in this manner found a way, within an established literary form, of expressing a complexity of feeling about her personal past that the form itself did not allow.[6]

The tradition of cultural criticism that has employed working-class lives, and their rare expression in literature, had made solid and concrete the absence of psychological individuality—of subjectivity—that Kathleen Woodward struggled against in *Jipping Street.* "In poor societies," writes Jeremy Seabrook in *Working Class Childhood,*

> where survival is more important than elaboration of relationships, the kind of ferocious personal struggles that lock people together in our own more leisured society are less known.[7]

But by making this distinction, the very testimony to the continuing reverberation of pain and loss, absence and desire in childhood, which is made manifest in the words of "the old working-class" people that make up much of *Working Class Childhood,* is actually denied.

It would not be possible, in fact, to write a book called "Middle Class Childhood" (this in spite of the fact that the shelves groan with psychoanalytic, developmental and literary accounts of such childhoods) and get the same kind of response from readers. It's a faintly titillating title, carrying the promise that some kind of pathology is about to be investigated. What is more, in *Working Class Childhood* the discussion of childhood and what our society has done to the idea of childhood becomes the vehicle for an anguished rejection of post-War materialism, the metaphor for all that has gone wrong with the old politics of class and the stance of the labour movement towards the desires that capitalism has inculcated in those who are seen as the passive poor. An analysis like this denies its subjects a particular story, a personal history, except when that story illustrates a general thesis; and it denies the child, and the child who continues to live in the adult it becomes, both an unconscious life, and a particular and developing consciousness of the meanings presented by the social world.

Twenty years before *Working Class Childhood* was written, Richard Hoggart explored a similar passivity of emotional life in working-class communities, what in *The Uses of Literacy* he reveal-

ingly called "Landscape with Figures: A Setting"—a place where in his own memories of the 1920s and 1930s and in his description of similar communities of the 1950s, most people lacked "any feeling that some change can, or indeed ought to be made in the general pattern of life."[8] All of Seabrook's corpus deals in the same way with what he sees as "the falling into decay of a life once believed by those who shared it to be the only admissable form that life could take."[9] I want to open the door of one of the terraced houses, in a mill town in the 1920s, show Seabrook my mother and her longing, make him see the child of my imagination sitting by an empty grate, reading a tale that tells her a goose-girl can marry a king.

Heaviness of time lies on the pages of *The Uses of Literacy.* The streets are all the same; nothing changes. Writing about the structure of a child's life, Seabrook notes that as recently as thirty years ago (that is, in the 1950s, the time of my own childhood) the week was measured out by each day's function—wash-day, market-day, the day for ironing—and the day itself timed by "cradling and comforting" ritual.[10] This extraordinary attribution of sameness and the acceptance of sameness to generations of lives arises from several sources. First of all, delineation of emotional and psychological selfhood has been made by and through the testimony of people in a central relationship to the dominant culture, that is to say by and through people who are not working class. This is an obvious point, but it measures out an immensely complicated and contradictory area of historical development that has scarcely yet been investigated. Superficially, it might be said that historians, failing to find evidence of most people's emotional or psychosexual existence, have simply assumed that there can't have been much there to find. Such an assumption ignores the structuring of late nineteenth- and early twentieth-century psychology and psychoanalysis, and the way in which the lived experience of the majority of people in a class society has been pathologized and marginalized. When the sons of the working class, who have made their earlier escape from this landscape of psychological simplicity, put so much effort into accepting and celebrating it, into delineating a background of uniformity and passivity, in which pain, loss, love, anxiety and desire are washed over with a patina of stolid emotional sameness, then something important, and odd, and possibly promising of startling revelation, is actually going on. This refusal of a complicated psychology to those living in conditions of material distress is a central theme of [my] book. . . .

The attribution of psychological simplicity to working-class people also derives from the positioning of mental life within Marxism:

> Mental life flows from material conditions. Social being is determined above all by class position—location within the realm of production. Consciousness and politics, all mental conceptions spring from material forces and the relations of production and so reflect these class origins.

This description is Sally Alexander's summary of Marx's "Preface to a Contribution to the Critique of Political Economy," and of his thesis, expressed here and elsewhere, that "the mode of production of material life conditions the general process of social, political and mental life."[11] The attribution of simplicity to the mental life of working people is not, of course, made either in the original, nor in this particular critique of it. But like any theory developed in a social world, the notion of consciousness as located within the realm of production draws on the reality of that world. It is in the "Preface" itself that Marx mentions his move to London in the 1850s as offering among other advantages "a convenient vantage point for the observation of bourgeois society," and which indeed he did observe, and

live within, in the novels he and his family read, in family theatricals, in dinner-table talk: a mental life apparently much richer than that of the subjects of his theories. Lacking such possessions of culture, working-class people have come to be seen, within the field of cultural criticism, as bearing the elemental simplicity of class-consciousness and little more.

Technically, class-consciousness has not been conceived of as *psychological* consciousness. It has been separated from "the empirically given, and from the psychologically describable and explicable ideas that men form about their situation in life," and has been seen rather as a possible set of reactions people might have to discovering the implications of the position they occupy within the realm of production.[12] Theoretical propositions apart though, in the everyday world, the term *is* used in its psychological sense, is generally and casually used to describe what people have "thought, felt and wanted at any moment in history and from any point in the class structure."[13] Working-class autobiography and people's history have been developed as forms that allow the individual and collective expression of these thoughts, feelings and desires about class societies and the effect of class structures on individuals and communities. But as forms of analysis and writing, people's history and working-class autobiography are relatively innocent of psychological theory, and there has been little space within them to discuss the *development* of class-consciousness (as opposed to its expression), nor for understanding of it as a *learned* position, learned in childhood, and often through the exigencies of difficult and lonely lives.

Children present a particular problem here, for whilst some women may learn the official dimensions of class-consciousness by virtue of their entry into the labour market and by adopting forms of struggle and understanding evolved by men,[14] children, who are not located directly within the realm of production, still reach understandings of social position, exclusion and difference. At all levels, class-consciousness must be learned in some way, and we need a model of such a process to explain the social and psychological development of working-class children (indeed, of all children).

When the mental life of working-class women is entered into the realm of production, and their narrative is allowed to disrupt the monolithic story of wage-labour and capital and when childhood and childhood learning are reckoned with, then what makes the old story unsatisfactory is not so much its granite-like *plot*, built around exploiter and exploited, capital and proletariat, but rather its *timing*: the precise how and why of the development of class-consciousness. But if we do allow an unconscious life to working-class children, then we can perhaps see the first loss, the earliest exclusion (known most familiarly to us as the oedipal crisis) brought forward later, and articulated through an adult experience of class and class relations.

An adult experience of class does not in any case, as Sally Alexander has pointed out, "produce a shared and even consciousness," even if it is fully registered and articulated.[15] This uneven and problematic consciousness (which my mother's life and political conviction represent so clearly) is one of the subjects of this book. A perception of childhood experience and understanding, used as the lineaments of adult political analysis, may also help us see, under the language and conflicts of class, historically much older articulations—the subjective and political expressions of radicalism—which may still serve to give a voice to people who know that they do not have what they want, who know that they have been cut off from the earth in some way.[16]

The attribution of psychological sameness to the figures in the working-class landscape has been made by men, for whom the transitions of class are at once more ritualized than they are

for women, and much harder to make. Hoggart's description of the plight of the "scholarship boy" of the thirties and forties, and the particular anxiety afflicting those in the working class

> who have been pulled one stage away from their original culture and have not the intellectual equipment which would then cause them to move on to join the 'declassed' professionals and experts,[17]

makes nostalgic reading now in a post-War situation where a whole generation of escapees occupies professional positions that allow them to speak of their working-class origins with authority, to use them, in Seabrook's words "as a kind of accomplishment."[18] By the 1950s the divisions of the educational establishment that produced Hoggart's description were much altered, and I, a grammar-school girl of the 1960s, was sent to university with a reasonably full equipment of culture and a relative degree of intellectual self-awareness. Jeremy Seabrook, some eight years older than me and at Cambridge in the late fifties, sat with his fellow travellers from working-class backgrounds "telling each other escape stories, in which we were all picaresque heroes of our own lives."[19]

But at the University of Sussex in 1965, there were no other women to talk to like this, at least there were none that I met (though as proletarianism was fashionable at the time, there were several men with romantic and slightly untruthful tales to tell). And should I have met a woman like me (there must have been some: we were all children of the Robbins generation), we could not have talked of escape except within a literary framework that we had learned from the working-class novels of the early sixties (some of which, like *Room at the Top*, were set books on certain courses); and that framework was itself ignorant of the material stepping-stones of our escape: clothes, shoes, make-up. We could not be heroines of the conventional narratives of escape. Women are, in the sense that Hoggart and Seabrook present in their pictures of transition, without class, because the cut and fall of a skirt and good leather shoes can take you across the river and to the other side: the fairy-tales tell you that goose-girls may marry kings.

The fixed townscapes of Northampton and Leeds that Hoggart and Seabrook have described show endless streets of houses, where mothers who don't go out to work order the domestic day, where men are masters, and children, when they grow older, express gratitude for the harsh discipline meted out to them. The first task is to particularize this profoundly ahistorical landscape (and so this book details a mother who was a parent, and a father who wasn't a patriarch). And once the landscape is detailed and historicized in this way, the urgent need becomes to find a way of theorizing the result of such difference and particularity, not in order to find a description that can be universally applied (the point is not to say that all working-class childhoods are the same, nor that experience of them produces unique psychic structures) but so that the people in exile, the inhabitants of the long street, may start to use the autobiographical "I," and tell the stories of their life.

There are other interpretative devices for my mother which, like working-class autobiographies of childhood, make her no easier to see. Nearly everything that has been written on the subject of mothering (except the literature of pathology, of battering and violence) assumes the desire to mother; and there are feminisms now that ask me to return Persephone-like to my own mother, and find new histories of my strength. When I first came across Kathleen Woodward's *Jipping Street,* I read it with the shocked astonishment of one who had never seen what she knows written down before. Kathleen Woodward's mother of the 1890s was the

one I knew: mothers were those who told you how hard it was to have you, how long they were in labour with you ("twenty hours with you," my mother frequently reminded me) and who told you to accept the impossible contradiction of being both desired and a burden; and not to complain.[20] This ungiving endurance is admired by working-class boys who grow up to write about their mother's flinty courage. But the daughter's silence on the matter is a measure of the price you pay for survival. I don't think the baggage will ever lighten, for me or my sister. We were born, and had no choice in the matter; but we were burdens, expensive, never grateful enough. There was nothing we could do to pay back the debt of our existence. "Never have children dear," she said; "they ruin your life." Shock moves swiftly across the faces of women to whom I tell this story. But it is ordinary not to want your children, to find them a nuisance.

I read the collection *Fathers: Reflections by Daughters,* or Ann Oakley's *Taking It Like a Woman*[21] and feel the painful and familiar sense of exclusion from these autobiographies of middle-class little-girlhood and womanhood, envy of those who belong, who can, like Ann Oakley, use the outlines of conventional romantic fiction to tell a life story. And women like this, friends, say: but it was like that for me too, my childhood was like yours; my father was like that, my mother didn't want me. What they cannot bear, I think, is that there exist a poverty and marginality of experience to which they have no access, structures of feeling that they have not lived within (and would not want to live within: for these are the structures of deprivation). They are caught then in a terrible exclusion, an exclusion from the experience of others that measures out their own central relationship to the culture. The myths tell their story, the fairy-tales show the topography of the houses they once inhabited. The psychoanalytic drama, which uses the spatial and temporal structures of all these old tales, permits the entry of such women to the drama itself. Indeed, the psychoanalytic drama was constructed to describe that of middle-class women (and as drama it does of course describe all such a woman's exclusions, as well as her relationship to those exclusions, with her absence and all she lacks lying at the very heart of the theory). The woman whose drama psychoanalytic case-study describes in this way never does stand to one side, and watch, and know she doesn't belong.

What follows is largely concerned with how two girl children, growing up in different historical periods, got to be the women they became. The sense of exclusion, of being cut off from what others enjoy, was a dominant sense of both childhoods, but expressed and used differently in two different historical settings. This detailing of social context to psychological development reveals not only difference, but also certain continuities of experience in working-class childhood. For instance, many recent accounts of psychological development and the development of gender treat our current social situation as astonishingly new and strange:

> On the social/historical level . . . we are living in a period in which mothers are increasingly living alone with their children, offering opportunities for new psychic patterns to emerge. Single mothers are forced to make themselves subject to their children; they are forced to invent new symbolic roles . . . The child cannot position the mother as object to the father's law, since in single parent households her desire sets things in motion.[22]

But the evidence of some nineteenth- and twentieth-century children used in this book shows that in their own reckoning their households were often those of a single female parent, sometimes because of the passivity of a father's presence, sometimes because of his physical absence. Recent feminisms have often, as Jane Gallop points out in *The Daughter's Seduction,* endowed men with "the sort of unified phallic sovereignty that characterises an absolute monarch, and which little resembles actual power in our social, economic structure."[23] We need a reading of history that reveals fathers mattering in a different way from the way they matter in the corpus of traditional psychoanalysis, the novels that depict the same familial settings and in the bourgeois households of the fairy-tales.

A father like mine dictated each day's existence; our lives would have been quite different had he not been there. But he didn't *matter,* and his singular unimportance needs explaining. His not mattering has an effect like this: I don't quite believe in male power; somehow the iron of patriarchy didn't enter into my soul. I accept the idea of male power intellectually, of course (and I will eat my words the day I am raped, or the knife is slipped between my ribs; though I know that will not be the case: in the dreams it is a woman who holds the knife, and only a woman can kill).

Fixing my father, and my mother's mothering, in time and politics can help show the creation of gender in particular households and in particular familial situations at the same time as it demonstrates the position of men and the social reality represented by them in particular households. We need historical accounts of such relationships, not just a longing that they might be different.[24] Above all, perhaps, we need a sense of people's complexity of relationship to the historical situations they inherit. In *Family and Kinship in East London,* the authors found that over half the married women they interviewed had seen their mothers within the preceding twenty-four hours, and that 80 per cent had seen them within the previous week. Young and Willmott assumed that the daughters wanted to do this, and interpreted four visits a week on average as an expression of attachment and devotion.[25] There exists a letter that I wrote to a friend one vacation from Sussex, either in 1966 or 1967, in which I described my sitting in the evenings with my mother, refusing to go out, holding tight to my guilt and duty, knowing that I *was* her, and that I must keep her company; and we were certainly not Demeter and Persephone to each other, nor ever could be, but two women caught by a web of sexual and psychological relationships in the front room of a council house, the South London streets stretching away outside like the railway lines that brought us and our history to that desperate and silent scene in front of the flickering television screen.

Raymond Williams has written about the difficulty of linking past and present in writing about working-class life, and the result of this difficulty in novels that either show the past to be a regional zone of experience in which the narrator cancels her present from the situation she is describing, or which are solely about the experience of flight. Writing like this, comments Williams, has lacked "any sense of the continuity of working class life, which does not cease just because the individual [the writer] moves out of it, but which also itself changes internally."[26]

This kind of cancellation of a writer's present from the past may take place because novels—stories—work by a process of temporal revelation: they move forward in time in order to demonstrate a state of affairs. The novel that works in this way employs contingency, that is, it works towards the revelation of something not quite certain, but *there*, nevertheless, waiting to be shown by the story,[27] and the story gets told without revealing the shaping force of the writer's current situation.

The highlighting not just of the subject matter of this book, but also of the possibilities of written form it involves, is important, because the construction of the account that follows has

something to say about the question that Raymond Williams has raised, and which is largely to do with the writing of stories that aren't central to a dominant culture. My mother cut herself off from the old working class by the process of migration, by retreat from the North to a southern country with my father, hiding secrets in—South London's long streets. But she carried with her her childhood, as I have carried mine along the lines of embourgeoisement and state education. In order to outline these childhoods and the uses we put them to, the structure of psychoanalytic case-study—the narrative form that Freud is described as inventing—is used in this book.[28] The written case-study allows the writer to enter the present into the past, allows the dream, the wish or the fantasy of the past to shape current time, and treats them as evidence in their own right. In this way, the narrative form of case-study shows what went into its writing, shows the bits and pieces from which it is made up, in the way that history refuses to do, and that fiction can't.[29] Case-study presents the ebb and flow of memory, the structure of dreams, the stories that people tell to explain themselves to others. The autobiographical section of this book, the second part, is constructed on such a model.

But something else has to be done with these bits and pieces, with all the tales that are told, in order to take them beyond the point of anecdote and into history. To begin to construct history, the writer has to do two things, make two movements through time. First of all, we need to search backwards from the vantage point of the present in order to appraise things in the past and attribute meaning to them. When events and entities in the past have been given their meaning in this way, then we can trace forward what we have already traced backwards, and make a history.[30] When a history is finally written, events are explained by putting them in causal order and establishing causal connections between them. But what follows in this book does not make a history (even though a great deal of historical material is presented). For a start, I simply do not know enough about many of the incidents described to explain the connections between them. I am unable to perform an act of historical explanation in this way.

This tension between the stories told to me as a child, the diffuse and timeless structure of the case-study with which they are presented, and the compulsions of historical explanation is no mere rhetorical device. There is a real problem, a real tension here that I cannot resolve (my inability to resolve it is part of the story). All the stories that follow, told as this book, aren't stories in their own right: they exist in tension with other more central ones. In the same way, the processes of working-class autobiography, of people's history and of the working-class novel cannot show a proper and valid culture existing in its own right, underneath the official forms, waiting for revelation. Accounts of working-class life are told by tension and ambiguity, out on the borderlands. The story—my mother's story, a hundred thousand others—cannot be absorbed into the central one: it is both its disruption and its essential counterpoint: this is a drama of *class*.

But visions change, once any story is told; ways of seeing are altered. The point of a story is to present itself momentarily as complete, so that it can be said: it does for now, it will do; it is an account that will last a while. Its point is briefly to make an audience connive in the telling, so that they might say: yes, that's how it was; or, that's how it could have been. So now, the words written down, the world is suddenly full of women waiting, as in Ann Oakley's extraordinary delineation of

the curiously impressive image of women as always waiting for someone or something, in shopping queues, in antenatal clinics, in bed for men to come home, at the school gates, by the playground swing, for birth or the growing up of children, in hope of love or freedom or re-employment, waiting for the future to liberate or burden them and the past to catch up with them.[31]

The other side of waiting is wanting. The faces of the women in the queues are the faces of unfulfilled desire; if we look there are many women driven mad in this way, as my mother was. This is a sad and secret story, but it isn't just hers alone.

What historically conscious readers may do with this book is read it as a Lancashire story, see here evidence of a political culture of 1890–1930 carried from the Northwest, to shape another childhood in another place and time. They will perhaps read it as part of an existing history, seeing here a culture shaped by working women, and their consciousness of themselves as workers. They may see the indefatigable capacity for work that has been described in many other places, the terrifying ability to *get by,* to cope, against all odds. Some historically conscious readers may even find here the irony that this specific social and cultural experience imparted to its women: "No one gives you anything," said my mother, as if reading the part of "our mam" handed to her by the tradition of working-class autobiography. "If you want things, you have to go out and work for them." But out of that tradition I can make the dislocation that the irony actually permits, and say: "If no one will write my story, then I shall have to go out and write it myself."

The point of being a Lancashire weaver's daughter, as my mother was, is that it is *classy*: what my mother knew was that if you were going to be working class, then you might as well be the best that's going, and for women, Lancashire and weaving provided that elegance, that edge of difference and distinction. I'm sure that she told the titled women whose hands she did when she became a manicurist in the 1960s where it was she came from, proud, defiant: look at me. (Beatrix Campbell has made what I think is a similar point about the classiness of being a miner, for working-class men.) [32]

This is a book about stories; and it is a book about *things* (objects, entities, relationships, people), and the way in which we talk and write about them: about the difficulties of metaphor. Above all, it is about people wanting those things, and the structures of political thought that have labelled this wanting as wrong. Later in the book, suggestions are made about a relatively old structure of political thought in this country, that of radicalism, and its possible entry into the political dialogue of the Northwest; and how perhaps it allowed people to feel desire, anger and envy—for the things they did not have.

The things, though, will remain a problem. The connection between women and clothes surfaces often in these pages, particularly in the unacknowledged testimony of many nineteenth- and twentieth-century women and girls; and it was with the image of a New Look coat that, in 1950, I made my first attempt to understand and symbolize the content of my mother's desire. I think now of all the stories, all the reading, all the dreams that help us to see ourselves in the landscape, and see ourselves watching as well. "A woman must continually watch herself," remarked John Berger some years ago.

> She is almost continually accompanied by her own image of herself. Whilst she is walking across a room or whilst she is weeping at the death of her father, she can scarcely avoid envisioning herself walking and weeping. [33]

This book is intended to specify, in historical terms, some of the processes by which we come to step into the landscape, and see ourselves. But the *clothes* we wear there remain a question. Donald Winnicott wrote about the transitional object (those battered teddies and bits of blanket that babies use in the early stages of distinguishing themselves from the world around them) and its usefulness to the young children who adopt it. The transitional object, he wrote, "must seem to the infant to give warmth, or to move, or to have texture, or to do something that seems to show it has vitality or reality of its own." [34] Like clothes: that we may see ourself better as we stand there and watch; and for our protection.

Notes

This chapter is the first chapter of Stedman's *Landscape for a Good Woman: A Story of Two Lives* (New Brunswick, Rutgers University Press, 1987).

1. John Berger, *About Looking* (Writers and Readers, 1972), 370–71.
2. Gareth Stedman-Jones, "Why is the Labour Party in a Mess?" in *Languages of Class: Studies in English Working Class History, 1832–1982* (Cambridge: Cambridge University Press, 1983), 239–56. Beatrix Campbell surveys critiques of the 1950s in *Wigan Pier Revisited* (Virago, 1984), 217–34. See also James Hinton, *Labour and Socialism: A History of the British Labour Movement, 1867–1974,* (Brighton: Wheatsheaf, 1983), 182–87.
3. "What actually happened is less important than what is felt to have happened. Is that right?" says Ronald Fraser to his analyst, and his analyst agrees. Ronald Fraser, *In Search of a Past* (Verso, 1984), 95.
4. Jeremy Seabrook, *Working Class Childhood* (Gollancz, 1982), 23–27, 33.
5. Catherine Cookson, *Our Kate* (Macdonald, 1969).
6. Kathleen Woodward, *Jipping Street* (1928; Virago, 1983).
7. Seabrook, *Working,* 140.
8. Richard Hoggart, *The Uses of Literacy* (Penguin, 1959), 91.

9. Jeremy Seabrook, *The Unprivileged* (1967; Penguin, 1973), Foreword.

10. Ibid., 102–3.

11. Sally Alexander, "Women, Class and Sexual Difference," *History Workshop Journal* 17 (1984): 125–49. Karl Marx, "Preface to 'A Contribution to the Critique of Political Economy'" (1859), *Early Writings*, Pelican Marx Library (Penguin, 1975), 474–78.

12. George Lukacs, *History and Class Consciousness* (Merlin Press, 1968), 46–82, especially 50–55. See also Eric Hobsbawm, "Notes on Class Consciousness," in *Worlds of Labour* (Weidenfeld and Nicolson, 1984), 15–32.

13. George Lukacs, 51.

14. Pauline Hunt, *Gender and Class Consciousness* (Macmillan, 1980), 171–79. A direct and simple learning isn't posited here; but it is the workplace and an existing backdrop of trade-union organization that provide for the expression of women's class consciousness.

15. Alexander, 131.

16. Carolyn Kay Steedman, "Exclusions," *Landscape for a Good Woman: A Story of Two Lives* (New Brunswick: Rutgers University Press, 1987), 119–21; and Gareth Stedman-Jones, "Rethinking Chartism" in Stedman-Jones, 90–178.

17. Hoggart, 293.

18. Jeremy Seabrook, *What Went Wrong?* (Gollancz, 1978), 260–61.

19. Ibid., 262.

20. To be told how difficult it was to give birth to you is an extremely common experience for all little girls, and as John and Elizabeth Newson point out in *Seven Years Old in the Home Environment* (Allen & Unwin, 1976), 186–87, chaperonage, and the consequent amount of time girls spend in adult company, are likely to make such topics of conversation accessible to them. But the punishment and the warning involved in telling girl children about the difficulties their birth presented to their mother are rarely written about. But see Carolyn Steedman, *The Tidy House: Little Girls Writing* (Virago, 1982), 34–35, 145–47.

21. Ursula Owen, ed., *Fathers: Reflections by Daughters* (Virago, 1983). Ann Oakley, *Taking It Like a Woman* (Cape, 1984).

22. E. Ann Kaplan, "Is the Gaze Male?" in *Desire: The Politics of Female Sexuality*, ed. Ann Snitow et al. (Virago, 1984), 335.

23. Jane Gallop, *Feminism and Psychoanalysis: The Daughter's Seduction* (Macmillan, 1982), xv.

24. For recent arguments concerning the necessity of historicization, see Jane Lewis, "The Debate on Sex and Class," *New Left Review* 149 (1985), 108–20.

25. Michael Young and Peter Willmott, *Family and Kinship in East London* (Penguin, 1962), 44–61.

26. Raymond Williams, *Politics and Letters* (NLB/Verso, 1979), 271–72. See also Seabrook, *What Went Wrong?* 261, where the same process is described: a working-class life, ossified by time, enacted in "symbolic institutional ways, by those who teach in poor schools, or who write novels and memoirs about a way of life which they have not directly experienced since childhood."

27. Seymour Chatman, *Story and Discourse: Narrative Structure in Fiction and Film* (Ithaca: Cornell University Press, 1978), 45–48.

28. See Steven Marcus, "Freud and Dora: Story, History, Case-History," in *Representations* (New York: Random House, 1976), 247–310, for the argument that Freud invented a new narrative form in his writing of the "Dora" case. See also Steedman, "Histories," *Landscape for a Good Woman*, 130–34.

29. For a brief discussion of the way in which historical writing masks the processes that brought it into being, see Timothy Ashplant, "The New Social Function of Cinema," *Journal of the British Film Institute* 79/80 (1981): 107–9, and Hayden White, "The Value of Narrativity in the Representation of Reality," *Critical Inquiry* 7, no. 1 (1980): 5–27.

30. Paul Ricoeur, *Time and Narrative* (Chicago: University of Chicago Press, 1984), 118, 157.

31. Ann Oakley, *From Here to Maternity: Becoming a Mother* (Penguin, 1981), 11.

32. Campbell, 97–115.

33. John Berger, *Ways of Seeing* (BBC/Penguin, 1972), 46.

34. Donald Winnicott, *Playing and Reality* (Penguin, 1974), 6.

20 Literary Domesticity and Women Writers' Subjectivities

Mary Jean Corbett

. . . Like the novel, the self-representing text is subject to circulation as a commodity: when one writes, prints, publishes, and markets an autobiography, one effectively sells oneself, one's own experience. Inserting oneself into that network of public circulation is as threatening in its way to Wordsworth and Carlyle as it is to Sherwood and Tonna. Those autobiographers, however, can report their experiences as a narrated history in which the "I" has an important, centering role, partly because of their different relation to commodity production, partly because literary and religious authority provide the necessary legitimation for self-representation. But with Martineau the exception to the rule, most secular woman autobiographers, who generally lack these two reference points, can master their anxiety about being circulated, read, and interpreted only by carefully shaping the personae they present and, more especially, by subordinating their histories of themselves to others' histories.

In this way, the middle-class woman writing autobiography both avoids self-exposure and attains a narrative stance closer to the fiction writer's: it is not her story she represents, but the story of others as she sees them. Underlying this strategy is a fundamental cynicism or pragmatism (depending on your point of view) about the way in which public representation operates:

as Eliza Lynn Linton asks in *My Literary Life* (1899), "could, indeed, any public man's life be transacted without myths and masks?"[1] Probably not, if one conceives of the public sphere, as [Margaret] Oliphant and Linton do, as the realm of inauthenticity and compromise. In their terms, self-representation becomes its writer's last performance of a role she writes to protect herself against the deformations of publicity and celebrity, the final mask that will survive her, a mask that can shield the private individual from public view.

Some middle-class women writing autobiography minimize their risk by laying little or nothing on the line, suppressing what they construct as the private feminine self. And as we will see in Oliphant's own autobiographical practice, even the knowledge that what they write will be read by strangers need not prevent them from representing intimate experience. But whether the autobiographer represents herself indirectly through reference to a familial network and a literary-historical context largely emptied of affective content, as some of the memoirists I will next consider do, or directly and personally, as Oliphant unexpectedly does, the sense of negotiating the boundary between public and private is particularly strong in these late-century texts even as that boundary begins to show signs of being constituted in new terms.

Subjectivity in Memoir

. . . Camilla Crosland (1812–95) begins her text, *Landmarks of a Literary Life 1820–1892* (1893), by offering a rationale for writing and publishing it, but her justification depends less on a sense of her own importance as a literary woman than on her position as a historian of the everyday:

> Probably no observant person ever reaches even middle age without being conscious of those changes of manners and modes, which taking place apparently but slowly, do yet, in the course of a decade or two, bring about silent social revolutions. It is for this reason that the recollections of any truth-loving, truth-telling individual who has passed the allotted three-score years and ten of life, mixing in the society of a great metropolis, ought to be worth recording. Swiftly the seasons pass by; old men and women drop into their graves, taking with them memories of the past which would be precious to historians and artists; and the young spring up to mount with measured steps or rapid strides to the world's high places, or to glide into the ranks of obscure workers.[2]

As one century passes into the next, the past as experienced by the individual can and should be conserved for future generations; this documentary record, Crosland asserts, plays a role in transmitting history from one age to another.

We see in this rationale for self-representation new concepts of history and subjectivity. Unlike Carlyle and his contemporaries, who saw history as the collective biography of great men, Crosland sees history happening in and through all individuals, each of whom has some story to tell. As Valerie Sanders puts it in describing this mode, "Everybody has 'recollections,' and even the humblest have their share of interest."[3] By conferring on everyone the potential capacity to tell life stories from particular points of view, Crosland suggests that the history of each individual, whether elite or obscure, has some value for readers. Every person is presumed to possess a distinct subjectivity, a particular vantage point depending on where that person stands in the world. Hence "the recollections of any truth-loving, truth-telling individual," and not only the story of the great man or the exceptional woman, "ought to be worth recording." Like Virginia Woolf, who wrote forty years later about her longing to read "the lives of the obscure," Crosland invests the record of ordinary experience with a historical value; she calls for life histories that will edify and represent both high and low.

The "democratic" impulse at work here does not imply, however, that sociocultural differences among individual subjects have disappeared: some readers will reach "the world's high places," while others will join "the ranks of obscure workers," just as the writer has occupied a particular place in the hierarchy. Gradually extending the legal and social status of the individual subject to include all men without respect to class position, liberal ideology in the nineteenth century thus creates a nominal equality among men which masks structural inequality, for high and low remain operative categories. Within the genre of autobiography, this means that all have access to writing the self, but that their contributions are differentially valued. Autobiography thus becomes the literary province of the great and the not-so-great alike: in an era in which the ideology of liberal individualism provides—as it continues to provide for the great many—the dominant model for middle-class subjectivity, the idea that "the thoughts and opinions of one human being," as Mary Ward puts it, "must always have an interest for some other human beings" makes the self-representing text a monument to the triumph of bourgeois ideology.[4]

Those who write autobiography, however, have particular relations to the liberal individualist model and those particularities depend in part on their positions in class and gender. By the end of the nineteenth century, middle-class women, too, formed a social group, each member of which could legitimately claim, as Crosland does, to be a participant-observer in and of public history. With the rise of fictional and actual "New Women" liberated from the domestic sphere and bent on taking their place in the public world—a place that had been partially prepared for them by the women's movement of the previous forty years—women were more able to position themselves textually as subjects in and of their histories. Middle-class women's autobiographies, then, underwent significant mutations once middle-class women's roles had been redefined to include possibilities for work outside the home, as autobiographies by Beatrice Webb, Annie Besant, and Frances Power Cobbe all testify; however, the dominant mode of autobiography among late Victorian literary women—the memoir—formally and thematically reflects the distinct historical experience of women as unequal and selfless subjects. In their practice as literary memoirists, Crosland and Eliza Lynn Linton (1822–98) exemplify this paradigm for autobiographical subjectivity. . . .[5]

Other Victorian women writers also write memoir rather than more self-centered narratives, perhaps because it allows them, as it does Crosland, to tell their stories between the lines, to narrate their histories as part of a larger story; the memoir legitimates the telling of their own lives without demanding that they commit full disclosure. As Valerie Sanders writes of such texts, "The speaker is often no more than a reporter of outmoded practices, funny experiences, or impressions of the great and famous," as in Crosland's *Landmarks*; "her audience's attention is focused on the told, rather than on the teller" (6). Writing the memoir can thus signify an utter unwillingness on the writer's behalf to speak of the self at all. The narrator must have a certain "name" (readers are unlikely to buy or read the recollections of someone they have never heard of) and convey an intimate look at celebrated public figures, but the memoir does not require that its narrator explicitly reveal herself. . . .

With the massive Victorian expansion of the popular press, which generated a bountiful supply of "private" information on "public" figures, personality became a marketable commodity on a scale that had never before been approached. The success of a work such as Edmund Yates's *Celebrities at Home* (1877–79) (a three-volume collection of vignettes that portrays an assortment of literary, artistic, and political figures *en famille*), the astounding circulation figures for papers such as the *Illustrated London News* and *Tit-Bits,* the popularity of autobiography itself, all testify to the extraordinary transformation of the relation between the private individual and the public world. Publishers consciously created and exploited the mass appeal that "sketches from the life" held for Victorian reading audiences. As early as the 1850s, for example, Mitford had been pressured by her publisher into giving her text its misnomer (*Recollections of a Literary Life*) because Richard Bentley believed, probably with some justification, that the titular suggestion of autobiography would sell more copies than the more accurate and less glamorous titles (*Readings of Poetry* and *Recollections of Books*) that she preferred.[6] The power of the celebrated name, Mitford's or Linton's, thus translates directly into market value.

The memoir, then, becomes a popular form because it purports to offer an insider's perspective on a sphere to which the common reader

ordinarily has little access. It can also be a pe-
culiarly appropriate form for a woman because
it allows her either to be silent about herself, as
in the case of Crosland or Linton, or to narrate
the self by indirection, as Anne Thackeray Ritchie (1837–1919) did. Her familial positioning
as Thackeray's daughter and her own literary
work make Ritchie an exemplary memoirist.
Just as Linton's text rarely ventures to assert a
textual "I," Ritchie's *Chapters from Some Unwritten Memoirs* (1895) suggests by its very title
an absence of the putative autobiographer. Ritchie does not narrate her story by making herself
the central character who stands out against the
"background" provided by her family and her
era. She instead establishes her place in the text
as the observer who takes all the different pieces
of which lives are made and by writing makes
them cohere. As Winifred Gerin states, "It is not
that she seeks to put herself in the picture, rather
that without her presence the picture would not
exist." . . .[7] The self Ritchie presents is a self in
process and in relation who is revealed only in
what she reveals about others.

Ritchie's autobiographical strategy, then, pos-
its the subject as knowable only through its interpersonal interactions, as part of a larger familial and historical framework.[8] Although she
writes this text for readers who seek the "true"
knowledge of character that can be located only
in private experience and that can be . . . best
understood only by the women who have made
character their primary study, she resists representing that knowledge as independent of her
personal, subjective perspective on it. What she
knows is a function of her familial position, yet
she does not portray herself as a centering subject of knowledge. . . . Ritchie represents herself
as the mediatrix who represents familial relationships to a world eager to know; like Ward,
she realizes "that not much detachment *is* possible" (Ward, 3) when what one tells is the story
of one's relation to the past and to others. But

for women writing themselves into memoir,
"detachment" is not a desirable position. The
goal of Ritchie's text is to represent the web of
relations that inhered between her life and her
father's, and among their other relatives' and
friends' lives, and not to tell a story in which she
stands apart from the context that has produced
and shaped her.

Family Histories: Public/Private, Euphoria/Dysphoria

Ritchie takes what is "private"—family life—
and makes it "public," yet she does not represent her "inner life"; nor does she give her
reader access to that sort of experience that
twentieth-century readers have labeled as the
"private," that is, the realm of the psychological. Neither does Mary Ward (1851–1920) in *A
Writer's Recollections* (1918). Alan W. Bellringer
complains that "it contains little of the usual autobiographical material on private stress"; "instead of inner drama . . . public information has
priority over private problems."[9] In the differences between what he understands as the relationship between "private" and "public" and
how Ward and Margaret Oliphant understand
that relationship lie clues to the differences between their historical moment and our own. For
what contemporary bourgeois criticism constitutes as the truly private takes place not in the
drawing room, or even in the bedroom, but only
within the expert analyst's office. The "private"
inhabits the interior of the body as consciousness and unconsciousness, an "inner space"
where all "inner dramas," including family psy-
chodramas, are performed by and for an audience of one. But for Ward and Oliphant, the last
two literary subjects I will consider, private consciousness is not conventional material for a
public text. While both senses of "private"—the
familial and the psychological—seem to be op-

erative in their texts, only Oliphant, who began recording her experience without intending to publish it, supplies any explicit detail on "private problems." And what Ward represents as private life—a familial history—does not center on the "inner realm," but rather publicizes a certain version of domestic life.

The "public information" to which Bellringer refers is the history of the Arnolds, their friends, and their associates, the famous people they knew and the famous movements in which they took part, which occupy a central place in Ward's history of herself. While one critic dismisses the text as "a series of anecdotal portraits and descriptions" (Sanders, 6), Bellringer rightly asserts that one of the functions of this material is "to form a texture of allusion to an eminent, indeed dominant literary tradition to which, unobtrusively, [Ward] claims the right to belong" (44). As a granddaughter of Thomas Arnold and one of "Uncle Matt's" favorite nieces, Ward is sensitive to the way in which their history shapes hers and how their eminence gives her a place in intellectual circles that, as the granddaughter and niece of "ordinary people," she would not have had. But Ward's text, as the "factual" feminine counterpart to Toni Brown's *Schooldays* (1857), also helps to ensure the preeminence of the Arnold family in Victorian cultural history. And her family history achieves the status of "public information" owing in part to the fact that such novels as Thomas Hughes's and such memoirs as her own were written and published for the marketplace; as Bellringer describes it, she establishes a "continuity in the network of intellectual families who sustain the 'history of ideas'" (43). Chronicling the private record as she knows it, personally and intimately, Ward supplies an insider's view which comes partially to constitute the publicly known, historically accessible story.

As in Ritchie's case but with a more historically and culturally conscious bent, Ward shapes

her recollections as a documentary account of an age; with a whole chapter on the origins of *Robert Elsmere* (1888), her first major success, and another on the circumstances surrounding its writing, publication, and enthusiastic reception, she places her own work in a context that stretches from her grandfather's era to the time of writing, in the midst of the Great War. Those who people her text—Charlotte Brontë, Harriet Martineau, George Eliot, Mark Pattison—pass through it, as the lesser lights do through Crosland's, making cameo appearances in the familiar roles they have taken on in the shared public imagination. It is thus not her own interior "drama" that Ward stages, but an external, historical, public one in which she plays her own part. From her privileged position, she conveys an intimate view of important personages, while always remaining "in role"—as granddaughter, niece, and wife, and as lady novelist as well. The memoir format, in other words, allows Ward to construct a text in which what we might think of as "private"—her family's story—can be made "public"; conversely, what is "public"—her work in literature—can be shown to have its genesis in her "private" experience.

In the meeting of the realms we see how these categories begin to lose their force once women can legitimately claim a place in the public sphere: while Ward continues to define herself in relation to the domestic, it is precisely that identification with the familial and the roles it assigns her that enables her public self-representation. Producing the private sphere for public consumption, Ward, like Ritchie, participates in the commodification of "ordinary" familial experience for a mass audience. The only "extraordinary" thing that separates middle-class readers from the celebrities they read about is the fact of celebrity itself, that mark of special talent and brilliance which only the fortunate few possess, that personal access to greatness which can bring Charlotte Brontë and Harriet Martineau into the Arnold family parlor for tea. . . . [T]he celebrity autobiographer . . . necessarily lays claim to being both an exceptional woman and an ordinary one, albeit for slightly different ends.

Ward's text does not enact an "inner drama," for interiority is not, as a rule, what the middle-class woman writing secular autobiography demonstrates. While the religious autobiographer could and was indeed expected to represent the spiritual progress of the religious subject, for Ward, whose autobiographical authority also rests on the claim that she is bringing the private out into public, engaging in that kind of self-scrutiny in public would be wholly inappropriate and perhaps impossible. Instead she narrates a bourgeois success story: she is a famous novelist, a worthy Arnold, and a Victorian mother, the descendent of a great family who has proven herself capable of carrying on the tradition.

By contrast, the posthumously published *Autobiography* (1899) of Margaret Oliphant (1828–97) demonstrates the devastating consequences for the writing subject who, imagining her narrative in those same middle-class terms, finds that her life has not met them. Brought up by her mother "with the sense of belonging (by her side) to an old, chivalrous, impoverished race," Oliphant "never got rid of the prejudice" in favor of her family's honor, although she recognizes that "our branch of the Oliphants was [not] much to brag of."[10] The history of this family, unlike Ward's, consists of one disaster after another, and Oliphant writes at length, if sometimes obliquely, of the family misfortunes: the slow demise of her two brothers (one an alcoholic, the other a bankrupt), the early loss of her husband and two daughters, as well as of her love and ambition for her surviving sons, both of whom died in the course of the ten or more years it took her to write the later sections of the *Autobiography* without fulfilling the destinies she had envisioned for them. Her family narra-

tive ironically counters Ward's euphoric family text with a vision of what the other story looks like. . . .

The question Oliphant hesitates to answer, and even to ask, is if under more fortuitous circumstances she could have written a first-class novel, a novel worthy of George Eliot's pen.[11] The question cannot be resolved, of course, but in her description of her life Oliphant makes a point of showing that the cards were overwhelmingly stacked against it. Always for her, writing "was . . . subordinate to everything, to be pushed aside for any little necessity," such as attending to the children, or nursing her sick husband, or sewing a shirt, yet it "ran through everything" (30). . . . Oliphant "had no table even to myself, much less a room to work in" (30), yet on her devolved all the financial responsibilities of a family that grew to include her older brother and his children. . . . Unlike Aurora Leigh, who "[put] down the woman's" instinct in her "[passion] to exalt / The artist's,"[12] Oliphant finds herself writing a dysphoric life that has not satisfied either urge. Neither art nor family can provide her with the story she seeks.

Oliphant began writing her text not for an anonymous reading audience or as a public monument to her family, but for the eyes of the sons who predeceased her.[13] Because she began it as a private journal and later redefined it as a personal legacy to her boys, once she decided to publish it, the change in her intended audience demanded she "change the tone of this record" (86) as well: "I used to feel that Cecco [her second son] would use his discretion,—that most likely he would not print any of this at all, for he did not like publicity, and would have thought his mother's story of her life sacred; but now everything is changed, and I am now going to try to remember more trivial things, the incidents that sometimes amuse me when I look back upon them" (87). Within a few pages, however, she questions her effort to write a popular memoir about "trivial things":

> How strange it is to me to write all this, with the effort of making light reading of it, and putting in anecdotes that will do to quote in the papers and make the book sell! It is a sober narrative enough, heaven knows! and when I wrote it for my Cecco to read it was all very different, but now that I am doing it consciously for the public, with the aim (no evil aim) of leaving a little more money, I feel all this to be so vulgar, so common, so unnecessary, as if I were making pennyworths of myself. . . . I must try to begin again. (95)

Conceptualizing the public in much the same way as Linton does, Oliphant is repelled at the idea of selling her life—"so vulgar, so common"—and her response is mitigated only by the need to make "a little more money," the hack's aim to which she has been dedicated throughout her literary career. She earmarks the proceeds from the *Autobiography* itself as payment for the debts she will leave at her death, as "something to make up deficiencies when I am gone."[14] But whatever value the text might come to possess for her publisher and her estate, it has none for her, for there is no one still living who will be able to read it rightly. "It is so strange to think that when I go it will be touched and arranged by strange hands," she wrote; possibly uncertain that her relatives would take on the duty of editing the text, she imagined that there would be "no child of mine to read with tenderness, to hide some things, to cast perhaps an interpretation of love upon others" (99). Implicitly identifying her life with her text, Oliphant (somewhat morbidly, to be sure) imagines herself going unmourned, unloved, misread. What has been vitally important to her, her domestic family life, is lost and what remains, the work of writing, is no longer of much moment.

The ironies that shape Oliphant's life shape her text as well. With an ear finely tuned to the voices of unknown readers who would probably have expected a very different text from someone who had sent forth nearly 100 novels into the marketplace, she speaks her own sentence on the *Autobiography*: "I need scarcely say that there was not much of what one might call a literary life in all this" (137). Even for middle-class women of the nineteenth century, living "a literary life," in the sense that term might hold for Mill or Dickens or Trollope, was almost impossible—and so, of course, was writing one. But middle-class women who worked for money, who spoke out publicly, and who tried to represent the difficulties of doing so even as they sought a form and an idiom that would enable them to represent themselves, these women autobiographers made the first rush at the invisible barriers that other workers, their contemporaries and their descendents, would continue to struggle to break down.

Notes

1. Eliza Lynn Linton, *My Literary Life* (London, 1899), 72.

2. Mrs. Newton [Camilla Toulmin] Crosland, *Landmarks of a Literary Life 1820–1892* (New York, 1893), 1.

3. Valerie Sanders, *The Private Lives of Victorian Women: Autobiography in Nineteenth-Century England* (New York: St. Martin's Press, 1989), 6.

4. Mrs. Humphry [Mary] Ward, *A Writer's Recollections* (London: W. Collins Sons, 1918), 2.

5. Avrom Fleishman describes the memoir as a "breed of writings designed to obscure their own artificiality" (37), by which he means that the absence of "the double focus" (192) of autobiography—in which "the interplay of I-past and I-present" (192) creates a complex psychological narrative structure—from the typical memoir keeps "the focus of attention . . . on the I-past" (192); this accounts for the lower generic status of this form (*Figures of Autobiog-*

raphy: *The Language of Self-Writing in Victorian and Modern England* [Berkeley: University of California Press, 1983]). This purely formal definition prizes the continuity of identity over time and the centrality of the writing subject; it also fails to take gender into account.

I use the term "memoir" to denote not an autobiographical text that tells a story about a centered self, but one in which the writing subject recounts stories of others and events or movements in which she and/or her other subjects have taken part. Valerie Sanders describes Victorian women's memoirs as often telling "the story of a generation" and offering "a slice of representative life in a specific period" (10–11), and I consider this a good way to think about these texts. While I do not care to make hard and fast distinctions any more than Fleishman does, I do want to suggest that the memoir form provides a fitting medium for Victorian women's self-representations.

6. For Mitford's response to Bentley's decision, see her letter of July 1851 to James T. Fields, quoted in his *Yesterdays with Authors* (1871; rpt. Boston, 1981), 291–93.

7. Winifred Gerin, *Anne Thackeray Ritchie: A Biography* (Oxford: Oxford University Press, 1981), 219. For a reading of Ritchie's biographical and autobiographical writings that deals in depth with the way in which she defined her position as narrating subject, see Carol Hanbery MacKay, "Biography as Reflected Autobiography: The Self-Creation of Anne Thackeray Ritchie," in *Revealing Lives: Gender in Autobiography and Biography*, ed. Marilyn Yalom and Susan Groag Bell (Albany: State University of New York Press, 1991).

8. Anne Thackeray Ritchie, *Chapters from Some Unwritten Memoirs* (New York, 1895).

9. Alan W. Bellringer, "Mrs Humphry Ward's Autobiographical Tactics: A Writer's Recollections," *Prose Studies* 8, no. 3 (December 1985): 41; all subsequent references to this article will be included in the text. In suggesting that what is expected of the woman autobiographer is a private story rather than a public account, Bellringer's critique indirectly repeats the psychological model for female identity to which the work of Erik Erikson once gave currency: as Judith Kegan Gardiner states of the Eriksonian account of fe-

male development, a woman's "unique 'inner space,'" her particular biological destiny as childbearer, is what "she seeks to fill and to protect . . . rather than forge into outward accomplishments" (350). Ward's focus on the public, then, appears particularly inappropriate to the psychoanalytically inclined male critic. See Erik Erikson, "Womanhood and the Inner Space," *Identity, Youth, and Crisis* (New York: W. W. Norton, 1968), 261–94, and Judith Kegan Gardiner, "On Female Identity and Writing by Women," *Critical Inquiry* 8, no. 2 (Winter 1981): 347–91.

10. *The Autobiography of Margaret Oliphant: The Complete Text*, ed. Elisabeth Jay (Oxford: Oxford University Press, 1990), 21–22; all subsequent references to this autobiography will be included in the text. Jay's new edition, which is based on the manuscript of *The Autobiography*, supersedes the recent University of Chicago Press reprint of the heavily edited 1899 edition. For an essay which covers much of the same ground as I do here but from a very different perspective, see Linda H. Peterson, "Audience and the Autobiographer's Art: An Approach to the *Autobiography* of Mrs. M. O. W. Oliphant," in *Approaches to Victorian Autobiography*, ed. George P. Landow (Athens: Ohio University Press, 1979), 158–74. Sanders includes a brief but perceptive reading of the text in *Private Lives*, 86–91. The most provocative recent reading is Gail Twersky Reimer, "Revisions of Labor in Margaret Oliphant's *Autobiography*," in *Life/Lines: Theorizing Women's Autobiography*, ed. Bella Brodzki and Celeste Schenck (Ithaca, NY: Cornell University Press, 1988), 203–20. Reimer expertly addresses the complicated issue of how Oliphant attempts to inscribe both maternal procreativity and literary creativity within the gendered generic boundaries of the form.

11. Oliphant's anxiety about Eliot was, as Elaine Showalter demonstrates, widespread among late Victorian novelists of both sexes; see "Queen George," in *Sexual Anarchy: Gender and Culture at the Fin de Siècle* (New York: Viking, 1990), 75.

12. Elizabeth Barrett Browning, *Aurora Leigh* (9.647, 645–46).

13. Peterson's essay speculates on how this shift in audience affects the text, and Jay's Introduction provides more information on this point. That the *Auto-*

biography began as a private journal without any "audience" other than Oliphant—and God—links her writing with the Protestant tradition of spiritual accounting. . . . See Treva Broughton, who also seems to have examined the unedited manuscript, for more commentary on the audience problem in "Margaret Oliphant: The Unbroken Self," *Women's Studies International Forum* 10, no. 1 (1987): 41–52.

14.   Quoted in Vineta Colby and Robert A. Colby, *The Equivocal Virtue: Mrs. Oliphant and the Victorian Literary Market Place* ([Hamden, CT]: Archon Books, 1966), 233.

21 The Literary Standard, Working-Class Autobiography, and Gender

Regenia Gagnier

. . . Feminist scholars have told the story of middle-class women's writing. Yet like the historical subjects themselves, they have rarely questioned the distinctions between mental and manual labor that first excluded women and they have rarely attempted to demystify the individualist "creative imagination" that women, as producers of concrete material life, were historically denied.[1]

In one of the most revealing cultural confrontations in modern British history, Virginia Woolf's 1931 Introduction to the autobiographical accounts of the Women's Co-Operative Guild illustrates the cross-purposes of individualist aesthetics and other uses of literacy.[2] Having been asked to write a preface, Woolf begins with the problem of prefaces for autonomous aesthetics—"Books should stand on their own feet" (xv)—and solves the problem of introducing the Co-Operativists' writing by writing not quite a Preface but rather a personal letter to the editor, another upper-class woman, Margaret Llewelyn Davies. Woolf wants the Co-Operativists to be individualists, to develop the self-expression and choices for things that are ends in themselves like "Mozart and Einstein" and not things that are means like "baths and money" (xxv–vi). She wants for them, in short, rooms of their own, private places for private thoughts, detached, as Bourdieu would say, from the necessities of the natural and social world.[3] Some

working-class women, indeed many upper domestic servants—the most ideologically "embourgeoised" workers—did want such pleasures; but the Guild women's accounts indicate that they wanted something different. They wanted commonality; and distance from the necessities of the natural and social world ("our minds flying free at the end of a short length of capital," as Woolf puts it [xxv]), had not led middle-class women to change society in that direction.

Rather, the Co-Operativists are especially grateful to the Guild for transforming shy, nervous women into "public speakers" (32, 48–49, 65, 100–101, 141): a woman can write forever in a room of her own without ever learning not to go dry-mouthed and shaking in public. Woolf writes sympathetically about the production of the Co-Operativists' texts, "a work of labour and difficulty. The writing has been done in kitchens, at odds and ends of leisure, in the midst of distractions and obstacles" (xxxix), but confined by her own aesthetics of individualism and detachment, she cannot imagine that "the self" can be communal, engaged, and dialogical as well as individual, detached, and introspective. . . .

Social historians (not to speak of socialist feminists) have made this point somewhat differently from middle-class feminists. The issue concerns normative dualism, the belief that the especially valuable thing about human beings is their mental capacity and that this capacity is a property of individuals rather than groups ("Mozart and Einstein"), and liberal rationality, the belief that rational behavior is commensurate with the maximization of individual utility.[4] Showing the astonishing "strategies" of married working-class women who lived at or below the poverty line in the late nineteenth and early twentieth centuries—working part or full-time outside the home, using children's wages, controlling household budgets, using the products of their families' allotments, and borrowing both goods and cash—Elizabeth Roberts writes that she is often asked what women themselves "got" out of their lives:

> It has been remarked that they gave to their families much more than they received in return. These questions and comments would not have been asked nor made by the women themselves. Their own individual concerns were of little importance to them. They appeared to have found their chief satisfaction in running their homes economically and seeing their children grow up. Their major preoccupations were (throughout the period) feeding, clothing and housing their families.[5]

In an article in the same collection, Diana Gittins writes of the three interrelated and often overlapping occupational spheres for working-class women from the mid-nineteenth century through the Second World War—paid work, unpaid domestic work in extended families, and marriage—as "strategies for survival, but survival for the household generally rather than for the individual women."[6] My reading of working women's autobiographies confirms that such strategies for the family household were, again, indistinguishable from self-actualization.

But nonindividualism comes in many forms, and working-class autobiography suggests that

that of women at home with their families in nineteenth-century Britain was the least conducive to the constitution of writing subjects. Contrary to the claims on behalf of a room of one's own, workers' autobiographies suggest that writing women were those whose work took them out of the home. Although some working people wrote to understand themselves, producing the kinds of texts I discuss in detail below, most wrote for communicative rather than introspective or aesthetic ends: to record lost experiences for future generations, to raise money, to warn others, to teach others, to relieve or amuse themselves. One functionalist, William Tayler, footman to a wealthy London widow in 1837, wrote his autobiographical journal "to improve my handwriting."[7]

Such functionalist uses of literacy contrast markedly with the aesthetic of detached individualism represented by literature (as it is represented in literature departments) in general and by the autobiographical canon in particular. The criteria we may deduce from the canon include a meditative and self-reflective sensibility; a faith in writing as a tool of self-exploration; an attempt to make sense of life as a narrative progressing in time, with a pronounced narrative structured upon parent-child relations and familial development; and a belief in personal creativity, autonomy, and freedom for the future. This is autobiography as the term is usually employed by literary critics, and it is also bourgeois subjectivity, the dominant ideology of the nineteenth and at least the first half of the twentieth century. It adds to assumptions of normative dualism and liberal rationality the assumption of abstract individualism, or the belief that essential human characteristics are properties of individuals independent of their material conditions and social environment. . . .

Discursive production must be understood in terms of the multifarious purposes and projects of specific individuals or groups in specific material circumstances. For example, I have often found it useful to adapt Roberto Mangabeira Unger's spectrum of personality (from longing to be with others to fear of others) to discourse, locating a text between the poles of discursive participation with and antagonism toward others.[8] All autobiographical "moves" in my sense are "interested," whether or not they are as intentionally political as those of the Guild Co-Operativists or Chartists. All display the features of two contexts, as cultural products in circulation with other cultural products (e.g., some music-hall performers wrote specifically for their writing's exchange value) and as articulations of participatory and antagonistic social relations. Sometimes these articulations are simultaneously participatory and antagonistic. Writers like Annie Kenney in *Memoirs of a Militant* (1924) and William Lovett in *Pursuit of Bread, Knowledge, and Freedom* (1876) are participatory with their respective movements, Suffrage and Chartism, while antagonistic to the hegemonic discourses of sexism and classism— "hegemonic" meaning dominant with respect to other discourses, preventing other discourses their full development and articulation. I read autobiography rhetorically, taking language as realist, not in the sense of metaphysical realism, direct isomorphism with reality (Thomas Nagel's "the view from nowhere"), but realist in the sense of projecting objectively real articulations of power in particular communities. Like reading itself, writing is a function of specific and community interactions.[9]

I want to emphasize that when I say "power" I intend its feminist as well as its Foucauldian associations: empowerment, "power to," as well as "power over." Autobiography is the arena of empowerment to represent oneself in a discursive cultural field as well as the arena of subjective disempowerment by the "subjecting" discourses of others. In the postmodern world we live in, "autobiography" as bourgeois subjec-

tivity may be dead except in academic or psychoanalytic circles; but as long as there is society, even cyborg society, there will be rhetorical projects of participation and antagonism in concrete material situations.[10] It is the responsibility of protectors of speech not to disqualify subhegemonic articulations, like women's, like workers', by evaluating them out of the game.

Gendered, Classed Subjects and Cultural Narratives

There is no "typical" Victorian working-class life or autobiography; rather, the forms of autobiography were as multifarious as the British laboring classes themselves. I have provided an anatomy of such writing elsewhere, based largely upon several hundred of the 804 texts indexed in John Burnett, David Vincent, and John Mayall's important bibliography *The Autobiography of the Working Class* (1984), but several salient points are worth reiterating here before focussing on gender.[11] First, loose "generic" groupings may be made according to the rhetorical approach outlined above; these indicate some uniformity in how texts are written, read, and historically assessed in terms of the participatory modes of value and consensus and the antagonistic modes of resistance, domination, and appropriation. Thus in nineteenth-century Britain, when working people began to include their occupations in titles of their work, as in *The Memories of a Working Woman, Confessions of a Strolling Player, Narrative of a Factory Cripple, In Service,* and *The Autobiography of a Private Soldier,* "memories" often came from southern agrarian workers who hoped to preserve local history for members of the community, or domestic workers whose trade had declined radically after the First World War; "narratives" from organized northern industrial workers who sought to empower other workers and compete historically with the bourgeoisie; and "confessions" from transients like stage performers who hoped to gain cash by giving readers immediate consumable sensation.[12] In other words, socioeconomic status, rhetorical purpose, status of labor, and geography were often heavily significant in the forms the autobiography took.

The second point that must be reiterated is that for working-class autobiographers, whether factory operatives (38% of the working population in 1861), agricultural laborers (18%), miners (4%), or domestic servants (19%—half of the population of women workers), subjectivity—the sense of being a significant agent worthy of the regard of others, a human subject, as well as an individuated "ego" distinct from others—was not a given.[13] In conditions of long work hours, crowded housing, and inadequate light, it was difficult enough for workers to contemplate themselves; as writers, they now had to justify themselves as being worthy of the attention of others. Thus I have written of what I call the "social atom" phenomenon: most working-class autobiography begins not with family lineage or a birthdate (conventional middle-class beginnings), but rather with a statement of its author's ordinariness, encoded in titles such as *One of the Multitude* (1911) by the pseudonymous George Acorn, a linguistically-conscious furniture builder who aspired to grow into an oak. The authors were conscious that to many potential readers they were but "social atoms" making up the undifferentiated "masses." As radical journalist William Adams put it in 1903, "I call myself a Social Atom—a small speck on the surface of society. The term indicates my insignificance. . . . I am just an ordinary person."[14] Depending upon the author's purpose in writing, such rhetorical modesty could signify any point within an affective range extending from defensive self-effacement through defiant irony, as in the "Old Potter" Charles Shaw's splendid, "We were a part of Malthus's 'superfluous population.' "[15] I have examined the sources of this rhetorical modesty in the writers' struggle, as *Homo laborans* rather than *Homo cogitans,* to distinguish themselves from "the masses" in order to present themselves as subjects worthy of the attention of others; their simultaneous resistance to embourgeoisement; and their competition with representations of themselves in middle-class fiction and its implicit, broadly Cartesian, assumptions about the self.

The relevance of gender appears with the structural differences between workers' autobiographies and the classic realist autobiography, in which gender plays a major structuring role. The classic realist autobiography includes such elements as remembered details of childhood, parent-child relations, the subject's formal education, and a progressive developmental narrative of self culminating in material well-being and "fame" within greater or lesser circles (whether the Old Boy's place among Old School fellows or John Stuart Mill's place in the democratic revolution). Most workers' autobiographies deviate from this narrative pattern for fairly obvious reasons: in A *Cornish Waif's Story* discussed below, Emma Smith was born in the workhouse, raised by a child molester, and educated in a penitentiary.

First, most of the writers were working outside the home by the time they were eight years old, so the period of "childhood" is problematic, the remembered details often truncated to the more common "first memory." This first memory is often traumatic; its significant positioning within the first paragraphs of the text operates and resonates differently from the evolutionary narrative of childhood familiar to readers of middle-class autobiography. Second, as will be demonstrated in detail below, parent-child relations among the working class often differed from those in the upper classes. Third, since the subject's formal education competed with the family economy, in most cases it was not limited to a particular period. In many working-class examples, education often continues throughout the book and up to the time of writing. And fourth, most working-class autobiographies do not end with success but rather *in medias res.* In this context it is worth noting that with the exception of political and religious-conversion autobiographies, most working-class texts do not have the crises and recoveries that are common to "literary" autobiography, just as they do not have climaxes. The bourgeois climax-and-resolution/action-and-interaction model presupposes an active and reactive world not always accessible to working-class writers, who often felt themselves passive victims of economic determinism. Working since the age of nine, Mrs. Wrigley writes a life consisting of a series of jobs, mentioning in the one sentence devoted to her marriage its maternal character and her childlike relations with her employers: "I was sorry to give up such a good home, and they was sorry for me to leave but my young man wanted to get married for he had no mother."[16]

What is "missing" then in much working-class autobiography is the structuring effect, apparent in any middle-class "plot," of gender dimorphism. In Britain, middle-class boys experienced and wrote of an ordered progress from pre-school at home to childhood and youth at school and university, through the Raj, diplomatic corps, or civil service, or through domestic life with equally genderized wives and daughters.[17] Middle-class women wrote of early life with fathers and afterlife with husbands. These two patterns—as central to the great nineteenth-century realist novels as to Victorian autobiography—represent middle-class gender construction of masculinity and femininity, power and domesticity. Whereas boys learned "independence" through extrusion from mothers and nannies and paternalism through elaborate forms of self-government in public

schools, middle-class girls, under constant supervision by parents and headmistresses, learned to be dependent upon and obedient to husbands. (Many, needless to say, also rebelled against this pattern. See especially Cecily Hamilton's trenchant and witty *Marriage As A Trade* [1909], recommended reading for every Victorian and feminist course.) Working-class women, on the other hand—from the time they were old enough to mind younger siblings, to their minding the children of the upper classes, to their noncompanionate (economically-oriented) marriages ("because my young man had no mother")—learned to be self-reliant and nurturing, and their husbands learned to be "matronized." "What I needed was a man who was master in his own house," writes Emma Smith, "upon whom I could lean. Instead of this, I always had to take a leading role."[18]

This difference in the practical sex-gender system leads to the major structural difference of working-class autobiography, but there are gender similarities that transcend class differences. Working women refer far more frequently to their husbands or lovers and children (their personal relationships) and working men to their jobs or occupations (their social status). Traditionally prevented from speaking in public, even women like the Guild Co-Operativists, who write with the explicit purpose of political reform, speak from within a material economic realm; yet politicized men, even before they gained full male suffrage in 1885, were accustomed to public speaking (for example, in pubs) and argued within the discourse of national politics.[19] Comparatively isolated within their homes (or others' as domestics), the Co-Operativists learned to internalize rhetorical values acceptable to the middle class, such as the catechism, criticizing personal injustices and inequalities within marriage and the family. On the other hand, from early experience in public and on the job with others, the men write movingly of specific material deprivations but predominantly of the "rights" of workers and the class struggle, explicitly attacking class structure.

This different understanding of injustice—one local and immediate, the other systemic—leads to different formulations of political goals. The Co-Operativists see politics as a forum for domestic demands, such as baths for miners or peace to save the life of one's remaining son. The radical men want what the middle class has. These may not in effect be different goals: what the middle class has is baths and sons comparatively safe from war; but because the women reason from personal example and moral lesson and the men launch discourses articulated within the democratic revolutions of the United States and France, even politically motivated autobiography is often informed differently by women and men.

Such differences, however, arise in the relative isolation of women's labor, as the highest paying and most independent employment was consigned to men as principal breadwinners and women were driven from the factories from the 1840s; and they may be dealt with by social historians concerned with the interrelations of gender, "private" and "public" spheres. For the literary or cultural critic, gender in working-class autobiography is most interesting when it shows itself as ideological hegemony—in Antonio Gramsci's sense of popular consent to the political order. Here the game is embourgeoisement. Although the texts to which I now turn by no means represent the majority of working-class autobiographies, there are enough like them to indicate how gender operates as a cultural narrative.

In such texts, one finds the cost of bourgeois familial or gender ideology to women and men who were not permitted bourgeois lives. They were often written by people with lives of unmitigated hardship, for whom writing is a form, more or less successful, of therapy. They are not trying to sell their work so much as to analyze and alleviate their pain; yet their narratives are derived from models, often literary models, more suitable to the conditions of middle-class authors. Unlike other working-class writers, they have also extensively adopted middle-class ideology: they have accepted the value of introspection and writing as tools of self-understanding; they seek to write their lives as middle-class narratives, especially with respect to the development of parent-child relations and material progress; and they believe that writing and self-understanding will help them succeed. Yet although they attempt self-analysis, their experience cannot be analyzed in the terms of their acculturation. This gap between ideology and experience leads not only to the disintegration of the narrative the writer hopes to construct, but, as the analyses below will show, to the disintegration of personality itself.

Discussion of these texts is inescapably reductive, for their characteristic is the authors' layered revisions of their experience, which contribute to an unusual density of signification. Literary readers will find them the most "literary" of working-class writers.[20] Here I shall focus upon the writers' attempts to structure their lives according to middle-class gender ideology.

The struggle between ideology and experience is inscribed, both micrologically and macrologically, in James Burn's *Autobiography of a Beggar Boy* (1855). At nine years old, Burn tracks down his biological father in Ireland, where the boy is humiliated to wear rags, endure lice, and work in isolation. In a fit of humiliation and self-hatred and a parody of primogeniture, he runs away, calling the dirt he associates with his father his patrimony. "I had neither staff, nor scrip, nor money in my pocket. I commenced the world with the old turf-bag. It was my only patrimony. In order that I might sever the only remaining link that bound me to my family, I tore two syllables from my name [i.e., from McBurney, his father's name]." [21] This minute detail of the boy's inability to meet a cultural code—his castration of his father's name as sign of his lack of father and patrimony in a patriarchal and propertied culture—prefigures the larger narrative distortion reflecting the insufficiency of his experience in the face of his society's master narrative of male progress.

When Burn summarizes the lesson of his life for his son at the end of his book (199–200), the summary corresponds to his preceding narrative only up to a point: he writes of his thoughtless wandering until he was 12 years old, of parental neglect ("I had been blessed with three fathers and two mothers, and I was then as comfortably situated as if I never had either one or the other" [106]), and of his lack of social connection for long periods. This summary corresponds to the episodic structure of his preceding story and to the fragmented nature of his childhood as itinerant beggar on the Scots border. Yet then Burn refers to the "grand turning point" of his life, when he learned a trade as hatter's apprentice. In fact, only a nominal change occurred with his apprenticeship: since there was no work, he was permitted to call himself a hatter rather than a beggar while on tramp for fourteen hundred miles (135). He makes much of a change of status from unemployable to employable, although no material change occurs—he remains unemployed. Similarly, he continues to insist upon the great happiness of his domestic life, despite the necessity of living apart from his family for long periods of tramping and the deaths of his wife and twelve of his sixteen children. The summary concludes with the assertion of his relative success in remaining respectable as a debt collector to the poor, a respectability reinforced by the bowdlerized version of 1882, in which he finally obliterated all references to sexual experiences and bodily functions.

This summary male middle-class narrative, beginning with the imaginary "grand turning point" of his trade, occludes, first, Burn's political activity, for which he was well known, and, second, much of his past. With the threat of the General Strike in 1839, he had turned against the Chartists and begun to conceive of his prior activism as "madness." In revising his life, this "madness" is excluded along with earlier madnesses, such as the madness of Scottish and Irish poetry. Due to its link with superstition and supernaturalism—and despite his opinion that English poetry is "dull and lifeless" in comparison—Burn must reject it as irreconcilable with "useful knowledge" (192–98). Similarly, the lively Dickensian style of the first two chapters shows his affection for society on the borders—for its lack of social differentiation and its extreme linguistic diversity. Yet this too disappears from his summary. He is left attempting to reconcile his proprietorship of taverns and spirit cellars with his hysterical temperance, and passing over the details of his job as debt collector to his former Chartist friends. Everything that must be repudiated in the service of class mobility—social tolerance, epistemological pluralism, the aspect of freedom of life on the borders as a beggar boy—is expunged from the summary. Yet in dutifully obliterating or rewriting his past, there is no indication that Burn is comfortable with his present or future. As he puts it, "Amid the universal transformation of things in the moral and physical world, my own condition has been tossed so in the rough blanket of fate, that my identity, if at any time a reality, must have been one which few could venture to swear to" (56); or, "All our antecedents are made up of so many yesterdays, and the morrow never comes" (185).

Moreover, despite the seasonal difficulties of the hatting trade and high unemployment among artisans in Glasgow in the 1830s and 1840s, and despite an active and successful life as spokesperson for hatters in the Glasgow United Committee of Trades Delegates, Burn blames himself for his failure in business. Assuming a liberal and masculine ethic of autonomy and progress, he concludes that he was personally deficient in the struggle to maintain either self or social position, and he therefore believes himself uneducable: "Although my teachers have been as various as my different positions, and much of their instruction forced upon me by the necessities of my condition, yet I have always been a dull dog" (196). Assuming individual responsibility for conditions beyond his control and de-identifying with other workers, he remains merely isolated, neither materially and socially residing in the middle class nor identifying with his own. The disturbing power of the first half of the text, with the boy's mystical worship of his stepfather; the disintegration of the later sections; the emphatic progress and rationality in tension with the obsessive memories of early days; and the mystified transition from anger against a negligent father to guilt as an unworthy native son all contribute to a nightmare of socio-psychic marginality. Nonetheless, the book was received as a gratifying example of self-improvement and respectability among the lower classes.[22] Today we can see it as releasing all the phantoms of an ideology of familialism and progress upon a child who was deprived of a family and a chance. Unlike other working-class writers, Burn attempts to narrate his experience according to upper-class models. The price he pays is narrative and psychological disintegration.

Whereas Burn's story shows the effects of Enlightenment narratives concerning material progress, the pursuit of knowledge, and political emancipation, presumably from his days as a Chartist, and masculine "success" stories combining with familial narrative, women's narratives of this type are correspondingly dominated by familialism and romance. In his *Annals of Labour*, the social historian John Burnett cites Louise Jermy's *Memories of a Working Woman* as

an example of a successful transition from a low-paying millinery position into domestic service and, ultimately, marriage.[23] Yet Jermy herself sees her life as a series of episodes failing to conform to her expectations of family and romance. Born in 1877, she is motherless before her second birthday. Her childhood and health are "bartered" by her father and stepmother when she is taken from school to do mangling at home in order for her parents to buy a house. Her adolescence is isolated, "not like other girls," between illness and an apprenticeship at fourteen to a dressmaker in "sweated" conditions (long hours in confined and crowded space, few and short breaks, low pay). Her education is continually frustrated as her stepmother destroys her books, and while in service to a married couple at Birmingham University "anything like deep thinking produced the dreadful headaches" (93).

Jermy's romantic life is also a series of noncorrespondences. A fragile betrothal conflicts with the long hours in service and the nine p.m. curfew of domestic servants, until her fiancé bolts and leaves her in a severe depression that endures two years. Finally she marries a farm laborer in 1911 but, like many husbands described by working-class wives, he is "delicate"; ill every spring, he lives only ten years. Jermy returns to work to raise her two sons.

She suffers from amnesia, ceases in childhood to confide in others, and bears a conviction of her awkwardness and unattractiveness. She leaves the millinery shop not, as Burnett implies, for better wages but in order to leave home; and she wears black—the "decent black" of domestic servants, as Mayhew put it, "no ringlets, followers, or scandals"—on and off the job.[24] While each episode fails to correspond to its middle-class analogue, Jermy nonetheless adopts middle-class standards and conventional narratives as her own. R. H. Mottram introduces *The Memories of a Working Woman* as the first autobiography written by a member of the Women's Institute. Yet Jermy never mentions the Institute: the dominant features of her life, at least prior to the Institute, were perverted familial relations (glorified dead mother, evil stepmother), aborted romance, and pronounced isolation.

In *A Cornish Waif's Story: An Autobiography,* the pseudonymous Emma Smith's life is also a sequence of noncorrespondences to middle-class norms. Born in 1894, Smith was the "illegitimate" daughter of one of the 23 children of a Cornish tin-miner blinded in a mining accident and retired without pension. As a child she is told that her mother is her sister. As accompanist to a hurdygurdy player, she is sexually molested by a man she calls "Fagin" and his friend Dusty the Sword Swallower. At eleven, she runs away and is sent to a convent penitentiary, a home for "errant" girls: "I was no more a prostitute than Dickens's Oliver Twist was a thief, if I may draw upon a character of fiction to illustrate what I mean. Yet here I was placed in the category, and indirectly it has affected my whole life" (108).

The convent penitentiary fails to prepare her for her reentry into society, especially for marriage and a family, while it equally denies her a "speakable" past. Upon release, "it was impressed upon me . . . that I was never to talk about the Home or let anyone know where I had come from . . . it was something to be very ashamed of (133). Working as a servant in a vicarage provides dissonances that are borne out by her own marriage—"Nothing was as I imagined it. The vicar was blessed with an unholy temper. His wife did not get on with her husband and took no pains to hide the fact" (134). Her marriage to a gardener is probably arranged by her employers—"If you have two servants, a man and a woman, the thing to do is to marry them up. Then you have two servants for the price of one" (152)—and she very quickly distances herself as a unique, reflective, psychologically rich self ("a complex piece of machinery") from her husband ("a simple country man"), who, as a transparent product of his class status, fails to fulfill her emotional, intellectual, and romantic aspirations (152–66).

Again echoing Oliver and Agnes, she obsessively attempts to reconcile with her mother (from an external point of view, always a nonexistent dyad), aborts an extramarital romance in Australia, and returns with her husband to Cornwall. Yet rather than a parish girl's progress to financial and domestic stability (she is a successful head laundress with three healthy daughters), Smith's is an "hysterical' narrative indicating her nonadjustment to married life and maternity. She is as unwilling a wife as a waif.

If personal identity is a function of a temporal unification of past, present, and future, Smith was as deprived as Foucault's "Herculine Barbin" (who, raised as a girl in a convent, was legally declared to be male as an adult) of the past she had had to repress, and as unprepared for the future entailed by her gender and family: "I would dream that I was an inmate of a convent . . . I was, or could have been, supremely happy if it were not for the knowledge that somewhere in the background I had a husband and children" (178). After several mental breakdowns, she twice attempts suicide (quietly, like a good servant, with aspirin and sleeping pills), but is finally convinced by her doctor that her responsibility is to live for her family. In her last paragraph Smith once again turns to fictive modes to mediate her experience, this time apparently unconsciously: "I should end my life story on a very happy note if I could honestly record that I have grown so well-balanced mentally that nothing now upsets or worries me. Such, however, is not the case. I am easily worried and upset over certain things, and for this reason as much as for others, I am anxious to find a little cottage somewhere in Cornwall with a bit of ground upon which we can grow vegetables and flowers. It would be a great thrill to me if my dream cottage had a view of both the sun rising and the sunset, for the sun rising fills me with hope, and the sunset fills me with peace" (188). Novel-readers will recognize this image of the rose-covered cottage as the standard ending of Dickens's domestic fiction, including the image and final resting place of the adopted orphan Oliver Twist.

What is common to these texts is the conscious desire on the part of the writers to write their lives according to middle-class narratives and the unconscious distance between those narratives—especially of financial success, familialism, and romance—and the facts of their existence, especially economic determinism, nonfamilialism, aborted romance, and noncompanionate marriage. What these narratives of disintegrated personality tell us about gender is that in circumstances of familial deprivation, familial ideology can only be assumed at great psychic cost.

Yet not all working-class autobiographers assumed familial ideology at such a cost. It was a cultural commonplace that many male radicals—for example, Thomas Hardy, William Lovett, Thomas Cooper, Robert Blatchford, Robert Lowery, James Watson, and Thomas Dunning—had been raised by women alone ("resourceful widows" was the technical term), and they resisted bourgeois ideology as much as Emma Smith suffered from it. Unlike the writers above, the male radicals were engaged in communities with common purpose, and they were engaged in the process of rearticulating their common experience through the progressive narratives of the Enlightenment—as Lovett put it, through their common pursuits of bread, knowledge, and freedom, or material well-being, education, and political status. Emma Smith, Louise Jermy, and the Chartist renegade James Burn, on the other hand, were as isolated, indi-

vidualistic, or unaffiliated as the middle-class subjects whose ideology they adopted—as isolated but not so autonomous. Smith maintained the forms of middle-class respectability and swallowed her pain like sleeping pills; Jermy was forced to return to work to support her fatherless sons; and as Burn said, whether or not there was work, his children were his "hostage to the State" (132).

Faced with such difficulties, the emotional health, or functional identities, of working-class writers was not dependent upon their politicization in any rigid sense so much as upon their participation in alternative articulations of their common experience. The indomitable Ellen Johnston, known to working people as Scotch Nell the "Factory Girl," could have been a Jermy or a Smith. Abandoned by her father, a stonemason, "tormented" by her stepfather, "deceived" by two lovers, and ostracized as a fallen woman, the power-loom weaver/poet's brief *Autobiography* (1867) is melodramatically modelled on Walter Scott and "those strange romantic ordeals attributed to the imaginary heroines 'of Inglewood Forest'"; her poems show the effects of literary hegemony, though often gender- and class-inverted, as in "Lines to a Young Gentleman of Surpassing Beauty."[25]

Yet Johnston also articulated a common experience of great value to herself and her fellow workers: for every epideictic lyric to a romantic young gentleman there are many more in praise of working men (she writes, she says, to relieve them from the toils of factory life), and her *Autobiography* concludes not with melancholy and melodrama but with her taking her foreman to court, indicating that the Factory Girl has learned to imitate the middle class in more than literary hegemony. She publishes proud poems on her "illegitimate" daughter "bonny Mary Auchinvole"; composes many—including love poems—on behalf of less literate coworkers; includes in her volume addresses and songs written for her from other workers (to which she often composes personal responses); goes international with "Welcome, Garibaldi" and "The Exile of Poland"; and writes with irresistible affection for the material life of the factory, as in "An Address to Napier's Dockyard" and "Kennedy's Dear Mill." "The Factory Girl's Farewell" concludes:

> Farewell to all the works around,
> The flaxmill, foundry, cooperage too;
> The old forge, with its blazing mound,
> And Tennant's stalk, farewell to you.
> Your gen'rous masters were so kind,
> Theirs was the gift that did excel;
> Their name around my heart is twined:
> So Gailbraith's bonnie mill, farewell!
>
> Farewell, my honour'd masters two,
> Your mill no more I may traverse;
> I breathe you both a fond adieu;
> Long may you live lords of commerce.
> Farewell unto my native land,
> Land of the thistle and blue-bell;
> Oh! wish me joy with heart and hand;
> So Gailbraith's bonnie mill, farewell! (95)

Johnston participated fully in public life in factories in England, Scotland, and Ireland. Familial and romantic ideology exacted the highest psychic cost to those who lived in isolation. It seems inescapable that the emotional health and flourishing self-image of working-class subjects whose lives did not conform to the patterns of the dominant culture were proportionate to the degree of participatory—as opposed to purely antagonistic—discursive engagement with others beyond the family in the home. The narrative and psychological disintegration of working-class writers who attempted to adopt middle-class narratives of self, and the relatively successful identities of those supported by alternative participatory articulations, indicate the significance of discourse—in this case, of gendered, familial discourse—in human identity, as well as discourse's inability entirely to override non-discursive material conditions.

Notes

I am very grateful to the Stanford Humanities Center and the Pew Memorial Trust for supporting the research for this essay; to Susan Groag Bell and Marilyn Yalom for inviting me to participate in the conference where it was first presented; and to the Institute for Research on Women and Gender at Stanford University, for being there.

1. See, however, Martha Vicinus, *The Industrial Muse: A Study of Nineteenth Century British Working-Class Literature* (London: Croom Helm, 1974), and Nan Hackett, *Nineteenth Century British Working-Class Autobiographies: An Annotated Bibliography* (New York: AMS, 1985).
2. Margaret Llewelyn Davies, ed., *Life As We Have Known It: By Co-Operative Working Women* (1931; New York: Norton, 1975). Further page references will be included in the text.
3. Pierre Bourdieu, *Distinction: A Social Critique of the Judgement of Taste* (Cambridge: Harvard University Press, 1984).
4. For full discussion of the philosophical concepts of normative dualism, liberal rationality, and abstract individualism, see Alison M. Jaggar, *Feminist Politics and Human Nature* (Sussex: Harvester Press, 1983).
5. Elizabeth Roberts, "Women's Strategies, 1890–1940," in *Labour and Love: Women's Experience of Home and Family, 1850–1940*, ed. Jane Lewis, (Oxford: Basil Blackwell, 1986), 243–44.
6. Diana Gittins, "Marital Status, Work and Kinship, 1850–1930," in *Labour and Love: Women's Experience of Home and Family, 1850–1940*, ed. Jane Lewis, (Oxford: Basil Blackwell, 1986), 265.
7. William Tayler in John Burnett, ed., *Annals of Labour: Autobiographies of British Working-Class People, 1820–1920* (Bloomington: Indiana University Press, 1974), 175.
8. See Roberto Mangabeira Unger, *Knowledge and Politics* (New York: Free Press, 1975), and *Passion: An Essay on Personality* (New York: Free Press, 1986).

9. See Chaim Perelman, *The New Rhetoric* (South Bend: University of Notre Dame Press, 1969) and Thomas Nagel, *The View from Nowhere* (New York: Oxford University Press, 1986).

10. For cyborg society, see Donna Haraway, "A Manifesto for Cyborgs: Science, Technology, and Socialist Feminism in the 1980s," *Socialist Review* 80 (March–April 1985), 65–107. Roughly, Haraway intends "cyborg" to represent the collapse of the distinction between organic and mechanical.

11. See John Burnett, David Mayall, and David Vincent, eds., *The Autobiography of the Working Class: An Annotated Critical Bibliography*, Volume 1, *1790–1900* (Brighton: Harvester, 1984); Regenia Gagnier, "Social Atoms: Working-Class Autobiography, Subjectivity and Gender," *Victorian Studies* (Spring 1987): 335–63. For the culmination of my comparative studies of autobiography, see Gagnier, *Subjectivities: A History of Self-Representation in Britain, 1832–1920* (New York: Oxford University Press, 1990). Also see Hackett.

12. Louise Jermy, *The Memories of a Working Woman* (Norwich: Goose and Son, 1934); Peter Paterson [James Glass Bertram], *Behind the Scenes: Being the Confessions of a Strolling Player* (London: Henry Lea, 1859); William Dodd, *Narrative of the Experience and Sufferings of William Dodd, A Factory Cripple, Written by Himself* (1841; rpt. London: Cass, 1968); Rose Gibbs, *In Service: Rose Gibbs Remembers* (Cambridge, UK: Archives for Bassingbourn and Comberton Village Colleges, 1981); Anon., *The Autobiography of a Private Soldier, Showing the Danger of Rashly Enlisting* (Sunderland: Williams and Binns, 1838).

13. For statistics, see R. Bairoch, *The Working Population and Its Structure* (New York: Gordon and Breach, 1968), 99. For detailed explanation see Burnett's introductory essays to the following sections of *Annals of Labour*: "The Labouring Classes," "Domestic Servants," and "Skilled Workers."

14. William Adams, *Memoirs of a Social Atom* (1903; rpt. New York: Augustus M. Kelley, 1968), xiii.

15. Charles Shaw, *When I Was a Child* (1893; rpt. East Ardsley, Wakefield: SR Publishers, 1969), 97.

16. Davies, 60.

17. For a cultural critique of the narratives of English public school boys, see Regenia Gagnier, "From Fag to Monitor; Or, Fighting to the Front: Art and Power in Public School Memoirs," *Browning Institute Studies* 16 (1988): 15–38, special volume on Victorian learning, ed. Robert Viscusi. Also see Gagnier, *Subjectivities*.

18. Emma Smith (pseud.), *A Cornish Waif's Story: An Autobiography* (London: Odhams, 1954), 154.

19. For the two modes, see Davies; and David Vincent, ed., *Testaments of Radicalism: Memoirs of Working Class Politicians, 1790–1885* (London: Europa, 1977). The fact that these primarily political and polemical documents represent a wide historical distance is less significant when it is realized that the gender difference alluded to is borne out by many "genres" of working-class autobiography throughout the period: e.g., conversion and gallows narratives as well as commemorative storytelling.

20. In *Victorian Writing and Working Women: The Other Side of Silence* (Cambridge: Polity Press, 1985), Julia Swindells also analyzes some working women's autobiographies in "Part 2: Working Women's Autobiographies" (115–207) in terms of what she calls "the literary": I see such "literary" effects controlling one kind of working-class writing, produced by men and women; whereas Swindells appears to find it characteristic of working women's writing exclusively and as a whole.

21. James Dawson Burn, *The Autobiography of a Beggar Boy* (1855), ed. David Vincent (London: Europa, 1978), 78.

22. See Vincent's Introduction, 28.

23. Burnett, *Annals of Labour*, 52; Louise Jermy, *The Memories of a Working Woman* (Norwich: Goose and Son, 1934).

24. Mayhew cited in John R. Gillis, *For Better or Worse: British Marriage, 1600 to the Present* (Oxford: Oxford University Press, 1985), 244.

25. Ellen Johnston, *The Autobiography, Poems, and Songs of "The Factory Girl"* (Glasgow: William Love, 1867), 5, 62.

22 The Construction of the Self in U.S. Latina Autobiographies

Lourdes Torres

In the 1980s we have witnessed a proliferation in the publication of literary works by U.S. Latina[1] writers. This growth, however, only begins to address the virtual absence of this literature on the marketplace and in the pages of literary journals. The sexism that predominates in both the Anglo and Latino presses has been a significant factor in its suppression. Since Anglo publishers rarely publish work by Latinas (or Latinos), the only recourse available has been Latino publishing concerns, which are male-run and until recently have shown little interest in the publication of Latina works (see Sánchez for a discussion of this situation). In the recent past, however, Latino publishers such as Arte Público Press and Bilingual Review Press have "discovered" Latina writers; in addition, since 1981 the Latina-run journal (and press) *Third Woman* has been dedicated exclusively to the writings of Latinas, both in the United States and internationally. Also, small feminist presses such as Kitchen Table: Women of Color Press and white feminist presses have begun to publish U.S. Latina titles.

In terms of what has been published thus far, poetry collections predominate, followed by short-story collections and, to a lesser extent, novels. Recently, a new genre has begun to be explored by U.S. Latina writers—the autobiography. To date three such collections exist: *Loving in the War Years: Lo Que Nunca Pasó Por Sus Labios,* by Cherríe Moraga (South End Press, 1983), *Getting Home Alive,* by Aurora Levins Morales and Rosario Morales (Firebrand Books, 1986), and *Borderlands/La Frontera,* by Gloria Anzaldúa (Spinsters/Aunt Lute Book Co., 1987).[2]

Seizing the Podium: Creating Latina Autobiography

These collections are both revolutionary and subversive at many levels. They challenge traditional notions about the genre of "autobiography" through their form and their content. They subvert both Anglo and Latino patriarchal definitions of culture. They undermine linguistic norms by using a mixture of English, Spanish, and Spanglish. All address the question of the politics of multiple identities from a position which seeks to integrate ethnicity, class, gender, sexuality, and language. The three texts appropriate a new space for Latinas where they too partake in the interpretation of symbols and the creation of meaning, and most important, they theorize a politics from which to forge the survival of Latinas and other women of color.

Both the form and the content of the three works being considered subvert conventions of canonized autobiographies. Estelle Jelinek (1980) in "Women's Autobiography and the Male Tradition" highlights differences of content and style in the autobiographies of men and women. One difference she notes is the degree of orderliness in the self-portraits; men's works generally are presented as chronologically linear wholes, while women's stories tend to consist of fragmented, disjunctive units. Recent autobiographies written by women of color, in addition to possessing these characteristics, tend to mix genres in a manner we have not seen in mainstream autobiographies. For example, *Zami* (1982) by Audre Lorde and *The Woman Warrior* (1979) by Maxine Hong Kingston combine biographical details with fictional tales, myths, and fantasies to tell their stories. Similarly, the three Latina autobiographies we are considering are composed of essays, sketches, short stories, poems, and journal entries. In all three, to a greater or lesser extent, there is no attempt to privilege any of the various genres. History— public and private—myth, fiction, and fantasy are all juxtaposed. As such, these collections are a fundamental subversion of mainstream autobiographies' traditions and conventions.

Getting Home Alive by Aurora Levins Morales and Rosario Morales encompasses yet another departure from typical autobiographies by bringing together the experiences and points of view of a mother and daughter. In this collection the two authors' words, stories, and poems are not separated into sections according to authors, but rather are all woven together. Occasionally a piece written by the mother is responded to by the daughter in the following piece, but this is not always the case. While conventional criticism might dismiss this ordering as fragmentary and confusing, the series of fragments and their apparent orderlessness can also be interpreted as a daring experiment with structure.

Moraga's text is likewise characterized by a mixture of genres. In her introduction, she states that her pieces are not arranged chronologically according to when they were written, but rather in terms of her political development. Anzaldúa,

on the other hand, presents her personal history and the history of her people in narrative sequences in the first half, and in the second half continues to explore these aspects in poetry. These autobiographies are a blending of the imagined and real; that is, myths and fantasies coexist with historical realities. The project of presenting the personal and collective selves takes precedence over conventional stylistics or established structures. In a sense the structure is parallel to the content, in that the main thematic concern of the texts, as in all autobiographies, is the question of identity and the presentation of the self, but in these texts is complicated by the problematic of the fragmented, multiple identity.

The use of fiction does not lessen the need of readers and critics to consider the extratextual conditions which produce the text—that is, the social and political forces that shaped the "self" who produced the text—although this reading practice is not fashionable in present-day literary criticism. In this context it is important to note that as people of color have begun to define and construct their subjectivity, the construction of a "subject" suddenly has become antitheoretical and problematic according to the dictates of current critical theory. However, as Elizabeth Fox-Genovese (1988) points out in an essay examining black women's autobiographies,

Feminist critics, like critics of Afro-American and Third World literatures, are beginning to refuse the implied blackmail of Western, white male criticism. The death of the subject and of the author may accurately reflect the perceived crisis of Western culture and the bottomless anxieties of its most privileged subjects—the white male authors who presumed to define it. Those subjects and those authors may, as it were, be dying. But it remains to be demonstrated that their deaths constitute the collective or generic deaths of the subject and author. There remain plenty of subjects and authors who, never having had much opportunity to write in their own names or the names of their kind, much less in the name of the culture as a whole, are eager to seize the abandoned podium. The white male cultural elite has not in fact abandoned the podium; it has merely insisted that the podium cannot be claimed in the name of any particular experience. And it has been busily trying to convince the world that intellectual excellence requires depersonalization and abstraction. The virtuosity, born of centuries of privilege, with which these ghosts of authors make their case, demands that others, who have something else to say, meet the ghosts' standards of pyrotechnics. (67)

Through their subversion of the autobiography, the Latina authors are seizing the podium, telling their own stories, creating new images, and contesting the often negative and degrading images which others have used to construct the Latina.

In a recent wave of feminist writings about women's autobiographies, male criteria for the construction of the autobiography are also being challenged. Susan Stanford Friedman (1988), for instance, argues that the traditional approach to autobiography which emphasizes the individual as a supreme and unique being is inappropriate to explain the creation of the female or "minority" self. Such an approach does not consider the externally imposed cultural identities of women and other oppressed groups and the particular socialization processes that women and people of color undergo in a racist and sexist culture. Women can never assume an individual identity because they are at every turn reminded of their gender (and color if they are not white). Meanwhile, since they personify the cultural categories privileged in Western culture

as human, those who are white, male, and heterosexual can think of themselves as individuals. Friedman states, "The emphasis on individualism as the necessary precondition for autobiography is thus a reflection of privilege, one that excludes from the canons of autobiography those writers who have been denied by history the illusion of individualism" (75, in this volume).

Like black autobiographers (Butterfield), Latina autobiographers do not create a monolithic self, but rather present the construction of the self as a member of multiple oppressed groups, whose political identity can never be divorced from her conditions. The subject created is at once individual and collective. For people who have been maligned or who have not had the power to name their own experience, the autobiography, as Sheila Rowbotham points out, is a means by which to "project its own image on to history" (27). This is, of course, far removed from the dominant and traditional autobiographical construction of the "superior" individual who seeks to separate himself from his community and perhaps, in part, accounts for why the works of women of color have been marginalized by the white male, heterosexual literary world.

Women's autobiographies generally challenge the male-imposed construction of their identity. As S. Smith states, "women approach autobiography from the position of speakers at the margins of discourse" (44). If this is true for white, heterosexual, middle-class women, what does it mean for the construction of self in the autobiographies of working-class, lesbian women of color? It is not enough to speak of double or triple oppression; rather, women of color are themselves theorizing their experience in radical and innovative terms. Their condition as women, as people of color, as working-class members, and in some cases as lesbians, has led them to reject partial, social, and political theories such as middle-class, white, mainstream feminism and Marxist socialism which have failed to develop an integrated analysis sensitive to the simultaneous oppression that women of color experience. Rather, Third World women are making connections between the forces of domination which affect their lives daily and are actively participating in the creation of a movement committed to radical social and political transformation at all levels.

Forging an Identity

In *Getting Home Alive, Loving in the War Years,* and *Borderlands/La Frontera,* the Latina authors engage in the process of claiming, as Michelle Cliff puts it, "an identity they have been taught to despise". In order to do this, they must work through all the cultural and gender socialization and misinformation which has left them in a maze of contradictions. This results in the fragmentation of identity, and the inability to speak from a unified, noncontradictory subject position. No existing discourse is satisfactory because each necessitates the repression of different aspects of the self. Moraga, Anzaldúa, Levins Morales and Morales create a new discourse which seeks to incorporate the often contradictory aspects of their gender, ethnicity, class, sexuality, and feminist politics. The radicalness of their project lies in the authors' refusal to accept any one position; rather, they work to acknowledge the contradictions in their lives and to transform difference into a source of power. They find that being marginalized by multiple discourses, and existing in a borderland, compels them to reject prescriptive positions and instead leads them to create radical personal and collective identities.

At this point, given that identity politics has become a popular target for criticism by feminists of all varieties (cf. Bourne; Kappeler; Adams), it is important to stress what identity politics means to these authors. All recognize that

the most radical, activist politics develop when one comes to understand the dynamics of how one is oppressed and how one oppresses others in her daily life. It is from this place that connections with other oppressed people are possible; when one comes to understand the basis of one's own pain and how it is connected to the pain of others, the possibility of forming coalitions with others emerges. As Moraga states, "Without an emotional, heartfelt grappling with the source of our own oppression, without naming the enemy within ourselves and outside of us, no authentic, non-hierarchical connection among oppressed groups can take place" (53). Identity politics, as conceived of by radical women of color (Moraga and Anzaldúa; B. Smith), has never meant bemoaning one's individual circumstances, or ranking oppressions, or a politics of defensiveness around one's issues. Rather, identity politics means a politics of activism, a politics which seeks to recognize, name, and destroy the system of domination which subjugates people of color.

In *Getting Home Alive,* Rosario Morales and her daughter Aurora explore the creation of their identities from an internationalist perspective. Rosario, daughter of Puerto Rican immigrants, was born and raised first in New York City, in the El Barrio community among Puerto Ricans, and then in a Bronx Jewish community. As an adult she became involved in the Communist movement. Early in her marriage to a white Jew, they decided to migrate to Puerto Rico to escape political difficulties. They remained there for thirteen years and raised two children. Aurora, coauthor of the autobiography, is thus the daughter of a Puerto Rican mother and a white, Jewish father. Interestingly, mother and daughter both identify with the Puerto Rican and Jewish struggles. Throughout the book the two women discuss the pull they feel to identify with one or the other identity. They refuse the pressure to choose, and in the last piece in their book, entitled "Ending Poem," the two authors fuse their voices and their histories and speak in a single voice. The first stanza reads:

I am what I am.
A child of the Americas.
A light-skinned mestiza of the Caribbean.
A child of many diaspora, born into this
    continent at a crossroads.
I am Puerto Rican. I am U.S. American.
I am New York Manhattan and the Bronx.
A mountain-born, country-bred, home-
    grown jibara child,
up from the shtetl, a California Puerto
    Rican Jew.
A product of New York ghettos I have
    never known.
I am an immigrant
and the daughter and granddaughter of
    immigrants.
We didn't know our forbears' names with
    a certainty.
They aren't written anywhere.
First names only, or hija, negra, ne,
    honey, sugar, dear. (212)

Through the joining of their different identities, the authors recognize that they are creating something new, something that is more than the sum of the parts of the identities they bring together.

In the texts by Moraga and Anzaldúa we again experience the intense pressure many people of color feel to choose between cultures. The most apparent options, assimilation to white culture or affirmation of native cultures, are paved with contradictions. For the Latina lesbian woman in the U.S. context, the discourses which claim her identity are multiple and the contradictions greater than those encountered by other, less marginalized groups. The two Latina lesbian writers, Moraga and Anzaldúa, attest to the "craziness" they felt growing up in a borderland situation where they were being pulled in many directions. They experienced conflicting expectations as women from white, Chicana, and Indian cultures, as well as from heterosexual and lesbian cultures. They describe feeling great self-hatred, feeling marginalized, and without a center to grasp onto because each center asks them to or makes them feel that they must choose. The pressure to choose between possible identities is experienced by both as maddening.

In *Loving in the War Years,* for example, Moraga explores the impact that being the child of a Mexican mother and a white Anglo father had on her development. As a light-skinned Chicana she was able to, and for a period of time did, pass as white. She explains that she moved away from Chicano culture and became anglicized in order to gain autonomy and be free of the sexual and gender restrictions placed upon her within her community. While she found Anglo society also to be sexist, she remarks that she still had less to risk in an Anglo context which did not hold personal power over her in the way that Chicano culture did.

The question of her sexuality increases the confusion felt by Moraga. Despite early attempts to repress her lesbianism, she seems always to have experienced the heterosexual identity she sought to live out as immensely contradictory. Although eventually she found the space to express her sexuality in an Anglo context, she was constantly forced to confront racism within the white, lesbian feminist community. Moraga felt that white women failed to acknowledge the privilege their skin color accorded them. The white feminist agenda ignored the concerns of Chicana and third world women such that Chicanas were invited to participate in the movement as followers but no space was provided to incorporate the culturally specific concerns or analyses of women of color. These contradictions within the white women's movement led her back to her mother and therefore to her Chicana roots, where she again feels the contradiction of being connected to, but simultaneously rejected by, her people. She writes:

> When I finally lifted the lid to my lesbianism, a profound connection with my mother reawakened in me. It wasn't until I acknowledged and confronted my own lesbianism in the flesh, that my heartfelt identification with and empathy for my mother's oppression—due to being poor, uneducated, and Chicana—was realized. My lesbianism is the avenue through which I have learned the most about silence and oppression, and it continues to be a tactile reminder to me that we are not free human beings. (52)

Similarly, Anzaldúa, failing to identify exclusively with either Mexican or Anglo-American culture, experiences a sense of being pulled by both identities. The tug of war is so strong as to make her feel totally annihilated: "I have so internalized the borderland conflict that sometimes I feel like one cancels out the other and we are zero, nothing, no one. A veces no soy nada, ni nadie. Pero hasta cuando no lo soy, lo soy" (63).

Discussing her sexuality, Anzaldúa declares that despite being brought up as a Catholic and socialized as straight, she made a conscious choice to be lesbian. Reflecting on this decision, she states,

> It is an interesting path, and one that continually slips in and out of the white, the Catholic, the Mexican, the indigenous, the instincts. In and out of my head. It makes for loquería, the crazies. It is a path of knowledge—one of knowing (and of learning) the history of oppression of our raza. It is a way of balancing, of mitigating duality. (19)

Both Moraga and Anzaldúa view their coming out as lesbians as a path that led them to become more politicized; it led them to explore how they are oppressed based on their sexuality and, crucially, how this particular type of oppression is related to other forms of oppression. The discussion of sexuality in Moraga and Anzaldúa is concerned with challenging the construction of female sexuality by the family, the state, and the church. Moraga's analysis of sexuality specifically considers how this construction affects the relationships between Chicano men and women, as well as between Chicana women; she explores how women are denied a right to their bodies through the repression of their sexuality, the lifelong threat of sexual violence, and the denial of reproductive rights.

The insistence on naming the specific oppression they experience as lesbians has earned writers such as Moraga and Anzaldúa the wrath of Marxists and Marxist feminists who argue that issues of sexuality, and particularly of lesbianism, are not central to the lives of third world women and should therefore not be discussed alongside the "real" issues such as hunger, poverty, imperialism, and liberation struggles (cf. Gilliam). One variation of this tired argument suggests that only U.S. women of color who are in a position of privilege relative to their third world sisters have the luxury of taking up these concerns, since third world women are more concerned with issues of basic survival and liberation struggles. These critiques often come from U.S.-based third world feminists who, despite their own location in the West, feel that they are somehow in a better position to articulate the "real" political agendas of women of color internationally. To suggest that third world women aren't grappling with issues of sexuality (yes, even of lesbianism), to suggest that these are merely the trivial concerns of indulgent bourgeois, middle-class white women and privileged Westernized third world women, is to condescendingly silence an essential part of the lives and struggles of third world women. As is clear from the work of Accad, Barroso and Bruschini, and Ramos, and from reports that have emerged from the various Latin American encuentros (see, for example, Yarbro-Bejarano), women internationally are recognizing the centrality of gender and sexuality to their lives and the importance of incorporating these issues into their politics.

The Politics of Language

The problem of identity again emerges in the three texts in discussions of language and how to give voice to a multiple heritage. The obvious and yet revolutionary answer is through the use of the mixing of the codes that have shaped their experience. Although all four authors engage in this process to a greater or lesser extent, the issue of language is played out differently for each writer. Moraga, for example, like many U.S. Latinos, lost her ability to use Spanish, one of the languages she grew up with, because she internalized the racism of the society around her and rejected her mother tongue. One of her most important concerns as she became politicized was to reclaim Spanish as an important part of her culture. Moraga's journal entry of September 1, 1981, reads:

> I called up Berlitz today. The Latino who answered refused to quote me prices over the phone. "Come down and talk to Mr. Bictner," he says. I want to know how much it's going to cost before I do any train riding into Manhattan. "Send me a brochure," I say, regretting the call.
>
> Paying for culture. When I was born between the legs of the best teacher I could have had. (141)

Moraga feels that she has been brainwashed and separated from her language; she feels that English does not speak the truth of her experience and that while she is fluent in it, English some-

how restricts her expression. Therefore, she struggles to regain her mother tongue, which she expects will allow her to express emotions and ideas which seem difficult for her to convey in English.

In contrast to Moraga's ambivalence about the use of the English language, both Aurora Levins Morales and Rosario Morales are comfortable with the fact that they are English-dominant. Unlike the Moraga and Anzaldúa collections, *Getting Home Alive* has few pieces that are written entirely in Spanish, although the work is sprinkled with Spanish words and phrases. The theme of Spanish as a lost tongue to be reclaimed does not permeate this text as it does the other two, yet the authors' uneasiness around their lack of fluency in Spanish emerges. Rosario Morales, who as an adult moved with her family to Puerto Rico for eleven years, remembers how difficult it was to reactivate her childhood Spanish, and she states that she will always be "clumsy with the language" (79). Most of her life has been more linked to English, as she was born in New York and associated primarily with English-speakers. She states, "I am Boricua as Boricuas come from the isle of Manhattan" (138), and in her case this means living in a predominantly English-speaking environment.

Her daughter, Aurora, born and raised in Puerto Rico, identifies more strongly with that island and claims that her first language is "Spanglish," although she, too, feels more comfortable with English. She refuses to apologize for this fact, which, as she acknowledges, is a product of her middle-class upbringing. In her "Class Poem" she proclaims that she will not feel guilty about the advantages that she has had. . . . and correctly anticipates that criticism will be leveled at her for not being fluent in Spanish and preferring English by those who argue that Latino/as who do not maintain their Spanish language are assimilating, and are forgetting their culture. Her class poem responds to this criticism by suggesting that she is using her middle-class advantage in the service of her people because denying her privilege and the skills that it implies would be an insult to those who came before her and struggled so that she would have the advantages that they have been denied.

Anzaldúa, in contrast to Levins Morales, Morales and Moraga, does not prioritize either Spanish or English; rather, she affirms the use of "Chicano Spanish," or "Tex-Mex." She speaks of "linguistic terrorism" as coming from all sides. Anzaldúa points out that Chicano Spanish is found to be deficient by Mexicans and Latin Americans, while Chicano English is scorned by Anglos, and she refers in this context to Chicanos as "linguistic orphans." Anzaldúa's concern is to highlight the damage that such criticism effects on the identity of the person. She writes,

> Until I can take pride in my language, I cannot take pride in myself. Until I can accept as legitimate Chicano Texas Spanish, Tex-Mex and all the other languages I speak, I cannot accept the legitimacy of myself. Until I am free to write bilingually and to switch codes without having always to translate, while I still have to speak English or Spanish when I would rather speak Spanglish, and as long as I have to accommodate the English speakers rather than having them accommodate me, my tongue will be illegitimate.
>
> I will no longer be made to feel ashamed of existing. I will have my voice: Indian, Spanish, white. I will have my serpent's tongue—my woman's voice, my sexual voice, my poet's voice. I will overcome the tradition of silence. (59)

Despite their differences, then, all four writers reject the dominant culture's attempts to silence them; and they insist on their right to use the language that best speaks to their experience, without having to translate for those who cannot

or will not understand. Readers, then, especially English monolingual readers, are shaken from their linguistic complacency, particularly when they read Moraga and Anzaldúa.

Cultural Genealogy

> Todavía soy la hija de mi mami. Keep thinking, it's the daughters. It's the daughters who remain loyal to the mother. She is the only woman we stand by. It is not always reciprocated. To be free means on some level to cut that painful loyalty when it begins to punish us. Stop the chain of events. La procesión de mujeres, sufriendo. . . . Free the daughter to love her own daughter. It is the daughters who are my audience. (Moraga, 34)

Moraga explores how this strong deference to Chicano men and traditional family structures seems a necessity given the history of oppression and the threat of genocide Chicanos have experienced in the U.S. She argues that only an honest examination and transformation of the rigid sex roles in Chicano families will create the strength and unity necessary to resist the dominant culture, but acknowledges that this self-criticism of Chicano culture is strongly resisted in the community.

New Modes of Consciousness: The Mestiza

The realization that a noncontradictory, unified self is impossible within the discourses they traverse opens up the possibility of radical change for these Latina writers. All four women reject the frustration, the madness, that comes from embracing a stifling subject position offered in one of the many discourses they are produced by and invited to take up. Instead they defy prescriptions and expectations and forge new possibilities. Anzaldúa, after experiencing the illness brought about by trying to repress contradictions, arrives at a state she describes as the new mestizaje. She states,

> The new *mestiza* copes by developing a tolerance for contradictions, a tolerance for ambiguity. She learns to be an Indian in Mexican culture, to be Mexican from an Anglo point of view. She learns to juggle cultures. She has a plural personality, she operates in a pluralistic mode—nothing is thrust out, the good the bad the ugly, nothing rejected, nothing abandoned. Not only does she sustain contradictions, she turns the ambivalence into something else. (79)

Moraga attempts to bring together the lesbian and "Chicana" elements of her experience through the creation of and participation in a third world women's feminist movement. Such a movement would strive for the liberation of all oppressed peoples. Moraga envisions a women's movement that does not insist that participants deny essential aspects of their identity in order to make "revolution" more acceptable to others. In this she concurs with the thinking of the Combahee River Collective (1983), a group of black feminists who in 1977 wrote,

> We are actively committed to struggling against racial, sexual, heterosexual, and class oppression and see as our particular goal the development of integrated analysis and practice based upon the fact that the major systems of oppression are interlocking. The synthesis of oppressions creates the conditions of our lives. (210)

The building of a women-of-color movement presents a new series of contradictions. The traditions, cultures, and priorities of third world women differ and make connections difficult. Rosario Morales, in a piece entitled "Double Oppression," discusses the difficulty of forging connections with other women. She reports that during a workshop to heal differences between women of color, participants argued about whose particular pain was the most damaging. She leaves the workshop devastated by this attempt to rank oppressions and determined to "sew" herself together with the "thread" spun from so many places. The Moraleses, similarly to Moraga and Anzaldúa, end up accepting and embracing difference as a positive factor which if confronted and analyzed could empower a third world women's movement.

Like Audre Lorde (*Sister Outsider*), all four authors find that it is not the differences between women that separate them, but the fear of recognizing difference, naming it, and understanding that we have been programmed to respond to difference with fear and loathing. Lorde suggests that radical change is possible only when we analyze difference and incorporate it into our lives and politics. She states,

> Advocating the mere tolerance of difference between women is the grossest reformism. It is a total denial of the creative function of difference in our lives. Difference must not be merely tolerated, but seen as a fund of necessary polarities between which our creativity can spark like a dialectic. Only then does the necessity for interdependency become unthreatening. Only within that interdependency of different strengths, acknowledged and equal, can the power to seek new ways of being in the world generate, as well as the courage and sustenance to act where there are no charters. (111)

While Lorde is speaking of acknowledging and transforming differences between women, Moraga and Anzaldúa suggest that a similar process must first occur at a personal, individual level. Latinas must come to terms with the contradictions inherent in their own beings as mestizas before connections with others become possible. This entails overcoming the learned self-hatred that renders them immobile and incapable of acting to transform the interrelated forces which oppress all women and people of color. The new being and the new movement these authors are theorizing will analyze differences and use them to enrich their analysis and develop strategies for change.

The contradictions and barriers experienced by all four Latinas bring them to similar positions. Levins Morales and Morales in the course of the text attempt to integrate all differences in their identity. In [their poetry] they trace their history and then declare themselves to be "new." They refuse to ignore who they are for anyone's convenience; their project is to integrate the various parts of their individual experiences and collective histories to create a new self. . . .

Similarly, Anzaldúa's new mestizaje and Moraga's third world women's movement are not stable, prescriptive positions but rather are radical because they are about producing a consciousness and a movement which does not insist on their fragmentation. The autobiographies produced by Levins Morales, Morales, Anzaldúa, and Moraga, through their form, language, and content, engage the reader in this radical, continual process. The reader also is prevented from fixing the authors in any stable position and must begin to question her desire to do so. The authors embrace a shifting and multiple identity which is in a state of perpetual transition. Anzaldúa best expresses the implications of such a politics when she predicts,

En unas pocas centuries, the future will belong to the mestiza. Because the future depends on the breaking down of paradigms, it depends on the straddling of two or more cultures. By creating a new mythos—that is, a change in the way we perceive reality, the way we see ourselves, the way we behave—la mestiza creates a new consciousness. (80)

In the work of all four authors, the power of this new consciousness is located in the continual creative motion that keeps breaking down the unitary aspect of all prescriptive paradigms offered to those who are marginalized. A narrow politics based exclusively on any of the forces that shape their experience (national origin, class, ethnicity, gender, or sexuality) is rejected, and a new "politics of the flesh" (Moraga and Anzaldúa) confronting all the conditions which shape the lives of U.S. Latinas is articulated.

The importance of such a contribution for U.S. Latinas is conveyed beautifully in the following quote from a letter by nineteen-year-old Alma Ayala to Gloria Anzaldúa, written to express appreciation for the book *This Bridge Called My Back: Writings by Radical Women of Color:*

The women writers seemed to be speaking to me, and they actually understood what I was going through. Many of you put into words feelings I have had that I had no way of expressing. . . . The writings justified some of my thoughts telling me I had a right to feel as I did. (Preface to 2d ed., xvii)

Like *This Bridge Called My Back,* the autobiographies are particularly empowering to the U.S. Latinas who rarely have the opportunity to encounter texts which speak to their lives and which seek to analyze the realities and complexities of living on the borderlands. The writers resist both silence and the lies and distortions that are offered to Latinas in dominant discourses. Instead, Anzaldúa, Moraga, Levins Morales, and Morales construct a politics of personal and collective transformation which is built on the strength of difference and a disentangling of the contradictions inherent in their multiple identities.

Notes

1. *U.S. Latina* refers to women of Latin American descent born in the United States, or those who have immigrated to the U.S. This paper considers work of two Chicanas: Cherrie Moraga and Gloria Anzaldúa, and two Puerto Ricans: Rosario Morales and Aurora Levins Morales.

Chicanas/os and Puerto Ricans are the largest Latina/o populations in the United States. Both peoples have a history of being colonized by the U.S. *Chicana/o* is a term of self-identification taken on by persons of Mexican ancestry in the U.S. context. The term may refer both to persons who were born in the U.S. but trace their background to Mexico, and to those whose families have lived for generations in what is today known as the Southwest, in the states (California, Texas, Arizona, New Mexico, Utah, and parts of Colorado) that were annexed by the U.S. from Mexico in 1848.

Puerto Rico has been a colony of the United States since 1898, when the U.S. took possession of the Caribbean island following the Spanish-American War. While the island has a population of over three million people, approximately two million Puerto Ricans reside in the continental United States. As citizenship was conferred on the Puerto Rican people in 1917, entry into the U.S. was facilitated. The history of the Puerto Rican people is characterized by periods of mass migration to the U.S. (especially following the two world wars) and cycles of back-and-forth migration primarily determined by economic factors. The following sources provide historical and sociocultural information on Chicana/os and Puerto Ricans: Acuña, Mirandé and Enríquez, Lewis, and Morales.

2. Given the revolutionary nature of these three texts, it is interesting to note which of the publishing houses have been prepared to take the risk of publishing feminist, bilingual, and, in the case of Moraga and Anzaldúa, lesbian works. While Latino presses have in the past published bilingual editions as works that have included code mixing, this has generally not been the case for non-Latino publishing houses. Yet these three texts, all of which to a greater or lesser ex-

tent alternate English and Spanish, were published by Anglo presses. Latino presses, which as stated before have only recently begun to publish the work of U.S. Latina women, were probably not excited by the prospect of publishing books such as Moraga's and Anzaldúa's which challenge not only the dictates of "Latino culture" but also the institution of heterosexuality. This is not to imply, however, that mainstream publishers are anxious to publish such texts either. All three texts were published by small presses. Two of the books were published by feminist concerns—Spinsters/Aunt Lute Company and Firebrand—which are relatively new women's presses, and Moraga's book was published by South End, a press that publishes leftist works.

Works Cited

Accad, Evelyne. "Sexuality and Sexual Politics: Conflicts and Contradictions for Contemporary Women in the Middle East." In *Third-World Women and the Politics of Feminism,* ed. Chandra T. Mohanty, Ann Russo, and Lourdes Torres. Bloomington: Indiana University Press, 1991. 237–50.

Acuña, Rodolfo. *Occupied America: The Chicano's Struggle toward Liberation.* San Francisco: Canfield Press, 1972.

Adams, Mary Louise. "There Is No Place like Home: On the Place of Identity in Feminist Politics." *Feminist Review,* no. 31 (Spring 1989).

Anzaldúa, Gloria. *Borderlands/La Frontera.* San Francisco: Spinsters/Aunt Lute, 1987.

Barradas, Efraín, and Rafael Rodríguez, eds. *Herejes y Mitificadores: Muestra de Poesía Puertorriqueña en los Estados Unidos.* Rio Piedras, P.R.: Ediciones Huracán, 1980.

Barroso, Carmen, and Christina Bruschini, "Building Politics from Personal Lives: Discussions on Sexuality among Poor Women in Brazil." In Mohanty, Russo, and Torres, 153–72.

Benstock, Shari, ed. *The Private Self: Theory and Practice of Women's Autobiographical Writings.* Chapel Hill: University of North Carolina Press, 1988.

Bourne, Jenny. "Homelands of the Mind: Jewish

Feminism and Identity Politics." *Race and Class* (Summer 1987).

Butterfield, Stephen. *Black Autobiography in America.* Amherst: University of Massachusetts Press, 1974.

Cliff, Michelle. *Claiming an Identity They Taught Me to Despise.* Watertown, MA: Persephone Press, 1980.

Combahee River Collective. "A Black Feminist Statement." In *This Bridge Called My Back,* ed. Cherríe Moraga and Gloria Anzaldúa. New York: Kitchen Table: Women of Color Press, 1983.

Fox-Genovese, Elizabeth. "My Statue, My Self: Autobiographical Writings of Afro-American Women." In Benstock, 63–89.

Friedman, Susan Stanford. "Women's Autobiographical Selves: Theory and Practice." In Benstock, (34–62). Excerpted in this volume.

Gilliam, Angela. "Women's Equality and National Liberation." In Mohanty, Russo, and Torres, 215–36.

Jelinek, Estelle C. "Introduction: Women's Autobiography and the Male Tradition." In *Women's Autobiography: Essays in Criticism,* ed. Estelle C. Jelinek. Bloomington: Indiana University Press, 1980.

Kappeler, Susanne. "Putting the Politics Back into Sex." *Trouble and Strife,* no. 15 (Spring, 1989).

Kingston, Maxine Hong. *The Woman Warrior: Memoirs of a Girlhood Among Ghosts.* New York: Knopf, 1976.

Lewis, Gordon K. *Puerto Rico: Freedom and Power in the Caribbean.* New York: Monthly Review Press, 1963.

Lorde, Audre. *Zami: A New Spelling of My Name.* Watertown, MA: Persephone Press, 1982.

Lorde, Audre. *Sister Outsider.* New York: Crossing Press, 1984.

Mirandé, Alfredo, and Evangelina Enríquez. *La Chicana.* Chicago: University of Chicago Press, 1979.

Moraga, Cherríe. *Loving in the War Years: Lo Que Nunca Por Sus Labios.* Boston: South End Press, 1983.

Moraga, Cherríe, and Gloria Anzaldúa, eds. *This Bridge Called My Back.* New York: Kitchen Table: Women of Color Press, 1983.

Morales, Aurora Levins, and Rosario Morales. *Getting Home Alive.* New York: Firebrand Books, 1986.

Morales, Julio. *Puerto Rican Poverty and Migration.* New York: Praeger Publishers, 1986.

Ramos, Juanita, ed. *Compañeras: Latina Lesbians.* New York: Latina Lesbian History Project, 1987.

Rowbotham, Sheila. *Women's Consciousness, Man's World.* London: Penguin, 1973.

Sánchez, Rosaura. "Chicana Prose Writers: The Case of Gina Valdés and Silvia Lizárraga." In *Beyond Stereotypes: The Critical Analysis of Chicana Literature,* ed. Maria Herrera-Sobek. Binghamton: Bilingual Press/Editorial Bilingue, 1985.

Smith, Barbara. *Home Girls.* New York: Kitchen Table: Women of Color Press, 1983.

Smith, Sidonie. *A Poetics of Women's Autobiography.* Bloomington: Indiana University Press, 1987.

Yarbro-Bejarano, Yvonne. "Primer Encuentro de Lesbianas Feministas Latinoamericanas y Caribeñas." *Third Woman* (1989).

23 Autobiography, Ethnography, and History: A Model for Reading

Anne E. Goldman

With respect to the narratives this study fore-grounds, I would argue that in privileging the "we" over the "I" recent responses which celebrate the collective in the theory and criticism of ethnic literature, autobiography, and gender studies run the risk of oversimplifying the relation between distinction and affiliation as surely as did the ethnographic publishing conditions under which these books were first produced.[1] My own concern is to move toward redressing this balance by retrieving those impulses toward self-presencing which I believe remain an essential characteristic of life writings. But I wish to hold to the notion of "balance" here, not to re-instate the idea of the isolationist "I" which lies at the heart of traditional definitions of the autobiographical canon. Rather than fix the subject of a given text as either illustrative of a privileged self, distinguished from others in bold relief, or as an example of the "we" that is metonymic of a collective, identity might more effectively be appraised with reference to a continuum. This flexible model has the advantage of supporting multiple self-positionings that can provide critiques of bipolar theories. Notwithstanding their different discursive and historical contexts, for instance, the texts I consider here all challenge conventional notions of the genre. Politically engaged, they tend to frame consciousness less as contemplative than as involved with social conditions, community affiliations, and historical circumstances. But drawing connections between "me" and "us" and maintaining distinctions between "us" and "them" . . . does not preclude the kind of self-formation traditionally considered autobiographical. The practice of self-contextualization, that is, does not prevent people from speaking their own idiosyncratic selves into textual existence. On the contrary, as I have already suggested in my comments on Fabiola Cabeza de Baca's *The Good Life*, acknowledgment of affiliation often provides the basis from which the "I" authorizes herself to speak.

Revising the Subject of Traditional Autobiography

I am interested here in amplifying such strategies toward self-presencing. My work could not have developed, however, without the two decades of committed attention to revising and enriching that earlier model. Susan Friedman cites Regina Blackburn as defining "The 'self' of black autobiography" as "a conscious political identity, drawing sustenance from the past experience of the group."[2] This contextualization is a crucial revision of earlier versions of subjectivity which refused to recognize how the "I" is implicated and informed by circumstances. Similarly, Arnold Krupat's description of Native

American autobiography as a tradition in which "the self most typically is not constituted by the achievement of a distinctive, special voice that separates it from others, but, rather, by the achievement of a particular placement in relation to the many voices without which it could not exist,"[3] if an overgeneralized critical portrait, corrects a monochrome version of personal narrative that defines only the self of the writings of the Puritans and their descendants—Jonathan Edwards, Benjamin Franklin, Henry Adams—as achieving autobiographical distinction.[4]

My own study builds upon this reevaluation of personal narrative. Critics like Blackburn and Krupat, as well as other scholars—William Andrews, Françoise Lionnet, Genaro Padilla, Joanne Braxton, Hertha D. Wong—have already responded to constricted definitions of the genre by delineating traditions of their own using more politically and historically engaged criteria of inclusion.[5] It seems to me time to examine more closely the range of self-representation exhibited by texts both within and across such critical categories. This project is historicist in that it honors the racial and cultural distinctions that underwrite, in part, the impulse toward self-formation in the writings of Jewish American, Chicana, and African American women, but it is more concerned with outlining the range of strategies particular narratives employ than it is in developing a general argument about a tradition of women's autobiography. My interest is in analyzing the strategies women with little access to textual positions of authority use to develop their voices, and, in keeping with this privileging of the will to autobiographical presence, I have tried to approach selected narratives as "agents as well as effects of cultural change," to adopt the phrase Carolyn Porter uses in her critique of the New Historicism.[6] In practice this has meant a focus more on the particular than on the general; a concern less with finding a textual common denominator than

with considering the range of rhetorical patterns distinct narratives provide and with redefining what constitutes writing about the self—always with an eye toward the discursive and historical contexts in which such scripting is conceived, produced, and read.

Cultural Engagement and Autobiographical Practice

Cogewea then told of an amusing incident. . . . The irrepressible camera man was there and he thought to obtain a rare picture of a band of stampeding buffaloes, bearing directly down upon him. He secured his negative alright, but with lowered horns the animals charged and he had scant time to spring into the branches of a nearby tree, where he hung, thus narrowly escaping his life. A noted "Cowboy Artist" was in close proximity and he drew a sketch of the discomfited man swinging to the tree with the rushing buffaloes passing under him. It was, perhaps, a more interesting picture than the camera could have secured.

—Mourning Dove, *Cogewea, the Half-Blood: A Depiction of the Great Montana Cattle Range*

Often locating the personal pronoun in cultural terms means writing it in language that appears self-defeating. Yet like the "amusing incident" relished by Cogewea in which an aspiring ethnographer finds himself caricatured by the "half-blood" cowboys whose way of life he expects to memorialize,[7] the anecdotes and memories related by the women often encode criticisms of the ethnographic scripts they appear to underwrite. Consider Cleofas Jaramillo, caustic on the subject of "Americans" who reproduce "Spanish" recipes without including all the ingredients necessary to make them edible; while furthering the commodification of nuevomexicano culture, she demands that it be orchestrated by Mexicanos themselves. Or Onnie Lee Logan, whose invocations of the editorial apparatus surrounding the telling of her story elide and call attention to the heavy-handed supervisory strategies by which two kinds of self-appointed "midwives"—medical and literary—seek to control her work. Or Rose Schneiderman, whose warmest recollections serve to reconfigure the insistently Jewish family life that is being whitewashed by the commercial frame within which her narrative of union labor is published.

At their most successful, the speakers and writers considered here maneuver between autobiographical and political-cultural texts, between "I" and various forms of "we." This study, then, documents those impulses toward self-presencing that counterpoint as well as contravene the pressures ethnographic discourse exerts upon autobiographers. In part, what enables such autobiographers simultaneously to represent culture and to write the self is their insistence on the work involved in both activities. Focusing on the reproduction of culture as a conscious labor rather than as "something . . . often unsuccessfully repressed or avoided,"[8] they often stress the extent to which the traditions of their particular communities have been appropriated by others—and therefore need to be reinterpreted by themselves. In an essay on African American women's autobiography, Elizabeth Fox-Genovese has suggested that "to write the account of one's self is to inscribe it in a culture that for each of us is only partially our own,"[9] but if they recognize the sociopolitical stakes involved in producing life history, these autobiographers are not content to cede discursive authority to cultural outsiders. And in the process of insisting that they retain the rights to represent cultural practice, such writers confer upon themselves the status to argue their claims. Cultural critique, that is, gives them their opportunity, as women, to speak at all. In voicing their opinions about a collective with which they are affiliated, whether they broadcast these opinions or argue them sotto voce, they accord themselves the agency and presence necessary for autobiographical distinction.[10]

Michael Omi claims that "where political opposition was banned or useless . . . transformation of the racial order, or resistance to it, was perforce military."[11] Yet the quiet but nonetheless decisive cultural engagement Evelyn Nakano Glenn describes suggests that this formulation is too narrow. According to Glenn, Japanese and Japanese American women acted not only as "conservators" but also as "mediators" of cultural change in the United States: "Employed women, especially those working as domestics, helped introduce selected aspects of American culture, such as home decoration and living arrangements."[12] Making changes in home decoration may seem a modest exercise of authority, but in an environment that is less than encouraging of self-articulation and that provides almost no leisure in which to create on a grander scale, that it happens at all is telling.

The recognition that Japanese American women can articulate a cultural polemic through their domestic practices demands a rethinking of the distinction between public domain and private sphere more generally and points toward the necessity of historicizing the private as thoroughly as the public. Yet postmortem theorists have denied the political efficacy of such resistive articulations. Fredric Jameson, for instance, mourns the apparent failure of all cultural critique: "Not only punctual and local countercultural forms of cultural resistance and guerrilla warfare but also even overtly political interventions . . . are all somehow secretly disarmed and reabsorbed by a system of which they themselves might well be considered a part, since they can achieve no distance from it."[13] The problem with such a systemic formulation, however, is that it denies the very real authority of individual agency—or it assumes a model of consciousness that credits its subjects with a singular incapacity to accommodate their speech to their listeners or to "speak out of both sides of their mouths" at once.[14] But, as the coded critique of Rose Pesotta, the ethnographic circumlocutions of Zora Neale Hurston, and the rhetorical wiliness of VertaMae Smart-Grosvenor's formulations of identity[15]—or even, to cite an older illustration of such strategizing, the Trojan Horse—make clear, resistance is often most potent when it is masked, most effective when it is formulated using the language of accommodation.

In order to evaluate the political work redefining culture does for personal narrative, we need a more nuanced conception of identity. Just as autobiography critics need not reduce the relation between distinction and affiliation to an either/or equation, identification of structural principles does not have to make individual lives irrelevant. Racial identity is, after all, as Michael Omi characterizes it, composed of a "complex of individual practices. . . . The panoply of individual attributes—from one's patterns of speech or tastes in food or music to the economic, spatial, familial, or citizenship 'role' one occupies—provides the essential themes for political organization."[16] Likewise, culture need not be formulated as an apocalyptic struggle between conqueror and conquered, but can instead be seen as a network of relations—hierarchically striated and often at odds, yes, but providing intellectual and spiritual sustenance nonetheless. As theorist John Brenkman articulates this: "Individuals . . . are members of several interlaced collectivities, so that their social identities are formed by and their discursive participation occurs within several potentially conflicting cultural practices/traditions at once."[17]

The narratives of the Jewish labor organizers . . . display a particularly curious working out of ethnic identity. In this instance, the language of class speaks on behalf of culture as well. Published during the First World War, when to act "American" meant to choose between a very limited number of cultural scripts, many Jewish writers—Elizabeth Hasanovitz, for instance, whose autobiography was initially serialized by *The Atlantic Monthly* in 1917 and 1918, and Rose Cohen, whose personal narrative was published in 1918 as part of George H. Doran Company's American Immigration Library—were able to construct American selves only by disaffiliating themselves from a Jewish culture identified as a political anachronism. In these books and others like them, the "Americanization" of the self, which requires a renunciation of Jewishness, is overtly framed as a story of class rise. Rose Pesotta's history of her involvement with the International Ladies' Garment Workers Union, *Bread upon the Waters* (1944), and Rose Schneiderman's recollections of struggle in *All for One* (1967) are equally class-conscious, but here working-class affiliations are celebrated rather than denied. In turn-of-the-century Russia, after all, to agitate for labor reform was virtually to announce yourself as Jewish-identified, since a disproportionately high number of Russian socialists were Jewish. This association, coupled with the fact that Jewish culture in the United States has historically been a working-class culture, suggests that those writers who choose steadfastly to represent themselves as part of the working poor express a kind of filial piety in the process. If there appears to be little explicit focus on Jewishness in these books, holding on to a working-class identity nonetheless enables these writers to maintain a secular kind of Jewish cultural practice.

What I wish to suggest by emphasizing the multiple and shifting nature of cultural forms and collective affiliations is that the identity that is predicated upon them is equally particularized. Its articulation takes different forms in different contexts, so that at various points in a narrative the same autobiographical subject may provide us with multiple formulations of, for instance, racial identity. The ethnic "I" of

VertaMae Smart-Grosvenor's culinary autobiography *Vibration Cooking,* for example, provides readers with what would be theorized as both essentialist and constructionist conceptions of blackness. Such apparently contradictory conceptions are a problem only when we consider race or other determinants of identity as pure categories. Dispense with this kind of abstraction, and what looks like inconsistency soon begins to read as flexibility, the kind of flexibility that allows for a richer conception of the "I" and a more nuanced version of the self's relation to ethnicity.

Smart-Grosvenor's refusal to generalize about racial identity—or, more specifically, her insistence on providing readers with multiple generalizations—is illustrative here. Denying both ethnography's claims on the subject as "representative" and an autobiographical model which would deprive the self of racial identity, she insists: "I don't have culinary limitations because I'm 'black.' On the other hand, I choose to write about 'Afro-American' cookery because I'm 'black' and know the wonderful, fascinating culinary history there is. And because the Afro-American cook has been so under-appreciated." Announcements like this one pull the complacent reader up short by making any easy formulation of race impossible. Or consider the following remark in which the autobiographer's insistence on her self-distinction is framed using a language that locates this idiosyncratic "I" squarely within black speech traditions: "Black people been eating that traditional New Year's Day dinner for years. That's why I'm not having no more open house on New Year's Day. I'm going to try something new" (4).

Ethnic identity may be a constant, but its forms are constantly changing, since this particular relationship between "I" and "we" depends upon a number of other factors, including geography and gender, work and sexuality, generation and class status and historical circumstance. In his celebrated study of Asian American history, Ronald Takaki explains how Korean children growing up on the sugar plantations of Hawaii begin to speak pidgin more fluently than Korean, creating "a new identity associated with Hawaii,"[18] while in Joss Villareal's novel *Pocho,* Richard's Mexican-born father simultaneously wonders at the racism of a high school teacher and affirms his own sense of mexicanidad: 'What the hell makes people like that, anyway? Always worried about his being Mexican and he never even thought about it, except sometimes, when he was alone, he got kinda funnyproud about it."[19]

What all of these examples are designed to suggest is that we conceptualize race—and every other determinant of identity—not as a pure and irreducible category, but instead as formed by and informing the whole range of social, historical, political, and cultural circumstances within which the subject locates herself. Evelyn Brooks Higginbotham questions the tendency of feminist criticism to privilege gender as the single most important determinant of identity. Gender, she suggests, was for nineteenth-century American women "both constructed and fragmented by race. Gender, so colored by race, remained from birth until death inextricably linked to one's personal identity and social status. For black and white women, gendered identity was reconstructed and represented in very different, indeed antagonistic, racialized contexts."[20] Her own counterprivileging of race as the more significant term of the equation runs the risk of creating different but equally significant overgeneralizations, however. As she herself indicates, any assessment of the ways in which race and gender inform identity must be framed historically. But privileging one term inevitably abstracts it in such a way as to render it ahistorical, reframing the contingent and material as a universal category that transcends the individual lives it sets out to explain.

This is not to suggest that I am interested in reinstating gender as the critical category of choice. Clearly, making "gender relations primary is to assume that they create a set of universal experiences more important than those of other inequalities," as Elizabeth Higginbotham, Maxine Baca Zinn, Lynn Weber Cannon, and Bonnie Thornton Dill maintain.[21] Privileging gender in this way is "inadequate," autobiography critic Julia Watson argues, given that women's positions "with respect to ethnicity and class and their modes of self-identification are not only divergent but organized within a structure of power relations."[22] While a certain number of globalizing statements are almost unavoidable in any discussion, I am more concerned to develop ad hoc, local observations about given narratives, privileging neither race nor gender as the dominant determinant of identity but instead acknowledging the range of inflections the combination of these factors—and others—can impart to different texts at different times. An ever more refined method of abstraction may be the mode of inquiry favored by much contemporary theory, but this study works instead toward a theory of the concrete, focusing closely on a series of individual voices and their permutations, refusing to make broad claims about autobiographical narrative by women but honoring the particular, distinct presences which the writers and speakers of individual narratives have worked so hard to achieve.

Generalizing statements are clearly useful in establishing the autonomy of particular autobiographical traditions, however. "Reading by ethnicity," as Sau-ling Wong argues, "is a necessary act of identity-building for those whose literatures have been rendered invisible by subsumption."[23] The distinction Elizabeth Fox-Genovese draws between personal narrative by black and by white women ("Much of the autobiographical writing of black women eschews the confessional mode—the examinations of personal motives, the searchings of the soul—that white women autobiographers so frequently adopt")[24] is helpful in establishing the work of African

American women as an autonomous narrative tradition that needs to be studied in its own right and on its own terms. Yet in circumscribing a given autobiographical genre, such statements run the risk of ignoring other narrative forms with which women experiment. To consider black women's writing, again, the meditations of Charlotte Forten in the journals she kept through the mid-1850s comment on the Port Royal experiment and the political circumstances of the freedmen living there but also develop a voice as rigorously "soul-searching" as are the reflections of Alice James in the diary she wrote some thirty years later. Marita Golden's 1983 autobiography oscillates between ethnographic description and an analysis of the "personal motives" that drew its author to Nigeria and back home following the birth of her son and a failed marriage. And Maya Angelou's 1986 appraisal of the relations between Africans and African Americans discloses as many personal "confessions" as political critiques.[25]

Delineating autobiographical traditions by particular groups of women requires, of necessity, limiting them as well. When scholars begin to make generalizations about the practices of women writers as a whole, however, the drawbacks attendant upon their conclusions are potentially more serious, their summarizing claims more likely to slight a greater range of self-representational strategies. The tendency of some feminist autobiography theory to celebrate the feminine self-in-relation rightly critiques the androcentric quality of much autobiography theory, but at the same time it leaves us with a model of the subject so abstracted as to transcend social conditions. Mary G. Mason's description, for instance, obscures as much as it reveals:

The self-discovery of female identity seems to acknowledge the real presence and recognition of another consciousness, and the disclosure of female self is linked to the identification of some "other." This recognition of another consciousness—and I emphasize recognition rather than difference—this grounding of identity through relation to the chosen other, seems . . . to enable women to write openly about themselves.[26]

For a great many women, as I have suggested earlier, the relation between "recognition" and "difference" is far more complicated, writing "openly" an impossibility—even with the authority affiliation provides. Take, for instance, the records of Jewish labor organizers considered in this study. If we assume, as does Margo Culley, that women writers in general "submerge the personal in some 'larger' purposes in order to become the vehicle for conveying a message about history,"[27] we are likely to hear these narratives only as voice-overs for the ongoing struggles of organized labor. Acknowledging the discursive constraints under which such activists as Rose Schneiderman and Elizabeth Hasanovitz labored leads to a different reading of their memoirs, a reading which in reaccentuating context underscores quality of voice as well.

Careful scrutiny thus suggests that we transform the terms of Culley's equation, identifying Schneiderman's and Pesotta's focus on their engagement in the collective labor contest as a means of justifying their interest as autobiographical subjects. Ostensibly celebrating the power of unified struggle, such writers thereby establish a sense of their singular authority. Elizabeth Hasanovitz's *One of Them: Chapters from a Passionate Autobiography* invokes the united response of hundreds of workers—in order to demonstrate how their solidarity supports her individual claim as shop steward.[28] Rose Schneiderman documents the founding of the National Women's Trade Union League but makes this bit of union history contingent upon personal history: "And so, with the blessings of la-

bor and laymen the National Women's Trade Union League was born, an organization which was to be the most important influence in my life."[29] And Rose Cohen's autobiography *Out of the Shadow* compares the anonymity of one form of collective consciousness—the dispirited sense of herself as one of the hospital "dependents"—to the recognition that working-class community gives to her as an individual.[30]

Recognizing the range of autobiographical models and the rhetorical strategies used to develop them in these three narratives alone—personal histories produced under similar publishing constraints by women of the same ethnic background—should not mean that we deny their interest as texts by women. If, as feminist critic Jill Mathews asserts, "There can be no unified history of women," the field of women's autobiography is only the more compelling for the number of different histories with which it does provide us.[31] Acknowledging each woman's narrative as a distinct working out of the "struggle of memory against forgetting"[32] suggests the need to theorize history differently as well, as Sarah Rice does in her autobiography *He Included Me*: "Right now what we are doing is making history. You might not ever be in a book, but you are making history. History is things that happened in the past, and things that you do every day, as long as you live, that's history."[33]

Fabiola Cabeza de Baca puts this another way in *We Fed Them Cactus*, when she glosses for us what constitute significant events in the llano country of Northeastern New Mexico:

Money in our lives was not important; rain was important. We never counted our money; we counted the weeks and months between rains. . . . We would remember an unusually wet year for a lifetime; we enjoyed recalling it during dry spells. Rain for us made history. It brought to our

minds days of plenty, of happiness and security, and in recalling past events, if they
fell on rainy years, we never failed to stress
that fact. The droughts were as impressed
on our souls as the rains. When we spoke
of the Armistice of World War 1, we always said, "The drought of 1918 when the
Armistice was signed." (11–12)

In this quiet but nevertheless radical statement,
Cabeza de Baca restructures the relation between history and personal narrative. Rather
than being a universal organizing principle, an
abstraction against which individual lives are
measured, history is redefined as a contingent
phenomenon, constructed, and constructed differently, by the very individual subjects it has
in more scholarly philosophical accounts found
wanting in authority. Accepting of the mundane
as well as the monumental, investing daily life
with the attention and dignity typically accorded
only to the sweeping changes of governments or
the rise and fall of civilizations, "history" in this
formulation is twin to life history, not the master
narrative engineered to supplant it. Explanations
like Rice's and Cabeza de Baca's and responses
like the one Ron Takaki records ("'What is it
you want to know?' an old Filipino immigrant
asked a researcher. 'Talk about history. What's
that . . . ah, the story of my life. . . . and how
people lived with each other in my time'") grant
a value to private life more commonly reserved
for the public sphere.[34] Perhaps this awareness
will make it easier not only for Gertrude Stein
but also for Rose Schneiderman—and Onnie
Lee Logan and Cleofas Jaramillo and Jesusita
Aragón—to receive the autobiographical recognition they deserve.

Notes

This chapter is from the introduction to Anne E.
Goldman's book, *Take My Word: Autobiographical In-*

novations of Ethnic American Women Writers (Berkeley: University of California Press, 1996).

1. For an example of this tendency to overcorrect
for the "existential" model of the subject by celebrating a wholly collaborative idea of identity, see bell
hooks: "I evoked the way of knowing I had learned
from unschooled Southern black folks. We learned
that the self existed in relation, was dependent for
its very being on the lives and experiences of everyone, the self not as signifier of one 'I' but the coining
together of many 'I's, the self as embodying collective reality past and present, family and community (*Talking Back: Thinking Feminist Thinking Black*
[Boston: South End Press, 1989], 30–31). This formulation seems to me to oversimplify the range of
representational strategies African American autobiography provides readers, but hooks's assertion that
we read the self historically ("Social construction of
the self in relation would mean . . . that we would be
in touch with what Paule Marshall calls 'our ancient
properties'—our history") is crucial. See Goldman,
Take My Word chapter 6, for a more sustained discussion of critical constructions of the relational self.

2. Susan Stanford Friedman, "Women's Autobiographical Selves: Theory and Practice," 72–82, in this
volume.

3. Arnold Krupat, *The Voice in the Margin: Native
American Literature and the Canon* (Berkeley: University of California Press, 1985), 133–34.

4. With our sometimes foreshortened scholarly
memories we may take such correctives for granted,
yet these revisions are both relatively recent and hard
won, and the ground they question remains a contested site. Thus as late as 1980, Roger Rosenblatt
supported what Krupat identifies as "egocentric individualism" (*Ethnocriticism: Ethnography, History,
Literature,* [Berkeley: University of California Press,
1992], 29) when he described autobiography as "one
person in relation to one world of that person's manu-
facture, which is that person in macrocosm, explained
and made beautiful by that same person in the distance, playing god to the whole unholy trinity"
("Black Autobiography: Life as the Death Weapon,"
in *Autobiography: Essays Theoretical and Critical,* ed.
James Olney [Princeton: Princeton University Press,
1980], 169), and in the same collection James Olney

rehearses the standard definition of autobiography as deriving from a tradition inaugurated by St. Augustine, celebrating the "dawning self-consciousness of Western man that found literary expression in the early moments of modern autobiography" ("Autobiography and the Cultural Moment: A Thematic, Historical, and Bibliographical Introduction," 13). It is pronouncements like these, by no means exceptional, that make the argument for the kind of more expansive definition advanced implicitly by Blackburn, and more explicitly by Krupat, so necessary.

5. See William L. Andrews, *To Tell a Free Story: The First Century of Afro-American Autobiography, 1760–1865* (Urbana: University of Illinois Press, 1986), and *Sisters of the Spirit: Three Black Women's Autobiographies of the Nineteenth Century* (Bloomington, Indiana University Press, 1986); Joanne M. Braxton, *Black Women Writing Autobiography: A Tradition within a Tradition* (Philadelphia: Temple University Press, 1989).

6. Carolyn Porter, "Are We Being Historical Yet?" *South Atlantic Quarterly* 87 (Fall 1988): 782.

7. Mourning Dove, *Cogewea, the Half-Blood. A Depiction of the Great Montana Cattle Range*, ed. Lucullus Virgil McWhorter, introduction by Dexter Fisher (Lincoln: University of Nebraska Press, 1981), 149.

8. Michael M. J. Fischer, "Ethnicity and the Post-Modern Arts of Memory," in *Writing Culture: The Poetics and Politics of Ethnography*, ed. James Clifford and George E. Marcus (Berkeley: University of California Press, 1988), 125. Fischer does not deny that cultural practice may be undertaken consciously, but his use of a psychoanalytic model of transference and of what he calls "dream-work" to explain ethnicity tends in practice to privilege unconscious mechanisms of transmittal as more "sophisticated"—and thus more worthy of study—than more direct means of cultural reproduction. See, for instance, the following weighted comparison: "Ethnicity is something reinvented and reinterpreted in each generation by each individual and . . . it is often something over which he or she lacks control. Ethnicity is not something that is simply *passed* on from generation to generation, taught and learned; it is something dynamic, often unsuccessfully repressed or avoided" (195; emphasis added).

9. Elizabeth Fox-Genovese, "My Statue, My Self: Autobiographical Writings of Afro-American Women," in *The Private Self: Theory and Practice of Women's Autobiographical Writings*, ed. Shari Benstock (Chapel Hill: University of North Carolina Press, 1988), 83.

10. Cf. Françoise Lionnet's discussion of ethnic and autobiographical authority in Hurston's *Dust Tracks*: "Despite its rich cultural content, the work does not authorize unproblematic recourse to culturally grounded interpretations. It is an orphan text that attempts to create its own genealogy by simultaneously appealing to and debunking the cultural traditions it helps to redefine" (*Autobiographical Voices: Race, Gender, Self-Portraiture* [Ithaca: Cornell University Press, 1989], 101). Orphan and affiliate, Hurston is at once a presence distinct from others and a cultural arbiter wholeheartedly engaged with a racial collective. According herself the power to revise the cultural standard also grants her more weight as an autobiographical subject.

11. Michael Omi, *Racial Formation in the United States from the 1960s to the 1980s* (New York: Routledge, 1986), 72–73.

12. Evelyn Nakano Glenn, *Issei, Nisei, War Bride: Three Generations of Japanese American Women in Domestic Service* (Philadelphia: Temple University Press, 1988), 38.

13. Fredric Jameson, *Postmodernism; Or, The Cultural Logic of Late Capitalism* (Durham: Duke University Press, 1990), 49.

14. This formulation is Genaro M. Padilla's in *My History, Not Yours: The Formation of Mexican American Autobiography* (Madison: University of Wisconsin Press, 1993). Padilla suggests that "ideologically subordinate speech . . . actually constitutes multi-addressed utterance in which pragmatic appeasement reads at one surface of language while anger and opposition read at other, and often within the same, surfaces. Such strategic utterance constitutes a form of rhetorical camouflage which first appropriates a public 'voice' for an individual from an otherwise 'silenced' group and then turns that voice to duplicitous purpose. Such discursive duplicity functions to communicate different stories to different audiences, with an implicit understanding that one's own people will . . . someday read them 'de una manera digna de

ellos'" (draft version of chapter 1, msp. 42). Given the all too common practice of figuring the speaker as "always already" silenced, the focus on speech is crucial here. Although her essay works in general to deconstruct reductive notions of oppressor/oppressed power relations, Chandra Talpade Mohanty's description of resistance as inhering "in the very gaps, fissures, and silences of hegemonic narratives" is illustrative of this tendency to deny voice to those who lack political authority (Introduction to her *Third World Women and the Politics of Feminism* [Bloomington: Indiana University Press, 1991], 38). This focus on silence may be an eloquent metaphor for oppression, but I would argue that it is inaccurate at the level of the literal and disabling as a trope.

15. VertaMae Smart-Grosvenor, *Vibration Cooking: Or, The Travel Notes of a Geechee Girl* (1970; New York: Ballantine, 1986), xv.

16. Omi, 67–68.

17. John Brenkman, *Culture and Domination* (Ithaca: Cornell University Press, 1988), 24. Mohanty makes a similar point in *Third World Women* when she suggests that "it is possible to retain the idea of multiple, fluid structures of domination which intersect to locate women differently at particular historical conjunctures, while at the same time insisting on the dynamic oppositional agency of individuals and collectives and their engagement in 'daily life'" (13).

18. Ronald Takaki, *Strangers from a Different Shore: A History of Asian Americans* (New York: Penguin, 1989), 168.

19. José Antonio Villareal, *Pocho* (New York: Doubleday, 1959), 108.

20. Evelyn Brooks Higginbotham, "African-American Women's History and the Metalanguage of Race," *Signs* 17 (Winter 1992): 258.

21. Maxine Baca Zinn, Lynn Weber Cannon, Elizabeth Higginbotham, and Bonnie Thornton Dill, "The Costs of Exclusionary Practices in Women's Studies," in *Making Face, Making Soul/Haciendo Caras: Creative and Critical Perspectives by Women of Color*, ed. Gloria Anzaldúa (San Francisco: Aunt Lute Foundation Books, 1990), 34. For another useful critique of Anglo-American feminism, see Norma Alarcón, "The Theoretical Subject(s) of *This Bridge Called My Back* and Anglo-American Feminism," in Hector Calderón and José David Saldívar, eds. *Criticism in*

the Borderlands: Studies in Chicano Literature, Culture, and Ideology* (Durham: Duke University Press, 1991). Alarcón argues that privileging gender effaces the ways in which "'one becomes a woman' in opposition to other women" as well as in "simple opposition to men" (33).

22. Julia Watson, "Toward an Anti-Metaphysics of Autobiography," in *The Culture of Autobiography: Constructions of Self-Representation* ed. Robert Folkenflik (Stanford: Stanford University Press, 1993), 71.

23. Sau-ling Cynthia Wong, "Immigrant Autobiography: Some Questions of Definition and Approach," 299–315, in this volume.

24. Fox-Genovese, 71.

25. Charlotte L. Forten [Grimké], *The Journal of Charlotte L. Forten: A Free Negro in the Slave Era*, ed. Ray Allen Billington (1953; New York: W. W. Norton, 1981); Alice James, *The Diary of Alice James*, ed. Leon Edel (New York: Penguin, 1964); Marita Golden, *Migrations of the Heart: An Autobiography* (New York: Ballantine, 1983); Maya Angelou, *All God's Children Wear Traveling Shoes* (New York: Random House, 1986).

26. Mary G. Mason, "The Other Voice: Autobiographies of Women Writers" 321–24, in this volume.

27. Margo Culley, "What a Piece of Work Is 'Woman'!" in her collection, *American Women's Autobiography: Fea[s]ts of Memory* (Madison: University of Wisconsin Press, 1992), 15–16.

28. Elizabeth Hasanovitz, *One of Them: Chapters from a Passionate Autobiography* (Boston: Houghton Mifflin, 1918).

29. Rose Schneiderman with Lucy Goldthwaite, *All for One* (New York: Paul S. Erikson, 1967), 76.

30. Rose Cohen, *Out of the Shadow* (New York: George H. Doran, 1918), 259.

31. Mathews's recognition of the specificity of women's lives is worth quoting in full: "Moreover, beyond acknowledgment of diversity among the groups of women, there is the need to acknowledge the diversity of each individual woman. . . . Each woman in any society is not simply a member of one definite social category, but is a unique and female focus of a multitude of coexisting and competing social groups and relationships" (as cited by Mary Jo Maynes, "Gender and Narrative Form in French and German

Working-Class Autobiography," in Personal Narratives Group, *Interpreting Women's Lives: Feminist Theory and Personal Narratives* [Bloomington: Indiana University Press, 1989], 40–41). Acknowledging the specificity of such narratives allows us a measure of defense against the critical complacency which can follow upon any sustained inquiry. It allows us, for instance, to read a critique of paternal authority encoded in a text that presents itself as all filial duty, without discrediting a more affirmative representational moment of the relation between father and daughter. Consider the irony with which Jade Snow Wong mocks this moment of fatherly self-importance: "One day when the family was at dinner, father broke the habitual silence by announcing a new edict: 'I have just learned that the American people commonly address their fathers informally as "Daddy"! The affectionate tone of this word pleases me. Hereafter, you children shall address me as "Daddy." No comment was required; the children mentally recorded this command" (*Fifth Chinese Daughter* [New York: Harper and Brothers, 1945], 12). Or this remembrance by Marita Golden: "My father was the first man I ever loved. He was as assured as a panther. His ebony skin was soft as the surface of coal. . . . In school he went as far as the sixth grade, then learned the rest on his own. . . . By his own definition he was 'a black man and proud of it.' Arming me with a measure of this conviction, he unfolded a richly colored tapestry, savored its silken texture and warned me never to forget its worth. Africa: 'It wasn't dark until the white man got there.' Cleopatra: 'I don't care WHAT they tell you in school, she was a black woman'" (*Migrations of the Heart: An Autobiography* [New York: Ballantine, 1983], 3).

32.   hooks, 4.

33.   Sarah Rice, *He Included Me: The Autobiography of Sarah Rice,* transcribed and ed. Louise Westling (Athens: University of Georgia Press, 1989), 77.

34.   Takaki, 9.

24 Immigrant Autobiography: Some Questions of Definition and Approach

Sau-ling Cynthia Wong

Introduction

Just as immigrants are often seen as less than fully American, immigrant autobiography has been customarily assigned to the peripheries of American autobiographical scholarship.[1] Of the many studies based implicitly or explicitly on the premise that autobiography is a characteristically American genre, few dwell at length, if at all, on works written by immigrants.[2] This state of affairs, which seems oddly incongruent with the widely acknowledged centrality of the immigrant experience in American history, has only recently been challenged by William Boelhower in *Immigrant Autobiography in the United States: Four Versions of the Italian American Self* (1982). Employing a heavily structuralist apparatus with a deconstructive twist, he makes a case for regarding immigrant autobiography as nothing less than a genotype of American autobiography. Boelhower's work is significant because it is, thus far, the only existing book-length study devoted to immigrant autobiography and attempting a coherent theoretical account of it. The following essay uses Boelhower's study as a focus to explore some fundamental

questions on how immigrant autobiography is to be defined and read.

Boelhower's Model of Immigrant Autobiography

. . . Boelhower sketches out a "macrotext, . . . a single story" (30), in which all immigrant autobiographies are presumed to participate. Beginning with a mythic moment of "dream anticipation" (28), the protagonist undertakes a journey from the Old World to the New and engages in a series of contacts and contrasts (40). During a process of "transformation" or "Americanization," the protagonist is "forced to confront the utopian grammar of the New World for what it actually represents" so that immigrant autobiography must "organize *two* cultural systems, a culture of the present and the future and a culture of memory, into a single model" (29; italics in original). The narrative possibilities are diagrammatically represented in figure 1:

299

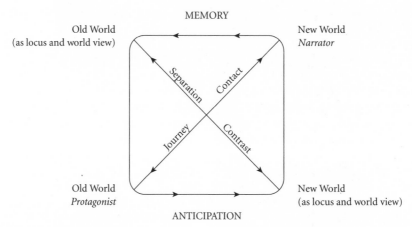

Old World
(as locus and world view)

New World
Narrator

Separation *Contact*

Journey *Contrast*

Old World
Protagonist

New World
(as locus and world view)

ANTICIPATION

Reversing the historical banishment of immigrant autobiographies to the outermost reaches of American literature Boelhower asserts that the model he propounds "can serve as the real epicenter for the larger category of ethnic autobiographies" (21–22). Further, he sees the theoretical implications of his work extending beyond the autobiographical genre, to challenge the commonsensically assumed ontological basis of American culture itself. Boelhower suggests that an analysis of immigrant autobiography may help uncover the "original metaphorical status" of the nation's reigning "monocultural paradigm": "the explicitiation [*sic*] of [the] marginal text [of the multiethnic paradigm] entails the deconstruction of the foundations of monocultural theory" (221). No matter how naturalized the dominant society's myths have been, how securely accorded the official status of history, "the multiethnic paradigm is necessarily copresent as a countertext and cancels the representational pretensions of monocultural theory" (226). Far from being the academic equivalent of political special-interest groups, therefore, ethnic literary scholarship, in Boelhower's view, assumes a centrality and dignity equal to, if not exceeding, that traditionally accorded mainstream literary scholarship. . . .[3]

This necessarily brief paraphrase of Boel-

hower's arguments makes his thesis more homogenizing than it is. He is careful to point out that "there are as many varieties as there are ethnic groups" and "in no way does the macrotext exhaust the . . . microtexts" (31). True to his deconstructive bent, he maintains that the American mythic language itself, as adopted by immigrant autobiographers, may serve a subversive rather than celebratory function:

> The immigrant actant, welcomed in on the basis of his appeal to a mythic language, actually smuggles into the house of American autobiography a Pandora's box of uncontrollable textual variants. As one passes from macrotext to microtexts, he finds that the actant fragments into actors of all races. . . . Through a deconstructive process, immigrant autobiography uses the cultural patterns on which the typology of American selves is based in order to shift the American cultural text towards the pole of diversity. (50, 51)

There is no denying, however, that *Immigrant Autobiography* intends its schema to be all-encompassing, capable of shedding light on details from highly diverse textual sources. . . .

. . . I will attempt to assess Boelhower's typology by testing its claims of broad applicability across generational, ethnic, and period boundaries, with Chinese-American immigrant autobiographies as my main sources.[4] My aims are to clarify the definition of American immigrant autobiography, whose distinctness Boelhower has labored to establish in his book, and to explore ways to approach autobiographies by immigrant authors from diverse backgrounds. Does the term immigrant autobiography adequately address the different historical experiences of both first- and second-generation ethnics, as Boelhower apparently intends it to? How does the immigrant autobiography "macrotext" hold up against "microtexts" from an ethnic group which is barely mentioned in *Immigrant Autobiography*[5] but has been in the United States for some 140 years of the nation's history? Do immigrants of all ethnic groups and all periods share, in some profound sense, a collective American experience? Does immigrant autobiography constitute a clearly marked subgenre of American autobiography? How useful is the concept of immigrant autobiography for scholars of ethnic literature?

The Foreign-Born and the American-Born

. . . To me, Boelhower's omnibus term immigrant autobiography signals a conceptually problematic telescoping of first and second generations into a single "immigrant experience." It suggests that the generational positioning of the narrator and the historical particulars of his life are relatively insignificant as long as the interactions between Old World and New are embodied in his narrative. In other words, while the immigrant generation actually spans the Old World and the New, the American-born may also be said to experience the "confrontation" of the two cultural systems—an indispensable element in Boelhower's schema—by having

been born into a family with an Old World culture. . . .

It seems to me that whereas directions on arrows can be manipulated in a diagram and matrices can be filled in to complete a set of theoretical possibilities, the historically-situated voyage that transforms foreign nationals into American immigrants separates the first and second generations quite drastically.[6] As a result, in spite of obvious biological and cultural continuities, first- and second-generation ethnics cannot be said to experience and perceive "Americanization" in the same way; to say that their autobiographies manifest an identical deep structure presupposes a rather static concept of culture.

Several arguments support a more scrupulous use of the term *immigrant autobiography*. To begin with, the American-born do not have direct memories of the Old World; their understanding of Old World culture is necessarily mediated by their parents, who themselves undergo inevitable transformations as a result of permanently relocating to the United States. This is not to say that the immigrants are always aware of how American they have become—such a realization can be psychologically threatening and is often resisted—or that, in front of their children, they don't gladly assume the authority of authentic representatives of the culture of origin. Moreover, immigrants and their children frequently do experience their family conflicts *in the form of* cultural confrontation; to that extent they are most likely incapable of deconstructing the rhetoric they use, and to that extent they can be said to share a common metaphor. Nevertheless, as critic, Boelhower could have gone through with (and beyond) *his* deconstructive analysis more rigorously, to reach an acknowledgment of different historical placements of the generations and the dynamic nature of cultural formation.[7] After all, autobiographies are often most fascinating to analysts when the protagonists think and say they are doing something but provide ample clues to the contrary.

Boelhower runs through various combinations of "Old World," "New World," "ideal" and "reality" as if they were pieces in a chess game. Closer to the truth, probably, is the more organic view that a new ethnic American culture has silently emerged even as its makers think they are busy with this or that end of a binarism, so that second-generation ethnics have to contend with three, not two, systems: "ideal" Old World values as presented (by parents who fancy themselves guardians of a beleaguered culture), "real" Old World values as actually mediated (by these same parents, Americans by adoption, who are rooted enough in America to produce children), and "real" New World values as seen from the vantage point of Americans by birth. . . .

Jade Snow Wong, author of *Fifth Chinese Daughter* (1945), couches her *Bildung* in terms of a rebellion against Old World values, yet the book abounds in details that show a more complex struggle. Her father, relentless traditionalist that he is in Jade Snow's eyes, speaks against footbinding and in favor of treating women as individuals with rights; subjectively, he feels no disjunction between word and deed, his deepseated Confucianism having been selectively fused with Western ideas (74–75). Jade Snow's mother reads "The Katzenjammer Kids" (73) and points out how Chinatown funeral practices have been altered to suit American conditions (78). The "after-hours" Chinese language school Jade Snow attends is an institution unknown in China proper, developed to meet the special cultural needs of Chinese on American soil.[8]

Finally, Maxine Hong Kingston's *The Woman Warrior* (1976) thematizes this very cultural dynamism.[9] The protagonist eventually realizes that she has no access to so-called genuine Chinese tradition, her mother's cultural mediations having been idiosyncratic, arbitrary, partial, and confusing. As a child, though, Maxine is capable only of posing a Chinese system against an American system: when aunt Moon Orchid goes mad, drawing curtains and locking doors against invisible enemies, Maxine and her siblings erroneously conclude, "Chinese people are very weird" (183). Such is the danger of a model premised on binary oppositions.

To echo Boelhower's terminology in the diagram, the Old World is both "locus" and "world view" for the immigrants prior to their relocation, but it has never been their children's "locus," and as "world view" it pervades the life of the latter in both a presented and a mediated form. In second-generation autobiography there is no "Old World protagonist" upon whom a "New World narrator" looks, for both narrator and protagonist are situated in the New World. The "culture of memory" of the foreign-born is not the same as the "culture of memory" of the American-born. All in all, a great deal of conflating appears to have taken place to make the elegance of Boelhower's model possible; in the process, some important historical realities have been obscured.

Two other ways in which the generations may experience and perceive "Americanization" differently—a difference inscribed in their autobiographies—can only be dealt with briefly here. America confers citizenship automatically on the native-born, whereas the foreign-born must naturalize (if, that is, the law allows them to).[10] The two groups do not really share the same expectations about the kind of place they can make for themselves in America. . . .

Secondly, immigrants, except for those from Anglophone areas, start out with an ethnic mother tongue and use English as a second language; on the other hand, their children, who may be bilingual to varying degrees, have an expected (if often frustrated) claim to the language of the nation unshared by the parents. Many second-generation ethnics have been brought up virtually English-monolingual, while others are not proficient enough in the mother tongue to compose in it with confidence. As a result of language shift, immigrant writers who compose in English tend to do so by choice; the American-born, by right and necessity. In Chinese-American literature, at least, there exists a fairly substantial body of immigrant autobiographies in the ethnic language, which suggests the possibility that immigrants who write their autobiographies in English are perhaps already predisposed to orient themselves to the dominant society in certain ways. . . .[11]

To conclude this part of my inquiry, I find Boelhower's comprehenive usage of the term immigrant autobiography more misleading than helpful. This is not to say that second-generation autobiographies should not be grouped together with first-generation ones in any kind of theoretical analysis; such insistence would lead to an infinite proliferation of categories that would make meaningful generalizations difficult. The point is that to use *immigrant*—a term so imbued with historicity—with the kind of liberty Boelhower desires calls for more justification than his structuralist schema can provide. I suspect that *autobiography of Americanization*—autobiography in which the Americanization process is explicitly in the foreground—may be a more appropriate description for Boelhower's subject matter, and I propose reserving *immigrant autobiography* for autobiography written by immigrants. (This distinction will be observed in the rest of the essay.) A change of name may catalyze a reconfiguration of Boethower's many insightful ideas; of itself, however, it cannot resolve the issues of ahistorical and reductionist conceptualization that I have raised.

Reading Immigrant Autobiographies across Ethnic and Period Boundaries

Having clarified the term immigrant autobiography, I will now turn to questions of approach.

How valid are the claims of transethnic and transhistoric applicability that Boelhower makes for his theoretical model? How are we to read immigrant autobiographies from widely divergent backgrounds and historical periods, all of them products of American experiences of one kind or another? By matching several major constitutive features of Boelhower's macrotext against Chinese-American microtexts, we may be able to test the usefulness of a universal interpretive grid for immigrant autobiography.

Boelhower identifies three "fabula moments" for immigrant autobiography which are indispensable ingredients of the macrotext: "anticipation" ("Old-World reality vs. New-World ideal"), "contact" (New-World ideal vs. New-World reality"), and "contrast" ("Old-World reality vs. New-World reality"). The seminal moment is that of "dream anticipation": "America was an idea before it was a geographical reality" (222).[12] Without the impetus of dream anticipation, there would be no journey; without the journey, no movement from the realm of myth to the realm of history; and without this movement, no "metacultural perspective" (29) which allows for cultural contrast. To Boelhower, "it is myth that has tended to construct history and not vice versa" (27).

Boelhower's analysis can readily be supported not only by the four exemplary Italian-American texts but also by a number of autobiographies by other European ethnics, such as Mary Antin's *The Promised Land* (1912), Edward Steiner's *From Alien to Citizen* (1914), Edward Bok's *The Americanization of Edward Bok* (1920), Louis Adamic's *Laughing in the Jungle* (1932), and Abraham Cahan's *The Education of Abraham Cahan* (1969), all of which are cited in the first chapter of *Immigrant Autobiography*. The language used in these autobiographies to evoke the dream image of America is heavily Biblical: "Edenic" and "Garden of Eden" (27, 41), "exodus" (33), the "heavenly city" or "sacred city" (33), and, naturally, "the Promised

Land." Of course, Boelhower quotes this language not to endorse it but rather to expose its instrumentality in constructing a fictive "monocultural paradigm" (221). Nevertheless, one might say his theory of immigrant autobiography depends on the idea that immigrant autobiographers celebrate, allude to, trope upon, challenge, subvert, or reject the dominant American myth: every time a new immigrant lands, the archetypal American drama of spiritual renewal that brought over the Puritans is supposed to be reenacted.

Are there immigrant autobiographies that are simply *indifferent* to this myth: works in which the requisite "fabula moments" are exhibited either not at all, or in so weak a form that they cannot convincingly be described as variants? If so, how would one account for them?

I have found a number of Chinese immigrant autobiographies that exhibit major deviations from the pattern proposed by Boelhower: "anticipation" is minimal, "contact" with the "utopian grammar" of America and its consequences hardly portrayed, and cultural "contrast" either not drawn or drawn more to enlighten Anglo readers than to map the protagonist's own "Americanization." Instead, the majority of the autobiography is devoted to the protagonist's pre-immigration life in China. In this category can be included Lee Yan Phou's *When I Was a Boy in China* (1887),[13] Helena Kuo's *I've Come a Long Way* (1942), Buwei Yang Chao's *Autobiography of a Chinese Woman* (1947), Su-ling Wong (pseud.) and Earl Herbert Cressy's *Daughter of Confucius* (1952), Katherine Wei and Terry Quinn's *Second Daughter* (1984), and Nien Cheng's *Life and Death in Shanghai* (1986). In none of these autobiographies have I found the kind of almost rhapsodic dreaming about America or meditation on an abstract idea of the New World that forms the basis of Boelhower's formulation in "The Brave New World of Immigrant Autobiography."[14] This is particularly striking in view of the Christian faith expressed (Wong and

Cressy) or missionary schooling described by some of the autobiographers (Kuo; Wong and Cressy; Wei and Quinn).

Among another group of works that do devote more space to life in America than in China—Huie Kin's *Reminiscences* (1932),[15] No-Young Park's *Chinaman's Chance* (1940),[16] and Anna Chennault's *The Education of Anna* (1980)—the majority also do not appear to take part in the symbolic discourse outlined by Boelhower. The closest thing to "dream anticipation" is found in Huie Kin's *Reminiscences*: the young boy had been so excited by relatives' reports of overnight fortunes in America that once, delirious with fever, he "talked of nothing else but wanting to go to Chinshan [Gold Mountain]" (18). His arrival in San Francisco in 1868 is described thus: "I wonder whether the ecstasy before the Pearly Gate of the Celestial City above could surpass what we felt at the moment we realized that we had reached our destination" (24). It is worth noting, however, that America is mentioned along with Australia, also associated with gold and also a destination for nineteenth-century Cantonese emigrants (18);[17] and that the Pearly Gate figure did not occur to the young Huie at the time of his arrival in America, for he converted to Christianity only later. The mythic rhetoric, therefore, is retrospectively applied, an overlay on an experience which at the time was felt in secular and psychological terms.

Huie's example points to a possible explanation of why Boelhower's macrotext fits Chinese-American microtexts so poorly: the historical situation of Chinese immigrants and their relationship to the Judaeo-Christian tradition are different from those of Italian, Jewish, and other European immigrants on whose autobiographies Boelhower builds his case. Thus the meaning of America may differ quite considerably for the two groups. A lost Golden Age or lost Eden to be recovered, a new Adam to be reborn, the Old World renewed, the New Jerusalem, the City on a Hill—these are European-origin fictions. For those coming from the real Orient it would be impossible to think of America as "a type of fabulous new Orient" (Boelhower, *Immigrant*, 19). The mysterious Cathay to which the European explorers sought passage was, to early Chinese immigrants, simply home. The kind of symbolic formula Boelhower establishes for Italian immigrant autobiography—"[the Italian immigrant] = Columbus = America-as-idea" (73)—would not work when extended to the literature of non-Europeans who were the victims rather than emissaries of an (at heart) imperialistic myth.

One must bear in mind how relatively recent an import Christianity is in China: although records of Christian activity date as far back as the eighth century, it wasn't until the nineteenth century that missionaries found a wider audience in China, along with other Western influences.[18] Contact with Christianity in China before the 1949 Communist Revolution was a function of, among other things, missionary activity (different nations and denominations in different spheres of influence, different styles of proselytization), geographical location (the southern and coastal provinces, the cities), and social class, (the severely disenfranchised or the socially ambitious who understood the advantages of consorting with the privileged missionaries) (Latourette, 825–31, 774, 479–80; Varg, 226–29).[19] For many of the Chinese immigrant autobiographers, the effects of a missionary education are limited to proficiency in English, familiarity with Western customs, association with foreigners in China which facilitated study abroad or emigration, and a general inclination to accept things Western. One's world view may or may not be recast.[20] The preponderance of Christianized authors among Chinese immigrant autobiographers stems from complex historical interactions between colonialism, religious institutions, emigration, and perhaps not the least, the American publishing industry and reading public.[21] It does not bespeak the kind of total immersion in the Judaeo-Christian tradition that informs Boelhower's cited works.

Overall, I detect a pragmatic, matter-of-fact attitude toward the idea of going to America on the part of Chinese immigrant autobiographers. America is one, albeit a particularly attractive one, of many destinations for Chinese emigrants, in a global scattering over a long period that some scholars call the Chinese diaspora.[22] Gold has few alchemic connotations for them, and fleeing war and upheaval does not necessarily spell conversion to the Enlightenment political ideals upon which the American nation was founded. Moreover, the Chinese were the first racial group to be singled out for exclusion from immigration, so that subterfuges had to be resorted to by many immigrants entering after 1882 and before 1965.[23] The Chinese exclusion period (1882–1943) overlapped and outlasted the period of great European immigration (1880–1920).[24] Chinese immigrants had no "passcard," comparable to a reminder that the American myth originated in Europe (Boelhower, 74), to present in defense of their difference. In such a historical context, it would hardly be surprising to find the "utopian grammar" of America exerting so negligible a structuring influence on Chinese immigrant autobiography.

Of course, Boelhower does acknowledge the existence of a cluster of symbolic equivalences operating alongside or beneath the theological language:

geographical (Old-World vs. New-World, closed space vs. open space); economic (poverty vs. wealth, static condition vs opportunity); psychological (despair vs. hope); religious and political (oppression vs. freedom, racial discrimination vs. racial equality). (42)

As theorist, he is less interested in real motives than cultural pieties, in sociological analysis than semiological speculations. But it is precisely the paucity of even *allusion* to American myths in Chinese immigrant autobiographies to which I wish to draw attention. (That the actual fate of minorities belies the governing pieties of the land is no news.) In a very broad sense, no one can deny that even for Chinese immigrants "America was an idea before it was a geographical reality"; this much can be said for any destination chosen by any emigrant for any reason. The Judaeo-Christian overtones of "idea" therefore admit of little dilution in Boelhower's theory, and I stress them advisedly.

Not only is "anticipation" weakly represented in Chinese immigrant autobiography, but whatever cultural "contact" and "contrast" take place appear to differ in kind from those found in the works cited by Boelhower. In Boelhower's model, the voyage is the turning point in the immigrant's life that makes the "juxtaposition of cultural spaces" (39) possible. "The journey literally breaks the immigrant autobiographical text in two" (39–40), at times into almost equal halves (151), with the arrival marking the beginning of Americanization. With those Chinese immigrant autobiographies whose center of gravity lies squarely in China, however, the journey is usually hastily narrated, while Americanization takes up a very small fraction of the textual space at the end.[25] In other words, while Boelhower implies immigrant autobiography and autobiography of Americanization to be more or less synonymous in a typological sense, a structurally recognizable cluster of Chinese immigrant autobiography indicates otherwise. Once again, the divergence is so marked that it would be far-fetched to call these Chinese works variants of the macrotext.

Several hypotheses on the Chinese counterexamples may be offered. To begin with, to immigrants who bore witness to the upheavals in recent Chinese history, the promise of America may mean simply a resting point, a clean, neutral space from which to look back on and take stock of their harrowing past. The autobiographies of Wei and Quinn and Cheng fit this pattern. Even though, in some minimalist sense, they have indeed come to America for a new beginning, these autobiographers are not particularly interested in an American fable of renewal attended by prospects of further questionings and struggles.

A second plausible explanation lies in the social class and educational background of many of the Chinese immigrant autobiographers, who learned English and became conversant in American ways before undertaking the journey (Kuo, Chao, Wong and Cressy, Wei and Quinn, Chennault, Cheng). An early immigrant from rural China like Huie fits more closely Boelhower's picture of the representative, early 1900s autobiographer: a "pre-metropolitan self" witnessing the birth of a modern, American self (17) and undergoing a movement from myth to history, "from an agricultural valley to the industrialized metropolis" (108). In contrast, many of the post–World War II Chinese immigrants fleeing Japanese invasion, civil war, the Communist Revolution, and the Cultural Revolution are already Americanized products of the metropolis, have already acquired what Boelhower calls a "metacultural" perspective. Physical relocation to America merely continues cultural "contact" begun in China.

This leads us to consider a third hypothesis: these Westernized autobiographers probably knew that the American reading public would not be very interested in their lives after immigration. (Their publishers almost certainly knew this.) It is traditional China (later, Communist China) that excites the American imagination, evokes mystery and alienness, and requires the service of knowledgeable insiders to explain terminology, kinship, manners, social organization, cultural practices, political ideology, . . . *differences.* Chao, whose autobiography was written in Chinese and rendered into English by her husband, explains in her foreword: "When I do publish the Chinese, it will not be the same book either. For, to a Chinese reader, there would be no point in telling what weddings and funerals are like in China" (x).[26]

To return to Boelhower's paradigm, no doubt a great deal of cultural "contrast" takes place in this kind of Chinese immigrant autobiography, but not in the form of "Old-World reality vs. New-World reality." Rather, it is "Old-World reality vs. New-World readers' expectations": what the audience wants to know, may misunderstand, may find incomprehensible, and so forth. If the Old-World account has a "folkloric" (105) element to it, it is anthropological instead of mythological. One observation provides ancillary evidence for this reading of China-centered Chinese immigrant autobiography: Huie, Park, and Kuo were all at one time or another paid lecturers on Chinese subjects, Park having been successful enough to be a regular on the Chautauqua circuit. (Huie writes of his Midwestern tour: "China was then little known among American people and Chinese lecturers were a rarity. So our tour was quite a success. Incidentally, my Oriental garb lent local color to my talks helping to fill the halls and churches in the towns and villages we visited, and, in turn, filling our pockets in a way beyond our equations" [39]). May it not be that the writing of autobiography for them is a kind of fixing in print of a sustained lecture?[27] If so, the autobiographer's New-World self is more a guide than an adventurer, more an interpreter than a discoverer.[28] The narrative elaboration of life in China and extreme foreshortening of life in America are a structural reflection of this function of the immigrant autobiographer.

If the intended audience could be a powerful shaper of narrative, one needs to revise the concept of the autobiographical project as an individual's negotiation of cultural forces. The audience's role has been taken into account only minimally in Boelhower's model (21, on "implied model reader"; 61, on [a particular Italian immigrant] as cultural diplomat). On the whole, he assumes "contrast" to originate in a (culturally structured) private impulse to attain understanding and coherence in the form of a constructed American identity. (The enterprise's eventual outcome is irrelevant to Boelhower's basic scenario.)

> The problem of identity springs from [the] displacement process, for [the immigrant autobiographer's] function is to personify, to map out, the cultures he journeys through while seeking his identity. (37)

Boelhower's emphasis on the tensions within the individual psyche can be seen in his choice of two poet figures (D'Angelo and Carnevali) as versions of a new American self. It can also be seen in his positing an inverse relationship between "anticipation" and "memory"; that is, if the American dream comes true for the immigrant protagonist, memory of the Old World tends to be weak, whereas a nightmarish New World would enhance memory (36). The China-centered autobiographies show, however, that what gets retrieved and presented as memory may be colored by what the autobiographer feels to be attractive to Anglo readers. In that sense, these texts are subtly "sponsored"; certainly they are not as self-authorized and inward-looking as one would be led to believe by Boelhower's theory.

Conclusion

There is strong evidence that the Chinese-American deviations from Boelhower's typology analyzed above are in fact characteristic of other Asian-American immigrant autobiographies.[29] While a handful of the latter, such as Buaken's *I Have Lived with the American People* (1948), may fit Boelhower's macrotext, the majority do not—for good historical reasons. The absolute number of Asian-Americans, especially before immigration reforms lifted racially based restrictions in 1965, has been small; geographically Asians have been concentrated on the west coast, away from the publishing centers of the east. These factors may have encouraged the writing of immigrant autobiographies set mostly in "exotic" Asia. Further, given the fact that Asians have traditionally been excluded from the American mainstream as "unassimilable aliens," upperclass, English-speaking, Christianized (or at least Westernized) immigrant autobiographers may have served as culture brokers.[30] Such a role would eclipse any effort to fashion the representative American self—to answer Crevecoeur's famous question, "What then is the American, this new man?"—which is commonly said to inform American autobiography. Sociologist Blauner, author of the theory of "internal colonialism," notes that because nineteenth-century Asians entered the United States under conditions ranging from the "colonial" (Filipinos) to the "semicolonial" (Chinese, Japanese), and because their group size and status were rigidly controlled, "it is misleading to equate the Asian experience with the European immigration pattern. . . . Even when, later on, some third world peoples were able to immigrate, the circumstances of the earlier entry affected their situation and the attitudes of the dominant culture toward them" (55).[31] As immigrant experiences differ, so must immigrant autobiographies.

The above investigation suggests that Boelhower's allegedly universal paradigm of immigrant autobiography is implicitly Eurocentric, derived as it is from a small corpus of works by European immigrants steeped in the Judaeo-Christian tradition, most of whom came during the great waves of immigration at the end of the nineteenth and the beginning of the twentieth century. When matched against immigrant autobiographies from a non-European, non-Christian ethnic group or a different historical period, Boelhower's macrotext proves inadequate, for his structuralist assumptions have foreclosed understanding of how profoundly historical realities may affect consciousness. To him, the autobiographers' situatedness in history pales before the mythic roles they incarnate and the symbolic drama their lives enact. Generational positioning, ethnic membership, historical period, and social class are little more than wrinkles on some pre-existing deep structure. The result of reasoning from axioms (one of Boelhower's favorite words) is a static if elegant model of limited applicability.

Rather than seeking some totalizing system in which autobiographers speak from a priori fixed positions and follow a finite set of trajectories, I believe it is less confining and more productive to conceive of multiple, provisional *axes of organization*: different salient features are revealed when an autobiography is read with different intertexts. In this approach, grouping autobiographies by immigrant status is only one of many possible strategies for eliciting insights; grouping them by treatment of Americanization is another. In Boelhower's case, despite the theoretical difficulties created by their conflation, both have yielded some fascinating observations. One could also group autobiographies by ethnicity, social class, gender, historical period, narrative point of view, or any number of other promising criteria (thematic options are numerous).[32] If there is truth in Bergland's proposed redefinition of the "I" of autobiography—"a speaking subject inscribed by multiple discourses, positioned in multiple subjectivities and situated in multiple historical contexts" (Bergland, 5)— then *immigrant autobiography* can no longer be conceived of as an unalterably demarcated segment of reality with a single set of inherent features. The term merely highlights a few of the many discourses, subjectivities and historical contexts in which immigrant autobiographers find themselves embedded.

Because of the critical role played by immigration in the making of America and the enduring potency of the immigrant myth of renewal in shaping the American imagination, the autobiographer's nativity may indeed, as Boelhower's innovative work gives us cause to hope, be an especially serviceable axis of organization. Boelhower has forced us to reassess the relevance of what appears to be a marginal literary concern, thence to rethink the nature of ideological myth itself. He has also demonstrated how the concept of immigrant autobiography can help reveal the lines of force that pattern "the American," much like a magnet drawn under a tray of iron filings. Provided that the critic exercises care in conceptualizing the "immigrant experience," employs a textually grounded rather than a schema-inspired approach, and pays attention to the historical particularities of various ethnic groups, the concept of immigrant autobiography should continue to be a fruitful one for the study of American autobiography.

A final remark: choice of reading strategy can be motivated as much politically as intellectually—as well it should be. This is actually a corollary of Boelhower's statement on the potential subversiveness of immigrant autobiography—the "Pandora's box of uncontrollable textual variants" smuggled into the "house of American autobiography"—though it is never fully explored in his book. (Ironically, in his own critical practice, Boelhower has underestimated the unruly diversity of the contents of the "Pandora's box.") To return to the methodological questions raised earlier about the implications of Boelhower's theoretical venture: when [Werner] Sollors deplores the current state of ethnic literary studies, he seems unaware that premature adoption of a transethnic approach, before the uniqueness of each group's historical situation and its manifestations in literature are

adequately understood, can be as static and ahistorical as any mechanically applied "group-by-group approach." So much for my intellectual objection to Sollors's critique. The political one is obvious: reading by ethnicity is a necessary act of tradition- and identity-building for those whose literatures have been rendered invisible by subsumption; this is true even for the reading of autobiography, a genre which often appears to oppose the personal to the political.

Notes

I am grateful to Gloria Chun, King-Kok Cheung, Paul John Eakin, Giulia Fabi, Him Mark Lai, Kathy Lo, Brian Niiya, Michael Omi, Shelley Wong, and Judy Yung for their help in the writing of this essay.

1. Following customary usage (Easterlin, 5), the term *immigrant* is used here to refer to those entering the United States after its establishment as an independent nation, even though, relative to Native Americans, the colonists could also be considered immigrants.

2. Little discussion of immigrant autobiography is found in studies that ponder the distinctiveness and continuities of the American autobiographical tradition beyond the colonial period, such as (in chronological order) Sayre, *Examined*; Spengemann and Lundquist, Cox; Cooley; Blasing; Couser; Sayre, "Autobiography," "Proper"; Stone, "Autobiography"; Bercovitch, "Ritual"; Stone, *Autobiographical*; and Taylor.

3. The idea that ethnic literature is prototypically American informs current scholarship on ethnic literature; Sollors (*Beyond*, 8) briefly traces the evolution of this idea in American studies.

4. Excluded from discussion are first-person works presented as sketches or impressions (e.g., Y. Chiang; Sze); autobiographies of "returned students" for whom sojourn in the United States was clearly a brief interlude (e.g., M. Chiang); and autobiographies by Chinese-Americans written in Chinese, such as those listed in Lai (85–105). The issue of choice of language is discussed in the text of this essay.

5. Boelhower briefly mentions Chinatowns in his introduction (*Immigrant*, 52).

6. There are always "gray areas" qualifying any generalization; those who immigrate in early childhood, those of mixed blood, those with one immigrant and one American-born parent, and other borderline cases must be left out of our discussion.

7. Sumida provides an interesting example of such deconstructive reading in his analysis of the conflict between first- and second-generation Japanese Americans portrayed in Murayama's story of Hawaiian plantation life, *All I Asking for Is My Body* [*sic*].

8. See S. C. Wong ("Language," 212–16) for a brief account of the "after-hours" Chinese language school as an evolving institution in America.

9. The generic ambiguity of this well-known work is a subject of great controversy within the Chinese-American community. In my essay, "Autobiography as Guided Chinatown Tour? Maxine Hong Kingston's *The Woman Warrior* and the Chinese American Autobiographical Debate," I have treated this complex matter at some length. The publication and widespread acceptance of *The Woman Warrior* as an autobiography are by now historical facts which have led to extensions of the concept of autobiography.

10. Ueda reviews legislation on naturalization and citizenship from the colonial period to the present. Note, in particular, various restrictions against the naturalization of Chinese as well as other ethnic groups judged unlikely or unwelcome candidates for assimilation (125–37). Lesser examines Supreme Court naturalization rulings affecting Asian-Americans, tracing the role of race in legal definitions of the undesirable "other."

11. Under "Biographies and Travel Accounts," Lai (85–105) lists a number of autobiographies in Chinese; life in America is depicted to various extents in these works.

12. An elaboration of this idea can be found in a section on cartography in Boelhower's *Through a Glass Darkly* (44–79).

13. Lee Yan Phou has retained the Chinese practice of placing the surname before the given name, as have other early immigrant writers discussed in this essay, such as Huie Kin and Yung Wing. (See notes 15 and 21.) Korean author New Il-Han (see note 30) follows a similar practice.

The basis for regarding Lee as an immigrant rather than a visitor can be found in LaFargue (14–18, 50–54). This evidence overrides the suggestion in X. Li (56–60) that Lee might have returned to China when his sponsoring organization, the Chinese Education Mission founded by Yung Wing, was closed down.

14. The single reference to the "Promised Land" that I found in Wei and Quinn (9) is more a cliché than part of an extensive network of mythic references.

15. Although Huie returned to and died in China (Yang, 53), he spent the majority of his life working and raising a family in the United States (Huie, 114). I think we may safely classify him as an American immigrant and his *Reminiscences* as an immigrant autobiography.

Boelhower himself includes the repatriated Carnevali in his discussion; to me, the practice is considerably more justifiable than combining the second generation with the first. Among immigrants, the subjective sense of belonging and the objective fact of residence do not always coincide, and intention and circumstances are always open to change, so that the sojourner-settler distinction cannot be absolute. Repatriation was common even during the "Great Wave" of European immigration; the 1911 Dillingham Commission Report estimated that two-fifths of the new immigrants returned to Europe after a relatively short time (Portes and Bach, 31).

16. Park's parents were Korean, but he was raised in Manchuria as a Chinese and later wrote of Chinese matters as a Chinese. For the purposes of this essay I consider *Chinaman's Chance* a Chinese-American autobiography. Cheung and Yogi's bibliography of Asian American literature, organized on the basis of ethnic origin alone, lists Park under "Korean-American writers."

17. One indication of the parallel perceptions of Australia and America can be seen in the Chinese names for San Francisco and Melbourne: *Old Gold Mountain* and *New Gold Mountain*. I am indebted to Chinese-American historian Him Mark Lai for this information.

18. According to Latourette, although missionary activities were recorded in China as early as the eighth and ninth centuries, it wasn't until the Qing, or Manchu, Empire began its precipitous decline in the mid-nineteenth century that Christianity penetrated Chi-

nese culture to any significant degree. The civil war and Japanese invasion of the 1930s and 1940s, the establishment of the Communist regime on the mainland in 1949, and periodic crackdowns by the Communists on organized religion all curtailed the spread of Christianity. See Brown for an account of the church since 1949. All in all, despite the church's continued presence in Taiwan and recent signs of religious revival on the mainland, the cumulative impact of Christianity on the life and thought of the majority of Chinese must be deemed extremely limited.

19. Gender may also have been a significant factor (Latourette, 449–51; Varg, 117).

20. Wei and Quinn (158–62) provide a vivid example of how Christian doctrine may be viewed by the Chinese simply as an inconvenience attached to an elite Western education. See also Latourette (683–84) and Varg (320). Note that even as partisan a Christian apologist as Latourette has to contend seriously with the criticism that "beyond aiding in the initial stages of the introduction of Western civilization, especially of the newer education, missions have made little impression upon the country as a whole" (831).

21. Chin, in "This Is Not an Autobiography," asserts that there is a Christianized or missionary tradition in Chinese-American literature, exemplified by autobiography and starting with Yung Wing's *My Life in China and America,* which has been disproportionately favored by white publishers.

22. Lai (17–22) lists sources that document the global presence of Chinese as well as their current status.

23. See, for example, Lyman (110–11) and Lai, Lim, and Yung (20, 22) for an account of the "paper son" system. Other fraudulent means of entry were also used. Immigration laws were liberalized in 1965 to eliminate previous biases in favor of northwestern European immigrants (Bernard, 103–5).

24. These dates are approximate but generally accepted. The year 1924 saw the passage of the restrictive Johnson-Reid Act which, among other provisions, set up a "national origins" system curtailing the entry of southern and eastern Europeans (Bernard, 96–98), who constituted the majority of immigrants in the 1890s. See Easterlin (11–18) for figures and trends in European immigration.

25. In Lee, the account of life in China up to departure for the United States takes up 98 out of 105

pages; in Wong and Cressy, 365 out of 379 pages; in Wei and Quinn, 232 out of 241 pages; in Cheng, 530 out of 533 pages.

26. According to Lai (86, 90, 95), Chennault, M. Chiang, and Chao have published autobiographical accounts in Chinese as well. It would be interesting to compare the Chinese and English versions to see what modifications, if any, the authors have made to accommodate different audiences.

27. Elbaz's thesis that the practice of autobiography is based on a concept of the self as "a commodity with an exchange value" (152) or "the exclusive property of its owner" (153) may be relevant here.

28. These terms allude to Boelhower's description of the "double self" in immigrant autobiography: "The protagonist-narrator is both emigrant and immigrant, exile and discoverer, and both these aspects enroll him under the sign of the voyager, the hero-adventurer" (*Immigrant Autobiography,* 37). My essay, cited in note 9, discusses the "tour guide" function of the ethnic autobiographer in greater detail.

29. Brian Niiya, personal communication, 2 Feb. 1989. This section of my essay relies heavily on Niiya's work on Asian-American autobiography for a master's thesis at the University of California, Los Angeles.

30. Kim (25–26) notes that Lee's *When I Was a Boy in China* and New Il-Han's *When I Was a Boy in Korea* were solicited by D. Lothrop Company of Boston as part of a series of books by young men from various lands. Kuo (344–45) writes of her meeting with American publishers to size up the market and the competition for first-person interpretations of Chinese culture after the manner of Lin Yutang. See Hsu and Palubinskas (10) and Chin et al. (xxiii–xxiv) for an analysis of the "publishability" of Asian-American autobiographies in a racial context.

31. I am indebted to Michael Omi and Brian Niiya for pointing out the relevance of Blauner's work to my thesis.

32. For example, if Mangione's *Mount Allegro,* Lowe's *Father and Glorious Descendant,* and Sone's *Nisei Daughter,* by children of immigrants from different ethnic groups, are read together, we might detect in their humorous tone an effort to fuse ridicule of and affection for the parents' Old World ways; this may lead to an inquiry into the cultural balancing strategies of second-generation autobiographers.

Second-generation autobiographies from the same

ethnic group, Chinese, might show another kind of similarity: *Father and Glorious Descendant, The Woman Warrior,* and L. Li's *Life Is for a Long Time* share an uncertainty of focus, in that the autobiographical label sometimes seems a cover for telling the immigrant generation's stories.

Titles like *Daughter of Confucius* (foreign-born), *Fifth Chinese Daughter* (American-born), and *Second Daughter* (foreign-born) should alert us to the importance of gender in Chinese-American autobiography. Almost all the autobiographies by women that I have cited in this essay allude to the author's awareness of the disadvantages of her sex, accompanied by an account of how she has come to be educated: an enlightened father or a wise grandmother or mother, the good fortune to be given the chance to acquire literacy, or to go to college, or to study English. From this one might make a leap across ethnic boundaries, contrasting the importance of literacy in the autobiographies of Chinese women and of blacks.

Works Cited

Abramson, Edward A. *The Immigrant Experience in American Literature.* BAAS Pamphlets in American Studies 10. Durham, England: British Association for American Studies, 1982.

Adamic, Louis. *Laughing in the Jungle: The Autobiography of an Immigrant in America.* New York: Harper & Bros., 1932.

Antin, Mary. *The Promised Land.* Boston: Houghton Mifflin, 1912.

Bercovitch, Sacvan. *The Puritan Origins of the American Self.* New Haven: Yale University Press, 1975.

Bercovitch, Sacvan. "The Ritual of American Autobiography: Edwards, Franklin, Thoreau." *Revue Française d'Etudes Américaines* 14 (1982): 138–50.

Bergland, Betty. "Postmodernism and the Autobiographical Subject: Reconstructing the 'Other.'" In *Autobiography and Postmodernism,* ed. Kathleen Oakley, Leigh Gilmore, and Gerald Peters. Amherst: University of Massachusetts Press, 1994, 130–66.

Bernard, William S. "A History of U.S. Immigration Policy." In Easterlin et al., 75–205.

Blasing, Mutlu Konuk. *The Art of Life: Studies in American Autobiographical Literature.* Austin: University of Texas Press, 1977.

Blauner, Robert. *Racial Oppression in America.* New York: Harper & Row, 1972.

Boelhower, William. *Immigrant Autobiography in the United States: Four Versions of the Italian American Self.* Verona, Italy: Essedue Edizioni, 1982.

Boelhower, William. *Through a Glass Darkly: Ethnic Semiosis in American Literature.* 1984. New York: Oxford University Press, 1987.

Bok, Edward. *The Americanization of Edward Bok: The Autobiography of a Dutch Boy Fifty Years After.* New York: Charles Scribner's Sons, 1920.

Buaken, Manuel J. *I Have Lived with the American People.* Caldwell, ID: Caxton, 1948.

Brown, G. Thompson. *Christianity and the People's Republic of China.* Rev. ed. Atlanta: Knox, 1986.

Cahan, Abraham. *The Education of Abraham Cahan.* Trans. Leon Stein, Abraham P. Conan, and Lynn Davison. Philadelphia: Jewish Publication Society of America, 1969.

Carnevali, Emanuel. *The Autobiography of Emanuel Carnevali.* Comp. Kay Boyle. New York: Horizon, 1967.

Chao, Buwei Yang. *Autobiography of a Chinese Woman.* [1947]. Trans. Yuenren Chao. Westport, CT: Greenwood, 1970.

Chen, Jack. *The Chinese of America.* San Francisco: Harper & Row, 1981.

Cheng, Nien. *Life and Death in Shanghai.* 1986. New York: Penguin, 1988.

Chennault, Anna. *The Education of Anna.* New York: Times, 1980.

Cheung, King-Kok, and Stan Yogi. *Asian American Literature: An Annotated Bibliography.* New York: Modern Language Association, 1988.

Chiang, Monlin. *Tides from the West: A Chinese Autobiography.* New Haven: University Press, 1947.

Chiang, Yee. *The Silent Traveller in New York.* New York: Day, 1950.

Chin, Frank. "This Is Not an Autobiography." *Genre* 18 (1985): 109–30.

Chin, Frank, et al. "An Introduction to Chinese- and Japanese-American Literature." [1974]. In

Aiiieeeee! An Anthology of Asian-American Writers. ed. Frank Chin et al. Washington, DC: Howard University Press, 1983. xxi–xiviii.

Cooley, Thomas. *Educated Lives: The Rise of Modern Autobiography in America.* Columbus: Ohio University Press, 1976.

Couser, G. Thomas. *American Autobiography: The Prophetic Mode.* Amherst: University of Massachusetts Press, 1979.

Cox, James M. "Autobiography and America." *Virginia Quarterly Review* 47 (1971): 252–77.

D'Angelo, Pascal. *Pascal D'Angelo, Son of Italy.* New York: Macmillan, 1924.

Demirturk, Emine Lale. "The Female Identity in Cross-Cultural Perspective: Immigrant Women's Autobiography." *DAI* 47 (1987): 2584-A.

DiPietro, Robert J., and Edward Ifkovic, eds. *Ethnic Perspective in American Literature.* New York: Modern Language Association, 1983.

Easterlin, Richard A. "Economic and Social Characteristics of the Immigrants." In Easterlin et al., 1–34.

Easterlin, Richard A., David Ward, William S. Bernard, and Reed Ueda. *Immigration.* Dimensions of Ethnicity: A Series of Selections from the Harvard Encyclopedia of American Ethnic Groups. Ed. Stephan Thernstrom, Ann Orlov, and Oscar Handlin. Cambridge: Harvard University Press, 1982.

Elbaz, Robert. *The Changing Nature of the Self: A Critical Study of the Autobiographic Discourse.* London: Croom Helm, 1988.

Fried, Louis. "Jacob Riis and the Jews: The Ambivalent Quest for Community." *American Studies* 20 (1979): 5–24.

Handlin, Oscar. *The Uprooted: The Epic Story of the Great Migrations That Made the American People.* Boston: Little, Brown, 1951.

Hansen, M. L. "The Problem of the Third Generation Immigrant." Rock Island, IL: Augustana Historical Society Publications, 1938.

Hansen, M. L. "The Third Generation in America: A Classic Essay in Immigration History." *Commentary* 14 (1952): 492–500.

Holte, James Craig. *The Ethnic I: A Sourcebook for Ethnic American Autobiography.* New York: Greenwood, 1988.

Holte, James Craig. "The Representative Voice: Autobiography and the Ethnic Experience." *MELUS* 9 (1982): 25–46.

Hsu, Kai-yu, and Helen Palubinskas. "Chinese American Literature." In *Asian-American Authors,* ed. Hsu and Palubinskas. Boston: Houghton, Mifflin, 1972. 7–12.

Huie, Kin. *Reminiscences.* Peiping: San Yu, 1932.

Kim, Elaine H. *Asian American Literature: An Introduction to the Writings and Their Social Context.* Philadelphia: Temple University Press, 1982.

Kingston, Maxine Hong. *The Woman Warrior: Memoirs of a Girlhood Among Ghosts.* 1976. New York: Knopf.

Kuo, Helena. *I've Come a Long Way.* New York: Appleton-Century-Crofts, 1942.

LaFargue, Thomas E. *China's First Hundred.* Pullman, WA: State College of Washington Press, 1942.

Lai, Him Mark, comp. *A History Reclaimed: An Annotated Bibliography of Chinese Language Materials on the Chinese of America.* Ed. Russell Leong and Jean Pang Yip. Los Angeles: Resource Development and Publications, Asian American Studies Center, University of California, 1986.

Lai, Him Mark; Genny Lim; and Judy Yung. *Island: Poetry and History of Chinese Immigrants on Angel Island, 1910–1940.* San Francisco: HOC DOI Project, 1980.

Latourette, Kenneth Scott. *A History of Christian Missions in China.* New York: Macmillan, 1929.

Lee, Yan Phou. *When I Was a Boy in China.* Boston: Lothrop, 1887.

Lejeune, Philippe. *Le pacte autobiographique.* Paris: Seuil, 1975.

Lesser, Jeff H. "Always 'Outsiders': Asians, Naturalization, and the Supreme Court." *Amerasia Journal* 12, no. 1 (1985–86): 83–100.

Li, Ling-Ai. *Life Is for a Long Time: A Chinese Hawaiian Memoir.* New York: Hasting, 1972.

Li, Xisuo. *Jindai Zongguo de liuxue sheng* [*Chinese students abroad in recent history*]. Beijing: Renmin, 1987.

Lowe, Pardee. *Father and Glorious Descendant.* Boston: Little, Brown, 1943.

Lyman, Stanford M. *Chinese Americans.* New York: Random House, 1974.

Mangione, Jerre. *Mount Allegro: A Memoir of Italian American Life.* [1942]. New York: Columbia University Press, 1981.

Murayama, Milton. *All I Asking for Is My Body.* San Francisco: Supa Press, 1975.

Neidle, Cecyle S. "The Foreign-Born View America: A Study of Autobiographies Written by Immigrants to the United States." Ph.D. diss., New York University, 1964.

New, Il-Han. *When I Was a Boy in Korea.* Boston: Lothrop, 1928.

Olney, James. ed. *Autobiography: Essays Theoretical and Critical.* Princeton: Princeton University Press, 1980.

Panunzio, Constantine M. *The Soul of an Immigrant.* New York: Macmillan, 1922.

Park, No-Yong. *Chinaman's Chance: An Autobiography.* Boston: Meador, 1940.

Portes, Alejandro, and Robert L. Bach. *Latin Journey: A Longitudinal Study of Cuban and Mexican Immigrants in the United States.* Berkeley and Los Angeles: University of California Press, 1985.

Reimers, David M. *Still the Golden Door: The Third World Comes to America.* New York: Columbia University Press, 1995.

Riis, Jacob. *The Making of an American.* New York: Macmillan, 1924.

Rodriguez, Richard. *Hunger of Memory: The Education of Richard Rodriguez.* Boston: Godine, 1981.

Rubin, Steven J. "Style and Meaning in Mary Antin's *The Promised Land*: Reevaluation." *Studies in American Jewish Literature* 5 (1986): 35–43.

Sayre, Robert F. "Autobiography and the Making of America ." In Olney, 146–68.

Sayre, Robert F. *The Examined Self. Benjamin Franklin, Henry Adams, Henry James.* Princeton: Princeton University Press, 1964.

Sayre, Robert F. "The Proper Study: Autobiographies in American Studies." In *The American Autobiography: A Collection of Critical Essays,* ed. Albert E. Stone. Englewood Cliffs, NJ: Prentice-Hall, 1981. 11–30.

Sollors, Werner. *Beyond Ethnicity: Consent and Descent in American Culture.* New York: Oxford University Press, 1986.

Sollors, Werner. "A Critique of Pure Pluralism." In *Reconstructing American Literary Theory,* ed. Sacvan Bercovitch. Cambridge: Harvard University Press, 1986. 250–79.

Sollors, Werner. "Literature and Ethnicity." In *Harvard Encyclopedia of American Ethnic Groups,* ed. Stephan Thernstrom, Ann Orlov, and Oscar Handlin. Cambridge: Harvard University Press, 1980. 647–65.

Sollors, Werner. "Nine Suggestions for Historians of American Ethnic Literature." *MELUS* 11 (1984): 95–96.

Sone, Monica. *Nisei Daughter.* [1953]. Seattle: University of Washington Press, 1979.

Spengemann, William C., and L. R. Lundquist. "Autobiography and the American Myth." *American Quarterly* 17 (1965): 501–19.

Steiner, Edward A. *From Alien to Citizen.* New York: Fleming H. Revell, 1914.

Stone, Alfred E. *Autobiographical Occasions and Original Acts: Versions of American Identity from Henry Adams to Nate Shaw.* Philadelphia: University of Pennsylvania Press, 1982.

Stone, Alfred E. "Autobiography in American Culture: Looking Back at the Seventies." *American Studies International* 19 (1981): 3–14.

Sumida, Stephen H. "First Generations in Asian American Literature: As Viewed in Some Second Generation Works." In *Issues in Asian and Pacific American Education,* ed. Nobuya Tsuchida. Minneapolis: Asian/Pacific Learning Resource Center, University of Minnesota, and National Association for Asian and Pacific American Education, 1986. 64–70.

Sze, Mai-mai. *Echo of a Cry: A Story Which Began in China.* New York: Harcourt, Brace, 1945.

Taylor, Gordon O. *Chapters of Experience: Studies in Twentieth-Century American Autobiography.* New York: St. Martin's, 1983.

Ueda, Reed. "Naturalization and Citizenship." In Easterlin et al., 106–54.

Varg, Paul A. *Missionaries, Chinese, and Diplomats: The American Protestant Missionary Movement in China, 1890–1952.* Princeton: Princeton University Press, 1958.

Wei, Katherine, and Terry Quinn. *Second Daughter: Growing Up in China, 1930–1949.* Boston: Little, Brown, 1984.

314

Wong, Jade Snow. *Fifth Chinese Daughter*. New York: Harper and Brothers, 1945.

Wong, Sau-ling Cynthia. "Autobiography as Guided Chinatown Tour? Maxine Hong Kingston's *The Woman Warrior* and the Chinese-American Autobiographical Controversy." In *American Lives:* Essays in Multicultural American Autobiography, ed. James Payne. Knoxville: Tennessee University Press, 1992. 248–79.

Wong, Sau-ling Cynthia. "The Language Situation of Chinese Americans." In *Language Diversity: Problem or Resource? A Social and Educational Perspective on Language Minorities in the United States.* ed. Sandra Lee McKay and Sau-ling Cynthia Wong. Cambridge: Newbury, 1988. 193–228.

Wong, Su-ling [pseud.], and Earl Herbert Cressy. *Daughter of Confucius: A Personal History*. New York: Farrar, Straus, and Giroux, 1952.

Yang, Qizhuang. "Xu Qin Mushi Zhuanlue" ["A Brief Biography of Huie Kin"]. In *The 100th Anniversary of the Founding, 58th Anniversary of the Naming of the First Chinese Presbyterian Church of the City of New York 1868–1968*. New York: First Chinese Presbyterian Church, 1968.

Yudkin, Leon Israel. *Jewish Writing and Identity in the Twentieth Century*. London: Croom Heim, 1982.

Yung, Wing. *My Life in China and America*. New York: Henry Holt, 1909.

PART V
Voice and Memory

French is my "stepmother" tongue. What is my long-lost mother-tongue, that aban-doned me and disappeared: . . . Burdened by my inherited taboos, I discover I have no memory of Arabic love songs . . . "L'amour, ses cris (s'écrit)" . . . it is no longer a question of writing only to survive . . . After more than a century of French occupa-tion, a similar no-man's-land still exists between the French and the indigenous lan-guages, between two national memories . . . the French tongue, with its body and voice, has established a proud presidio *within me, while the mother tongue, all oral tradition, resists and attacks . . . I am alternately the besieged foreigner and the native swaggering off to die, so there is seemingly endless strife between the spoken and writ-ten word.*

— Assia Djebar, *Fantasia: An Algerian Cavalcade*, trans. Dorothy S. Blair
(London: Quartet, 1989), 214–15

The world's earliest archives or libraries were the memories of women.

— Trinh T. Minh-ha, "Grandma's Story," in *Woman, Native, Other*
(Bloomington: Indiana University Press, 1989), 121

For me—a writer in the last quarter of the twentieth century, not much more than a hundred years after Emancipation, a writer who is black and a woman—the exercise is very different. My job becomes how to rip that veil drawn over "proceedings too terrible to relate." The exercise is also critical for any person who is black, or who belongs to any marginalized category, for, historically, we were seldom invited to par-ticipate in the discourse even when we were its topic.

Moving that veil aside requires, therefore, certain things. First of all, I must trust my own recollections. I must also depend on the recollections of others. Thus memory weighs heavily in what I write, in how I begin and in what I find to be significant. Zora Neale Hurston said, "Like the dead-seeming cold rocks, I have memories within that came out of the material that went to make me." These "memories within" are the subsoil of my work. But memories and recollections won't give me total access to the unwritten interior life of these people. Only the act of the imagination can help me.

— Toni Morrison, "The Site of Memory," in *Inventing the Truth: The Art and Craft of Memoir*, ed. William Zinsser (Boston: Houghton Mifflin, 1987), 110–11

25 The Other Voice: Autobiographies of Women Writers

Mary G. Mason

. . . In these four works—Julian's *Revelations* or *Showings*,[1] *The Book of Margery Kempe*,[2] Margaret Cavendish's *True Relation*,[3] and Anne Bradstreet's spiritual account "To My Dear Children"—we can discover not only important beginnings in the history of women's autobiography in English as a distinct mode of interior disclosure but also something like a set of paradigms for life-writing by women right down to our time. And while there are some obvious disadvantages inherent in distinguishing literary works by gender, in the specific instance of autobiography, where a life is so intimately joined to the act of writing, one can achieve certain important insights into the possibilities and necessities of self-writing if one first isolates according to gender and then brings female and male autobiographical types back into proximity in order that they may throw light (at times by sheer contrast) on one another. Nowhere in women's autobiographies do we find the patterns established by the two prototypical male autobiographers, Augustine and Rousseau; and conversely male writers never take up the archetypal models of Julian, Margery Kempe, Margaret Cavendish, and Anne Bradstreet. The dramatic structure of conversion that we find in Augustine's *Confessions,* where the self is presented as the stage for a battle of opposing forces and where a climactic victory for one force—spirit defeating flesh—completes the drama of the self, simply does not accord with the deepest realities of women's experience and so is inappropriate as a model for women's life-writing. Likewise, the egoistic secular archetype that Rousseau handed down to his Romantic brethren in his *Confessions,* shifting the dramatic presentation to an unfolding self-discovery where characters and events are little more than aspects of the author's evolving consciousness, finds no echo in women's writing about their lives. On the contrary, judging by our four models, the self-discovery of female identity seems to acknowledge the real presence and recognition of another consciousness, and the disclosure of female self is linked to the identification of some "other." This recognition of another consciousness—and I emphasize recognition rather than deference—this grounding of identity through relation to the chosen other, seems (if we may judge by our four representative cases) to enable women to write openly about themselves. . . .

Both Julian and Margery Kempe, writing in the mystical tradition of personal dialogue with a divine being who is Creator, Father, and Lover, discover and reveal themselves in discovering and revealing the Other. Speaking in the first person, with a singleness of vision that allows for no distractions or ambivalences, Julian establishes an identification with the suffering Christ on the cross that is absolute; yet, while such a total identification might seem to suggest a loss of self, the fact is that Julian is in no way obliterated as a person, for her account is shot through with evidence of a vivid, unique, and even radical consciousness. Margery Kempe, by way of contrast, speaks in the third person (she figures throughout her narrative as "þis creatur") to a Christ who, when he is not her infant ("for þu art to me a very modir," he once tells her [91]) is her manly bridegroom. Unlike Julian's single visioned *Revelations*, *The Book of Margery Kempe* displays a dual sense of vocation: the wife-mother, pilgrim-mystic roles, which were continuous throughout Margery Kempe's life, represent a rather more common pattern of women's perception of themselves as maintaining two equally demanding identities, worldly and otherworldly, both of which, however, are ultimately determined by their relation to the divine.

Like Julian's, Anne Bradstreet's brief retrospection is possessed of a singleness of focus, but because her spiritual autobiography comes out of the Puritan tradition and out of the early days of the New England colonies, its intense focus falls not on a personal figure but on a spiritual community. When we place Anne Bradstreet's prose autobiography alongside her autobiographical poetry, we can observe in both a unique harmonizing of the divine, the secular, and the personal, a unifying of a public and a private consciousness.

Margaret Cavendish, author of the first important secular autobiography by a woman, limns her own portrait in a double image, herself and her husband, the Duke of Newcastle. (Here, incidentally, the history of women's lifewriting parallels the history of men's life-writing, secular autobiography being in both cases a latter-day development out of or away from religious self-examination.) The focus of the *True Relation* might better be called duo than dual, and while Margaret Cavendish does not exactly

subordinate herself to her husband's image, she obviously identifies herself most sharply when she is identifying him too. The full-length biography of her husband was written some ten years after the Duchess produced her own short autobiography, and at about the same time that she was writing the life of her husband she also wrote a utopian fantasy, *The Blazing World*, in which she once again splits and reunifies the self-image, appearing both as Duchess of Newcastle and as Empress of the Blazing World—as both herself and another. As we shall see, this duo pattern is a fairly common one in women's autobiographies (indeed in Margaret Cavendish's time two other well-known women, Lucy Hutchinson and Lady Anne Fanshawe, wrote their memoirs and actually appended them to their husbands' biographies).

The Duchess of Newcastle was insistently and prolifically literary, which might seem to set her *True Relation* off from the three spiritual autobiographies; likewise, those three spiritual and didactic documents might not appear amenable to consideration as works of literature. However, as with Margaret Cavendish, the assertion of self in Julian, Margery Kempe, and Anne Bradstreet is accompanied by a strong sense of themselves as authors. Julian's literary intentions were obviously not primary, but even she shows consciousness of being an author, and the book she produced has gradually assumed its rightful place in the great lyrical-mystical tradition of English literature. Margery Kempe, though she was illiterate and was therefore obliged to dictate her story to others, nevertheless took her role as author very seriously indeed—so seriously that the composing and transcribing and the recomposing and retranscribing of her book became a major obsession. But in the end she found the satisfaction of that obsessive need to be both creative and curative: "And sche was many tyme seke whyl þis tretys was in writyng, and, as sone as sche wolde gon a-bowte þe writyng of þis tretys, sche was heil & hoole sodeynly in a maner" (219). Like Julian, Margery Kempe made a contribution not only to the development of autobiography in English but to other literary modes as well: the eclectic structure of her Book draws on a number of literary conventions of the time—voyage and pilgrimage literature, lives of saints, fables—and in its strung-along plot of dramatized episodes, it moves toward fiction and the picaresque novel.

Margaret Cavendish leaves the reader in no doubt about her sense of a literary calling. In the *True Relation* she tells us that she was conscious of her vocation in childhood, and was even then "addicted . . . to write with the pen [rather] than to work with the needle" (172). This longstanding addiction to "scribbling" (as she herself called it) eventually made the Duchess one of the first "literary ladies" of England: she published thirteen books in her lifetime, and as she makes very clear in the epistle prefatory to the *True Relation,* she will not have it that any hand other than her own was involved in the production of these volumes. Moreover, besides being a very early secular autobiography, her *Life* also foreshadowed later developments both in the novel of education and in social novels. Anne Bradstreet, though she was vastly different from Margaret Cavendish both as a woman and as an author, nevertheless echoes her contemporary in the prologue to "The Four Elements" when she declares her fondness for the "poet's pen," and writes that "I am obnoxious to each carping tongue / Who says my hand a needle better fits."[4] In its distilling of a spiritual story to its essence, the little autobiography that came from that pen can be seen as a paradigm of the Puritan "way of the soul," and of course Anne Bradstreet's contribution to the American poetic tradition requires no demonstration. It was important for each of the four autobiographic ex-

emplars to consider herself in one way or another an author, or else her days would have been consigned to work with the needle, and her story, with its self-discovery and self-expression achieved through "other" reference, would have gone untold. . . .

Julian's intensity of focus on a single divine figure and a corresponding intensity of being realized through relationship to that figure; Margery Kempe's dual vocation in this world and in another and her dual focus on these two separate, secular/religious worlds; Margaret Cavendish's pairing of her image with another, equal image and her doubling of the self-image whether in husband or in fantasy creation; and Anne Bradstreet's harmonious merger and identification with a collective consciousness and a corporate other—these are the four great originals, the lived and recorded patterns of relationship to others that allowed these women, each in her own characteristic way, to discover and delineate a self and to tell the story of that self even as it was being uncovered and coming into existence.

Notes

1. Julian of Norwich, *Showings,* trans. Edmund Colledge and James Walsh (New York, 1978), chapter 6 ("short text"), 135. This edition of the "Shewing of God's Love" or the "Sixteen Revelations of Divine Love" includes both the "short text," written shortly after Julian experienced the revelations, and the "long text," written some twenty years after; it supersedes all previous editions and will hereafter be cited in the text.

2. *The Book of Margery Kempe,* ed. Sanford Brown Meech (London, 1940), 1. Citations in the text are to this edition.

3. *A True Relation of My Birth, Breeding and Life,* appended to *The Life of William Cavendish, Duke of Newcastle,* ed. C. H. Firth, 2d ed. (London, n.d.), 178. Citations in the text are to this edition. The "carping

tongues" and "malicious censurers" are in an "epistle" on 154. *A True Relation* first appeared in 1656 as part of *Natures Pictures Drawn by Fancies Pencil to the Life* and was republished as an appendix to *The Life of William Cavendish* in 1667.

4.   *The Works of Anne Bradstreet,* ed. Jeanine Hensley (Cambridge, MA, 1967), 16. All references to Anne Bradstreet's writing in the text will be to this edition. "Carping tongue(s)" is also, interestingly enough, Margaret Cavendish's phrase in much the same context.

26 The Politics and Aesthetics of Métissage

Françoise Lionnet

The Cultural Politics of *Métissage*

. . . There is a long Western tradition, from Plato to Maurice Blanchot, including Augustine and Montaigne, which conceives of writing as a system that rigidifies, stultifies, kills because it imprisons meaning in "la rigidité cadavérique de l'écriture [the cadaverous rigidity of the written sign]" instead of allowing a "parole vive [living *logos*]" to adjust fluidly to the constantly changing context of oral communication in which interlocutors influence each other: Derrida has studied how this relation of opposition between *écriture* and *parole* becomes established in Plato, and is thenceforth central to Western discourse.[1] It is worth noting that Montaigne was the first to use the same phrase—"la parole vive et bruyante [a lively and noisy way of speaking]"—in a secular context. He was discussing his efforts to write the way he speaks, instead of using Latin, to use the lively figurative language of his native Gascogne, however hyperbolic, rather than be stifled either by a dead language or by a literal style that follows the "vérité nayfve . . . nue et crue [the simple truth . . . the naked and unvarnished truth]."[2] These central questions of orality and literacy, speech and writing, truth and hyperbole, transparency and obscurity have become the cornerstone of the cultural aesthetics of many postcolonial writers. As Edouard Glissant, the Martinican poet, novelist, and theorist, spells it out:

For us it is a matter of ultimately reconciling the values of literate civilizations and the long repressed traditions of orality. . . .

This practice of cultural creolization [pratique de *métissage*] is not part of some vague humanism, which makes it permissible for us to become one with the other. It establishes a cross-cultural relationship, in an egalitarian and unprecedented way, among histories which we know today in the Caribbean are interrelated. . . . We also know that there is an obscure residue of something unexpressed deep within every spoken word, however far we may push our meaning and however hard we may try to weigh our acts [il est au fond de toute parole . . . la matière obscure d'un informulé].[3]

For Glissant, the *métissage* or braiding of cultural forms through the simultaneous revalorization of oral traditions and reevaluation of Western concepts has led to the recovery of occulted histories. In the effort to recover their unrecorded past, contemporary writers and critics have come to the realization that opacity and obscurity are necessarily the precious ingredients of all authentic communication: "il est au fond de toute parole . . . la matière obscure d'un informulé."[4] Since history and memory have to be reclaimed either in the absence of hard copy or in full acknowledgment of the ideological distortions that have colored whatever written documents and archival materials do exist, contemporary women writers especially have been interested in reappropriating the past so as to transform our understanding of ourselves. Their voices echo the submerged or repressed values of our cultures. They rewrite the "feminine" by showing the arbitrary nature of the images and values which Western culture constructs, distorts, and encodes as inferior by feminizing them.[5] All the texts I will be discussing interrogate the sociocultural construction of race and gender and challenge essentializing tendencies that perpetuate exploitation and subjugation on behalf of those fictive differences created by discourses of power.

For those of us who are natives of the so-called Third World, it has become imperative to understand and to participate fully in the process of re-vision begun by our contemporary writers and theorists. The latter are engaged in an enterprise which converges toward other efforts at economic and political survival but which is unique in its focus on memory—the oral trace of the past—as the instrument for giving us access to our histories. These recovered histories have now become the source of creative explosions for many authors, male and female, who are being nurtured and inspired by the phenomenon applauded by Glissant, the egalitarian interrelations in which binary impasses are deconstructed.

Within the conceptual apparatuses that have governed our labeling of ourselves and others, a space is thus opened where multiplicity and diversity are affirmed. This space is not a territory staked out by exclusionary practices. Rather, it functions as a sheltering site, one that can nurture our differences without encouraging us to withdraw into new dead ends, without enclosing us within facile oppositional practices or sterile denunciations and disavowals. For it is only by imagining nonhierarchical modes of relation among cultures that we can address the crucial issues of indeterminacy and solidarity. These are the issues that compel us in this fin de siècle, for our "green dirt-ball" will survive only if we respect the differences among its peoples.[6] We can be united against hegemonic power only by refusing to engage that power on its own terms, since to do so would mean becoming ourselves a term within that system of power. We have to articulate new visions of ourselves, new concepts that allow us to think *otherwise*, to bypass the ancient symmetries and dichotomies that have governed the ground and the very condition of possibility of thought, of "clarity," in all of Western philosophy. *Métissage* is such a concept and a practice: it is the site of undecidability and indeterminacy, where solidarity becomes the fundamental principle of political action against hegemonic languages. . . .

For me *métissage* is a praxis and cannot be subsumed under a fully elaborated theoretical system. *Métissage* is a form of *bricolage*, in the sense used by Claude Lévi-Strauss, but as an aesthetic concept it encompasses far more: it brings together biology and history, anthropology and philosophy, linguistics and literature. Above all, it is a reading practice that allows me to bring out the interreferential nature of a particular set of texts, which I believe to be of fundamental importance for the understanding of many postcolonial cultures. If, as Teresa de Lauretis has pointed out, identity is a strategy, then *métissage* is the fertile ground of our heterogeneous and heteronomous identities as postcolonial subjects.[7] The reactionary potential of a separatist search for a unitary and naturalized identity is a well-known danger on which I shall not dwell here. Only a well-understood feminist politics of solidarity can protect us from such a danger.[8]

Solidarity calls for a particular form of resistance with built-in political ambiguities. These ambiguities allow gendered subjects to negotiate a space within the world's dominant cultures in which the "secretive and multiple manifestations of Diversity," in Edouard Glissant's words, will not be anticipated, accommodated, and eventually neutralized.[9] A politics of solidarity thus implies the acceptance of *métissage* as the only racial ground on which liberation struggles can be fought. For the five women writers [I discuss in *Autobiographical Voices*], the possibility of emancipation is indeed linked to an implicit understanding of métissage as a concept of solidarity which demystifies all essentialist glorifications of unitary origins, be they racial, sexual, geographic, or cultural. . . .

Métissage and Language

. . . It is my suspicion that our common and current perception of what constitutes a "race" can be tested by the terms we use to define various "subcategories" within those races and by the way language responds to and accommodates the fact of *métissage*. There is always a certain cultural relativism at work in those terms; because language is molded by the politics and ideology of a community, it influences—in turn—the way a given community comes to think about the world. I would go so far as to argue that in the absence of scientific or experiential grounding, it is language that conditions our concept of race and that the boundaries of that concept change according to cultural, social, and linguistic realities.[10]

The analysis of French, English, Portuguese, or Spanish terms used to define racial categories reveals that those words do not readily translate into one another because they do not cover the same reality, hence have only local significance and are not interchangeable: their semantic values and connotative fields do not overlap.[11] In the French colonial context, for example, the

métis constitutes a distinct but unstable racial category, which varies according to geography: in Canada, the word denotes a "half-breed" of French and Native American descent only. In the late eighteenth century, however, in the capital of the Senegal, St.-Louis, the *métis* were generally persons of French and African descent who then constituted one-fourth of the total population of the town. In the island colonies of the Indian Ocean and the West Indies—as in New Orleans—the *métis* are also called *créoles, mulâtres, cafres* and *cafrines,* although the term may apply indifferently to people who are ostensibly white (*créoles*) or black (*cafres*); the words have even wider semantic ranges in the local creole languages.

The very notion of *métissage,* then, is something culturally specific. The word does not exist in English: one can translate *métis* by "half-breed" or "mixed-blood" but these expressions always carry a negative connotation, precisely because they imply biological abnormality and reduce human reproduction to the level of animal breeding. "Mulatto" is sometimes used, but usually refers to a certain kind of fictional character, the "tragic mulatto," as in William Faulkner's *Go Down Moses* and *Light in August* or Mark Twain's *Puddin' Head Wilson.*[12] But here again, the connotations are totally negative and the referent is the animal world, namely, the generally sterile mule. In English, then, there is no real equivalent for the word *métis* and we could infer that for all English-speaking peoples the very concept of race is different from that of the French, Spanish, or Portuguese speakers. Indeed, in the United States, even an "octoroon" is technically supposed to be a "nonwhite," and those who "look" white but have (some) black "blood" were said to be able to "pass" for white. What does this tell us about the social construction of "race" within different linguistic contexts? That language, in effect, can create reality, since certain categories, such as *créole* and *métis,* are not part of any visible racial difference for the average English speaker. The Anglo-American consciousness seems unable to accommodate miscegenation positively through language. It is a serious blind spot of the English language which thus implies that persons of indeterminate "race" are freaks. It is another way of making invisible, of negating, the existence of nonwhites whose racial status remains ambiguous.

When we attempt to understand the full range of connotations of our racial terminologies, we are forced to reexamine the unconscious linguistic roots of racial prejudice and to face the fact that language predetermines perception. This is why a word like *métis* or *mestizo* is most useful: it derives etymologically from the Latin *mixtus,* "mixed," and its primary meaning refers to cloth made of two different fibers, usually cotton for the warp and flax for the woof: it is a neutral term, with no animal or sexual implication. It is not grounded in biological misnomers and has no moral judgments attached to it. It evacuates all connotations of "pedigreed" ascendance, unlike words like *octoroon* or *half-breed.*

Furthermore, its homonym in ancient Greek, *mētis,* is the allegorical "figure of a function or a power," a cunning intelligence like that of Odysseus, which opposes transparency and the metaphysics of identity and is thus closely related, in practice, to the meaning of *métissage* as I understand it here—and as Glissant uses it too. Within the Greek context, the reality of *mētis* as a form of *techne* projects itself on a plurality of practical levels but can never be subsumed under a single, identifiable system of diametric dichotomies. It is a form of savoir faire which resists symbolization within a coherent or homogeneous conceptual system since it is also the power to undo the logic and the clarity of concepts.

And as Marcel Détienne and Jean Pierre Vernant point out, Mētis is also a proper name: that

of the wife of Zeus, who swallowed her when she was about to give birth to Athena. Mētis is subjugated by Zeus, who appropriates her power of transformation, "thereby guaranteeing his paternal authority for eternity." [13] We may thus appropriate the term for our own feminist pantheon, thanks to the fortuitous nature of this link between the Greek representation of subjugated female power and the elusive semantic field of the French term *métis*: the very polyvalence of the word dictates and legitimates my own heterogeneous approach.

Finally, the use of *métissage* as an analytical tool forces us to reevaluate certain key concepts of literary history as well, for even Leopold Sédar Senghor, whose name is synonymous with the term *négritude,* also claims to be a defender of *métissage* and considered himself a pan-African *métis.*[14] Negritude has borne the brunt of much criticism because of the essentialistic racial ideology implicit in the term, although both Senghor and Aimé Césaire have argued that the criticism was based in a reductive appropriation of the concept of negritude, which came to be interpreted as a purely reactive gesture against white supremacy, without regard for the polysemic potential intended by its originators.[15]

By contrast, in Cuba, it is the concept of *mestizaje* which has long been used by politicians and poets alike (José Marti or Nicolás Guillén, for example) as an enabling metaphor of transculturation with revolutionary potential because it is capable of generating broad support, of enlisting and encouraging solidarity among different ethnic groups against a common enemy, namely the hegemonic discourse of racialism. As Cuban poet Nancy Morejón explains it, "*Transculturation* means the constant interaction, the transmutation between two or more cultural components with the unconscious goal of creating a third cultural entity—in other words, a culture that is new and independent even though rooted in the preceding elements. Reciprocal influence is the determining factor here, for no single element superimposes itself on another; on the contrary, each one changes into the other so that both can be transformed into a third. Nothing seems immutable."[16]

In this constant and balanced form of interaction, reciprocal relations prevent the ossification of culture and encourage systematic change and exchange. By responding to such mutations, language reinforces a phenomenon of creative instability in which no "pure" or unitary origin can ever be posited. A linguistic and rhetorical approach to the complex question of *métissage* thus points to the ideological and fictional nature of our racial categories while underlining the relationship between language and culture. A linguistic approach shows how and why racial difference is a function of language itself. I suggest that any successful strategy of resistance to the totalizing languages of racism must be based in the attempt to create a counterideology by exposing our rhetorical conventions. . . .

The art of *mētis* thus rejoins the signifying practices familiar to all oppressed peoples, in particular to the descendants of slaves in the New World. Such practices had to be learned by the slaves as survival tactics within a hostile environment that kept them subjugated, relegated them to the margins.

Reading the Writers

From Augustine to Marie-Thérèse Humbert, writers I discuss are examples of "divergent" individuals, living on borderlines. They use linguistic and rhetorical structures that allow their plural selves to speak from within the straightjackets of borrowed discourses. The five women authors represent specific examples of creative *métissage* grounded in the historical and geopolitical realities that motivate and inspire them. In order to make clear the complex lineage that influences both their writing and my reading of

their work, I have . . . found it necessary to go back to Augustine and Nietzsche. My point is not to use them as male paradigms or antimodels to be criticized and refuted: I want to examine how dimensions of their work that might be called feminine tend to be either ignored or coded in reference to a more "masculine" and hierarchical framework, even though these texts explicitly reject the possibility of such unproblematic appropriation by critics blind to the biases of their own disciplines and unreceptive to the subversive rhetorical features of language.

But dealing with Augustine and Nietzsche poses a problem opposite to that of the women writers. Far from being neglected, they have been buried under such a bulk of critical interpretation that it is sometimes difficult to approach their texts without preconceived notions colored by nineteenth-century misreadings of their work. What I attempt to do in [my book] amounts to a feminist reappropriation of the covertly maternal elements of both the *Confessions* and *Ecce Homo*. I contrast those with the metaphors of death and disease which permeate the authors' language and structure their narratives. I discuss the problematic status of orality in Augustine's text and the procreative symbolism of Nietzsche's. My reading of Augustine will thus lead to the deconstruction of the notion of gender as we commonly understand it in contemporary terms, and my use of Nietzsche will do the same with regard to the concepts of race and nationality.

Augustine's mother tongue was a North African patois, New Punic, spoken until about A.D. 550 in his hometown of Thagaste, near Carthage, a colony of the western Roman Empire. The classical Latin in which he wrote was a second language, learned in school. Instruction was dispensed by a grammarian who relied on corporal punishment to train his pupils. Augustine also learned Greek, but as he explains in the *Confessions*, that language was odious to him and so hard to understand that "[he] was constantly subjected to violent threats and cruel punishments to make [him] learn" it. Of his native language, he says that he learned it simply, without threats of punishments "while my nurses fondled me and everyone laughed and played happily with me."[17] For him, then, the language he would come to use as a writer—Latin—had done violence to his body and to his soul. This pain explains in part the ambiguous relationship he would maintain with all forms of discourse and his search for a silent resting point, a state of total metaphysical communion, where communication transcends language, is not circumscribed by it.

Nietzsche struggles with the languages of reason and unreason, the silences of hysteria and madness within the monologues of what Michel Foucault terms "the merciless language of non-madness."[18] He is acutely aware of the tyranny of rationalism, the conflicts of consciousness, and the symbolic structures that artificially order perception, feelings, selfhood. Nietzsche stages his life as *Ecce Homo,* a text of rupture and fragmentation. Operating in the space between being and becoming and as heir to Heraclitean and Darwinian notions of multiplicity, Nietzsche undercuts all our illusions about self-possession and self-appropriation: his "autobiography" is an interpretive reading of his corpus, a commentary on his linguistic selves. In many ways, Nietzsche reverses Augustine: the *imitatio Christi* collapses into the figure of the Antichrist, self-dissolution in the transcendent other becomes Dionysian metamorphosis. The last line of *Ecce Homo,* "Have I been understood?—Dionysus versus the Crucified—" is a proclamation and a promise of life against a Christian redemption in death. It is, however, the point at which writing ceases, since madness can only cancel out all possibilities of pursuing an oeuvre. In Foucault's words, "Nietzsche's last cry . . . is the very annihilation of the work of art, the

point where it becomes impossible and where it must fall silent; the hammer has just fallen from the philosopher's hands."[19]

The five women writers also struggle with metaphors of death and disease or madness and silence as the ambivalent foci of their efforts at self-writing. Some of the women—Maya Angelou, Marie Cardinal, and Marie-Thérèse Humbert—ultimately succeed in achieving a reaffirmation of life through the emancipatory potential of writing, with admittedly varying degrees of optimism and triumph. But for Zora Neale Hurston and Maryse Condé, who have experienced the lethal effects of historical contradictions, writing is an unrelenting search for a different past, to be exhumed from the rubble of patriarchal and racist obfuscations. The women's narratives thus dramatize relations of overwhelming indenture. As colonized subjects of patriarchy and racism, these authors are also acutely aware of and profoundly ambivalent about the literary and vernacular traditions within which they implicitly situate themselves as writers. This ambivalence is of particular interest to me because it reveals the damaging process of human internalization of negative stereotypes. I will try to uncover and analyze some of the (Nietzschean) dissimulating strategies these writers use to subvert generic or critical canons and to address social or cultural prejudices.

The women belong to widely different cultural backgrounds. Yet they share a profound concern for the rhetoric of selfhood, for the processes of self-reading and self-writing as facilitated or impeded by the styles and languages in which they are compelled to write. Two are Afro-Americans: Zora Neale Hurston and Maya Angelou, both raised in the South. Three are Francophone: Maryse Condé was raised in Guadeloupe, Marie Cardinal in Algeria, and Marie-Thérèse Humbert in Mauritius. But all are cultural *métis, créoles* whose socioideological horizons are marked by the concrete layerings or stratifications of diverse language systems. The textual space where these layers interact and enter into dialogue is the "autobiographical" theme that will be my generic focus in this book.

Because the path of creativity is particularly tortuous for those who must straddle the interval between different and hierarchized cultural universes, each of the writers examined here has a different relationship to his/her chosen means of expression (the language in which s/he writes) as well as to the style and mode of discourse s/he chooses to adopt within the broader generic configurations of "autobiography." In other words, language is problematic for all of them, not simply because no one ever has a transparent relationship to a given linguistic frame of reference but more specifically because their frames of reference are cultural worlds apart. The space of writing in which these frames intersect positions the writing subject at the confluence of complex and sometimes conflicting creative impulses, which complicate both the writer's and the implied reader's relations in (and to) the text under scrutiny. Thus the denotative and connotative layers of the text can either undermine, contradict, and sabotage each other or reinforce and strengthen patterns of address which allow the subject to speak the language of the other—the implied reader—without risk of abandoning a privileged position within the semiotic field of the mother tongue. By implication, under the articulated, written, organized surface of the narrative there exists a certain energy that can alternatively disrupt the surface layer (as is the case with Condé, Cardinal, and Humbert) or pull together and unify seemingly contradictory or discontinuous narrative modes (as is the case with Augustine, Hurston and Angelou). Hence, I have chosen texts constituted by multilayered nestings, corresponding to their plural languages. These languages can only enter into dialogue when the interval between the textual layers is allowed to

function as "third man," "demon," or "noise" to use Michel Serres's terminology.

For Serres, discourse—in whatever discipline—succeeds in producing meaning by exclusionary binary tactics: "The most profound dialectical problem is not the problem of the Other, who is a variety—or a variation—of the Same, it is the problem of the third man. We might call this third man the *demon,* the prosopopeia of noise." So that if we think of Western history and culture as one long dialogue between interlocutors who are united in one common goal—the search for knowledge or, as Serres has also said, "the hunt" for knowledge and the aggressive appropriation of truth and meaning by two partners in discourse who battle against "noise"—then this "third man" is more often than not a "she-devil," a figure constructed variously as "woman" or as "*Third World*," the better to negate or abolish the multifarious differences among women, peoples, and countries not aligned with the dominant ideologies and conceptual systems of the West. The progressive historical marginalization of this "third" term is a direct consequence of the paradigm of struggle that Serres's metaphor of the hunt aptly summarizes: "Dialectic makes the two interlocutors play on the same side; they do battle together to produce a truth on which they can agree, that is, to produce a successful communication," and thus to expel nomad or evacuate all interference from "the powers of noise" which become the excluded middle, the marginalized peoples, the silent but paradoxically "noisy" gender.[20]

In contrast to this dialectic of struggle in the autobiographical texts analyzed here a different kind of dialogue occurs *because* of the "noise" (the unfiltered, mumbled, "demonic" mother tongue) and thanks to the interferences between contradictory strategies, not in spite of them. Starting with Augustine's *Confessions,* for example, we discover under the apparent structures of the text a different system of organization: I establish the presence of a form of coherence that belies the initial impression of discontinuity. And in *A l'autre bout de moi*, I show how the autobiographical novel, which seems to foreclose interpretation if we remain in the realm of linguistic coherence and read it as a "French" text, is inhabited by another tongue, which turns it into a palimpsest—a verbal rather than a visual one. Indeed, when a verbal sign hides another, to find the underlying structure of a given work, the most useful procedure is not to "look" for it but rather to "listen" for it, since speech acts are a matter of *parole* and not of static visual signs. Augustine and Nietzsche both offer clues, following which I develop the art of listening for "noise." In my approaches to Angelou and Cardinal, I then analyze the painful process of creativity for women writers who are also mothers and seem to have with words as complicated a relationship as they do with their children, thus reproducing their initial ambivalent relationships to their own parents and to the literary tradition that shapes their access to language. Following Hurston and Condé, I argue that the search for past connections must not be allowed to dissolve into negative mythic identifications but must be a thorough reinterpretation of the texts and of the other "noisy" voices of history. If, as critic, I can attempt to read the textual layers while occupying the interval where this otherness speaks, then perhaps I shall succeed in doing justice to strata that might otherwise go unnoticed, remaining masked under superficial and epidermic structures of address.

The metaphors Marie Cardinal uses in her description of the Algerian civil war graphically summarize the tragedy of clashing colonial monolithic systems in their struggle to eliminate noise and heteroglossia. The hideous consequences of war on the lives of those who are caught under the wheels of history are a func-

tion of the abstract, mathematical itinerary traced by the discourses of power in their efforts to silence undesirable, hysterical, or "demonic" elements, that is, blood: "And yet, it was still the shameful agony of French Algeria. The degradation of everything was in the blood of civil war which ran into the gutters and overflowed onto the sidewalks, *following the geometric patterns in the cement of civilization.*"[21] When empirical considerations—such as pain or torture—are geometrically ordered so as not to disturb the intelligence-gathering powers in their search for "truth," war becomes a metaphor for all the great instruments of social codification which, in Deleuze's terms, fight against "thought,"[22] or as Cardinal herself puts it, against the "divagations" that alone can free one from "the yoke of truth" (215). For Cardinal, the path to social self-consciousness is the crooked one of hysteria: only hysteria can transform the dominant codes through and by which we become self-aware as a collective body politic. Because wars need heroes and heroes must die, ancient patterns of honorable conduct and sacrificial victimization are repeated in all patriarchal conflicts. . . . Life, on the other hand, belongs in a different realm from truth, in that in intermediate space where distinctions are effaced, divergence occurs, and one's fate can follow an unheroic, muddy, and noisy path: that is ultimately the perspective adopted by Cardinal.

Like Augustine, Angelou and Humbert write a rich and classical prose (English and French respectively) in a language that is not exactly their "mother tongue." Angelou grew up in the American South during the Depression and learned to read and write in a very religious community where the language of the Bible was familiar to all. For her, to acquire a personal style was to combine the English literary tradition with old-fashioned southern idioms, biblical phrases and rural as well as urban dialects. Unlike other black American writers who choose to express themselves in dialect only, Angelou makes a conscious political decision to master "the King's English" in order to reach a wider audience but also, as she recognizes honestly, because "insecurity can make us spurn the persons and traditions we most enjoy."[23] But what she dispenses with on the level of language, she recuperates in the mythic dimensions of her narrative, which becomes a vast historical and allegorical fresco of the lives of black American women. The use of an eighteenth-century picaresque model, which she succeeds in subverting with humor and irony, is a distinctive feature of her style. She appropriates traditional patterns to her own distinctive ends, thus modifying our perception of what constitutes both "autobiography" and "fiction" in black and Anglo-American literatures.

For Humbert, writing is possible in the psychic space where three languages intersect. The Mauritian creole dialect of her native island seldom surfaces as such in the text or in the mouth of the characters, but it is crucial to a full understanding of the narrative layers and of the Nietzschean operation of self-dissimulation that her text performs on itself. Traces of English (the official political language of Mauritius) are frequent in a novel that rewrites Miranda's (and Caliban's and Ariel's) story in Shakespeare's *Tempest*. And finally, there is French, the "literary" language of Mauritius, which the Francophone population prides itself on cultivating and refining, the more so because it is by no means the language of the majority or the official language. On one level, Humbert's novel is a romantic melodrama with two traditional heroines, one tragic and one romantic, whose fates follow the patterns ascribed to such characters in the canonical texts of the genre. But under the surface structure of the narrative is a complex self-portrait that deconstructs the notion of "heroine," allowing the narrator to assume control and to reject the tradition of female passivity inscribed in the dominant scripts of her legacy.

Hurston and Condé are consumed by the need to find their past, to trace lineages that will empower them to live in the present, to rediscover the histories occluded by History. The impasse in which Condé's Véronica finds herself at the end of her stay in Africa is an allegory of the impasse of *départementalisation* in the French West Indies. As a figure for the failure of Antilleans to embrace their fate as *Caribbean* peoples (instead of "French" Antilleans), she epitomizes the cultural problems of her island. As Glissant points out, "The nation is not based on exclusion; it is a form of dis-alienated relationship with the other who in this way becomes our fellow man [qui ainsi devient autrui]."[24] Condé's disturbing pessimism is a reflection of the political morass of her people, who continue to live under the thumb of the *métropole,* thus entertaining an alienated relationship with the French other, who cannot, under those circumstances, become an *autrui,* that is, a peer and an equal.

So, unlike that of the other women writers, Hurston's and Condé's concern for the past remains linked to a certain pessimism about the future. Their narrators are the lost daughters, orphaned offspring, of an imaginary Africa. For Hurston, anthropological field research becomes a way to rediscover and study lost siblings, to learn about the transformations, transculturations, and cultural *métissages* at work in various areas of the New World. She succeeds in showing the value of "dialect" as a sophisticated means of expression, dispensing once and for all with sentimental or condescending attitudes toward so-called primitivism. But Condé's Véronica makes the trip back to Africa to discover the emptiness within, the false solutions of exile and nomadism. Her narrative presents the most disturbing questions about race and origin, sexuality and domination, intellectual honesty and political engagement. These are questions we must face with great urgency if we believe that intellectual work can have any kind of effect on reality, if we do not want our words to be "dust tracks on a road," aimless detours or strategies of deferral, and would rather choose to have them function as means of transforming our symbolic systems, for the symbolic is real, and in symbols lies our only hope for a better world. To reinterpret the world *is* to change it.

If Nietzsche and Augustine seem to write themselves into silence, the silence of madness or religion, by contrast, Angelou, Cardinal, and Humbert write in an attempt to break out of the prison house of colonizing languages: writing becomes the only key to the (utopian?) creation of a different, heterogeneous, and multicolored future, a future in which the "principle of divergence" is recognized as valid and functional not only in nature but in all our cultural institutions as well, from language to politics. It is no accident that this emphasis on a life-affirming view of writing and creativity is common to three women who are also mothers but whose articulation of the "maternal," as we shall see, is more problematic than Augustine's search for the kind of elusive plenitude that Julia Kristeva has termed the "Eternal Phallic Mother," although it will remain quite close to Nietzsche's writing of the (pro)creative body.[25] Augustine's search for plenitude and coherence leads him to emphasize wholeness and completeness, whereas for the women writers, it will become clear that the human individual is a fundamentally relational subject whose "autonomy" can only be a myth. In the context of our postcolonial history, this view inevitably implies a critique of the myth of economic and political independence of the so-called Third World nations whose survival depends on the "First" World's understanding of *inter*dependence, of "global relations [la relation planétaire]."[26]

. . . Throughout my discussions, I rely on *mé-tissage* as an aesthetic concept to illustrate the relationship between historical context and individual circumstances, the sociocultural construction of race and gender and traditional genre theory, the cross-cultural linguistic mechanisms that allow a writer to generate polysemic meanings from deceptively simple or seemingly linear narrative techniques. I thus establish the need for a kind of Geertzian "thick description" of those texts.[27] Indeed, the use women writers make of both Western literary (or religious) traditions and vernacular cultures (or dialects) contributes to a form of intertextual weaving or *mé-tissage* of styles. This, I believe, is a fundamentally emancipatory metaphor for the inevitably relational and interdependent nature of peoples, nations, and countries hoping to enter into a peaceful "relation planétaire" at the threshold of the twenty-first century.

Notes

This chapter is from the introduction to Lionnet's *Autobiographical Voices: Race, Gender, Self-Portraiture* (Ithaca: Cornell University Press, 1989).

1. Jacques Derrida, "La Pharmacie de Platon," in *La Dissémination* (Paris: Seuil, 1972), 89, *Dissemination,* trans. Barbara Johnson (Chicago: University of Chicago Press, 1981), 114–15.

2. See Michel de Montaigne, *Essais,* "Des boyteux" and "Sur des vers de Virgile," in *Oeuvres complètes* (Paris: Gallimard/La Pléiade, 1962), 1005 and 853. *The Complete Works of Montaigne,* trans. Donald Frame (Stanford: Stanford University Press, 1948), 786 and 667. For a more detailed discussion of this aspect of Montaigne's style, see Claude Blum, "La Peinture du moi et l'écriture inachevée: Sur la pratique de l'addition dans les 'Essais' de Montaigne," *Poétique* 53 (1983), 60–71.

3. Edouard Glissant, *Le Discours antillais* (Paris: Seuil, 1981), 462–63. All further references are given in the text. The English translation by J. Michael Dash, *Caribbean Discourse,* is published by the University Press of Virginia (1989). Whenever possible, I have used this translation. But I have frequently had

to alter it in order to stress nuances of the French text which are indispensable to my analyses. For example, Dash translates *métissage* by the word "creolization" which is perfectly acceptable when dealing with cultural mixing but not appropriate when referring to the racial context. That is why I shall retain the word *métissage* here. I shall indicate "trans. mod." whenever I alter the English text.

4. See, for example, Sarah Kofman's stimulating discussion of what can be problematic in "the will to clarity," in "Nietzsche and the Obscurity of Heraclitus," *Diacritics* 17 (Fall 1987).

5. Sander Gilman has studied the common denominator shared by negative stereotypes in the West and shown how the "other" is always sexualized and racialized: blacks, Jews, women, the mad are described as inferior because they are the reductive antithesis of what is set up as "normal." *Difference and Pathology: Stereotypes of Sexuality, Race, and Madness* (Ithaca: Cornell University Press, 1985).

6. To use Zora Neale Hurston's humorous phrasing. *Dust Tracks on a Road,* ed. Robert Hemenway, 2d ed. (Urbana: University of Illinois Press, 1984), 147.

7. Teresa de Lauretis, "Issues, Terms and Contexts," *Feminist Studies/Critical Studies,* ed. de Lauretis (Bloomington: Indiana University Press, 1986), 9.

8. See, for example, Sandra Harding, *The Science Question in Feminism* (Ithaca: Cornell University Press, 1986), chap. 7; and Frantz Fanon's critique of negritude as I discuss it briefly in chapters 2 and 3 of my *Autobiographical Voices.*

9. GIissant, 12, trans. mod.

10. Twentieth-century science has shown that it is impossible to define with any kind of accuracy the genetic frontiers that might permit the classification of humans into a set of well-defined "races." See, for example, Masatoshi Nei and Arun K. Roychoudhury, "Genetic Relationship and Evolution of Human Races," *Evolutionary Biology* 14 (1983); Albert Jacquard, "A la recherche d'un contenu pour le mot 'race': La réponse du généticien," and François Jacob, "Biologie-Racisme-Hiérarchie," both in *Le Racisme: Mythes et sciences,* ed. Maurice Olender (Paris: Complexe, 1981). Both Jacquard and Jacob emphasize that the attempt to classify and hierarchize human beings is the consequence of an *ideological* parti pris.

11. According to anthropologist Marvin Harris,

the comparative study of race relations in Brazil and the United States illuminates important ambiguities in "culturally controlled systems of 'racial' identity." His inventory of Portuguese lexical terms which define Brazilian "acial" types number 492, and do not correlate with precise usage: which is to say that there is no objective agreement among native Brazilians as to the "racial" status of a given person. Full siblings who look different phenotypically are identified by heterogeneous terms, and there is no such thing as a single "sociocentric racial identity," even within the same community or family. (Some of the 492 Portuguese expressions listed by Harris translate as: white African, white Negro, black Negro, black Indian, Indian mulatto, yellow white, white mulatto, white yellow, blond black, mestizo black, and so on. This highly subjective terminology is by no means static.) And Harris argues that Brazilian ambiguity could allow for a much broader base of support among oppressed groups, unlike the situation in the United States, where racial splits fragment the lower classes. "Referential Ambiguity in the Calculus of Brazilian Racial Identity," in *Afro-American Anthropology: Contemporary Perspectives,* ed. Norman E. Whitten and John F. Szwed (New York: Free Press, 1970), 75.

12. As Sondra O'Neale has argued, the mulatto figure is "the most discussed black female character in American literature." Such women are "perceived as totally Europeanized, not only in facial features but in acculturation, as well." "Inhibiting Midwives, Usurping Creators: The Struggling Emergence of Black Women in American Fiction," in *Feminist Studies/ Critical Studies,* ed. Teresa de Lauretis (London: Macmillan, 1988), 139–156 (147). It should be clear that what I am stressing in my use of the term *métissage* is quite different from the assimilationist tendencies criticized by O'Neale.

13. See Marcel Détienne and Jean Pierre Vernant, *Les Ruses de l'intelligence: La Mētis des grecs* (Paris: Flammarion, 1974); and the review by Richard Klein, "The Mētis of Centaurs," *Diacritics* 16 (Summer 1986): 2–13 (4–5).

14. See, for example, Senghor's "Preface to Marie-Madeleine Marquet," *Le Métissage dans la poésie de Léopold S. Senghor* (Dakar: Nouvelles Editions Africaines, 1983).

15. But see also the arguments against monolithic views of race put forth by René Depestre, *"Les Aspects créateurs du métissage culturel,"* and Anthony Phelps, "Moi, Nègre d'Amérique . . . ," in *Notre Librairie* 74 (April–June 1984): 61–65 and 53–60.

16. Nancy Morejón, *Nacion y mestizaje en Nicolás Guillén* (Havana: Unión, 1982), 23. My translation.

17. Augustine, *Confessions,* trans. R. S. Pine-Coffin (New York: Penguin Books, 1979), 35.

18. Michel Foucault, *Madness and Civilization: A History of Insanity in the Age of Reason,* trans. Richard Howard (New York: Random House, 1965), ix.

19. Ibid., 287.

20. See Michel Serres, *Hermes: Literature, Science, Philosophy,* ed. Josué V. Harari and David F. Bell (Baltimore: Johns Hopkins University Press, 1982), 65–70 (67). In *The Parasite,* trans. Lawrence R. Schehr (Baltimore: Johns Hopkins University Press, 1983), Serres also develops the question of noise and the figures it assumes. In "The Algebra of Literature: The Wolf's Game," in *Textual Strategies: Perspectives in Post-Structuralist Criticism,* ed. Josué Harari (Ithaca: Cornell University Press, 1979), 276, he speaks of the "hunt" for knowledge.

21. Marie Cardinal, *The Words to Say It,* trans. Pat Goodheart (Cambridge, MA.: VanVactor and Goodheart, 1984), 88, my italics. I have modified the translation.

22. Gilles Deleuze, "Nomad Thought,' in *The New Nietzsche: Contemporary Styles of Interpretation,* ed. David B. Allison (Cambridge: MIT Press, 1985), 142–49.

23. Maya Angelou, *Singin' and Swingin' and Gettin' Merry like Christmas* (New York: Random House, 1976), 94.

24. Glissant, 463.

25. For an excellent feminist psychoanalytic approach to the issues that concern me here, see Shirley N. Garner et al., eds. *The (M)other Tongue: Essays in Feminist Psychoanalytic Interpretation* (Ithaca: Cornell University Press, 1985). I am more interested in the cross-cultural repressive linguistic mechanisms that "colonize" a writer's access to his/her (m)other tongue. I will be analyzing how this repressed linguistic layer resurfaces in the text, creating echoes of another discourse, another sensitivity under the apparent simplicity of the narrative.

26. Glissant, 465.

27. See Clifford Geertz, *The Interpretation of Cultures* (New York: Basic Books, 1973), chap. 1.

27 Forbidden Gaze, Severed Sound

Assia Djebar

I

On 25 June 1832, Delacroix disembarks in Algiers for a short stopover. He has just spent a month in Morocco, immersed in a universe of extreme, visual richness (the splendor of the costumes, reckless frenzy of *fantasias*, the pomp of a royal court, the rapture of Jewish weddings or of street musicians, the nobility of royal felines: lions, tigers, and so forth). . . .

Delacroix spends only three days in Algiers. This brief stay in an only recently conquered capital city directs him, thanks to a felicitous combination of circumstances, toward a world that had remained foreign to him during his Moroccan trip. For the first time, he penetrates into a world that is off-limits: that of the Algerian women. . . .

Upon his return to Paris, the painter will work for two years on the image of a memory that teeters with a muted and unformulated uncertainty, although well-documented and supported by authentic objects. What he comes out with is a masterpiece that still stirs questions deep within us.

Women of Algiers in Their Apartment: three women, two of whom are seated in front of a hookah. The third one, in the foreground, leans her elbow on some cushions. A female servant, seen three quarters from the back, raises her arm as if to move the heavy tapestry aside that masks this closed universe; she is an almost minor character, all she does is move along the edge of

the iridescence of colors that bathes the other three women. The whole meaning of the painting is played out in the relationship these three have with their bodies, as well as with the place of their enclosure. Resigned prisoners in a closed place that is lit by a kind of dreamlike light coming from nowhere—a hothouse light or that of an aquarium—Delacroix's genius makes them both near and distant to us at the same time, enigmatic to the highest degree. . . .

II

During the time of the Emir Abdelkader, nomadic tribes loyal to him, the Arbaa and the Harazeli, found themselves besieged in 1839 in Fort Ksar el Hayran by their traditional enemy, the Tedjini. On the fourth day of the siege, the assailants are already scaling the walls, when a young Harazeli girl, named Messaouda ("the happy one"), seeing that her men are ready to turn their backs, calls out:

> "Where are you running like that? The enemies are on this side! Must a young girl show you how men are supposed to behave? Well then, take a look!"

She climbs onto the ramparts, lets herself slide down the other side, facing the enemy. Thus exposing herself willingly, she speaks these words at the same time:

"Where are the men of my tribe?
Where are my brothers?
Where are those who used to sing songs
      of love to me?"

Thereupon the Harazeli came running to her aid and tradition reports they did so while clamoring this war cry that was also a cry of love:

"Be happy, here are your brothers, here are your lovers!"

Electrified by the young girl's call, they pushed back the enemy.

Messaouda was brought back in triumph, and ever since, the "Song of Messaouda" has been sung by the tribes in the Algerian south, recalling these facts and ending with this exact exaltation of the heroic wound:

"Messaouda, you shall always be a wrench for pulling teeth!"

In the history of Algerian resistance struggles during the last century, numerous episodes, indeed, show women warriors who left the traditional role of spectator. Their formidable look would prod the men's courage, but suddenly also, right where the ultimate despair dawns, their very presence in the boiling movement of battle decides the outcome.

Other accounts of feminine heroism illustrate the tradition of the feudal queen-mother (intelligent, a tactician of "virile" courage), for example, the distant Berber woman Kahina.

The story of Messaouda, more modest, seems to me to present a newer aspect: surely a variant on heroism and tribal solidarity, but above all it is here connected with a body in danger (in completely spontaneous motion), with a voice that calls, challenges, and abrades. In short, it heals the temptation of cowardice and allows a victorious outcome.

"Be happy, here are your brothers, here are your lovers!" Are these brothers-lovers more upset to see the completely exposed body, or are they more "electrified" by the feminine voice that runs off? This sound at last comes forth from the entrails, brushing past the blood of death and of love. And this is the revelation: "Be happy!" The song of Messaouda is the only one that consecrates this happiness of women, completely inside a mobility that is improvised and dangerous at the same time: in short, that is creative.

Very few Messaoudas, alas, in our recent past of anti-colonial resistance. Before the war of liberation, the search for a national identity, if it did include a feminine participation, delighted in erasing the body and illuminating these women as "mothers," even for those exceptional figures who were recognized as women warriors. But when, in the course of the seven years of the national war, the theme of the heroine becomes exalted, it is exactly around the bodies of young girls, whom I call the "fire carriers" and whom the enemy incarcerates. Harems melted for a while into so many Barberousse prisons, the Messaoudas of the Battle of Algiers were called Djamila.

Since that call by Messaouda and the antiphonal response of the "brothers-lovers," since that race forward of woman's pride set free, what do we have as a "story" of our women, as feminine speech?

Delacroix's painting shows us two of the women as if surprised in their conversation, but their silence has not stopped reaching us. The halting words of those who have half-lowered their eyelids or who look away in the distance in order to communicate. As if it concerned some secret, the enlightenment of which the servant is watching for, and we cannot quite tell whether she is spying on them or is an accomplice to them.

From childhood on, the little girl is taught "the cult of silence, which is one of the greatest powers of Arabic society."[1] What a French general, "friend to the Arabs," calls "power," is something we feel as a second mutilation.

Even the yes that is supposed to follow the fatiha of the marriage ceremony and that the father must ask of his daughter—the Koran requires this of him—is ingeniously squelched almost everywhere (in Moslem regions). The fact that the young girl may not be seen uncovered in order to utter her acquiescence (or her nonacquiescence), obliges her to go through the intermediary of a male representative who speaks in "her place." A terrible substitution for the word of one by another, which, moreover, opens the way to the illegal practice of the forced marriage. Her word deflowered, violated, before the other deflowering, the other violation intervenes.

Besides, even without the *ouali,* it has been agreed that this yes, which they are waiting for directly from her, may be expressed, because of her "modesty" in front of her father and the man of the law, through her silence or through her tears. It is true that in ancient Persia, an even more characteristic practice has been noted:[2] to consecrate the marriage, the boy makes his agreement heard loudly and clearly; the fiancée, the girl, is put in the next room amid other women, near the door over which a curtain falls. In order to make the necessary yes audible, the women hit the young girl's head against the door, causing her to moan.

Thus, the only word the woman must pronounce, this yes to submission under the pretense of propriety, she breathes out with discomfort, either under the duress of physical pain or through the ambiguity of silent tears.

It is told that in 1911, during various Algerian campaigns, the women (mothers and sisters) would come and roam around the camps where the so-called indigenous conscripts were penned in, would come to weep and tear at their faces.

The image of the tearful woman, lacerating her cheeks to the point of hysteria, becomes for the ethnologists of the time the only image "in motion": no more women warriors, no more women poets. If it doesn't concern invisible and mute women, if they're still an integral part of their tribe, they can only appear as powerless furies. Silence even of the dancer-prostitutes of the Ouled Naïls, their bodies covered down to their feet, their idol-like faces weighed down by jewels, their only sound the rhythmic one of their ankle bands.

Thus, from 1900 to 1954 in Algeria, there is a closing down of an indigenous society, more and more dispossessed of its vital space and its tribal structures. The orientalizing look—first with its military interpreters and then with its photographers and filmmakers—turns in circles around this closed society, stressing its "feminine mystery" even more in order thus to hide the hostility of an entire Algerian community in danger.

However, this has not prevented the spatial tightening from leading to a tightening of family relationships during the first half of the twentieth century: between cousins, brothers, etc. And in the relationships between brothers and sisters, the latter have been most often—always thanks to the "yes-silence of the tears"—disinherited to the advantage of the males in the family: here is another face of that immemorial abuse of trust, of that alienation of material goods and bed and board.

Thus, doubly imprisoned in that immense jail, the woman has the right to no more than a space that is doomed to become ever smaller. Only the mother-son relationship has grown stronger to the point of obstructing all other exchanges. As if the attachment to the roots, which grows more and more difficult for these new proletarians without any land and soon without a culture, should again pass through the umbilical cord.

But beyond this tightening within the families, by which only the males benefit, there is the attachment to the oral roots of history.

The sound of the mother who, woman without a body and without an individual voice, finds once again the sound of the collective and obscure voice, which is necessarily asexual. For in the spinning around of the defeat that ended in tragic immobility, the models for finding a second wind and oxygen have been sought elsewhere,[3] in places other than this kind of immense nourishing womb in which the long chain of mothers and grandmothers, shaded by patios and shacks, nurtured the emotional memory. . . .

The echoes of the battles lost in the last century, details of color very much worthy of a Delacroix, reside among the illiterate storytellers: the whispered voices of those forgotten women have developed irreplaceable frescoes from these, and have thus woven our sense of history.

In this way, the enlarged presence of the mother (woman without body or, conversely, of multiple bodies) finds itself to be the most solid knot in the almost complete incommunicability between the sexes. But at the same time, in the realm of the word, the mother seems, in fact, to have monopolized the only authentic expression of a cultural identity—admittedly limited to the land, to the village, to the popular local saint, sometimes to the "clan," but in any case, concrete and passionate with affectivity.

As if the mother, recoiling on this side of procreation, were masking her body from us, in order to return as the voice of the unknown ancestress, timeless chorus in which history is retold. But a history from which the archetypal image of the feminine body has been expelled.

A hesitant sketch in stipples floats on the surface, all that's left of a culture of women, now slowly suffocating: songs once sung by young girls on their verandas,[4] quatrains of love from the women of Tlemcen,[5] magnificent funereal threnodies from the women of Laghouat, an entire literature that, unfortunately, is becoming further and further removed, only to end up by resembling those mouthless wadis that get lost in the sands. . . .

Ritual lament of the Jewish and Arabic women folksingers who sing at Algerian weddings, this outdated tenderness, this delicately loving nostalgia, barely allusive, is transmitted little by little from the women to the adolescent girls, future sacrificial victims, as if the song were closing in upon itself.

We, children in the patios where our mothers still seem young, serene, wearing jewelry that doesn't crush them—not yet—that often adorns them in inoffensive vanity, we, in the faint murmuring of those lost feminine voices, we still feel its old warmth . . . but rarely its withering. These islets of peace, this intermission to which our memory clings, are these not a small part of that plant life autonomy of the Algerian women in the painting, the totally separate world of women?

A world from which the growing boy removes himself, but from which today's young, self-emancipating girl distances herself as well. For her in particular, the distancing amounts to shifting the location of her muteness: she exchanges the women's quarters and the old community for an often deceptive one-on-one with the man.

Thus, this world of women, when it no longer hums with the whisperings of an ancillary tenderness, of lost ballads-in short, with a romanticism of vanished enchantments—that world suddenly, barrenly, becomes the world of autism.

And just as suddenly, the reality of the present shows itself without camouflage, without any addiction to the past: sound has truly been severed.

III

As the war of liberation in Algeria was just barely getting started, Picasso, from December 1954 to February 1955, goes to live every day in the world of Delacroix's "Women of Algiers." There he comes face-to-face with himself and erects around the three women, and with them, a completely transformed universe: fifteen canvases and two lithographs carrying the same title.

It moves me to think that the Spanish genius presides in this manner over a changing in the times.

As we entered our "colonial night," the French painter offered us his vision that, the admiring Baudelaire notes, "breathes I don't know what heady perfume of evil haunts that leads us rather quickly toward the unplumbed limbo of sadness." That perfume of evil haunts came from quite far off and will have become even more concentrated.

Picasso reverses the malediction, causes misfortune to burst loose, inscribes in audacious lines a totally new happiness. A foreknowledge that should guide us in our everyday life.

Pierre Daix remarks: "Picasso has always liked to set the beauties of the harem free." Glorious liberation of space, the bodies awakening in dance, in a flowing outward, the movement freely offered. But also the preservation of one of the women, who remains hermetic, Olympian, suddenly immense. Like a suggested moral, here, of a relationship to be found again between the old, adorned serenity (the lady, formerly fixed in her sullen sadness, is motionless from now on, but like a rock of inner power) and the improvised bursting out into an open space.

For there is no harem any more, its door is wide open and the light is streaming in; there isn't even a spying servant any longer, simply another woman, mischievous and dancing. Finally, the heroines—with the exception of the queen, whose breasts, however, are bursting out—are totally nude, as if Picasso was recovering the truth of the vernacular language that, in Arabic, designates the "unveiled" as "denuded" women. Also, as if he were making that denuding into a sign not of an "emancipation," but rather of these women's rebirth to their own bodies.

Two years after this intuition of the artist, there appeared the descendants, the carriers of the bombs, in the Battle of Algiers. Are these women merely the sisters-companions of the nationalist heroes? Certainly not, for everything takes place as if the latter, in isolation, outside of the clan, had made a long trek back, from the 1920s to almost 1960, in order to find their "sisters-lovers" again, and that in the shadow of the prisons and the brutal treatment by the legionnaires.

As if the guillotine and those first sacrificed in the coldness of the dawn were needed for young girls to tremble for their blood brothers and to say so.[6] The ancestral accompaniment had, until then, been the ululation of triumph and of death.

It is a question of wondering whether the carriers of the bombs, as they left the harem, chose their most direct manner of expression purely by accident: their bodies exposed outside and they themselves attacking other bodies? In fact, they took those bombs out as if they were taking out their own breasts, and those grenades exploded against them, right against them. Some of them came back later with their sex electrocuted, flayed through torture.

If rape, as a fact and a "tradition" of war, is in itself horribly banal ever since wars have existed, it became—when our heroines were its victims of expiation—the cause of painful upheaval, experienced as trauma by the whole of the Algerian collective. The public condemnation of it through newspapers and legal intervention certainly contributed to the spread of scandalous repercussions: the words that named it became, where rape was concerned, an explicit and unanimous condemnation. A barrier of words came down in transgression, a veil was shredded in front of a threatened reality, but one whose repression was too strong not to return. Such repression submerged a solidarity in misery that for a moment had been effective. What words had uncovered in time of war is now being concealed again underneath a thick covering of taboo subjects, and in that way, the meaning of a revelation is reversed. Then the heavy silence returns that puts an end to the momentary restoration of sound. Sound is severed once again. As if the fathers, brothers, or cousins were saying: "We have paid plenty for that unveiling of words!" Undoubtedly forgetting that the women have inscribed that statement into their martyred flesh, a statement that is, however, penalized by a silence that extends all around.

Sound severed once again, the gaze once again forbidden, these are what reconstruct the ancestral barriers. "A perfume of evil haunts," Baudelaire said. There is no seraglio any more. But the "structure of the seraglio"[7] attempts to impose its laws in the new wasteland: the law of invisibility, the law of silence.

Only in the fragments of ancient murmuring do I see how we must look for a restoration of the conversation between women, the very one that Delacroix froze in his painting. Only in the door open to the full sun, the one Picasso later imposed, do I hope for a concrete and daily liberation of women.

Notes

1. See *La Femme arabe* (The Arab woman) by General Daumas, written shortly before the author's death in 1871 and published in 1912.

2. See P. Raphaël du Mans, *Etat de la Perse en 1660* (The state of Persia in 1660) (Paris, 1890).

3. Elsewhere because the origin of political nationalism is as much due to the emigration of workers to Europe in the 1920s as to the movement of the new ideas from the Arabic East where large numbers of educated Arabic speakers and Moslems are trained (the Parti Progressiste Algérien—P.P.A.—and the *ulema* movements).

4. The "songs . . . from the verandas" are those of the Bokala game, in which the young girls respond to each other in rhyming couplets, as signs of portent.

5. These are the *hawfis,* a kind of popular, feminine poetry that is sung. Ibn Khaldoun already mentions this traditional genre, which he calls *mawaliya.* This same kind of feminine literature is found in places other than Tlemcen, but always in small towns of the Algerian north.

6. See, before 1962, Zora Drif, *La mort de mes frères* (The death of my brothers).

7. *La structure du serail,* by Alain Grosrichard (1979).

28 Speaking in Tongues: Dialogics, Dialectics, and the Black Woman Writer's Literary Tradition

Mae Gwendolyn Henderson

I am who I am, doing what I came to do, acting
upon you like a drug or a chisel to remind you of your me-ness,
as I discover you in myself.
　　　　　　　—Audre Lorde, *Sister Outsider* (emphasis mine)

There's a noisy feelin' near the cracks
crowdin' me . . .
It spooks my alley, it spooks my play,
more nosey now than noisy,
　　lookin' for a tongue
　　lookin' for a tongue
　　to get holy in.
Who can tell this feelin' where to set up church?
Who can tell this noise where to go?. . . .
　　　　　　　—Cherry Muhanji, *Tight Spaces*

Some years ago, three black feminist critics and scholars edited an anthology entitled *All the Women Are White, All the Blacks Are Men, But Some of Us Are Brave,*[1] suggesting in the title the unique and peculiar dilemma of black women. Since then it has perhaps become almost commonplace for literary critics, male and female, black and white, to note that black women have been discounted or unaccounted for in the "traditions" of black, women's, and American literature as well as in the contemporary literary-critical dialogue. More recently, black women writers have begun to receive token recognition as they are subsumed under the category of woman in the feminist critique and the category of black in the racial critique. Certainly these "gendered" and "racial" decodings of black women authors present strong and revisionary methods of reading, focusing as they do on literary discourses regarded as marginal to the dominant literary-critical tradition. Yet the "critical insights" of one reading might well become the "blind spots" of another reading. That is, by privileging one category of analysis at the expense of the other, each of these methods risks setting up what Fredric Jameson describes as "strategies of containment," which restrict or repress different or alternative readings.[2] More specifically, blindness to what Nancy Fraser describes as "the gender subtext" can be just as occluding as blindness to the racial subtext in the works of black women writers.[3]

Such approaches can result in exclusion at worst and, at best, a reading of part of the text as the whole—a strategy that threatens to replicate (if not valorize) the reification against which black women struggle in life and literature. What I propose is a theory of interpretation based on what I refer to as the "simultaneity of discourse," a term inspired by Barbara Smith's seminal work on black feminist criticism.[4] This concept is meant to signify a mode of reading which examines the ways in which perspectives of race and gender, and their interrelationships, structure the discourse of black women writers. Such an approach is intended to acknowledge and overcome the limitations imposed by assumptions of internal identity (homogeneity) and the repression of internal differences (heterogeneity) in racial and gendered readings of works by black women writers. In other words, I propose a model that seeks to account for racial difference within gender identity and gender difference within racial identity. This approach represents my effort to avoid what one critic describes as the presumed "absolute and self-sufficient" *otherness* of the critical stance in order to allow the complex representations of black women writers to steer us away from "a simple and reductive paradigm of 'otherness.'"[5]

Discursive Diversity: Speaking in Tongues

What is at once characteristic and suggestive about black women's writing is its interlocutory,

or dialogic, character, reflecting not only a relationship with the "other(s)," but an internal dialogue with the plural aspects of self that constitute the matrix of black female subjectivity. The interlocutory character of black women's writings is, thus, not only a consequence of a dialogic relationship with an imaginary or "generalized Other," but a dialogue with the aspects of "otherness" within the self. The complex situatedness of the black woman as not only the "Other" of the Same, but also as the "other" of the other(s) implies, as we shall see, a relationship of difference and identification with the "other(s)."

It is Mikhail Bakhtin's notion of dialogism and consciousness that provides the primary model for this approach. According to Bakhtin, each social group speaks in its own "social dialect"—possesses its own unique language—expressing shared values, perspectives, ideology, and norms. These social dialects become the "languages" of heteroglossia "intersect[ing] with each other in many different ways . . . As such they all may be juxtaposed to one another, mutually supplement one another, contradict one another and be interrelated dialogically."[6] Yet if language, for Bakhtin, is an expression of social identity, then subjectivity (subjecthood) is constituted as a social entity through the "role of [the] word as medium of consciousness." Consciousness, then, like language, is shaped by the social environment. ("Consciousness becomes consciousness only . . . in the process of social interaction.") Moreover "the semiotic material of the psyche is preeminently the word—*inner speech.*" Bakhtin in fact defines the relationship between consciousness and inner speech even more precisely: "Analysis would show that the units of which inner speech is constituted are certain *whole entities . . . [resembling] the alternating lines of a dialogue.* There was good reason why thinkers in ancient times should have conceived of inner speech as *inner dialogue.*"[7]

Thus consciousness becomes a kind of "inner speech," reflecting "the outer word" in a process that links the psyche, language, and social interaction.

It is the process by which these heteroglossic voices of the other(s) "encounter one another and coexist in the consciousness of real people—first and foremost in the creative consciousness of people who write novels,"[8] that speaks to the situation of black women writers in particular, "privileged" by a social positionality that enables them to speak in dialogically racial and gendered voices to the other(s) both within and without. If the psyche functions as an internalization of heterogeneous social voices, black women's speech/writing becomes at once a dialogue between self and society and between self and psyche. Writing as inner speech, then, becomes what Bakhtin would describe as "a unique form of collaboration with oneself" in the works of these writers.[9]

Revising and expanding Teresa de Lauretis's formulation of the "social subject and the relations of subjectivity to sociality," I propose a model that is intended not only to address "a subject engendered in the experiencing of race," but also what I submit is *a subject "racialized" in the experiencing of gender*.[10] Speaking both to and from the position of the other(s), black women writers must, in the words of Audre Lorde, deal not only with "the external manifestations of racism and sexism," but also "with the results of those distortions internalized within our consciousness of ourselves and one another."[11]

What distinguishes black women's writing, then, is the privileging (rather than repressing) of "the other in ourselves." Writing of Lorde's notion of self and otherness, black feminist Barbara Christian observes of Lorde what I argue is true to a greater or lesser degree in the discourse of black women writers: "As a black, lesbian, feminist, poet, mother, Lorde has, in her own life, had to search long and hard for her people. In responding to each of these audiences, in which a part of her identity lies, she refuses to give up her differences. In fact she uses them, as woman to man, black to white, lesbian to heterosexual, as a means of conducting creative dialogue."[12]

If black women speak from a multiple and complex social, historical, and cultural positionality which, in effect, constitutes black female subjectivity, Christian's term "creative dialogue" then refers to the expression of a multiple *dialogic of differences* based on this complex subjectivity. At the same time, however, black women enter into a *dialectic of identity* with those aspects of self shared with others. It is Hans-Georg Gadamer's "dialectical model of conversation," rather than Bakhtin's dialogics of discourse, that provides an appropriate model for articulating a relation of mutuality and reciprocity with the "Thou"—or intimate other(s). Whatever the critic thinks of Gadamer's views concerning history, tradition, and the like, one can still find Gadamer's emphases—especially as they complement Bakhtin's—to be useful and productive. If the Bakhtinian model is primarily adversarial, assuming that verbal communication (and social interaction) is characterized by contestation with the other(s), then the Gadamerian model presupposes as its goal a language of consensus, communality, and even identification, in which "one claims to express the other's claim and even to understand the other better than the other understands [him or herself]." In the "I-Thou" relationship proposed by Gadamer, "the important thing is . . . to experience the 'Thou' truly as a 'Thou,' that is, not to overlook [the other's] claim and to listen to what [s/he] has to say to us." Gadamer's dialectic, based on a typology of the "hermeneutical experience," privileges tradition as "a genuine partner in communication, with which we have fellowship as does the 'I' with a 'Thou.'" For black and women writers such an avowal of tradition in the subdominant order, of course, constitutes an operative challenge to the dominant order. It is this rereading of the notion of tradition within a field of gender and ethnicity that supports and enables the notion of community among those who share a common history, language, and culture. If Bakhtin's dialogic engagement with the Other signifies conflict, Gadamer's monologic acknowledgment of the Thou signifies the potential of agreement. If the Bakhtinian dialogic model speaks to the other within, then Gadamer's speaks to *the same within*. Thus, "the [dialectic) understanding of the [Thou]" (like the dialogic understanding of the other[s]) becomes "a form of self-relatedness."[13]

It is this notion of discursive difference and identity underlying the simultaneity of discourse which typically characterizes black women's writing. Through the multiple voices that enunciate her complex subjectivity, the black woman writer not only speaks familiarly in the discourse of the other(s), but as Other she is in contestorial dialogue with the hegemonic dominant and subdominant or "ambiguously (non)-hegemonic" discourses.[14] These writers enter simultaneously into familial, or *testimonial* and public, or *competitive* discourses—discourses that both affirm and challenge the values and expectations of the reader. As such, black women writers enter into testimonial discourse with black men as blacks, with white women as women, and with black women as black women.[15] At the same time, they enter into a competitive discourse with black men as women, with white women as blacks, and with white men as black women. If black women speak a discourse of racial and gendered difference in the dominant or hegemonic discursive order, they speak a discourse of racial and gender identity and difference in the subdominant discursive order. This dialogic of difference and dialectic of identity characterize both black women's subjectivity and

black women's discourse. It is the complexity of these simultaneously homogeneous and heterogeneous social and discursive domains out of which black women write and construct themselves (as blacks and women and, often, as poor, black women) that enables black women writers authoritatively to speak to and engage both hegemonic and ambiguously (non)hegemonic discourse.

Janie, the protagonist in Zora Neale Hurston's *Their Eyes Were Watching God*, demonstrates how the dialectics/dialogics of black and female subjectivity structure black women's discourse.[16] Combining personal and public forms of discourse in the court scene where she is on trial and fighting not only for her life but against "lying thoughts" and "misunderstanding," Janie addresses the judge, a jury composed of "twelve more white men," and spectators ("eight or ten white women" and "all the Negroes [men] for miles around" [274]). The challenge of Hurston's character is that of the black woman writer—to speak at once to a diverse audience about her experience in a racist and sexist society where to be black and female is to be, so to speak, "on trial." Janie speaks not only in a discourse of gender and racial difference to the white male judge and jurors, but also in a discourse of gender difference (and racial identity) to the black male spectators and a discourse of racial difference (and gender identity) to the white women spectators. Significantly, it is the white men who constitute both judge and jury, and, by virtue of their control of power and discourse, possess the authority of life and death over the black woman. In contrast, the black men (who are convinced that the "nigger [woman] kin kill . . . jus' as many niggers as she please") and white women (who "didn't seem too mad") read and witness/oppose a situation over which they exercise neither power nor discourse (225, 280).

Janie's courtroom discourse also emblematizes the way which the categories of public and private break down in black women's discourse. In the context of Janie's courtroom scene, testimonial discourse takes on an expanded meaning, referring to both juridical, public, and dominant discourse as well as familial, private, and nondominant discourse. Testimonial, in this sense, derives its meaning from both "testimony" as an official discursive mode and "testifying" defined by Geneva Smitherman as "a ritualized form of . . . communication in which the speaker gives verbal witness to the efficacy, truth, and power of some experience in which [the group has] shared." The latter connotation suggests an additional meaning in the context of theological discourse where testifying refers to a "spontaneous expression to the church community [by whomever] feels the spirit." [17]

Like Janie, black women must speak in a plurality of voices as well as in a multiplicity of discourses. This discursive diversity, or simultaneity of discourse, I call "speaking in tongues." Significantly, glossolalia, or speaking in tongues, is a practice associated with black women in the Pentecostal Holiness church, the church of my childhood and the church of my mother. In the Holiness church (or as we called it, the Sanctified church), speaking unknown tongues (tongues known only to God) is in fact a sign of election, or holiness. As a trope it is also intended to remind us of Alice Walker's characterization of black women as artists, as "Creators," intensely rich in that spirituality which Walker sees as "the basis of Art." [18]

Glossolalia is perhaps the meaning most frequently associated with speaking in tongues. It is this connotation which emphasizes the particular, private, closed, and privileged communication between the congregant and the divinity. Inaccessible to the general congregation, this mode of communication is outside the realm of public discourse and foreign to the known tongues of humankind.

But there is a second connotation to the notion of speaking in tongues—one that suggests not glossolalia, but heteroglossia, the ability to speak in diverse known languages. While glossolalia refers to the ability to "utter the mysteries of the spirit," heteroglossia describes the ability to speak in the multiple languages of public discourse. If glossolalia suggests private, nonmediated, nondifferentiated univocality, heteroglossia connotes public, differentiated, social, mediated, dialogic discourse. Returning from the trope to the act of reading, perhaps we can say that speaking in tongues connotes both the semiotic, presymbolic babble (baby talk), as between mother and child—which Julia Kristeva postulates as the "mother tongue"—and also the diversity of voices, discourses, and languages described by Mikhail Bakhtin.

Speaking in tongues, my trope for both glossalalia and heteroglossia, has a precise genealogical evolution in the Scriptures. In Genesis 11, God confounded the world's language when the city of Babel built a tower in an attempt to reach the heavens. Speaking in many and different tongues, the dwellers of Babel, unable to understand each other, fell into confusion, discord, and strife, and had to abandon the project. Etymologically, the name of the city Babel sounds much like the Hebrew word for "babble"—meaning confused, as in baby talk. Babel, then, suggests the two related, but distinctly different, meanings of speaking in tongues, meanings borne out in other parts of the Scriptures. The most common is that implied in 1 Corinthians 14—the ability to speak in unknown tongues. According to this interpretation, speaking in tongues suggests the ability to speak in and through the spirit. Associated with glossolalia—speech in unknown tongues—it is ecstatic, rapturous, inspired speech, based on a relation of intimacy and identification between the individual and God.

If Genesis tells of the disempowerment of a

people by the introduction of different tongues, then Acts 2 suggests the empowerment of the disciples who, assembled on the day of Pentecost in the upper room of the temple in Jerusalem, "were filled with the Holy Spirit and began to speak in other tongues." Although the people thought the disciples had "imbibed a strange and unknown wine," it was the Holy Spirit which had driven them, filled with ecstasy, from the upper room to speak among the five thousand Jews surrounding the temple. The Scriptures tell us that the tribes of Israel all understood them, each in his own tongue. The Old Testament, then, suggests the dialogics of difference in its diversity of discourse, while the New Testament, in its unifying language of the spirit, suggests the dialectics of identity. If the Bakhtinian model suggests the multiplicity of speech as suggested in the dialogics of difference, then Gadamer's model moves toward a unity of understanding in its dialectics of identity.

It is the first as well as the second meaning which we privilege in speaking of black women writers: the first connoting polyphony, multivocality, and plurality of voices, and the second signifying intimate, private, inspired utterances. Through their intimacy with the discourse of the other(s), black women writers weave into their work competing and complementary discourses—discourses that seek both to adjudicate competing claims and witness common concerns.[19]

Also interesting is the link between the gift of tongues, the gift of prophecy, and the gift of interpretation. While distinguishing between these three gifts, the Scriptures frequently conflate or conjoin them. If to speak in tongues is to utter mysteries in and through the Spirit, to prophesy is to speak to others in a (diversity of) languages which the congregation can understand. The Scriptures would suggest that the disciples were able to perform both. I propose, at this juncture, an enabling critical fiction—that it is black

women writers who are the modern day apostles, empowered by experience to speak as poets and prophets in many tongues. With this critical gesture, I also intend to signify a deliberate intervention by black women writers into the canonic tradition of sacred/literary texts. . . .[20]

It is this quality of speaking in tongues, that is, multivocality, I further propose, that accounts in part for the current popularity and critical success of black women's writing. The engagement of multiple others broadens the audience for black women's writing, for like the disciples of Pentecost who spoke in diverse tongues, black women, speaking out of the specificity of their racial and gender experiences, are able to communicate in a diversity of discourses. If the ability to communicate accounts for the popularity of black women writers, it also explains much of the controversy surrounding some of this writing. Black women's writing speaks with what Mikhail Bakhtin would describe as heterological or "centrifugal force" but (in a sense somewhat different from that which Bakhtin intended) also unifying or "centripetal force."[21] This literature speaks as much to the notion of commonality and universalism as it does to the sense of difference and diversity.

Yet the objective of these writers is not, as some critics suggest, to move from margin to center, but to remain on the borders of discourse, speaking from the vantage point of the insider/outsider. As Bakhtin further suggests, fusion with the (dominant) Other can only duplicate the tragedy or misfortune of the Other's dilemma. On the other hand, as Gadamer makes clear, "there is a kind of experience of the 'Thou' that seeks to discover things that are typical in the behaviour of [the other] and is able to make predictions concerning another person on the basis of [a commonality] of experience."[22] To maintain this insider/outsider position, or perhaps what Myra Jehlen calls the "extra-terrestrial fulcrum" that Archimedes never acquired, is to see the other, but also to see what the other cannot see, and to use this insight to enrich both our own and the other's understanding.[23]

As gendered and racial subjects, black women speak/write in multiple voices—not all simultaneously or with equal weight, but with various and changing degrees of intensity, privileging one *parole* and then another. One discovers in these writers a kind of internal dialogue reflecting an *intrasubjective* engagement with the *intersubjective* aspects of self, a dialectic neither repressing difference nor, for that matter, privileging identity, but rather expressing engagement with the social aspects of self ("the other[s] in ourselves"). It is this subjective plurality (rather than the notion of the cohesive or fractured subject) that, finally, allows the black woman to become an expressive site for a dialectics/dialogics of identity and difference.

Unlike Bloom's "anxiety of influence" model configuring a white male poetic tradition shaped by an adversarial dialogue between literary fathers and sons (as well as the appropriation of this model by Joseph Skerrett and others to discuss black male writers), and unlike Gilbert and Gubar's "anxiety of authorship" model informed by the white woman writer's sense of "dis-ease" within a white patriarchal tradition, the present model configures a tradition of black women writers generated less by neurotic anxiety or dis-ease than by an emancipatory impulse which freely engages both hegemonic and ambiguously (non)hegemonic discourse.[24] Summarizing Morrison's perspectives, Andrea Stuart perhaps best expresses this notion:

> I think you [Morrison] summed up the appeal of black women writers when you said that white men, quite naturally, wrote about themselves and their world; white women tended to write about white men because they were so close to them as husbands, lovers and sons; and black men

wrote about white men as the oppressor or the yardstick against which they measured themselves. Only black women writers were not interested in writing about white men and therefore they freed literature to take on other concerns.[25]

In conclusion, I return to the gifts of the Holy Spirit: 1 Corinthians 12 tells us that "the [one] who speaks in tongues should pray that [s/he] may interpret what [s/he] says." Yet the Scriptures also speak to interpretation as a separate gift—the ninth and final gift of the Spirit. Might I suggest that if black women writers speak in tongues, then it is we black feminist critics who are charged with the hermeneutical task of interpreting tongues?

Notes

1. Gloria Hull, Patricia Bell Scott, and Barbara Smith, eds., *All the Women Are White, All the Blacks Are Men, But Some of Us Are Brave* (Old Westbury, NY: Feminist Press, 1982).

2. Fredric Jameson, *The Political Unconscious: Narrative as a Socially Symbolic Act* (Ithaca: Cornell University Press, 1981), 53.

3. The phrase "gender subtext" is used by Nancy Fraser (and attributed to Dorothy Smith) in Fraser's critique of Habermas, "What's Critical about Critical Theory?" in *Feminism as Critique*, ed. Seyla Benhabib and Drucilla Cornell (Minneapolis: University of Minnesota Press, 1987), 42.

4. See Barbara Smith, ed., *Home Girls: A Black Feminist Anthology* (New York: Kitchen Table: Women of Color Press, 1983), xxxii.

5. John Carlos Rowe, "'To Live Outside the Law, You Must Be Honest': The Authority of the Margin in Contemporary Theory," *Cultural Critique* 1 (2): 67–68.

6. Mikhail Bakhtin, "Discourse in the Novel," reprinted in *The Dialogic Imagination: Four Essays by M. M. Bakhtin*, ed. Michael Holquist (Austin: University of Texas Press, 1981), 292. Bakhtin's social groups are designated according to class, religion, generation,

region, and profession. The interpretative model I propose extends and rereads Bakhtin's theory from the standpoint of race and gender, categories absent in Bakhtin's original system of social and linguistic stratification.

7. V. N. Volosinov (Mikhail Bakhtin), *Marxism and the Philosophy of Language* (New York: Seminar Press, 1973), 11, 29, 38. Originally published in Russian as *Marksizm I Filosofija Jazyka* (Leningrad, 1930). Notably, this concept of the "subjective psyche" constituted primarily as a "social entity" distinguishes the Bakhtinian notion of self from the Freudian notion of identity.

8. Bakhtin, "Discourse in the Novel," 292.

9. According to Bakhtin, "The processes that basically define the content of the psyche occur not inside but outside the individual organism . . . Moreover, the psyche enjoys extraterritorial status . . . [as] a social entity that penetrates inside the organism of the individual personal" (*Marxism and the Philosophy of Language*, 25, 39). Explicating Caryl Emerson's position on Bakhtin, Gary Saul Morson argues that selfhood "derives from an internalization of the voices a person has heard, and each of these voices is saturated with social and ideological values." "Thought itself," he writes, "is but 'inner speech,' and inner speech is outer speech that we have learned to 'speak' in our heads while retaining the full register of conflicting social values." See Gary Saul Morson, "Dialogue, Monologue, and the Social: A Reply to Ken Hirshkop," in *Bakhtin: Essays and Dialogues on His Work*, ed. Morson (Chicago: University of Chicago Press, 1986), 85.

10. Teresa de Lauretis, *Technologies of Gender* (Bloomington: Indiana University Press, 1987), 2.

11. Audre Lorde, "Eye to Eye," included in *Sister Outsider* (Trumansburg, NY: Crossing Press, 1984), 147.

12. Barbara Christian, "The Dynamics of Difference: Book Review of Audre Lorde's *Sister Outsider*," in *Black Feminist Criticism: Perspectives in Black Women Writers* (New York: Pergamon Press, 1985), 209.

13. While acknowledging the importance of historicism, I can only agree with Frank Lentricchia's conclusion that in some respects Gadamer's "histori-cist argument begs more questions than it answers. If we can applaud the generous intention, virtually unknown in structuralist quarters, of recapturing history for textual interpetation, then we can only be stunned by the implication of what he has uncritically to say about authority, the power of tradition, knowledge, our institutions, and our attitudes." See Frank Lentricchia, *After the New Criticism* (Chicago: University of Chicago Press, 1980), 153. Certainly, Gadamer's model privileges the individual's relation to history and tradition in a way that might seem problematic in formulating a discursive model for the "noncanonical" or marginalized writer. However, just as the above model of dialogics is meant to extend Bakhtin's notion of class difference to encompass gender and race, so the present model revises and limits Gadamer's notion of tradition. See Hans-Georg Gadamer, *Truth and Method* (New York: Seabury Press, 1975), 321–25. My introduction to the significance of Gadamer's work for my own reading of black women writers was first suggested by Don Bialostosky's excellent paper entitled "Dialectic and Anti-Dialectic: A Bakhtinian Critique of Gadamer's Dialectical Model of Conversation," delivered at the International Association of Philosophy and Literature in May 1989 at Emory University in Atlanta, Georgia.

14. I extend Rachel Blau DuPlessis's term designating white women as a group privileged by race and oppressed by gender to black men as a group privileged by gender and oppressed by race. In this instance, I use "ambiguously (non)hegemonic" to signify the discursive status of both these groups.

15. Black women enter into dialogue with other black women in a discourse that I would characterize as primarily testimonial, resulting from a similar discursive and social positionality. It is this commonality of history, culture, and language which finally constitutes the basis of a tradition of black women's expressive culture. In terms of actual literary dialogue among black women, I would suggest a relatively modern provenance of such a tradition, but again, one based primarily on a dialogue of affirmation rather than contestation. As I see it, this dialogue begins with Alice Walker's response to Zora Neale Hurston. Although the present article is devoted primarily to the contestorial function of black women's writing,

my forthcoming work (of which the present essay constitutes only a part) deals extensively with the relationships among black women writers.

16.   Zora Neale Hurston, *Their Eyes Were Watching God* (1937; rpt., Urbana: University of Illinois Press, 1978). All subsequent references in the text.

17.   Geneva Smitherman, *Talkin and Testifyin: The Language of Black America* (Detroit: Wayne State University Press, 1996), 58.

18.   Alice Walker, "In Search of Our Mothers' Gardens," in *In Search of Our Mother's Gardens. Womanist Prose* (New York: Harcourt Brace Jovanovich, 1984), 232.

19.   Not only does such an approach problematize conventional categories and boundaries of discourse, but, most importantly, it signals the collapse of the unifying consensus posited by the discourse of universalism and reconstructs the concept of unity in diversity implicit in the discourse of difference.

20.   The arrogant and misogynistic Paul tells us, "I thank God that I speak in tongues more than all of you. But in church I would rather speak five intelligible words to instruct others [i.e., to prophesy] than ten thousand words in a tongue." Even though we are perhaps most familiar with Paul's injunction to women in the church to keep silent, the prophet Joel, in the Old Testament, speaks to a diversity of voices that includes women: "In the last days, God says, I will pour out my Spirit on all people. Your sons and *daughters* will prophesy . . . Even on my servants, both men and *women,* I will pour out my Spirit in those days, and they will prophesy" (emphasis mine). I am grateful to the Rev. Joseph Stephens whose vast scriptural knowledge helped guide me through these and other revelations.

21.   Bakhtin, "Discourse in the Novel," 271–72.

22.   Gadamer, *Truth and Method,* 321.

23.   Myra Jehlen, "Archimedes and the Paradox of Feminist Criticism," reprinted in *The Signs Reader: Women, Gender and Scholarship* ed. Elizabeth Abel and Emily K. Abel (Chicago: University of Chicago Press, 1983).

24.   See Harold Bloom, *The Anxiety of Influence: A Theory of Poetry* (New York: Oxford University Press, 1973); Sandra M. Gilbert and Susan Gubar, eds., *The Madwoman in the Attic: The Woman Writer and the Nineteenth-Century Literary Imagination* (New Haven: Yale University Press, 1979); and Joseph T. Skerrett, "The Wright Interpretation: Ralph Ellison and the Anxiety of Influence," *Massachusetts Review* 21 (Spring 1980): 96–212.

25.   Andrea Stuart in an interview with Toni Morrison, "Telling Our Story," *Sparerib* (April 1988): 12–15.

29 The Recovery of Memory, Fantasy, and Desire in Women's Trauma Stories: Feminist Approaches to Sexual Abuse and Psychotherapy

Janice Haaken

I hadn't so much forgot as I couldn't bring myself to remember. Other things were more important.

—Maya Angelou

After decades of feminist gains in achieving public recognition of the widespread incidence of sexual abuse, the women's movement confronts a new wave of coordinated opposition in the 1990s. The False Memory Syndrome (FMS) Foundation is a group of parents who have organized to defend themselves against what they claim to be false accusations of sexual abuse—accusations frequently based on the recovery of memories in psychotherapy. Many clinicians who specialize in treating victims of abuse dismiss FMS as part of the backlash against feminism and the movement for children's rights (H. Armstrong; Wasserman; Herman, "Abuses"; Wylie, "Shadow"; Cronin; Bass and Davis).

As a psychoanalytic clinician and a feminist, I share these concerns over societal resistances to recognizing sexual abuse. But the debate has raised unsettling questions for me, ones that are not satisfactorily answered by rallying around sloganistic appeals to "believe survivors." The political interests behind the FMS Foundation are important to analyze, and these interests are sometimes obscured by the emotionally charged stories of "families destroyed by false accusations" (Goldstein). But we need to widen the field of our critical vision, here, and not use the term "backlash" reflexively.

This essay is an effort to concede some of the ground claimed by the other side—by skeptics and critics of recovered memory—while reclaiming it through a psychoanalytic-feminist analysis of two central themes. First, in the rush to defend the authority of women's voices, both patients and therapists have lost an important area of feminine struggle: the right of women to recognize the role of fantasy and desire in mental life, capacities that are fundamental to resisting patriarchal control and imagining a world beyond it. Second, the centrality of trauma memory in the clinical elaboration of sexual disturbances has imposed a new silencing on women. Women have been limited in the kinds of stories that can be told and on the areas of conflict which may be explored, including that between women patients and therapists.

Sexual Abuse and the Trauma/ Dissociation Model

As women begin to speak about the past and to become authors of their own lives, their audiences shape the process through which fragments of memory are woven into autobiographical accounts. In psychotherapy no less than in politics, the project of converting private knowledge into a narrative form is a social one, where speakers and listeners mutually influence the story that gets told.

In the early period of mobilization around incest, women spoke out publicly and in consciousness-raising groups, supporting each other in defiance of cultural mandates to remain silent (see Alcoff and Gray; L. Armstrong). As women entered the mental health professions in larger numbers, the climate of therapeutic receptivity to child abuse allegations shifted as well. Women turned private remembrances into social testimonials, refusing to remain the guardians of the fathers' secrets.

Over the past decade, the clinical literature on sexual abuse has extended this stance of "believing women's stories" to include clinical exploration of sexual abuse that is hidden behind the presenting clinical symptoms. A vast literature has developed to identify sexual abuse survivors who do not recognize the imprint of their abuse experiences in their clinical symptoms (Bass and Davis; Courtois and Sprei; Maltz; Fredrickson). While this emerging emphasis upon "disguised presentation" expands the possibilities for recognizing women who may have been abused, it also raises important issues about the influence of therapists in accessing memory and in interpreting ambiguous indicators of abuse.

There has been a shift from the early feminist clinical literature on sexual abuse, which situated abuse within a broad configuration of relationships in the patriarchal family, to contemporary approaches based on the trauma/dissociation model. This latter model underlies current treatment approaches focusing on traumatic memory retrieval. In understanding the political implications of this transition, Judith Lewis Herman's work is important because it bridges these two traditions of feminist inquiry. While there is currently an extensive clinical literature based on the trauma/dissociation model, my analysis centers on the development of Herman's work because it illustrates a set of problems confronted by feminist therapists in reconciling psychiatric and political conceptions of female maladies.

Herman's early book, *Father-Daughter Incest* (1981), combined psychodynamic and feminist thought and shaped feminist discourse on sexual abuse during the early 1980s. Her second book, *Trauma and Recovery* (1992), represents a significant departure from her earlier formulations and an adoption of the trauma/dissociation model. While the adoption of this new model reflects the growing recognition in the mental health field of the impact of childhood abuse on adult psychopathology, this shift introduces new blindspots in conceptualizing the disturbing side of female development under patriarchy.

Father-Daughter Incest (1981) is based on an analysis of two groups of women: incest survivors and daughters of "seductive fathers." In describing commonalities between the two groups, Herman notes that patriarchal family dynamics include both an eroticized father-daughter relationship and intense anxiety over sexuality. "Bodies, particularly women's bodies, were considered dirty" (110). She also describes the tendency of women in both groups to idealize the father. The daughter's conflictual relationship with the father included guilty gratification in displacing the mother as the father's primary love object, as well as fear and helplessness in response to his sexual interest in her. In contradistinction to the idealized relationship with the father, the relationship with the mother was marked by pronounced hostility and rivalry. The adult daughters' descriptions of mothers similarly had an oedipal cast, suggestive of triangular rivalries within the nuclear family:

> Mothers were often suspicious and resentful of this special relationship . . . The mothers' resentment made the daughters feel guilty but could not entirely extinguish the pleasure they derived from their favored status. Some even exulted in their mothers' mortification.

The psychological legacy of incestuous and seductive father-daughter relationships included an idealization of men and a profound distrust of and contempt for women. In *Father-Daughter Incest,* the emotional suffering of daughters encompasses both real and imagined terrors, along a continuum from overt abuses to more subtle, erotically-toned invasions of childhood. In Herman's exploration of family dynamics, the very ambiguities and uncertainties attached to terms such as incest and sexual abuse implicitly allow for a range of interpretations of early sexual experiences.

Herman's caveats suggest that "validating" women's abuse experiences involves engaging women around conflictual alliances, including the legacy of mother/daughter antagonisms. In her more recent book, these conflictual themes in women's relationships—both familial and therapeutic—are notably minimized. In the following discussion, I attempt to "recover" conflictual aspects of feminine experience that are themselves dissociated from awareness by the use of the trauma/dissociation model.

In the clinical literature on sexual abuse, the problem of disguised presentation is increasing-

ly framed by the link between trauma and dissociation (Cornell and Olio; Davies and Frawley, "Dissociative," "Treating"; Briere; Herman, *Trauma*). The theory that the experience of extreme childhood trauma leads to a dual consciousness or splits in consciousness was initially advanced by Pierre Janet in the late 19th century (van der Kolk, *Psychological*). In order to survive emotionally overwhelming experiences, the individual splits off the memory of the traumatic experience from consciousness. The dissociated memories are preserved in an alter ego state, or latent state of consciousness, through an amnesic barrier protecting one part of the personality from knowledge of the abuse (van der Kolk, *Psychological*; Spiegel).

Freud's early theory of hysteria developed along similar lines in suggesting the presence of a "double consciousness," conceptualized as the coexistence of internally coherent, yet separate and autonomous operations within the ego. This conception of dissociation as vertical splits in consciousness was later supplanted in Freud's theorizing by the concept of repression—or horizontal splits separating levels of consciousness, i.e., the System Conscious and the System Unconscious. Repression involved reversals, substitutions, and transpositions of images and ideas. From this perspective, all memory is "screen memory." Freud abandoned the idea that an original, pristine memory of a traumatic scene could be psychotherapeutically unearthed in the search for a single cause of the patient's difficulties.

The dissociation model asserts that traumatic memory is preserved in split-off ego formations and emerges over time in a fragmentary re-experiencing of the trauma, often through self-hypnotic trance states, flashbacks, or fluctuating identity states (van der Kolk, *Psychological*; Shengold; Davies and Frawley, *Treating*). Whereas the repression model assumes that infantile desires and conflicts inevitably shape the process of remembering—both at the level of the initial encoding of events and in their later retrieval—dissociation implies a more orderly, "rational" unconscious with closer access to consciousness (Spiegel).

The trauma model represents a revolt against biological psychiatry, with its traditional emphasis on pathological symptoms as deficits, as well as a reaction against Freudian psychoanalysis. Given the oppressiveness of the "faulty machine" model of biological psychiatry, diagnoses that restore the humanity of mental patients are an advance. The capacity of the mind to preserve a coherent representation of a past disorganizing event, a premise of the trauma model, means that the patient carries within him/her the "key to the kingdom," the hidden source of later difficulties. The task of the therapist is to aid the patient in accessing the memory of the traumatic event, buried in the recesses of the mind.

Feminists have a special affinity with the trauma/dissociation model because of its emphasis on the ability of the survivor to preserve trauma memories as veridical accounts of external events, despite the devastating effects of the trauma (Root). The model provides a language for articulating the pain and injury of women, then, while preserving the position of women's essential rationality. However, the subsuming of a broad range of sexually disturbing recollections under the rubric of psychic trauma has led to a certain slippage in how feminist therapists understand power within the family. The concept of power is now less apt to be anchored in material differences in fathers' privileges or access to resources, including the capacity to make use of others toward some identifiable end, as it is described as a primary drive to dominate or a spiritual impulse toward evil.

Herman's elaboration of the trauma model illustrates this trend in feminist literature. On the one hand, trauma theory permits a uniting of male and female victimization around a common redemptive project. The male abuser, constructed through the lens of post-traumatic stress disorder (PTSD), is reenacting his own victimization. The Vietnam vet, for example, is viewed as a trauma survivor who suffers from the same condition of captivity as do abused girls and women. On the other hand, the male abuser, as archetypal perpetrator, takes on an altogether different cast: "The perpetrator's first goal appears to be the enslavement of his victim . . . He appears to have a psychological need to justify his crimes, and for this he needs the victim's affirmation . . . His ultimate goal appears to be the creation of a willing victim. Hostages, political prisoners, battered women, and slaves have all remarked upon the captor's curious psychological dependence upon his victim" (*Trauma*, 75–76).

Herman's use of extreme trauma and absolute captivity as paradigmatic of women's oppression generally obliterates attention to *degrees* of harm or positions along a continuum of perpetrator/victim relations. The master/slave dialectic does involve a life and death struggle over the "master's" disavowed dependency, as Herman points out, one that places the "slave" in a paradoxical position of power. Yet when we move from situations of total captivity to those involving some degrees of freedom, women's own motivations and fantasies may more readily come into play.

There are two realities that must be recognized in interpreting women's experiences of sexuality and imagery of bodily invasion. One is the material reality of sexual abuse and its often traumatic consequences for women. The other is the seductive and intrusive presence of the symbolic phallus in the course of "normal" female development. To suggest, as Andrea Dworkin does, that "all men are rapists" does express a reality. Women often do "discover" their sexuality initially through the intrusive presence of the phallus, metaphorically or literally. It is not surprising, then, that many women do identify with the testimonies in the sexual abuse literature, whether or not incest ever occurred.

This fixation on trauma does, of course, counter the cultural legacy of denial or minimizing of the injuries of women. The assertion that "regardless of its form and the child's response, incest is a devastating experience and leaves a devastating mark on its victims" (Manlowe, 10), finds a responsive chord among women patients and therapists who resist the traditional injunction to suffer silently. While this claim of "inevitable effects" of sexual abuse has been strenuously challenged in recent clinical research (Russell; Steiger and Zanko; Edwards and Alexander), it remains a legendary truth because it operates collectively as a refusal to be appeased.

As a self-organizing belief, however, this assertion has its downside. The notion that psychological devastation inevitably results from objectively abusive experiences may predispose therapists and women patients to understand a range of emotional responses as evidence of psychic trauma. This is not so very far from the idea that virginal women are "ruined" by early, culturally unauthorized sexual experiences, as well as by sexual abuse (see Nathanson). The use of trauma metaphors in the service of emotional suffering may be a Trojan horse. Under the guise of validating women's injuries, the old idea of an inherent female vulnerability can be imported into the therapeutic field. The therapist who assumes that psychic devastation follows from particular life events may be operating under the sway of an archaic fantasy: that an original "castratedness"—a primal "wound"—leaves the female psyche perpetually vulnerable to injury.

Trauma Stories and Clinical Practice

Within a society that vacillates between hysteria and denial around all forms of "sexual transgression," sexual abuse has tremendous evocative power. As the public becomes inured to violence and images of victimization, the survivor's ability to mobilize support comes increasingly to depend on the dramatic power of the trauma story. To be a trauma survivor is to have one's suffering recognized and to be entitled to special forms of social support that would otherwise not be available. The trauma story anoints the survivor with a heroic status—as the bearer of unspeakable truths.

Within feminism, trauma stories also have become a unifying vehicle for expressing female disturbances within a narrative that wards off exploration of potentially disunifying differences. In the recovery literature, therapists and other group members are repeatedly described as bearing witness to the trauma, which often depends on the recovery of trauma memories. Herman (*Trauma*) states that while members of trauma-focused groups are encouraged to choose a concrete goal to achieve, most members choose recovery of trauma memories or the telling of the trauma story. Herman doesn't consider the possibility of group pressure to produce a trauma memory, or the influence of therapists on the retrieval of memory (see Loftus and Ketchum; Ofshe and Watters; Yapko).

The subsuming of a broad range of experiences and symptoms under the rubric of trauma provides a unifying basis for group identity, but one that forecloses the exploration of many aspects of female experience, including conflict among women. Herman's description of the groups illustrates this avoidance of conflict:

> The work of the group focuses on the shared experience of trauma in the past, not on interpersonal difficulties in the present. Conflicts and differences among group members are not particularly pertinent in the group; in fact, they divert the group from the task. The leaders must intervene actively to promote sharing and minimize conflict. (*Trauma*, 223)

The potential of the trauma memory to serve as a kind of psychological container for the disturbing side of female experience, including conflict with other women, is heightened by this focus on the recovery of the trauma memory. Through the story, women are able to speak about the forbidden: sexuality, aggression, rivalry and fantasies of submission and domination. Because all of these feelings are assumed to be derived from the trauma, the retrieval of the trauma memory becomes essential to the validating and normalizing of women's responses.

Although Herman notes that sexual abuse stories may stir sexual responses in therapists, particularly in male therapists, discussion of the evocative power of the trauma story in recovery groups is limited to its overt meaning as a testimonial. Implicit in her analysis is the assumption that women are not aroused by such stories, nor do they experience voyeuristic interest in such dramas. Herman does recognize, however, the potential for the retrieval of trauma memories to reenact the original trauma for the patient:

> The patient may imagine a kind of sadomasochistic orgy, in which she will scream, cry, vomit, bleed, die, and be reborn cleansed of the trauma. The therapist's role in this reenactment comes uncomfortably close to that of the perpetrator, for she is invited to rescue the patient by inflicting pain. (*Trauma*, 172)

The potentially invasive aspects of "inflicting pain," and the possibility that the patient's emerging memory is a symbolic communication of her own position in relation to an intrusive therapist, are not considered here. Herman is more apt to describe the therapist's interventions in heroic terms, just as the survivor is described heroically.

Another problematic issue in traumatic memory retrieval is the therapist's unconscious resistance to material that may be disturbing or disruptive to the fantasied unity of therapist and patient. The negative meaning attached to fantasy in the sexual abuse literature contributes to its destabilizing effects in psychotherapy. If fantasy is equated with "making things up" and is devoid of significance in understanding the past, then it does appear as a barrier to achieving an authentic sense of self and introduces a disturbing source of uncertainty.

The devaluation of fantasy can close off a range of indeterminate meanings about the past. Patient and therapist may unconsciously experience anxiety over any fantasies that go beyond reenactment of the trauma, so that all disturbing mental images are interpreted *a priori* as "flashbacks." This is particularly problematic in that sexual fantasies are as much (perhaps more) a source of shame for women as are revelations around sexual abuse. In constructing memory as a literal representation of past events, the comingling of disturbing events and their fantasy elaborations is closed off.

Memories of sadistic invasion may result from a range of experiences, including those not directly attributable to childhood sexual abuse. Other developmental factors can underlie abuse memories, including dynamics associated with emotional deprivation which can be elaborated intrapsychically as sadomasochistic fantasy (Benjamin). It is significant to note that while reports of physical abuse and *neglect* have always been included in the literature on dissociative disorders (Frankel), the issue of parental neglect has received little clinical discussion. This inattention to neglect is particularly problematic given the pervasiveness of neglect—and particularly paternal neglect—in female development (Johnson). Emotional neglect and abandonment themes are even more difficult to construct through the narrative of memory than are abuse experiences. It is easier to struggle against a demonic presence than a perniciously absent one.

Herman describes the process of memory retrieval as transformative "only in the sense of [the memories] becoming more present and more real" (*Trauma*, 181). It is important to recognize in this formulation, however, the potential for an intrusive therapeutic demand for memories of abuse and for self-knowledge that is clear in meaning. While Herman has noted a tendency in the field of sexual abuse treatment to focus too exclusively on the retrieval of trauma memory, her therapeutic suggestions focus primarily on the importance of regulating the pace of memory retrieval rather than on the complex and variable meanings of emerging images of the past. For example, she describes a woman who experiences a "flashback" during sexual intercourse that is assumed to signal the emergence of repressed memories of early sexual abuse:

> I was having sex with my husband, and I had come to a place in the middle of it where I felt like I was three years old. I was very sad, and he was doing the sex, and I remember looking around the room and thinking, "Emily" (who's my therapist), "please come and get me out from under this man." I knew "this man" wasn't my husband, but I didn't yet say dad. (185)

I wonder, here, whether the therapist considered the range of potential meanings of "please get me out from under this man" (including, perhaps, her relationship with her husband). The reference to the therapist might be usefully explored, as well as the developmental significance of being in the position of a three-year-old girl, caught between her desire for her mother (evoked in the imagery of turning to the therapist) and her position in relation to the father.

When the therapist can only respond to the good, hurt child within the patient, there is po-tential for the perpetrator to serve as a projective vehicle for disturbing, destructive impulses that are experienced as threatening to the therapeutic relationship and, unconsciously, to the therapist. This would seem to be an important therapeutic issue to explore, given that conflict over maternal abandonment and rage toward the mother are often associated with child sexual abuse (Herman, *Father-Daughter*; Starzecpyzel; Jacobs, "Victimized," *Victimized*). This theme of mother/daughter conflict, central to Herman's early work on incest survivors, has been displaced by an overriding emphasis on locating the event that destroyed a pre-existing state of harmony. The use of the trauma/dissociation model may be employed defensively, then, in warding off the disturbing and conflictual aspects of feminine experience, including those that emerge in the therapeutic encounter between women.

The use of the trauma model may also "contain" political conflicts within feminism. The focus on retrieval of the trauma memory places the perpetrator securely in the past. As some women achieve authority within public life, and yet find themselves continuing to be subjugated to more powerful men, it may be less dangerous to confront the "dead" fathers of early childhood than the living ones. The trauma model also unifies women in a common project that evades differences between those who have achieved authority and those who are subject to that authority. It defends against the struggle to recognize the various and divergent grievances among women, including the ways in which women may be implicated in the suffering of other women. And further, it permits political mobilization around the least controversial issue within feminism: child sexual abuse. Given the history of anxiety over sexuality in the culture, however, particularly when the image of the innocent child is invoked, there are tremendous gains that follow from the victory—gains that are harder to achieve on other grounds. But it is a victory with significant costs.

Conclusions

In *Possessing the Secret of Joy,* Alice Walker struggles with the difficulty of achieving an authentic account of the past. In one passage, she raises questions about how we separate the revelatory and defensive aspects of storytelling:

> I mean, if I find myself way off into an improbable tale, imagining it or telling it, then I can guess something horrible has happened to me and that I can't bear to think about it. Wait a minute, I said, considering for the first time, do you think this is how storytelling came into being? That the story is only the mask for the truth? (130)

Where women's fiction explores the ambiguity in chronicling the mythopoetic and historical aspects of memory, clinical and political practice creates anxieties around such ambiguities. Raising questions about women's memories of sexual abuse is particularly anxiety-provoking when the feminist movement is on the defensive. Those who work with abuse survivors and in the anti-violence movement experience directly the damaged side of women's lives and confront as well the difficulties in mobilizing a unified response to patriarchal domination.

The trauma/dissociation model has been important in bridging feminist clinical and political practice and in holding onto a conception of women both as rational agents and as damaged victims. At the same time, this model reinforces traditional constructions of feminine experience that can be debilitating. One problem involves the centering of female disturbances on trauma memories, and of recovery on the retrieval of those memories. The therapeutic preoccupation with the recovery of trauma memory engages women, paradoxically, in a quest that reaffirms their fragility and position of non-recognition. Both therapist and patient assume that women's untold stories are more important than the remembered ones, and that the unrevealed drama provides the key to the kingdom. There is a real possibility here for the trauma story to become a kind of Gothic fairytale, or a Cinderella story with the prince as the perpetrator. The reversals are important but the narrative elements are the same: the fantasy of discovering the missing object (the memory, the phallus) that will make women whole.

Feminists may argue that exploring the ambiguities in women's accounts of abuse, and the problematic aspects of an emerging feminine authority within the professions, is a luxury that the movement cannot yet afford. But if feminism is not able to engage these questions and to shape the terms of public debate, groups hostile to feminism will continue to claim this ground and use it against us.

Feminist discourse on sexual abuse has both sustained inquiry into the long-term, destructive effects of women's sexual victimization and simultaneously had a defensive cast. Ultimately, the trauma model gives over too much to the perpetrator, and leaves women, as survivors, with too little of their own. The alternative is not to jettison the tenuous gains feminism has made in public recognition of the pervasive effects of childhood sexual abuse, but, rather, to insist on the cultural space for a broader range of stories and on multiple readings of those stories.

Works Cited

Alcoff, Linda, and Laura Gray. "Survivor Discourse: Transgression or Recuperation?" *Signs: Journal of Women in Culture and Society* 18, no. 2 (1993): 260–90.

Angelou, Maya. *I Know Why the Caged Bird Sings.* New York: Bantam, 1969.

Armstrong, Helen. "Awareness Grows but Incest Victims Still Mostly Keep to Themselves." *NOW* (Toronto), 1–7 October 1992, 16.

Armstrong, Louise. *Rocking the Cradle of Sexual Politics.* New York: Addison-Wesley, 1994.

Bass, Ellen, and Laura Davis. *The Courage to Heal: A Guide for Women Survivors of Child Sexual Abuse.* 1988. New York: Harper Perennial, 1992.

Benjamin, Jessica. *The Bonds of Love: Psychoanalysis, Feminism, and the Problem of Domination.* New York: Pantheon Books, 1988.

Briere, John N. *Child Abuse Trauma.* Newbury Park: Sage, 1992.

Cornell, William, and Karen A. Olio. "Integrating Affect in Treatment with Adult Survivors of Physical and Sexual Abuse." *American Journal of Orthopsychiatry* 61 (1991): 59–69.

Courtois, C. A., and J. E. Sprei. "Retrospective Incest Therapy for Women." In *Handbook on Sexual Abuse of Children,* ed. Lenore Walker. New York: Springer, 1988.

Cronin, James. "False Memory." *Z Magazine,* April, 1994, 31–37.

Davies, Jody M., and Mary G. Frawley. "Dissociative Processes and Transference-Countertransference Paradigms in the Psychoanalytically Oriented Treatment of Childhood Sexual Abuse." *Psychoanalytic Dialogues* 2 (1991): 5–36.

Davies, Jody M., and Mary G. Frawley. *Treating the Adult Survivor of Childhood Sexual Abuse: A Psychoanalytic Perspective.* New York: Basic Books, 1994.

Edwards, James J., and Pamela C. Alexander. "The Contributions of Family Background to the Long Term Adjustment of Women Sexually Abused as Children." *Journal of Interpersonal Violence.* 7 (1992): 306–20.

Frankel, Fred N. "Adult Reconstructions of Childhood Events in the Multiple Personality Literature." *American Journal of Psychiatry* 150 (1993): 954–58.

Fredrickson, Renee. *Repressed Memories: A Journal of Recovery from Sexual Abuse.* New York: Simon & Schuster, 1992.

Freud, Sigmund. "The Aetiology of Hysteria" (1897). In *The Standard Edition* of *the Complete Works of Sigmund Freud,* ed. James Strachey. London: Hogarth, 1964. 3:189–221.

Goldstein, Eleanor. *Confabulations.* Boca Raton, FL: SIRS Books, 1992.

Herman, Judith Lewis. "The Abuses of Memory." *Mother Jones,* March–April (1993): 3.

Herman, Judith Lewis. *Father-Daughter Incest.* Cambridge: Harvard University Press, 1981.

Herman, Judith Lewis. *Trauma and Recovery.* New York: Basic Books, 1992.

Jacobs, Janet Liebman. "Victimized Daughters: Sexual Violence and the Empathic Female Self." *Signs: Journal of Women in Culture and Society* 19 (1993): 126–45.

Jacobs, Janet Liebman. *Victimized Daughters.* New York: Routledge, 1994.

Johnson, Miriam M. *Strong Mothers, Weak Wives.* Berkeley: University of California Press, 1988.

Loftus, Elizabeth, and Katherine Ketchum. *The Myth of Repressed Memory.* New York: St. Martin's, 1994.

Maltz, Wendy. "Identifying and Treating the Sexual Repercussions of Incest: A Couples Therapy Approach." *Journal of Sex and Marital Therapy* 14 (1988): 142–170.

Manlowe, Jennifer. *Faith Born of Seduction.* New York: New York University Press, 1995.

Nathanson, Constance. *Dangerous Passage.* Philadelphia: Temple University Press, 1991.

Ofshe, Richard, and Ethan Watters. *Making Monsters: False Memories, Psychotherapy, and Sexual Hysteria.* New York: Scribner, 1994.

Root, Maria. "Reconstructing the Impact of Trauma of Personality." In *Personality and Psychopathology: Feminist Reappraisals,* ed. Laura S. Brown and May Ballou. New York: Guilford, 1992. 229–65.

Russell, Diana E. H. *The Secret Trauma: Incest in the Lives of Girls and Women.* New York: Basic Books, 1986.

Shengold, Leonard. *Soul Murder.* New Haven, CT: Yale University Press, 1989.

Spiegel, David. "Hypnosis, Dissociation, and Trauma: Hidden and Overt Observers." In *Repression and Dissociation,* ed. Jerome Singer. Chicago: University of Chicago Press, 1990. 121–42.

Starzecpyzel, Eileen. "The Persophone Complex: Incest Dynamics and the Lesbian Preference." In *Lesbian Psychologies,* ed. Boston Lesbian Psychologies Collective. Urbana and Chicago: University of Illinois Press, 1987. 261–82.

Steiger, Howard, and Maria Zanko. "Sexual Trauma among Eating-Disordered, Psychiatric, and Normal Female Groups: Comparison of Prevalences and Defense Styles." *Journal of Interpersonal Violence* 5 (1990): 74–86.

Van der Kolk, Bessel A. "The Body Keeps the Score: Memory and the Evolving Psychobiology of Posttraumatic Stress." *Harvard Review of Psychiatry* 1 (1994): 253–65.

Van der Kolk, Bessel A. *Psychological Trauma.* Washington, DC: American Psychiatric Press, 1987.

Walker, Alice. *Possessing the Secret of Joy.* New York: Harcourt, Brace, Jovanovich, 1992.

Wasserman, Cathy. "FMS: The Backlash against Survivors." *Sojourner: The Women's Forum,* November 1992, 18–19.

Wylie, Mary Sykes. "Revising the Dream." *Networker,* July/August 1992, 11–23.

Wylie, Mary Sykes. "The Shadow of Doubt." *Networker* September/October 1993, 18–29, 70–73.

Yapko, Michael. *Suggestions of Abuse: True and False Memories of Childhood Sexual Trauma.* New York: Simon and Schuster, 1994.

PART VI
Bodies and Sexualities

By writing her self, woman will return to the body which has been more than confiscated from her, which has been turned into the uncanny stranger on display—the ailing or dead figure, which so often turns out to be the nasty companion, the cause and location of inhibitions. Censor the body and you censor breath and speech at the same time.

Write your self. Your body must be heard. Only then will the immense resources of the unconscious spring forth. Our naphtha will spread, throughout the world, without dollars—black or gold—nonassessed values that will change the rules of the old game.

To write. An act which will not only "realize" the decensored relation of woman to her sexuality, to her womanly being, giving her access to her native strength; it will give her back her goods, her pleasures, her organs, her immense bodily territories which have been kept under seal; it will tear her away from the superegoized structure in which she has always occupied the place reserved for the guilty (guilty of everything, guilty at every turn: for having desires, for not having any; for being frigid, for being "too hot"; for not being both at once; for being too motherly and not enough; for having children and for not having any; for nursing and for not nursing . . .)—tear her away by means of this research, this job of analysis and illumination, this emancipation of the marvelous text of her self that she must urgently learn to speak. A woman without a body, dumb, blind, can't possibly by a good fighter. She is reduced to being the servant of the militant male, his shadow. We must kill the false woman who is preventing the live one from breathing. Inscribe the breath of the whole woman.

Hélène Cixous, "The Laugh of the Medusa," in *New French Feminisms,* ed. Elaine Marks and Isabelle de Courtivron (New York: Schocken Books, 1981), 250

People are starting to ask me about fashion. I love that! Maybe they think the doctor sewed in some fashion sense during my genital conversion surgery.

I see fashion as a proclamation or manifestation of identity, so, as long as identities are important, fashion will continue to be important. The link between fashion and identity begins to get real interesting, however, in the case of people who don't fall clearly into a culturally-recognized identity—people like me. My identity as a transsexual lesbian whose female lover is becoming a man is manifest in my fashion statement; both my identity and fashion are based on collage. You know—a little bit from here, a little bit from there? Sort of a cut-and-paste thing.

—Kate Bornstein, *Gender Outlaw* (New York: Vintage Books, 1995), 3

30 Introduction to *Bodies That Matter*

Judith Butler

Why should our bodies end at the skin, or include at best other beings encapsulated by skin?

       —Donna Haraway, *A Manifesto for Cyborgs*

If one really thinks about the body as such, there is no possible outline of the body as such. There are thinkings of the systematicity of the body, there are value codings of the body. The body, as such, cannot be thought, and I certainly cannot approach it.

    —Gayatri Chakravorty Spivak, "In a Word," interview with Ellen Rooney

There is no nature, only the effects of nature: denaturalization or naturalization.

       —Jacques Derrida, *Donner le Temps*

Is there a way to link the question of the materiality of the body to the performativity of gender? And how does the category of "sex" figure within such a relationship? Consider first that sexual difference is often invoked as an issue of material differences. Sexual difference, however, is never simply a function of material differences which are not in some way both marked and formed by discursive practices. Further, to claim that sexual differences are indissociable from discursive demarcations is not the same as claiming that discourse causes sexual difference. The category of "sex" is, from the start, normative; it is what Foucault has called a "regulatory ideal." In this sense, then, "sex" not only functions as a norm, but is part of a regulatory practice that produces the bodies it governs, that is, whose regulatory force is made clear as a kind of productive power, the power to produce—demarcate, circulate, differentiate—the bodies it controls. Thus, "sex" is a regulatory ideal whose materialization is compelled, and this materialization takes place (or fails to take place) through certain highly regulated practices. In other words, "sex" is an ideal construct which is forcibly materialized through time. It is not a simple fact or static condition of a body, but a process whereby regulatory norms materialize "sex" and achieve this materialization through a forcible reiteration of those norms. That this reiteration is necessary is a sign that materialization is never quite complete, that bodies never quite comply with the norms by which their materialization is impelled. Indeed, it is the instabilities, the possibilities for rematerialization, opened up by this process that mark one domain in which the force of the regulatory law can be turned against itself to spawn rearticulations that call into question the hegemonic force of that very regulatory law.

But how, then, does the notion of gender performativity relate to this conception of materialization? In the first instance, performativity must be understood not as a singular or deliberate "act," but, rather, as the reiterative and citational practice by which discourse produces the effects that it names. What will, I hope, become clear in what follows is that the regulatory norms of "sex" work in a performative fashion to constitute the materiality of bodies and, more specifically, to materialize the body's sex, to materialize sexual difference in the service of the consolidation of the heterosexual imperative.

In this sense, what constitutes the fixity of the body, its contours, its movements, will be fully material, but materiality will be rethought as the effect of power, as power's most productive effect. And there will be no way to understand "gender" as a cultural construct which is imposed upon the surface of matter, understood either as "the body" or its given sex. Rather, once "sex" itself is understood in its normativity, the materiality of the body will not be thinkable apart from the materialization of that regulatory norm. "Sex" is, thus, not simply what one has, or a static description of what one is: it will be one of the norms by which the "one" becomes viable at all, that which qualifies a body for life within the domain of cultural intelligibility.[1]

At stake in such a reformulation of the materiality of bodies will be the following: (1) the recasting of the matter of bodies as the effect of a dynamic of power, such that the matter of bodies will be indissociable from the regulatory norms that govern their materialization and the signification of those material effects; (2) the understanding of performativity not as the act by which a subject brings into being what she/he names, but, rather, as that reiterative power of discourse to produce the phenomena that it regulates and constrains; (3) the construal of "sex" no longer as a bodily given on which the construct of gender is artificially imposed, but as a cultural norm which governs the materialization of bodies; (4) a rethinking of the process by which a bodily norm is assumed, appropriated, taken on as not, strictly speaking, undergone *by a subject,* but rather that the subject, the speaking "I," is formed by virtue of having gone through such a process of assuming a sex; and (5) a linking of this process of "assuming" a sex with the question of *identification,* and with the discursive means by which the heterosexual imperative enables certain sexed identifications and forecloses and/or disavows other identifications. This exclusionary matrix by which subjects are formed thus requires the simultaneous production of a domain of abject beings, those who are not yet "subjects," but who form the constitutive outside to the domain of the subject. The abject[2] designates here precisely those "unlivable" and "uninhabitable" zones of social life which are nevertheless densely populated by those who do not enjoy the status of the subject, but whose living under the sign of the "unlivable" is required to circumscribe the domain of the subject. This zone of uninhabitability will constitute the defining limit of the subject's domain; it will constitute that site of dreaded identification against which—and by virtue of which—the domain of the subject will circumscribe its own claim to autonomy and to life. In this sense, then, the subject is constituted through the force of exclusion and abjection, one which produces a constitutive outside to the subject, an abjected outside, which is, after all, "inside" the subject as its own founding repudiation.

The forming of a subject requires an identification with the normative phantasm of "sex," and this identification takes place through a repudiation which produces a domain of abjection, a repudiation without which the subject cannot emerge. This is a repudiation which creates the valence of "abjection" and its status for the subject as a threatening spectre. Further, the materialization of a given sex will centrally concern *the regulation of identificatory practices* such that the identification with the abjection of sex will be persistently disavowed. And yet, this disavowed abjection will threaten to expose the self-grounding presumptions of the sexed subject, grounded as that subject is in a repudiation whose consequences it cannot fully control. The task will be to consider this threat and disruption not as a permanent contestation of social norms condemned to the pathos of perpetual failure, but rather as a critical resource in the struggle to rearticulate the very terms of symbolic legitimacy and intelligibility.

Lastly, the mobilization of the categories of sex within political discourse will be haunted in some ways by the very instabilities that the categories effectively produce and foreclose. Although the political discourses that mobilize identity categories tend to cultivate identifications in the service of a political goal, it may be that the persistence of disidentification is equally crucial to the rearticulation of democratic contestation. Indeed, it may be precisely through practices which underscore disidentification with those regulatory norms by which sexual difference is materialized that both feminist and queer politics are mobilized. Such collective disidentifications can facilitate a reconceptualization of which bodies matter, and which bodies are yet to emerge as critical matters of concern.

From Construction to Materialization

The relation between culture and nature presupposed by some models of gender "construction" implies a culture or an agency of the social which acts upon a nature, which is itself presupposed as a passive surface, outside the social and yet its necessary counterpart. One question that feminists have raised, then, is whether the discourse which figures the action of construction as a kind of imprinting or imposition is not tacitly masculinist, whereas the figure of the passive surface, awaiting that penetrating act whereby meaning is endowed, is not tacitly or—perhaps—quite obviously feminine. Is sex to gender as feminine is to masculine?[3]

Other feminist scholars have argued that the very concept of nature needs to be rethought, for the concept of nature has a history, and the figuring of nature as the blank and lifeless page, as that which is, as it were, always already dead, is decidedly modern, linked perhaps to the emergence of technological means of domination. Indeed, some have argued that a rethinking of "nature" as a set of dynamic interrelations suits both feminist and ecological aims (and has for some produced an otherwise unlikely alliance with the work of Gilles Deleuze). This rethinking also calls into question the model of construction whereby the social unilaterally acts on the natural and invests it with its parameters and its meanings. Indeed, as much as the radical distinction between sex and gender has been crucial to the de Beauvoirian version of feminism, it has come under criticism in more recent years for degrading the natural as that which is "before" intelligibility, in need of the mark, if not the mar, of the social to signify, to be known, to acquire value. This misses the point that nature has a history, and not merely a social one, but, also, that sex is positioned ambiguously in relation to that concept and its history. The concept of "sex" is itself troubled terrain, formed through a series of contestations over what ought to be decisive criteria for distinguishing between the two sexes; the concept of sex has a history that is covered over by the figure of the site or surface of inscription. Figured as such a site or surface, however, the natural is construed as that which is also without value; moreover, it assumes its value at the same time that it assumes its social character, that is, at the same time that nature relinquishes itself as the natural. According to this view, then, the social construction of the natural presupposes the cancellation of the natural by the social. Insofar as it relies on this construal, the sex/gender distinction founders along parallel lines; if gender is the social significance that sex assumes within a given culture—and for the sake of argument we will let "social" and "cultural" stand in an uneasy interchangeability—then what, if anything, is left of "sex" once it has assumed its social character as gender? At issue is the meaning of "assumption," where to be "assumed" is to be taken up into a more elevated sphere, as in "the Assumption of the Virgin." If gender consists of the social meanings that sex assumes, then sex does not *accrue* social meanings as additive properties but, rather, *is replaced by* the social meanings it takes on; sex is relinquished in the course of that assumption, and gender emerges, not as a term in a continued relationship of opposition to sex, but as the term which absorbs and displaces "sex," the mark of its full substantiation into gender or what, from a materialist point of view, might constitute a full *de*substantiation.

When the sex/gender distinction is joined with a notion of radical linguistic constructivism, the problem becomes even worse, for the "sex" which is referred to as prior to gender will itself be a postulation, a construction, offered within language, as that which is prior to language, prior to construction. But this sex posited as prior to construction will, by virtue of being posited, become the effect of that very positing, the construction of construction. If gender is the social construction of sex, and if there is no access to this "sex" except by means of its construction, then it appears not only that sex is absorbed by gender, but that "sex" becomes

something like a fiction, perhaps a fantasy, retroactively installed at a prelinguistic site to which there is no direct access.

But is it right to claim that "sex" vanishes altogether, that it is a fiction over and against what is true, that it is a fantasy over and against what is reality? Or do these very oppositions need to be rethought such that if "sex" is a fiction, it is one within whose necessities we live, without which life itself would be unthinkable? And if "sex" is a fantasy, is it perhaps a phantasmatic field that constitutes the very terrain of cultural intelligibility? Would such a rethinking of such conventional oppositions entail a rethinking of "constructivism" in its usual sense?

The radical constructivist position has tended to produce the premise that both refutes and confirms its own enterprise. If such a theory cannot take account of sex as the site or surface on which it acts, then it ends up presuming sex as the unconstructed, and so concedes the limits of linguistic constructivism, inadvertently circumscribing that which remains unaccountable within the terms of construction. If, on the other hand, sex is a contrived premise, a fiction, then gender does not presume a sex which it acts upon, but rather, gender produces the misnomer of a prediscursive "sex," and the meaning of construction becomes that of linguistic monism, whereby everything is only and always language. Then, what ensues is an exasperated debate which many of us have tired of hearing: Either (1) constructivism is reduced to a position of linguistic monism, whereby linguistic construction is understood to be generative and deterministic. Critics making that presumption can be heard to say, "If everything is discourse, what about the body?" or (2) when construction is figuratively reduced to a verbal action which appears to presuppose a subject, critics working within such a presumption can be heard to say, "If gender is constructed, then who is doing the constructing?"; though, of course, (3) the most pertinent formulation of this question is the following: "If the subject is constructed, then who is constructing the subject?" In the first case, construction has taken the place of a godlike agency which not only causes but composes everything which is its object; it is the divine performative, bringing into being and exhaustively constituting that which it names, or, rather, it is that kind of transitive referring which names and inaugurates at once. For something to be constructed, according to this view of construction, is for it to be created and determined through that process.

In the second and third cases, the seductions of grammar appear to hold sway; the critic asks, Must there not be a human agent, a subject, if you will, who guides the course of construction? If the first version of constructivism presumes that construction operates deterministically, making a mockery of human agency, the second understands constructivism as presupposing a voluntarist subject who makes its gender through an instrumental action. A construction is understood in this latter case to be a kind of manipulable artifice, a conception that not only presupposes a subject, but rehabilitates precisely the voluntarist subject of humanism that constructivism has, on occasion, sought to put into question.

If gender is a construction, must there be an "I" or a "we" who enacts or performs that construction? How can there be an activity, a constructing, without presupposing an agent who precedes and performs that activity? How would we account for the motivation and direction of construction without such a subject? As a rejoinder, I would suggest that it takes a certain suspicion toward grammar to reconceive the matter in a different light. For if gender is constructed, it is not necessarily constructed by an "I" or a "we" who stands before that construction in any spatial or temporal sense of "before." Indeed, it is unclear that there can be an "I" or a "we" who

has not been submitted, subjected to gender, where gendering is, among other things, the differentiating relations by which speaking subjects come into being. Subjected to gender, but subjectivated by gender, the "I" neither precedes nor follows the process of this gendering, but emerges only within and as the matrix of gender relations themselves.

Such attributions or interpellations contribute to that field of discourse and power that orchestrates, delimits, and sustains that which qualifies as "the human." We see this most clearly in the examples of those abjected beings who do not appear properly gendered; it is their very humanness that comes into question. Indeed, the construction of gender operates through *exclusionary* means, such that the human is not only produced over and against the inhuman, but through a set of foreclosures, radical erasures, that are, strictly speaking, refused the possibility of cultural articulation. Hence, it is not enough to claim that human subjects are constructed, for the construction of the human is a differential operation that produces the more and the less "human," the inhuman, the humanly unthinkable. These excluded sites come to bound the "human" as its constitutive outside, and to haunt those boundaries as the persistent possibility of their disruption and rearticulation.[4]

Paradoxically, the inquiry into the kinds of erasures and exclusions by which the construction of the subject operates is no longer constructivism, but neither is it essentialism. For there is an "outside" to what is constructed by discourse, but this is not an absolute "outside," an ontological thereness that exceeds or counters the boundaries of discourse;[5] as a constitutive "outside," it is that which can only be thought—when it can—in relation to that discourse, at and as its most tenuous borders. The debate between constructivism and essentialism thus misses the point of deconstruction altogether, for the point has never been that "everything is discursively constructed"; that point, when and where it is made, belongs to a kind of discursive monism or linguisticism that refuses the constitutive force of exclusion, erasure, violent foreclosure, abjection and its disruptive return within the very terms of discursive legitimacy.

And to say that there is a matrix of gender relations that institutes and sustains the subject is not to claim that there is a singular matrix that acts in a singular and deterministic way to produce a subject as its effect. That is to install the "matrix" in the subject-position within a grammatical formulation which itself needs to be rethought. Indeed, the propositional form "Discourse constructs the subject" retains the subject-position of the grammatical formulation even as it reverses the place of subject and discourse. Construction must mean more than such a simple reversal of terms.

There are defenders and critics of construction, who construe that position along structuralist lines. They often claim that there are structures that construct the subject, impersonal forces, such as Culture or Discourse or Power, where these terms occupy the grammatical site of the subject after the "human" has been dislodged from its place. In such a view, the grammatical and metaphysical place of the subject is retained even as the candidate that occupies that place appears to rotate. As a result, construction is still understood as a unilateral process initiated by a prior subject, fortifying that presumption of the metaphysics of the subject that where there is activity, there lurks behind it an initiating and willful subject. On such a view, discourse or language or the social becomes personified, and in the personification the metaphysics of the subject is reconsolidated.

In this second view, construction is not an activity, but an act, one which happens once and whose effects are firmly fixed. Thus, constructivism is reduced to determinism and implies the evacuation or displacement of human agency.

This view informs the misreading by which Foucault is criticized for "personifying" power: if power is misconstrued as a grammatical and metaphysical subject, and if that metaphysical site within humanist discourse has been the privileged site of the human, then power appears to have displaced the human as the origin of activity. But if Foucault's view of power is understood as the disruption and subversion of this grammar and metaphysics of the subject, if power orchestrates the formation and sustenance of subjects, then it cannot be accounted for in terms of the "subject" which is its effect. And here it would be no more right to claim that the term "construction" belongs at the grammatical site of subject, for construction is neither a subject nor its act, but a process of reiteration by which both "subject" and "acts" come to appear at all. There is no power that acts, but only a reiterated acting that is power in its persistence and instability.

What I would propose in place of these conceptions of construction is a return to the notion of matter, not as site or surface, but as *a process of materialization that stabilizes over time to produce the effect of boundary, fixity, and surface we call matter*. That matter is always materialized has, I think, to be thought in relation to the productive and, indeed, materializing effects of regulatory power in the Foucaultian sense.[6] Thus, the question is no longer, How is gender constituted as and through a certain interpretation of sex? (a question that leaves the "matter" of sex untheorized), but rather, Through what regulatory norms is sex itself materialized? And how is it that treating the materiality of sex as a given presupposes and consolidates the normative conditions of its own emergence?

Crucially, then, construction is neither a single act nor a causal process initiated by a subject and culminating in a set of fixed effects.

Construction not only takes place *in* time, but is itself a temporal process which operates through the reiteration of norms; sex is both produced and destabilized in the course of this reiteration.[7] As a sedimented effect of a reiterative or ritual practice, sex acquires its naturalized effect, and, yet, it is also by virtue of this reiteration that gaps and fissures are opened up as the constitutive instabilities in such constructions, as that which escapes or exceeds the norm, as that which cannot be wholly defined or fixed by the repetitive labor of that norm. This instability is the *de*constituting possibility in the very process of repetition, the power that undoes the very effects by which "sex" is stabilized, the possibility to put the consolidation of the norms of "sex" into a potentially productive crisis.[8]

Certain formulations of the radical constructivist position appear almost compulsively to produce a moment of recurrent exasperation, for it seems that when the constructivist is construed as a linguistic idealist, the constructivist refutes the reality of bodies, the relevance of science, the alleged facts of birth, aging, illness, and death. The critic might also suspect the constructivist of a certain somatophobia and seek assurances that this abstracted theorist will admit that there are, minimally, sexually differentiated parts, activities, capacities, hormonal and chromosomal differences that can be conceded without reference to "construction." Although at this moment I want to offer an absolute reassurance to my interlocutor, some anxiety prevails. To "concede" the undeniability of "sex" or its "materiality" is always to concede some version of "sex," some formation of "materiality." Is the discourse in and through which that concession occurs—and, yes, that concession invariably does occur—not itself formative of the very phenomenon that it concedes? To claim that discourse is formative is not to claim that it originates, causes, or exhaustively composes that which it concedes; rather, it is to claim that there

is no reference to a pure body which is not at the same time a further formation of that body. In this sense, the linguistic capacity to refer to sexed bodies is not denied, but the very meaning of "referentiality" is altered. In philosophical terms, the constative claim is always to some degree performative.

In relation to sex, then, if one concedes the materiality of sex or of the body, does that very conceding operate—performatively—to materialize that sex? And further, how is it that the reiterated concession of that sex—one which need not take place in speech or writing but might be "signaled" in a much more inchoate way—constitutes the sedimentation and production of that material effect?

The moderate critic might concede that *some part* of "sex" is constructed, but some other is certainly not, and then, of course, find him or herself under some obligation not only to draw the line between what is and is not constructed, but to explain how it is that "sex" comes in parts whose differentiation is not a matter of construction. But as that line of demarcation between such ostensible parts gets drawn, the "unconstructed" becomes bounded once again through a signifying practice, and the very boundary which is meant to protect some part of sex from the taint of constructivism is now defined by the anti-constructivist's own construction. Is construction something which happens to a ready-made object, a pregiven thing, and does it happen *in degrees?* Or are we perhaps referring on both sides of the debate to an inevitable practice of signification, of demarcating and delimiting that to which we then "refer," such that our "references" always presuppose—and often conceal—this prior delimitation? Indeed, to "refer" naively or directly to such an extra-discursive object will always require the prior delimitation of the extra-discursive. And insofar as the extra-discursive is delimited, it is formed by the very discourse from which it seeks to free itself. This delimitation, which often is enacted as an untheorized presupposition in any act of description, marks a boundary that includes and excludes, that decides, as it were, what will and will not be the stuff of the object to which we then refer. This marking off will have some normative force and, indeed, some violence, for it can construct only through erasing; it can bound a thing only through enforcing a certain criterion, a principle of selectivity.

What will and will not be included within the boundaries of "sex" will be set by a more or less tacit operation of exclusion. If we call into question the fixity of the structuralist law that divides and bounds the "sexes" by virtue of their dyadic differentiation within the heterosexual matrix, it will be from the exterior regions of that boundary (not from a "position," but from the discursive possibilities opened up by the constitutive outside of hegemonic positions), and it will constitute the disruptive return of the excluded from within the very logic of the heterosexual symbolic.

The trajectory of this text, then, will pursue the possibility of such disruption, but proceed indirectly by responding to two interrelated questions that have been posed to constructivist accounts of gender, not to defend constructivism per se, but to interrogate the erasures and exclusions that constitute its limits. These criticisms presuppose a set of metaphysical oppositions between materialism and idealism embedded in received grammar which, I will argue, are critically redefined by a poststructuralist rewriting of discursive performativity as it operates in the materialization of sex.

Performativity as Citationality

When, in Lacanian parlance, one is said to assume a "sex," the grammar of the phrase creates the expectation that there is a "one" who, upon waking, looks up and deliberates on which "sex" it will assume today, a grammar in which "assumption" is quickly assimilated to the notion of a highly reflective choice. But if this "assumption" is *compelled* by a regulatory apparatus of heterosexuality, one which reiterates itself through the forcible production of "sex," then the "assumption" of sex is constrained from the start. And if there is *agency,* it is to be found, paradoxically, in the possibilities opened up in and by that constrained appropriation of the regulatory law, by the materialization of that law, the compulsory appropriation of and identification with those normative demands. The forming, crafting, bearing, circulation, signification of that sexed body will not be a set of actions performed in compliance with the law; on the contrary, they will be a set of actions mobilized by the law, the citational accumulation and dissimulation of the law that produces material effects, the lived necessity of those effects as well as the lived contestation of that necessity.

Performativity is thus not a singular "act," for it is always a reiteration of a norm or set of norms, and to the extent that it acquires an act-like status in the present, it conceals or dissimulates the conventions of which it is a repetition. Moreover, this act is not primarily theatrical; indeed, its apparent theatricality is produced to the extent that its historicity remains dissimulated (and, conversely, its theatricality gains a certain inevitability given the impossibility of a full disclosure of its historicity). Within speech act theory, a performative is that discursive practice that enacts or produces that which it names.[9] According to the biblical rendition of the performative, i.e., "Let there be light!" it appears that it is by virtue of *the power of a subject or its will* that a phenomenon is named into being. In a critical reformulation of the performative, Derrida makes clear that this power is not the function of an originating will, but is always derivative:

Could a performative utterance succeed if its formulation did not repeat a "coded" or iterable utterance, or in other words, if the formula I pronounce in order to open a meeting, launch a ship or a marriage were not identifiable as conforming with an iterable model, if it were not then identifiable in some way as a "citation"? . . . in such a typology, the category of intention will not disappear; it will have its place, but from that place it will no longer be able to govern the entire scene and system of utterance [*l'énonciation*].[10]

To what extent does discourse gain the authority to bring about what it names through citing the conventions of authority? And does a subject appear as the author of its discursive effects to the extent that the citational practice by which he/she is conditioned and mobilized remains unmarked? Indeed, could it be that the production of the subject as originator of his/her effects is precisely a consequence of this dissimulated citationality"? Further, if a subject comes to be through a subjection to the norms of sex, can we read that "assumption" as precisely a modality of this kind of citationality? In other words, the norm of sex takes hold to the extent that it is "cited" as such a norm, but it also derives its power through the citations that it compels. And how it is that we might read the "citing" of the norms of sex as the process of approximating or "identifying with" such norms?

Further, to what extent within psychoanalysis is the sexed body secured through identificatory practices governed by regulatory schemas? Identification is used here not as an imitative activity by which a conscious being models itself after another; on the contrary, identification is the assimilating passion by which an ego first emerges.[11] Freud argues that "the ego is first and foremost a bodily ego," that this ego is, further,

"a projection of a surface,"[12] what we might re-describe as an imaginary morphology. Moreover, I would argue, this imaginary morphology is not a presocial or presymbolic operation, but is itself orchestrated through regulatory schemas that produce intelligible morphological possibilities. These regulatory schemas are not timeless structures, but historically revisable criteria of intelligibility which produce and vanquish bodies that matter.

If the formulation of a bodily ego, a sense of stable contour, and the fixing of spatial boundary are achieved through identificatory practices, and if psychoanalysis documents the hegemonic workings of those identifications, can we then read psychoanalysis for the inculcation of the heterosexual matrix at the level of bodily morphogenesis? What Lacan calls the "assumption" or "accession" to the symbolic law can be read as a kind of *citing of* the law, and so offers an opportunity to link the question of the materialization of "sex" with the reworking of performativity as citationality. Although Lacan claims that the symbolic law has a semi-autonomous status prior to the assumption of sexed positions by a subject, these normative positions, i.e., the "sexes," are only known through the approximations that they occasion. The force and necessity of these norms ("sex" as a symbolic function is to be understood as a kind of commandment or injunction) are thus functionally *dependent on* the approximation and citation of the law; the law without its approximation is no law or, rather, it remains a governing law only for those who would affirm it on the basis of religious faith. If "sex" is assumed in the same way that a law is cited . . . then "the law of sex" is repeatedly fortified and idealized as the law only to the extent that it is reiterated as the law, produced as the law, the anterior and inapproximable ideal, by the very citations it is said to command. Reading the meaning of "assumption" in Lacan as citation, the law is no longer given in a fixed form *prior* to its citation, but is produced through citation as that which precedes and exceeds the mortal approximations enacted by the subject.

In this way, the symbolic law in Lacan can be subject to the same kind of critique that Nietzsche formulated of the notion of God: the power attributed to this prior and ideal power is derived and deflected from the attribution itself.[13] It is this insight into the illegitimacy of the symbolic law of sex that is dramatized to a certain degree in the contemporary film *Paris Is Burning*: the ideal that is mirrored depends on that very mirroring to be sustained as an ideal. And though the symbolic appears to be a force that cannot be contravened without psychosis, the symbolic ought to be rethought as a series of normativizing injunctions that secure the borders of sex through the threat of psychosis, abjection, psychic unlivability. And further, this "law" can only remain a law to the extent that it compels the differentiated citations and approximations called "feminine" and "masculine." The presumption that the symbolic law of sex enjoys a separable ontology prior and autonomous to its assumption is contravened by the notion that the citation of the law is the very mechanism of its production and articulation. What is "forced" by the symbolic, then, is a citation of its law that reiterates and consolidates the ruse of its own force. What would it mean to "cite" the law to produce it differently, to "cite" the law in order to reiterate and coopt its power, to expose the heterosexual matrix and to displace the effect of its necessity?

The process of that sedimentation or what we might call *materialization* will be a kind of citationality, the acquisition of being through the citing of power, a citing that establishes an originary complicity with power in the formation of the "I."

In this sense, the agency denoted by the performativity of "sex" will be directly counter to any notion of a voluntarist subject who exists

quite apart from the regulatory norms which she/he opposes. The paradox of subjectivation (*assujetissement*) is precisely that the subject who would resist such norms is itself enabled, if not produced, by such norms. Although this constitutive constraint does not foreclose the possibility of agency, it does locate agency as a reiterative or rearticulatory practice, immanent to power, and not a relation of external opposition to power.

As a result of this reformulation of performativity, (a) gender performativity cannot be theorized apart from the forcible and reiterative practice of regulatory sexual regimes; (b) the account of agency conditioned by those very regimes of discourse/power cannot be conflated with voluntarism or individualism, much less with consumerism, and in no way presupposes a choosing subject; (c) the regime of heterosexuality operates to circumscribe and contour the "materiality" of sex, and that "materiality" is formed and sustained through and as a materialization of regulatory norms that are in part those of heterosexual hegemony; (d) the materialization of norms requires those identificatory processes by which norms are assumed or appropriated, and these identifications precede and enable the formation of a subject, but are not, strictly speaking, performed by a subject; and (e) the limits of constructivism are exposed at those boundaries of bodily life where abjected or delegitimated bodies fail to count as "bodies." If the materiality of sex is demarcated in discourse, then this demarcation will produce a domain of excluded and delegitimated "sex." Hence, it will be as important to think about how and to what end bodies are constructed as it will be to think about how and to what end bodies are *not* constructed and, further, to ask how bodies which fail to materialize provide the necessary "outside," if not the necessary support, for the bodies which, in materializing the norm, qualify as bodies that matter.

How, then, can one think through the matter

of bodies as a kind of materialization governed by regulatory norms in order to ascertain the workings of heterosexual hegemony in the formation of what qualifies as a viable body? How does that materialization of the norm in bodily formation produce a domain of abjected bodies, a field of deformation, which, in failing to qualify as the fully human, fortifies those regulatory norms? What challenge does that excluded and abjected realm produce to a symbolic hegemony that might force a radical rearticulation of what qualifies as bodies that matter, ways of living that count as "life," lives worth protecting, lives worth saving, lives worth grieving?

Notes

This chapter is the first part of the "Introduction" to *Bodies That Matter: On the Discursive Limits of "Sex,"* Judith P. Butler (New York and London: Routledge, 1993).

1.   Clearly, sex is not the only such norm by which bodies become materialized, and it is unclear whether "sex" can operate as a norm apart from other normative requirements on bodies. This will become clear in later sections of this text.

2.   Abjection (in latin, *ab-jicere*) literally means to cast off, away, or out and, hence, presupposes and produces a domain of agency from which it is differentiated. Here the casting away resonates with the psychoanalytic notion of *Verwerfung*, implying a foreclosure which founds the subject and which, accordingly, establishes that foundation as tenuous. Whereas the psychoanalytic notion of *Verwerfung*, translated as "foreclosure," produces sociality through a repudiation of a primary signifier which produces an unconscious or, in Lacan's theory, the register of the real, the notion of *abjection* designates a degraded or cast-out status within the terms of sociality. Indeed, what is foreclosed or repudiated within psychoanalytic terms is precisely what may not reenter the field of the social without threatening psychosis, that is, the dissolution of the subject itself. I want to propose that certain abject zones within sociality also deliver this threat, con-

stituting zones of uninhabitability which a subject fantasizes as threatening its own integrity with the prospect of a psychotic dissolution ("I would rather die than do or be that"). See the entry under "Forclusion" in Jean Laplanche and J.-B. Pontalis, *Vocabulaire de la psychanalyse* (Paris: Presses Universitaires de France, 1967), 163–67.

3.   See Sherry Ortner, "Is Female to Male as Nature Is to Culture?" in *Woman, Culture, and Society,* ed. Michelle Rosaldo and Louise Lamphere (Stanford: Stanford University Press, 1974), 67–88.

4.   For different but related approaches to this problematic of exclusion, abjection, and the creation of "the human," see Julia Kristeva, *Powers of Horror: An Essay on Abjection,* trans. Leon Roudiez (New York: Columbia University Press, 1982); John Fletcher and Andrew Benjamin, eds., *Abjection, Melancholia and Love: The Work of Julia Kristeva* (New York and London: Routledge, 1990); Jean-François Lyotard, *The Inhuman: Reflections on Time,* trans. Geoffrey Bennington and Rachel Bowlby (Stanford: Stanford University Press, 1991).

5.   For a very provocative reading which shows how the problem of linguistic referentiality is linked with the specific problem of referring to bodies, and what might be meant by "reference" in such a case, see Cathy Caruth, "The Claims of Reference," *Yale Journal of Criticism* 4, no. 1 (Fall 1990): 193–206.

6.   Although Foucault distinguishes between juridical and productive models of power in *The History of Sexuality, Volume One,* trans. Robert Hurley (New York: Vintage, 1978), I have argued that the two models presuppose each other. The production of a subject—its subjection (*assujetissement*)—is one means of its regulation. See my "Sexual Inversions" in Domna Stanton, ed., *Discourses of Sexuality* (Ann Arbor: University of Michigan Press, 1992), 344–61.

7.   It is not simply a matter of construing performativity as a repetition of acts, as if "acts" remain intact and self-identical as they are repeated in time, and where "time" is understood as external to the "acts" themselves. On the contrary, an act is itself a repetition, a sedimentation, and congealment of the past which is precisely foreclosed in its act-like status. In this sense an "act" is always a provisional failure of memory. In what follows, I make use of the Lacanian notion that every act is to be construed as a repetition, the repetition of what cannot be recollected, of the

irrecoverable, and is thus the haunting spectre of the subject's deconstitution. The Derridean notion of iterability, formulated in response to the theorization of speech acts by John Searle and J. L. Austin, also implies that every act is itself a recitation, the citing of a prior chain of acts which are implied in a present act and which perpetually drain any "present" act of its presentness. See note 9 below for the difference between a repetition in the service of the fantasy of mastery (i.e., a repetition of acts which build the subject, and which are said to be the constructive or constituting acts of a subject) and a notion of repetition-compulsion, taken from Freud, which breaks apart that fantasy of mastery and sets its limits.

8.   The notion of temporality ought not to be construed as a simple succession of distinct "moments," all of which are equally distant from one another. Such a spatialized mapping of time substitutes a certain mathematical model for the kind of duration which resists such spatializing metaphors. Efforts to describe or name this temporal span tend to engage spatial mapping, as philosophers from Bergson through Heidegger have argued. Hence, it is important to underscore the effect of *sedimentation* that the temporality of construction implies. Here what are called "moments" are not distinct and equivalent units of time, for the "past" will be the accumulation and congealing of such "moments" to the point of their indistinguishability. But it will also consist of that which is refused from construction, the domains of the repressed, forgotten, and the irrecoverably foreclosed. That which is not included—exteriorized by boundary—as a phenomenal constituent of the sedimented effect called "construction" will be as crucial to its definition as that which is included; this exteriority is not distinguishable as a "moment." Indeed, the "moment" may well be nothing other than a retrospective fantasy of mathematical mastery imposed upon the interrupted durations of the past.

To argue that construction is fundamentally a matter of iteration is to make the temporal modality of "construction" into a priority. To the extent that such a theory requires a spatialization of time through the postulation of discrete and bounded moments, this temporal account of construction presupposes a spatialization of temporality itself, what one might, following Heidegger, understand as the reduction of temporality to time.

The Foucaultian emphasis on *convergent* relations of power (which might in a tentative way be contrasted with the Derridean emphasis on iterability) implies a mapping of power relations that in the course of a genealogical process form a constructed effect. The notion of convergence presupposes both motion and space; as a result, it appears to elude the paradox noted above in which the very account of temporality requires the spatialization of the "moment." On the other hand, Foucault's account of convergence does not fully theorize what is at work in the "movement" by which power and discourse are said to converge. In a sense, the "mapping" of power does not fully theorize temporality.

Significantly, the Derridean analysis of iterability is to be distinguished from simple repetition in which the distances between temporal "moments" are treated as uniform in their spatial extension. The "betweenness" that differentiates "moments" of time is not one that can, within Derridean terms, be spatialized or bounded as an identifiable object. It is the non-thematizable *différance* which erodes and contests any and all claims to discrete identity, including the discrete identity of the "moment." What differentiates moments is not a spatially extended duration, for if it were, it would also count as a "moment," and so fail to account for what falls between moments. This "entre," that which is at once "between" and "outside," is something like non-thematizable space and non-thematizable time as they converge.

Foucault's language of construction includes terms like "augmentation," "proliferation," and "convergence," all of which presume a temporal domain not explicitly theorized. Part of the problem here is that whereas Foucault appears to want his account of genealogical effects to be historically specific, he would favor an account of genealogy over a philosophical account of temporality. In "The Subject and Power" (*Michel Foucault: Beyond Structuralism and Hermeneutics,* ed. Hubert Dreyfus and Paul Rabinow [Chicago: Northwestern University Press, 1983]), Foucault refers to "the diversity of . . . logical sequence" that characterizes power relations. He would doubtless reject the apparent linearity implied by models of iterability which links them with the linearity of older models of historical sequence. And yet, we do not receive a specification of "sequence": Is it the very notion of "sequence" that varies historically, or are there configurations of sequence that vary, with sequence itself remaining invariant? The specific social formation and figuration of temporality is in some ways unattended by both positions. Here one might consult the work of Pierre Bourdieu to understand the temporality of social construction.

9.   See J. L. Austin, *How to Do Things with Words,* ed. J. O. Urmson and Marina Sbisà (Cambridge: Harvard University Press, 1955), and *Philosophical Papers* (Oxford: Oxford University Press, 1961), especially 233–52; Shoshana Felman, *The Literary Speech-Act: Don Juan with J. L. Austin, or Seduction in Two Languages,* trans. Catherine Porter (Ithaca: Cornell University Press, 1983); Barbara Johnson, "Poetry and Performative Language: Mallarmé and Austin," in *The Critical Difference: Essays in the Contemporary Rhetoric of Reading* (Baltimore: Johns Hopkins University Press, 1980), 52–66; Mary Louise Pratt, *A Speech Act Theory of Literary Discourse* (Bloomington: Indiana University Press, 1977); and Ludwig Wittgenstein, *Philosophical Investigations,* trans. G. E. M. Anscombe (New York: Macmillan, 1958), part 1.

10.   Jacques Derrida, "Signature, Event, Context," in *Limited, Inc.,* ed. Gerald Graff, trans. Samuel Weber and Jeffrey Mehlman (Evanston: Northwestern University Press, 1988), 18.

11.   See Michel Borch-Jacobsen, *The Freudian Subject,* trans. Catherine Porter (Stanford: Stanford University Press, 1988). Whereas Borch-Jacobsen offers an interesting theory of how identification precedes and forms the ego, he tends to assert the priority of identification to any libidinal experience, where I would insist that identification is itself a passionate or libidinal assimilation. See also the useful distinction between an imitative model and a mimetic model of identification in Ruth Leys, "The Real Miss Beauchamp: Gender and the Subject of Imitation" in *Feminists Theorize the Political,* ed. Judith Butler and Joan Scott (New York: Routledge, 1992), 167–214; Kaja Silverman, *Male Subjectivity at the Margins* (New York: Routledge, 1992), 262–70; Mary Ann Doane, "Misrecognition and Identity," in *Explorations in Film Theory: Selected Essays from Ciné-Tracts,* ed. Ron Burnett (Bloomington: Indiana University Press, 1991), 15–25; and Diana Fuss, "Freud's Fallen Women: Identification, Desire, and 'A Case of Homosexuality in a Woman,'" in *Yale Journal of Criticism* 6, no. 1 (1993): 1–23.

12.   Sigmund Freud, *The Ego and the Id,* ed. James Strachey, trans. Joan Riviere (New York: Norton, 1960), 16.

13.   Nietzsche argues that the ideal of God was produced "[i]n the same measure" as a human sense of failure and wretchedness, and that the production of God was, indeed, the idealization which instituted and reinforced that wretchedness; see Friedrich Nietzsche, *On the Genealogy of Morals,* trans. Walter Kaufmann (New York: Vintage, 1969), section 20. That the symbolic law in Lacan produces "failure" to approximate the sexed ideals embodied and enforced by the law is usually understood as a promising sign that the law is not fully efficacious, that it does not exhaustively constitute the psyche of any given subject. And yet, to what extent does this conception of the law produce the very failure that it seeks to order, and maintain an ontological distance between the laws and its failed approximations such that the deviant approximations have no power to alter the workings of the law itself?

31 Lesbian Identity and Autobiographical Difference(s)

Biddy Martin

No theoretical reading of "lesbian autobiography" can fail to take up the question of the category itself. Under the circumstances, it seems almost obligatory to begin with a set of questions designed to introduce some margin of difference into that apparently airtight package. To write about lesbian autobiography or even lesbian autobiographies as if such a totalizable, intelligible object or its multiplication simply existed would be to beg a number of questions, for example, what a lesbian life is, what autobiography is, and what the relation between them could possibly be. There is no singular answer to such questions, however ingenious the attempt to mask partial, provisional, interested responses with claims to generality, universality, or authority. Any attempt to give a definitive or singular answer to these three questions must be rendered suspect.

Much recent lesbian writing is autobiographical, often taking the form of autobiographical essay and coming-out stories, and I will return to that writing. There are full-blown, bound autobiographies by authors who define themselves quite explicitly as lesbians. If we lend credence to the lesbian reader's sensitivity to the ways in which lesbianism is encoded in only apparently "straight" autobiographical accounts, then there are many more lesbian autobiographies. And if we abandon the obsession with the author's identity, the text's mimetic function and the

reader's necessary identification, if we then consider the reader's pleasure, the ways in which she feels addressed, her desire engaged, then the question of what is lesbian about a life or an account of a life shifts much more dramatically. In 1977 Bertha Harris suggested that lesbian writing engaged a desire and an excess that defied the fixity of identity, the boundaries drawn round individual subjects, around all forms of categorization and normalization. Her lobbying efforts for an avant-garde or modernist writing included the infamous and curious claim that *Jaws,* in its celebration of unassimilable monstrosity, was a far more lesbian novel than the far more "conventional" fiction written in the 1970s by self-declared lesbians.[1] In 1987 there are surely (lesbian) readers who would find, say, a Roland Barthes to be a far more "lesbian" autobiographer than some explicitly lesbian writers. I would not ordinarily go so far, but here, under the weight of that certain identification "lesbian autobiography," such extreme claims acquire a certain allure. They also constitute a certain danger, given the institutional privileges enjoyed by those who can afford to disavow "identity" and its "limits" over against those for whom such disavowals reproduce their invisibility.

Of course, "lesbian autobiography," in its bound singularity, could appear to be a match made in a rather conventional heaven, plagued as both terms are historically by "facile assumptions of referentiality."[2] Their combination brings out the most conventional interpretation in each, for the *lesbian* in front of *autobiography* reinforces conventional assumptions of the transparency of autobiographical writing. And the *autobiography* that follows *lesbian* suggests that sexual identify not only modifies but essentially defines a life, providing it with predictable content and an identity possessing continuity and universality. Set apart in a volume on women's life stories, "lesbian autobiography" suggests that there is something coherently different about lesbians' lives vis-à-vis other lives and that there is something coherently the same about all lesbians. We could attempt to introduce difference into the category by speaking of lesbians' autobiographies and emphasizing the differences between the experiences of various lesbians. Many of the collections of coming-out stories and autobiographical narratives are organized on this very principle. However, differences, for example, of race, class, or sexuality, are finally rendered noncontradictory by virtue of their (re)presentation as differences between individuals, reducible to questions of identity within the unifying context of feminism. What remains unexamined are the systemic institutional relationships between those differences, relationships that exceed the boundaries of the lesbian community, the women's movement, or particular individuals, and in which apparently bounded communities and individuals are deeply implicated.

The isolation of lesbian autobiography here may have strategic political value, given the continued, or perhaps renewed, invisibility of lesbians even in feminist work, but it also marks lesbianism in a way that gives "women's autobiography" a curiously unmarked and unifying quality, reproducing the marginality of lesbianism and its containment in particular types of people. Lesbianism loses its potential as a position from which to read against the grain of narratives of normal life course, and becomes simply the affirmation of something separated out and defined as "lesbian." Of course, the problem of essentialism inevitably plagues not only scholarly volumes committed to representing differences among women; it has plagued and continues to plague lesbian and gay politics and writing as well. In fact, it is the risk taken by any identity politics. Claims to difference conceived in terms of different identities have operated and continue to operate as interventions in facile assumptions of "sisterhood," assumptions that have tended to mask the operation of white, middle-class, heterosexual "womanhood" as the hidden but hegemonic referent. Challenges to the erasure of difference in the name of another identity, however, limit the potential for subversion and critique by recontaining the discursive/ institutional operations of "differences" in discrete categories of individuals, thereby rendering difference a primarily psychological "problem." A number of marginalized communities now face important questions about the possibility of reconceptualizing identity without abandoning it and its strategic deployment altogether. I suggest that such reconceptualizations of identity and of community have emerged in recent autobiographical writing and on the very grounds of identity and community.

The work of Michel Foucault has been essential in gay studies to a critique of identity politics, of the ways in which sexuality comes to constitute the ground of identity, and autobiographical gestures the exclusive ground of politics.[3] Several chains have made their way into gay historiography and into discussions of the politics of "coming out": first, that homosexual identity, the "homosexual" as a particular type of personality was an invention of the late nineteenth century, and further, that the creation of the homosexual as type was, in the words of Jeffrey Minson, part of "the efforts in the human sciences to regulate and control by way of the construction of definite categories of personality."[4] At the same time that "deviance" and "perversion" were located and confined in marginal types and communities, sexual pathologies of all kinds were discovered to be potentials in "the normal family," justifying the intervention of pedagogical, medical, psychiatric, and social welfare experts. At stake in late nineteenth-century Europe was the health of the "family" and its role in securing the health of the "race." Foucault locates the deployment of sexuality at the center of a racist eugenics.[5]

In contrast, then, to conventional assumptions that the Victorian age was characterized by the repression of sexuality, Foucault argues that sexualities and discourse on sexuality proliferated in the late nineteenth century; moreover, he asserts that the deployment of sexuality as an apparatus of normalization and control involved the inducement to speak the truth of one's sexuality, to locate the truth of one's self in a buried sexual essence, and to confuse autobiographical gestures with liberation. The "repressive hypothesis" itself served to mask the actual workings of power. Laying claim, then, to one's sexuality and the rights associated with it, insisting on the freedom to speak freely of one's sexuality, risks subjection to regulation and control. Foucault's critique of the association of sexuality and truth and their location in the depths of the only apparently autonomous individual externalizes questions presumed to be internal and psychological by throwing them onto social and discursive axes. Hayden White characterizes Foucault's challenge to the illusions of the bourgeois subject: "Foucault resists the impulse to seek an origin or transcendental subject which would confer any specific 'meaning' on human life. Foucault's discourse is willfully superficial. And this is consistent with the larger purpose of a thinker who wishes to dissolve the distinction between surfaces and depths, to show that wherever this distinction arises, it is evidence of the

play of organized power."[6] Foucault challenges any belief in the autonomy of the psychological, thereby contesting what Arthur Brittan and Mary Maynard have called the derivation of both racism and sexism "from the operation of the irrational, from the hidden depths of the human psyche."[7] Foucault's critique pushes "identity politics" off the exclusive grounds of identity to questions of alternative social and communicative forms, away from claims to "rights" and "choice" to questions about "the social relationships in which choice becomes meaningful."[8] It may also, however, as a number of feminist critics have noted, work to suppress questions of subjective agency, indeed, to render self-determination unthinkable.

Teresa de Lauretis remains one of the most persistent critics of Foucault and discourse theory for neutralizing gender by conceiving it as pure discursive effect and for suppressing questions of subjective agency and self-representation. In her introduction to *Technologies of Gender,* de Lauretis also uses Foucault's work to criticize American cultural feminists for reproducing conceptions of gender as "sexual difference," i.e., woman's difference from man.[9] She identifies the heterosexual social contract and its constant assumption in feminist as well as nonfeminist writing as a primary site for the reproduction of "just two neatly divided genders." Such assumptions obscure the ways in which gender is constructed across a range of discursive and institutional lines, and always at the intersections of class, race, and ethnicity. Drawing on Foucault's technologies of sexuality, de Lauretis's conception of the "technologies of gender" serves not only to separate gender from any apparent continuity with biology but also to suggest that there is no one monolithic ideology of gender.

De Lauretis's double-edged critique of American feminist identity politics and of Foucault points to the importance of reconceptualizing "experience" and "identity" without abandoning attention to "the semiotic interaction of 'outer world' and 'inner world,' the continuous engagement of a self or subject in social reality.'"[10] To her earlier formulation of the tensions between that ideological distillate "Woman" and historical, empirical "women," de Lauretis adds a third term, "the subject of feminism," the space of an "elsewhere," in order to point to the irreducibility of "women" to any one ideology of gender:

By the phrase "the subject of feminism" I mean a conception or an understanding of the (female) subject as not only distinct from Woman with the capital letter . . . but also distinct from women, the real historical beings and social subjects who are defined by the technology of gender and actually engendered in social relations. The subject of feminism I have in mind is one *not* so defined, one whose definition or conception is in progress.[11]

According to de Lauretis, this subject must be sought not in particular persons or groups— i.e., not in identities—but in "micropolitical practices," practices of self-representation which illuminate the contradictory, multiple construction of subjectivity at the intersections, but also in the interstices of ideologies of gender, race, and sexuality.

De Lauretis draws on the autobiographical writing of women of color to suggest that identity can be reconceptualized on its very grounds. She is one of several feminist critics who read recent autobiographical writing by women of color in the United States as "representational practices" that illuminate the "contradictory, multiple construction of subjectivity." This autobiographical writing actually complicates de Lauretis's own earlier formulation of the inevitable tensions between the negativity of theory and the positivity of politics by robbing theory of its exclusive claim to negativity and suggesting a new imbrication of theory and personal history.

I am interested here in recent autobiographical writings that work against self-evidently homogeneous conceptions of identity, writings in which lesbianism comes to figure as something other than a "totalizing self-identification" and to be located on other than exclusively psychological grounds.[12] These recent writings necessarily take up, even as they work against, already conventional lesbian-feminist narratives of lesbian experience. Encounters between and among feminists over racism and anti-Semitism have played a crucial role in pushing identity politics, generally, and lesbian identity, in particular, beyond the apparent impasses of the late 1970s and early 1980s. The autobiographical contributions to *This Bridge Called My Back*, edited by Cherríe Moraga and Gloria Anzaldúa (1981), serve as a concrete example of how the politics of identity has been challenged on its very grounds. For the writings of Moraga, Anzaldúa, and others participate in attempts to attend to the irreducibly complex intersections of race, gender, and sexuality, attempts that both directly and indirectly work against assumptions that there are differences within the "lesbian self" and that lesbian authors, autobiographical subjects, readers, and critics can be conflated and marginalized as self-identical and separable from questions of race, class, sexuality, and ethnicity. I will conclude with a discussion of how the encounter with racism and its complexities has informed the autobiographical writing of two southern white lesbian writers, Minnie Bruce Pratt and Mab Segrest. In the exchange between the work of women of color and that of white lesbian writers, only apparently discrete and unified identities are rendered complex by attention to the imbrications of different personal and community histories.

Before I take up these exchanges in more detail, let me recall the forms of lesbian identity against which recent autobiographical texts implicitly, when not explicitly, react and on which they necessarily rely. In her review of the most widely read collections of coming-out stories and autobiographical essays of the 1970s and early 1980s, Bonnie Zimmerman argues that the centrality of autobiography in lesbian writing is fundamentally connected with the emergence of a lesbian-feminist politics of experience and identity.[13] Self-worth, identity, and a sense of community have fundamentally depended on the production of a shared narrative or life history and on the assimilation of individuals' life histories into the history of the group. This autobiographical writing has specific purposes in the (not always synchronous) histories of the community and of the individuals who write or read them; it aims to give lesbian identity a coherence and legitimacy that can make both individual and social action possible. The coming-out stories and autobiographical essays collected in such volumes as *The Coming Out Stories, The Lesbian Path, The New Lesbians* are responses to the at least implicit question of what it means to be a lesbian, how lesbianism figures in a life, what it means to come out. In a stricter sense, they are accounts of the process of becoming conscious of oneself as a lesbian, about accepting and affirming that identity against enormous odds, including, of course, the authors' own resistance to the label. Hence, lesbianism becomes the central moment around which women's lives are reconstructed. These narratives appear in journals and anthologies committed quite explicitly to making the realities of lesbians' lives visible in accessible terms, committed, in short, to presence. They are addressed to a reading community assumed to be (or to have the potential to be) lesbian. They assume a mimetic relationship between experience and writing and a relationship of identification between the reader and the autobiographical subject. Moreover,

they are explicitly committed to the political importance of just such reading strategies for the creation of identity, community, and political solidarity.

In an important sense, these written stories are imitations of oral narratives, the coming-out stories at the heart of community building, at the most everyday level. Indeed, many of the stories read as if they had been transcribed from taped accounts. But the oral exchange of stories is, of course, impossible to reproduce, despite the obviously dialogic quality of the individuals' written narratives, which identify the lesbian community as their origin and end. Like all spoken language, the language of many written coming-out stories is necessarily reductionist, all the more so in published accounts, for the pleasures and subtleties of oral exchange and storytelling traditions are eradicated. Here the communicative, performative, and provisional aspects of coming-out stories are subordinated to the claims of recorded speech; in print, the coming-out story appears to hold more claims on the "truth" of the life as a whole.

Telling, writing, and reading autobiographical stories are linked to the perceived importance of countering representations that have rendered homosexuality invisible, perverse, aberrant, or marginal. In her collection of autobiographical essays titled *My Mama's Dead Squirrel: Lesbian Essays on Southern Culture*, Mab Segrest attempts to link antiracist literary traditions with lesbian writing by suggesting that autobiography constitutes a critical "decolonization of self" in the lesbian community. Further, she defines lesbian storytelling as part of larger struggles for self-determination among oppressed and silenced groups.

Now this literature I stumbled into was very different, you had better believe it, from what I had been reading while struggling to acquire a Ph.D. in English. . . .

Most of the "great works" of this century traced the dissolution of Western white male culture, by male writers who could only identify with its demise.... With lesbian literature I remembered how it's supposed to be. No lesbian in the universe, I do believe, will tell you there's nothing left to say. We have our whole lives to say, lives that have been censored, repressed, suppressed and depressed from millennia from official versions of literature, history and culture.... The lesbian's knowledge that we all have stories to tell and that each of our cultures produces its own artists lessens the suicidal modern alienation between writer and audience. Lesbian literature, like all the best women's writing, is fueled by the knowledge that what we have to say is essential to our own survival and to the survival of the larger culture which has tried so hard to destroy us. The lesbian's definition of herself is part of the larger movement by all oppressed people to define ourselves.[14]

Rendering lesbianism natural, self-evident, original, can have the effect of emptying traditional representations of their content, of contesting the only apparent self-evidence of the "normal" (read heterosexual) life course. Lesbian autobiographical narratives are about remembering differently, outside the contours and narrative constraints of conventional models. Events or feelings that are rendered insignificant, mere "phases"—or permanent aberrations when a life is organized in terms of the trajectory toward adult heterosexuality, marriage, and motherhood—become differently meaningful in lesbian stories. They become signs that must be reread on the basis of different interpretive strategies. Whether the emphasis is on a tomboyish past, on childhood friendships, or on crushes on girl friends, teachers, or camp counselors—all now the stock-in-trade of lesbian humor—these narratives point to unsanctioned discontinuities between biological sex, gender identity, and sexuality.

But lesbian autobiographical writing has an affirmative as well as a critical relationship to questions of identity and self-definition. And lesbian identity comes to mean quite particular things in the seventies under the impact of feminist struggles for conceptual and political unity. It is now quite common to reconstruct the history of those struggles among American feminists as a shift from a "radical" to a "cultural" feminism concerned only with psychology and identity and guilty of reproducing the very gender divisions radical feminism set out to question.[15] A particular construction of lesbianism as a political stance for all women is seen to be at the heart of that shift, to have enabled and supported it. "Elevating" lesbianism to the status of a "sign" of political solidarity with women worked to challenge the homophobic reduction of lesbianism to sex. Alice Echols has argued that the "desexualization" of questions of lesbianism may have been the condition of possibility for any unity between lesbians and feminists at all, given the virulent homophobia in the women's movement and the use of homophobia to attack the movement from without.[16] It also had more positive effects, providing a name and a visibility for interpersonal and political solidarity among women and for the pleasures that women, whatever their sexuality, take in each other's company. As a political fantasy, it allowed for the convergence of legitimate (because not explicitly sexual) desire and political liberation. And it provoked and enabled analyses of the intersection of gender division and a heterosexist social contract. In the place of the "sexual minority," however, another figure emerged, one that could encompass both lesbians and heterosexual women, the "woman-identified woman" with a legacy in the history of (romantic) female friendship, a figure that proved disabling and reductionist in its own way. By the late 1970s, when pornography and sexual violence had become the focus of what are now called "cultural feminist analyses," heterosexuality itself, not just particular institutionalized forms and normalizations of heterosexuality, had been identified as the source of women's dependence and oppression. In the context of this emerging critique of heterosexuality, lesbianism came to figure more and more significantly as what Katie King has called "feminism's magical sign of liberation."[17] For the key to opposing male supremacy and the forms of false consciousness imposed on women through the myths of heterosexual desire and pleasure was withdrawal from men, now named lesbianism.

One of the effects of the monolithic and universal division between men and women suggested by this work was the disappearance of institutional analyses, a focus on psychology, and the suggestion that politics could be derived directly from experience or identity. In King's words, "Identifying with lesbianism falsely implies that one knows all about heterosexism and homophobia magically through identity or association. . . . The power of lesbianism as a privileged signifier makes analysis of heterosexism and homophobia difficult since it obscures the need for counter-intuitive challenges to ideology."[18] At the heart of the division is a conception not only of an inside and outside of oppression but of an inside and outside of ideology. Drawing on the work of the Furies Collective in the mid-1970s, Zimmerman suggests that the unity constructed between lesbianism and feminism and the links established between "the personal" and "the political" resulted in "a radically rationalistic rewriting of personal history" to conform to political stance[19]—hence, the often formulaic and noncontradictory quality of some autobiographical writing, hence, too, the forms of moralism and voluntarism that inhere

in such demands for the identity of sexuality, subjectivity, and political stance.

As many critics have now argued, Adrienne Rich's "Compulsory Heterosexuality and Lesbian Existence" (1980) constitutes the ultimate formulation of a particular conception of the relationship between sexuality and politics, explicitly marking off lesbianism as an issue of gender identification and contrasting the interests of gay men and lesbians.[20] Indeed, Rich's essay can be read as the culmination of a textual and political tendency that begins with the Furies Tracts of the early 1970s, namely, the construction of lesbianism as "feminism's magical sign of liberation." Rich uses Freud himself to argue for the primacy and naturalness of women's erotic bond with another woman. The daughter is violently separated from the mother by the imperative of heterosexuality, a social imperative and a form of violence which serves to consolidate male power and to blind women to their own supposedly "essential" love or desire. The ultimate formulation of a politics of nostalgia, of a return to that state of innocence free of conflict conceived as women's primary emotional bonds with one another, enacts its own violence, as all dreams of perfect union do. A number of lesbian critics have remarked that Rich's lesbian continuum effectively erases sexuality and robs lesbianism of any specificity. As Hilary Allen argues, "In conventional terms, whatever is sexual about Political Lesbianism appears to be systematically attenuated: genitality will yield to an unspecified eroticism, eroticism to sensuality, sensuality to 'primary emotional intensity,' and emotional intensity to practical and political support."[21]

Many of the coming-out stories and autobiographical narratives collected in the 1970s quite clearly display the effects of feminist rhetoric on definitions of lesbianism. The narratives are written against the notion that lesbianism can be explained in terms of "penis envy" or the desire to be or imitate a man. And indeed, sexual desire is often attenuated and appears as "love" in these narratives. Lesbianism, understood to be first and foremost about love for other women and for oneself as a woman, becomes a profoundly life-saving, self-loving, political resistance to patriarchal definitions and limitations in these narratives. Virtually every contributor to *The Lesbian Path* and *The Coming Out Stories* acknowledges her debt to feminism for giving lesbianism the meaning it has come to have. A feminist analysis of the suppression of love and solidarity among women in a sexist society and the ensuing celebration of women's relationships with one another provide the lever with which many of the authors pry lesbianism loose from its homophobic reduction to sex, suggesting that the reduction of their desires and their relationships to sex stood in the way of their ability or willingness to accept a lesbian identity. Feminism and the collective rereadings and redefinitions it facilitated are credited with having created the possibility of taking on and redefining the label.

The debt is particularly clear in the editors' presentations of these collections. *The Coming Out Stories* are organized, according to the editors, on the basis of each author's access to a language for her feelings and desires.[22] The book begins with the stories of those contributors who came out when there were no words for the feelings they had, or only words that rendered them perverse, sick, or male; they end with the stories of those who could name their experience woman identification. The cover blurb of *The New Lesbians* makes the impact of feminist politics even more apparent; it suggests that "a majority of lesbians are woman-identified: they do not want to act like or look like men or to practice role-playing."[23] *The Lesbian Path* is introduced as "the book I never had: true stories of strong, women-identified women."[24] The opposition between negative stereotypes and new "truths" about the majority of lesbians masks the role of rhetoric in constructing this majority. The "old" lesbians, those who came out prior to feminism, are rendered invisible, made anachronistic, or converted.

Clearly, access to lesbian and feminist communities, to the collective interpretive strategies and rhetoric developed there has made positive self-definition, and political activism, possible. As Joan Nestle suggests in her contribution to *The Lesbian Path*, self-definition shifts and changes as lesbian communities shift and grow. Nestle describes her own transformation under the impact of feminism from the bar butch/fem culture of the 1950s and 1960s to a lesbian-feminist culture of woman identification.[25] Joan Nestle has since become one of the most articulate critics of the constraints imposed on what it means to be a lesbian by the woman-identified woman, the rhetorical figure that effaced the subtleties of legacies other than romantic female friendship.[26] In the context of the "sexuality debates," renewed interest in butch/fem relationships, in role playing, and in sadomasochism has restored attention to the discontinuities of sex, gender, sexual desire, sexual object choice by introducing the elements of fantasy and play. This work not only has fractured the unity achieved in the woman-identified woman between lesbianism and feminism but has exposed the absence of any consensus about the definition of lesbian identity and its relation to politics.[27]

Many of the coming-out stories are tautological insofar as they describe a process of coming to know something that has always been true, a truth to which the author has returned. They also describe a linear progression from a past shrouded in confusion or lies to a present or future that represents a liberation from the past. Coming out is conceived, then, as both a return to one's true self and desire and a movement beyond distortion and constraints, grounding identity and political unity in moral right and truth. The titles alone, according to Zimmerman—*The Lesbian Path, Lesbian Crossroads, The Coming Out Stories*—point to the conception of lesbianism and of life story as a journey, as a "metaethical" journey à la Mary Daly from patriarchal distortion to a woman-identified consciousness, a choice, finally, to be who one is in a new world of women.[28] The "happy end" to internal struggles, doubts, and contradictions in many coming-out stories depends, in part, on forgetting that "the community" and the feminist literature on which it relies construct rather than simply reflect the truth of experience and identity. It depends, moreover, on suppressing the fact that the past has been rendered not more diverse but homogeneous in a new way. Despite the dialogic exchange between individual and community, these narratives tend to erase the individual's and the group's active participation in their formation as social beings by relying on apparently transcendent "essences" lying in wait for discovery and language. The increasingly exclusive focus on shifts in consciousness and on identification with women leads Zimmerman to conclude that "although lesbian feminism evolved during the 1970's as a politics of transliteration, this power of the word has been used primarily to name, and thereby control, individual and group identity."[29]

In her review of lesbian autobiographical writing, Zimmerman points out that the critiques of lesbian-feminist unities by women of color, Jewish women, and sex radicals have themselves proceeded by way of autobiographical texts committed to the affirmation of multiple identities. In some sense, according to Zimmerman, anthologies like Evelyn Torton Beck's *Nice Jewish Girls* and Moraga and Anzaldúa's *This Bridge Called My Back* reproduce a cultural politics that places its faith in identity and in writing.[30] Zimmerman warns against the fragmentation that results from the search for more authentic unities based on multiplication of identities. Like other critics of "cultural feminism" and identity politics, she concludes with an appeal for institutional analyses in place of the focus on identity. Challenges to increasingly identical constructions of the unity of "women" have at times simply expanded the conception of personal and group identities arithmetically without changing entrenched notions of identity and without furthering what Barbara Smith has called "our ability to analyze complicated intersections of privilege and oppression."[31] The autobiographical writings of women of color, however—indeed, the conception of that category itself—also have the potential to challenge conventional assumptions of identity and its relationship to politics and writing.[32]

I would like to look more closely at *This Bridge Called My Back: Writings by Radical Women of Color,* a collection of autobiographical essays, poems, and letters that move questions of identity off exclusively psychological ground. *This Bridge Called My Back* is a collection of writings by and for radical women of color which also addresses white feminists both directly and indirectly. *This Bridge* is a provocation to white feminists to educate themselves about racism, about the material lives and realities of communities other than their own, about the relationship between the histories of their communities or growing-up places and those of people of color in the United States and elsewhere. It also insists that we cease locating "race" in those individuals or groups in whom it is supposedly embodied, that we abandon the notion that to be "white" is to be unmarked by race. And further, it is a provocation to white feminists and lesbians to render their own histories, subjectivities, and writing complex by attending to their various implications in overlapping social/discursive divisions and their histories.

By demonstrating the complex discursive and institutional intersections of race, class, gender, and sexuality and their inscription on the bodies and psyches of women, these autobiographical essays, poems, and letters relate psychic and political struggles in ways that make "identity" irreducible to consciousness. Not all the contributors to *This Bridge* are lesbians; even for those who identify themselves as lesbians, sexual identity is not a singular focus. *This Bridge* is conceived as a discussion, between and among "women of color," of the contradictions, conflicts, and possibilities in that constructed but "potent fusion of outsider identities."[33] It is a text committed to exposing the complexities of "race" in the United States, complexities too often reduced to a black/white divide. The contributions of women from a range of racial, ethnic, even national communities complicate "race" by focusing on the relationship between the histories and the current situations of different communities and individuals. The category "women of color," as it is elaborated in *This Bridge*, stands in a critical relation to assumptions of unity based on identity, assumptions of a "unity of the oppressed." For the forms of solidarity forged here are based on shared but not identical histories, shared but not identical structural positions, shared but not identical interests. Moreover, the forms of solidarity suggested here are grounded not in claims to victimization but, as Chela Sandoval has argued, in the convergence of shared perspectives, shared competences, and shared pleasures. For Sandoval, the very category "women of color" eschews reference to an essential, pregiven, natural, or self-evident "home" or whole; it is a category that operates as a form of "oppositional consciousness" as well as a source of new political unities, new pleasures and communities.[34] In her critique of Susan Krieger's work on lesbian communities, Sandoval formulates the challenge: "United States Third World feminists are painting out the differences that exist among all women not in order to fracture any hope of unity among women but to propose a new order—one that provides a new possibility for unity without the erasure of differences. This new order would draw attention to the construction and ideological consequences of every order, of every community, of every identity."[35] The category "women of color" amounts to an acknowledgment of what Erica Carter, in her introduction to the work of a German feminist collective on ideology, has called "the disappearance of *any* one coherent subject whose history (individual or collective) might be mobilized as a force for political action," this without abandoning personal histories or politics altogether. . . .[36]

[Martin proceeds to discuss *This Bridge* in more depth and then to turn to autobiographical works by Minnie Bruce Pratt[37] and Mab Segrest, both of whom write as white lesbians struggling to understand the imbrications of sexuality and race in identity de/formation. She concludes as follows.]

Mab Segrest's work participates in attempts to remove questions of identity from the exclusive ground of the psychological or interpersonal and to open up questions about the relations between psychic and social life, between intrapsychic, interpersonal, and political struggles. Identity is thrown onto historically constructed discursive and social axes that crisscross only apparently homogeneous communities and bounded subjects. Experience itself, now exposed as deeply ideological, no longer guarantees knowledge and political correctness. In fact, experience and the identities on which it is presumed to rely stand in the way of analysis and solidarity. The circuits of exchange between the work of Moraga, Anzaldúa, Pratt, and Segrest, whether direct or indirect, have moved autobiographical writing in this context onto a different plane. In these exchanges there is no longer a simple side by side, but a provocation to examine the complication of "my" history in "yours," to analyze the relations between.

As a consequence of these developments, lesbianism ceases to be an identity with predictable contents, to constitute a total political and self-identification, and yet it figures no less centrally for that shift. It remains a position from which to speak, to organize, to act politically, but it ceases to be the exclusive and continuous ground of identity or politics. Indeed, it works to unsettle rather than to consolidate the boundaries around identity, not to dissolve them altogether but to open them to the fluidities and heterogeneities that make their renegotiation possible. At the same time that such autobiographical writing enacts a critique of both sexuality and race as "essential" and totalizing identifications, it also acknowledges the political and psychological importance, indeed, the pleasures, too, of at least partial or provisional identifications, homes, and communities. In so doing, it remains faithful to the irreducibly complex and paradoxical status of identity in feminist politics and autobiographical writing.

Notes

1. Bertha Harris, "What We Mean to Say: Notes toward Defining the Nature of Lesbian Literature," *Heresies: A Feminist Publication on Art and Politics-Lesbian Art and Artists* (Fall 1977): 5–8. Harris's distinction between a literature of the grotesque and a literature of "winkieburgers" is certainly unsatisfying. For those, however, who felt somewhat isolated in 1977–78 in our critical response to increasingly homogeneous narratives of lesbian experience, Bertha Harris's pleas for monstrosity had particular polemical value.

2. Paul de Man, "Autobiography as Defacement," *MLN* 94 (Dec. 1979): 920.

3. I am interested here in the impact of Michel Foucault's *The History of Sexuality*, vol. 1 (New York: Pantheon Books, 1978).

4. Jeffrey Minson, "The Assertion of Homosexuality," *m/f* 5 (1981): 22. Also see Minson, *Genealogies of Morals: Nietzsche, Foucault, Donzelot and the Eccentricity of Ethics* (New York: St. Martin's Press, 1985).

5. I have argued this point in more detail in "Feminism, Criticism and Foucault," *New German Critique* 27 (Fall 1982): 3–10.

6. Hayden White, "Michel Foucault," *Structuralism and Since,* ed. John Sturrock (Oxford: Oxford University Press, 1979), 82.

7. Arthur Brittan and Mary Maynard, *Sexism, Racism, and Oppression* (Oxford: Basil Blackwell, 1984), 29. Brittan and Maynard use the work of Foucault to critique orthodox Marxism, Frankfurt School critical theory, and radical feminists for treating racism and sexism as derivative of more primary contradictions.

8. Jeffrey Weeks, *Sexuality and Its Discontents: Meaning, Myths, and Modern Sexualities* (London: Routledge and Kegan Paul, 1985), 218. I agree with Weeks's reading of the strategic political implications for gay politics in Foucault's work, in particular his emphasis on reconceptualizing rights and choices in terms of the social conditions that make such notions meaningful.

9. Teresa de Lauretis, *Technologies of Gender: Feminism, Film, and Fiction* (Bloomington: Indiana University Press, 1987), 1. De Lauretis works with and against Louis Althusser as well as Foucault. Her critique of Althusser draws on the interesting and important work of Wendy Hollway, "Gender Difference and the Production of Subjectivity," Julian Henriques, Wendy Hollway, Cathy Urwin, Couze Venn, and Valerie Walkerdine, *Changing the Subject: Psychology, Social Regulation and Subjectivity* (London: Methuen, 1984), 225–63. For an excellent discussion by the German feminist Argument Collective of the uses of and problems with Foucault for feminists, see *Female Sexualization,* ed. Frigga Haug et al., trans. Erica Carter (London: Verso, 1987). Haug et al. make a critique of the suppression of subjective agency in Foucault's work which is very similar to that made by de Lauretis. The Argument Collective is interested in mobilizing historical memory in order to expose both processes of "individualization" and possibilities of resistance. See also *Feminism and Foucault,* ed. Irene Diamond and Lee Quinby (Boston: Northeastern University Press, 1988).

10. Teresa de Lauretis, *Alice Doesn't: Feminism, Semiotics, Cinema* (Bloomington: Indiana University Press, 1984), 182.

11. De Lauretis, *Technologies of Gender,* 9–10.

12. I am indebted to Jeffrey Minson's "Assertions

of Homosexuality" for this formulation and for his use of that formulation to criticize particular forms of the politics of coming out.

13. Bonnie Zimmerman, "The Politics of Transliteration: Lesbian Personal Narratives," in *The Lesbian Issue: Essays from Signs,* ed. Estelle B. Freedman, Barbara C. Gelpi, Susan L. Johnson, and Kathleen M. Weston (Chicago: University of Chicago Press, 1985), 251–70.

14. Mab Segrest, *My Mama's Dead Squirrel: Lesbian Essays on Southern Culture* (Ithaca, NY: Firebrand Press, 1985), 101–2.

15. For two of the most influential reconstructions, see Alice Echols. "The Taming of the Id: Feminist Sexual Politics, 1968–83," in *Pleasure and Danger: Exploring Female Sexuality* (Boston: Routledge and Kegan Paul, 1984), 50–72; and Echols, "The New Feminism of Yin and Yang," in *Powers of Desire: The Politics of Sexuality,* ed. Ann Snitow, Christine Stansell, and Sharon Thompson (New York: Monthly Review Press, 1993), 439–59; see also Hester Eisenstein, *Contemporary Feminist Thought* (Boston: G. K. Hall, 1983). Ellen Willis, "Feminism, Moralism and Pornography," in *Powers of Desire,* 460–67, has also popularized a narrative that moves from "radical" to "cultural" feminism. To the extent that these reconstructions rely on only apparently self-evident taxonomies, even as a position from which to assess the use of certain taxonomies, they tend to reproduce the problems they expose. Despite the importance of Echols's critique of what she calls "cultural feminism," the danger exists that all manner of cultural practices will be ossified as mere symptoms of a feminism gone wrong. It is also not clear what the status of "culture" is in many of these critical reconstructions. Since at least some such reconstructions have emerged in the context of a self-identified "socialist feminism," there is some danger that conventional distinctions between "real politics" and "cultural preoccupations" are reproduced in another guise.

16. Echols, "The Taming of the Id," 55–56.

17. Katie King, "The Situation of Lesbianism as Feminism's Magical Sign: Contests for Meaning and the U.S. Women's Movement, 1968–1972," *Communication* 9 (1986): 65–91. King's work provides an explicit and implicit critique of historical reconstructions of feminism that rely on taxonomic identification and linear historical narratives.

18. King, 85.

19. Zimmerman, 255.

20. Adrienne Rich, "Compulsory Heterosexuality and Lesbian Existence," *Signs* 5 (1980): 631–60.

21. Hilary Allen, "Political Lesbianism and Feminism—Space for Sexual Politics?" *m/f* 7 (1982): 15–34.

22. *The Coming Out Stories,* ed. Julia Penelope Stanley and Susan J. Wolfe (Watertown, MA: Persephone Press, 1980).

23. *The New Lesbians,* ed. Laurel Galatia and Gina Cavina (Berkeley: Moon Books, 1977).

24. *The Lesbian Path,* ed. Margaret Cruikshank (San Francisco: Grey Fox Press, 1985).

25. Joan Nestle, "An Old Story," in *Cruikshank,* 37–39.

26. For more detailed autobiographical accounts and analyses of the lesbian culture of the 1950s, see Joan Nestle's collected essays, *A Restricted Country* (Ithaca, NY: Firebrand Press, 1997).

27. Gayle Rubin has gone as far as to suggest that sexuality constitutes a separate axis, which intersects with but is irreducible to gender, so that feminism becomes inadequate to an analysis or politics of sexuality. Though Rubin's work on lesbian sadomasochism has become legitimately criticized for reproducing identity politics in the name of a different sexual community and for tending toward a sexual essentialism, it has served to contest the only apparent hegemony of particular constructions of lesbianism by introducing a complicating axis. See in particular Rubin's "Thinking Sex: Notes for a Radical Theory of the Politics of Sexuality," in *Pleasure and Danger,* 267–319. For a critical assessment of the "prosex" and "antisex" divisions in the sexuality debates, see the review of the texts and major conferences of the so-called sexuality debates by B. Ruby Rich, "Feminism and Sexuality in the 1980s," *Feminist Studies* 12 (Fall 1986): 525–63.

28. Mary Daly, *Gyn/ecology: The Metaethics of Radical Feminism* (Boston: Beacon Press, 1978).

29. Zimmerman, 270.

30. Zimmerman characterizes *Nice Jewish Girls: A Lesbian Anthology,* ed. Evelyn Torton Beck (Watertown, MA: Persephone Press, 1982) and *This Bridge Called My Back: Writings by Radical Women of Color,* ed. Cherríe Moraga and Gloria Anzaldúa (Watertown, MA: Persephone Press, 1981), both now published by

Firebrand Books, as "more political" than *The Coming Out Stories* or *The Lesbian Path,* both of which include work primarily by white, middle-class women. According to Zimmerman, however, "it is the intensity and power of self-affirmation that dominates these volumes" (265). I am less interested in contesting Zimmerman's assessment of the differences, an assessment with which I basically agree, than in specifying the differences between conceptions of identity in the two sets of texts in terms other than "political" versus "self-affirmative." Zimmerman also points to a number of what she calls imaginative personal narratives or autobiographical texts by women of color, which are producing "a new, more inclusive, and more accurate politics" (264). She notes, in particular, Audre Lorde, *Zami: A New Spelling of My Name* (Trumansburg, NY: Crossing Press, 1982); Michelle Cliff, *Claiming an Identity They Taught Me to Despise* (Watertown, MA: Persephone Press, 1980); Anita Cornwall, *Black Lesbian in White America* (Tallahassee, FL: Naiad Press, 1983); Cherríe Moraga, *Loving in the War Years* (Boston: South End Press, 1983); and Gloria Anzaldúa, *Borderlands/La Frontera: The New Mestiza* (San Francisco: Spinsters/Aunt Lute, 1987).

31.   Barbara Smith, "Between a Rock and a Hard Place," in Elly Bulkin, Minnie Bruce Pratt, and Smith, *Yours in Struggle: Three Feminist Perspectives on Anti-Semitism and Racism* (New York: Long Haul Press, 1984), 81.

32.   For an excellent discussion of the possibilities of "postmodern autobiography," see Caren Kaplan, "The Poetics of Displacement in Buenos Aires," *Discourse: Journal of Theoretical Studies in Media and Culture* 8 (Fall–Winter 1986–87): 84–102.

33.   I am indebted for this formulation to Donna Haraway's discussion of "women of color" as a category and a form coalition in "A Manifesto for Cyborgs: Science, Technology, and Socialist Feminism in the 1980s," *Socialist Review* 80 (April 1985): 93.

34.   Chela Sandoval, "Dis-illusionment and the Poetry of the Future: The Making of Oppositional Consciousness," Ph.D. qualifying essay, University of California-Santa Cruz, 1984, quoted in Haraway, 73.

35.   Sandoval, "Comment on Susan Krieger's 'Lesbian Identity and Community: Recent Social Science Literature,'" in Freedman et al., 241–44.

36.   Erica Carter, Introduction to Haug et al., 15.

37.   Minnie Bruce Pratt, "Identity: Skin Blood Heart," in Bulkin, Pratt, and Smith.

32 Unspeakable Differences: The Politics of Gender in Lesbian and Heterosexual Women's Autobiographies

Julia Watson

The Unspeakable

In women's autobiographies, naming the unspeakable is a coming to voice that can create new subjects, precisely because women's marginality may be unnameable within the terms or parameters of the dominant culture.[1] Maxine Hong Kingston introduces the category of the unspeakable in *The Woman Warrior* to describe the lack of identity that surrounds the first-generation Chinese-American children who want to name and therefore erode the boundaries of ghostly silence that guard the old culture's hegemony:

> Those of us in the first American generations have had to figure out how the invisible world the emigrants built around our childhoods fit in solid America. . . . [The emigrants] must try to confuse their offspring as well, who, I suppose, threaten them in similar ways—always trying to get things straight, always trying to name the unspeakable.[2]

Refusing to name the unspeakable not only protects what is sacred in Chinese tradition by enshrouding it in silence, guarding it from the uninitiated, it also marks cultural boundaries within which what is operative does not need to be spoken. For the immigrant or multicultural daughter, naming the unspeakable is at once a transgressive act that knowingly seeks to expose and speak the boundaries on which the organization of cultural knowledge depends and a discursive strategy that, while unverifiable, allows a vital "making sense" of her own multiple differences.[3]

The unspeakable is a category that has also been used to designate sexual differences that remain unspoken, and therefore invisible. In a heterosexual order, the homosexual woman has been both unrepresented and unrepresentable within sanctioned cultural fictions. Since the early 1970s, Adrienne Rich's essays have underscored the unspeakability of lesbian women and their texts.

> Whatever is unnamed, undepicted in images, whatever is omitted from biography, censored in collections of letters, whatever is misnamed as something else, made

difficult-to-come-by, whatever is buried in the memory by the collapse of meaning under an inadequate or lying language—this will become, not merely unspoken, but *unspeakable*.[4]

Indeed, many fictions of female development structure the incorporation of sexuality as the internalization of the only sexual identity to be spoken—that of female heterosexuality defined as the other of heterosexual masculinity. In autobiography, which as a genre has functioned as the keeper of the "law" of patriarchal identity, women's sexuality has usually been presumed as heterosexual except when spoken otherwise.[5] When it is spoken as lesbian in autobiography, it has been read as voicing a transgressive sexuality—as the naming of an unspeakable—whose difference is read as deviance.[6]

That is, in autobiography, only homosexuals have sexuality. Heterosexuality, because it does not have to be named, retains some of the disciplinary power that Adrienne Rich attributed to it in delineating its "compulsory" mechanisms.[7] But it should be possible to locate women's autobiographies with respect to sexual demarcations along an axis of sexualities, and to read their speaking of sexual identity as complex statements that may challenge or rethink contemporary ideologies of gender. I propose to begin from lesbian markings of sexuality, and to read these articulations of the "unspeakable" against autobiographies of women whose sexuality is assumed to be normatively heterosexual at the same time that it is repressed as superfluous, the object of another's desire. Reading sexual difference as, in Audre Lorde's phrase, "the house of difference" in lesbian autobiographies, we may trace a trajectory of naming the unspeakable. This voicing may in turn be read against autobiographies in which the presumption of heterosexuality makes trouble within and across cultures. Can the repressive unspeakables

of heterosexuality be named or unknotted without a critique of sexuality such as lesbian manifestos and other feminist critiques of patriarchy enable? While the texts I will discuss are recent (from the 1950s to the present in the United States), much has changed during the four decades since the first of them was published. What was formerly unspeakable may now no longer be transgressive, as critiques of heterosexuality have begun to be named from several points within its "system." My project is, then, a double one: to read women's autobiographies not just as acts of coming to voice but as negotiations in naming the unspeakable, and to claim a critical location from which to read the sexual unspeakable from outside a polarized framework in which normative heterosexuality and oppositional homosexuality operate as authorized and mutually exclusive discourses.

I do this in part in the interest of my own autobiographical project, to locate myself with respect to the discourses of lesbian and feminist identity politics, which have been positioned as inimical at several points, and to consider my investment in each.[8] If in my own life these categories have seemed inadequate to describe the complexities of experience, if the formulas of sexual and identity politics and the fixities of gender have seemed insufficiently articulated for the particulars of relationships, perhaps the polarized discourse of gender itself needs to be renegotiated through the specifics of personal affiliation. Reading women's autobiographies of lesbian and heterosexual orientations, declared or not declared, against one another may help to frame a politics of reading that undoes their simple opposition. This speaking may be located at an Archimedean point, but it is one that frames the possibility of women's affiliation through, and not despite, sexual difference. To read outside a framework of either heterosexual or homosexual identity politics focuses our attention on the possibility of becoming, in a sense, the sexually "decolonized" readers that both alternative texts and non-dominant theories of autobiography propose.

Framing the Unspeakable

Carolyn Heilbrun, in *Writing a Woman's Life,* has observed the difficulty of negotiating and describing women's friendships outside a patriarchal framework by calling eloquently for reading and writing affiliation with other women as a focus of women's autobiography. Heilbrun states that affiliations have been conceived in women's writing as "this sense of identification with women alone, not as fellow sufferers but as fellow achievers and fighters in the public domain" and "the sole saving grace of female friendship." [9] In seeing Toni Morrison's *Sula* and Audre Lorde's *The Cancer Journals* as models of such friendship, Heilbrun both identifies and elides the differential politics of such affiliations: between remorseful heterosexuality that gestures toward a nonrepresentable elsewhere (Sula) and lesbianism that reads relationships to women through its multiple, exclusionary differences (Lorde). Though Heilbrun does not expand on this interplay between sexual ideologies and women's affiliations, her characterization of the dilemma extends into women's autobiography generally. She leaves open a space for asking what the possible practices and politics of women's affiliation are that could undo the rhetoric and claims to power of both heterosexual and lesbian hierarchies.

There are justifications for reading from outside the heterosexual framework within feminist theory as well as in the autobiographical practices of many women writers. Teresa de Lauretis, in analyzing how the technologies of gender collude in maintaining a repressive status quo, has called for disengaging gender from the binary terms of patriarchy and repositioning it in a necessarily unspecified elsewhere:

To envision gender (men and women) otherwise, and to (re)construct it in terms other than those dictated by the patriarchal contract, we must walk out of the male-centered frame of reference in which gender and sexuality are (re)produced by the discourse of male sexuality. [10]

De Lauretis cites Monique Wittig's claim that "the discourses of heterosexuality oppress in the sense that they prevent us from speaking unless we speak in their terms" as justification for her argument that women's desire is unspeakable within current gender arrangements. If women are to forge an identity politics that would not simply reproduce the terms of patriarchy, the multiplicity of women's differences must be spoken in terms other than the heterosexist concepts that designate "feminist" and "lesbian" as forms of difference from its norms. [11]

Arguments in support of de Lauretis's call for women to position themselves in an "elsewhere" outside the heterosexual framework are made from two positions, that of lesbian readings of women's texts and that of revisionist gender theory. In "Lesbian Identity and Autobiographical Difference(s)" Biddy Martin argues powerfully against what she sees as an emerging hegemonic discourse in women's autobiography that threatens to silence female difference in the name of "woman." [12] White heterosexual feminists, she argues, have replicated a politics of marginalization in which lesbian autobiography is rendered invisible by being presented as a unitary other. Martin points out that lesbian autobiography has been represented as different from all other life writing and as the same for all lesbians, its difference localized reductively in sexual practice (380–92, in this volume). The coming-out story is, she argues, not only a genre of writing, but a way of reading that reduces and institutionalizes lesbian difference. Its conventions, including the representation of a homogeneous, repressive past and the subject's discovery of her lesbian "essence" and desire, make for an oversimplified story. In suppressing their own and the larger group's active participation in creating a community through internal and external struggle, the authors of coming-out stories may help to sustain a unitary and polarized construct of lesbian identity.

In challenging this univocity in the representation of lesbian life writing, Martin argues against reading lesbianism as "a totalizing self-identification" (000, in this volume).[13] To relocate its differences, the concept of gender must be expanded and filtered through the multiple differences and intersecting sites of oppression that characterize women's life writings, particularly those of women of color. In turning to the politics of experience to indict the narrowness of theory, Martin focuses on the important anti-academic feminist text *This Bridge Called My Back: Writings by Radical Women of Color,* a collection of autobiographical poems, essays, stories, and sketches.[14] In *Bridge,* the many autobiographical writers point to their systematic exclusion from the dominant white—including white academic feminist—culture and invoke collective identification of women of color across multiple differences as a community in unspeakability. In *Bridge,* Martin argues, lesbianism is "less an identity than a desire that transgresses the boundaries imposed by structures of race, class, ethnicity, nationality . . . and figures as a provocation that . . . desires different kinds of connections" (000, in this volume). Martin's relocation of lesbian desire frees it from the polarized opposition to a dominant heterosexuality that has characterized much earlier theorizing.

Women such as the writers in *Bridge,* in voicing experiences of invisibility, necessarily write against the norms of autobiography, traditionally understood as an institutionalized discourse of patriarchal authority that has rendered their differences unspeakable. Martin argues that les-

bian autobiography has to be rethought not as a genre of writing, but as a rhetorical figure of the negotiations around identity and difference in which many autobiographers are engaged. It is, then, exemplary of new-model autobiographies when it is least like the fixed genre of lesbian autobiography. Like other autobiographers of marginality, the woman writer has to break silence to question dominant structures of meaning. Martin's textual readings free lesbianism from its own generic orthodoxy, in the "law" of the coming-out story, and refigure it as a transgressive desire and a provocation to heretofore unspeakable connections and affiliations.

In ways that complement Martin's rethinking of lesbian difference and particularize and revise de Lauretis's analysis, Judith Butler critiques the system of gender by showing how established models of both heterosexuality and homosexuality are constructed around binary oppositions. Butler argues that "heterosexuality" is a falsely naturalized coherence that acts as a regulatory fiction to police and deny more complex constructions of cultural identity.[15] The implications of her argument for women's autobiography are considerable. Butler argues that Lacanian and feminist post-Lacanian critiques of the subject are rooted in a binary matrix in which variants of two heterosexual desires underlie all available notions of gender. She notes:

> Under Lacanian and anti-Lacanian story lines about gender acquisition gender meanings are circumscribed within a narrative frame which both unifies certain legitimate sexual subjects and excludes from intelligibility sexual identities and discontinuities which challenge the narrative beginnings and closures offered by these competing psychoanalytic explanations. (329)

That is, representations of identity have been polarized within a binary matrix that prohibits what Butler terms "the subversive recombination of gender meanings" observable in historical subjects (335). What Freud posited as a pre-Oedipal primary bisexuality turns out to be subsumed and refigured within a paternally organized culture. To achieve gender identity is to achieve coherent heterosexuality, according to both Lacanian and Freudian analyses. Gender has been a falsely stabilized category that acts to regulate and maintain heterosexuality as a fiction of great cultural power. That constituted coherence, Butler argues, conceals the gender discontinuities within any sexuality, whether its context be heterosexual, bisexual, gay, or lesbian. In none of these does gender necessarily follow from sex, nor desire from gender (336). A coherent fiction of sexual identity and an oppositional model in which heterosexuality is the norm and all other sexualities are deviant, while claiming to describe sexuality, regulate it as a developmental law.

Equally important to Butler's argument is her claim that critics of "compulsory heterosexuality," notably Monique Wittig and Adrienne Rich, have categorically criticized being "straight" as a compulsory ideology and argued for the necessity of an oppositional politics and praxis. Butler both learns from and revises Wittig's attack on fixed gender identities rooted in heterosexual ideology and her use of gendered homosexuality as a critical instrument to examine the negotiations of women's bodies. In so doing, Butler "makes trouble" by opening up a space within the oppositional representation of hetero/homosexuality for undoing and complicating the definitional claims of both heterosexual and lesbian as categories of gender identity. Butler's challenge cuts both ways. On the one hand, she criticizes the power of heterosexuality as a norm that levels and marginalizes the diversity and fluidity of sexual possibilities. On the other hand, she criticizes the discourse of lesbian identity as replicating the oppositional structure of heterosexuality by imitating and inverting its binary oppositions, suggesting that radical feminist critics have not been able to undo its fundamental power. For Butler the notion of multiple, fragmentary, fluid postures around a set of dissonant sexual roles opens up an interplay between hetero- and homosexual categories that destabilizes both. Such a theory would have potential for a politics of reading identity differently—reading it, that is, as a negotiation among fixed possibilities that both resists and remakes the representation of human experience. In such a negotiation the unspeakable would be mapped as what becomes speakable when boundaries are traversed, articulated, confused, and undone.

The Unspeakable and "Colonization"

Both de Lauretis's insistence on reading gender outside the terms of the patriarchal contract and Martin's and Butler's loosening of "heterosexuality" and "lesbian" from their competing claims to delimit women's sexuality offer us a language for reading the sexual identities of women's autobiographies other-wise. Such reforms speak to a claim within lesbian theory and, for that matter, much feminist theory, namely, that women's autobiographical projects are "sexual self-decolonization," which seems to me problematic. *Sexual decolonization* refers to a recurrent debate among feminists about whether women are "colonized" by compulsory heterosexuality in ways that only decolonizing strategies and the practice of critical consciousness can undo. Such critiques of heterosexuality need not inevitably point outside it to a primary "lesbian continuum" or a lesbian refiguring of sexuality, as the consciousness-raising groups of the 1970s—which could be understood as collective acts aimed at liberation from sexist ideology—showed. But the rhetoric of sexual decolonization has been employed primarily by lesbian writers in the context of their "unspeakability" to argue that the situation of women in patriarchy is in some ways analogous to that of colonized peoples.

Adrienne Rich uses the "unspeakable" to name how women's love for and affiliation with one another, which she sees as primary, are silenced by the colonizing practices exerted literally upon the bodies of women in Western culture: "There is the heterosexist, patriarchal culture which has driven women into marriage and motherhood through every possible pressure—economic, religious, medical, and legal—and which has literally colonized the bodies of women." [16] To counter that "colonization," Rich calls upon women to resist gynephobia and affirm the radical complexity of women's bonds without reverting to a simpler "dyke separatism." [17] Affirming a primary affiliation as women and naming it "lesbian" is, Rich argues in several essays, necessary to undo both the unspeakables and the "colonizing" practices of heterosexism: "The word *lesbian* must be affirmed because to discard it is to collaborate with silence and lying about our very existence; with the closet-game, the creation of the *unspeakable*." [18] Rich insists on the "primary intensity" of woman-to-woman relationships as a way of "desiring . . . and choosing oneself" and on naming that focus "lesbian" as a way of resisting collaboration with the "unspeakable" or forbidden status of women's relationships under patriarchy. [19]

Similarly, Mab Segrest, who describes her autobiographical project as "self-decolonization," intends to divest herself of the inherited cultural baggage of heterosexism, along with that of "good" English literature and southern conservative politics. Segrest observes: "If much of it is rooted in autobiography, much of this decade of lesbian-feminist writing has undertaken the work of decolonizing the self." [20] Within an American lesbian feminist context, then, "decolonization" has been used as a metaphor for

self-investigation of sexual difference, by definition an autobiographical divestiture of the unspeakables that police sexuality. Before exploring how colonization, as a metaphor and a discursive strategy, is used in lesbian women's autobiographies and considering whether such a condition can be read back into autobiographies of heterosexual women, where it is often not marked, it is important to situate the American feminist use of "decolonization" within the framework of postcolonial critique. Is a concept of colonization even viable outside a network of political, externally imposed, repressive practices that operate on entire peoples? Or is "sexual decolonization" an indication of the decadent and depoliticized discourse of American feminism, which has often been criticized by its non-European "Third World" sisters for being mired in personal and bourgeois issues rather than addressing the exploitation of entire classes of women workers characteristic of late capitalism?

Nigerian expatriate novelist Buchi Emecheta takes up these concerns in denouncing Western feminism's preoccupation with issues of sexuality as a kind of exoticism when projected onto non-Western women:

I have not been relating well with Western feminists and have found myself at loggerheads with them from time to time. They are only concerned with issues that are related to themselves and transplant these onto Africa. Their own preoccupations—female sexuality, lesbianism, and female circumcision—are not priorities for women in Africa. . . . Many African women are involved in food production in the rural areas and are far removed from lesbianism. . . . Western feminists are often concerned with peripheral topics and do not focus their attention on major concerns like the exploitation of women by Western multi-national companies. They think that by focusing on exotic issues in the "third world" they have internationalized their feminism.[21]

For Emecheta, colonization, and particularly the neocolonization of African countries, creates macropolitical issues that are obscured or distorted by a preoccupation with sexual politics at the micropolitical level. While indifference to social responsibility might be entertained by educated Western women, African women, situated in networks of family responsibility, must resist it. Emecheta's critique strikes at the heart of the feminist dictum "The personal is political," by reading the phrase as a substitution of the personal for the political. For Emecheta, as for other African women writers, a critique of sexual politics is not a sufficient act of "self-decolonization," and practicing heterosexuality does not necessarily signify the absence of a critique of how sexual organization intersects macrosocial organization.

Similar critiques of sexual politics as exoticizing and trivializing women's primary and proper concerns with economic and political exploitation have been made with reference to women autobiographers outside the Euro-American frame. Barbara Harlow notes that in many women's autobiographies of resistance the personal tends to disappear into the political, or to be renounced for it in specific historical situations.[22] Harlow recalls Gayatri Spivak's observation on the "inbuilt colonialism of First World feminism toward the Third" and Hazel Carby's criticism of the participation of Western feminists in "the self-proclaimed 'civilizing mission' of European and United States colonialism and imperialism" as indictments of Western feminist claims to a global sisterhood. Harlow also notes that Western readers of women's autobiography deemphasize that many resistance women writers have relocated their lives to the public

sphere, where the historic struggles of their people are taking place (187). The discussion of sexual colonization as an aspect of "de/colonizing the subject," therefore, needs to be bracketed as a problematic and potentially misleading concept within the privileged discourse of Western identity politics that autobiography has helped to create and sustain, while it has refused to read the real and devastating effects of economic and political colonization. As the critics mentioned above persuasively argue, *sexual colonization* is too historically specific a term to apply to the situation of all women or even to the heterosexism that oppresses lesbians when that is not complicated by racial or ethnic oppression of a class of people.

The case for sexual colonization, however, has been made persuasively at some sites by radical women of color writing in the United States. A situation of colonial domination was assuredly represented in Harriet Jacobs's *Incidents in the Life of a Slave Girl*.[23] Notably, in the autobiographies of Chicana feminists Cherríe Moraga (*Loving in the War Years*) and Gloria Anzaldúa (*Borderlands/La Frontera*) and in *This Bridge Called My Back*, the interpellation of marginalizations by gender, race/ethnicity, class, and sexual orientation may inform a postcolonial situation.[24] The writers in *Bridge* read the isolation and invisibility imposed on them by their self-proclaimed lesbianism not as analogous to their marginalization as women of color, but as another outcome of heterosexist domination in American life. By claiming Audre Lorde's proclamation, "The master's tools will never dismantle the master's house," in an essay of the same title published in *Bridge,* they look to a restructuring that is political and economic, as well as interpersonal.

Autobiography, then, has been in recent years a productive site for rewriting the arrangements of gender. In an influential essay, Barbara Smith points to the unspeakability of lesbian women of color in feminist theory and urges white women to "a sane accountability to all the women who write and live on this soil." Smith calls for "what has never been" in saying:

> I . . . want to express how much easier both my waking and my sleeping hours would be if there were one book in existence that would tell me something specific about my life. One book based in Black feminist and Black lesbian experience.[25]

Writing in the late 1970s, Smith asks that autobiography resituate black women's experience outside cultural sanctions. Although canonical lesbian texts such as Gertrude Stein's *The Autobiography of Alice B. Toklas* had long been in print, they remained texts of privileged white women whose major identification was with male expatriate writers and the cult of genius. (In fact, in the 1970s Stein's writings were not yet being read as lesbian texts—not surprisingly, given Stein's own equivocation about homophobia and her "ventriloquist" silencing of Alice in the text.)[26] Barbara Smith points out a gap that oppresses by what it does not permit to be spoken. The project of naming the unspeakable is an effort to pose the problem of the relationship between personal experience and political goals as an instrument for change.[27]

In this way, rereading women's autobiographies both for their voicing of oppressed identities and *against* a misapplied concept of decolonization may enable a reformulation of sexual identity in autobiography. Reading lesbian autobiographies as, in Judith Butler's term, "complex sites of dissonance around sexual identity" (338) implicitly dislodges heterosexual women's autobiographies from a fixed concept of gender as stable heterosexuality. Displacing the rhetoric of binary and polarized sexual orientations in autobiography and understanding that as a strategy that keeps attempting to, in Hong Kingston's phrase, "name the unspeakable" may open up that dissonance.[28]

Notes

1. Rita Felski argues that feminist autobiographies, linking the personal and the political, have been an important moment for the self-definition of formerly voiceless groups in recent years by creating a "counter-public sphere" as a genre of autobiography that both interrogates and affirms gendered subjectivity. Such autobiographies of marginality thus create *new subjects. Beyond Feminist Aesthetics* (Cambridge: Harvard University Press, 1989), 121.

2. Maxine Hong Kingston, *The Woman Warrior: Memoirs of a Girlhood Among Ghosts* (New York: Knopf, 1976), 6. Kingston again refers to the unspeakable as the unnamed of traditional Chinese discourse: "If we had to depend on being told, we'd have no religion, no babies, no menstruation (sex, of course, unspeakable), no death. I thought talking and not talking made the difference between sanity and Insanity. Insane people were the ones who couldn't explain themselves" (216). Writing the book *names* the "secrets" on whose repression the perpetuation of traditional culture depends; figuring them out is both a transgression and, for the emigrants, a way of making sense of one's life. Compare this with the remark by Lena St. Clair in *The Joy Luck Club*: "I always thought it mattered, to know what is the worst possible thing that can happen to you, to know how you can avoid it, to not be drawn by the magic of the unspeakable." Amy Tan, *The Joy Luck Club* (New York: G. T. Putnam's Sons, 1989), 103.

3. Similarly, James Baldwin remarks, "Growing up in a certain kind of poverty is growing up in a certain kind of silence." The facts and injustices of everyday life cannot be named because "no one corroborates it. Reality becomes unreal because no one experiences it but you." Baldwin also attests to the power of another's witnessing to what seems unspeakable: "Life was made bearable by Richard Wright's testimony. When circumstances are made real by another's testimony, it becomes possible to envision change." Quoted by Margaret Spillane in a

review, "The Culture of Narcissism," *Nation*, 10 December 1990, 739.

4.   Adrienne Rich, " It is the Lesbian in Us . . . ," in *On Lies, Secrets, and Silence: Selected Prose 1966–1978* (New York: W. W. Norton, 1979), 199.

5.   See Caren Kaplan's essay, "Resisting Autobiography: Out-Law Genres and Transnational Feminist Subjects," in *De/Colonizing the Subject: The Politics of Gender in Women's Autobiography,* ed. Sidonie Smith and Julia Watson (Minneapolis: University of Minnesota Press, 1992). Excerpted in this volume.

6.   Assuredly, as Sidonie Smith, Carolyn Heilbrun, and others have shown compellingly, women autobiographers are always writing against a history of their own cultural silencing, producing texts whose multiple, fragmentary discourses stand in no easy relationship to the empowered, coherent subjectivity that has been taken as a norm of autobiography. In the last ten years, a series of canons have emerged in women's autobiography, initially privileging texts by literary women autobiographers (Mary McCarthy, Lillian Hellman, Virginia Woolf, and Gertrude Stein, as well as earlier spiritual autobiographers), that has now shifted toward autobiographies of marginality (the work of Maxine Hong Kingston, Zora Neale Hurston, Maya Angelou, women's slave narratives). Significantly, Stein's texts have appeared in this canon as well, becoming a site of lesbian discourse/marginality. See Sidonie Smith, *A Poetics of Women's Autobiography: Marginality and the Fictions of Self-Representation* (Bloomington: Indiana University Press, 1987); Carolyn Heilbrun, *Writing a Woman's Life* (New York: W. W. Norton, 1988).

7.   Adrienne Rich, "Compulsory Heterosexuality and Lesbian Existence," in *Blood, Bread, and Poetry: Selected Prose 1979–1985* (New York: W. W. Norton, 1986), 23–75. In her 1980 foreword to this essay (which first appeared in *Signs* in 1978), Rich notes, "I continue to think that heterosexual feminists will draw political strength for change from taking a critical stance toward the ideology which demands heterosexuality, and that lesbians cannot assume that we are untouched by that ideology and the institutions founded upon it" (26). Rich goes on to note that the intent of such a critique is not to make women into victims, but to voice the grounds for their resistance.

8.   For valuable suggestions and help in hearing out and framing the perplexities of issues raised in this essay, I am indebted to Sidonie Smith.

9.   Heilbrun, 72, 75.

10.   Teresa de Lauretis, *Technologies of Gender* (Bloomington: Indiana University Press, 1987), 17. Subsequent references to this book will be in parentheses in the text.

11.   It is clear from de Lauretis's recent work that her own practice requires that she situate herself critically toward the claims of heterosexual feminism and speak from a lesbian position that she distinguishes from feminist ones and glosses autobiographically, as she did in papers presented at the 1989 meeting of the Philological Association of the Pacific Coast and at the 1990 Modern Language Association convention.

12.   Biddy Martin, "Lesbian Identity and Autobiographical Differences," in *Life/Lines: Theorizing Women's Autobiography,* ed. Bella Brodzki and Celeste Schenck (Ithaca: Cornell University Press, 1988), 77–103. Excerpted in this volume.

13.   Similarly, in reviewing recent books on lesbian writing, Julie Abraham calls for reconsidering the contention of many lesbian critics that lesbian sexuality is central to lesbian representation and that the lesbian's marginality is the major factor informing her writing. Abraham asks, "How far do [these propositions] constitute an acceptance of the dominant culture's definitions?" Abraham calls for distinguishing "between representations of the lesbian and lesbian representations," and argues that "lesbian representation would be a theoretically infinite set of possibilities for lesbian cultural . . . expression." "Criticism Is Not a Luxury," *Nation,* 3 December 1990, 711–12.

14.   Cherríe Moraga and Gloria Anzaldúa, eds., *This Bridge Called My Back: Writings by Radical Women of Color* (New York: Kitchen Table: Women of Color Press, 1981).

15.   Judith Butler, "Gender Trouble, Feminist Theory, and Psychoanalytic Discourse," in *Feminism/Postmodernism,* ed. Linda J. Nicholson (New York: Routledge, 1990), 338–39. All subsequent references to this essay appear in parentheses in the text. Butler's *Gender Trouble* (New York: Routledge, 1990) has also been informative for my analysis.

16. Adrienne Rich, "The Meaning of Our Love for Women Is What We Have Constantly to Expand," in *On Lies, Secrets, and Silence: Selected Prose, 1966–1978* (New York: W. W. Norton, 1979), 225. Similarly, Rich considers how women internalize the values of colonialism and participate in carrying out the colonization of self and sex in *Of Woman Born* (New York: W. W. Norton, 1976); see especially "The Kingdom of the Fathers."

17. Rich, "Meaning of Our Love," 227.

18. Rich, "It Is the Lesbian in Us," 202.

19. Ibid., 201.

20. Mab Segrest, *My Mama's Dead Squirrel: Lesbian Essays on Southern Culture* (Ithaca, N.Y.: Firebrand, 1985), 126. Segrest reads lesbian coming-out stories as analogous to African American slave narratives because both are narratives of victimization, resistance, and transformation through the power to name oppressions. My attention was drawn to this essay by Biddy Martin's "Lesbian Identity and Autobiographical Difference(s)." While Segrest's analogy between lesbians and African American slaves as oppressed peoples seems to be untenable, her emphasis on the process of coming to speech is helpful.

21. Thelma Ravell-Pinto, "Buchi Emecheta at Spelman College" (interview), *SAGE* 2 (Spring 1985): 50–51. Emecheta states, "My novels are not feminist; they are part of the corpus of African literature" (50). The editor points out that "[Emecheta's] perspective on women as portrayed in her novels is most definitely feminist" (51).

22. Barbara Harlow, *Resistance Literature* (New York: Methuen, 1987). Subsequent references to this book are in parentheses in the text.

23. Harriet Jacobs, *Incidents in the Life of a Slave Girl*, ed. Jean Fagan Yellin (Cambridge: Harvard University Press, 1967; first published in 1861). See "The Changing Moral Discourse of Nineteenth-Century African American Women's Autobiography: Harriet Jacobs and Elizabeth Keckley," by William L. Andrews, in *De/Colonizing the Subject.*

24. Cherríe Moraga, *Loving in the War Years* (Boston: South End, 1983); Gloria Anzaldúa, *Borderlands/La Frontera* (San Francisco: Spinsters/Aunt Lute, 1987); Moraga and Anzaldúa, *This Bridge Called My Back.* For discussions of *Bridge*'s relevance as autobiography, see Martin, "Lesbian Identity," especially 388–89, in this volume. I am indebted to this essay and to discussion with Biddy Martin in July 1989 in formulating the concerns of my essay. My review of *This Bridge Called My Back* (*a/b: Auto/Biography Studies* 4 [Fall 1988]: 77–79) also considers the collection as women's autobiographical writing.

25. Barbara Smith, "Toward a Black Feminist Criticism," in *The New Feminist Criticism*, ed. Elaine Showalter (New York: Pantheon, 1985), 183–84.

26. See Sidonie Smith, "The Impact of Critical Theory on the Study of Autobiography: Marginality, Gender, and Autobiographical Practice," *a/b: Auto/Biography Studies* 3 (Fall 1987). See also Catherine Stimpson's insightful essays on the complexities of Stein's position as a lesbian in drag in *The Autobiography of Alice B. Toklas,* notably the essay "Gertrude Stein and the Lesbian Lie," in *American Women's Autobiography: Fea(s)ts of Memory,* ed. Margo Culley (Madison: University of Wisconsin Press, 1992).

27. Rita Felski discusses the force of women's confessional autobiography, in which women write self-consciously and explicitly as women, as a mode of shifting autobiography away from idiosyncratic individualism and toward a concept of representative communal identity of the sort Barbara Smith calls for. See 83–95, in this volume.

28. Mary Jacobus calls for a similar rupturing of women's confinement in urging that women, while necessarily inscribed within "male" discourse, "work ceaselessly to deconstruct it: to write what cannot be written." Quoted in Heilbrun, 41.

33 Mystical Bodies and the Dialogics of Vision

Laurie A. Finke

The mystic is by no means that which is not political. It is something serious, which a few people teach us about, and most often women.

—Jacques Lacan

The soul is the prison of the body.

—Michel Foucault

In his discussion of torture in *Discipline and Punish*, Michel Foucault reverses one of the central beliefs of Christianity—the belief that the body is the prison of the soul, a miserable container that constrains the freedom of its far more valuable contents. One lesson Christianity since Augustine has consistently drawn from the Genesis story of the Fall is that humans have bodies that experience pain, desire, and mortality; God does not. The body is a limit; its vulnerability and weakness impede the soul in its progress toward God.[1] Foucault challenges these beliefs by suggesting that the body has instead been constrained by—been the prisoner of—its representations that necessarily follow from Christian dualism and the privileging of the soul. What Foucault misses in his analysis, however, is that this dualism has a gender component that guarantees that men and women experience the limits of their bodies in quite different ways. Medieval Christianity construed man as spirit and woman as body. Like the body, woman is accident to man's essence, despite claims of the spiritual equality of all believers.

This essay explores some of the consequences of this difference for women of the later Middle Ages who attempted to achieve spiritual authority through mystical experiences.

Women in the later Middle Ages were more likely than men to gain a reputation as spiritual leaders based on their mystical experiences.[2] Perhaps because they were in an "oppressed social situation," women were especially drawn to radical forms of religious experience. Some scholars have argued that, because religion was the dominant mode of expression in medieval Europe and the church such a powerful socioeconomic institution, political dissent almost invariably took the form of religious dissent—heresy, but also the kinds of extreme religious practices associated with even orthodox mystics.[3]

My concern in this essay, then, is the discourse of late medieval mysticism as it exhibits at least some women's ability to speak and be heard within a patriarchal and forthrightly misogynistic society. My point is not to make outlandish claims for these women's anticipation of feminist concerns or to condemn ahistorically their conservatism or slavish capitulation to patriarchal religion. Rather, I wish to examine the discourse of mysticism as a site of struggle between the authoritative, monologic language of a powerful social institution and the heteroglossia[4] of the men and women who came under its sway and sometimes resisted it. Mysticism, as I describe it, is not a manifestation of the individual's internal affective states but a set of cultural and ideological constructs that both share in and subvert orthodox religious institutions. Furthermore, linguistic empowerment for women was tied to certain attitudes about the body prevalent in the Middle Ages. The discourse of the female mystic was constructed out of disciplines designed to regulate the female body, and it is, paradoxically, through these disciplines that the mystic consolidated her power. Specifically, I examine the ways in which several mystics of the thirteenth and fourteenth centuries developed a means of transcending their own secondariness out of cultural representations of the body and technologies designed to contain and suppress it. Although the women I look at in this essay are widely separated by time, geography and class, and while further research will undoubtedly disclose many of these differences, I wish to consider them as a single group for several reasons. These women did not live and write in total isolation. They were aware of the existence of other famous mystics. Indeed, they saw themselves as part of a tradition of exceptional religious women. Younger mystics often modeled their lives and writings on those of their predecessors.[5] I want to insist upon this dialogism—this "intense interaction of one's own and another's voice"—that I see as central to the visionary experience.[6] Furthermore, I want to emphasize the continuous power of the cultural representations that paradoxically confined these women and enabled them to challenge their cultural figurations.

Although it falls outside of the scope of this essay, the *Life of St. Leoba*—written by a monk of Fulda named Rudolph about an eighth-century Anglo-Saxon nun who participated in the Christianization of Germany—recounts a curious visionary dream that strikingly illustrates the major concerns of this essay. One night the saint sees a purple thread issuing from her mouth, "as if it were coming from her very bowels." When she tries to draw it out with her hand, she cannot reach the end of it. As she pulls it out she begins to roll the thread into a ball. Finally, "the labour" of doing this becomes so tiresome that through sheer fatigue she wakes from her sleep and begins to wonder what the meaning of the dream might be.[7] Because this is a "true vision," the dream demands authoritative interpretation. Its meaning must be made publicly manifest by someone, empowered to reveal the "mystery hidden in it." It is another woman—an older nun residing in the same monastery at Wimborne, "who was known to possess the spirit of prophecy"—who offers the definitive gloss on this dream:

"These things," she went on, "were revealed to the person whose holiness and wisdom makes her a worthy recipient, because by her teaching and good example she will confer benefits on many people. The thread which came from her bowels and issued from her mouth, signifies the wise counsels that she will speak from the heart. The fact that it filled her hand means that she will carry out in her actions whatever she expresses in her words. Furthermore, the ball which she made by rolling it round and round signifies the mystery of divine teaching, which is set in motion by the words and deeds of those who give instruction and which turns earthwards through active works and heavenwards through contemplation, at one time swinging downwards through compassion for one's neighbour, again swinging upwards through the love of God. By these signs God shows that your mistress will profit many by her words and example, and the effect of them will be felt in other lands afar off whither she will go."[8]

Two things strike me as noteworthy about this vision, a rather obscure example from the so-called dark ages of a woman's speech empowered to produce consequences in a man's world. First, it calls into question our usual stereotypes of women in the Middle Ages either as the subject of a clerical misogyny that saw woman as the incarnation of every evil, on the one hand, or as the docile and virginal saint and martyr, on the other, suggesting that the dichotomy between Eve and Mary oversimplifies women's position in the Middle Ages. The dream reveals that St. Leoba's words will be powerful and authoritative. Her "wise counsels" will not only be spoken publicly and listened to, they will be realized in actions—hers and others'. More importantly, her words—the ball which she fashions from the purple thread—become the means by which "the mystery of divine teaching" are realized in human and social terms; they mediate between the human and divine (turning "earthwards through active works and heavenwards through contemplation"). According to the male author of the Life, Leoba's speech will have powerful material effects on the social institutions of which she is a part—in this case the institutions of nascent Christianity. The dream's prophecy is indeed fulfilled. At the request of Saint Boniface, Leoba travels to Germany as a missionary to aid in its Christianization. She presides over a convent at Bischofsheim. Her miracles include the calming of a storm, and the exposing of an infanticide. In the latter episode, her assumption of the authority of a judge in what is virtually a trial by ordeal exonerates an accused sister and saves the reputation of her convent. Leoba

counted among her powerful friends not only spiritual leaders like Saint Boniface, but temporal rulers as well, including the emperor Charlemagne and his queen, Hiltigard.

The second striking aspect of this vision is the fact that it locates Leoba's power to speak specifically in her body. The thread "issues from her very bowels." Leoba regurgitates her powerful words in a process that has its source in her body but seems beyond her control. This episode violates our sense of the decorum required of religious speech, which traditionally separates the disembodied voice of spirituality from the material body. It also transgresses the ideological boundaries between the classical "discursive" body—viewed as closed, homogenous, and monumental—and the grotesque body, with its materiality, orifices, and discharges. Leoba (or some other because the dream challenges the autonomy of the individual subject) speaks the body of her text through the text of her body.

Saint Leoba is only one of a number of women throughout the Middle Ages whose mystical visions gave them an unprecedented authority to speak and write, indeed to preach and instruct. This fact may come as a surprise to feminists more used to proclaiming women's historical silences. Saint Leoba's biography suggests that the "fact" of women's exclusion from the discourses of power in any period may be more complicated than it originally appears. But although they share the condition of patriarchy, as well as the misogynist attitudes inherited from early Christianity, there is much that separates an eighth-century visionary like Leoba from her counterparts in the thirteenth and fourteenth centuries.

Religious women in the eighth century enjoyed more institutional power, better education, and were more likely to assume duties and privileges that after the twelfth century would be reserved solely for men. Women could preside over convents and even over double monasteries, as the Saxon abbess Hugeberc did. The range of their learning was remarkable for the so-called dark ages, including Latin, the classics, Scriptures, the church fathers, and canon law. Often they were instructed not by men but by other women. Leoba was sent to Wimborne to study under its erudite abbess, Mother Tetta. Perhaps because the early church afforded women—at least aristocratic women—a greater scope for their talents and abilities, these women were less likely to indulge in abuses of their bodies. On the contrary, they preached—and practiced—moderation in all things pertaining to the body. Leoba's biographer, Rudolph, for instance, stresses her moderation in eating, drinking, and sleeping, in everything, indeed, except her studies.[9]

The twelfth, thirteenth, and fourteenth centuries produced an even larger number of texts by and about women whose speech was imbued with an authority of divine origins. "This is the only place in the history of the West," the French theorist Luce Irigaray writes hyperbolically, "in which a woman speaks and acts so publicly."[10] While it is possible to argue that female mystics merely ventriloquized the voice of a patriarchal religion,[11] it is worth asking why and how these particular women were empowered to speak with an authority that rivaled, and at times seemed to surpass, that of the misogynist male clerics who ruled the institutional church.

Elizabeth Petroff gives a sense of the kind of social and political power women with the status of orthodox mystic enjoyed. "Visions led women to the acquisition of power in the world while affirming their knowledge of themselves as women. Visions were a socially sanctioned activity that freed a woman from conventional female roles by identifying her as a genuine religious figure. They brought her to the attention of others, giving her a public language she could use to teach and learn. Her visions gave her

the strength to grow internally and to change the world, to build convents, found hospitals, preach, attack injustice and greed, even within the church."[12] Even heterodox mystics like Marguerite Porète and more marginal religious figures like Margery Kempe enjoyed something of the same privileged status and following.[13] As Petroff's analysis makes clear, the basis of the power the female mystic enjoyed was both discursive and public, not private and extralinguistic. The mystic's possession of a "public language" gives her the ability to act not just within a "woman's culture," but in a "man's world" as well.

What Petroff's analysis fails to make clear, however, is how the mystic's identification as a "genuine religious figure" freed her from "conventional female roles" that mandated docility, passivity, subservience, and reticence and how her public activities came to be "socially sanctioned" by a church anxiously guarding its spiritual and temporal power. These questions can only be answered by examining the relation of mystical discourse, institutional structures, and ideology by taking into account not only the subversiveness of mystical discourse but also its cooptation by the institutional church. It is, after all, not just a matter of discovering why women were turning to mysticism and other kinds of religious experience—both sanctioned and condemned—but also why the church, in certain cases, tolerated and even encouraged the female visionary, who occasionally seemed to undermine its own claims to authority. The needs served by mysticism must be understood in the context of a Foucauldian *disposatif,* or "grid of intelligibility," a nexus of social, cultural, and historical practices, both discursive and nondiscursive, encompassing not only institutional morality, theological statements, and philosophical propositions but such things as architectural arrangements, the arts, regulations, laws, administrative procedures, medicine, and customs as well.[14] In the case of mysticism, such a *dispositif* might be constructed from three primary sources: the political situation of the church after the twelfth century that resulted in the institutionalization of religious women, the cultural representations of the female body, and the disciplinary technologies that attempted to realize these representations. Within the *dispositif* these three threads form an interconnected web; but to see each of the various strands, it will be necessary to unravel them and treat each separately.

The political situation of the church in the thirteenth century bore little resemblance to that of its eighth-century counterpart. Concerned with consolidating its own authority by stressing the special power of the priesthood, the Catholic church, from the twelfth century on, had little use for women in official positions of either spiritual or temporal power. The church's jealous guarding of its prerogatives is evident in its numerous calls to pastoral care, its emphasis on the sacraments, particularly the Eucharist and confession where the priest most directly exercised his authority, and in conflicts between advocates of a monastic life of contemplation and those of an active life of pastoral care that often erupted into full-scale political conflicts over spiritual "turf." The growing distance between the clergy and the laity coincided with a resurgence of lay piety that left both men and women searching for outlets to express their own religious sentiments. The privileged status of the mystic reflected this tension between clerical centralization and lay expressions of piety. On the one hand, her claims of authority could easily be seen as subversive of clerical prerogatives. On the other, they could, when necessary, be co-opted by the church to strengthen its own spiritual and temporal authority. Although women were officially banned from preaching or administering sacraments (like penance), many of the female visionaries had disciples and followers whom they instructed, counseled, and even reprimanded for their sins. The line between preaching and instructing, between hearing confessions and concern for the sinfulness and spiritual welfare of others is thinly drawn in the writings of many of the medieval mystics. . . .

But if the mere existence of female mystics enjoying an unmediated relationship with the divine successfully subverted clerical authority, it could do so, paradoxically, only from within the institutional church and only to further that institution's ends—the consolidation of its power. The church strictly defined and controlled the nature and content of mystical experience. While it is easy for the twentieth-century reader to see the mystic's visionary claims as a reflection of highly private and personal experiences brought on by heightened affective and psychological states, for the Middle Ages, mysticism was a public discourse. It was neither private nor passive, but communal, dialogic, and active. The mystical experience was highly structured, and it was the church that provided both structure and content because it controlled through various means the lives and learning of women in religious communities. Increasingly after the twelfth century, the church attempted through strict cloistering to bring religious women more firmly under its control, to enforce women's silence, to institutionalize their powerlessness, and, most importantly from its own point of view, to isolate itself from women's supposedly corrupting influence.[15] Orthodox mystics with few exceptions were, after the twelfth century, cloistered, in keeping with the church's sense of women's spiritual role. To be sure, not all mystics were nuns. A mystic could express her religious ecstasies as a nun, abbess, wife, mother, tertiary, anchoress, Beguine, or itinerant. Often, when they were not cloistered, religious women tended to be tertiaries—like Catherine of Siena—or Beguines. But the model upon which all spiritual organizations for women were based was the cloister. And quite clearly its primary purpose was isolation. The rule Pope Honorius III handed down to Saint Clare, for instance, required that "no sister is to go out of the convent for any purpose whatever except to found a new community. Similarly, no one, religious or secular, is to be allowed to enter the monastery. Perpetual silence is imposed on all members of the community, and continuous fasting, often on bread and water." [16] Architecturally, the convent fostered maximum isolation from the society outside it, and access to these communities of cloistered women was strictly controlled. Life within the convent was structured by the liturgy and rituals of the church including "the seven canonical hours of daily prayers that followed the cycle of the liturgical year . . . [and] specific prayers for special saints' days and major feasts." [17] The spiritual disciplines that filled out this life included such practices as mantric prayer, flagellation, fasting, and vigils which, when carried to excesses, as they sometimes were, seemed designed to produce an emotional state conducive to mystical experience.

These technologies both resulted from and fed back into medieval cultural representations of the female. Woman had to be enclosed, restricted, and isolated because, in the eyes of the church, she was the quintessence of all fleshly evil, a scapegoat whose expulsion allowed the church to purge itself of the corruption of the body. [18] This loathing for the female flesh, expressed in countless official church documents, must be understood in light of its cultural meaning. To do so, we must abandon our usually biologistic understanding of the human body. Ordinarily we attribute to the body an *a priori* material existence without considering how our experience of our bodies is organized by cultural representations of them. Such representations are not universal but have historical specificity. Similarly, the material body can itself

be one of those discursive practices. It is itself a sign, imbued with meaning that can be glossed. We might argue, then, drawing upon Mikhail Bakhtin's distinction between the "classical body" and the "grotesque body," that two antithetical representations of the body structure discursive norms in any culture. [19] This opposition between the classical and grotesque bodies is meant to draw attention to those discursive practices that may have structured medieval women's understanding of their bodies. As I use it, the classical body denotes the form of official high culture. Medieval "high" culture was Latin, male, and extremely homogeneous, including such discourses as philosophy, theology, canon law, and liturgy. In the medieval church, the classical body was harmonious, proportionate, and monumental; it attempted to represent a sort of disembodied spirituality and, as such, it never existed except as cultural representation. The grosser, more material aspects of "the body" were displaced onto the "grotesque body." Woman (along with other marginal social groups, the lower classes, for example) is constructed by this dominant culture as the grotesque body, the other, whose discursive norms include heterogeneity, disproportion, a focus on gaps, orifices, and symbolic filth.

This sketch describes accurately the writings of many female mystics whose emotionalism and intense personal involvement, polyglot mixture of genres, and open-endedness contrast markedly with the monumental rationalism and harmonious proportion of classical theological writing by men. [20] Indeed, the emotionalism so often attributed to female piety, its so-called affective nature, as compared to the rationalistic nature of male piety, may in fact be expressed through violence on the body—tears, inflicting of elaborate injuries, screams, and howls.

. . . Their writings feature representations of grotesque bodies that open up and spill forth their contents—blood, milk, excrement—bodies that endure wounding and mutilation. The mystic's own body becomes the site of contested discourses about the body—and about culture.

Frequently, these conflicts emerge in rituals designed to chastise the flesh. In this passage from Angela's *Liber,* for instance, we see an intense loathing for the "lower-bodily stratum" and the grotesqueness of the physical body expressed through the desire to inflict humiliation on it. "I do not blush to recite before the whole world all the sins that I ever committed. But I enjoyed imagining some way in which I could reveal those deceptions and iniquities and sins. I wanted to go through the squares and the towns naked, with fish and meat hanging about my neck, saying, 'Here is that disgusting woman, full of malice and deception, the sewer of all vices and evils, . . . behold the devil in my soul and the malice of my heart.'" [21] The metonymic association of the female body with the corruption of rotting meat and fish invokes the grotesque body paradoxically to exorcize it. The female mystic's only means of escaping her body was to indulge in an obsessive display and denouncing of its most "grotesque" features. This suggests the extent to which, in her writing, the female mystic has internalized the discursive norms of the dominant "high" culture.

The mystic internalized the disciplinary technologies evolved by the church to subject and contain the female body, not just discursively, but physically as well. As one might guess, these technologies, misogynistic in their intent, were designed to suppress and control a female body the church deemed disruptive. In the case of the most famous mystics, these disciplines often became spectacular examples of self-torture in which the mystic indulged in extravagant abuses of her body. Rudolph Bell described Angela of Foligno's struggle to control her flesh.

Demons filled her head with visions of her soul being strung upside down so that all her virtues turned to vices; in anger, pain, tears, desperation, she pinched herself so hard that her head and body were covered with bruises, and still the torture continued. Human vices, even ones she never had known before, tormented every member of her body. Even when these desires may have shifted away from her "intimate parts" to places where she felt the pain less, so on fire was she that until Friar Arnaldo prohibited it, she used natural fire to extinguish the internal burning. As her spiritual understanding deepened, her wish changed from instant death to a drawn out physically painful and tormenting ending, one in which she would experience all the sufferings of the world in her every limb and organ. Her love had sacrificed and so would she. Earlier she had undertaken a detailed examination of each part of her body, judging them member by member and assigning to each its due penance. [22]

One can only assume that those penances would have been much like those practiced by Catherine of Siena, another Italian visionary, who wore rough wool clothing, an iron chain bound around her hips so tightly that it inflamed her skin, and flagellated herself three times a day with an iron chain for one and one-half hours. Angela of Foligno's obsession with the grotesqueness of the body is strikingly illustrated by another anecdote, also related by Bell. "She and her companion one Holy Thursday had gone to the local hospital of San Feliciano to wash the feet of sick women and the hands of men who were there. One leper they tended had flesh so putrefied and rotten that pieces peeled off into the wash basin they were using, Angela then proceeded to drink this mixture, giving her almost the sensation of receiving communion, and when a bit of flesh got stuck in her throat she tried to swallow it too until against her will she choked it out."[23] In this anecdote, the juxtaposition of the putrefied rotten flesh and the Eucharist calls up again the opposition between the grotesque and the classical bodies.[24] Indeed, it vividly and powerfully merges these two cultural representations of the body.

What, one might be tempted to ask, does the female mystic gain from such spectacles of self-abuse? My initial answer might be, like Petroff's, quite simply, power. But I would like to explore more specifically the nature of the power claimed by the female mystic, beginning, as I began this essay, with a reminder of just how audacious some female mystics' claims to power proved to be. If Marguerite Porète was burned at the stake for self-deification, several orthodox mystics made strikingly similar statements: "My Me is God," wrote Catherine of Genoa; Hadewijch of Brabant wished "To be God with God"; Angela of Foligno wrote that "The Word was made flesh to make me God." Surely these are not the statements of women who have accepted the traditional religious roles allotted to women. These women claim a virtually divine authority that they frequently exercised. Nevertheless, I am not suggesting that these women "intended" in any conscious way to seek their temporal or spiritual power. Rather my analysis depends upon what Paul Ricoeur has called a "hermeneutics of suspicion." The fact that none of the mystics says her intention is empowerment cannot be accepted at face value; it must be interrogated. I am assuming that these women were capable of entertaining as part of their cultural ideology motives of which they were not fully conscious. The whole point of embedding the discourse of medieval mysticism within a network of other discourses, within the Foucauldian *disposatif*, is precisely to interrogate "intention" from the perspective of cultural ideology.

Mystics took disciplines designed to regulate and subject the body and turned them into what Michel Foucault has called "technologies of the self," methods of consolidating spiritual power and authority, perhaps the only ones available to women.[25] Foucault argues that individuals often effect by their own means a certain number of operations on their bodies, souls, thoughts, and conduct—all to transform themselves and to attain a certain state of perfection, happiness, purity, and supernatural power.[26] Although he is describing the medieval Catholic discipline of confession, he might just as well be describing the lives of many medieval mystics. Michel de Certeau takes Foucault's argument about technologies of the self even further and argues that these mechanisms, which he calls "poaching," enable those subjected to disciplinary technologies to manipulate and evade them, or even shape them to their own ends, by seeming to conform to them.[27]

To understand how self-torture could become a technology of the self, a means of empowerment, we must understand the place of torture in medieval society. In the Middle Ages, torture was not regarded simply as a form of punishment. It was, as Foucault has shown, a technique and a ritual, a semiotic system which "must mark the victim."[28] Torture inscribed on the victim's body the "signs" of the ruler's power. It was one of the most visible displays of that power, an art, "an entire poetic" that competed with other visual displays of theocratic rule.[29] The marking of the victim's body signifies the power that punishes. "In the 'excesses' of torture, a whole economy of power is invested."[30] In her excesses, the mystic becomes at once both torturer and victim. This, it seems to me, is the whole point. The mystic's pain—her inflicting of wounds upon herself—grants her the authority to speak and be heard, to have followers, to act as a spiritual advisor, to heal the sick, and to found convents and hospitals. Her body bears the marks, the "signs," of her own spiritual power. The mystic's progress, then, is discursively organized by the disciplines authorized by religious tradition and performed on her body. She changes, however, the meaning of the physical forces that oppress her. She assumes for herself the power to define what they mean. It is important to recognize that the church at no time advised or condoned such severe fasting and self-flagellation. It advised moderation in all penance. In fact, the mystics themselves did not urge such extremes on others. The mystics were never seen as models to be imitated. They were always special instances of God's grace because they chose their own suffering and thus were free to define what it meant. That is why Angela of Foligno could desire such a violent and painful death, why Julian of Norwich could beg God for a terrible illness, and why Catherine of Siena starved herself to death. Technologies which, in the hands of a powerful church, were meant to limit severely the autonomy and authority of women became for the mystics a source of self-determination, virtually the only one available to women during this period.

It is this power to construct cultural meanings that creates the mystical text's dialogism—the interanimation of its words, its signs, with other ambiguous words and signs. The mystic does not merely call upon what she has read or seen to give words to an essentially wordless experience; I am not invoking here merely a one-way form of intertextuality. Rather these "spiritual exercises," and the meanings she gives them, are constitutive of her visions, as the following example from the Long Text of Julian of Norwich's *Showings* demonstrates. The fourteenth-century English mystic meditates on Christ's suffering during the Crowning with Thorns.

And during the time that our Lord showed me this spiritual vision which I have now described, I saw the bodily vision of the copious bleeding of the head persist. The great drops of blood fell from beneath the crown like pellets, looking as if they came from the veins, and as they issued they were a brownish red, for the blood was very thick, and as they spread they turned bright red. And as they reached the brows they vanished; and even so the bleeding continued until I had seen and understood many things. Nevertheless, the beauty and the vivacity persisted, beautiful and vivid without diminution.

The copiousness resembled the drops of water which fall from the eaves of a house after a great shower of rain, falling so thick that no human ingenuity can count them. And in their roundness as they spread over the forehead they were like a herring's scale.[31]

At first glance, this passage seems idiosyncratic, its metaphors positively bizarre. What perhaps most repels the twentieth-century reader is the disjunction between Christ's pain and suffering at the hands of his torturers, the ostensible subject of the vision, and the artifice with which it is conveyed. The images of the pellets, the rain drops falling from the eaves of a house, and particularly the herring's scales work against the impression of suffering; they detach the reader from any realistic sense of pain. Instead, they point to the symbolic nature of Christ's suffering. In Julian's vision, although the torturers attempt to leave their mark of temporal power on Christ's body, she shows that the "signs" contain messages other than those intended by the torturers, symbols of divine power that transcend mere physical pain, that shade over into the decorative, into art.

Indeed, the scene reminds me of nothing so much as a painting. Although Julian calls it a "bodily vision," suggesting a vision appearing to her eyes, reading the passage one is put in mind of an intense meditation upon a visual image— a picture in a book of hours, a station of the cross or some other church painting Julian might have seen. As she meditates ever closer on particular details, they lose their relationship to the whole composition and begin to remind her of other inanimate objects. As she traces the brush strokes, following the change in color from brownish red to bright red, finally vanishing from the canvas, other images—pellets, rain drops, herring's scales—suggest themselves to her, transforming the suffering into something artistic. Hence the contradictory description of the vision as "beautiful and vivid," "hideous and fearful," "sweet and lovely." The mystical vision, seen from this perspective, takes on the character less of a chance event, whether the sign of psychosis or spiritual grace, than of a calculated event, carefully prepared for and highly structured by the religious experiences available to medieval women, including those designed to chastise the flesh and imitate Christ's suffering.

The female mystic of the Middle Ages did not claim to speak in her own voice. Because women could serve no ministerial or sacerdotal functions within the church, they could claim no spiritual authority in and of themselves, nor could they claim it—as the clergy did—from the institutional church. Rather, the source of the mystic's inspiration was divine; she was merely the receptacle, the instrument of a divine will. Hildegard of Bingen, for example, describes her authorship in precisely those terms: "She . . . utters God's miracles not herself but is being touched by them, even as a string touched by a lutanist emits a sound not of itself but by his touch."[32] But women like Hildegard of Bingen, Angela of Foligno, and Julian of Norwich were not nearly as disingenuous as they had to appear in order to win the church's toleration and acceptance. Any visionary experience made public is always, *ipso facto*, a revisioning of that experience, an attempt to represent the unrepresentable. These women claimed the power to

shape the meaning and form of their experiences. Their words, and even their bodies when necessary, became the sites of a struggle to redefine the meaning of female silence and powerlessness.

Notes

I wish to thank Robert Markley, Valerie Lagorio, and Ulrike Wiethaus for their helpful comments on earlier drafts of this essay.

1. Michel Foucault, *Discipline and Punish: The Birth of the Prison,* trans. Alan Sheridan (New York: Vintage, 1979), 3–69, esp. 30. For an important discussion of the relationships between the body and the forms of divine power in the Hebraic Scriptures, esp. Genesis, see Elaine Scarry, *The Body in Pain: The Making and Unmaking of the World* (New York: Oxford University Press, 1985), esp. chap. 4, "The Structure of Belief and Its Modulation into Material Making," 181–243. For a discussion of early Christian commentaries on Genesis 1–3, see Elaine Pagels, *Adam, Eve, and the Serpent* (New York: Random House, 1988).

2. Caroline Bynum, *Jesus as Mother: Studies in the Spirituality of the High Middle Ages* (Berkeley: University of California Press, 1982), 172.

3. Gottfried Koch, *Frauenfrage und Ketzertum im Mittelalter,* 1962; quoted in Richard Abels and Ellen Harrison, "The Participation of Women in Languedocian Catharism," *Medieval Studies* 41 (1979): 215–51.

4. This term is a rough translation of Mikhail Bakhtin's term—*raznojazychie*—for the ideologically contested field of utterances.

5. In her notes to *The Book of Margery Kempe,* for example, Hope Emily Allen points out many instances of intertextuality between Margery's writing and that of several continental mystics (edited with Sanford Meech, London: Oxford University Press, 1940). Kempe describes her visit to her contemporary, Julian of Norwich, with whom she enjoyed lengthy conversations.

6. M. M. Bakhtin, *The Dialogic Imagination,*

trans. Caryl Emerson and Michael Holquist (Austin: University of Texas Press, 1981), 354.

7. Elizabeth Petroff, *Medieval Women's Visionary Literature* (New York: Oxford University Press, 1986), 108.

8. Ibid., 108–9.

9. Ibid., 110. On the position of women in the early church, see Jo Ann McNamara and Suzanne F. Wemple, "Sanctity and Power: The Dual Pursuit of Medieval Women," in *Becoming Visible: Women in European History,* ed. Renate Bridenthal and Claudia Koontz (Boston: Houghton Mifflin, 1977), 96–109.

10. Luce Irigaray, *Speculum of the Other Woman,* trans. Gillian C. Gill (Ithaca: Cornell University Press, 1985), 191. Irigaray's psychoanalytic reading of mysticism in "La Mystérique" regards the mystical experience as belonging in some essential way to women, or at least to the female; "the poorest in science and the most ignorant were the most eloquent, the richest in revelations. Historically, that is women. Or at least the female" (192). Irigaray's somewhat romanticized idealizations place the mystical experience outside language and representation, aligning it ahistorically, I would argue, with hysteria and madness. Irigaray's opposition of mystical discourse to the "dry desolation of reason" denies the historical complexity of women's participation in mysticism as a public, not solipsistic, discourse that thrived in a dialogic relationship with medieval culture.

11. To my knowledge, no one has made this argument specifically about the medieval mystics, although someone might. For the dangers in appropriating medieval women writers for feminism, see Sheila Delany, "Mothers to Think Back Through," in *Medieval Texts and Contemporary Readers,* ed. Laurie A. Finke and Martin Schichtman (Ithaca: Cornell University Press, 1987), 177–97.

12. Petroff, 6.

13. Although Marguerite was burned at the stake in 1310 and her book, *The Mirror of Simple Souls,* ordered burned by the Inquisition, the *Mirror* survived her death; its popularity is attested to by the number of translations made during the fourteenth century, including one in English. See Peter Dronke, *Women Writers of the Middle Ages: A Critical Study of Texts from Perpetua (203) to Marguerite Porète (1310)* (Cam-

bridge: Cambridge University Press, 1984), 217. Margery Kempe during her religious life alternately suffered accusations of madness and heresy and enjoyed the patronage and support of powerful ecclesiasts.

14. Hubert L. Dreyfus and Paul Rabinow, *Michel Foucault: Beyond Structuralism and Hermeneutics* (Chicago: University of Chicago Press, 1982), 120–25.

15. For a discussion of these changes in the twelfth-century church, see McNamara and Wemple, 110–16.

16. John Moorman, *A History of the Franciscan Order from Its Origins to the Year 1517* (Oxford: Clarendon, 1968), 35.

17. Petroff 6.

18. For an illuminating analysis of medieval misogyny as evidence of a "deep mistrust of the body and of the materiality of the sign," see Howard Bloch, "Medieval Misogyny," *Representations* 2 (1987): 14.

19. See M. M. Bakhtin, *Rabelais and His World,* trans. H. Iswolsky (Cambridge: MIT Press, 1968), 19; and Peter Stallybrass and Allon White, *The Politics and Poetics of Transgression* (Ithaca: Cornell University Press, 1986), 9–26.

20. On the effective nature of female piety in the fourteenth century, see Richard Kieckhefer, *Unquiet Souls: Fourteenth-Century Saints and Their Religious Milieu* (Chicago: University of Chicago Press, 1984).

21. Ibid., 7.

22. Rudolph M. Bell, *Holy Anorexia* (Chicago: University of Chicago Press, 1985), 107–8. Although I want to distance myself from its conclusions, Bell's book, like Bynum's *Holy Feast and Holy Fast: The Religious Significance of Food to Medieval Women,* 209–11, provides numerous examples of this kind of self-torture.

23. Bell, 108.

24. Bynum writes that the drinking of pus was a common practice among female saints (*Holy Feast and Holy Fast,* 144–45). For another argument on the "hidden alliances" between mysticism and torture, see Michel de Certeau, "Mystic Speech," in *Heterologies: Discourse on the Other,* trans. Brian Massumi (Minneapolis: University of Minnesota Press, 1986), 80–100.

25. Michel Foucault, "Sexuality and Solitude," in *On Signs,* ed. Marshall Blonsky (Baltimore: Johns Hopkins University Press, 1985), 43.

26. Ibid., 367.

27. Michel de Certeau, *The Practice of Everyday Life,* trans. Steven Rendall (Berkeley: University of California Press, 1984).

28. Foucault, *Discipline and Punishment,* 34.

29. Ibid., 45.

30. Ibid., 35.

31. Julian of Norwich, *Showings,* ed. Edmund Colledge and James Walsch (New York: Paulist, 1978), 287–88.

32. Dronke, 160.

34 Autobiography, Bodies, Manhood

Shirley Neuman

*And so at last we come down to it, the body—that small hot engine at the
centre of all these records and recollections.*

—David Malouf

Autobiography, or,
Life (Dis)Embodied

Despite David Malouf's getting "down" to the
fact that the lives represented in autobiographies
are embodied, he gives only a few brief pages to
his own body. Nonetheless, in this his *12 Edmonstone Street* does more than most autobiographies, which almost completely efface the bodies in which the lives they describe were lived.
We can cite many reasons for this, chief among
them a Platonic tradition which opposes the
mental/spiritual to the corporeal and then identifies "self" with the spiritual. The same opposition informs the elevation of soul over body in
Christian theology and operates powerfully in
confession which, in its careful eliciting of precise details of the desires of the flesh, particularly
in its early practice, aimed at mastery of that
same flesh. Autobiography, Georges Gusdorf
showed us some time ago, grew out of confession and it inherited both the legislation toward
the incorporeal codified in confession and the
increasing reserve in the questions asked, particularly about sex, counselled in confessors'
manuals from the late seventeenth century on
(Foucault, 18–19). By the eighteenth century,
Foucault notes, the practice of confession had
been transformed and extended to relationships
such as those between child and parent, student
and teacher, patient and doctor, and much of its
use aimed at the regulation of sexuality (63). The
ultimate goal of these confessional practices remained, however, the transcendence, through
regulation, of the corporeal: witness Descartes'
definition of "man" as "a thing or substance
whose whole essence or nature is only to think,
and which, to exist, has no need of space nor of
any material thing or body" (Foucault, 25). The
body, defined as "natural," functioned as the binary opposite of and as a metaphor by which the
spiritual was understood; it remained necessary
to this understanding at the same time that it
had, necessarily, to be transcended in philosophy and effaced in representation. Freud's work
would seem to constitute a definitive break
in this binarism of body and mind insofar as
it theorizes a libido-driven consciousness and
elaborates a somatic symptomology of psychic
disturbances. In fact, much in its analytic procedures is continuous with confession and its
diversification into post-Enlightenment pedagogical and medical practices. Like these earlier
practices, Freud's is preoccupied above all with
the sexed body, and, like theirs, his aims at con-

415

structing an interiorized experience of the self and somatic manifestations of that experience consonant with public, cultural values. The hysteric's symptoms analyzed away, the body as signifier once again cedes to the life of the mind.

Confession, whether practised in the church or by means of one of its avatars in childrearing, tutoring, or medical consultation, remains an intimate and *private* discourse, one of the aims of which, as Foucault has shown, is to manage the body, to make it conform with *public* and *cultural* values. In the traditions of life-writing, therefore, bodies, in all their aches and illnesses, as sites of unease, and, more modestly and fleetingly, in their beauties or their desires, are far more apt to make an appearance in the private genre of the diary than in the avowedly public and cultural genre of the autobiography. Redirected into autobiography and its criticism, not the practice but the goal of confession determines the narrative which, like others in western "high" cultures, establishes access to public discourse about the self as synonymous with spiritual quest and defines the "self" or "identity" as synonymous with continuity and coherence of consciousness rather than of the physical body. That western cultures assume an analogy between mind, masculinity, and culture, and between body, femininity, and "nature," only reinforces the disembodiment of the self characteristic of most autobiographies.

In what follows I will look at [one] anomalous moment in which a masculine body ruptures and exceeds the discursive effacement of the corporeal which is characteristic of autobiography. I will do so neither from the long-held assumption that anatomy determines and defines sexuality and gender nor from the more recent distinction between biological sex and social gender. Rather, I hold, as Bryan Turner, who follows Foucault, puts it, that our bodies are both material and "the effects of cultural, historical activity" (49)—codified by adornment, exercise,

surgery, gestures, pleasures, performances, diet, labors, punishments, idealizations, etc. These mediated bodies are in themselves representations of social values. They are "*always already cultural*" (Grosz, "Notes," 7), socially constructed and codified from before birth. Their codification or "inscription," to use Grosz' metaphor, is "directed towards the acquisition of appropriate cultural attitudes, beliefs and values," that is, toward the production of a body's "interiority." Rather than standing opposed to mind, then, the body becomes a medium, or an "*interface* between 'privatised' experience and signifying cultures" ("Notes," 10). One of the main effects of this process in western cultures is that sexed bodies whose biological and material characteristics and capacities and whose psychosexual experiences and drives exist on a broad continuum have been socially coded into the categories of male and female, and this polarization of heterosexual difference has been at the expense of many possible positions along the continuum.[1] Finally, and again along with recent feminist theorists of the body, in what follows I conceive of bodies not only as produced or constructed by social power but also as potentially resistant to that power and productive of other ideologies and other social powers. The question for the reader of the rare autobiography which represents the body becomes, then, one of the extent to which that representation reiterates and reinforces the social codes constructing bodies or the extent to which it reconfigures them,

The *Memoirs* of the nineteenth-century French hermaphrodite, Herculine Barbin . . . foreground the masculine body by representing its penis metonymically. However reductive this seems, it is not, I would suggest, the equivalent of the fragmentation of female bodies which, historically, has characterized much erotic representation of women, nor does it anticipate Lacan by asking the Phallus as transcendental signifier to stand up for a more or less (in)effective penis. The direct, if obvious, metonymy for masculine bodies, used in autobiography, does constitute an explicit subversion of the social relegation of penises to folktales, locker room talk, jokes, pornography, sex manuals, soldiers' songs, colloquial idiom, profanity, and the intimacy of the therapist's office, a relegation concomitant with a minimalization of the penis in "high" culture, particularly in the classical traditions of the visual arts. The motivation to that subversion, the autobiographers' understanding of the social construction of their "masculine" bodies, the extent and kinds of agency which the written representation of their masculine bodies produces for Barbin . . . and the implications for our understanding of gender of that agency are my subject in the remainder this essay.

Law, the Hermaphrodite, and the Gender of Style

Adélaide Herculine Barbin, called Alexina, was born in France in 1838 and grew up about equally, if incompletely, endowed with male and female sexual morphology. Registered at birth as a girl, she was educated in a convent and at a normal school, and, nineteen but "completely ignorant of the facts of life" (Barbin, 33), went on to teach in a girls' boarding school. There she fell in love with, and made love to, the daughter of the school's proprietess, with whom she lived, to all appearances, on sisterly terms. Alerted to her anomalous situation by the surprised remarks of a doctor whom she consulted about abdominal pains, she sought the advice of a bishop who referred her to a Dr. Chesnet. He, after examining her, counselled her to apply to the courts to "rectify" her "civil," that is, her gender, status (Barbin, 78). On the basis of his recommendation, the courts ruled her a man. Moved by "disgust," "shame," and a "vast de-

sire for the unknown" which "made [him] egotistic" (80–81), Abel, as he now became legally, or Herculine as the literature usually refers to him, or Camille as he names the narrator of his *Memoirs,* broke with her lover, went to Paris where he worked in railroad administration and, in 1868, asphyxiated himself by means of the fumes from a charcoal stove.[2] The following year, Dr. E. Goujon published his report of the autopsy he performed on the body, and Professor Auguste Tardieu edited and published in the medical literature in 1872 and 1874 the *Memoirs* of Herculine Barbin, written between the time Barbin assumed a masculine identity and his death.

Two aspects of this instance of hermaphroditism and of Barbin's description of it in the *Memoirs* can tell us something about the ways in which various discourses shaped understanding of the sexed body at this particular historical juncture. One is to be found in the religious, medical and legal decisions and discourses about her gender, that is, her "civic" status, as well as in Alexina's own reaction to having made love to a woman: all these constructed Barbin's hermaphroditic body as masculine. The second is to be found in the rhetoric of the *Memoirs.*

The medical reports both of Dr. Chesnet's examination of Alexina and of Dr. Goujon's autopsy of Abel continuously assert and simultaneously deny her/his hermaphroditic and female sexual morphology, assimilating both to the morphology of the male body. Dr. Goujon's autopsy report characterizes Abel as "one of the most typical cases of *masculine* hermaphroditism" but then goes on in the next sentence to note that "it is difficult . . . to discover a more extreme mixture of the two sexes, as concerns everything relating to the external genital organs" (129, my emphasis). It details a narrow vagina two and one-half inches long and a "penis" which, flaccid, is two inches long and one inch in diameter. Although the autopsy report concludes that this "was a large clitoris rather than a penis" (131), it nonetheless consistently calls it a penis. Both reports note that Barbin's "penis" is imperforate, making it homologous to her vagina which is closed at its nether end. Neither manual examination nor autopsy reveals a uterus. What Dr. Chesnet first describes as labia majora, he later concludes is "only the two halves of a scrotum that remained divided" (126). Both doctors note sperm ducts descending on either side of the vagina; the autopsy report indicates that the "seminal fluid . . . did not contain spermatozoa" (143). The vaginal mucous membrane Dr. Goujon found "very congested" (135) and full of ducts indicating that it produced the fluids characteristic of sexual arousal in a woman. The urethra is definitely feminine. Secondary sexual characteristics are absent or, minimally present, tend to the "masculine": there is no breast development nor is there hair on the chest, and the beard is sparse, although hair is abundant on the buttocks and thighs.

Barbin lived out this hermaphroditism at a historical juncture when two contradictory paradigms defining masculinity, femininity and the relation between them were culturally current.[3] The *psychology* of masculinity, femininity and heterosexuality, since the seventeenth century, had increasingly been defined in terms of the *differences* between the sexes. Moreover, nineteenth-century culture represented sexuality as a specific "problem" which needed to be "faced" by means of the investigative and theorizing capabilities of the medical profession (Heath, 16). The "problem" was largely the political and social one of control of female sexuality, and its "solution" depended largely on medical confirmation that conception could take place without orgasm, allowing for the idealized gendering of women as "different" from men in being both "maternal" and "passionless."

At the same time, however, the medical discourse of sexual morphology was still formulated, as it had been from the time of Aristotle and Galen and through the Renaissance, in terms of the *similarities* between the sexes. For the long tradition growing out of Greek medicine, generative organs and "substances" were homologous and "incontrovertible elements in the economy of a single-sex body" which was then socially gendered into a higher, male and a lower, female form (Laqueur, *Making*, 42). Moreover, by the mid-nineteenth century the discoveries of embryogeny had confirmed that the penis and the clitoris develop out of what begins as an undifferentiated embryonic structure, as do the testicles and the ovaries, and the labia and the scrotum (Laqueur, *Making*, 10, 169). Indeed, the precision brought to sexual morphology by nineteenth-century medical discoveries meant that "true sex"—as Dr. Goujon would have it—was decided on more rigorously and narrowly anatomical grounds than ever before. With reference to Barbin, for example, Professor Tardieu insisted that sex "is a pure question of fact that can and ought to be resolved by the anatomical and physiological examination of the person in question" (cited in Laqueur, *Making*, 136, 278–79 n. 41). Morphology and not experience decided the question of sex, as the case of Herculine Barbin so graphically demonstrates; in Thomas Laqueur's succinct formulation, "The autopsy, not the interview, was the moment of truth" (*Making*, 188). The simultaneous development and entrenchment of a psychology of gender *difference*, however, exerted enormous pressure on the interpretation of anatomical evidence and virtually precluded an understanding of the sexed body that would have allowed for a place somewhere between the heterosexual poles of male and female: the object of the examination was to decide which was the "true sex," not to decide where, on a continuum, the individual experienced his or her body and sexuality. This tension between a same-sex model and a different-sex model for the human body remained an unresolved part of the medical and legal discourses which exercised such a decisive role in Alexina's life. Only when Freud, ignoring the considerable medical evidence pointing to the paucity of nerve endings susceptible to erotic stimulation in the vagina as compared to the clitoris, relocated mature female sexual pleasure from the clitoris to the vagina did a complete shift in sexual definition from the establishment of similarities to the establishment of differences between the sexes seem to have taken place.[4] Freud displaces morphological evidence in order to theorize a different female body stamped by the imprimatur of his new psychological "science." What he theorizes is a female body whose mature sexuality is ineluctably in the service of reproduction, a body purged of the temptations to self-pleasuring or homoeroticism that had always lurked within the "one sex/flesh" model.

Alexina was diagnosed a man, then, at an historical juncture when the medical discourse of men and women as sexually homologous, if socially different, had partially but not entirely given way to both a medical and a social discourse of sexual difference. That her sexuality and her body were constructed and represented in religious, medical and legal discourses in terms of the *confusion* of this (rather prolonged) historical moment is nowhere so evident as in the two medical reports, the details of which imply a place on a sexual continuum between male and female which both doctors' conclusions emphatically deny. Dr. Chesnet, in the report which became the basis of the legal decision, after listing the anatomical details I have cited above, sums up:

What shall we conclude from the above facts? Is Alexina a woman? She has a vulva, labia majora, and a feminine urethra, in-

dependent of a sort of imperforate penis, which might be a monstrously developed clitoris. She has a vagina. True, it is very short, very narrow; but after all, what is it if it is not a vagina? These are completely feminine attributes. Yes, but Alexina has never menstruated; the whole outer part of her body is that of a man, and my explorations did not enable me to find a womb. Her tastes, her inclinations draw her toward women. At night she has voluptuous sensations that are followed by a discharge of sperm; her linen is stained and starched with it. Finally, to sum up the matter, ovoid bodies and spermatic cords are found by touch in a divided scrotum. *These are the real proofs of sex.* We can now conclude and say: Alexina is a man, hermaphroditic, no doubt, but with an obvious predominance of masculine sexual characteristics. (127–28, emphasis mine)

And on the basis of his autopsy, Dr. Goujon suggests that the

formation of the external genital organs of this individual permitted him, *although he was manifestly a man,* to play either the masculine or the feminine role in coitus, without distinction; but he was sterile in both cases. He could play the role of the man in this act by virtue of an imperforate penis that was capable of erection. . . . As we shall see later when it is described, this organ was a large clitoris rather than a penis. . . . As he tells us in his memoirs, it was possible for the erection to be accompanied by an ejaculation and voluptuous sensations. (131–32, my emphasis)

There are two sticking points for Goujon, both of which he finesses. The first is Alexina's female urethra, which leads the doctor into a discussion of the uses of the male urinary canal as an "analogue of the vaginovulvar canal of the female": "As a matter of fact, it is above all the propulsor of the semen. It only *lends itself* to the excretion of urine." Men, this argument runs, have "no urethral canal, strictly speaking"; instead they have a seminal canal. Only women have a urethra (142, his emphasis). Alexina, therefore, is not, in a "strict" sense, missing a male urethra. Instead, because she has not one, but two, ejaculatory canals, albeit uncharacteristically displaced from the penis to the sides of the vagina, she is clearly male: "Procreation is the natural goal of marriage, and Alexina possessed the organs that are characteristic of his sex and whose functions he exercised" (143). But this raises the second sticking point: the absence of spermatazoa. Goujon sets that difficulty aside with the observation that "this state of affairs might well have been only temporary . . . and at another time one might well have noted the presence of spermatozoa in his seminal fluid" (144).

The confused nomenclature of these accounts, the sleights of hand by which ambiguous sexual morphology is assimilated to the masculine, the heterosexual assumption that because Alexina is attracted to women she is male: all make plain that there is no more provision in these medical readings of morphological evidence for a continuum of sexuality between "male" and "female" than there is in the era's psychology of heterosexual difference. Instead, two assumptions underlie the reading of the evidence which ensure that the subject's "true sex" can be discovered and that, in cases of ambiguity, that sex will be "male."

The first assumption is not stated but is clearly operative in the priority given to "masculine" over "feminine" morphology when it comes time to draw conclusions. Despite Chesnet's observation that "this little member . . . because of its dimensions is as far removed from

the clitoris as it is from the penis" (126); despite Goujon's conclusion that the penis was in fact a clitoris; despite the fact that French medical literature of the nineteenth century held that the clitoris was the locus of female sexual pleasure and the vagina only a comparatively uninteresting passage of ingress and egress for reproductive purposes;[5] despite the fact that Alexina/Abel is able "to play either the masculine or the feminine role in coitus, without distinction"; and despite the fact that s/he is sterile in either role, the "penis" becomes the dominant signifier of sexuality. Masculinity is the "norm" against which sexuality and gender are defined, and the clerical, medical and legal practitioners can, quite simply, only see a penis. In this, their interpretation is entirely consistent with the history of medical discourse about the sexed body; they read the evidence before them in terms of "the classical one-sex model" (Laqueur, "Amor," 104) which shaped medical discourse from the Greeks to Freud, a model which sustained "only one canonical body and that body was male" (Laqueur, *Making*, 63). Combined with the still-lingering Aristotelian (and Renaissance) conviction that all forms tended toward the more perfect, this model ensured that medical science could see the ambiguously sexed hermaphroditic body only as tending toward and needing to be assimilated into the canonical male body.

The second assumption determining the physicians' conviction that Alexina is a "man" is stated by Goujon. "Procreation is the natural goal of marriage" (i.e., sex), he begins his concluding remarks which will be about Alexina's capacity to ejaculate. Here, "evidence" so imprecise as to be retrospectively undecidable is used as a determinant of masculinity. It is worth noting that Barbin's *Memoirs* do not, as we saw Goujon suggesting earlier, tell us that he ejaculates. At their most precise, they tell us that she is "dominated . . . completely" by *an incredible sensation,* also described as "nervous trembling" (32). The detail of ejaculation Goujon actually takes from Dr. Chesnet's report that "At night she has voluptuous sensations that are followed by a discharge of sperm; her linen is stained and starched with it." We have, of course, no way of knowing what Alexina told Dr. Chesnet about these nocturnal emissions; however, given either the terms of their description by Dr. Chesnet (voluptuousness, an emission staining and starching her underwear), or the terms in which she describes her orgasms in the *Memoirs,* there is no *a priori* or *necessary* reason to read the "incredible sensation" as male orgasm or the emission as spermatic. (Orgasm during sleep, sometimes as a consequence of dreams, remains a subject passed over in silence by medical discourse about female sexuality.) Once again, the medical profession can only see a penis and its products. Not to do so, in this case, would be to acknowledge that Alexina's hermaphroditism might include something of an impassioned woman, one outside male heterosexual control and one capable of orgasmic dreams and of "tribadism."

Alexina's experience of "real passion" (48) for Sara, at least as "Abel" recounts it in the *Memoirs,* falls into the same pattern. She approaches Sara as a woman to another woman, but, having made her her "lover" (52), she conceptualizes the situation in terms of illicit heterosexuality, terming her "my *mistress!!!*" (54), and fearing she has impregnated her. Given the euphemistic style of the narrative, as well as Alexina's own avowal that she was still ignorant of the facts of life at the time that she moved from normal school to Sara's boarding school, one perhaps cannot take this heterosexual language or her fears too literally. Neither Alexina's knowledge nor Abel's literary conventions and language equip her/him to describe with precision the physical aspects of the relationship. What is clear is that, once the dalliance had passed beyond the sisterly, Alexina thinks of it heterosexually. To make love to a woman is to be a man, for her as for the medical profession.

For both Alexina and her doctors, all rests then on the penis and its reproductive function, even if organ and function are separated as in the case of Barbin's genitals. Hence the particular unease caused Dr. Goujon by the fact that there are no spermatozoa in the vesicles of the deceased Barbin and his need to hypothesize their possible presence at other times. To firmly ensure not only the canonicity but the unassailable priority and perfection of the male body in this heterosexual narrative of hermaphroditism (to ensure in effect that, as Dr. Goujon asserts, "hermaphroditism does not exist in man" [139]), the cause of that unease must be rationalized away. Goujon, constrained by the facts of the autopsy, can only hypothesize other, more reproductively virile, moments for Barbin. But one Oscar Panizza, psychiatrist turned soft-porn writer, took the license of fiction to insure that all was right with the world when he used Barbin's case history as the basis of his "Alexina Besnard" in "A Scandal at the Convent." His directive epigraph cites the reproductive mandate from Genesis 1:27–28: "male and female created he them. . . . and God said unto them, Be fruitful, and multiply" (155). And his conclusion quotes a report of the doctor's examination of his protagonist which relies for most of its details on the actual medical reports about Barbin but from which he also makes significant departures. These increase the "masculinity" of Alexina's secondary sexual characteristics, render the vagina so tight as to make penetration impossibly painful, suppress all suggestions of a clitoris in favor of "a succulent body, perforated at the tip, which proves to be a well-defined *membrum virile*" (198). The perforation, he makes plain, is the opening of the urethra which, for this fictional Alexina, performs both its usual functions: "he had, in the course of the examination, . . . an involuntary emission of semen, which proved under the microscope to contain normal, mobile spermatozoa" (199). Lest any doubt remain about the virile capacities of the "male hermaphrodite," Panizza's final paragraph tells us that Alexina's lover "found it necessary to leave [the convent] after about six months, for the home of an aunt in a distant part of the country" where, we are to conclude, she had Alexina's child in more privacy than the convent permitted (199). One of the ideological mandates of this fiction, then, is to resolve, in favor of maleness and more conclusively than the medical reports could, the crisis of reference and representation produced by Barbin's ambiguously sexed body.

On the evidence of the church, the law, medicine and of fiction, Alexina is a man, and a changed codification of her sexed body is simultaneous with this decision. He gives up her job as schoolmistress, adopts masculine dress, takes up a masculine job, and, in the last words of the *Memoirs,* determines on spiritual quest out of his "thirst for the unknown, which is so natural to man" (115).

The effects of this gendering of the body are nowhere so evident in Barbin's memoirs as in her/his style. Throughout, the style adopts the gendered rhetoric of the romantic novels of the period, which frequently interpret sexuality in terms of obstacle-ridden love and characterize women in terms of excesses of sensibility, in an overwrought and euphemistic rhetoric which Barbin imitates (Butler, 98–99; Porter, 127–28). Describing her experience as a woman, Barbin tells us about her anxieties about her physical appearance (26–27), about her physical shame, about her feelings for her mother, her protector, her girlfriends, her lover, her employer. A reticence sometimes obscures her self-representation as when she describes her refusal to take part in a bathing party with her schoolmates, but she is retrospectively clear that this reticence re-

flects her own innocence at the time of what restrained her and that she was motivated by (appropriately "feminine") modesty (39). But her language also marks her emotional connectedness to others, and it is, above all, intimate as to her feelings.

This style changes decisively at the juncture in the manuscript at which Herculine, now a "man," departs for Paris, when these details and this intimacy fall away and a pained rhetoric of Olympian spiritual superiority and Promethean defiance begins to dominate. We do not know precisely what adjustments of attitude and manner Alexina makes to become Abel. We do see him become more summary, and more alienated, aloof, and judgmental than was the Alexina who engaged her emotions and others directly. Of others, he concludes, "There is an abyss between them and myself, a barrier that cannot be crossed . . . I defy them all" (102). Most particularly, Abel/Herculine no longer speaks of his body. Instead he sets the "degraded women," "hideous copulations," "faithless" wives and "filthy sores" of those "enchained here below by the thousand bonds of . . . gross, material senses" against his own participation in "the nature of the angels" and his spirit's "plunge into that limpid Ocean of the infinite, where . . . my soul drinks deep" (99). Any conclusion about the gendered construction of the self or about its embodiment in life or in autobiography that we might wish to draw from this rhetoric must be tempered by a recognition of the fact that someone redefined as masculine at twenty-two is hardly gender-representative and by a recognition of the real alienation Herculine experiences as an object of curiosity and newly burdened with specific medical knowledge, as well as with a sense of moral opprobrium with regard to her lover. His rhetoric is shaped by suffering, self-pity, isolation, shame, regret and a compensatory arrogance at least as much as by his considerable awareness of the ways in which gender, and even the sexed body, are socially constructed.

Moreover we do not know that this repression of the "material senses" for a rhetoric of the spirit plunging into the "limpid Ocean of the infinite"—lying perhaps across the boundary of suicide—is entirely Barbin's doing for we have for his life as a man only the incomplete and edited version of the manuscript presented in the medical literature by Auguste Tardieu. His editing, as Michel Foucault describes it, "neglected the recollections of Alexina's final years—everything that in his opinion consisted only of laments, recriminations, and incoherencies" (Barbin, 119). Which is to say: Tardieu excised precisely that content and rhetoric which, in the misogynist traditions of literature and medicine, have been associated with women's writing and women. Moreover, Barbin writes his memoirs from the knowledge and the perspective of his "masculinity"; the extent to which his depictions of his life as a girl and his life as a man are the result of a gendered perspective assumed along with the legal status of manhood is impossible to determine. We do not know, therefore, whether Barbin's disembodiment within his own memoirs once he reaches the point in the narrative of being *legally* identified as masculine is an effect of his own narrative, and what motivated it if it is, or whether it is an effect of Tardieu's editing of it to conform with the discourse of the medico-legal venue in which he published it. But whichever is the case, both the medical reports and the edited version of Barbin's life as a man enact a reading of hermaphroditism which strongly suggests that the masculine body is constructed *as always already seen*. The edited *Memoirs* also suggest that because what is always already seen becomes the "canonical body," it need not be represented for it is what the reader knows is there. The reader himself is indisputably masculine: Herculine addresses "Men!" in their relations to women (99). We *see* Alexina's body because she is painfully aware that its thin gracelessness, its "sickly pallor," its "hardness" of feature, and its hairiness "all struck the eye" (26–27) as deviating from the norm of female beauty as object of the gaze. Once that body is medically and judicially defined as male, has been made to conform, however ambiguously or inadequately, to *the* sexual body, Barbin, or Tardieu, can assume rather than display it in the *Memoirs*. Masculinity, as rhetoric, consists precisely in this disembodiment. Alexina may have gained a voice by assuming masculinity, as Roger Porter has suggested . . . , but she has lost her body to discourse and to death. Alexina Barbin's suicide is but the logical extension of the understanding of gender that church, state, law, medicine and literature have effected on and by means of her body.

Notes

1. Cf. Wendy Hollway (in Henriques et al.) and Teresa de Lauretis' discussion of her argument (15–17); also Weeks; Laqueur; Butler (8); and Grosz ("Inscriptions," 72–73).

2. In my use of masculine and feminine pronouns for Alexina, I follow her/his own practice in the French text. See the translator's note (Barbin, xiv).

3. 1 am indebted to the work of Foucault, Laqueur, Weeks, and Heath for what follows on the history of the discursive construction of sex and gender.

4. Freud, however, could not have posited vaginal sexuality as a basis of female sexual difference without nineteenth-century medicine's discovery of the embryonic homology of clitoris and penis. Early medical science held that the vagina, not the clitoris, was the inverted homologue of the penis. It held, therefore, that men's and women's sexual morphology was the same, rather than different, precisely because, like Freud, it located female sexual pleasure in the vagina. (See Laqueur, *Making Sex,* for a detailed account

of these changing representations of female sexual morphology in relation to the male. And see his "Amor Veneris" for a discussion of the clitoris as the most frequently new found, and lost again, land of female sexuality.)

5. Laqueur, *Amor,* 99–100, summarizes some of this literature.

Works Cited

Barbin, Herculine. *Herculine Barbin: Being the Recently Discovered Memoirs of a Nineteenth-Century French Hermaphrodite.* Intro. Michel Foucault. Trans. Richard McDougall. New York: Pantheon Books, 1980. [*Herculine Barbin dite Alexina B.* Paris: Gallimard, 1978.]

Butler, Judith. *Gender Trouble: Feminism and the Subversion of Identity.* New York and London: Routledge, 1990.

Chesnet, Dr. "The Question of Identity; the Malformation of the External Genital Organs; Hypospadias; an Error about Sex." In Barbin, 124–28.

De Lauretis, Teresa. "The Technology of Gender." *Technologies of Gender: Essays on Theory, Film, and Fiction.* Bloomington: Indiana University Press, 1987. 1–30.

Foucault, Michel. *The History of Sexuality.* Vol. 1: *An Introduction.* Trans. Robert Hurley. New York: Vintage, 1990. *[La volonté de savoir.* Paris: Gallimard, 1976.

Freud, Sigmund. "Medusa's Head." *The Standard Edition of the Complete Psychological Works of Sigmund Freud.* Vol. 18 (1920–22). Ed. James Strachey. London: Hogarth, 1955. 273–74.

Goujon, E. "A Study of a Case of Incomplete Hermaphroditism in a Man." In Barbin, 129–44.

Grosz, Elizabeth. "Inscriptions and Body Maps: Representations and the Corporeal." In *Feminine, Masculine, and Representation,* ed. Terry Threadgold and Anne Cranny-Francis. Sydney: Allen and Unwin, 1990. 62–74.

Grosz, Elizabeth. "Notes towards a Corporeal Feminism." In *Feminism and the Body,* ed. Judith Allen and Elizabeth Grosz. Special issue of *Australian Feminist Studies* 5 (1987): 1–16.

Gusdorf, Georges. "Conditions and Limits of Autobiography." Trans. James Olney. In *Autobiography: Essays Theoretical and Critical,* ed. James Olney. Princeton: Princeton University Press, 1980. 28–48.

Heath, Stephen. *The Sexual Fix.* London: Macmillan, 1982.

Henriques, Julian, Wendy Hollway, Cathy Urwin, Couze Venn, and Valerie Walkerdine, eds. *Changing the Subject: Psychology, Social Regulation, and Subjectivity.* London: Methuen, 1984.

Laqueur, Thomas W. "Amor Veneris, vel Dulcedo Appelatur." *Fragments for a History of the Human Body. Part Three.* Ed. Michel Feher with Ramona Naddaff and Nadia Tazi. New York: Zone, 1989. 90–131.

Laqueur, Thomas W. *Making Sex: Body and Gender from the Greeks to Freud.* Cambridge: Harvard University Press, 1990.

Malouf, David. *12 Edmonstone Street.* London: Chatto and Windus, 1985.

Panizza, Oscar. "A Scandal at the Convent." Trans. Sophie Wilkins. In Barbin, 153–99.

Porter, Roger. "Figurations and Disfigurements: Herculine Barbin and the Autobiography of the Body." In *Autobiography and Questions of Gender,* ed. Shirley Neuman. London: Frank Cass, 1991. 122–36.

Turner, Bryan S. *The Body and Society: Explorations in Social Theory.* Oxford: Basil Blackwell, 1984.

Weeks, Jeffrey. *Sexuality.* London: Tavistock; Chichester: Ellis Horwood, 1986.

PART VII
Politics and Pedagogy

That is my cause. As I've already said, it wasn't born out of something good, it was born out of wretchedness and bitterness. It has been radicalized by the poverty in which my people live. It has been radicalized by the malnutrition which I, as an Indian, have seen and experienced. And by the exploitation and discrimination which I've felt in the flesh. And by the oppression which prevents us performing our ceremonies, and shows no respect for our way of life, the way we are. At the same time, they've killed the people dearest to me, and here I include my neighbors from my village among my loved ones. Therefore, my commitment to our struggle knows no boundaries nor limits. This is why I've traveled to many places where I've had the opportunity to talk about my people. Of course, I'd need a lot of time to tell you all about my people, because it's not easy to understand just like that. And I think I've given some idea of that in my account. Nevertheless, I'm still keeping my Indian identity a secret. I'm still keeping secret what I think no-one should know. Not even anthropologists or intellectuals, no matter how many books they have, can find out all our secrets.

    —Rigoberta Menchú, *I, Rigoberta Menchú: An Indian Woman in Guatemala*, ed. Elisabeth Burgos-Debray, trans. Ann Wright (London: Verso, 1984), 246–47

Sometimes I feel I have seen too long from too many disconnected angles: white, Jewish, anti-Semite, racist, anti-racist, once-married, lesbian, middle-class, feminist, expatriate southerner, split at the root—*that I will never bring them whole. . . . Yet we can't wait for the undamaged to make our connections for us; we can't wait to speak until we are perfectly clear and righteous. There is no purity and, in our lifetimes, no end to this process.*

    —Adrienne Rich, "Split at the Root," in *Blood, Bread, and Poetry: Selected Prose, 1979–85* (New York: Norton & Co., 1986), 122–23

35 writing autobiography

bell hooks

To me, telling the story of my growing up years was intimately connected with the longing to kill the self I was without really having to die. I wanted to kill that self in writing. Once that self was gone—out of my life forever—I could more easily become the me of me. It was clearly the Gloria Jean of my tormented and anguished childhood that I wanted to be rid of, the girl who was always wrong, always punished, always subjected to some humiliation or other, always crying, the girl who was to end up in a mental institution because she could not be anything but crazy, or so they told her. She was the girl who sat a hot iron on her arm pleading with them to leave her alone, the girl who wore her scar as a brand marking her madness. Even now I can hear the voices of my sisters saying "mama make Gloria stop crying." By writing the autobiography, it was not just this Gloria I would be rid of, but the past that had a hold on me, that kept me from the present. I wanted not to forget the past but to break its hold. This death in writing was to be liberatory.

Until I began to try and write an autobiography, I thought that it would be a simple task this telling of one's story. And yet I tried year after year, never writing more than a few pages. My inability to write out the story I interpreted as an indication that I was not ready to let go of the past, that I was not ready to be fully in the present. Psychologically, I considered the possibility that I had become attached to the wounds and sorrows of my childhood, that I held to them in a manner that blocked my efforts to be self-realized, whole, to be healed. A key message in Toni Cade Bambara's novel *The Salteaters*, which tells the story of Velma's suicide attempt, her breakdown, is expressed when the healer asks her "are you sure sweetheart, that you want to be well?"

There was very clearly something blocking my ability to tell my story. Perhaps it was remembered scoldings and punishments when mama heard me saying something to a friend or stranger that she did not think should be said. Secrecy and silence—these were central issues. Secrecy about family, about what went on in the domestic household was a bond between us— was part of what made us family. There was a dread one felt about breaking that bond. And yet I could not grow inside the atmosphere of secrecy that had pervaded our lives and the lives of other families about us. Strange that I had always challenged the secrecy, always let something slip that should not be known growing up, yet as a writer staring into the solitary space of paper, I was bound, trapped in the fear that a bond is lost or broken in the telling. I did not want to be the traitor, the teller of family secrets—and yet I wanted to be a writer. Surely, I told myself, I could write a purely imaginative work—a work that would not hint at personal private realities. And so I tried. But always there were the intruding traces, those elements of real life however distinguished. Claiming the freedom to grow as an imaginative writer who connected for me with having the courage to open, to be able to tell the truth of one's life as I had experienced it in writing. To talk about one's life—that I could do. To write about it, to leave a trace—that was frightening.

The longer it took me to begin the process of writing autobiography, the further removed from those memories I was becoming. Each year, a memory seemed less and less clear. I wanted not to lose the vividness, the recall and felt an urgent need to begin the work and complete it. Yet I could not begin even though I had begun to confront some of the reasons I was blocked, as I am blocked just now in writing this piece because I am afraid to express in writing the experience that served as a catalyst for that block to move.

I had met a young black man. We were having an affair. It is important that he was black. He was in some mysterious way a link to this past that I had been struggling to grapple with, to name in writing. With him I remembered incidents, moments of the past that I had completely suppressed. It was as though there was something about the passion of contact that was hypnotic, that enabled me to drop barriers and thus enter fully, rather re-enter those past experiences. A key aspect seemed to be the way he smelled, the combined odors of cigarettes, occasionally alcohol, and his body smells. I thought often of the phrase "scent of memory," for it was those smells that carried me back. And there were specific occasions when it was very evident that the experience of being in his company was the catalyst for this remembering.

Two specific incidents come to mind. One day in the middle of the afternoon we met at his place. We were drinking cognac and dancing to music from the radio. He was smoking cigarettes (not only do I not smoke, but I usually make an effort to avoid smoke). As we held each other dancing those mingled odors of alcohol, sweat, and cigarettes led me to say, quite without

thinking about it, "Uncle Pete." It was not that I had forgotten Uncle Pete. It was more that I had forgotten the childhood experience of meeting him. He drank often, smoked cigarettes, and always on the few occasions that we met him, he held us children in tight embraces. It was the memory of those embraces—of the way I hated and longed to resist them—that I recalled.

Another day we went to a favorite park to feed ducks and parked the car in front of tall bushes. As we were sitting there, we suddenly heard the sound of an oncoming train—a sound which startled me so that it evoked another long-suppressed memory: that of crossing the train tracks in my father's car. I recalled an incident where the car stopped on the tracks and my father left us sitting there while he raised the hood of the car and worked to repair it. This is an incident that I am not certain actually happened. As a child, I had been terrified of just such an incident occurring, perhaps so terrified that it played itself out in my mind as though it had happened. These are just two ways this encounter acted as a catalyst breaking down barriers enabling me to finally write this long-desired autobiography of my childhood.

Each day I sat at the typewriter and different memories were written about in short vignettes. They came in a rush, as though they were a sudden thunderstorm. They came in a surreal, dreamlike style which made me cease to think of them as strictly autobiographical because it seemed that myth, dream, and reality had merged. There were many incidents that I would talk about with my siblings to see if they recalled them. Often we remembered together a general outline of an incident but the details were different for us. This fact was a constant reminder of the limitations of autobiography, of the extent to which autobiography is a personal story telling—a unique recounting of events not so much as they have happened but as we remember and invent them. One memory that I would have sworn was "the truth and nothing but the truth" concerned a wagon that my brother and I shared as a child. I remembered that we played with this toy only at my grandfather's house, that we shared it, that I would ride it and my brother would push me. Yet one facet of the memory was puzzling, I remembered always returning home with bruises or scratches from this toy. When I called my mother, she said there had never been any wagon, that we had shared a red wheelbarrow, that it had always been at my grandfather's house because there were sidewalks on that part of town. We lived in the hills where there were no sidewalks. Again I was compelled to face the fiction that is a part of all retelling, remembering. I began to think of the work I was doing as both fiction and autobiography. It seemed to fall in the category of writing that Audre Lorde, in her autobiographically-based work *Zami,* calls bio-mythography. As I wrote, I felt that I was not as concerned with accuracy of detail as I was with evoking in writing the state of mind, the spirit of a particular moment.

The longing to tell one's story and the process of telling is symbolically a gesture of longing to recover the past in such a way that one experiences both a sense of reunion and a sense of release. It was the longing for release that compelled the writing but concurrently it was the joy of reunion that enabled me to see that the act of writing one's autobiography is a way to find again that aspect of self and experience that may no longer be an actual part of one's life but is a living memory shaping and informing the present. Autobiographical writing was a way for me to evoke the particular experience of growing up southern and black in segregated communities. It was a way to recapture the richness of southern black culture. The need to remember and hold to the legacy of that experience and what it taught me has been all the more important since I have since lived in predominantly white communities and taught at predominately white col-

leges. Black southern folk experience was the foundation of the life around me when I was a child; that experience no longer exists in many places where it was once all of life that we knew. Capitalism, upward mobility, assimilation of other values have all led to rapid disintegration of black folk experience or in some cases the gradual wearing away of that experience.

Within the world of my childhood, we held onto the legacy of a distinct black culture by listening to the elders tell their stories. Autobiography was experienced most actively in the art of telling one's story. I can recall sitting at Baba's (my grandmother on my mother's side) at 1200 Broad Street—listening to people come and recount their life experience. In those days, whenever I brought a playmate to my grandmother's house, Baba would want a brief outline of their autobiography before we would begin playing. She wanted not only to know who their people were but what their values were. It was sometimes an awesome and terrifying experience to stand answering these questions or witness another playmate being subjected to the process and yet this was the way we would come to know our own and one another's family history. It is the absence of such a tradition in my adult life that makes the written narrative of my girlhood all the more important. As the years pass and these glorious memories grow much more vague, there will remain the clarity contained within the written words.

Conceptually, the autobiography was framed in the manner of a hope chest. I remembered my mother's hope chest, with its wonderful odor of cedar and thought about her taking the most precious items and placing them there for safekeeping. An autobiographical narrative seemed an appropriate place. Each particular incident, encounter, experience had its own story, sometimes told from the first person, sometimes told from the third person. Often I felt as though I was in a trance at my typewriter, that the shape of a particular memory was decided not by my conscious mind but by all that is dark and deep within me, unconscious but present. It was the act of making it present, bring it into the open, so to speak, that was liberating.

From the perspective of trying to understand my psyche, it was also interesting to read the narrative in its entirety after I had completed the work. It had not occurred to me that bringing one's past, one's memories together in a complete narrative would allow one to view them from a different perspective, not as singular isolated events but as part of a continuum. Reading the completed manuscript, I felt as though I had an overview not so much of my childhood but of those experiences that were deeply imprinted in my consciousness. Significantly, that which was absent, left out, not included also was important. I was shocked to find at the end of my narrative that there were few incidents I recalled that involved my five sisters. Most of the incidents with siblings were with me and my brother. There was a sense of alienation from my sisters present in childhood, a sense of estrangement. This was reflected in the narrative. Another aspect of the completed manuscript that is interesting to me is the way in which the incidents describing adult men suggest that I feared them intensely, with the exception of my grandfather and a few old men. Writing the autobiographical narrative enabled me to look at my past from a different perspective and to use this knowledge as a means of self-growth and change in a practical way.

In the end I did not feel as though I had killed the Gloria of childhood. Instead I had rescued her. She was no longer the enemy within, the little girl who had to be annihilated for the woman to come into being. In writing about her, I reclaimed that part of myself I had long ago rejected, left uncared for, just as she had often felt alone and uncared for as a child. Remembering was part of a cycle of reunion, a joining of fragments, "the bits and pieces of my heart" that the narrative made whole again.

36 Autobiographical Manifestos

Sidonie Smith

Decolonization never takes place unnoticed, for it influences individuals and modifies them fundamentally. It transforms spectators crushed with their inessentiality into privileged actors, with the grandiose glare of history's floodlights upon them. It brings a natural rhythm into existence, introduced by new men, and with it a new language and new humanity. Decolonization is the veritable creation of new men. But this creation owes nothing of its legitimacy to any supernatural power; the "thing" which has been colonized becomes man during the same process by which it frees itself.
—Frantz Fanon, *The Wretched of the Earth*

In the process of putting their bodies in the picture, Cherríe Moraga [in *Loving in the War Years*] and Jo Spence [in *Putting Myself in the Picture*] extract the "I" from traditional narrative frames, those histories and myths that censor certain bodies and affect complicit self-censorship. Both women thus engage in overtly political writing practices. As resisting subjects, they require and develop resisting forms. Moraga incorporates poetry, prose analysis, journal entries, and sketches as well as multiple languages in a dialogic engagement with history and fantasy.[1] Spence incorporates bare chronological data with exhibition catalogs, interviews, articles, and photographs in a textual montage of self-portraiture and its politics. These hybrid forms join other recent anti-"autobiographical" forms, what Caren Kaplan calls "out-law genres,"[2] autobiographical but eclectically "errant" and culturally disruptive writing practices. Kaplan includes *testimonio*, prison narratives, collective autoethnography, biomythography, and regulative psychobiography in her discus-

sion of out-law genres. I want to look . . . at another one of these out-law genres, what I call the autobiographical manifesto.

By way of introduction to this last autobiographical gesture, let me consider briefly what kinds of autobiographical strategies lead to what kinds of political empowerment. One strategic move we might label mimesis. In this move the autobiographer positions herself as the subject of traditional autobiography: that is, she mimes the subjectivity of universal man. Speaking from this location proffers authority, legitimacy, and readability. It also proffers membership in the community of the fully human. For oppressed peoples, such membership can be psychologically and politically expedient and potent. Unselfconsciously embraced, however, mimesis invites recuperation as well as the promise of power, the maintenance of subjection to the self-definitions that bind.

Yet there is another side to this mirroring, the nitrate of mimicry, for something may be exposed here: an unauthorized speaker positions herself in the locale of the universal subject, thereby introducing a menacing suspicion of inexact correlation between representations. "As incomplete mirrors, as the waste of the system that produced the identity of the white male," suggests Linda Kintz, "[an unauthorized speaker] can only reflect back to the male subject a partial representation of himself, a reflection that is askew, flawed, not specular."[3] As a result, autobiographical mimicry may subtly contest the "natural," "commonsensical," "universal" categorizations of difference. In addition to its treacherous invitation to recuperation, then, mimesis may promise escape from an exclusionary configuration of subjectivity.

A second strategy for a contestatory autobiographical practice looks to the politics of fragmentation as the means to counter the centrifugal power of the old unitary self of western rationalism. Promoting the endless possibilities of self-fragmentation, the politics of fragmentation reveals the cultural constructedness of any coherent, stable, and universal subject. It may also reveal how problematic it is to maintain a decisive, unified point of departure for identity as the ground of a liberatory autobiographical practice, since the exclusions of unified points are legion. But shattering the old notion of the unitary individual in favor of the split and multiply fragmented subject may not always serve emancipatory objectives; rather, it may serve further oppressive agendas, as Judith Butler cautions: "If oppression is to be defined in terms of a loss of autonomy by the oppressed, as well as a fragmentation or alienation within the psyche of the oppressed, then a theory which insists upon the inevitable fragmentation of the subject appears to reproduce and valorize the very oppression that must be overcome."[4] Any autobiographical practice that promotes endless fragmentation and a reified multiplicity might be counterproductive since the autobiographical subject would have to split itself beyond useful-

ness to be truly nonexclusionary. And it is difficult to coalesce a call to political action founded upon some kind of communal identity around a constantly deferred point of departure.[5]

Other strategies for oppositional autobiographical practice are grounded in conceptions of "experiential" politics. Difficulties negotiating the terrain of "the real" lead in fact to opposing orientations to experience. For some there is an experience outside representation to which the autobiographical text refers. And there is an ontological basis to identity in this experience. So a potentially emancipatory practice would be one that seeks to uncover the "true" self and the "truth" about that self's experience, the sources of oppression and strength, the essential difference in body, psyche, and modes of knowing and being in the world. For others such a positivist approach to experience neglects the relationship of experience to discourse, the artifactual nature of representation, the operations and apparati of cultural determinations. From this perspective, there is no subject outside language as textuality displaces any transparent experience. And since language operates to fix subjects, the subject of resistance can only engage in a drama of negativity, to allude to Julia Kristeva's theoretical frame, a drama of the what-I-am-not.[6] Now the resisting autobiographer lingers in the space of negativity where she refuses attempts to universalize any "us," "we," or "I." But once again she may be caught in an endless self-qualification that takes her further away from any community of interest and political action.

However problematic its strategies, autobiographical writing has played and continues to play a role in emancipatory politics. Autobiographical practices become occasions for restaging subjectivity, and autobiographical strategies become occasions for the staging of resistance. Thus within what Judith Butler calls "this conflicted cultural field"[7] the autobiographer can lay out an agenda for a changed relationship to subjectivity, identity, and the body. We see this agenda in recent texts by women who pursue self-consciously political autobiographical acts, who issue calls for new subjects, in texts I call autobiographical manifestos. Purposeful, bold, contentious, the autobiographical manifesto contests the old inscriptions, the old histories, the old politics, the *ancien régime,* by working to dislodge the hold of the universal subject through an expressly political collocation of a new "I." In service to a new "social reality," what Donna Haraway describes as "our most important political construction, a world-changing fiction,"[8] the manifesto offers an arena in which the subject can insist on identity in service to an emancipatory politics, even if, as Robert K. Martin argues, that identity is "assumed."[9]

The Subject of Manifesto

Dictionary definitions suggest that a manifesto is a proof, a piece of evidence, a public declaration or proclamation, usually issued by or with the sanction of a sovereign prince or state, or by an individual or body of individuals whose proceedings are of public importance, for the purpose of announcing past actions and explaining the reasons or motives for actions announced as forthcoming. Within this definitional context six constituent aspects of manifesto affect our discussion.

To appropriate/to contest sovereignty

As noted in the introduction, the universal subject consolidates sovereignty through exclusionary practices. These practices figure "others" as "not-an-individualized-'I,'" persons whose humanity is opaque, and whose membership in the human community is negated by relegation to what Nancy Hartsock describes as "a chaotic, disorganized, and anonymous collectivity."[10] Autobiographical manifestos issue from persons assigned to this anonymous collectivity who vig-

orously reject the sovereignty of this specular *ancien régime* and the dominance of the universal subject. Through the manifesto, the autobiographical subject confronts the ghost of the identity assigned her by the old sovereign subject, what Paul Smith terms the ideological "I," a fixed object position representing culturally intelligible and authorized performances of identity. These fixed identifications (of "woman," "black," "lesbian," etc.) function as cultural templates for repetition. Repetition, however, breeds contempt; that is to say, repetition brings with it alterations precisely because, as Smith suggests, "imaginary identifications . . . are continually vulnerable to the registration of ever renewed and contradictory interpellations."[11] The autobiographical manifesto confronts this process directly: the tensions set in motion by contradictory identity assignments incite, to use revolutionary rhetoric, self-conscious encounters with the politics of identification and catalyze subjectivity around specific and oppositional contours of "I-ness." Resisting "the taken-for-granted ability of one small segment of the population to speak for all,"[12] the autobiographer purposefully locates herself as a subject, leaving behind the object status to which cultural identities have confined her.

To bring to light, to make manifest (literally struck with the hand)

Since awareness of the pressures to repeat certain cultural identifications is the ground of resistance to repetition, the difficult road to a liberatory autobiographical practice lies through the terrain of cultural critique. And so, when Cherríe Moraga comments in *Loving in the War Years* that "the Third World lesbian brings colored female sexuality with all its raggedy edges and oozing wounds—for better or for worse— into the light of day," she captures colloquially the political agenda of the autobiographical manifesto: to force issues "into the light of day."[13] Intent on bringing culturally marginalized experiences out from under the shadow of an undifferentiated otherness, the autobiographical manifesto anchors its narrative itinerary in the specificities and locales of time and space, the discursive surround, the material ground, the provenance of histories.

To bring things "into the light of day," to make manifest a perspective on identity and experience, affects an epistemological breakage of repetition. The legitimacy of a new or alternative knowledge located in the experiences of the margins is affirmed.[14] The autobiographical manifesto thus attempts to develop what Hartsock describes as "an account of the world as seen from the margins, an account which can expose the falseness of the view from the top and can transform the margins as well as the center. . . . an account of the world which treats our perspectives not as subjugated or disruptive knowledges, but as primary and constitutive of a different world." The individual story becomes the occasion for what Hartsock calls "standpoint epistemologies," analyses of specific confluences of social, psychological, economic, and political forces of oppression.[15] The trajectories, strategies, and tools of these analyses take various forms, some of which I will explore below as part of the enabling myths and motivating metaphors of resistance.

To announce publicly

Autobiographical writing is always a gesture toward publicity, displaying before an impersonal public an individual's interpretation of experience. The very impetus for contemporary autobiographical manifestos, however, lies in the recognition of a vexed relationship between what too easily becomes the binary opposition of the political and the personal. The early rallying cry of the white, middle-class feminist movement was "The personal is political." And through the last two decades the politics of personal relationships, the economics of reproduction, and the politics of psychosexual develop-

ment have been central to feminist analyses in many fields. In challenging the hegemony of white middle-class feminism, however, theorists of multiple differences have differentiated the personal stakes and psychological impacts of systems of colonization, focusing on the personal experiences of multiple oppressions, of class, caste, race, gender, sexuality, nationality. In this more heterogeneous context, "the private" requires reconceptualization, as Aida Hurtado suggests when she emphasizes that "the political consciousness of women of Color stems from an awareness that the public is *personally* political. . . . There is no such thing as a private sphere for people of Color except that which they manage to create and protect in an otherwise hostile environment."[16] And so a cautionary gesture is necessary here. Different autobiographers come at the private/public duality from different experiences of oppression, from different locales in discourse. As a result the mapping of private/public politics may proceed to lay out different borderlines.

Hurtado argues that we need to attend to the relative positionality of specific women vis-à-vis the "middle-class white man," the prototype for the universal subject who stands centrally in the public space and whose standpoint determines the places of power, the margins of meaning, the geographies of knowledge. As a result the cartography of private space takes its contours from multiple spaces of adjacency. For instance, the white middle-class woman exists alongside "public man," sharing his private spaces. But the woman of color exists separately from that man, generally at a distance from his private space. Different alignments toward the dominant private space condition different cultural constructions of "woman," different cultural practices for women.[17]

The autobiographical manifesto asserts unqualifiedly, even exuberantly, both the politicization of the private and the personalization of the public, effectively troubling the binary complacencies of the *ancien regime* of selfhood with its easy dichotomization of private and public.[18] But the trajectory of its mappings must be considered in the specific cultural locations of the woman who issues the manifesto's call to action.

To perform publicly

While it might seem strange to repeat the former aspect of the autobiographical manifesto with a change of one word, it is important to note separately the performative aspect of the autobiographical manifesto. Expressly a public performance, the manifesto revels in the energetic display of a new kind of subject. The manifesto engages directly the cultural construction of identities and their sanctioned and legitimated performances, engaging the ideological systems pressing specific identities on specific persons. It takes a public stand on behalf of purposeful deflections, intervening in oppressive identity performances, troubling culturally authorized fictions.[19] Historicizing identity, the autobiographical manifesto implicitly, if not explicitly, insists on the temporalities and spatialities of identity and, in doing so, brings the everyday practices of identity directly into the floodlights of conscious display.

To speak as one of a group, to speak for a group

In the manifesto group identification, rather than radical individuality, is the rhetorical ground of appeal. During her public performance the manifesto speaker positions herself expressly as a member of a group or community, an auto/ethnographer, so to speak.[20] The "I" anchored in collectivity is the "I" of what Rita Felski à la Jurgen Habermas labels a counter-public sphere.[21] Counter-public spheres are multiple, invoking identification around various experiences of oppression and exclusions from the central or centrifugal bourgeois public sphere and its ideology of the universal subject. While Felski's particular interest focuses on the dynamics of the feminist counter-public sphere,

which she says "does not claim a representative universality but rather offers a critique of cultural values from the standpoint of women as a marginalized group within society," for the purposes of this discussion we need to emphasize the existence of multiple counter-public spheres that operate along analogous lines and generate their specific critiques of universalizing spheres of influence.[22]

Critique in this instance is motivated by the autobiographical subject's desire to contest dominant discourses surrounding the subject, discourses through which the subject is objectified in strategic difference and rendered abnormative. Moreover, the subject in this instance of the autobiographical manifesto speaks as a member of a nonhegemonic group or counter-public sphere, and that group too has what Mikhail Bakhtin suggests is its own "social dialect," its languages. For Bakhtin it is through the conflictual, supplementary, consonant action of heteroglossia that consciousness emerges. Psyche, sociality, language converge to link consciousness to critique. But critique does not proceed univocally. Critique is accompanied by what Mae Gwendolyn Henderson describes as "testimony." According to Henderson, testimony derives from the subject's "dialectic of identity," that is, from her acknowledgment of a commonality of "history, language, and culture" with others of the group.[23]

In the manifesto communitarian auto/ethnography functions as a kind of "nationalism." Bernice Johnson Reagon captures the nationalism inherent in communitarian politics when she suggests that a liberatory space "should be a nurturing space where you sift out what people are saying about you and decide who you really are. And you take the time to try to construct within yourself and within your community who you would be if you were running society . . . [this is] nurturing, but it is also nationalism. At a certain stage, nationalism is crucial to a people if you are ever going to impact as a group in your own interest."[24] Nationalism determines the specific moves through which the manifesto negotiates the landscapes of identity and difference. Postulating a testimonial nationalism, the manifesto quarrels with "competitive discourses"[25] and through its narrative itinerary stages a breakage in repetitions. As it does so it struggles to resist the totalizing agenda of the universal subject and proclaims the viability of a nonuniversal position.[26]

To speak to the future

The generic contracts of western literary practices promise something, but what exactly they promise is subject to various theoretical interpretations. Traditionally, western autobiography involves a contractual obligation in which the autobiographer engages in a narrative itinerary of self-disclosure, retrospective summation, self-justification. Thus critics of autobiography, including such contemporary theorists as Philippe Lejeune, emphasize the retrospective aspect of autobiography. Postmodern theorists have shifted the trope to the autobiographical text as the site of a deadly specularity. Paul de Man, for instance, argues that "autobiography veils a defacement of the mind of which it is itself the cause."[27] As a result, "the autobiographical project" becomes, according to Paul Smith, "a privileged kind of impossibility, always given over to uncertainty, undecidability, and, finally, to death."[28] But other theorists resist what they consider the dead end of death in autobiography. For instance, Kathleen Woodward talks of the writing of autobiography as taking place not under the sign of death, defacement, or desire but under the sign of anxiety, "a state of expecting a danger and preparing oneself for it, although the danger may be unknown to oneself, that is, not consciously known." Attempting to suggest a difference between male and female narratives, Woodward suggests that where men may write under the sign of desire and its "em-

phasis . . . on past loss," women write under the sign of anxiety for future loss.[29]

The autobiographical manifesto offers another sign. Here the "I" does not write under the sign of desire or the sign of anxiety. Rather the "I" writes under the sign of hope and what Hélène Cixous calls "the very possibility of change," emphasizing the generative and prospective thrust of autobiography.[30] Calling the subject into the future, the manifesto attempts to actively position the subject in a potentially liberated future distanced from the constraining and oppressive identifications inherent in the everyday practices of the *ancien régime*. Thus while the manifesto looks back in what Teresa de Lauretis terms "the critical negativity" of theoretical critique, it also gestures forward in "the affirmative positivity of its politics" to new spaces for subjectivity.[31]

Since new interpretations and hopeful futures are "crucially bound up with power," the manifesto always foregrounds the relationship of subjectivity to power.[32] It insists on new interpretations as a means of wresting power, resisting universalized repetitions that essentialize and naturalize. In service to that political cause, the autobiographer issues the call for a new, revolutionary subject, offers an agenda for "I" transformations. Ultimately, then, the manifesto proffers a utopian vision, "a 'waking dream' of the possible," writes Françoise Lionnet, "which might inspire us to see beyond the constraints of the here and now to the idealized vision of a perfect future."[33]

. . . The autobiographical manifesto is a revolutionary gesture poised against amnesia and its compulsive repetitions. It is not quite anamnesis (or reminiscence) so much as a purposeful constitution of a future history, the projection of anamnesis into the future. Moreover, the manifesto offers a point of departure for the current generation (of women, of people from the borderlands, of cyborgs) to resist a former generation imposing its multifarious technologies of identity. Through compelling myths and metaphors . . . manifestos map alternative futures for the "I" in the late twentieth century. They point to blurred boundaries, crossed borderlands of multiplicity, differences and divergences, political possibilities and pitfalls, strategies for intervention. They offer fascinating performances of the revolutionary subject, performances which, as Frantz Fanon noted, effectively "transform spectators crushed with their inessentiality into privileged actors, with the grandiose glare of history's floodlights upon them." Whether we follow them or not, whether we pursue some other kind of alternative subjectivity, such performances hold out hope by insisting on the possibility of self-conscious and imaginative breaks in cultural repetitions of the universal subject.

Notes

1. Lourdes Torres, "The Construction of the Self in U. S. Latina Autobiographies," page 277, in this volume.

2. Caren Kaplan, 208–16, in this volume.

3. Linda Kintz, "In-Different Criticism: The Deconstructive 'Parole,'" in The Thinking Muse: Feminism and Modern French Philosophy, ed. Jeffner Allen and Iris Marion Young (Bloomington: Indiana University Press, 1989), 131.

4. Judith Butler, "Gender Trouble, Feminist Theory, and Psychoanalytic Discourse," in Feminism/Postmodernism, ed. Linda J. Nicholson (New York: Routledge, 1990), 327.

5. For a critique of postmodern fragmentation, see Susan Bordo, "Feminism, Postmodernism, and Gender-Scepticism," in Nicholson, 133–56.

6. See Julia Kristeva, "A New Type of Intellectual," in The Kristeva Reader, ed. Toril Moi (Oxford: Basil Blackwell, 1986), 292–300.

7. Judith Butler, Gender Trouble: Feminism and the Subversion of Identity (New York: Routledge, 1990), 145.

8. Donna Haraway, "A Manifesto for Cyborgs: Science, Technology, and Socialist Feminism in the 1980s," in Nicholson, 191.

9. Robert K. Martin, "Is Anybody There? Critical Practice and Minority Writing," paper delivered at MLA convention, Washington, DC, December 1989.

10. Nancy Hartsock, "Foucault on Power: A Theory for Women?" in Nicholson, 160–61.

11. Paul Smith, Discerning the Subject (Minneapolis: University of Minnesota Press, 1988), 106.

12. The phrase comes from Hartsock, 171.

13. Cherríe Moraga, Loving in the War Years (Boston: South End Press, 1983), 138.

14. "Knowledge" is "essentially the making visible of material," writes Edward W. Said in Orientalism (New York: Random House, 1979), 127. See also Elspeth Probyn, "Travels in the Postmodern: Making Sense of the Local," in Nicholson, 178.

15. Hartsock, 171–72.

16. Aida Hurtado, "Relating to Privilege: Seduction and Rejection in the Subordination of White Women and Women of Color," Signs 14 (Summer 1989): 849.

17. Hurtado argues that "for white women, the first step in the search for identity is to confront the ways in which their personal, individual silence endorses the power of white men that has robbed them of their history. For women of Color, the challenge is to use their oral traditions for specific political goals" (848–49).

18. See also Haraway, 205.

19. See Judith Butler's discussion of the relationship of acts to idea: "Because there is neither an 'essence' that gender expresses or externalizes nor an objective ideal to which gender aspires," Butler says, "and because gender is not a fact, the various acts of gender create the idea of gender, and without those acts, there would be no gender at all. Gender is, thus, a construction that regularly conceals its genesis; the tacitly collective agreement to perform, produce, and sustain discrete and polar genders as cultural fictions is obscured by the credibility of those productions—and the punishments that attend to agreeing to believe in them; the construction 'compels' our belief in its necessity and naturalness. The historical possibilities materialized through various corporeal styles are nothing other than those punitively regulated cultural

fictions alternately embodied and deflected under duress" (*Gender Trouble*, 140).

20. See Françoise Lionnet, *Autobiographical Voices: Race, Gender, Self-Portraiture* (Ithaca: Cornell University Press, 1989), 99.

21. Rita Felski, *Beyond Feminist Aesthetics: Feminist Literature and Social Change* (Cambridge: Harvard University Press, 1989), 166.

22. Felski, 167. What Felski says of the internal and external dynamics of the feminist counter-public sphere applies to these multiple spheres: "*Internally,* it generates a gender-specific identity grounded in a consciousness of community and solidarity among women; *externally,* it seeks to convince society as a whole of the validity of feminist claims, challenging existing structures of authority through political activity and theoretic critique" (168).

23. Mae Gwendolyn Henderson, "Speaking in Tongues: Dialogics, Dialectics, and the Black Woman's Literary Tradition," 343–51, in this volume.

24. Bernice Johnson Reagon, "Coalition Politics: Turning the Century," in *Home Girls,* ed. Barbara Smith (New York: Kitchen Table/Women of Color Press, 1983); quoted in Hartsock, 163.

25. Henderson, in this volume.

26. The collective identification of the manifesto's speaker is perhaps the most problematic aspect of this autobiographical form precisely because the postulation of a counter-public sphere, of "women" for instance, functions yet again as a gesture of universalization, if a universalization whose application is narrower than the hegemonic center's universalization. As recent theorists have argued, community is a problematic utopian ideal. (See Iris Marion Young, "The Ideal of Community and the Politics of Difference," in Nicholson, 300–323; Felski, chap. 5; and Hartsock, 171.) Posited on exclusivities, or blindnesses to complex material realities, an idealized community erases differences and contradictory experiences. As Felski notes, "The ideal of a free discursive space that equalizes all participants is an enabling

fiction which engenders a sense of collective identity but is achieved only by obscuring actual material inequalities and political antagonisms among its participants" (168). Thus, however attractive the ideal of "a unified collective subject" might be, we must constantly remind ourselves that the price we pay for celebrating collectivity may be "the actual activities and self-understanding of women, in which gender-based divisions frequently conflict with a whole range of other alliances, such as those based on race or class, and work against any unproblematic notion of harmonious consensus" (Felski, 169).

27. Paul de Man, "Autobiography as Defacement," *Modern Language Notes* 94 (1979): 930.

28. Smith, 103.

29. Kathleen Woodward, "Simone de Beauvoir: Aging and Its Discontents," in *The Private Self: Theory and Practice of Women's Autobiographical Writings,* ed. Shari Benstock (Chapel Hill: University of North Carolina Press, 1988), 108–9.

30. Hélène Cixous, "The Laugh of the Medusa," in *New French Feminisms: An Anthology,* ed. Elaine Marks and Isabelle de Courtivron (New York: Schocken Books, 1981), 249. All further citations will appear in the text.

31. Teresa de Lauretis calls these future spaces the "space off"—"those other spaces both discursive and social that exist . . . in the margins . . . of hegemonic discourse and in the interstices of institutions, in counterpractices and new forms of community," in de Lauretis, *The Technologies of Gender: Essays on Theory, Film, and Fiction* (Bloomington: Indiana University Press, 1987), 26.

32. Tania Modleski, "Feminism and the Power of Interpretation: Some Critical Readings," in *Feminist Studies/Critical Studies,* ed. Teresa de Lauretis (Bloomington: Indiana University Press, 1986), 136.

33. Lionnet, 110. As Lionnet has suggested, "Utopian thinking is perhaps the only way out of the impasse created by the neocolonialist strangulation of nations and peoples" (247).

37 Semiotics, Experience, and the Material Self: An Inquiry into the Subject of the Contemporary Asian Woman Writer

Shirley Geok-lin Lim

This chapter is not a scholarly examination of native-language or English-language Asian women's materials and strategies for survival and acceptance in their colonized and indigenous societies. Nor will it analyse the struggles of a later generation of women poets and writers whose works display like scars the deleterious effects of multiplying marginalizations. Asian women writers in the twentieth century were and continue to be marginalized first by gender, in socio-political structures that have no functions for women except as nurturers (nurses, teachers, lovers, mothers, what is called the helping professions). They are marginalized, also, in nations where national identity has been forcibly equated with a national language policy, by their choice of writing in English. If members of a minority ethnic or regional group they are further marginalized by a majority ethnic power structure. Generally also women who write in English are Western-educated members of a professional middle-class, a narrow segment in basically peasant societies still undergoing development. A woman writing and publishing English-language poems and fiction in India, Pakistan, the Philippines, Hong Kong or Malay-

sia in the 1980s (and perhaps even more in the year 2000?) is still a freak, like that spelling dog. (Only in Singapore is there a mercantile and manufacturing base, a national language policy in which English has a place, and a substantial middle-class population, factors that make publishing by women more acceptable.) In many of these countries, the publishing women writers can be counted on one hand; two at the most.

It is precisely because there are so few of us (and I use the plural first-person as a problematic, occasioned by the definitions of this essay, and in the context of time past, which is always present in time present and time future) that I defer the analysis of sisterhood in the examination of self and the Asian woman writer, and revert instead to a meditation, a prologue, an open and sundried inquiry into what only I and no one else has as much acquaintance with, that primary subjectivity of my "self." Nor do I offer this yet-to-be-shaped because yet-to-be-written "self" as representative, type, or allegorical figure; it is the concrete particular, the specific facticity, the materiality, "earth," through only which any abstraction can take color, size and shape.

And yet what will be offered is as abstract as architecture; for it is only through having read enormous bodies of literature, some offered as poetry, some as fiction, some yet as ideas or theory, and much believed to be knowledge, that I am able to "see" this ground, to "smell" this sensate life, to offer in language, that most abstract of symbolic discourse, the specificity of "self." So I will begin with the abstract, the "theory" that having been pieced together through unrelated readings across gaps in time, space, and societies appears to me now to make a pattern of the whole. I stress the temporality of this signifying pattern; it may be a conjunction of lack of sleep, increased caffeine intake, and the particular although accidental texts I had been reading just this past week that has produced an illusion of clarity, as tired eyes see entertaining designs on worn walls that disappear with rest. Or it may be that the pattern is inscribed within myself, to be obsessively projected on worn walls whenever fatigue, leisure, and over-stimulated nerves combine to break down that efficient corporate eye and leave it prey to the mute projectionist who will madly play and replay the same primal scenes to ever-changing music.

I shall provide the commentary by which you will approach the script and its editing. As the shapes begin to form on those blank worn walls, as director and sole survivor in the plot I shall provide the voice-over. For the "self" can be imaged as a movie in which one is producer, scriptwriter, director, actor being directed by other two-bit directors, projectionist, and audience.

I would argue that "self" cannot be, has never been, that unitary imperial "I" of Kantian thought. Freud, for all his masculinist orientation, pointed the way to areas of self that are outside the knowing "I": the concept of the unconscious self that works so deeply on behavior, feeling, and thought has shattered forever the myth of self as understandable, graspable,

integrated, a positive agent defined by its colonization of experience, and negative only in its absence. After Freud, philosophers and psychologists such as Sartre and Laing accept the notion of self as divided, fragmented, in conflict, composed of contradictions, acting in bad faith, encompassing its own double, displaying the energy of a dialectic between presence and absence. Feminists such as Kristeva have seized upon these descriptions of the subject as more accurate of female experience: fractured between Others in their biological/maternal circumstance; the boundaries between mother and self entangled in the pre-Oedipal bond; their consciousness of self engendered as female desire or lack (a notion Lacan has popularized among some feminists).[1] Writers such as Tillie Olsen and Doris Lessing have portrayed this suffering experience of female subjectivity in stories such as "Tell Me a Riddle" and "To Room Nineteen." To the unitary conception of the subject, as Domna C. Stanton tells us, "Kristeva opposes one already in process and in question, 'no longer simply explaining, understanding, and knowing, but an ungraspable subject because it is transforming the real'" (74). Kristeva postulates a female principle—the semiotic—that predates the symbolic, a preverbal locus situated at the moment when the child is bound up with the mother's body; and she conceptualizes this as a stage of silent production in which instinctual drives are organized. "Only the eruption of the semiotic into the symbolic can give rein to heterogenous meaning, to difference, and thus subvert the existing systems of signification" (Stanton, 74).

Kristeva's postulation of the semiotic female principle articulates what many writers, male and female, have acknowledged, a principle, spirit, or agent in the self that is preverbal, a-logical, ungraspable, but whose violence to existing symbolic systems is the self's most significant because most transforming act upon "reality." This is the principle that acts upon the material subject to produce the "auto" in autobiography, transforming a life to the specificity of a subject.

Of course, that other aspect of self, the "bio"graphy which includes history, society, community, family, gender, race, class, geography, the materiality of a particular situated world, is as important a counterbalance to my view of self. These can be rendered as organized rather than organizing entities, like items listed for a Who's Who, identifying without bestowing identity; as untransformed facticity. It is and is not the material of literature, although the Asian woman writer suffers greater constraints from it. Her ambitions must be narrower, for her freedoms are less. Her energies, which for writers are inscribed in writing, in the "graphic" creations of self, must necessarily be dispersed or dispensed on material "creations"—childbirth and childcare, the planting of gardens, preparations of meals, weaving and sewing of clothing. The Asian man is not free of material constraints either, but there has long been in Asian societies a tradition of male as writer that was denied to women: the Confucian scholar; Brahmin priest; court advisors; government bureaucrats; recorders of social action and journalists; privileged nationalists selected for foreign education and service. These roles had been male prerogatives for centuries, and from these traditions have been drawn the majority of English-language writers from Asia.

For the Asian woman poet, therefore, her "bio" must largely remain on the ground floor of experience. The semiotic presses on life as experience, the daily unfolding of smells, bustle, sensations, endless movement, those pressures of personalities on the self as receiver. According to de Lauretis, experience is "the general sense of a process by which, for all social beings, subjectivity is constructed. Through that process one places oneself or is placed in social reality,

and so perceives and comprehends as subjective (referring to, even originating in, oneself) those relations—material, economic, and interpersonal—which are in fact social and in a larger perspective historical" (159).

The Asian woman, however, is seldom an active agent except in the most domestic of situations, so for her the subject is often emptied of political content. For this subject to change its centuries-old separation from the political, a revolution must take place. Ding Ling's portrayal of woman, in "Shanghai in the Spring of 1930," as material self resisting ideological transformation—in the character of Mary (Mother of us all)—acknowledges that a psychological transformation must occur before the political can take place.[2] Mary is a nonconformist student from a wealthy Chinese family: "She had talked a lot, been very lively, conspicuously drunk a great deal . . . her proud and free ways, her charming insolence, had particularly captivated him" (66). Her lover, Wang-wei, adores her, but when she comes to live with him in Shanghai, she discovers that he is absorbed in his work in a socialist organization. Mary rejects the social stereotypes for women, but Ding Ling points to the vacuity in the selfish individualism of her rebellion:

> But she loved nobody other than herself. She knew that she depended entirely on the beauty that youth had given her . . . From all the novels she had read and films she had seen she knew that once a woman married her life was over. To be a docile housewife, then a good mother, loving her husband and her children, losing all other forms of happiness for the so-called warmth of a family, then in an instant find your hair turned white and your hopes all dashed when your husband was still healthy enough to be going out and feeling around. All you could do then was

cultivate benevolence and wait patiently to become a grandmother. What was the point of it? . . . She was very satisfied with her present freedom. (81)

Wangwei attempts to involve her in political activism, but her half-awareness of the moral vitality of these socialist activities only pains her by illuminating the ugliness of her "debauchery, idleness" (98).

For Mary, "love"—the sexual bond between man and woman—was the meaning of her existence. Ding Ling contrasts Wangwei's devotion to the political cause with Mary's apolitical self-centered subjectivity. To remain with Wangwei, Mary would have to "obliterate her own self to turn herself into someone with a head like his" (112). Wangwei himself had been transformed by the political process: "He was so ruthless now. She had no idea what could have given him the strength to be like that. It terrified her. She could not make the change with him. Her circumstances and her character were too different" (112). This "difference" is not simply that of male and female but rather one of class. Ding Ling suggests in the minor characters of Feng and the condustress an idealized proletarian male/female relationship uncorrupted by liberal subjective values. Wangwei, the bourgeois male, makes the successful transformation to a revolutionary consciousness, but Mary, encumbered by her ideas of individual freedom, happiness, and capitalist consumption of goods, cannot change. The story ends with Wangwei in a Black Maria, arrested for demonstrating, seeing Mary with her arms full of shopping by the entrance of a department store (120–121). As Kristeva points out and Ding Ling's short story portrays, "no sociopolitical transformation is possible which does not constitute a transformation of subjects" (Stanton, 73).

Self as the semiotic principle that constitutes

the subject; self as experience in which both agent and receiver act and are acted upon; and self finally as constituted by the Other, which is the field of the political. Together they form not layers of a self like the flesh of an onion easily peeled apart but rather types of chemicals whose different properties bind to produce for each individual a unique process, reaction, and alchemical substance.

The Asian woman writer, like women everywhere, continues to be constituted by a Male Other. When we look at ourselves in maturity, the gaze we have re-constituted from our culture is male. Our valuation of our selves, our femininity, learned from our mothers, is inexorably the market value of the male world. Our physical size and shape, our choice of coverings, the pitch of our speech, our gestures and walk, the life of our eyes, our abilities and capacities are always measured against male-constituted desires. We learn to desire for ourselves what men desire in us, an endless regression of desire in which the self cannot separate from the Other except with the most violent repercussions (as portrayed in Doris Lessing's *The Summer before the Dark*). For Asian women, therefore, not only is the personal political, but sex is often the field in which the political is waged.[3] In the absence of a tradition of political engagement in the world, they articulate political engagement of their most private encounters with the Male Other. . . .

In looking for the selves in Asian women's literature, however, one is more usually frustrated to find something one may not wish to recognize because it has been mutilated by an Other which imposes weakness, marginality, inferiority, and absence of being. . . . As many critics have pointed out, colonial and post-colonial women have suffered a double colonization, alienated from the free exercise of their power by a foreign race and also by a native patriarchal society.[4] When the society is Confucian, Hindu,

Muslim, Christian, animistic, Jain, Parsi, Buddhist, the female is always already a colonized subject.

In order for the woman to write in this doubly colonial world, the self must be in exile; she has to leave the rule of her community and become, if only in her writing, undomesticated, wild. Thus I begin with myself as the feral child.

If my mother had not abandoned us, five sons and a daughter, when I was eight, I may never have become a writer. I remember her then as a feminine mother, that is, she liked fine clothes, gold jewelry, creams and powders, to visit friends and gossip. She had prepared herself for an idle life. Her collection of sarongs was of the most expensive batiks, handblocked with vivid Javanese birds and flower motifs, crisp with starch. Her *kebayas* were fine transparent voile, their seams worked painstakingly by hand, and the front openings and sleeves pieced into delicate lace. Such *kebayas* are hardly ever seen in Malaysia now that Malay women conceal their bodies under Arab purdahs and Nonyas like my mother have become Westernized and copy dresses and pants from British Hong Kong. When she dressed carefully to visit her friends in Malacca, she wore three or four gold bangles on each wrist. They were brassy twenty-three carat gold, patterned with vines and petals. A thick gold chain, closely linked, circled her round throat. Like other Nonyas, she wore a modest chemise under the airy *kebaya,* and fastened the blouse with *kerosong* in the shape of a trailing string of flowers. In the hot afternoons at home she mixed a paste of rice powder and water, and this *bedak* she smoothed on her face to keep her complexion white and unlined. But for night before bed she had large jars of Ponds Cold Cream which smelled like sugar syrup.

Did I love my mother then? I don't know. Her luxuries made her a distant figure, organized for a different world. Between a girl child not yet constituted in this version of the feminine and a mother absorbed in preparations for a presentation in the economic world, little can bind them beyond the biological. And even that was not conscious, for she had three sons after me, a fact that now strikes me as totally significant but which then passed before me as unremarkable. Her continuous pregnancies must have been unwelcome and unpleasant, for I can recall no festivity associated with any of them. The last son was handed over to an aunt at two weeks of age. There was some explanation that a fortune teller had warned the infant would harm his mother's health, and at four I had no curiosity over a displaced brother. That she did give over the last child now falls into a signifying act, for a few years later she gave us over to our father and left the small town for Singapore City.[5] The childbirth weeks impressed me then only as food sensations: chicken feet boiled in soy and sugar; pork kidneys scored like graph paper and tasting of rice wine and ginger; rice porridge rich with minced pork and scallions. These were foods for after-birth. I can taste them still in memory even though no pictures of baby brothers or maternal bliss appear.

In this way I must have been a cold child, already separated from the mother and plunged into experience. This very early indifference to my mother can be explained by my strong attraction to the sensate world, the world of play, activity, intervention, the rough, coarse world of my brothers who ran wild in the narrow back lanes of Kampong Pantai. The street in front of my father's shoe-shop carried its Malay name, Beach Village (Pantai for beach-front), from ancient days, but it was a thoroughly South Seas Chinese street. On our side, the side I travelled every day, trailing behind the boys as they ran past the shop-fronts, were piles of discarded damaged cans and foodstuffs from the two sundry shops on the right. On the far right the street was anchored by a small Chinese temple behind a walled open-air courtyard which you entered through an ungated entrance. A large red clay urn, closed on the top but with apertures on the sides, stood beside the entrance, and here the worshippers burned silver and gold paper money. The urn was always full of ash and blackened leaves of burned paper not yet consumed to ash.

One day my brothers found some battered, rusted cans of grapes among the rubbish pile in front of the sundry stores. I still recall the pale, peeled fruit loggy in thick syrup, an exotic, exciting taste made dangerous because it had been discarded, then discovered, like hidden treasure. . . .

I was never a delicate child, and it seems to me now that my father, so abundant with male sperm, having eight sons from two women, must have created a half-boy in me. I wanted to play my brothers' games and would stand in tears, outside a locked door, listening to them whispering inside the magic room of their boys' companionship, wailing for entry. It was not love I wanted from my brothers, only admission to their games. When they made catapults out of whittled, crooked branches and rubber bands and shot at each other with hard unripe berries from waste bushes, all scavenged from visits to relatives who lived outside the town, I wanted to learn to shoot also. I wanted to cheer and dodge, to hit a target, to be triumphant. But on the rare occasions that they permitted me to join their game, I was never handed a catapult; I was always the hunted, hurtling from the whooping savages with winded lungs, and crunched behind a box or pillar with painfully thudding heart. When I was allowed to play their games, I was always clumsy, fumbling, falling behind, half in tears, terrified. I would hold a catapult for that brief precious time it was loaned to me when the game was over. The wood had been

sanded smooth, the two arms of the weapon strengthened by rubber bands lashed around them. The cradle from which the pellet-berries were slung had been cut out of the inner tubes of bicycle rubbers. The catapult was a crafted artifact, solid, powerful, and I was never taught how to draw back the cradle, how to position the berry, how to throw it with such force that it would fly for yards and sting your enemy on the cheek.

Earnestly following after my brothers, crying at their curt demands that I leave them, terrified when they let me play, whether I was hiding or seeking, my mother was nowhere in my mind. Or rather she was that female self I did not desire, that repressed consciousness into which was thrown everything that I rejected: the bland and vain behavior; petty, narrow concerns; boring social meetings; passive pregnancies; repetitious, meaningless gestures of motherhood. She was my negative, my brothers my positive model.

But I myself was a vacuum of energy, restless, unsettled, unbelonging, neither girl nor boy. Subjectivity is still to me a kind of drift, an active withholding of identity, when you don't know who you are because the world is still too new, and you can only know yourself, if at all, by letting the world be, and letting the shape of your experience of this world shape your knowledge of your self. This active withholding of identity appears like a kind of passivity but needs a high intensity of observing without prior sight, like an articulate baby with all the tools of a mature language looking at things for the first time.

This must have been my experience of my brothers' half-familiar, half-alien world. My sense of my self was always in abeyance, under their interrogation, and in the experience of my failure as a boy. It is the failure of this kind of identity which has created the consciousness of a gap between myself and others (that is, unlike

Freudians, I do not believe that female subjectivity is simply penis envy, but when successfully past the stage of recognition of difference, an active and self-creative energy). It is this consciousness of the eternal separation reproduced in myself that has involuntarily organized my instincts to be an observer and a writer.

The feral child and the coldness of an intense, isolated subjectivity are elements of my self that only I can know. But there are elements of a life that are there for public record. My father had lost his business because he had invested the little money he had on a get-rich scheme presented to him by one of his best friends, a pawnbroker whose shop was across the street from my father's shoe-store. When my mother abandoned the family, for a few years we were dreadfully poor. After my grandfather's house was sold and my father's extended family broke into separate households scattered over the town, my father, brothers, and I, six members in all, finally settled into a tiny two-bedroom house in a row of four such houses, all roofed with the same long sheets of zinc that burned in the afternoons as if to bake our brains and rattled in the monsoon storms like an unending army of red ants invading our eardrums.

Those years were vividly full. I was finally in a situation, a game, just like my brothers. In our wild, abandoned state, we had become equals. We were always hungry, usually having only one meal in the evening each day. One of my brothers would ride his bicycle to a cheap restaurant set up in one of the shacks jumbled together by the river beside the town-market. We waited impatiently for his return with the three-tiered tiffin carrier. The bottom container was filled with rice, although never enough rice for us; the second container held soup, a waterish liquid flavored with dried anchovies, a few pieces of cabbage; if we were lucky some strips of gray pork intestine or tripe. The top container was only half-filled, with bony ribs or fatty pork with thin strips of lean or chunks of ray meat which we chewed, cartilage and all. The family dinner was our civilized hour, after which father would start a sing-a-long or some of us completed our homework or studied for exams, then went to bed. . . .

There was never enough fruit to fill me up. I walked two-and-a-half miles to the missionary school to save the five cent bus-fare and schemed on what it could buy that had the biggest bulk. A wonderful day came when I discovered that five cents would buy a large handful of dried dates, the very sweet, sticky dates that came in sacks, clumped together and matted with straw, rope, pebbles, and who knows what else. Chinese Malaysians never ate these dates, for they were the food of fasting Malay Muslims, and the Chinese stores carried them only for the Malays, many of whom were as indigent as we were.

Was I unhappy? Hunger is a drive, and like all drives it gives meaning to the world. I was too hungry to be unhappy, and remember above all the pure joy of discovering food and having food. Moving from gathering area to gathering area, animals do not stop to wonder what it all adds up to. The smell of a ripe banana appearing as it were from one's search in the world gives rise to an emotion of concentrated pleasure that has nothing to do with our usual associations with deprivation and hunger. There is a resilience in the human animal beyond psychological understanding, taking place at the level of instinct, a pleasure in surviving which explains the laughter of refugee children, the ability of raped women to love the children of the rapists. . . .

Of course, unless one is practising a kind of Zen meditation, it is difficult for the mind to be emptied of content. The kind of withholding of identity while one looks at the world easily spills over into a looking at the self; into self-consciousness. What is commonly described as woolgathering, staring into space, being lost in thought is that process by which the subject separates the observer/subject from the object/subject, transforming subjectivity itself into mental objects for study. The self-conscious subject, when it uses its capacity for reflection, is in the process of claiming its own subjectivity.

But this claim as autonomous subject is often not legitimized for the Asian woman writer. Where women are situated as objects for others' possession, their attempts to observe, reflect, and articulate their subjectivity in art and literature are seen as dangerous or decadent. Expressions of female subjectivity are most accepted only in the domestic world; hence women's art historically is seen in weaving, pottery, basketmaking, home decoration and so on. Written discourse which is in the public domain—history, fiction, poetry (as opposed to letters and diaries)—is traditionally seen as the realm of male expression, and women attempting to use such discourse are perceived as competing with men and unwomanly. In Asia, women writers must face the possibility of social ridicule, censure, and distrust. Ding Ling, for example, was silenced and exiled to the Great Northern Wilderness from 1958 to 1979 for, among other things, the decadence of themes in her early stories (stories which deal explicitly with sexual self-consciousness and self-conflicts in young women). Kamala Das has been excoriated by both male and female critics for the strongly sexual nature of her work, its subjective autobiographical scale. . . .

The pressure of social inhibition (self-exposure presented as suicidal) on the Asian woman writer marks her expressions of her self. The chief marker is the kinds of silences evident in the literary history of her society. Feuerwerker points out, for example, that although "women had been relatively visible in traditional [Chinese] literature . . . they had been presented less

as subjects in their own right than as objects or images catering to the needs, desires, and projections of a preponderantly male authorship" (20).

Beginning with the twentieth century, Asian women's literature displays the marks of what I have described as a female experience of consciousness, including an intense subjectivity which is extremely sensitive to sensual experiences while at the same time cold and isolated. It is a kind of subjectivity which has been criticized as self-indulgent, fragmented, or ideologically rightist because selfishly preoccupied with subjective needs. When the Asian woman writer becomes conscious of her own subjectivity, she becomes conscious first of the fracture between her desire for the sensual world in which her being is grounded and the isolated signifying self which grasps the social oppression of the female but cannot overcome its internalized meaning. . . .

Even when Asian women become conscious of strengths, these strengths are often seen as male qualities or as betrayals of a feminine self. With the dawning of liberation for women in Asia, the woman as autonomous subject, maker of her own destiny, separate from the traditional roles of mother and sexual possession, will become increasingly the topic of women's writing. Yet Asian women may not be comfortable with these changes; without, as Kristeva says, a radical transformation of the psychological subject, there can be no social revolution. It is understandable therefore that, faced with the choice of claiming their subjectivity, many women have retreated instead into the anonymity of purdah (as in Egypt or Malaysia) or the counterclaims of total maternal consciousness (as in Japan, where many women stop working to devote themselves to their children's education).

The contemporary Asian woman writer is shadowed by this double, of active self seen in the background of traditional social expectations that continue to complicate and subvert the process of claiming subjectivity. This scene of self and society, like a visual trick, can shift foreground and background, and the Asian woman will alternately place self first, then place family and community before self, with hardly a sense of the contradictions involved. But the writer who becomes conscious of this doubling of moral vision can be tormented by inconsistency, self-contempt and hatred. . . .

The modern Asian woman writer is least likely to acknowledge a self as material, which is the field of politics for the empowered male. Because she has had little experience with political power, receiving the vote late and even now very seldom included in governmental roles, her imagination has not absorbed the material reality of consciousness. The Other to her has not moved beyond the first barrier of the Male Other. The Asian woman for centuries has been used by a patriarchal society as an object of economic exchange, de-centered in traditional customs such as arranged marriages, child brides, dowries, polygamy, and prostitution. Not possessing economic power, she has been able to value herself only in the biological and domestic reproductive system, as mother and home-maker, values that rest on her ability to attract a mate, on her sexuality. As I've said earlier, for Asian women writers like Ding Ling, Kamala Das, or Gauri Deshpande, the sexual is the political.

Ding Ling was able to move out of her early sexual themes to a consciousness of the material world, expressed in novels such as *The Sun Shines Over the Sanggan River,* a rare development only matched by Western women writers such as Doris Lessing and Adrienne Rich. The future of self for the Asian woman writer must lie in this vision (or re-vision as Rich calls it in her essay "When We Dead Awaken: Writing as Re Vision"), in which the material world emerges from its possession by males to the grasp of the woman. . . .

For me, to recognize a material self is to begin to write politically, with a sense of history and larger forces at work outside the subject. It is to begin to understand how remote history and politics have been for women and how totalizing in their lives. So my father's precipitate decline into bankruptcy was a story of greed, betrayal and stupidity, but more than that it was the common story of small private businesses failing in the face of new, aggressive corporate companies that began entering Malaysia after the end of World War II. It was the story of family businesses destroyed by familial rivalries, and of the harsh laws of bankruptcy imposed by a British colonial government still meting out a Dickensian punishment to the impoverished and unlucky. So too my mother's sudden flight to Singapore, abandoning six children heedlessly, is a tale of selfishness, egotism, an unforgiving resentment of the woman for the man who has abused her. But it is also a tale of an Asian woman influenced by Western mores of individualism, the sociological story of women from the provinces departing for the metropolitan centers and for new economic opportunities.

My story as a writer is also that of a colonized education in which the essential processes of identity formation are ironically the very processes stripping the individual of Asian tradition and communal affiliation. All writers begin as readers, and what I read for British external exams administered in Cambridge and Oxford and for pleasure in the cool thick-walled Malacca library were William Shakespeare, Jane Austen, Alfred Lord Tennyson, T. S. Eliot, Mills' and Boone's books, Barbara Cartland and Agatha Christie.[6] At that voracious age before puberty, I did not reflect that Hamlet was hardly a character a Chinese Malaysian girl could understand; after all, he was presented as universal. So we chanted, "To be or not to be, that is the question," and watched Laurence Olivier in black and white, impressed most by the daring of his exposed stockinged legs. Years later, I read the graffiti on the bathroom walls of a second-hand book store in New York, "Shakespeare: To be or not to be; Sartre: To do is to be; Sinatra: Doobeedoobeedoo" and realized that some native wag had Americanized an Anglo wit. But in Malacca in the 1950s, English literature was a very solemn affair, reflecting the seriousness with which the British undertook to inculcate their civilization in us. "The White Man's Burden" was still taken by white men as their responsibility in the Far East, and while we were gifted with the splendid weight of the English language and its poetry, we were also burdened with their images, assumptions, values, history, and ideology, not to mention their prosodic forms, rhymes, silly poses, cheap sentimentality, Cliff Richards songs, tinned crackers, boiled sweets, Cadbury chocolates, all the colonial trivia of Malaysian daily life which adds up to a crackpot culture.

Of course it was a yellow culture we received, whether it was Thomas Peacock's unutterably dull satires canonized by the Cambridge Exams or Denis Robin's ladylike because suggestive pornography for teenage girls and frustrated wives. But then no open society is safe from yellow culture; to put it more positively, from the undesirable influences of other cultures. We were, however, not an open society. We were caged in British colonial culture and like the mynah learned to repeat the master's phrases, a song that we hear in the poems of the early Indian women writers such as Toru Dutt and Sarojini Naidu. The Asian woman writer, once the colonial screen has been lifted, is not yet a free individual, for colonial education has shaped both the spirit of independence and the language of independence that are to free her, and, as Audre Lorde asks, how is the master's house to be dismantled by the master's tools?

When the Asian woman looks to the West for social and economic liberation, she is exchanging a traditional social oppression for a new cultural oppressiveness. Filipino women who advertise for and marry aging European males are acting out of the ancient role of women as economic possessions to be bought and sold to the highest bidder. When Chinese girls in Beijing deliberately seek Western men to marry, they are moving from one level of colonized mentality to another. . . .

There are other selves not yet created in English literature and culture. The story of the Asian woman writer is the yet-to-be-told story of these selves which are dense with facticity, intersected by history and politics. The material self is the most Asian; rejects universality as the lesson of the master's tools; and insists on political realism as the space for self-creation. For me as a Chinese-Malaysian woman writer whose ethnicity marks her as subject to a new colonialism in the name of nationalism, this realism must be deeply insisted upon. To continue to write in English about a Chinese-Malaysian self and world, to insist on the validity of my material history, is the most revolutionary act possible in a society which seeks to deny autonomy or value to people like me.

In naming her experiences, the modern Asian woman writer is existentialist. To write is to inscribe original identity; "Asian" is a term that is still filling with meaning. The material world is the political world; and the self, which is always already in exile, is also always already in birth.

Notes

I thank Nancy K. Miller for insights shared during the 1987 NEH Summer Seminar at Barnard; and Wimal Dissanayake for his support during my 1988 summer residency at the East-West Center, Honolulu, which resulted in this chapter.

1. See feminist critics' discussion of Lacan's ideas on the language of desire or female self inscribed as lack; for example, Toril Moi's succinct summary of Lacan's theories on the Imaginary and Symbolic Orders, the Mirror Stage, and the usages of the Other as "the locus of the constitution of the subject"; she points out that "If, for Lacan, it is the entry into the Symbolic Order that opens up the unconscious, this means that it is the primary repression of the desire for symbolic unity with the mother that creates the unconscious."

2. Ding Ling, "Shanghai in the Spring of 1930," *Miss Sophie's Diary*, 1985. All references to the story are taken from this edition.

3. After writing the bulk of this essay, I came across Teresa de Lauretis's summary of Catharine MacKinnon's essay which expresses a similar although larger argument: "To feminism, the personal is epistemologically the political, and its epistemology is its politics" (535).

4. See, for example, the anthology *A Double Colonialism: Colonial and Post-Colonial Women's Writing*, ed. Anna Rutherford.

5. I have written on my mother's abandonment of the family in an earlier essay, "When East Meets West: Second Mothers and Abandoned Daughters."

6. I have written of the colonial reading experience in previous essays, especially in "Interview with Norman Simms" and "The Dispossessing Eye: Reading Wordsworth on the Equatorial Line."

Works Cited

Das, Kamala. *Alphabet of Lust*. New Delhi: Orient Paperbacks, 1976.

Das, Kamala. *The Old Playhouse and Other Poems*. New Delhi: Orient Longman, 1973.

de Lauretis, Teresa. *Alice Doesn't: Feminism, Semiotics, Cinema*. Bloomington: Indiana University Press, 1984.

Dutt, Toru. *Ancient Ballads and Legends of Hindustan*. London: Kegan Paul, 1882.

Dutt, Toru. *A Sheaf Gleaned in French Fields*. 3d ed. London: Kegan Paul, 1880.

Feuerwerker, Yi-tsi Mei. *Ding Ling's Fiction*. Cambridge: Harvard University Press, 1983.

Gilbert, Sandra M., and Susan Gubar. *The Norton Anthology of Literature by Women*. New York: Norton, 1985.

Kristeva, Julia. "La Femme, ce n'est jamais ça," *Polylogue*. Paris: Editions du Seuil, 1977.

Lessing, Doris. *The Summer before the Dark*. New York: Knopf, 1973.

Lessing, Doris. *To Room Nineteen*. London: Jonathan Cape, 1978.

Lim, Shirley Geok-lin. "The Dispossessing Eye: Reading Wordsworth on the Equatorial Line." In *Discharging the Canon: Cross-Cultural Readings in Literature*, ed. Peter Hyland. Singapore: Singapore University Press, 1985, 126–32.

Lim, Shirley Geok-lin. "Interview with Norman Simms." *NZASIA*, Hamilton: New Zealand Asian Studies Society, 1983: 28–46.

Lim, Shirley Geok-lin. *No Man's Grove*. Singapore: National University of Singapore English Department Press, 1985.

Lim, Shirley Geok-lin. "When East Meets West: Second Mothers and Abandoned Daughters." In *Women and Stepfamilies: Voices of Anger and Love*, ed. Nan Bauer Maglin and Nancy Schiedewind. Philadelphia: Temple University Press, 1989. 162–69.

Ling, Ding. *The Sun Shines over the Sanggan River*. Trans. by Yang Xianyi and Gladys Yang. Beijing: Foreign Languages Press, 1984.

Ling, Ding. "Miss Sophie's Diary" and "Shanghai in the Spring of 1930." In *Miss Sophie's Diary and Other Stories*. Trans. W. J. F. Jenner. Beijing: Panda Books, 1985.

Lorde, Audre. "The Master's Tools Will Never Dismantle the Master's House." *Sister Outsider*. Trumansburg, NY: Crossing Press, 1984. 110–13.

Moi, Toril. *Sexual/Textual Politics*. London and New York: Methuen, 1985.

Naidu, Sarojini. *The Golden Threshold*. With an introduction by Arthur Symonds. New York: John Lane, 1905.

Naidu, Sarojini. *The Sceptred Flute Songs of India*. New York: Dodd and Mead, 1928.

Olsen, Tillie. *Tell Me a Riddle*. New York: Dell, 1981.

Parthasarathy, R., ed. *Ten Twentieth-Century Indian Poets*. Delhi: Oxford University Press, 1976.

Rich, Adrienne. "When We Dead Awaken: Writing as Re-Vision," *College English* 34 (October 1973): 18–30.

Rutherford, Anna, ed. *A Double Colonialism: Colonial and Post-Colonial Women's Writing*. Aarhus, Denmark: Kunapipi, 1985.

Stanton, Domna C. "Language and Revolution." In *The Future of Difference,* ed. Hester Eisenstein and Alice Jardine. New Brunswick, NJ: Rutgers University Press, 1987.

38 From the Women's Prison: Third World Women's Narratives of Prison

Barbara Harlow

Women's prison writings from the Third World present a twofold challenge to Western theoretical developments, both literary critical and feminist. What may seem to be incidental as the common feature among them, that they are written by women in the Third World and deal with the experience of prison, is in fact potentially constructive of a discursive category. Generically, these writings defy traditional categories and distinctions and combine fictional forms with documentary record. Furthermore, the women's collective experience and political development that they describe emerge out of their position within a set of social relations giving rise to a secular ideology, one not based on bonds of gender, race, or ethnicity—which may be shared by men and may not be shared by all women. It is this twofold challenge of these writings that this paper proposes to examine.

Political forces and economic pressures are radically altering the structure of women's lives in Third World societies, transforming not only their relationship to men within the family setting but their role in the larger social order as well. Just as the Baluch woman will bear an increased social burden following the death of her husband, her brother, her son, so too will the women of other peoples engaged in national liberation struggles or resistance movements find their political responsibilities reorganized, either by the necessity of their assuming the place of the absent men or by their taking up arms beside them. Following the departure of the Palestine Liberation Organization (PLO) fighters from Beirut after the Israeli invasion of Lebanon in 1982, for example, the Palestinian women—mothers, wives, daughters, and sisters—took over, as they had done before, the supervision and maintenance of many of the social services provided by the resistance organization.[1] Similarly, in Guinea-Bissau, women participated in the armed struggle led by Amilcar Cabral (who was himself later assassinated by members of his movement in collaboration with the Portuguese) that culminated finally in 1974 in liberation from Portuguese imperialism and national independence. The role of these women, however, unlike that of Angolan women, was not that of combatants in active fighting but developed primarily in areas of service and support. This distinction, according to the leaders of the revolution, was generated less out of a patriarchal system than as a response to the circumstances and conditions of the country itself, its population, the nature of its terrain, and the immediate and long-range needs of the struggle.[2] In South Africa, the mass removals of populations under various apartheid laws, such as the pass laws restricting the freedom of movement and choice of occupation, have succeeded not only in separating families but in politicizing women as well.[3] In *One Day of Life*, the banned novel by the El Salvadoran writer Manlio Argueta, Lupe and her granddaughter Adolfina must carry on the political struggle when Lupe's husband, José, is murdered by Salvadoran death squads.[4]

No less than political repression and popular resistance to it, economic pressures and the consequences of migrant labor, as well as rural-urban migration and the failures of postcolonial governments are also forcing a reconstruction of traditional female roles and family patterns. Like Wanja in *Petals of Blood,* the Kenyan novel of neocolonialism by Ngugi wa Thiong'o, African women are leaving the family structure to join forces in the beginnings, not always successful, of a new social order.[5] The absence of men, whether through struggle, death, migration, or abandonment, is critical to the position of women in many developing countries. . . .

Women's writings from the Third World, which are representative of the social and political struggle in those countries, challenge certain presuppositions of Western critical theory as well as the literary and ideological conventions that organize the articulation of these issues. The popularity in the Arab world and in Latin America of the short story, as a major literary form, the genre, according to Frank O'Connor, of a "submerged population group,"[6] is significant as a potential reordering of the canonical hierarchy of forms presided over by the Western literary critical establishment. For these critics generally, it is the novel and the psychological development of its individualized hero or heroine which, among narrative forms, occupies the most elevated ranks in the literary order. As Masao Miyoshi has pointed out, however, with regard even to the novel, "as geopolitical hegemony is to the state, so is traditionalism to its culture. The first-world tradition is to be the universal norm and the inevitable future of every culture in the world."[7] Miyoshi's article, "Against the Grain: Reading the Japanese Novel

in America," insists on the cultural and historical specificity of literary production and warns U.S. readers against the danger of either "domestication" or "neutralization" in reading non-Western works of literature. The "Japanese novel," he maintains, is influenced as much by the *Monogatari* tales and the stylized *Noh* dramas of Japan and their concept of character as it is by European narrative forms. The construction of the subject as well as the conventions of form is implicit in the use by writers of the short story in "marginalized" cultures.

Like the demands of the short story's collective protagonist, the subject of autobiography poses a similar challenge to formal authority and its legitimacy. Although genealogists of the form trace its ancestry often back as far as Saint Augustine's *Confessions,* "all autobiography," maintains Roger Rosenblatt, citing its importance in Black literature in the United States, "is minority autobiography." "Minority autobiography and minority fiction," he goes on, "deserve their minority status not because of comparative numbers, but because of the presence of a special reality, one provided for the minority by the majority, within which each member of the minority tries to reach an understanding both of himself and the reality into which he has been placed."[8] The role played by autobiography in Black literature is paralleled by its place in women's writings. In both cases, furthermore, the very presence of the autobiography and its persistent continuation are sustained by the same historical and ideological conditions as those that underwrite Michael Sprinker's proposition on the "end of autobiography," that "no autobiography can take place except within the boundaries of a writing where concepts of subject, self and author collapse into the act of producing a text."[9] In the prison memoirs of Third World political detainees, the challenge to the literary conventions of autobiography is concomitant with the refusal of filial ties based exclusively on gender or race, sexuality, or ethnicity. As H. Bruce Franklin concluded in his study of the writings of prisoners, especially Blacks, in U.S. jails,

People who have become literary artists because of their imprisonment tend to write in an autobiographical mode. The reason is obvious: it is their own personal experience that has given them both their main message and the motive to communicate it. The works of today's prisoners, though predominantly autobiographical, are rarely intended as a display of individual genius. Whereas the literary criteria dominant on campus exalt what is extraordinary or even unique, with "originality" as the key criterion, most current autobiographical writing from prison intends to show the readers that the author's individual experience is not unique or even extraordinary.[10]

The same can be said of writers who are imprisoned because they write.

In the same way that institutions of power—whether established from within the society or political order or imposed as a result of external hegemonic practices and domination—are subverted by the demand on the part of dispossessed groups for an access to history, power, and resources, so too are the narrative paradigms and their textual authority being transformed by the historical and literary articulation of those demands. The women of Pakistan, like Palestinian women, black and white South African women, Bolivian or Egyptian women—whose husbands have died, been imprisoned, migrated, or joined the resistance movement, or who perhaps have never married—are writing their autobiographies. Like Kate Chopin, they have embarked on new careers. Many of their autobiographies, however, are being written out of the experience of prison.

For women in the Third World, imprisonment by the authoritarian states and repressive regimes within which they live and work is a real possibility as the outcome of their private and public struggles. Their case histories, most often suppressed by their own governments, have been documented by international human rights organizations such as Amnesty International.[11] But the women themselves have provided textual accounts, narratives and autobiographies of their prison experiences. Their personal itineraries, which have taken them through struggle, interrogation, incarceration, and, in many cases, physical torture, are attested to in their own narratives as part of a historical agenda, a collective enterprise. These writings, taken collectively, suggest the emergence of a new literary corpus out of contemporary conditions in the Third World of political and social repression. Located in a specific historical context, this corpus continues nonetheless to develop as those conditions of global repression are perpetuated. In this article, however, I will concentrate on seven examples, each of which combines, in different and sometimes experimental ways, the formal questions of literary convention with the urgent demand for documentation and records. These texts, which include short story, novel, autobiography, diary, and "testimony," are integral in compiling the chapters of what Gayatri Chakravorty Spivak has designated in her critique of psychoanalysis and the Third World as the social and "psychobiographies that constitute the subject effect of these [Third World] women."[12] The main texts to be discussed are Bessie Head's short story "The Collector of Treasures"; Nawal el-Saadawi's novelistic testimony, *Woman at Point Zero*, followed by el-Saadawi's own *Memoirs from the Women's Prison*; the prison diaries of Akhtar Baluch, "Sister, Are You Still Here?"; the autobiography, *Let Me Speak*, of Domitila Barrios de Chungara; and the prison memoirs of Ruth First, *117 Days*, and of Raymonda H. Tawil, *My Home, My Prison*. These texts have begun to emerge as a collective corpus, a common statement, which embodies the challenge to authoritarian structures and state apparatuses.[13] Based exclusively neither on issues of gender or race nor, strictly speaking, on questions of class, they outline the possibilities of new secular forms of social organization.

The question of the significance of categories other than gender—such as race, ethnicity, religion and class—in determining issues of international solidarity and collective struggle is vital to the contemporary debates and controversy within the feminist movement in the West. The priority of sex as an analytic category is being subjected to reformulation from more than one perspective. As Joan Kelly-Gadol maintains, "in seeking to add women to the fund of historical knowledge, women's history has revitalized theory, for it has shaken the conceptual formulations of historical study," and, furthermore, "it has done this by making problematical three of the basic concerns of historical thought: (1) periodization, (2) the categories of social analysis, and (3) theories of social change."[14] On the other hand, feminism and feminist theory have also been accused of universalism, a lack of historical consciousness, and a refusal to consider the specificity of material conditions influencing the women's struggle from within different societies and cultural traditions. The problematization of the sexual category through the introduction of questions of racial oppression is still further rearticulated and complicated by, to take just one example, the battered women's movement, which has obliged feminist theoreticians to reconsider the role of class in discriminating among women who are being discriminated against.[15] Thus, too, Domitila Barrios de Chungara, leader of the Housewives Committee organized in support of Bolivia's miners, is dismayed to discover that Western feminists attending the 1975 United Nations-sponsored In-

ternational Women's Tribunal held in Mexico City were more concerned that she participate in their sisterhood than they were with supporting the Bolivian miners' struggle in which Barrios de Chungara saw herself as first of all and most importantly a participant. "For us," she writes, "the first and main task isn't to fight against our compañeros, but with them to change the system we live in for another."[16] Similarly, Iranian women found it necessary to distinguish the priorities of their roles in the Iranian revolution from those of many Western women. As one woman put it, in the West, "men allegedly separated women from each other, so feminism took up this as an arena of struggle and made it a principle to promote women's 'sisterhood and solidarity.' But this aspect was absent from the Iranian picture. All-women groups were the *only* possibility in Iran and in fact it was the demand for the coming together of the sexes that preoccupied women's struggles, and was considered its most outrageous character."[17] Finally, Gloria Joseph, the black West Indian feminist, insists that "to speak of women, all women categorically, is to perpetuate white supremacy—white female supremacy," and she concludes her critique not only of feminism but also of classical Marxism by heralding the idea that "the fight against white supremacy and male domination over women is directly linked to the worldwide struggles for national liberation. Protracted struggle must take place on an international level."[18]

What characterizes the writings of women like Domitila Barrios de Chungara, Nawal el-Saadawi, Ruth First, or Raymonda Tawil, what they have in common—despite the specificity of their concerns rooted in the unique material conditions of their lives and the differing forms taken by oppression in their respective societies—is their secularism. This secularism is articulated in their challenge to a genealogy of authority based exclusively on ties of filiation.

Although legitimacy, according to Edward Said, who introduces the distinction in *The World, the Text, and the Critics,* can be transferred "from filiation to affiliation," it is also possible, he maintains, "for the critic to recognize the difference between instinctual filiation and social affiliation, and to show how affiliation sometimes reproduces filiation, sometimes makes its own forms."[19] It is this second alternative, that of a "secular critical consciousness," which distinguishes the writing of these women and their efforts, through political struggle and personal and collective testimony, to elaborate new bases of affiliation. . . .

Although the prison writing of Third World women does not necessarily conform to generic criteria and specifications as formulated by a Western critical or literary tradition, ranging as that writing does from short story to autobiographical testimony or political documentary and confounding thereby even the categorical distinction between fiction and nonfiction, it does nonetheless propose alternative parameters for the definition and articulation of literary conventions. Ngugi wa Thiong'o, the Kenyan writer and academic, maintained in his essay "Literature in Schools" that "in literature there have been two opposing aesthetics: the aesthetics of oppression and exploitation and of acquiescence with imperialism and that of human struggle for total liberation." Formal criteria are thus obliged to yield to the insistence of ideological and political exigencies in deciding the ascendancy of form and the alliances among texts and writers. But these formal categories, literary or textualized, are not without a parallel set of distinctions imposed on the prisoners from within the prison system itself. Important among these distinctions concerning the classification of prisoners is that maintained by the state judicial apparatus and manipulated by the prison authorities between common law inmates and political detainees, between those serving sentences for criminal offenses, that is, and those being held on account of their political activities. These activities include the act of writing itself. In Egypt's el-Qanatir prison for women where Nawal al-Saadawi was held in 1981 by the Sadat regime, it was "forbidden to speak with politicals." On Robben Island, however, South Africa's notorious penitentiary, the prison officials began their punitive practice by attempting to use common law prisoners to factionalize and divide the political prisoners among themselves. Indres Naidoo, a South African Indian who served a ten-year sentence in the prison for his subversive activities against the apartheid government as a member of the African National Congress, describes in his memoirs, *Robben Island,* the defeat engineered by the political prisoners of these divisive tactics on the part of the authorities. The common law prisoners ended by being convinced of the political programs of their fellow inmates.[20] So, too, al-Qanatir's common law prisoners formed alliances, albeit ambiguous, with the political detainees, even at times acting as conduits for messages and communications to and from the outside world. No more than common law or criminal prisoners can be separated from political detainees can literary genres be isolated from their political and ideological context and consequences. . . .

The merging of the categories of common law prisoners and political detainees entails as well the emergence of a mutual and reciprocal relationship between writer and character. The distance between the two positions which had been maintained in Head's story of Dikeledi Mokopi, or even in el-Saadawi's life history of Firdaus, is collapsed when writing itself becomes an offense against the state punishable by law and a prison sentence. El-Saadawi, unlike either Dikeledi Mokopi or Firdaus, is arrested because she writes, and the very act of writing assumes a different, less conventional significance. Writing, on the one hand, no longer distinguishes her from other women in the society but, rather, links her to them in their respective opposition to the reprisals of authoritarian structures. On the other hand, it is still through her writing that the isolated acts of violent aggression or vengeance of these women find collective meaning as the expression of a popular struggle. If, as Fredric Jameson maintains in his analysis of "magical narratives" in *The Political Unconscious,* "the strategic value of generic concepts for Marxism clearly lies in the mediation function of the notion of genre, which allows the co-ordination of immanent formal analysis of the individual text with the twin diachronic perspective of the history of form and the evolution of social life,"[21] then just as clearly these prison writings by women from the different regions of the Third World are attempting the complicated task not only of rearticulating the "history of form" as received or imposed but of reorganizing as well the "evolution of social life" with its attendant distinctions of political/nonpolitical and the categories of gender, race, and class within their communities. . . .

The relationship between family and other forms of collectivity remains significant, indeed crucial, to the prison memoirs of political detainees. Furthermore, this effort to reformulate the authoritarian imposition of familial obligations as part of a collective political struggle is not specific to women's prison narratives. Mu'in Basisu—the Palestinian poet held in Egyptian jails for his political activities in the 1950s—and the Kenyan writer Ngugi wa Thiong'o—arrested by Jomo Kenyatta on 31 December 1977—recount in their prison diaries the programmatic manipulation by the state prison apparatus of the prisoners' family ties and loyalties as a means of coercion. In Basisu's *Descent into the Water* and in *Detained* by Ngugi, Egyptian authorities and their Kenyan counterparts promise the subjugated but still defiant prisoners visits from their wives if they will at last agree

to cooperate with the states' investigations. Their continued refusal to participate in these repressive conventions, however, bespeaks a continued commitment to the reconstruction of the ideological system. According to Louis Althusser, the ideological state apparatuses, such as prisons, the army, the police, and the courts—regardless of whether they operate on religious, educational, familial, legal, political, trade-union or cultural levels—"may be not only the *stake,* but also the *site* of the class struggle." . . .[22]

For many Third World women, feminism means women's liberation and women's liberation is seen as part of a popular struggle against the forces of oppression. Such a struggle must have its roots in the material conditions of the people themselves but must also contain the possibilities for a larger collective vision. The active role of women in the national liberation struggles and resistance movements of the Third World has contributed significantly to an articulation of political ideology in their countries which transcends the distinctions of gender, race, and ethnicity. According to Samora Machel, for example, now president of Mozambique, in his essay "The Liberation of Women Is a Fundamental Necessity for the Revolution," "the antagonistic contradiction is not between women and men, but between women and the social order, between all exploited people, both men and women, and the social order. . . . Therefore, just as there can be no revolution without the liberation of men, the struggle for women's emancipation cannot succeed without the victory of the revolution."[23] This reciprocal relationship is further articulated by Ghassan Kanafani in "The Case of Abu Hamidu,"[24] the last article he wrote before he was assassinated in 1972 in a carbomb explosion in Beirut. In this article, the Palestinian writer reiterated the necessity within the revolutionary movement itself for social and ideological reeducation, not only of the people but of the commandos as well. Abu Hamidu was a Palestinian guerrilla in southern Lebanon in 1971 when he was accused by the villagers of raping one of their daughters. The commando was tried for his crime, found guilty, and sentenced to death by the resistance organization. The girl in question was killed by her brother, because, according to tradition, a stain on her honor was a stain as well on the honor of the entire family. The authoritarian traditions and social structures which lead women to kill their husbands, brothers to seek blood vengeance from their sisters, must be revised. National liberation, the writer maintains, must be a part of a larger social revolution. In his radical critique of the Abu Hamidu incident, Kanafani insists on the need for the revolutionary movement to educate its own members, female and male, to a practice that would transform systems of exploitation—whether based on gender, race, or class—into a collective solidarity, an active alliance with a secular vision. There is, in the end, as the Baluch poet wrote, "no other way of saying this gently."[25]

Notes

1. For an account of Palestinian women in the refugee camps of Lebanon in the year immediately preceding the invasion, see Ingela Bendt and James Downing, *We Shall Return: Women of Palestine*, trans. Ann Henning (London: Zed Press, 1982).

2. See Stephanie Urdang, *Fighting Two Colonialisms: Women in Guinea-Bissau* (New York: Monthly Review, 1979).

3. See Hilda Bernstein, *For Their Triumphs and for Their Tears: Women in Apartheid South Africa* (London: International Defense and Aid Fund, 1978).

4. Manlio Argueta, *One Day of Life*, trans. Bill Brow (New York: Random House, 1983). Ngugi wa Thiong'o, *Petals of Blood* (New York: E. P. Dutton, 1978).

5. See Christine Obbo, *African Women: Their Struggle for Economic Independence* (London: Zed Press, 1980). See also the special issue of *MERIP Reports* 14, no. 5 (1984) on migrant labor and its effects on women in Egypt and Yemen.

6. Frank O'Connor, *The Lonely Voice* (Cleveland: World, 1960).

7. Masao Miyoshi, "Against the Grain: Reading the Japanese Novel in America," in *Critical Perspectives in East Asian Literature*, ed. Peter H. Lee (Seoul: International Cultural Society of Korea, 1984), 223.

8. Roger Rosenblatt, "Black Autobiography: Life as the Death Weapon," in *Autobiography: Essays Theoretical and Critical*, ed. James Olney (Princeton: Princeton University Press, 1980), 168, 171.

9. Michael Sprinker, "The End of Autobiography: Fictions of the Self," in Olney, 342.

10. H. Bruce Franklin, *The Victim as Criminal and Artist: Literature from the American Prison* (New York: Oxford University Press, 1978), 249–50.

11. In addition to reports on individual countries and regimes, see also *Torture in the Eighties* (London: Amnesty International, 1984). For a discussion by writers who face imprisonment, whether as threat or reality, see *The Writer and Human Rights*, ed. Toronto Arts Group for Human Rights (New York: Doubleday, 1983).

12. Gayatri Chakravorty Spivak, "Rethinking the Political Economy of Women," paper presented at Pembroke Center Conference on Feminism, Theory Politics, Providence, Rhode Island, 14–16 March 1985.

13. Bessie Head, "The Collector of Treasures," in *The Collector of Treasures* (London: Heinemann, 1977); Nawal el-Saadawi, *Woman at Point Zero*, trans. Sherif Hetata (London: Zed Press, 1983), and *Memoirs from the Women's Prison* (Cairo: Dar al-Mustaqbal al-Arabi, 1984); in Arabic, translations my own. See also Akhtar Baluch, "Sister, Are You Still Here? The Diary of a Sindhi Woman Prisoner," with introduction and notes by Mary Tyler, in *Race and Class* 18 (1977): 219–45; Domitila Barrios de Chungara and Moema Viezzer, *Let Me Speak: Testimony of Domitila, A Woman of the Bolivian Mines*, trans. Victoria Ortiz (New York: Monthly Review, 1978); Ruth First, *117 Days* (New York: Stein & Day, 1965); Raymonda H. Tawil, *My Home, My Prison* (London: Zed Press, 1983. Other examples include Mary Tyler, *My Years in an Indian Prison* (London: Victor Gollanz, 1977); Etel Adnan, *Sitt Marie Rose*, trans. Georgina Kleege (Sau-

salito, CA: Post Apollo Press, 1982); and Rosemary Sayigh, "The Mukhabarat State: Testimony of a Palestinian Woman Prisoner," *Race and Class* 26 (1984).

14. Joan Kelly-Gadol, "The Social Relation of the Sexes: Methodological Implications of Women's History," in *The Signs Reader: Women, Gender, and Scholarship,* ed. Elizabeth Abel and Emily Abel (Chicago: University of Chicago Press, 1983), 11.

15. See Susan Schechter, *Women and Male Violence: The Visions and Struggles of the Battered Women's Movement* (Boston: South End Press, 1983).

16. Chungara, 194–206.

17. Nahid Yeganeh, "Women's Struggles in the Islamic Republic of Iran," in *In the Shadow of Time: The Women's Movement in Iran,* ed. Azar Tabari and Nahid Yeganeh (London: Zed Press, 1982), 34.

18. Gloria Joseph, "The Incompatible Ménage à Trois: Marxism, Feminism, and Racism," in *Women and Revolution: A Discussion of the Unhappy Marriage of Marxism and Feminism,* ed. Lydia Sargent (Boston: South End Press, 1981), 95, 106.

19. Edward Said, *The World, the Text, and the Critic* (Cambridge: Harvard University Press, 1983), 74.

20. Indres Naidoo and Albie Sachs, *Robben Island: Ten Years as a Political Prisoner in South Africa's Most Notorious Penitentiary* (New York: Vintage, 1983). Indres Naidoo was held in the Robben Island penal institution from 1963 to 1973.

21. Fredric Jameson, *The Political Unconscious: Narrative as a Socially Symbolic Act* (Ithaca: Cornell University Press, 1981), 105.

22. Louis Althusser, "Ideology and Ideological State Apparatuses," in *Lenin and Philosophy,* trans. Ben Brewster (New York: Monthly Review, 1971), 147.

23. Samora Machel, "The Liberation of Women Is a Fundamental Necessity for the Revolution," in *Mozambique: Sowing the Seeds of Revolution* (London: Committee for Freedom in Mozambique, Angola, and Guinée, 1974). Also cited in Introduction, "Sister, Are You Still Here?"

24. Ghassan Kanafani, "The Case of Abu Hamidu," in *Shu'un filastiniyya* 12 (August 1972): 8–18.

25. Balach Khan, "I Have No Way of Saying This Gently" (unpublished poem). Three other poems by Khan have been published in *Seneca Review* 14 (1984): 48–53.

39 Teaching Autobiography

Nancy K. Miller

What I have written strains to be true but nevertheless is not true enough.
Truth is anecdotes, narrative, the snug opaque quotidian.

John Updike, *Self-Consciousness*

This essay was written for a conference devoted to the subject of autobiography. The fact of that focus—the knowledge that the participants in the event and the audience were already convinced of the genre's importance (whether autobiography should be defined as a genre is of course another matter)—seems to have authorized me (in a reflection here about self-authorization) to go further in the mode I'm calling narrative criticism than I had been willing to go before. Writing autobiographically about autobiography—which is less common than one might imagine—also led me (before the fact) to include the occasion as biographeme in the structure of the writing.

At the conference itself there was something exhilarating in the effects of a common frame of reference that by its very nature was both constructed and embodied. And there was something irresistible for me in the chance to write for a context in which it was not necessary to prepare the ground before advancing. Nonetheless, rereading it now well after the fact, I see that the essay still struggles defensively with the problems left unsolved in "Dreaming, Dancing": the waltz of the "as a"s; the obligatory dance cards of representativity—even, or perhaps especially, at the heart of feminism's self-writing.

August 23, 1989.

I'm on leave in Paris. Sitting here, at the end of summer, trying to get back there, to what was I thinking of when I picked the title "Teaching Autobiography." Find the abstract in the computer:

"Teaching Autobiography"
This will be a paper about contemporary (after mid-1970s) U.S. minority feminist autobiographies—*The Woman Warrior, The House on Mango Street, Fierce At-* tachments, etc. Specifically, I want to talk about my experience teaching this literature to adult-degree students (primarily women) in a large, urban public university. I'm especially interested in questions of identification: to what extent does reading autobiography require the ability (the desire?) to identify with "the other"? Is a common gender, ethnicity, class location, racial identity, etc. the basis of the connection? Or are certain themes more powerful than location: the struggle with the

mother, the desire to become a writer, the need to resist the "maternal" culture, etc.? Is it possible to theorize the reading of autobiography, women's reading of women's autobiography, etc.? Is it desirable? I may also consider the current autobiographical mode in feminist criticism as a way of shaping the question of reading and theory.

Yes, well. All true, but how to go about writing such a paper? Do I even *want* to write it? The abstract, whatever excuses one can make for the necessary pretentiousness of the genre, seems to have been produced by a feminist computer: mine is of course responsible, but any number of other feminist computers could have generated it. All the buzzwords are there; the language oozes political correctness while nonetheless falling into the trap of condescension through implicit self-positioning (the worst kind): the first-world, majority "theorist" who will, in the interest of politicizing the field of theory, have recourse to experience: her own, and presumably—through hers—her students'. Poor students.

Still, I did teach the course; it was pretty interesting; the students, they said it themselves, "learned a lot," "got a lot out of it," and I've promised to write something on the subject because I got a lot out of it, too. What I got of course is less easy to say than what I think they got.

The difficulty I experience around writing this paper is inseparable from a problem about the language to say it in: saying the right thing, in this instance, about teaching for the first time in a non-elite institution. Anxiety about sounding classist—which, positioned as I am here, I cannot fail to do—but also at the same time irritation with the language police and impatience with my introjected feminist correctness.

In the spring of 1988, I left Barnard College and Columbia University where I had taught in vari-

ous capacities for almost twenty years and where I had also done my undergraduate and graduate studies. I left a campus located in walking distance of the apartment in which I had grown up. It would not be putting too fine a point on the matter to say that I was finally leaving home. Home, but not New York, since I was changing institutions but not cities. That's not quite right either. I did change boroughs. The new job at Lehman College required going from Manhattan to the Bronx—almost an hour by subway.

The question I am most often asked about Lehman—especially by New Yorkers from Manhattan like me—is about location: where is it? The question itself is more significant than its answer, because in fact there is no good answer beyond saying: it's in the Bronx. No one who asks the question ever seems to know where anything else in the Bronx is. The Bronx is a place without landmarks for the people who don't live there. There are famous exceptions of course: there's the Bronx Zoo, Yankee Stadium, and Loehmann's. But unless you have small children, love baseball, or shop for bargains you can't return, you will not be helped by these local toponyms. And it would be possible, moreover, to go to any of these places and still not know where they are, except in relation to a subway station. There's Riverdale, of course, which is the Bronx, too; only the nice part near the Hudson River that gets not to call itself the Bronx (and where a new Loehmann's has just opened).

The Bronx is also a place that people "from" Manhattan often come from (as opposed to move to), or once had relatives in. One of my grandmothers lived in the Bronx and I visited her there—but where?—when I was a child. In that sense, the Bronx is a place that historically one leaves, without leaving it behind. The myth of the old Bronx—a myth of immigrant community: Jewish, Italian, and Irish—is still powerful for New York writers as a scene in which questions of cultural identity and individual autonomy are staged with particular intensity. I'm thinking most recently of the memoirs of life in the old Bronx by two women writers: Kate Simon published the first installment of her autobiography under the title *Bronx Primitive* in 1983, and Vivian Gornick a memoir called *Fierce Attachments* in 1987.

In the spring of 1989 I taught a course I called—expanding on Carolyn Heilbrun's recent book title—"Reading and Writing Women's Lives" to women in an adult-degree program at night. According to the unwritten mandate of the adult-degree program, students were above all to be encouraged to believe that they could undertake and complete a B.A., a process, measured by the accumulation of credits, that might take a dauntingly long number of years. The life time this commitment represented was a fact the women all emphasized during their initial self-presentations. And it is perhaps this perspective (in addition to their age—twenty-eight to sixty-eight) that most radically distinguishes these women from what are called "traditional" students. This difference further complicated for me the already complicated traditional teacher/student relationship between women that I had grown accustomed to at Barnard, where the students, especially over the last few years, had begun to confuse me with their mothers (their "mom" as they would say). But outside those familial categories, which I in fact had come to find dangerously immobilizing, how to find the right distance, which is also to say closeness? What structured the relations between me as the teacher and the students at Lehman, it seemed to me finally, was a borough and a generation of classing—my parents went to CUNY. What joined us? . . .

August 30.

I open the program for the conference at random, casting about hopefully for inspiration, and see the question: "Why Is There No Class in Women's Autobiography?" This is in a session called "Bourgeois Subjects"; surely a session for me, an exemplary case. The question belongs to Carolyn Kay Steedman and perhaps it's not by chance that her question catches my eye because I have just read her *Landscape for a Good Woman*. In fact, I had considered beginning this reflection with a quotation from the book. The narrative is framed by an episode in which a health worker who has visited her mother's home, presumably on the occasion of the birth of the author's baby sister, declares: "This house isn't fit for a baby." Steedman, who recounts the anecdote in a preface entitled "Death of a Good Woman," comments fiercely:

> I will do everything and anything until the end of my days to stop anyone ever talking to me like that woman talked to my mother. It is in this place, this bare, curtainless bedroom that lies my secret and shameful defiance. I read a woman's book, meet such a woman at a party (a woman now, like me) and think quite deliberately as we talk: we are divided: a hundred years ago I'd have been cleaning your shoes. I know this and you don't. (2)

What I most struggled with, and wondered about when I taught this group of students, was precisely the power of that divide and the range of its effects. But from the other side; and knowing it. Knowing also that, at the same time, the divide is unstable: a hundred years ago I would have been a tailor's daughter. What then?

I don't think there is "no class in women's autobiography," if, minus any further context, I understand what that phrase means.[1] If the discussion of class seems absent from current discussions of women's autobiography, the inscription of class is certainly, even insistently, present in many contemporary autobiographical works. In any event, recalling Richard Terdiman's reformulation of the famous Stanley Fish theory/anecdote "Is There a Text in This Class" as "Is There Class in This Class?" we might ask here how, in teaching in a class on women's autobiography, one is also teaching class. If, as Terdiman argues, following Pierre Bourdieu, class is "a mode of vision and of division," if *"in classes we learn to class"* (227), what is the fate of power relations between, for instance, a bourgeois subject/teacher and her students in a non-elite classroom? Not only, how do I resist classing their reading (I'm sure that I don't), but how, as a bourgeois subject and a teacher, I negotiate with my students a working relation to autobiographical narratives that emerge from class and race positions not one's own? How, finally, do they class me? These are questions I put forward awkwardly because I dread the language I find myself obliged to cast them in. It immediately sounds false.

We began with *A Room of One's Own.*

I almost always begin with Woolf in courses dealing with women and literature. By its themes and analysis of the relations between making art and the concrete conditions of its production, *A Room* in a course on reading and writing women's lives is exemplary. In this case, moreover, I was particularly eager to begin with a text that addressed the issue of women and poverty, and the inequities between women and men in matters of education and access to culture. But Woolf's collective, fictional, historical autobiography did not play in the Bronx. This group of women found Woolf too foreign; too—the only word for it—elite. *A Room* came to life, I think, finally when I had dragged it through the rest of the semester: Judith Shakespeare everywhere. But for many of them, there was no pleasure of the text.

Despite the massive, and finally neither uninteresting nor wholly unjustified resistance to *A Room of One's Own,* Louise de Salvo's "A Portrait of the *Puttana* as a Middle-Aged Woolf

Scholar" was a big hit (we read not only straight autobiography in the course, but personal essays, poetry, and first-person fiction). It is always difficult to know why certain books work in a course and others don't; impossible to generalize about, moreover, because there are too many variables. But my hunch about the success of the de Salvo essay is that it embodied for the students a desire for self-authorization which also modeled a way to enact its consequences. (There is notably a scene that the students loved in which de Salvo makes a connection between watching her deaf child learning painfully to speak and her equally painful struggle to finish her dissertation.) De Salvo, writing explicitly as a working class Italian woman (and a mother of sons), writes at the same time as a scholar who can define herself outside those origins and categories; this doubleness offered a parable of possibility to women also doing something not foreseen for them, and liking it.

If many of these students were put off by the *figure* of Woolf's lecturer and moved by de Salvo's *puttana,* they all loved Jane Eyre, triumphant heroine of a fictional autobiography. But what grounded these reactions is complex: neither purely sociological—class, ethnicity, etc.— nor purely textual, or generic. In Brontë's novel, the students admired the rooftop speech that Woolf laments; they vibrated to the rage in Brontë, in Jane, for entitlement in the world: what women are allowed to claim as their domain of experience. Cast in another set of codes, what I think happened in these reading events is that the students found a language of empowerment for themselves—as women. In this sense, I would argue, reading as women and feminists, in a highly psychologized take on this dazzling fiction of female self-realization, they cut across, while reading through, the social and cultural specificities of—let's call it in shorthand—the Bronx. We could also say they read as feminist critics, Gilbert and Gubar avant la lettre, recognizing in Brontë's story the autobiography of generations of women whose desires had been transformed into fiction.

August 31.

A while ago I read a call for papers for a volume of personal essays on "the making of feminist scholarship." The editors warn the potential contributors that there will be "no room for untheorized narrative or the merely personal anecdote." The stringency of their language haunts me as I write this piece. How can you tell the difference between the merely personal and the theoretically acute? What are the grounds for establishing the difference? Who decides?

For instance. Since I wrote the last segment of the paper, it's been arranged for me to spend three weeks in Brazil after the conference, lecturing and doing seminars on women and literature, on feminist criticism. This excites and distracts me. I suppose talking about this could be what they meant by merely personal anecdote. But let's take a more postmodern view. As the author of this paper, I also know what's coming next, Gloria Anzaldúa's "Speaking in Tongues: A Letter to Third World Women Writers." So if I leave in the anecdote about going to Brazil here, it both gives me a thematic transition and lets me make the argument through narrative. . . .

September 1.

In the official U.S. government materials sent to prepare me for my trip to Brazil I read this sentence in a description of life in Brasilia, one of the three cities in which I will be working: "Servants are necessary." [2]

The passage below from Anzaldúa's essay, which deals with questions of women and entitlement, is also the bridge to my discussion of writing in the context of a course on autobiography:

Who gave us permission to perform the act of writing? Why does writing seem so unnatural for me? I'll do anything to postpone it—empty the trash, answer the telephone. The voice recurs in me: *Who am I, a poor Chicanita from the sticks, to think I could write?* How dared I even consider becoming a writer as I stooped over the tomato fields bending, bending under the hot sun, hands broadened and calloused, not fit to hold the quill, numbed into an animal stupor by the heat.

How hard it is for us to think we can choose to become writers, much less feel and believe that we can. What have we to contribute, to give? Our own expectations condition us. Does not our class, our culture as well as the white man tell us writing is not for women such as us?

The white man speaks: *Perhaps if you scrape the dark off of your face. Maybe if you bleach your bones. Stop speaking in tongues, stop writing left-handed. Don't cultivate your colored skins nor tongues of fire if you want to make it in a right-handed world.* (166)

In a course on feminist theory, I would juxtapose Anzaldúa's prose to Hélène Cixous's rhetoric in "The Laugh of the Medusa" where Cixous, speaking now famously from the place of high Continental theory, exhorts her female readers: "Write! Writing is for you . . . I know why you haven't written . . . Because writing is at once too high, too great for you, it's reserved for the great—that is for 'great men' and it's 'silly'" (246). When Cixous rebels against the male theorists' vision of women as the "dark continent," a topography in psychoanalytic terms constructed on lack, do her metaphors join or erase Anzaldúa's record of work and physical oppression?

Let's go back briefly to the issue of self-authorization, the permission to write. To be sure, a world of material and symbolic difference separates the histories of these two writers, Anzaldúa and Cixous: they come from different places, as we used to say. At the same time, to the extent that the history of women's writing is also a history of a same reiterated struggle in the face of institutionalized exclusions based on gender, to appropriate language and to rework one's place in its turns, it seems to me that it is precisely at this place of common struggle that women's autobiography takes root. I locate here the site of my own doubts of self-authorization, my own longing for permission to write: going public with private desires. And here, perhaps, we should also be more careful: isn't, for instance, postponing writing by emptying the trash or answering the telephone a strategy of avoidance that cuts across the divide of class (not to say gender) lines? Have I been doing anything else in trying to write this essay?

This returns us to the question of where in autobiographical writing to place the emphasis: the culture in the woman or the woman in the culture. As de Lauretis has widely argued, in imagining the construction of feminist subjects, the future of their difference, the goal is not to try to determine competitively, self-righteously, however ringingly, what is more constraining, or excluding, race, class, sexual preference, or gender; or in what combination. It is neither useful nor really interesting finally to decide who had the most difficulty coming to writing. As Anzaldúa, later in the essay, says with some impatience: "Forget the room of one's own—write in the kitchen, lock yourself up in the bathroom" (170). Rather, coming back now to the question of identity pedagogy, to the extent that in a course on autobiography, in which women, who like Anzaldúa's and Cixous's rhetorical sisters, find it hard to believe that writing is *for them,* the question becomes how to find a way to answer the letter. In the classroom, the issues of permission and self-authorization present them-

selves with another, practical, and material emphasis: discovering a parable of possibility.

I am not a teacher of writing, but I was asked to have the students write. And then, having asked them to write, and announced that I was not a writing teacher, corrected their writing. And performed my part as a force for anti-writing in Anzaldúa's script. About teachers and correction, she writes: "The schools we attended or didn't attend did not give us the skills for writing nor the confidence that we were correct in using our class and ethnic languages. I, for one, became adept at, and majored in English to spite, to show up, the arrogant racist teachers who thought all Chicano children were dumb and dirty" (165–66). I found myself one day, having taught the Anzaldúa essay, returning a set of papers, most of them scrawled over in the margins with *awk, diction, tone, sentence structure,* etc. Seeing myself in their eyes as that teacher, I could not fail to point out my enactment of the role; they nodded with a certain jubilation. But that of course did not solve the writing problem.

Was it absolutely necessary to insist upon "critical writing" in a course on autobiography? For whom is critical writing produced, besides for us and graduate students wanting to replace us? And to what end? So, on the assumption that the main thing was to write something, instead of a second critical essay I assigned the writing of what I called "autobiographical fragments." My notion in asking for short takes of personal experience was to bypass both the problem of institutional writing, with its canonized standards of correctness, and the plot of becoming that characterizes canonical autobiography. I wanted a short text, two to three pages, that would be read aloud—and to ask for an emblematic episode within those constraints seemed unfair, although, as it turned out, not undoable. To reduce the panic level the assignment of self-representation raised in some of the students, I suggested the mode of self-portrayal through the portrait of another (they had the examples of Colette's portraits of her father, and the characters of *The House on Mango Street*). This was the solution most of the students chose.

I want to describe briefly two of the pieces written that spring to evoke some of the drama of what happened with this writing experiment. By what happened I mean more specifically the language through which these students—many of whom had to struggle with themselves to return to school in the first place—found a way to construct some form of public self-representation: through writing.

The first example, which in fact was the first piece read in the class, was ominously entitled "Letter to My Unborn Children." In the seconds that elapsed between the announcement of the title and the actual reading of the essay I panicked internally and regretted I had so quickly given up on compare and contrast. The student, a woman in her late thirties, was as far as I knew, the only gay woman in the group, and I wondered whether this was going to be the occasion of a coming out, or maybe an account of abortions, or both. I was more worried about a coming out because hints of a generalized homophobia had from time to time punctuated class discussion. Instead we heard an articulate account explaining why a woman, looking back on her life, felt that the other things she had wanted for herself did not seem to include a context in which to have children; that it wasn't that she hadn't wanted children or that she wouldn't have loved them—sufficiently imagined to be the addressees of this text—rather, that she hadn't seen how to do this, and that now it was too late; she lacked the energy, and, she thought, had become too selfish. The class listened in awed silence and finally burst into applause (also into tears). I felt that she had in some ways told my

story, but at the same time that I couldn't say anything because "I was the teacher." I had decided I had to remain publicly as neutral as possible: not to reward someone's life, especially if it resembled my own, with pedagogic approval, not to say a good grade.

The second instance was the portrait of a greatly beloved grandmother by a mother in her mid-thirties. When she read the last line of her text which came to conclude her feelings for this grandmother—"I wish she had been my mother"—she choked, and, as though horrified by her own words, apologized to the class, trying to take them back. By this time, we were all fishing around in our purses for handkerchiefs.

Not all of the pieces of course were successful; nor were they all poignantly delivered; some were ironic and funny; some were solemn, conventional and fell a little flat. But these students—*almost* all of them—could write; they heard it in each other, and in themselves. I would never have known this if I had kept on assigning conventional paper topics; they might never have known it, either.

At the end of the semester, when we were reviewing the course, the author of the portrait of the grandmother said she wanted to say two things: the first, that what she had learned in the course was that it was OK to have mixed feelings about your mother (my own mother would not have been surprised to learn that this was the net effect of my teaching!); and the second, that her boss had given her a desk calendar and that she had begun writing something in it—something for herself—every day.

What I come back to as I try to locate the specific point of *teaching* autobiography—as a social and institutional activity distinct from merely reading autobiography or theorizing it—is that teaching autobiography provides texts for reading that engender the coming to writing in others. Perhaps the essence of autobiography as a genre—or rather one of its most valuable effects—is to enable this process. To say this is also to say that autobiography in *its performance as text* complicates the meaning and reading of social identity, and hence of the writing subject.

September 3.

The day before Labor Day and I see on my American calendar a slightly dowdy female figure, drawn by Roz Chast, my favorite *New Yorker* cartoonist, standing in the countryside, wearing a pair of shorts and wondering with an air of pursed bewilderment: "Where has Summer gone?"

Here it already feels like autumn; I'm wearing a sweater, and feeling glad not to be returning to teaching. I'm not sure I really enjoy teaching, even when I can give myself (and others) a self-congratulatory account of it. Teaching makes me anxious and teaching autobiography is no exception. I worried all semester, a little like former Mayor Koch: "How am I doing?" Do they like this? Or are they just jollying me along: telling me what they are learning that I like to hear? *They know that I want them to want to write.* How should I be with them? Am I being elitist? Am I asking them to choose my values? Denying their own? Agonies of self-positioning: am I othering them? myself? In particular, I also worried, in a course on women's lives, what to say about my own. Should I have read a piece of my own autobiographical writing?

My compromise in self-revelation was to teach, probably with more feeling than critical distance, a book I have come to think of as "my" autobiography—its "I" is New York, Jewish, middle-aged, intellectual, difficult, etc.—*Fierce Attachments*. And by way of shaping a conclusion to this reflection, I want to describe my sense of personal connection with the work as *writing*, and what the effects of this hyper-identification might have to add to a discussion

of understanding the experience of reading and teaching autobiography.

I should say first that the ways in which, according to the checkpoints of locational identity, I am like her are also ways in which I'm not like her at all: I am not the daughter, but the granddaughter of Jewish immigrants; we were not working-class but middle-class; I grew up in Manhattan, not the Bronx; there was no erotic female figure like Nettie in my life; my father didn't die when I was young; I didn't have a brother but a sister, etc. And yet despite these important differences, I felt written by this book. The place of identification for me, or rather the point of entry into the deepest rhythms of the text, was in the particular intensity of the relationship to the mother, a long, violent, and ongoing war, though perhaps evolving at the end into a more complex and productive antagonism. . . .

September 5.

I've written myself into a bind: like the daughter in the hot room, listening to the noise of the street: half in, half out. I don't want to end "theoretically" in a piece so grounded in the accidents of practice. I probably should do more with this slightly reworked (I had typed: reworded) concept of identification, bring in Nancy Chodorow, for instance; with class in the (Women's Studies) classroom, but it doesn't seem worth it (I also think it's been done).[3] I don't want to add further to the wonderful set of commonplaces about autobiography we all already trade in (I will leave the task to the younger and more aerobic). Maybe dealing with autobiography binds one irretrievably to the commonplace. Maybe that's the whole point.

I would rather end personally, but I'm afraid to go too far, though it may be worse not to go far enough: what does a woman, no longer a daughter, who does not enter the maternal, turn into?

What remains, I think, is to give the last word,

or almost, to the autobiography that made me want to teach autobiography, and also to write one. This is a passage that was widely excerpted when *Fierce Attachments* was published:

> We became, my mother and I, all women conditioned by loss, unnerved by lassitude, bound together in pity and anger. After Hiroshima dead bodies were found of people who had been wearing printed kimonos when they were killed. The bomb had melted the cloth on their bodies, but the design on the kimonos remained imprinted in the flesh. It seemed to me in later years the deep nerveless passivity of that time together had become the design burned into my skin while the cloth of my own experience melted away. (129)

Perhaps the question of teaching autobiography remains precisely the task of negotiating in the public space of the classroom what remains, must remain unsaid and most intensely private—the unanswered question of another's life: "Why don't you go already?" The task of teaching autobiography, we know, like the reading of it, entails learning to make out the texture of one's own experience—one's own blank, suffering immobility—beneath the other's imprint; in order to walk away and move on; but to do this requires first recognizing the radical separateness of the other's design, the sound of another's voice; to do this in the classroom may require writing it down for the others to hear.

Separateness, but not fixed in otherness: a sustained and self-consciously performed oscillation between the two, as between two distinct places, like Manhattan and the Bronx, an island and a mainland that are no less connected by the dirt and noise of public transportation. To produce this in the classroom demands an almost impossible tact.

By now it must be clear that I have been turning around another quotation in my effort to find a place to stop. It is the last line from Luce Irigaray's violent first-person, perhaps autobiographical, daughter/mother dialogue, "And the One Doesn't Stir Without the Other": "And what I wanted from you, Mother, was this: that in giving me life, you still remain alive" (67).[4]

I will end here for now. . . .

Notes

I am grateful to Kathleen Ashley for inviting me to "The Subject of Autobiography," a conference held at the University of Southern Maine in September 1989.

1. Steedman did not come to the conference, and so I don't know how she would have glossed her title.

2. As it turned out, most of the women I met—middle-class academics like me—employed servants who lived with them, cared for their children, and took care of their houses. This was perhaps the single point that most feminists I spoke to identified as the problem within Brazilian feminism, and the place of contradiction in their own lives.

3. Susan Stanford Friedman has used Chodorow's work productively in her illuminating chapter "Women's Autobiographical Selves: Theory and Practice" (72–82, in this volume).

4. The French reads: "Et ce que j'attendais de toi, c'est que, me laissant naître, tu demeures aussi vivante."

Works Cited

Anzaldúa, Gloria. "Speaking in Tongues: A Letter to Third World Women Writers." In *This Bridge Called My Back: Writings by Radical Women of Color,* ed. Cherríe Moraga and Gloria Anzaldúa. New York: Kitchen Table: Women of Color Press, 1983.

Cisneros, Sandra. *The House on Mango Street.* New York: Random House, 1989.

Cixous, Hélène. "The Laugh of the Medusa." Trans. Keith Cohen and Paula Cohen. In *New French Feminisms,* Elaine Marks and Isabelle de Courtivron, eds. New York: Schocken, 1981. 245–64.

de Salvo, Louise. "Portrait of the *Puttana* as Middle-Aged Woolf Scholar." In *Between Women,* Carole Ascher, Louise de Salvo, Sara Ruddick, eds. Boston: Beacon Press, 1984.

Friedman, Susan Stanford. "Women's Autobiographical Selves: Theory and Practice." In *The Private Self: The Theory and Practice of Women's Autobiographical Writings,"* ed. Shari Benstock. Chapel Hill and London: University of North Carolina Press, 1988.

Gornick, Vivian. *Fierce Attachments.* New York: Farrar, Straus, Giroux, 1987.

Heilbrun, Carolyn. *Writing a Woman's Life.* New York: W. W. Norton, 1988.

Irigaray, Luce. "And the One Doesn't Stir Without the Other." Trans. Hélène Vivienne Wenzel. *Signs* 7, no. 1 (Autumn 1981): 56–67.

Kingston, Maxine Hong. *The Woman Warrior: Memoirs of a Girlhood Among Ghosts.* New York: Knopf, 1976.

Miller, Nancy K. *Getting Personal: Feminist Occasions and Other Autobiographical Acts.* New York: Routledge, 1991.

Simon, Kate. *Bronx Primitive.* New York: Harper Colophon, 1983.

Steedman, Carolyn Kay. *Landscape for a Good Woman: A Story of Two Lives.* New Brunswick: Rutgers University Press, 1987.

Terdiman, Richard. *Discourse/Counter-discourse: The Theory and Practice of Symbolic Resistance in Nineteenth-Century France.* Ithaca: Cornell University Press, 1985.

Woolf, Virginia. *A Room of One's Own.* New York: Harcourt, Brace, and World, 1967.

40 The Way In

Nancy Mairs

The body itself is a dwelling place, as the Anglo-Saxons knew in naming it *banhus* (bonehouse) and *lichama* (bodyhome), and the homeliness of its nature is even livelier for a woman than for a man. Bachelard speaks of "inhabited space" as the "non-I that protects the I." Woman may literally become that inhabited space, containing, in Cixous's words, "a thousand and one fiery hearths" of erotic desire and experiencing in childbirth "the not-me within me," thereby becoming the non-I that protects the I of the unborn child. Still, forced to function as man's Other and thus alienated from her self, "she has not been able to live in her 'own' house, her very body. . . . Women haven't had eyes for themselves. They haven't gone exploring in their house. Their sex still frightens them. Their bodies, which they haven't dared enjoy, have been colonized." Through writing her body, woman may reclaim the deed to her dwelling.

The reverberations of these texts have coalesced for me into the project of exploring my own "felicitous space," to use Bachelard's phrase, the houses where I once lived and where, time collapsing through dreams, I continue to live today. I return to them, reenter them, in order to discover the relationships they bear to my own erotic development and thus perhaps—because I'm ever aware of my self as a cultural, not merely a personal, construct—to feminine erotic development in general.

Admittedly, "eroticism" has a more global meaning for me than language in its present state permits. This dissonance between idiosyncratic meaning and meaning that everyone can agree upon causes me problems with all the good-hearted people who inquire after my new book with much the same solicitude they might summon for my ailing puppy or my recently widowed mother-in-law. "An erotics of place and space," I tell them, waiting for the wince, the furrow, the grin—the responses vary, but plainly they all assume that I'm writing "a dirty book." Well, maybe I am. I mention my body, certainly, quite a lot, even its secret places. Here and there I kiss, stroke, press, squeeze, even engage in sexual intercourse. Not as often, though, as I lie in bed, run across a playground, eat favorite foods, listen to the radio, tease my sister, roll in new snow. All these acts, happening to me as a body, shaping my awareness of my embodied self, form my erotic being. It is that process I'm seeking to capture and comprehend: how living itself takes on an erotic tone.

For a woman saturated to the bone in Calvinist tradition, such an exploration necessitates the healing of a classic Western patriarchal bifurcation: body/mind or body/spirit. I grew up in the belief that my intellectual-spiritual life, reflective of my "true" self, was separate from and superior to my life as a body. My body's appearance, which preoccupied me, was dismissed as beneath my concern: "Handsome is as handsome does," I was told whenever I seemed to think well of my looks. Its urges were denied, or at least deferred: I was "saving" myself for marriage, when I would "give" myself to my husband, the reward for which seemed to be not physical bliss but spiritual satisfaction at having him appreciate my "purity." As an adult, apparently, my bodily life might begin, and I suppose it did, at least in sexual terms. After I was married, I deliberately masturbated for the first time, so I must have believed myself entitled to my body's sensations in a new way. But I got through two pregnancies and childbirths, several sexual affairs, a couple of serious suicide attempts, and the onset of a devastating degenerative disease locked almost entirely in my head.

My body, of course, was going through all these experiences, whether "I" was holding my "self" aloof from it or not. Fortunately, one simply cannot *be* without being a body. One simply *is* inches of supple skin and foot after foot of gut, slosh of blood, thud of heart, lick of tongue, brain humped and folded into skull. And it is as a body that one inhabits the past and it inhabits one's body: "But over and beyond our memories, the house we were born in is physically inscribed in us. It is a group of organic habits," Bachelard writes. "After twenty years, in spite of all the other anonymous stairways, we would recapture the reflexes of the 'first stairway,' we would not stumble on that rather high step. . . . The word habit is too worn a word to express this passionate liaison of our bodies, which do not forget, with an unforgettable house." Whether or not I permitted myself to think of my self as a body at some earlier time, I cannot deny the identity today. That identity offers my only means of entering and literally making sense of my past.

The search for lost time necessitates spatial, not merely temporal, recall. As Bachelard tells us, memory "does not record concrete duration"; rather, "we think we know ourselves in time, when all we know is a sequence of fixations in the spaces of the being's stability. . . ." We can impose a grid of time onto our memories, much as we sketch lines of latitude and longitude on a globe, a useful device for knowing when or where we are in relation to some event or spot

used as a reference point. But the memories won't yield up their freight in response. For that we have to let go of lifelines and plunge into the multiple modalities—sensory, emotional, cognitive—which have encoded the past and will release it, transformed, into the present. To this end, I prefer to work in the fragmented form of essays; each concentrating on a house or houses important to my growth as a woman. Each house contains its own time, of course. But in emphasizing the spatial rather than the temporal elements in my experience, I attempt to avoid what critic Georges Gusdorf calls, in "The Conditions and Limits of Autobiography," the "original sin of autobiography" (and, one might add, the outstanding feature of phallocentric discourse in general)—that is, "logical coherence and rationalization."

To avoid these qualities, their reassuring rigidity and muscularity beloved by all of us who are products of the ivory phallus. To abandon the phallic narrative structure inculcated there: exposition, complication, climax, denouement. To refuse its critical questions: What does this mean? Why does it matter? To embrace the past as "meaningless," as "matterless," without "worth" in an economy based on the scarcity of resources, on the fear of running out: of reasons, of memories, of precious time. To seduce the impatient reader boldly: *Here, let's take our time. We've got plenty more where it came from.* To dare to dally. These are the risks of a woman who experiences her past—the past in which she lived as a body, which dwells in her body still—as a bower.

> When we were children, we formed
>   an enclosure of hands linked
>   into arches and sang:
> Go in and out the window.
> Go in and out the window.
> Go in and out the window
> As you have done before.

Writing my past as a body enacts that circle game, I invite you through my openings because

I have been schooled in hospitality: you, my strangers, my guests. *Mi casa es su casa.* "Writing," says Cixous, "is the passageway, the entrance, the exit, the dwelling place of the other in me. . . ." Writing itself is space. It is a populated house.

In the houses of my past which I write about, I often felt alone; now, in writing about them, I am never alone. I cannot write my self without writing you, my other. I don't believe literally that, in writing my "life," I am writing yours as well. On the contrary, I feel certain I am not. You didn't get bitten on the foot by red ants when you were four, did you? You didn't sing "Lullay, Thou Little Tiny Child" in the fourth-grade Christmas pageant? Your baby bunny wasn't chewed up and swallowed, hind legs last, by your Irish setter, Pegeen? You don't eat the same thing for breakfast every morning of your life? You're not still scared of the dark? These are my details. And heaven knows I have enough trouble getting them straight without keeping track of yours as well.

In fact, this is one of the problems that pursue and daunt me in autobiographical work: I can never get the details right to the satisfaction of everyone who shows up in the telling. The French philosopher Maurice Merleau-Ponty comments that "all action and all love are haunted by the expectation of an account which will transform them into their truth." My mother's expectation in particular! She wants to check over my essays to make sure I've told things as they "really" happened this time, since I missed the mark mightily in an earlier book. Others who find themselves presented here will no doubt wish the same.

But the past, that ramshackle structure, is a fabrication. I make it up as I go along. The only promise I can state about its "reality" is that I "really" remember (reembody? flesh out anew?) the details I record; that is, I haven't deliberately invented any of them. But on the whole I haven't sought historical accuracy. Instead, I have tried, in Merleau-Ponty's words, "to give the past not a survival, which is the hypocritical form of forgetfulness, but a new life, which is the noble form of memory." In these terms, I can't even tell my own truth, much less anyone else's. I can only settle the problem in the manner of Clément's sorceress: "She is true because she believes her own lies."

And yet, in a deeper sense of the word, I hope that I've spoken truthfully about all our lives. Because I think that my "story," though intensely personal, is not at all private. Beneath its idiosyncrasies lie vast strata of commonality, communality. I don't see how anyone engaged in self-representation can fail to recognize in the autobiographical self, constructed as it is in language, all the others whom the writing self shelters. The not-me dwells here in the me. We are one, and more-than-one. Our stories utter one another.

Think, for example, of your houses: the one you live in now, if you have one, and the ones you have inhabited before. I am writing a book about your houses. You never lived in a yellow house on the coast of Maine? No matter. You have had such a house, perhaps a long time ago, not perhaps your chief house, the one you spent the most time in, but the one that you return to now most frequently in dreams, whether you remember them or not, a locus for you, inexplicably, of mystery and desire. I will write about the yellow house. You will read about your house. If I do my job, the book I write vanishes before your eyes. I invite you into the house of my past, and the threshold you cross leads you into your own.

Notes

This chapter is excerpted from the introduction to Mairs' *Remembering the Bone House: An Erotics of Place and Space* (New York: Harper & Row, 1989).

A Selected List of Women's Autobiographies

(Many more autobiographies are mentioned in individual essays.)

Addams, Jane. *Twenty Years at Hull House.* New York: Macmillan, 1910.

Alderson, Nannie, as told to Helena Huntington Smith. *A Bride Goes West.* 1942. Lincoln: University of Nebraska Press, 1969.

Amrouche, Fadhma. *My Life Story: The Autobiography of a Berber Woman.* Trans. Dorothy Blair. New Brunswick: Rutgers, 1989.

Alexander, Meena. *Fault Lines: A Memoir.* New York: Feminist Press, 1993.

Allende, Isabel. *Paula.* Trans. Margaret Sayers Peden. New York: HarperCollins, 1994.

Anderson, Margaret C. *My Thirty Years' War.* New York: Covici, 1930.

Anderson, Marion. *My Lord, What a Morning!* New York: Viking, 1956. Intro. Nellie Y. McKay. Madison: University of Wisconsin Press, 1992.

Angelou, Maya. *Gather Together in My Name.* Random House, 1974.

Angelou, Maya. *The Heart of a Woman.* New York: Random House, 1981.

Angelou, Maya. *I Know Why the Caged Bird Sings.* New York: Random House, 1969.

Angelou, Maya. *Singin' and Swingin' and Gettin' Merry like Christmas.* Random House, 1976.

Antin, Mary. *The Promised Land.* Boston: Houghton Mifflin, 1912.

Anzaldúa, Gloria. *Borderlands/La Frontera.* San Francisco: Spinsters/Aunt Lute, 1987.

Ashbridge, Elizabeth. "Some Account of the Four Parts of the Life of Elizabeth Ashbridge." In *Journeys in New Worlds,* ed. William L. Andrews. Madison: University of Wisconsin Press, 1990. 147–80.

Ashton-Warner, Sylvia. *Teacher.* New York: Simon and Schuster, 1963.

Austin, Mary. *Earth Horizon: Autobiography.* 1932. Albuquerque: University of New Mexico Press, 1991.

Austin, Mary. *A Woman of Genius.* Garden City, NY: Doubleday, 1912.

Baker, S. Josephine. *Fighting for Life.* New York: Macmillan, 1939.

Barreno, Maria Isabel, Maria Teresa Horta, and Maria Velhoda Costa. *The Three Marias: New Portuguese Letters.* 1973. Trans. Helen R. Lane. Garden City, NY: Doubleday, 1975.

Barrios de Chungara, Domitila. *Let Me Speak! Testimony of Domitila, a Woman of the Bolivian Mines.* New York: Monthly Review Press, 1978.

Bashkirtseff, Marie. *Journal.* Paris: Charpentier, 1887.

Beauvoir, Simone de. *Memoirs of a Dutiful Daughter.* Cleveland: World, 1959.

Beauvoir, Simone de. *The Prime of Life.* Cleveland: World, 1962.

Beauvoir, Simone de. *A Very Easy Death.* Trans. Patrick O'Brian. New York: Pantheon, 1965.

Bernard, Jessie. *Self-Portrait of a Family.* Boston: Beacon Press, 1978.

Bhutto, Benazir. *Daughter of Destiny: An Autobiography.* New York: Simon and Schuster, 1989.

Bird, Isabella. *A Lady's Life in the Rocky Mountains.* Norman: University of Oklahoma Press, 1960.

Blakely, Mary Kay. *Wake Me When It's Over: A Journey to the Edge and Back.* New York: Ballantine Books, 1989.

Blew, Mary Clearman. *All but the Waltz.* New York: Penguin, 1991.

Blodgett, Harriet, ed. *Centuries of Female Days: English Women's Private Diaries.* New Brunswick: Rutgers, 1988.

Blunt, Lady Anne. *A Pilgrimage to Nejd, the Cradle of the Arab Race.* London: Cass, 1968.

Bogan, Louise. *Journey around My Room.* Ed. Ruth Limmer. New York: Viking Press, 1980.

Bornstein, Kate. *Gender Outlaw: On Men, Women, and the Rest of Us.* New York: Routledge, 1994.

Bourke-White, Margaret. *Portrait of Myself.* New York: Simon and Schuster, 1963.

Bowen, Catherine. *Family Portrait.* Boston: Little, Brown, 1970.

Bradstreet, Anne. "To My Dear Children." *The Works of Anne Bradstreet,* ed. Jeannine Hensley. Cambridge: Harvard University Press, 1967.

Brittain, Vera. *Testament of Youth.* London: Virago Press, 1985.

Brown, Elaine. *A Taste of Power.* New York: Doubleday, 1992.

Buck, Pearl. *My Several Worlds: A Personal Record.* New York: John Day, 1954.

Bulkin, Elly, Minnie Bruce Pratt, and Barbara Smith. *Yours in Struggle: Three Feminist Perspectives on Anti-Semitism and Racism.* Ithaca: Firebrand Books, 1984.

Burney, Fanny. *Journals and Letters,* Vol. 3. Ed. Joyce Hemlow. Oxford: Clarendon Press, 1973.

Cabeza de Baca, Fabiola. *The Good Life: New Mexico Traditions and Food.* 1949. Sante Fe: Museum of New Mexico Press, 1982.

Caldéron de la Barca, Frances. *Life in Mexico, During a Residence of Two Years in That Country.* 1843. London: Dent, 1970.

Callisher, Hortense. *Herself.* New York: Dell, 1972.

Campbell, Maria. *Halfbreed.* 1973. Toronto: Goodread Biographies, 1983.

Cardinal, Marie. *The Words to Say It.* 1975. Trans. Pat Goodheart. Cambridge, MA: VanVactor & Goodheart, 1983.

Cary, Lorene. *Black Ice.* New York: Random House, 1991.

Carrington, [Dora]. *Letters and Extracts from Her Diaries.* Ed. David Garnett. New York: Holt, Rinehart & Winston, 1971.

Cassady, Carolyn. *Off the Road: My Years with Cassady, Kerouac, and Ginsberg.* New York: William Morrow, 1990.

Cavendish, Margaret, Duchess of Newcastle. *The Life of William Cavendish, Duke of Newcastle, to Which is Added The True Relation of My Birth, Breeding, and Life.* London: G. Routledge & Sons, 1903

Chang, Jung. *Wild Swans: Three Daughters of China.* New York: Doubleday, 1991.

Charke, Charlotte. *A Narrative of the Life of Mrs. Charlotte Charke (Youngest Daughter of Colley Cibber, Esq.), Written by Herself.* Ed. Leonard R. Ashley. N. Gainsville: Scholars' Fascimiles & Reprints, 1969.

Cheng, Nien. *Life and Death in Shanghai.* New York: Penguin, 1986.

Chernin, Kim. *In My Mother's House.* New York: Harper and Row, 1983.

Chesnut, Mary Boykin. *Mary Chesnut's Civil War.* Ed. C. Vann Woodward. New Haven: Yale University Press, 1981.

Chicago, Judy. *Through the Flower: My Struggle as a Woman Artist.* New York: Doubleday, 1975.

Christie, Agatha. *An Autobiography.* London: William Collins & Son, 1977.

Cisneros, Sandra. *The House on Mango Street.* New York: Random House, 1989.

Clark, Septima Poinsette. *Echo in My Soul.* New York: Dutton, 1962.

Cliff, Michelle. *Abeng.* New York: Penguin Books, 1991.

Cliff, Michelle. *No Telephone to Heaven.* New York: Vintage Books, 1989.

Clifton, Lucille. *Generations: A Memoir.* New York: Random House, 1976.

Coleridge, Sara. *Memoirs.* London: H. S. King, 1873.

Colette, Sidonie Gabrielle. *My Apprenticeships.* Trans. Helen Beauclerk. London: Martin, Secker & Warburg, 1957.

Collected Black Women's Narratives. Schomberg Library of Nineteenth-Century Black Women Writers. New York and Oxford: Oxford University Press, 1988.

Conway, Jill Ker. *The Road from Coorain.* New York: Vintage Books, 1989.

Crowdog, Mary. *Lakota Woman.* New York: G. Weidenfeld, 1990.

Cuero, Delfina. *The Autobiography of Delfina Cuero. As Told to Florence Shipek.* Trans. Rosalie Pinto Robertson. Morongo Indian Reservation: Malki Museum Press, 1970.

Danica, Elly. *Beyond Don't: Dreaming Past the Dark.* Charlottetown: Gynergy Books, 1996.

Danica, Elly. *Don't: A Woman's Word.* Charlottetown: Gynergy Books, 1988.

Davis, Angela. *With My Mind on Freedom: An Autobiography.* New York: Bantam, 1975.

Day, Dorothy. *The Long Loneliness.* New York: Harper and Row, 1952.

Delany, Sarah, and A. Elizabeth Delany, with Amy Hill Hearth. *Having Our Say: The Delany Sisters' First 100 Years.* New York: Kodansha International, 1993.

De Salvo, Louise. *Vertigo: A Memoir.* New York: Dutton, 1996.

Diallo, Nafissatou. *A Dakar Childhood.* 1975. Trans.

Dorothy Blair. London; Longman Drumbeat, 1982.

Dillard, Annie. *An American Childhood.* New York: Harper and Row, 1987.

Dinesen, Isak. *Out of Africa.* 1937. New York: Random House, 1989.

Djebar, Assia. *Fantasia, an Algerian Cavalcade.* 1985. Trans. Dorothy S. Blair. London: Quartet Books, 1988.

Djebar, Assia. *Women of Algiers in Their Apartment.* 1980. Trans. Marjolijn de Jager. Charlottesville: University Press of Virginia, 1992.

Doolittle, Hilda. [H.D.]. *Asphodel.* Durham: Duke University Press, 1992.

Duncan, Isadora. *My Life.* New York: Boni & Liveright, 1927.

Duras, Marguerite. *The Lover.* Trans. Barbara Bray. New York: Pantheon, 1985.

Durova, Nadezhda, *The Cavalry Maiden.* Trans. Mary Fleming Zirin. Bloomington: Indiana University Press, 1988.

Eberhardt, Isabelle. *The Passionate Nomad: The Diary of Isabelle Eberhardt.* Trans. Nina De Voogd. London: Virago Press, 1987.

Ellis, Anne. *The Life of an Ordinary Woman.* Boston: Houghton Mifflin, 1931.

Emecheta, Buchi. *Head above Water.* Oxford: Heinemann, 1986.

Ernaux, Annie. *A Woman's Story.* New York: Ballantine, 1991.

Fairbanks, Evelyn. *The Days of Rondo.* St. Paul: Minnesota Historical Society Press, 1990.

Fanshawe, Ann. *The Memoirs of Anne, Lady Halkett, and Ann, Lady Fanshawe.* New York: Oxford University Press, 1979.

Ferber, Edna. *A Peculiar Treasure.* Garden City, NY: Doubleday, 1960.

Fields, Mamie. *Lemon Swamp and Other Places: A Carolina Memoir.* New York: Free Press, 1983.

Fisher, M. F. K. *As They Were.* New York: Alfred A. Knopf, 1982.

Flynn, Elizabeth Gurley. *The Rebel Girl: An Autobiography.* 1955. New York: International Publishers, 1973.

Forten, Charlotte L. *The Journals of Charlotte Forten Grimké.* Ed. Brenda Stevenson. New York: Oxford University Press, 1968.

Fossey, Dian. *Gorillas in the Mist.* Boston: Houghton Mifflin, 1983.

Frame, Janet. *An Autobiography.* New York: G. Braziller, 1991.

Frank, Anne. *The Diary of a Young Girl.* Trans. B. M. Mooyaart-Doubleday. Garden City, NY: Doubleday, 1952.

Franklin, Miles. *My Brilliant Career.* 1901. New York: Washington Square Press, 1980.

Gardiner, Muriel. *Code Name "Mary."* New Haven: Yale University Press, 1983.

Gilman, Charlotte Perkins. *The Living of Charlotte Perkins Gilman.* 1935. Madison: University of Wisconsin Press, 1990.

Gilman, Charlotte Perkins. *The Yellow Wallpaper.* Old Westbury: Feminist Press, 1973.

Giovanni, Nikki. *Gemini: An Extended Autobiographical Statement on My First Twenty-Five Years of Being a Black Poet.* New York: Bobbs-Merrill, 1971.

Glasgow, Ellen. *The Woman Within.* New York: Harcourt Brace, 1954.

Glückel. *The Memoirs of Glückel of Hameln.* Trans. Marvin Lowenthal. New York: Schocken, 1977.

Golden, Marita. *Migrations of the Heart: An Autobiography.* New York: Ballantine, 1983.

Goldman, Emma. *Living My Life.* 1931. New York: New American Library, 1977.

Gornick, Vivian. *Fierce Attachments.* New York: Farrar, Straus & Giroux, 1987.

Goulianos, Joan, ed. *'By a Woman Writt': Literature from Six Centuries by and about Women.* Baltimore: Penguin, 1973.

Grealy, Lucy. *Autobiography of a Face.* Boston: Houghton Mifflin, 1994.

Greenberg, Joanne. *I Never Promised You a Rose Garden.* Garden City, NY: Holt, Rinehart & Winston, 1964.

Gunn, Janet Varner. *A West Bank Memoir.* Minneapolis: University of Minnesota Press, 1995.

Hahn, Emily. *China to Me.* Garden City, NY: Country Life Press, 1944.

Haizlip, Shirlee Taylor. *The Sweeter the Juice.* New York: Simon & Schuster, 1994.

Hale, Janet Campbell. *Bloodlines: Odyssey of a Native Daughter.* New York: Random House, 1993.

Halkett, Anne. *The Autobiography of Anne, Lady Hal-*

kett. Ed. John Gough Nichols. Westminster: Camden Society, 1875.

Hampl, Patricia. *A Romantic Education.* Boston: Houghton Mifflin, 1981.

Hansberry, Lorraine. *To Be Young, Gifted, and Black.* Englewood Cliffs, NJ: Prentice-Hall, 1969.

Hayslip, Lely, *When Heaven and Earth Changed Places.* New York: Penquin, 1989.

Head, Bessie. *A Question of Power.* London: Heinemann Educational, 1974.

Hejinian, Lyn. *My Life.* Los Angeles: Sun & Moon Press, 1987.

Hellman, Lillian. *Pentimento.* Boston: Little, Brown, 1976.

Hellman, Lillian. *Scoundrel Time.* Boston: Little, Brown, 1973.

Hellman, Lillian. *An Unfinished Woman.* Boston: Little, Brown, 1969.

Hepburn, Katharine. *Me.* New York: Random House, 1991.

Hildegard of Bingen. "Vita." *Women Writers of the Middle Ages: A Critical Study of Texts from Perpetua (d. 203) to Marguerite Porète (d. 1310),* ed. Peter Dronke. Cambridge: Cambridge University Press, 1984. 144–201, 231–64.

Hoffman, Eva. *Lost in Translation.* New York: Penguin, 1989.

Holiday, Billie, with William F. Dufty. *Lady Sings the Blues.* New York: Doubleday, 1956.

hooks, bell [Gloria Watkins]. *Talking Back: Thinking Feminist, Thinking Black.* Boston: South End Press, 1989.

Houston, Jeanne Wakatsuki, and James D. Houston. *Farewell to Manzanar.* Boston: Houghton Mifflin, 1973.

Hunter-Gault, Charlayne. *In My Place.* New York: Farrar, Straus & Giroux, 1992.

Hurston, Zora Neale. *Dust Tracks on a Road.* 2d ed. Ed. Robert Hemenway. Urbana and Chicago: University of Illinois Press, 1984.

Hutchinson, Lucy. *Memoirs of the Life of Colonel Hutchinson, with the Fragment of an Autobiography by Mrs. Hutchinson.* Ed. James Sutherland. London: Oxford University Press, 1973.

Huxley, Elspeth. *The Flame Trees of Thika.* 1959. London: Penguin, 1962.

Jacobs, Harriet A. *Incidents in the Life of a Slave Girl Written by Herself.* Ed. Jean Fagan Yellin. Cambridge: Harvard University Press, 1987.

James, Alice. *The Diary of Alice James.* New York: Dodd Mead, 1964.

Jameson, Kay Redfield. *An Unquiet Mind.* New York: Knopf, 1995.

Jaramillo, Cleofas M. *Romance of a Little Village Girl.* San Antonio: Naylor, 1955.

Johnson, Joyce. *Minor Characters.* Boston: Houghton Mifflin, 1983.

Jones, Hettie. *How I Became Hettie Jones.* New York: Dutton, 1990.

Juana Inéz de la Cruz, Sor. *The Answer/La Respuesta.* 1691. Trans. Electa Arenal and Amanda Powell: The Feminist Press, 1994.

Julian of Norwich. "Revelations of Divine Love." *Julian of Norwich: An Introductory Appreciation,* ed. P. Franklin Chambers. London: Victor Gollancz, 1955.

Kahlo, Frida. *The Diary of Frida Kahlo.* Ed. Sarah M. Lowe. New York: Harry N. Abrams, 1995.

Kaplan, Alice. *French Lessons.* Chicago: University of Chicago Press, 1993.

Kaysen, Susanna. *Girl, Interrupted.* New York: Vintage Books, 1993.

Keckley, Elizabeth. *Behind the Scenes: Or Thirty Years a Slave and Four Years in the White House.* New York: G. W. Carlton, 1868.

Keller, Helen. *The Story of My Life.* 1902. New York: Penguin, 1988.

Kempe, Margery. *The Book of Margery Kempe.* London: Penguin, 1994.

Ken Bugul [Marietou M'baye]. *The Abandoned Baobab.* 1982. Trans. Marjolijn De Jager. Brooklyn: Lawrence Hill Books, 1991.

Kingston, Maxine Hong. *The Woman Warrior: Memoirs of a Girlhood Among Ghosts.* New York: Knopf, 1976.

Klein, Gerda Weissmann. *All but My Life.* New York: Hill & Wang, 1957.

Knight, Sarah Kemble. "The Journal of Madame Knight." *Journeys in New Worlds,* ed. William L. Andrews et al. Madison: University of Wisconsin Press, 1990. 85–116.

Koller, Alice. *An Unknown Woman.* New York: Holt Rinehart & Winston, 1982.

Larcom, Lucy. *A New England Girlhood.* 1889. Boston: Northeastern University Press, 1986.

Leduc, Violette. *La Bâtarde.* Trans. Derek Coltman. New York: Farrar, Straus & Giroux, 1965

Lee, Mary Paik. *Quiet Odyssey: A Pioneer Korean Woman in America.* Ed. Sucheng Chan. Seattle: University of Washington Press, 1990.

Lessing, Doris. *The Memoirs of a Survivor.* London: Octagon, 1974.

Lim, Shirley Geok-lin. *Among the White Moon Faces.* Old Westbury: Feminist Press, 1996.

Lindbergh, Anne Morrow. *Bring Me a Unicorn.* New York: New American Library, 1971.

Lindbergh, Anne Morrow. *Gift from the Sea.* New York: Random House, 1955.

Lispector, Clarice. *An Apprenticeship, or The Book of Delights.* Austin: University of Texas Press, 1986.

Logan, Onnie Lee. *Motherwit: An Alabama Midwife's Story. As Told to Katherine Clark.* New York: E. P. Dutton, 1989.

Lorde, Audre. *The Cancer Journals.* San Francisco: Spinsters/Aunt Lute, 1980.

Lorde, Audre. *Zami: A New Spelling of My Name.* Trumansberg, NY: Crossing Press, 1982.

Luhan, Mabel Dodge. *Intimate Memoirs.* New York: Harcourt Brace, 1933.

MacLaine, Shirley. *You Can Get There from Here.* New York: W. W. Norton, 1975.

MacLane, Mary. *The Story of Mary MacLane.* 1902. In *Tender Darkness,* ed. Elizabeth Pruitt. Belmont, CA: Abernathy & Brown, 1993.

Madeleine. *Madeleine: An Autobiography.* 1919. New York: Persea Books, 1986.

Mairs, Nancy. *Carnal Acts.* New York: Harper & Row, 1990.

Mairs, Nancy. *Plaintext: Essays.* Tucson: University of Arizona Press, 1986.

Mairs, Nancy. *Remembering the Bone House: An Erotics of Place and Space.* New York: Harper & Row, 1989.

Mairs, Nancy. *Voice Lessons: On Becoming a (Woman) Writer.* Boston: Beacon Press, 1994.

Malkiel, Theresa. *The Diary of a Shirtwaist Striker.* 1910. New York: IRL Press/Cornell University Press, 1990.

Mandela, Winnie. *Part of My Soul Went with Him.* New York: Norton, 1985.

Mankiller, Wilma. *Mankiller, A Chief and Her People.* New York: St. Martin's Press, 1993.

Markham, Beryl. *West with the Night.* San Francisco: North Point Press, 1983.

Marshall, Paule. *Brown Girl, Brownstones.* New York: Random House, 1959.

Martineau, Harriet. *Harriet Martineau's Autobiography.* Ed. Maria Weston. Boston: James R. Osgood, 1877.

Maynard, Joyce. *Looking Back.* New York: Doubleday, 1971.

McCarthy, Mary. *How I Grew.* New York: Harcourt Brace Jovanovich, 1987.

McCarthy, Mary. *Memories of a Catholic Girlhood.* New York: Harcourt Brace, 1957.

Mead, Margaret. *Blackberry Winter.* New York: William Morrow, 1972.

Mebane, Mary. *Mary, Wayfarer.* New York: Viking Press, 1983.

Menchú, Rigoberta. *I, Rigoberta Menchú: An Indian Woman in Guatemala.* Ed. Elisabeth Burgos-Debray. Trans. Ann Wright. London: Verso, 1984.

Mernissi, Fatima. *Dreams of Trespass: Tales of a Harem Girlhood.* Reading, MA: Addison-Wesley, 1994.

Millett, Kate. *Flying.* New York: Knopf, 1974.

Millett, Kate. *The Looney Bin Trip.* New York: Simon and Schuster, 1990.

Millett, Kate. *Sita.* New York: Farrar, Straus & Giroux, 1977.

Munro, Eleanor. *Memoir of a Modernist's Daughter.* New York: Penguin, 1988.

Montagu, Lady Mary Wortley. *The Letters and Works of Lady Mary Wortley Montagu.* Ed. Lord Wharncliffe. New York: AMS Press, 1970.

Moody, Anne. *Coming of Age in Mississippi.* New York: Dell, 1968.

Moraga, Cherríe. *Loving in the War Years.* Boston: South End Press, 1983.

Morgan, Sally. *My Place.* Freemantle: Freemantle Arts Press.

Morris, Mary. *Nothing to Declare.* New York: Penguin, 1988.

Mother Jones. *The Autobiography of Mother Jones.* Chicago: Charles H. Kerr, 1972.

Mountain Wolf Woman. *Mountain Wolf Woman, Sister of Crashing Thunder: The Autobiography of a Winnebago Indian.* Ed. Nancy Lurie. Ann Arbor: University of Michigan Press, 1961.

Mourning Dove. *Mourning Dove: A Salishan Autobiography.* Ed. Jay Miller. Lincoln: University of Nebraska Press, 1990.

Mowatt, Anna Cora. *Autobiography of an Actress; or, Eight Years on the Stage.* Boston: Ticknor, Reed & Fields, 1854.

Murasaki, Shikibu. *The Tale of Genji.* Trans. Arthur Waley. New York: Modern Library, 1960.

Nestle, Joan. *A Restricted Country.* Ithaca: Firebrand Books, 1987.

Nightingale, Florence. *Cassandra.* Old Westbury: Feminist Press, 1979.

Nin, Anaïs. *The Diary of Anaïs Nin.* Ed. Gunther Stuhlman. New York: Swallow Press, 1966–80.

Nisa. *Nisa: The Life and Words of a !Kung Woman.* Ed. Marjorie Shostak. Cambridge: Harvard University Press, 1981.

Njeri, Itabari. *Every Good-Bye Ain't Gone: Family Portraits and Personal Escapades.* New York: Times Books, 1990.

Norris, Kathleen. *Dakota: A Spiritual Geography.* Boston: Houghton Mifflin, 1993.

Oliphant, Margaret. *The Autobiography of Margaret Oliphant.* Ed. Elisabeth Jay. Oxford: Oxford University Press, 1990.

Ossoli, Margaret Fuller. *Memoirs of Margaret Fuller Ossoli.* 2 vols. Boston: Phillips, Sampson, 1852.

Pankhurst, Emmeline. *My Own Story.* London: E. Nash, 1914.

Pemberton, Gayle. *The Hottest Water in Chicago: Notes of a Native Daughter.* New York: Anchor Doubleday, 1993.

Pilkington, Laetitia. *Memoirs of Mrs. Laetitia Pilkington, 1712–1750, Written by Herself.* London: George Routledge & Sons, 1928.

Piozzi, Hester Lynch Thrale. *Thraliana.* Ed. Katherine C. Balderston. Oxford: Clarendon Press, 1951.

Plath, Sylvia. *The Journals of Sylvia Plath.* Ed. Ted Hughes. New York: Doubleday, 1982.

Qoyawayma, Polingaysi/Elizabeth Q. White. *No Turning Back: A True Account of a Hopi Woman's Struggle to Bridge the Gap between the World of Her People and the World of the White Man.* Al-buquerque: University of New Mexico Press, 1964.

Rama Rau, Santha. *Remember the House.* New York: Harper, 1956.

Reagan, Nancy. *My Turn: The Memoirs of Nancy Reagan.* New York: Random House, 1989.

Rhys, Jean. *Smile, Please: An Unfinished Autobiography.* New York: Harper & Row, 1979.

Rich, Adrienne. *What Is Found There.* New York: Norton, 1993.

Richardson, Laurel. *Fields of Play: Constructing an Academic Life.* New Brunswick: Rutgers University Press, 1997.

Robertson, Adele Crockett. *The Orchard.* New York: Henry Holt, 1995.

Roosevelt, Eleanor. *The Autobiography of Eleanor Roosevelt.* New York: Harper, 1961.

Rowlandson, Mary. "A True History of the Captivity and Restoration of Mrs. Mary Rowlandson." *Journeys in New Worlds,* ed. William L. Andrews et al. Madison: University of Wisconsin Press, 1990. 27–65.

El Saadawi, Nawal. *My Travels around the World.* Trans. Shirley Eber. London: Methuen, 1991.

El Saadawi, Nawal. *Woman at Point Zero.* 1975. Trans. Sherif Hetata. New Jersey: Zed Books, 1983.

Sand, George. *My Life.* Trans. Daniel Hofstadter. New York: Harper & Row, 1979.

Sanger, Margaret. *An Autobiography.* New York: W. W. Norton, 1938.

Sarraute, Nathalie. *Childhood.* Trans. Barbara Wright. New York: G. Brazilier, 1983.

Sarton, May. *I Knew a Phoenix: Sketches for an Autobiography.* New York: W. W. Norton, 1959.

Sarton, May. *Journal of a Solitude.* New York: Norton, 1977.

Schlissel, Lillian. *Women's Diaries of the Westward Journey.* New York: Schocken Books, 1982.

Sedgwick, Catharine Maria. *The Power of Her Sympathy.* 1872. Ed. Mary Kelley. Boston: Northeastern University Press, 1993.

Segrest, Mab. *My Mama's Dead Squirrel.* Ithaca: Firebrand Books, 1985.

Sévigné, Marie de Rabutin Chantal. *Letters of Madame de Sevigné to Her Daughter and Her Friends.* Ed. R. Aldington. New York: Brentano's, 1927.

Sexton, Anne. *Anne Sexton: A Self-Portrait in Letters.* Boston: Houghton Mifflin, 1977.

Sigourney, Lydia H. *Letters of Life.* New York: D. Appleton, 1866.

Silko, Leslie Marmon. *Storyteller.* New York: Seaver Books/Grove Press, 1981.

Simon, Kate. *Bronx Primitive.* New York: Harper & Row, 1982.

Sisters of the Spirit: Three Black Women's Autobiographies of the Nineteenth-Century [Jarena Lee, Zilpha Elaw, Julia Foote]. Ed. William L. Andrews. Bloomington: Indiana University Press, 1986.

Smart-Grosvenor, Vertamae. *Vibration Cooking or the Travel Notes of a Geechee Girl.* 1970. New York: Ballantine, 1992.

Smith, Lillian. *Killers of the Dream.* New York: Norton, 1949.

Sone, Monica. 1953. *Nisei Daughter.* Seattle: University of Washington Press, 1987.

Sorensen, Virginia Eggertsen. *Where Nothing Is Long Ago: Memories of a Mormon Childhood.* New York: Harcourt, Brace & World, 1955.

Spence, Jo. *Putting Myself in the Picture.* Seattle: Real Comet Press, 1988.

Stanton, Elizabeth Cady. *Eighty Years and More (1815–1897): Reminiscences of Elizabeth Cady Stanton.* New York: European, 1898.

Steedman, Carolyn K. *Landscape for a Good Woman.* 1986. New Brunswick: Rutgers University Press, 1987.

Stein, Gertrude. *The Autobiography of Alice B. Toklas.* 1933. New York: Vintage, 1960.

Stein, Gertrude. *Everybody's Autobiography.* New York: Random House, 1937.

Stewart, Elinore Pruitt. *Letters of a Woman Homesteader.* 1914. Boston: Houghton Mifflin, 1982.

Tarbell, Ida. *All in the Day's Work: An Autobiography.* New York: Macmillan, 1939.

Tawil, Raymonda Hawa. *My Home, My Prison.* New York: Holt, Rinehart, and Winston, 1980.

Taylor, Susie King. *Reminiscences of My Life in Camps, with the 33rd United States Colored Troups Late 1st S.C. Volunteers.* Boston: By the author, 1902.

Terésa de Lisieux, Saint. *The Autobiography of Terésa de Lisieux.* Trans. John Beevers. Garden City: Doubleday, 1957.

Teresa of Avila, Saint. *The Life of Teresa of Jesus.* Trans. E. Allison Peers. Garden City: Doubleday, 1960.

Terhune, Mary Virginia Hawes. *Marion Harland's Autobiography: The Story of a Long Life.* New York: Harper & Brothers, 1910.

Terrell, Mary Church. *A Colored Woman in a White World.* Washington, DC: Ransdell, 1940.

Tillich, Hannah. *From Time to Time.* New York: Stein & Day, 1973.

Torgovnick, Marianna de Marco. *Crossing Ocean Parkway: Readings by an Italian American Daughter.* Chicago: University of Chicago Press, 1994.

Trist, Elizabeth House. "The Travel Diary of Elizabeth House Trist: Philadelphia to Natchez, 1783–84." *Journeys in New Worlds,* ed. William L. Andrews. Madison: University of Wisconsin Press, 1990. 201–32.

Truitt, Anne. *Daybook: The Journal of an Artist.* New York: Pantheon Books, 1982.

Turner, Tina, with Kurt Loder. *I, Tina.* New York: Avon, 1986.

Walker, Alice. *In Search of Our Mothers' Gardens: Womanist Prose.* San Diego: Harcourt Brace Jovanovich, 1983.

Webb, Beatrice. *My Apprenticeship.* New York: Longmans, Green, 1926.

Wells-Barnett, Ida B. *Crusade for Justice: The Autobiography of Ida B. Wells.* Chicago: University of Chicago Press, 1970.

Welty, Eudora. *One Writer's Beginnings.* New York: Warner Books, 1983.

West, Rebecca. *Family Memories.* New York: Penguin, 1988.

Wharton, Edith. *A Backward Glance.* New York: Appleton-Century, 1934.

Whitman, Narcissa. In *First White Women over the Rockies: Diaries, Letters, and Biographical Sketches of the Six Women of the Oregon Mission Who Made the Overland Journey in 1836 and 1838.* Introduced and edited by Clifford Merrill Drury. Glendale, CA: A. H. Clark, 1963–66.

Williams, Donna. *Nobody Nowhere.* New York: Times Books, 1992.

Williams, Donna. *Somebody Somewhere: Breaking Free from the World of Autism.* New York: Times Books, 1994.

Williams, Terry Tempest. *Refuge: An Unnatural History of Family and Place.* New York: Vintage Books, 1992.

Wolf, Christa. *Patterns of Childhood.* 1976. Trans. Ursula Molinaro. New York: Farrar, Straus & Giroux, 1980.

Wong, Jade Snow. *Fifth Chinese Daughter.* New York: Harper and Brothers, 1945.

Woolf, Virginia. *Moments of Being: Unpublished Autobiographical Writings.* New York and London: Harcourt Brace Jovanovich, 1976.

Wurtzel, Elizabeth. *Prozac Nation.* Boston: Houghton Mifflin, 1994.

Yezierska, Anzia. *Bread Givers.* 1925. New York: Persea Books, 1975.

Yourcenar, Marguerite. *Dear Departed.* Trans. Maria Louise Ascher. New York: Farrar, Straus & Giroux, 1991.

Zitkala-Sä [Gertrude Bonnin]. "An Indian Teacher among Indians," "Impressions of an Indian Childhood," "The School Days of an Indian Girl," "Why I Am a Pagan," 1900–1902. In *Classic American Autobiographies,* ed. William L. Andrews. New York: Mentor, New American Library, 1992.

Contributors

Shari Benstock is the author and editor of ten books in the fields of autobiography, biography, critical theory, and modernist studies. These include *Women of the Left Bank: Paris 1900–1940* (1986), *The Private Self* (1988), *Textualizing the Feminine* (1991), *No Gifts from Chance: A Biography of Edith Wharton* (1994), and *On Fashion* (1994). She is chair of the Department of English at the University of Miami and co-editor of the series "Reading Women Writing" at Cornell University Press.

Bella Brodzki teaches comparative literature at Sarah Lawrence College. She is the co-editor of *Life/Lines: Theorizing Women's Autobiography* (1988) and the author of articles on Borges, contemporary criticism, francophone and anglophone African and Caribbean literature, and feminist theory. Her current project is a book-length study that links translation, survival, and cultural memory across a range of theoretical, biographical, and fictional texts.

Helen M. Buss is Professor of English at the University of Calgary where she teaches life writing and Canadian literature. Her book, *Mapping Our Selves: Canadian Women's Autobiography in English* (1993), won the Gabrielle Roy Prize for best critical study on a Canadian topic. She has authored many articles and monographs on life writing and at present is working on a study of contemporary women's uses of the memoir form, as well as preparing a settler woman's memoir for publication and completing a memoir about her own childhood in Newfoundland.

Judith Butler is Chancellor's Professor of Rhetoric and Comparative Literature at the University of California, Berkeley. She is the author of *Subjects of Desire: Hegelian Reflections in Twentieth Century France* (1987), *Gender Trouble: Feminism and the Subversion of Identity* (1990), *Bodies That Matter* (1993), *Excitable Speech: A Politics of the Performative* (1997), and *The Psychic Life of Power: Theories in Subjection* (1997), as well as numerous essays on the philosophical analysis of gender and identity. She is also co-editor of *Feminists Theorize the Political* (1992) and *Erotic Welfare: Sexual Theory and Politics in the Age of Epidemic* (1993).

Mary Jean Corbett is Associate Professor of English and an affiliate of the Women's Studies Program at Miami University in Oxford, Ohio, where she teaches courses in nineteenth-century British literature and culture. She is the author of *Representing Femininity: Middle-Class Subjectivity in Victorian and Edwardian Women's Autobiographies* (1992), and of essays on Mary Shelley, Maria Edgeworth, Sydney Owenson, and George Eliot. Her current book project is entitled "Family Likeness: English Writing and Irish History, 1790–1886."

Margo Culley is Professor of English and Associate Director of Graduate Studies at the University of Massachusetts in Amherst, where she teaches courses in American women's literature with particular emphases on personal narrative and ethnicity. In addition to *A Day at a Time: The Diary Literature of American Women from 1763 to the Present* (1985), she is the editor of the Norton Critical Edition of Kate Chopin's *The Awakening* and of *American Women's Autobiography: Fea(s)ts of Memory* (1992). She is in her third term as a member of the Selectboard in the town of Wendell, Massachusetts.

Assia Djebar is an eminent Algerian writer now living in Paris. She has made two films in Arabic and published fiction and essays in French, many of which have been translated into English, including *Fantasia: An Algerian Cavalcade* (1985), *A Sister of Sheherazade* (1987), and *Women of Algiers in Their Apartment* (1980), a volume of short stories from which the excerpt in this book is taken. She won the 1996 Neustadt International Prize for Literature sponsored by *World Literature Today* and the University of Oklahoma.

Rita Felski is Professor of English at the University of Virginia. She is the author of *Beyond Feminist Aesthetics* (1989) and *The Gender of Modernity* (1995) and co-editor of a recent issue of *Cultural Studies* on Australian feminisms.

Laurie A. Finke is Professor of Women's and Gender Studies at Kenyon College. She is the author of *Feminist Theory, Women's Writing* (1987) and articles on feminist theory and medieval women.

Susan Stanford Friedman is the Virginia Woolf Professor of English and Women's Studies at the University of Wisconsin–Madison. She is the author of *Psyche Reborn: The Emergence of H. D.* (1981) and *Penelope's Web: Gender, Modernity, H. D.'s Fiction* (1990); co-editor of *Signets: Reading H. D.* (1990); editor of *Joyce: The Return of the Repressed* (1993); and co-author of *A Woman's Guide to Therapy* (1979). She has published many articles on feminist theory and pedagogy, narrative theory, women's poetry, modernism, psychoanalysis, autobiography, women's studies, and multiculturalism. She is at work on a critical study on modernism, a collection of her essays on feminism, and an edited volume on the new modernist studies.

Regenia Gagnier is Professor of English at the University of Exeter in England, where she teaches Victorian studies, social theory, feminist theory, and interdisciplinary studies. Her books include *Idylls of the Marketplace: Oscar Wilde and the Victorian Public* (1986), *Subjectivities: A History of Self-Representation in Britain, 1832–1920* (1991), and an edited collection, *Critical Essays on Oscar Wilde* (1992). Most recently she has published essays on the histories of economics and aesthetics in market society.

Leigh Gilmore is Associate Professor of English at the Ohio State University. She is the author of *Autobiographics: A Feminist Theory of Women's Self-Representation* (1994) and co-editor of *Autobiography and Postmodernism* (1994). Her current interest in self-representation focuses on limit cases. She is also working on a study of obscenity law and the representation of sexuality and "sexual offenses" in the United States.

Anne E. Goldman is Assistant Professor of English at the University of Colorado, Boulder, where she teaches African American, Chicana/o, and ethnic American literatures. Her book, *Take My Word: Autobiographical Innovations of Ethnic American Working Women*, was published in 1995. Currently she is completing a project on region, nation, and race in nineteenth-century fiction, provisionally titled "Racing: Toward a More Dialogical Model for American Studies."

Sara Suleri Goodyear was educated at Punjab University and received her Ph.D. from Indiana University. She has taught at Williams College and is currently at Yale University. She has written two books, *Meatless Days* (1989) and *The Rhetoric of English India* (1992), and is founding editor of the *Yale Journal of Criticism*.

Janice Haaken is Professor of Psychology at Portland State University. She is the author of *Pillar of Salt: Women and the Perils of Looking Back* (1998). She has published essays in *Signs*, *Social Text*, and *Psychiatry*.

Barbara Harlow is Professor of English at the University of Texas, Austin. She is the author of *Resistance Literature* (1987), *Barred: Women, Writing, and Political Detention* (1992), and *After Lives: Legacies of Revolutionary Writing* (1996), and co-editor with Ferial J. Ghazoul of *A View from Within: Writers and Critics on Contemporary Arabic Literature* (1994).

Mae Gwendolyn Henderson is Professor of English at the University of North Carolina at Chapel Hill. Author of numerous articles on African American and feminist criticism and theory, she is also co-editor of the five-volume *An Annotated Index of Letters, 1817–1871* (1980) and editor of the English Institute volume *Borders, Boundaries, and Frames: Cultural Criticism and Cultural Studies* (1995). Her collected essays, *Speaking in Tongues: The Voices of Black Women Writers*, will be published by Oxford University Press. Also forthcoming is her monograph on black expatriate writers in France.

bell hooks is Professor of English at CUNY–Graduate Center. She is the author of numerous books of cultural criticism, including *Ain't I a Woman: Black Women and Feminism* (1981), *Feminist Theory: From Margin to Center* (1984), *Talking Back: Thinking Feminist, Thinking Black* (1989), *Black Looks: Race and Representation* (1992), *Outlaw Culture: Resisting Representations* (1994), *Yearning: Race, Gender, and Cultural Politics* (1990); *Teaching to Transgress: Education as the Practice of Freedom* (1994), and *Killing Rage, Ending Racism* (1995).

Caren Kaplan is Associate Professor in the Department of Women's Studies at the University of California, Berkeley. She is the author of *Questions of Travel: Postmodern Disclosures of Displacement* (1996) and the co-editor with Inderpal Grewal of *Scattered Hegemonies: Postmodernity and Transnational Feminist Practices* (1994).

Shirley Geok-lin Lim is Professor of English and Women's Studies at the University of California, Santa Barbara, and has published four books of poetry, two collections of stories, and two critical books. She received the Commonwealth Poetry Prize for her first book of poems, *Crossing the Peninsula* (1980), and the American Book Award for her memoir, *Among the White Moon Faces* (1996). Currently writing a study of Asian American literature, she has also published in journals such as *Feminist Studies, Signs, New Literary History*, and *MELUS*.

Françoise Lionnet is the author of *Autobiographical Voices: Race, Gender, Self-Portraiture* (1989) and *Postcolonial Representations: Women, Literature, Identity* (1995). She is the co-editor of special issues of *Yale French Studies* (1993) and *Signs* (1995).

Nancy Mairs is the author of multiple memoirs, including *Plaintext: Essays* (1986), *Remembering the Bone House: An Erotics of Place and Space* (1989), *Carnal Acts* (1990), *Ordinary Time: Cycles in Marriage, Faith, and Renewal* (1993), *Voice Lessons: On Becoming a*

(Woman) Writer (1994), and *Waist High in the World: A Life among the Nondisabled* (1996). She lives in Tucson, Arizona.

Biddy Martin is Professor of German and Women's Studies at Cornell University. She is the author of *Woman and Modernity: The Life Styles of Lou Andreas Salome* (1991) and *Femininity Played Straight: The Significance of Being Lesbian* (1996), as well as numerous articles on feminist theory and sexuality.

Mary G. Mason is Professor of English at Emmanuel College. She has published several articles on women writers, and especially on women's autobiographical writing. With Carol Hurd Green, she co-edited *American Women Writers: A Critical Reference Guide, Supplement* (1994), and *Journeys: Autobiographical Writings by Women* (1979). She is writing a memoir, *LifePrints: Memories of a Poster Child.*

Nellie Y. McKay is Professor of American and African American Literature at the University of Wisconsin–Madison. Her scholarship on black women's autobiographies appears in many books and journals. She is also General Co-Editor with Henry Louis Gates, Jr., of *The Norton Anthology of African American Literature* (1996); author of *Jean Toomer, Artist: A Study of His Literary Life and Work* (1984); and editor of *Critical Essays on Toni Morrison* (1989).

Nancy K. Miller is Distinguished Professor of English at the Graduate School and Lehman College, CUNY. Her most recent book is *Bequest and Betrayal: Memoirs of a Parent's Death* (1996). She is currently working on a memoir about New York and Paris at the end of the fifties.

Shirley Neuman is Professor of English and Dean of Arts at the University of British Columbia. In other lives she has chaired the Women's Studies Programme at the University of Alberta, where she taught for many years and helped found and run small literary publishing houses. She continues to teach and write about autobiography, Canadian literature, and women's writing.

Felicity A. Nussbaum, Professor of English at UCLA, has published most recently *Torrid Zones: Maternity, Sexuality, and Empire* (1995). She is currently a National Endowment for the Humanities Fellow while completing a book, tentatively entitled "A Generation of Amazons," on the conjunctions of race, gender, and deformity in mid-eighteenth-century texts.

Jeanne Perreault is Associate Professor of English at the University of Calgary. She is the author of *Writing Selves: Contemporary Feminist Autography* (1995) and has co-edited an anthology of Western Canadian Native women's writing entitled *Writing the Circle* and a special issue of *Ariel* (1994) on Native writing and writers. Her critical articles include "White Feminist Guilt, Abject Scripts, and (other) Transformative Necessities" in *West Coast Line* (1994) and "Writing White" in *English Writing in Canada*. She is currently working on literary hysteria and the construction of whiteness in American women's prose.

Joan W. Scott is Professor of Social Science at the Institute for Advanced Study at Princeton. She is the author most recently of *Only Paradoxes to Offer: French Feminists and the Rights of Man* (1996).

Contributors

Sidonie Smith is Director of Women's Studies and Professor of English and Women's Studies at the University of Michigan. She is the author most recently of *Subjectivity, Identity, and the Body: Women's Autobiographical Practices in the Twentieth Century* (1993); co-editor with Julia Watson of *De/Colonizing the Subject: The Policies of Gender in Women's Autobiography* (1992), and *Getting a Life: Everyday Uses of Autobiography* (1996); and co-editor with Gisela Brinker-Gabler of *Writing New Identities: Gender, Nation, and Immigration in Contemporary Europe* (1997).

Doris Sommer is Professor of Latin American literature at Harvard University. She is the author of *Foundational Fictions: The National Romances of Latin America* (1991), *One Master for Another: Populism as Patriarchal Discourse in Dominican Novels* (1984), and a forthcoming book about the "rhetoric of particularism" that develops the approach she learned from reading Rigoberta.

Patricia Meyer Spacks is the author of many books on subjects ranging from eighteenth-century poetry to gossip. She has taught for extended periods at Wellesley, Yale, and Virginia and chaired the English Department at each institution. Her most recent book is *Boredom: The Literary History of a State of Mind* (1995).

Domna C. Stanton is Professor of French and Women's Studies at the University of Michigan. The first woman editor of *PMLA*, she has edited *The Female Autograph* (1984), *The Defiant Muse: French Feminist Poems from the Middle Ages to the Present* (1986), *Discourses of Sexuality: From Aristotle to AIDS* (1992), and recently co-edited *Feminisms in the Academy: Rethinking the Disciplines*. Her book, *Women Writ, Women Writing: Gendered Discourses and Differences*, will appear in 1998.

Carolyn Kay Steedman is Professor in the Centre for Social History at the University of Warwick. Her most recent book is *Strange Dislocations: Childhood and the Idea of Human Interiority, 1780–1930* (1995). She is currently working on a history of servants, service, and servitude in the period 1750–1820.

Lourdes Torres is Associate Professor of Spanish Linguistics at the University of Kentucky. Her teaching and research interests include sociolinguistics, Spanish varieties in the United States, and U.S. Latina/o literature. She is the author of *Puerto Rican Discourse: A Sociolinguistic Study* and co-editor of *Third World Women and the Politics of Feminism*. She is currently working on a book on U.S. Latina lesbian literature.

Julia Watson directs the comparative literature program in the Division of Comparative Studies at The Ohio State University. She has co-edited two books with Sidonie Smith, *De/Colonizing the Subject: The Politics of Gender in Women's Autobiography* (1992), and *Getting a Life: Everyday Uses of Autobiography* (1996). She is working on a study of women's autoethnographic writing in African and American contexts.

Hertha D. Sweet Wong is Associate Professor in the English Department at the University of California, Berkeley, where she teaches courses in autobiography, Native American literatures, and American cultures. She is the author of *Sending My Heart Back across the Years: Tradition and Innovation in Native American Autobiography* (1992), as well as numerous essays on Native American authors and indigenous responses to American nature writing. In addition, she is co-editor with John Elder of *Family of Earth and Sky: Indigenous Tales of Nature from around the World* (1994).

Sau-ling Cynthia Wong is the author of *Reading Asian American Literature: From Necessity to Extravagance* (1993); co-founding editor of *Hitting Critical Mass: A Journal of Asian American Cultural Criticism;* and co-editor of *MLA Resource Guide to Asian American Literature* (forthcoming). She has published extensively on such topics as gender, ethnicity, and nationalism in Chinese immigrant and diasporic writing; Maxine Hong Kingston's *The Woman Warrior;* the "Amy Tan phenomenon"; Asian American masculinity; and filmic images of "mothering" caregivers of color.

Sources

The following chapters are drawn from these sources: Benstock chapter excerpted from Shari Benstock, "Authorizing the Autobiographical," from *The Private Self: Theory and Practice of Women's Autobiographical Writings*, edited by Shari Benstock. Copyright © 1988 by the University of North Carolina Press. Used by permission of the publisher. Brodzki chapter excerpted from Bella Brodzki, "Mothers, Displacement, and Language in the Autobiographies of Nathalie Sarraute and Christa Wolf," in *Life/Lines: Theorizing Women's Autobiography*, ed. Bella Brodzki and Celeste Schenck. Copyright © 1988 by Cornell University. Used by permission of the publisher, Cornell University Press. Buss chapter reprinted from Helen M. Buss, "A Feminist Revision of New Historicism to Give Fuller Readings of Women's Private Writing," from *Inscribing the Daily: Critical Essays on Women's Diaries*, edited by Suzanne L. Bunkers and Cynthia A. Huff (Amherst: The University of Massachusetts Press, 1996). Copyright © 1996 by the University of Massachusetts Press. Butler chapter reprinted from *Bodies That Matter: On the Discursive Limits of "Sex,"* by Judith Butler. Copyright © 1993 by Routledge. Reproduced by permission of the publisher, Routledge, Inc. Corbett chapter excerpted from Mary Jean Corbett, "Literary Domesticity and Women Writers' Subjectivities," from *Representing Femininity: Middle-Class Subjectivity and Victorian and Edwardian Women's Autobiography*. New York: Oxford University Press, 1992. Reprinted by permission of Oxford University Press. Culley chapter reprinted and excerpted, by permission, from Margo Culley, "Introduction," in *A Day at a Time: The Diary Literature of American Women from 1764 to the Present* (New York: The Feminist Press at The City University of New York, 1985). Copyright © 1985 by Margo Culley. Djebar chapter reprinted from Assia Djebar, "Forbidden Gaze, Severed Sound," in *Women of Algiers in Their Apartment*. Trans. Marjolijn de Jager. Charlottesville: University of Virginia Press, 1992. Reprinted with permission of the University Press of Virginia.

Felski chapter, "On Confession," excerpted with permission of the publisher from *Beyond Feminist Aesthetics: Feminist Literature and Social Change* by Rita Felski, Cambridge, Mass.: Harvard University Press, copyright © 1989 by Rita Felski. Finke chapter reprinted from Laurie A. Finke, "Mystical Bodies and the Dialogics of Vision," from *Maps of Flesh and Light: The Religious Experience of Medieval Women Mystics*, ed. Ulrike Wiethaus. Syracuse: Syracuse University Press, 1993. Reprinted by permission of the publisher, Syracuse University Press. Friedman chapter excerpted from Susan Stanford Friedman, "Women's Autobiographical Selves: Theory and Practice," from *The Private Self: Theory and Practice of Women's Autobiographical Writings*, edited by Shari Benstock. Copyright © 1988 by the University of North Carolina Press. Used by permission of the publisher. Gagnier chapter excerpted from Regina Gagnier, "The Literary Standard, Working-Class Autobiography, and Gender," from *Textual Practice* 3, no. 1 (Spring 1989). Copyright © 1989. Reproduced by permission of Routledge, Inc. Gilmore chapter excerpted from Leigh Gilmore, *Autobiographics: A Feminist Theory of Women's Self-Representation*. Copyright © 1994 by Cornell University. Used by permission of the publisher, Cornell University Press. Goldman chapter reprinted from Anne E. Goldman, "Autobiography, Ethnography, and History: A Model for Reading," from *"Take My Word": Autobiographical Innovations by Ethnic American Working Women* (University of California, 1995). Copyright © 1995. Used by permission of the Regents of the University of California. Haaken chapter reprinted from Janice Haaken, "The Recovery of Memory, Fantasy, and Desire in Women's Trauma Stories: Feminist Approaches to Sexual Abuse and

Index

Wisconsin Studies in American Autobiography

William L. Andrews
General Editor

Robert F. Sayre
The Examined Self: Benjamin Franklin, Henry Adams, Henry James

Daniel B. Shea
Spiritual Autobiography in Early America

Lois Mark Stalvey
The Education of a WASP

Margaret Sams
Forbidden Family: A Wartime Memoir of the Philippines, 1941–1945
Edited, with an introduction, by Lynn Z. Bloom

Journeys in New Worlds: Early American Women's Narratives
Edited by William L. Andrews

Mark Twain
Mark Twain's Own Autobiography:
The Chapters from the "North American Review"
Edited, with an introduction, by Michael J. Kiskis

American Autobiography: Retrospect and Prospect
Edited by Paul John Eakin

Charlotte Perkins Gilman
The Living of Charlotte Perkins Gilman: An Autobiography
Introduction by Ann J. Lane

Caroline Seabury
The Diary of Caroline Seabury: 1854–1863
Edited, with an introduction, by Suzanne L. Bunkers

Cornelia Peake McDonald
A Woman's Civil War: A Diary with Reminiscences of the War, from March 1862
Edited, with an introduction, by Minrose G. Gwin

Marian Anderson
My Lord, What a Morning
Introduction by Nellie Y. McKay

American Women's Autobiography: Fea(s)ts of Memory
Edited, with an introduction, by Margo Culley

Frank Marshall Davis
Livin' the Blues: Memoirs of a Black Journalist and Poet
Edited, with an introduction, by John Edgar Tidwell

Joanne Jacobson
Authority and Alliance in the Letters of Henry Adams

Kamau Brathwaite
The Zea Mexican Diary
Foreword by Sandra Pouchet Paquet

Genaro M. Padilla
My History, Not Yours: The Formation of Mexican American Autobiography

Frances Smith Foster
Witnessing Slavery: The Development of Ante-bellum Slave Narratives

Native American Autobiography: An Anthology
Edited, with an introduction, by Arnold Krupat

American Lives: An Anthology of Autobiographical Writing
Edited, with an introduction, by Robert F. Sayre

Carol Holly
Intensely Family: The Inheritance of Family Shame and the Autobiographies of Henry James

People of the Book: Thirty Scholars Reflect on Their Jewish Identity
Edited by Jeffrey Rubin-Dorsky and Shelley Fisher Fishkin

John Downton Hazlett
My Generation: Collective Autobiography and Identity Politics

William Herrick
Jumping the Line: The Adventures and Misadventures of an American Radical

Women, Autobiography, Theory: A Reader
Edited by Sidonie Smith and Julia Watson